Susan Riley

MADAME DE STAËL

MARIA FAIRWEATHER

2006

Other books by the author

Pilgrim Princess: A Life of Princess Zinaida Volkonsky

MADAME DE STAËL

MARIA FAIRWEATHER

ROBINSON
London

For my daughters,
Catherine and Natasha

Constable & Robinson Ltd
3 The Lanchesters
162 Fulham Palace Road
London W6 9ER
www.constablerobinson.com

First published in the UK by Constable,
an imprint of Constable & Robinson Ltd 2005

This paperback edition published by Robinson,
an imprint of Constable & Robinson Ltd 2006

A copy of the British Library Cataloguing in Publication Data is available from the British Library

ISBN 13 978-1-84529-227-0
ISBN 10 1-84529-227-8

Printed and bound in the EU

Contents

PART FOUR The Sword and the Spirit

~

Illustrations

Madame de Staël's father, Jacques Necker (1732–1804), (oil on canvas), Jean-Sifred Duplessis, Coppet Collection.

Her mother Suzanne Necker (1737–1794), (oil on canvas), Jean-Sifred Duplessis, Coppet Collection.

Fourteen-year-old Germaine Necker, the future Madame de Staël (1766–1817), Coppet Collection.

The Château de Coppet, Coppet Collection.

Madame de Staël's bedroom at Coppet, Coppet Collection.

Madame de Staël's eldest son, Auguste de Staël (1790–1827), (oil on canvas), Anne-Louis Girodet-Trioson, Coppet Collection.

Her second son Albert de Staël (1792–1813), (pencil with highlights in white chalk), by Firmin Massot, Coppet Collection.

Her daughter Albertine, duchesse de Broglie (1797–1838), (oil on wood), Ary Schaeffer, Coppet Collection.

Her first husband, Baron Eric-Magnus de Staël-Holstein (1749–1802), (oil on canvas), Adolphe-Ulrich Wertmüller, Coppet Collection.

Charles Maurice de Talleyrand-Périgord (1754–1838), James Sharples, (c.1751–1811) © Bristol City Museum and Art Gallery, UK/www.bridgeman.co.uk

Benjamin Constant (1767–1830), (pencil with highlights in white chalk), by Firmin Massot, Coppet Collection.

Madame Récamier (1777–1849), (oil on canvas), Eulalie Morin, Coppet Collection.

Portrait of Friedrich Schlegel (1772–1829), (oil on panel), German School, (19th century) Goethe Museum, Frankfurt, Germany, INTERFOTO/BRIDGEMAN ART LIBRARY/www.bridgeman.co.uk

Napoleon Bonaparte (1769–1821), (oil on canvas), Baron Francois Pascal Simon Gerard, (1770–1837) Southampton City Art Gallery, Hampshire, UK/www.bridgeman.co.uk

Madame de Staël with her daughter Albertine (oil on canvas), Madame Vigée-Lebrun, Coppet Collection.

Madame de Staël as 'Corinne', (oil on wood), by Firmin Massot, Coppet Collection.

Madame de Staël's second husband, John Rocca (1788–1818), (oil on canvas), Pierre-Louis Bouvier, Musée d'Art et d'Histoire, Genève.

Portrait of the Duke of Wellington (1769–1852), Henry Perronet Briggs, (1792-1844) Royal Pavilion, Libraries & Museums, Brighton & Hove/www.bridgeman.co.uk

Acknowledgements

Almost two hundred years after her death, Madame de Staël, once encountered, is as impossible to forget as she was in her lifetime. Indeed, it is hard to think of her as dead at all, so alive are her letters, so lively and compelling her observations, so illuminating her analysis. The six years spent in her company, researching and writing my version of the story of her life, have been endlessly fascinating, stimulating and totally absorbing. As a self-invited guest, I always felt strangely at home and welcome. Madame de Staël's generous and inclusive spirit survives in her writing. I have been as profoundly interested, touched, maddened, warmed and above all instructed by her as by any living person, and I part with her now with immense gratitude. I have tried to show her in all her complexity, but I cannot deny that I am a friend. My aim was to write a general biography of her life, introducing her to new generations of readers, at a time when I believe her ideals are more needed than ever. I have discussed her work only where it was necessary to clarify her thinking or explain the consequences on her life, leaving detailed literary analysis to those better qualified.

Writing a life of Madame de Staël is a little like trying to control a coach driven by several horses each one pulling in different directions. Benjamin Constant once said of her that there were enough talents in Madame de Staël to have made ten or a dozen distinguished men. She certainly lived enough for several lives. My task has been made immeasurably easier by the wonderfully presented and annotated volumes of Madame de Staël's general correspondence, edited and commented on by the late Madame Beatrice Jasinski. I have used several other collections of her letters which are all mentioned in the bibliography. I am very much indebted to the great number of scholars from several countries whose work has been published under the auspices of the *Société des études staëliennes*, in the fifty-four volumes of *Cahiers staëliens*, most of which I read. Several have been of particular value and I have cited the authors, I hope without exception, in the endnotes. Of the biographies about her, all of which are mentioned in the bibliography, I owe a particular debt to Madame Necker-de Saussure's *Notice*, written immediately after Madame de Staël's death, by one who was not only her cousin and close friend, but also exceptionally intelligent and a fine writer. I am indebted to Sainte-Beuve as well as for a fascinating account of Madame de Staël written a generation after her death, for his accounts of many of her contemporaries and successors and of the times in general and for the unalloyed pleasure of reading him. Lady Blennerhassett's three-volume biography, published in English in 1889, and several important works published at the beginning of the twentieth century, of which Pierre Kohler's *Madame de Staël et la Suisse* (1916) and Paul Gautier's *Madame de Staël et Napoléon* (1903), have been particularly useful.

Madame de Staël's descendants have inherited many of her gifts. The body of work by successive generations of the family – Panges, d' Haussonvilles, d'Andlaus and Broglies – based on family archives, are indispensable to any biographer of Madame de Staël. All are listed in the bibliography. I owe a particular debt to Madame de Staël's living descendants: to Comtesse Hélène d'Andlau for her kind help and interest, and to Comte Othenin d'Haussonville who is the present Master of Coppet as well as executive president of the *Société des études staëliennes*, for his kind hospitality at Coppet, his help with illustrations and corrections for this edition, and his own work on Madame de Staël and her children and on Coppet. Not least of the debts I owe him is an introduction to the late Madame Simone Balayé, doyenne of Staëlien scholarship, whose untimely death robbed us not only of the foremost expert on all matters relating to Madame de Staël but also of a delightful presence, at once stern and encouraging, who in spirit reminded me forcibly of Madame de Staël herself. I count myself truly fortunate to have been able to meet her in her charming fifth-floor flat in rue Vaneau in Paris, not far from where Madame de Staël once lived herself, and I treasure her letters of encouragement and advice. Her great body of work on Madame de Staël, particularly her intellectual biography, *Madame de Staël, Lumières et Liberté*, is beyond price.

Among the more recent biographies of Madame de Staël and her family special mention must be made of Christopher Herold's *Mistress* to *An Age* (1958), which first sparked an interest in her when I was still at school; Jean-Denis Bredin's *Une singulière famille* (1999); and Ghislain de Diesbach's prize-winning biographies of Madame de Staël, (1983), of her father, *Necker ou la faillite de la vertu* (1978), and his fascinating history of the emigration during the French Revolution, *Histoire de l'Émigration* (1975).

On the history of the period in English, among the many books listed in the bibliography, the following were particularly illuminating: Alfred Cobban's three-volume *History of France*, Norman Davies's *Europe*, Eric Hobsbawm's *The Age of Revolution 1789–1848*, Colin Jones's *The Great Nation*, Philip Mansel's *Paris Between Empires 1814–1852*, and Simon Schama's *Citizens*. In French, apart from Madame de Staël's own *Considérations sur la Révolution française*, I have relied on François Furet's *La Révolution*, Georges Lefebvre's *La Révolution française* and *Napoléon*, Michelet's *Histoire de la Révolution française*, and Alexis de Toqueville's *l'Ancien Régime et la Révolution*.

A number of people have helped me over the years that this book has been in preparation. Without their help, encouragement and introductions, without the loan of their books and the snippets they sent me that led to unknown treasures or threw light on a particular moment in Madame de Staël's life, this would have been a much harder enterprise and a more lonely one. Some of them have read large parts of the book and made important suggestions. All those who read the manuscript corrected my punctuation and often each other's! I thank my friends particularly, for putting up with my need to talk about Madame de Staël, her world and her times. Few were indifferent to her and I found their various reactions fascinating and illuminating. My warmest thanks in London go to many of the usual suspects: to Marina and Adrian Camrose for all of the above and much more besides; to Lawrence and Linda Kelly, who generously lent their books to me for years, among them Linda's excellent *Juniper Hall* and *Women of the French Revolution*; to Ingela Evans, Shusha Guppy, Prof. Stephen Graubard, Jenny Johnson, Tessa and Henry Keswick, who kindly allowed me to use their painting by Orchardson among the illustrations, Jan de Staël Holstein, my cousin Gérard Legrain for his help with corrections, George Loudon, John Prideaux, Gaia Servadio, Christine Sutherland, David Sulzberger and Ben Whitaker. My special thanks for their advice and support to my agent, Christopher Sinclair-Stevenson, and to my publishers: to Ben Glazebrook and Nick Robinson and to Carol O'Brien, Roger Hudson and Jane Robertson for their editorial help, as well as to all at Constable & Robinson.

My warmest thanks to my friends in Paris, whose company and hospitality added immeasurably to the pleasure of research there. I am most grateful to Emanuela Pallesi for sharing my enthusiasm for Madame de Staël, for her encouragement from the very beginning and for her generous hospitality in Rome and in Paris; to Meredith Shelton for lending me her charming flat in Paris; to Jacqueline de Ponton d'Amécourt for her help and interest and her always stimulating company; to Marie Noêle and Didier Sicard, for their hospitality, and especially to Marie Noêle for initiating me into the mysteries of the Bibliothèque nationale and for finding rare books, just as I needed them, and to Didier for his help in deciphering eighteenth-century medical practice.

I would like to thank the helpful staff of the Bibliothèque nationale, the Bibliothèque de l'Arsenal and the Honoré Champion bookshop in Paris; the Château de Coppet in Switzerland; and in London, the library of the French Institute, the British Library, and especially the invariably kind and helpful staff of the London Library – surely one of the most agreeable places on earth.

Last, but foremost, I should like to thank my family. My warmest thanks to my mother, Isabelle Merica, my first supplier of books, among whose many gifts to me, that of a large part of my father's library of French literature and history, after his death, has been invaluable in the writing of this book. I take this opportunity to salute his shade with love. Special thanks to my daughters, Catherine and Natasha, to whom I dedicate this book, for their invariable support and enthusiasm and for their editorial expertise.

Above all I should like to thank my husband, Patrick. He has not only shared me with Madame de Staël these past six years, but also shared with me his experience of diplomacy and knowledge of history. He has supported me in every way, contributing greatly to the final draft and rearranging my punctuation. All translations unless otherwise stated are my own, as of course are any mistakes, apart from those of punctuation, which are now mostly my husband's.

Chronology

1732 Birth of Jacques Necker, Madame de Staël's father, in Geneva.

1737 Birth of Suzanne Curchod, Madame de Staël's mother, at Crassier, Vaud.

1764 Neckers' marriage in Paris.

1766 Birth of Anne Louise Germaine Necker in Paris, 22 April.

1767 Birth of Benjamin Constant in Geneva.

1774 Louis XVI ascends the throne.

1776 Neckers visit London with Germaine.

1777 Necker made Director General of Finance.

1778 Eric de Staël, Swedish diplomat, asks for twelve-year-old Germaine Necker's hand in marriage.
March: Germaine visits Voltaire with her mother.
30 May: death of Voltaire in Paris.
3 July: death of Rousseau.
Germaine suffers a nervous breakdown. Convalescence at Saint-Ouen.
She writes a comedy, *Les inconvénients de la vie à Paris*.

1781 Necker publishes his *Compte rendu au Roi*. The King asks for his resignation.

1783 Germaine refuses to contemplate marriage with William Pitt.

1784 Necker buys the Château of Coppet near Geneva. He publishes *De l'administration des Finances de la France*. Travels in the south of France.

1785 Germaine Necker keeps a journal and writes stories – *Mirza*, and *Histoire de Pauline*. Her marriage to Staël is agreed.

1786 January: The marriage contract is signed at Versailles in the presence of the royal family and takes place at the Swedish Embassy.
Madame de Staël is presented at court on 31 January. She

begins sending her news bulletins to the King of Sweden, Gustavus III.
She writes a play: *Sophie ou les sentiments secrets* and begins her *Lettres sur J.-J. Rousseau*.
1787 Louis XVI exiles Necker.
Madame de Staël gives birth to her daughter Gustavine, god-child of the king and queen of Sweden.
She writes a play: *Jane Grey*.
1788 Necker publishes *De l'importance des idées religieuses*. He returns to take charge of the Ministry of Finance.
Announcement of the recall of the Estates General.
Affair with Talleyrand.
She meets Louis de Narbonne and publishes *Lettres sur les ouvrages de Jean-Jacques Rousseau*.
1789 7 April: Death of Gustavine de Staël.
5 May: Madame de Staël witnesses the opening of the Estates General.
June: Third Estate becomes the National or Constituent Assembly.
11 July: Necker is again sent into exile. He leaves for Belgium with Madame Necker. The Staëls join the Neckers and travel to Switzerland.
14 July: Fall of the Bastille.
Necker is recalled a few days later and returns in triumph, accompanied by the Staëls.
August: Declaration of the Rights of Man.
October days: march of women on Versailles. The royal family is brought to Paris and installed in the Tuileries.
1790 14 July: Madame de Staël is present at the Fête de la Fédération, the 1st anniversary of the Revolution.
She writes her *Éloge de Monsieur de Guibert* after his death in May.
31 August: birth of her son Auguste.
3 September: Necker resigns and leaves for Coppet.
King addresses the Assembly – Civil Constitution of the Clergy.
1791 Her salon is the meeting place for the moderates including Sieyès.
She publishes her first article (unsigned) in *Les Indépendents*.
20 June: flight of the royal family to Varennes.
25 June: return of the royals to Paris. King suspended from his functions.

September: king accepts Constitution and is restored to his place.
October: meeting of the Legislative Assembly.
November: king uses his right of veto.
December: Narbonne becomes Minister of War, reorganizes the army.

1792 March: Narbonne falls.
16 March: Gustavus III is assassinated. One of the conspirators is Count Ribbing.
April: War declared on Austria–Prussia.
June: mob invades Tuileries.
July: Madame de Staël, Narbonne and Malouet offer a plan of escape to the royals, which is turned down by Marie-Antoinette.
August: proclamation of the first Republic.
August: Madame de Staël saves the lives of several of her aristocratic friends who escape to England.
2 September: the September massacres. Mme de Staël narrowly avoids death and leaves for Coppet.
September: Prussian Army crosses into France and is beaten at the battle of Valmy. The Assembly becomes the National Convention, abolishes the monarchy, establishes revolutionary calendar, orders trial of Louis XVI. French Army occupies Nice.
November: birth of her second son, Albert, at Rolle in Switzerland.
December: she leaves to join Narbonne in England.

1793 January: execution of Louis XVI.
Madame de Staël spends January–May in England at Juniper Hall in Surrey where she becomes friendly with Fanny Burney.
February: France declares war against England and Holland.
March: war declared against Spain. Revolt in the Vendée.
Madame de Staël works on *De l'influence des passions*, her study on the influence of the passions.
May: fall of the Girondins. Beginning of the Reign of Terror.
She returns to Coppet in June. Meets Count Adolph Ribbing who is in exile.
Saves many friends from the Terror.
Publication of her *Réflexions sur le procès de la Reine (Reflections on the Queen's Trial)*.
October: the trial and execution of Marie-Antoinette. Beginning of the Republican calendar.

1794 She rescues several more people from the Terror. Publishes *Zulma*, travels with Ribbing.
April: execution of Danton.
15 May: death of Madame Necker.
June, July: Terror rages in France.
Arrest and death of Robespierre. End of the Terror.
18 September: she meets Benjamin Constant.
December: publication in Switzerland by François de Pange of her *Réflexions sur la Paix (Reflections on Peace)*.

1795 Publication in Paris of *Reflections on Peace*.
Spring publication of *Essai sur les fictions*.
Madame de Staël and Constant arrive in Paris where she reopens her salon. In an article in the newspapers she accepts the Republic. Constant publishes his first article in Suard's journal *Les Nouvelles politiques*.
Madame de Staël is attacked in the Convention by Legendre and exiled by the Committee for Public Safety. She leaves Paris for Forges les Eaux.
The Convention is dissolved. Inauguration of the Directory. She leaves for Switzerland with Constant.

1796 She is threatened with arrest if she returns to Paris. She spends the year in Switzerland. In September she publishes *De l'influence des passions*. Returns to France at the end of the year to stay with Constant until May at Hérivaux where he has bought a house.
Bonaparte becomes General of the Army of Italy.

1797 Necker publishes *De la Révolution française*.
January to May: she stays with Constant at Hérivaux.
8 June: birth of their daughter Albertine in Paris.
Club de Salm (Constitutional circle) founded by Madame de Staël, Constant and others.
Having ensured the return of Talleyrand from America she persuades Barras to name him Foreign Minister.
The coup of 18 Fructidor.
December: first meeting with General Bonaparte whom she tries to dissuade from invading Switzerland.

1798 She returns to Coppet where she spends the whole year.
Proclamation of Roman Republic.
French army invades Canton of Vaud. Proclamation of Helvetian Republic.

She writes *Des circonstances actuelles pour terminer la Révolution* (*On the present circumstances for ending the Revolution*) which she does not publish. Begins work on *De la Littérature* (*On Literature considered in its relations with Social Institutions*).

1799 Declaration of War with Austria–Parthenopian Republic in Naples.
May – mid-July at Saint-Ouen. She is expelled by the Directory.
July to October at Coppet.
She returns to Paris on 18 Brumaire (9 November), the eve of the *coup d'état* of Brumaire.
She meets Madame Récamier for the first time.
Constant nominated to the Tribunate by Sieyès.
Bonaparte becomes First Consul.

1800 Constant's speech at the Tribunate annoys the First Consul.
April: publication of *De la Littérature*. She is strongly attacked in the press.
May: return to Coppet. She begins *Delphine* that summer and starts learning German.
July–August: works on the second edition of *De la Littérature*, which is published in mid-November.
Necker publishes *Cours de morale religieuse* in October.
Madame de Staël returns to Paris in December. Separation from her husband.

1801 She returns to Coppet where she meets Sismondi.
November: return to Paris.

1802 Bonaparte sacks moderates in Tribunate, Constant among them.
March: Peace of Amiens.
April: celebration of the Concordat.
Madame de Staël is part of the Moreau/Bernadotte Conspiracy.
May: return to Coppet with Staël who is incapacitated by a stroke. He dies on the way and is buried at Coppet.
Bonaparte is made Consul for life.
December: publication of her novel *Delphine*. Bonaparte banishes her from Paris.

1803 May: resumption of war with England.
September: she arrives at Maffliers and in October is ordered to stay outside forty leagues from Paris.
October: at the end of the month she leaves for Germany, accompanied by her children and Benjamin Constant.

Arrival at Weimar – meetings with Schiller, Wieland and Goethe.

1804 General Moreau banished, Cadoudal and Pichegru executed as a result of their plot uncovered at the end of 1803.
20–21 March: the kidnap and murder of the Duc d'Enghien.
March: departure from Weimar. Madame de Staël goes to Berlin alone where she meets August Wilhelm Schlegel whom she persuades to come back with her as tutor to her children and help her with her book on Germany. Constant returns to Lausanne.
9 April: death of Necker. Believing her father to be merely ill Madame de Staël sets out from Berlin. Constant returns to her at Weimar and announces the news of Necker's death.
19 May: return to Coppet where she spends the summer working on a eulogy of her father. She refuses Constant's proposal of marriage.
May: the Empire is proclaimed.
Autumn: publication of *Du caractère de M. Necker et de sa vie privée.*
2 December: Napoleon is crowned Emperor.
She leaves for Italy, accompanied by Schlegel, where they are joined by Sismondi. She meets the poet, Vincenzo Monti, in Milan at the end of December.

1805 February: arrival in Rome.
On to Naples until early March.
Mid-March to May: Rome. Romance with a young Portuguese diplomat, Don Pedro de Souza, future Duke of Palmella.
May – 15 June: Florence, Venice and Milan where she arrives after the Emperor's coronation.
4 June: Napoleon's coronation as King of Italy.
15 June: return to Coppet. Refuses Constant again.
First gathering of scholars and writers at Coppet. She begins work on her novel *Corinne ou l'Italie*, meets the young future historian Prosper de Barante, with whom she starts a five-year relationship.
She writes a play *Agar dans le désert* (*Hagar in the desert*).
August: Chateaubriand visits Coppet. Her son Auguste leaves for Paris to prepare for the École Polytechnique. He passes his exams with the highest marks possible.

2 December: Napoleon's victory at Austerlitz.

1806 Madame de Staël takes the château de Vincelles near Auxerre where she entertains many of her friends. After Schlegel's illness in July, she moves to Rouen.
Constant falls in love with Charlotte du Tertre (formerly Hardenberg). He begins his novel, *Adolphe*, joining Madame de Staël at Rouen while she finishes *Corinne*.

1807 Napoleon warns Fouché repeatedly to keep Madame de Staël away from Paris. She nevertheless manages to spend a few days there at the beginning of April.
May: publication of *Corinne* which is a resounding success.
June: the treaty of Tilsit.
Madame de Staël spends the summer at Coppet – another brilliant gathering of European talent.
She writes *Geneviève de Brabant.*
December: She leaves for Vienna with Schlegel. Auguste meets the Emperor at Chambéry and pleads for permission for his mother to return to Paris, which is refused.

1808 Winter in Vienna. She sees a great deal of the Prince de Ligne and has an affair with Maurice O'Donnell, a young Austrian officer of Irish extraction whom she had met in Venice.
23 May: abolition of the slave trade in Britain and later that year by the United States (though not yet of slavery).
June: secret marriage of Constant and Charlotte.
July: at Coppet, Madame de Staël begins work on *De l'Allemagne*.
July: Napoleon invades Spain.

1809 In May Madame de Staël learns of Constant's secret marriage. He nevertheless follows Madame de Staël to Coppet.

1810 April: Madame de Staël rents the château de Chaumont. Her publisher, Nicolle, begins to set *De l'Allemagne*.
Censorship is made more strict in France. Savary replaces Fouché as Minister of Police.
Napoleon marries Marie-Louise of Austria.
On Napoleon's orders, Savary orders the confiscation of *De l'Allemagne* and banishes Madame de Staël from France. Madame de Staël manages to smuggle two copies of the book out to Coppet with her.
October: *De l'Allemagne* is pulped.
November: she meets John Rocca.

1811 Problems with the new *Préfet*. Schlegel leaves for Vienna with a copy of *De l'Allemagne*. Madame de Staël begins work on *Dix années d'exil*, writes *Sapho* and begins research on her projected 'Richard Coeur de Lion'.
May: Madame de Staël and Rocca exchange vows to marry before a Protestant pastor.
Visits by Mathieu de Montmorency and Madame Récamier, which result in the exiling of both from Paris.

1812 January to March: in Geneva.
7 April: she gives birth secretly at Coppet, to John Alphonse, her son by Rocca.
Leaving the baby in the care of a Swiss pastor, she escapes to England, via Austria, Russia and Sweden – the only way open to her.
June: in Vienna.
14 July: she crosses into Russia as Napoleon's armies do the same.
August: Moscow then St Petersburg where she has several interviews with the Tsar and meets General Kutuzov. Crosses into Finland on 7 September on the same day as French and Russian armies meet at Borodino.
14 September: the occupation of Moscow by Napoleon's troops. Moscow torched.
18 October: the Grande Armée begins the retreat from Russia.
December: Napoleon returns to Paris.
24 September: Madame de Staël arrives in Stockholm where she is welcomed by General Bernadotte, Crown Prince of Sweden, and where remains until the following summer. She begins work on *Considérations sur la Révolution* and on the second part *of Dix années d'exil*. She actively promotes Bernadotte as Napoleon's successor in France.
General Malet's conspiracy in France.

1813 Publication of *Réflexions sur le Suicide*.
June: Madame de Staël, her son Auguste and her daughter Albertine arrive in England. They are fêted by the British establishment and literary world. Madame de Staël meets Byron, Coleridge, James Mackintosh and Wilberforce.
12 July: her younger son, Albert, who is an officer in the Swedish army, is killed in a duel in Germany.

De l'Allemagne is published to great acclaim, in French and then in English by John Murray in London.
16–19 October: Napoleon is defeated at Leipzig by the allied armies.

1814 January: the Allies invade France.
30 March: Allied entry into Paris.
6 April: Napoleon abdicates.
April: Soult defeated at the battle of Toulouse. End of Peninsular War.
12 May: Madame de Staël arrives in Paris. She opens her salon and receives the Tsar and all the ministers and diplomats, reluctantly supporting the restoration of the Bourbons when Bernadotte's candidacy is rejected.
Summer at Coppet when she receives all her English friends.
September: return to Paris.
September: the Congress of Vienna assembles.

1815 1 March: Napoleon leaves Elba.
10 March: Madame de Staël leaves Paris for Coppet.
20 March: Napoleon enters Paris. Constant helps Napoleon to draft the *Acte additionel* during the Hundred Days.
9 June: final Act of the Congress of Vienna.
18 June: battle of Waterloo.
22 June: Napoleon abdicates for the second time and is exiled to St Helena.
Madame de Staël returns to Paris. She supports the second restoration of Louis XVIII. Her father's money is repaid. Albertine is engaged to the Duc de Broglie.
Madame de Staël, her children, Rocca and Schlegel leave for Italy.

1816 January in Milan where she publishes *De l'esprit des traductions*, then Pisa for the rest of the winter, where Albertine is married to the Duc de Broglie on 20 February.
Publication of Constant's *Adolphe* in London.
Summer at Coppet: Byron is a frequent visitor.
October: Madame de Staël and Rocca are married secretly and return to Paris.

1817 February: Madame de Staël suffers a stroke.
14 July: death of Madame de Staël in Paris.
28 July: she is buried at Coppet. After the reading of her will her marriage and her son Alphonse are officially recognized.

1818 January: death of John Rocca.
Auguste and Albertine publish Madame de Staël's *Considérations sur la Révolution française*.
1820 Publication of *Dix années d'exil* and of her *Complete Works*.
1821 5 May: death of Napoleon on St Helena.
1824 April: death of Lord Byron in Missolonghi, Greece.
1825 Marriage of Auguste de Staël and Adèle Vernet.
December: death of Alexander I of Russia.
1826 24 March: death of Mathieu de Montmorency in Paris.
1827 17 November: death of Auguste de Staël, followed by that of his infant son.
1830 December: death of Benjamin Constant in Paris.
1832 Death of Goethe.
Slavery abolished throughout the British Empire.
1838 Death of Albertine de Broglie, direct ancestress of all Madame de Staël's descendants.
May: death of Talleyrand.
1841 Death of Madame Necker-de Saussure.
1842 Death without issue of Louis-Alphonse Rocca.
1844 March: death of Bernadotte (King Charles XIV of Sweden).
1845 Death of Schlegel in Bonn.
1848 July: death of Chateaubriand.
1849 May: death of Madame Récamier.
1852 September: death of the Duke of Wellington.
1870 Death of Madame de Staël's son-in-law and political heir, Victor de Broglie.

~

Prologue

'POLITICS, THE DEMANDING love of an eighteen-year-old, the need for society, the need for glory, melancholy as a desert, the need to influence, the need to shine, everything paradoxical and complicated . . . yet she unites the most outstanding qualities of mind and heart,' wrote Benjamin Constant, the only one of Madame de Staël's lovers who was her intellectual equal. He also called her 'the most famous person of our age through her writing and her conversation'.

Germaine de Staël was, indeed, the most remarkable and the most famous woman of her time, whose work was read all over Europe and who influenced many of her contemporary writers, including Byron. She remains a major writer of the revolutionary and Napoleonic period in France. It was politics that brought about her eclipse, which began in the 1870s. The message of the author of *De l'Allemagne*, who had championed German culture, was unwelcome in the long period of repeated Franco–German conflict. As Napoleon's liberal opponent and stern critic, her reputation fluctuated in opposition to his. Misogyny also played its part. Rich, independent and unconventional, Germaine de Staël was nevertheless considered ugly – an unforgivable sin in a woman and one compounded by her intellectual brilliance and determination to play an active part in the affairs of her time. A difficult combination, even in our day, it earned her at best, accusations of meddling and intriguing, at worst, the most crude and blatant forms of sexual vilification.

'Literary glory was not her chief ambition,' wrote her cousin and closest friend, Albertine Necker-de Saussure. 'Her books are the natural result of that prodigious abundance of thoughts that passed through her head and which could not be linked or fully developed unless they were fixed on paper. She did not think because she wished to write; she wrote because she had thought . . . Madame de Staël cannot be considered separately from her work.'

An impetuous and passionate nature, a penetrating intellect, an original and fertile imagination, relentless drive and extraordinary vitality were never more clear than in her unmatched talent for conversation, which was remarked on by all her contemporaries throughout her life, at a time when the art of conversation really mattered. 'If I were Queen,' wrote one contemporary, 'I would command her to talk to me always.'

Born into the world of the Paris salons, which she dominated with effortless ease, she was no more a mere salon hostess than Napoleon, her great adversary, was a mere general. She not only drew to her salons men who wielded power but was able to influence them. In her youth she helped Talleyrand to write his speeches, she wrote them for Narbonne when he was Minister of War, she collaborated with Benjamin Constant on most of his major writing, and persuaded Wellington that it was right to withdraw the army of occupation from France after Napoleon's downfall.

And yet her awareness of her own intellectual brilliance was balanced by a great generosity of spirit and a warm curiosity. Almost all her contemporaries speak of her unique ability to make everyone around her shine, and of her passionate desire to persuade people to come to an agreement through rational argument. 'I know of no woman, nor of any man more convinced of their immense intellectual superiority over everyone else, nor of one who allowed this conviction to weigh less on others,' Chateaubriand wrote of her.

Hers was not a long life – she died at the age of fifty-one – but she filled it to the brim. Her life and work span the eighteenth and nineteenth centuries. There were few aspects of the new world emerging after the French Revolution which escaped her notice. Persecuted and exiled by Napoleon, who recognized her as a genuine threat, she became an exemplary 'dissident', turning her Château of Coppet in Switzerland, already a centre of European thought, into one of liberal resistance. And she travelled – to Italy, Germany, Austria, Poland, Russia, Sweden and England. Poor health or political events prevented her from adding Spain, Greece, Constantinople, Syria and the United States to this list, depriving posterity of unique historical insights. She lived to witness Napoleon's downfall, a downfall to which she had undoubtedly contributed, just as she had contributed to a rising nationalist consciousness in Europe, not in its narrow and aggressive sense but by encouraging, through her writing, all peoples to value and understand their own customs and history and to develop their own authentic literature. This was acknowledged by figures like Goethe, Pushkin, Leopardi and Foscolo. Her network of political and intellectual contacts was such that in 1815 it was popularly said: 'There are three great powers in Europe: England, Russia and Madame de Staël.'

Her life is full of contradictions. She was born to great riches and power: her father Jacques Necker became Louis XVI's influential Minister of Finance, while her mother presided over one of the most important intellectual salons of the *ancien régime*. Yet her middle-class Swiss background and Protestant faith ensured that she remained forever an outsider. Painfully aware of the limitations imposed by society on women, particularly women of talent, she had scant regard for the conventions of her day. She dealt with this problem head-on in her novels, exposing herself to scurrilous vilification. She was alternately accused of masculinity or sluttishness, not only in the press but by some of the great men of her time, chief among them Napoleon. Terrified of loneliness, longing for love and a perfect marriage, she repeatedly risked her reputation in love affairs with ever younger men. She was also terrified of old age. In spite of her fears and anxieties – an undercurrent of deep melancholy ran through her nature – she lived life with extraordinary courage and zest. Egotistical and demanding at times, she was compassionate and generous to a fault, repeatedly risking her life to save friends during the Revolution, offering them shelter and sparing neither time nor money to help them. She risked her own freedom, and sacrificed her greatest pleasure – living in Paris – in the cause of liberty.

Perhaps the greatest contradiction of all is between her cool and practical mind and her passionate and unruly heart, the former seemingly able to function to perfection even when she was floored by her emotions. Eminently self-disciplined in her work, she was incapable of self-control – as her lapses in tact and her repeated hysterical rows with her lovers demonstrate.

But it was her full-blooded personal experience of life which enabled her to write books which were ground-breaking in her day and still have much to offer. *De L'influence des passions* (*On the Influence of Passions on the Happiness of Individuals and of Nations* (1796)) bears all the marks of her own suffering through her first great love affair and of living through the Terror in France. Of all her books, it is the one most truly 'written on the body'. Her novels, *Delphine*

(1802) and especially *Corinne* (1807), the model for all celebrated women, as Sainte-Beuve called it, helped to bring to public notice the injustices suffered by women. *Corinne* was also influential in raising national consciousness in Italy. *De l'Allemagne* (*On Germany* (1810)), a magisterial account of German culture, did the same for Germany and also brought the new German Romantic philosophy to the attention of the French for the first time. Madame de Staël is generally credited with the birth of the French Romantic movement. Two of her most important books were published posthumously. *Dix années d'exil* (*Ten Years of Exile* (1820)) remains a wonderful personal account of her travels through Napoleonic Europe, particularly in Russia on the eve of Borodino, as well as a personal account of Napoleon. Her combination of great erudition, intellectual curiosity and the personal warmth which enabled her to make easy contact with all kinds of people, makes her an exciting travel writer and anecdotist. The *Considérations sur la Révolution française* (*Considerations on the French Revolution* (1818)) is both a comprehensive history of the period by an exceptional frontline eyewitness, and an examination of its causes and its consequences. In this work she views Napoleon in a more historical context, acknowledging his greatness, but balancing the good he did against the great harm. Above all Madame de Staël made a case for liberal values, the worth and welfare of the individual and individual freedom, earning herself a place as one of the principal founders of French liberalism.

It is perhaps as a moralist that Madame de Staël is still entirely relevant today. In all her works, in her letters and journals, in the accounts of her contemporaries, friends and enemies there is a common thread: her advocacy of reason and tolerance in the face of fanaticism and violence, her belief in action and her optimism in the face of despair, as important in our day as it was in hers.

PART ONE

An Extraordinary Family

'What an extraordinary family is that of Madame de Staël; all three on their knees in constant adoration of one another.'

Napoleon

Chapter 1

Madame Necker's Salon

> 'She had needed that unique being, she found him and spent her life with him.'
>
> Madame de Staël on her mother's marriage

A SMALL GIRL DRESSED in the stiff clothes of the eighteenth century, her black curls bouncing, her great, dark eyes sparkling with laughter, races an elderly lady to her special chair across her mother's salon. Her mother, usually so prim and proper, looks on with amusement, sometimes even joins in the race. It is a joke between the three of them. The ambitious young hostess knows better than to reprove her high-spirited daughter, when her elderly friend is pleased to approve. The child – Minette to her familiars – is the future Madame de Staël; her mother, Madame Necker, is a rising star of the Paris salons; the old lady, Madame Geoffrin, is one of the two most important *salonnières* of her time in Paris. She is a frequent guest of the Neckers and likes to send a favourite chair ahead, perhaps even two, 'to prevent her [Madame Necker] from beating me to my chair as her little girl does, and to keep the peace'.[1]

In the early 1770s, when this scene takes place, young Minette's father, Jacques Necker was already well on the way to being among the richest bankers in Paris. Her mother, Suzanne, meanwhile was establishing an intellectual salon which was to be the last and most important of the pre-revolutionary era. Their double achievement, remarkable enough in itself, was all the more so in the Paris of the *ancien régime*, for Jacques Necker and his wife were not French, Catholic or aristocratic, but Swiss, Protestant and bourgeois.

But they had arrived at the right time. Although the aristocratic and xenophobic traditions of the *ancien régime*, which made life for Protestants difficult and sometimes dangerous, were still largely in place in the middle of the eighteenth century – there had been a wave of Huguenot emigration as recently as 1752 – France was beginning to open up to foreigners. Indeed, thanks to Voltaire and Rousseau foreigners were in fashion: a matter of the utmost importance in a country where fashion was king. Since Louis XIV's time, when the Sun King had looked to the great financiers and bankers to pay for his wars and foreign expeditions, the newly rich had become an important force in French society. While the old aristocracy was wary and jealous of the new men, the King and his ministers received them at court. They built splendid town houses which they filled with treasures, entertained in princely fashion, married their daughters into the aristocracy, and bought titles of nobility for their sons. Paris expanded rapidly as the fashionable new *faubourgs* of Saint-Honoré and Saint-Germain grew on either bank of the Seine. By the middle of the eighteenth century, when Jacques Necker arrived in Paris as a simple bank clerk, the city's population had grown to half a million.

Jacques Necker was born in Geneva in 1732. His father, Karl Friedrich, came from Küstrin in Brandenburg, a descendant of a line of Lutheran clergymen who, according to a doubtful family legend, traced their roots to aristocratic Norman-Irish origins. Karl Friedrich Necker's talents, via the usual route for impoverished but clever young men of tutoring the sons of the aristocracy, had brought him to Geneva, where he became professor of German law at the University of Geneva, and a burgher of the city. (At that time, the small but influential Republic of Geneva was ruled by an oligarchy whose members alone enjoyed full citizenship. Below them came the burghers, who might one day aspire to citizenship, though this honour was jealously guarded.) His marriage in 1726 to Jeanne-Marie Gautier, daughter of the First Syndic of the Republic, ensured him full citizenship as well as entry into the ruling elite as a member of the 'Two Hundred' and of the Consistory. Charles-Frédéric, as he now called himself, and his wife were well into middle age – he was forty-six and she was forty – at the time of the birth of their elder son Louis in 1730. Another son was born two years later, on 30 September 1732. They named him Jacques.

Although both boys were studious and clever, it was the charming Louis who seemed by far the more brilliant of the two, winning a chair in mathematics at an early age. When Jacques finished school at the age of sixteen, he was denied his wish to pursue a life of literature, to which some early, unpublished fragments of a play and a novel bear witness,[2] and was placed instead in the bank of his father's friend, Isaac Vernet, as a clerk. Two years later, in 1750, he had done sufficiently well to be sent to the bank's headquarters in Paris, with his modest salary doubled. By 1756, when the bank was reorganized, Vernet's nephew and successor Georges-Tobie de Théllusson, in recognition of Jacques Necker's outstanding talents and capacity for hard work, gave him a quarter share in the bank of which he was now one of three managers. By the age of thirty, the heavy-set, quiet young workaholic, who had even taught himself Dutch the better to follow the bank's business in the Netherlands, found himself the co-director of the Banque Vernet, with special expertise in the grain trade – vitally important to governments in those times of recurring wheat shortages. While almost nothing is known about Jacques Necker's private life between his arrival in Paris and his marriage (perhaps because he hardly had one), he managed in those years to build up a considerable personal fortune, as well as doing extremely well by his bank. The exact provenance of Necker's fortune is not clear. Probably it was built on speculation in grain, especially wheat, and on transactions following the liquidation of French possessions in Canada and the sale of English and French treasury bonds. There was no suggestion of financial skulduggery, indeed Necker always enjoyed a reputation for exceptional honesty, but in later years he would never refer to the origins of his fortune, perhaps because he did not wish to recall his modest beginnings.

In 1760 a family scandal must surely have disturbed Jacques Necker's peaceful and industrious life. A widower since 1759, Jacques's jovial and fast-living older brother Louis had found consolation in the arms of Madame Vernes, wife to the brother of the austere Pastor Vernes, a friend of Voltaire and a member of one of Geneva's oldest families. Unfortunately for Louis, the pastor's brother was a man of old-fashioned views. Surprising Louis in bed with his wife, he shot and almost killed him, broadcasting the affair to the whole of Geneva for good measure. Voltaire, who had been following events from his house at Ferney, was vastly amused and lost no time in relaying news of the scandal to his friends in Paris. But the Consistory of Geneva was not amused at all. Louis was deprived of his chair, had to grovel to the city fathers, and was banished from the Republic for a year. He was hurriedly dispatched to Paris to join his younger brother, his reputation going before him, although in that city it did him no harm. From Paris Louis, on the advice of his brother Jacques, went to Marseilles, which was then a free port. Here, in his turn, success in grain speculation made his fortune. Quite forgiven his youthful indiscretions, the rich financier was welcomed home a few years later, took the name of Monsieur de Germany, after a country property near Rolle, which his father had acquired in 1762 and called 'Germanie' in honour of his origins, and founded the financial house of Germany & Girardot.

In the summer of 1764, his own fortune made, Jacques Necker too began to think of marriage. His eye first alighted on a relation of the Thellussons, Madame Germaine de Vermenoux, the twenty-six-year-old widow of a Swiss officer, not only pretty, witty and rich, but like him, a Protestant. Necker began to pay her serious court, even venturing to propose. But, unwilling to lose her freedom after an unhappy marriage, and bored by the earnest young banker, she turned him down. His frequent appearances usually signalled her disappearance on some slender excuse, and she would leave him to be entertained by Suzanne Curchod, her son's serious and attractive Swiss governess.

Suzanne was the only child of Louis-Antoine Curchod, Calvinist Pastor of the village of Crassier in the canton of Vaud, and his wife Madeleine d'Albert de Nasse, the beautiful daughter of a French Huguenot lawyer from Montélimar, whose family had taken refuge in the Vaud after the revocation of the Edict of Nantes. She was born at the vicarage of Crassier on 2 June 1737. Later, she tried hard but unsuccessfully to prove that her mother's family was of the minor nobility.[3] Whatever the case, her father the Pastor, though of solid old bourgeois stock, intelligent and well educated, was poor. Suzanne was brought up modestly and devoutly, although she was unusually well educated by her father. She knew Latin and even some Greek, and was taught mathematics and physics, for which she had a particular aptitude, as well as the more usual female accomplishments – she painted, played the harpsichord and the violin. Suzanne had also inherited her mother's beauty and for all her modest upbringing was held to be something of a flirt. Well aware of her charms and accomplishments she set her sights high, looking down on the hopeful young curates who gathered at her father's vicarage. She later described herself at the time as having 'a face which announced youth and gaiety, fair hair and a fair complexion animated by blue eyes full of laughter, vivacity and sweetness, a small but well-turned nose, a pretty mouth which smiled in graceful accompaniment to the eyes; a tall and well proportioned figure, but without that elegance which might have added to its value'.[4]

Only a few miles from the parsonage of Crassier lay Lausanne, then a charming town set among orchards and vineyards on the hillside above Lake Geneva. Less stuffy than Calvinist Geneva, described by Voltaire as '*petitissime, parvulissime et pedantissime*',[5] Lausanne society was ideal for a young woman of serious education but slender means. 'La belle Curchod' became a frequent visitor. As 'Themire' she shone at several of the literary and discussion societies with names such as 'The Society of Spring' and 'The Academy of the Waters', which were then fashionable among the young. It was in Lausanne that Suzanne, still unmarried at twenty, met a young Englishman of good birth and exceptional intelligence. He signed himself with youthful affectation as Edouard de Guibon, though he is better known as plain Edward Gibbon, the future author of *The Decline and Fall of the Roman Empire*. Dispatched to Lausanne by his exasperated father, a Hampshire squire of traditional and unbending views, because of his decision while at Oxford to 'enter without delay into the pale of the Church of Rome', Gibbon 'was immediately settled under the roof and tuition of M. Pavilliard, a Calvinist Minister'.[6] Hardly handsome, even at the age of twenty – although he had not yet reached the monstrous proportions of his later years when one wag remarked that when he needed exercise he walked three times around Edward Gibbon – the young man had charming manners as well as notable erudition. He in turn was much taken by Suzanne. 'The personal attractions of Mademoiselle Suzanne Curchod were embellished by the virtues and talents of the mind. Her fortune was humble but her family was respectable', he wrote, adding, 'In her short visits to some relations at Lausanne, the wit and beauty and the erudition of Mademoiselle Curchod were the theme of universal applause. The report of such a prodigy awakened my curiosity; I saw and loved.'

Suzanne's parents, who were anxious to see their beloved only child take her place on a wider stage than their village could offer, 'honourably encouraged a connection which might raise their daughter above want and dependence', Gibbon wrote after several visits to the vicarage. Suzanne herself, if not in love (Gibbon thought her beyond 'the gay vanity of youth') none the less 'listened to the voice of truth and passion'.[7]

But Edward Gibbon had reckoned without his father. In April 1758 he returned to England where 'the romantic hopes of youth and passion were crushed' by his father's refusal to countenance this marriage to a penniless foreigner, and threats to cut him off from his inheritance. Perhaps secretly relieved, for as he later admitted, he was not made for marriage, Gibbon wrote to Suzanne from the family house at Beriton. His distraught and self-dramatizing protestations must have sounded as hollow to her as they do now: 'I cannot begin! And yet I must. I take up my pen. I put it down, I take it up again. You perceive at once what I am going to say. Spare me the rest; yes I must give you up for ever.' In the face of his father's refusal, after wrestling with himself for all of two hours alone in his room, 'I went to tell my father that I would sacrifice all the happiness of my life to him.'[8]

Suzanne's reply points to a proud, highly strung, passionate nature, a considerable histrionic talent, and a manipulative and calculating head. Hurt, furious and anxious for her future, for Gibbon was by far the best matrimonial prize that had so far been presented to her, she had retained hopes that after his father's death he might yet change his mind: 'Am I to believe that I will never see you again? . . . I am not afraid to write to you, the state into which your letter has plunged me puts me beyond all care . . . you are the only man I have ever cried over, the only one whose loss has torn me apart with sobbing . . . I have never felt my solitude more bitterly and yet you have sacrificed me to duty with an exemplary firmness. Could I have lived with one to whom the sensitivity of my heart was a burden? . . . I had flattered myself that it would contribute to your happiness, it was that which was, I think, the reason for my attachment to you.' She had been prepared to abandon her own country for him. After several more pages in this vein, she begs him to burn her letter.[9]

Five years later, when Gibbon returned to Lausanne, he might well have considered the affair at an end. For him, as he put it, 'the remedies of absence and time were at length effectual'. Suzanne – still unmarried though not unsought – felt differently. No sooner had she heard of his arrival than she sent off a long letter. She believed, she wrote, that she 'owed it to my peace of mind to approach you. If I fail to take this chance there can be no possible peace for me; could I enjoy peace if my heart, ever ready to torture me, was convinced that your apparent coldness was merely proof of your delicacy? . . . Admit your complete indifference and my soul will resign itself to its fate; certainty will give me the tranquillity I long for.'[10]

Gibbon's answer must have dashed any further hopes she had of marriage, although certainty about his intentions failed to give her the promised tranquillity. Whatever his excuses of filial duty, the breaking off of an engagement was a serious matter, particularly in a small town like Lausanne. Gibbon had broken his word and Suzanne had no intention of letting him off lightly. 'Five years of separation could not work the change which has taken place in me. It might have been better if you had spoken earlier,' she writes, 'do not however grieve over my fate. My parents are dead – what is outward prosperity to me now?' She was thinking of going to England as a lady's companion, she wrote, or perhaps to one of the German courts: 'You could help me to a decision. I depend as much upon your judgement as your taste.'[11]

Suzanne's situation was indeed difficult. Her father had died in 1761, leaving his wife and daughter all but penniless. Her mother, with whom she had moved to Geneva, had died a few months before Gibbon's return in 1763 and with her loss had gone her tiny pension. Suzanne, who had been obliged to work to supplement it and keep them both, now had no funds at all. Fortunately, Pastor Moultou, a childhood friend and former admirer, took Suzanne in as governess to his children, becoming her friend and protector. It was he who introduced the clever young woman to Voltaire and Rousseau. A talented actress with a passion for theatre – both gifts she was to pass on to her daughter – Suzanne often took part in Voltaire's productions.

Suzanne and Gibbon were to meet several more times in Lausanne, where in spite of her poverty she went about in the best circles of society with a cheerful face, while writing long, anguished letters, full of recriminations, to Gibbon. Much admired for her wit and beauty, Mademoiselle Curchod's tendency to pedantry, her lack of spontaneity and warmth, was already being noticed. Gibbon noted in his diary that he believed her to be insincere, with a 'false, affected character', while the writer Charles-Victor de Bonstetten described her as 'tall, handsome, but rather affected'.[12]

In Geneva at that time lived Dr Théodore Tronchin, a highly respected doctor, famous throughout Europe, an early practitioner of inoculation, but also very popular with rich women suffering from various fashionable and unspecified ailments. It was now that Madame de Vermenoux, the charming widow pursued in Paris by Jacques Necker, decided to visit the eminent physician and happened to take lodgings in Geneva in the same house as Pastor Moultou. The good Pastor lost no time in introducing his young friend. In the spring of 1764, when the time came for Madame de Vermenoux to return to Paris, she asked Suzanne Curchod to accompany her as companion and governess to her young son.

Suzanne knew that for young women in her situation marriage was the only way out of genteel poverty. There was no shortage of suitors, indeed, a lawyer from Yverdon, a Monsieur Correvon, had recently proposed. While utterly disinclined to marry him, Suzanne kept him dangling in the hope that something more interesting might turn up and save her from a life of obscurity and boredom. Here was just such a chance – an opportunity to visit Paris, then the centre of the world and perhaps to escape from her sad fate. Encouraged by Moultou, Suzanne accepted. The Duchesse d'Enville, who, during one of her visits to her friend Voltaire in Geneva, had befriended Suzanne, wrote to Moultou from Paris: 'I am glad that Mademoiselle Curchod has found a position, but I doubt that she will be as happy here as in Geneva. Do simplify her before she arrives! She won't go far with her metaphysics or with her coiffure! For Heaven's sake simplify her!'[13] There was always something awkward and rigid about her: studied good manners but no warmth, a mixture of defensive pride and arrogance, an inability to be herself, a steely and calculating ambition, understandable in one with such a precarious social position, but hardly attractive.

Suzanne's first weeks in Paris were indeed difficult. Her stiff manners, her provincial clothes and her position as governess made life hard for the proud young woman. The necessary purchase of 'dresses, bonnets etc.' out of her tiny salary had left her very short of money. In a desperate and bitter letter to Moultou, she admitted that she might, after all, have to marry 'in spite of all my inclinations'. The company she found at Madame de Vermenoux's salon in the rue Neuve-Grange-Batelière, was a great disappointment too. 'We see no men of letters . . . our little circle is neither particularly brilliant nor intellectual,' she wrote to a friend. She remained with Madame de Vermenoux, however, began to acquire some town polish, was taught to curtsy properly, and took her mother's maiden name of de Nasse, which seemed to her grander and more appropriate to the society in which she now found herself. For all the petty humiliations of life as a governess, Suzanne had not been wrong in thinking she might do better. Her life was about to change spectacularly.

In July 1764, in one of her many letters to Moultou, Suzanne refers to a Monsieur Necker (who still courting Madame de Vermenoux) in approving tones: 'I am very pleased with Necker's intelligence and with his character.' She had already assessed his possibilities.[14] Rejected by Madame de Vermenoux, and his mind made up to marry, the rising young banker lost no time in turning his attention to the admiring and handsome young governess, who, like himself, was both Swiss and a Protestant. Suzanne, after her experiences with Gibbon, was wary of counting too much on the dazzling prospects now opening up before her. Later that summer, when the prudent Necker went to Geneva to check on her reputation and background, she obviously still feared that she might lose him. 'This is my plan,' she wrote to her confidant, Moultou: 'I will follow your advice exactly; although, but for a miracle, I despair of success. If our brilliant chimera evaporates, I shall marry Correvon next summer.'[15]

But on his return, Necker wrote, asking Suzanne for a meeting, leaving no doubt that he would propose marriage. She replied at once: 'And so I must write what I dared not say to you. If your happiness depends on my sentiments, I fear that you may have been happy before you desired it. I shall be at home all evening and my door will be closed [to other callers].'[16] It was done. At last Suzanne was able to inform the patient M. Correvon that she could not marry him.

Jacques Necker, who could not fail to be aware that his future wife was considered by one and all to be extremely lucky to have landed such a catch, wrote loftily to Moultou, the chief promoter of the match, to thank him for his good wishes: 'Yes Monsieur, your friend was kind enough to accept me and I consider myself to be as happy as a man can be. I cannot understand why it is you who is being congratulated, unless it is as my friend. Is money always to be what matters most? How pitiful! If one marries a virtuous, amiable and sensitive woman, has one not done well, whether or not one is sitting on sacks of money? Poor humans, what poor judges you are!'[17] Even at the early age of thirty Monsieur Necker was apt to see himself as a being apart.

Jacques Necker and Suzanne Curchod were married almost furtively, at midnight in the chapel of the Embassy of the Netherlands on 30 September 1764. Madame de Vermenoux, Suzanne's benefactress and the object of Jacques Necker's earlier affections, was not invited. A letter from the new Madame Necker was delivered to her the next day full of convoluted protestations of loyalty: 'A thousand pardons, Madame, for the slight trick I have played on you but my heart could not bear the prospect of the sorrow of parting with you. Had you been at the marriage ceremony you would have made me forget that I was being united to the one man dearest to me. I would have perceived what a separation that union was costing me . . . My illness decided M. Necker to put our marriage forward. I will call on you tomorrow if my health permits. Ah! What a friend I am leaving and how hard M. Necker will have to try to compensate me for such a loss.'[18]

Madame de Vermenoux might well have felt that her companion owed her a little more frankness, and there was undoubtedly some irritation at the thought that her erstwhile governess was now much richer and would soon be much grander than herself. She was clever enough, however, to pretend that it had all been her doing, dismissing the matter lightly by telling her friends that the Neckers would bore each other so much that it would be an occupation in itself for them. In spite of a certain edge in their relations, they remained friends. Jacques Necker took over the management of Madame de Vermenoux's finances, while she was invited to be godmother to the Necker's only child, named Germaine after her.

Suzanne Necker never got over her gratitude to her husband for saving her from a life of obscurity, a gratitude that grew into a passionate and demanding adoration. 'I am the wife of one I would take for an angel, if his liking for me did not betray his weakness,' she wrote to a friend, Madame de Brenles, soon after her marriage.[19] Jacques Necker, who did not number humility among his many virtues, had at last found someone who shared his own very high opinion of himself, a trait to which his new wife alludes playfully in a letter to her sister-in-law – which, she makes clear, Jacques Necker was reading over her shoulder. 'Imagine the most literal creature in the world, so happily convinced of his own superiority that he fails to notice mine; so convinced of his understanding that he is constantly caught out; so sure that he combines every talent to the highest degree, that he never deigns to look elsewhere for models. He never notices the insignificance of others because he so sure of his own greatness . . . I am hoping that the harmless medicine of reading this letter will cure him of this insufferable malady.'[20]

But in truth, Madame Necker had no wish to cure her husband. On the contrary, she would turn even his faults to his advantage. Her own vanity must have been constantly flattered by the thought that such a great man had chosen her. She was to become his chief publicist, ready to sacrifice her every wish and ambition to his glory, determined to subsume her own considerable talents to his, wishing to be everything to him, jealous of anyone who might have the slightest claim on him. Her depressive nature, which she passed on to her daughter and granddaughter, her abiding insecurity, her morbid fear of death and her wish to control everything around her even made her fear his possible remarriage in the event of her death. In time this jealousy would be turned on her daughter, but for the moment she longed for a child as a way of further attaching him. 'I've been married eight months and still no sign of pregnancy,' she wrote to a friend; 'this upsets me for I love my husband passionately, and if I die without children, I shall leave him a prey to greedy heirs, or to another . . . I cannot go on . . .'[21]

With no need to worry ever again about the cost of dresses, bonnets or anything else, Madame Necker now turned her attention to her new life in Paris. In spite of her husband's considerable fortune, the Neckers had no social connections. Life was not easy. While her intelligence, exceptional learning and love of intellectual pursuits made her anxious to take a leading role as a salon hostess, she was at first disappointed, considering most of those she met shallow and frivolous, though she was not unaware of the narrow provincialism of her own views. From the beginning of her married life in their apartment on the second floor of the Hôtel d'Hallwyl in the rue Michel Leconte in the Marais, adjoining the offices of the bank, young Madame Necker began to establish the rigid discipline which she maintained all her life, writing down her thoughts under a variety of headings, including a daily account of her activities in a special journal, so that she might check how she had spent her time at the end of each month. God Himself, was allocated twenty minutes in the morning and ten at night, 'so as not to importune Him excessively', while her husband, later her child, her household, the poor, her social life and her toilette were given so many hours a week or a day.[22]

Poor Madame Necker! For all her efforts, her intelligence and her good looks, for all Monsieur Necker's growing importance, her starchiness and his aloofness did not endear them as a couple to many. She was trying too hard. If, secretly, there were things she despised about the society she now found herself in, she passionately wanted to succeed in it. She set about her task with her customary thoroughness, as her niece remarked, 'she studied herself, she studied society, individuals, the art of writing, the art of conversation and of housekeeping'.[23] A friend mentioned that she might try to be a little more natural. Earnestly, she confided to her journal: 'Let us try therefore to let ourselves go a little more, this fault stems from inattention, from dealing with other things and not following the conversation properly, so that when I get back to the subject I say things which I've prepared, I lack that spontaneity which is a part of graceful manners and which no amount of finesse can remedy. I am not naturally graceful, but deliberately so.'[24]

In many ways she was most admirable as herself – the highly intelligent daughter of a Calvinist Pastor with solid values, one who consistently gave financial support to many of her poor relations and befriended several institutions – a self only ever unveiled to her few friends at home. Soon after her marriage she wrote to one: 'The only advantage of this country is in the forming of taste, but it is at the expense of genius; a phrase might be turned in a thousand ways, an idea looked at from every angle. If a metaphor is not exactly right, if an expression is not quite right, if a term is not precise, if the harmony is not perfect; then the beauty or greatness of the thought, the courage of the attempt to put it across counts for nothing . . . people will still say "this is in poor taste".'[25]

While deafness in one ear must have contributed to her troubles, she was never able to change her natural stiffness, or disguise her snobbery which came naturally to one so insecure. Many years later, when Necker was the most important man in France after the King, the Baroness d'Oberkirch, still found her pedantic and conceited beyond all bounds: 'When God created Madame Necker, he dipped her first, inside and out in a bucket of starch,' she wrote, adding that Madame Necker was, 'handsome but not agreeable, benevolent but not loved. Her body, her mind, her heart are deficient in grace. In a word, she knows neither how to weep or smile.'[26]

Whatever others thought of them, Suzanne and Jacques Necker's marriage turned out to be a source of infinite satisfaction and happiness to them both, setting an unattainable example of marital bliss to their only child, on whom, for good and ill, they both exercised a major and lifelong influence: 'She had needed that unique being, she found him and spent her life with him.'[27] Madame de Staël wrote of her mother.

Chapter 2

~

Minette

> 'It would seem that Madame de Staël has always been young, but never a child.'[1]
>
> Madame Necker-de Saussure

MADAME NECKER'S FEARS had proved groundless. The longed-for child, a daughter, born on 22 April 1766, was christened Anne Louise Germaine in the embassy chapel of the United Provinces, in the presence of the Dutch Ambassador, M. Lestevenon de Berkenroodee,[2] five days after her birth. Her godparents, after whom she was named, were her paternal uncle, Louis Necker, who was absent, and her mother's former employer, Madame Anne Germaine Larrivée de Vermenoux.

Madame Necker had longed for a child, but the horror of giving birth made an indelible impression on her and, for whatever reason, she never repeated the experience. 'I must confess that my terrified imagination fell far short of the truth,' she wrote to a friend soon after her daughter's birth. 'For three days and two nights, I suffered the tortures of the damned. Death was ever at my bedside, assisted by people far more terrible than the Furies, specially designed to repel all modesty and revolt nature. The very word '*accoucheur*' still makes me shudder! I would have expired in their infernal talons, had it not been necessary to send them away, for the harm they were doing me, and call a midwife . . . Such care had been taken to hide the revolting details of childbirth from me that I was as surprised as I was horrified. I can't help reflecting that the vows most women make are foolhardy. I doubt they would willingly go to the altar to swear their readiness to be broken on the wheel every nine months.'[3]

As a disciple of Rousseau, whose book *Émile*, published in 1762, had set a fashion for bringing up children in a natural way, beginning with maternal breast-feeding, Madame Necker resolved to breast-feed her baby herself. She should have heeded Dr Tronchin's wise advice 'that breast-feeding should be like fasting during Lent – obligatory only for those who can bear it'.[4] Three months later a starving baby and her own exhaustion convinced her to give up the Rousseauist ideal. The baby, nicknamed Minette, was handed over to a big Flemish wet-nurse with an inexhaustible supply of milk – 'very pretty and a great chatterbox' – and soon thrived under the watchful eye of her mother.[5]

When the child was just over two, Madame Necker sent to her friend Madame Reverdil, in Switzerland for a Bible and books of piety. 'Having given some thought to the education of my dear little one, I realized that I could undertake it myself. Nurses are always a problem. If they are any good they come between the love of the child for its mother; what I would like is a simple housemaid; a Protestant, sweet-natured, flexible and well mannered, who can read perfectly and has been well schooled in her religion.'[6] The question of religion was to continue to worry Madame Necker for the next few years; she was much afraid of Catholic influence on her daughter.

Emerging from babyhood, Minette charmed all around her, as she was to do for the rest of her life. Her great expressive, dark eyes, shining with intelligence and goodness, her one truly beautiful feature, struck all those who saw her. Her childish prattle was encouraged by her father, though not by her mother.

In the year after Minette's birth, the Neckers, no doubt now cramped in their Marais apartment, moved to 27 rue de Cléry. This much grander house boasted a splendid façade with a rotunda and a beautiful wrought iron staircase which led to the salons on the first floor, whose ceilings were decorated with mythological subjects and the walls covered with medallions and arabesques.[7] In the following year, 1768, Necker took the first steps in his political career, when he was asked by the Council of Geneva to represent the Republic at the French court as minister: a post he accepted, taking no salary. He also gave up his position at the bank to his brother, at least nominally, to avoid any conflict of interest. The post proved to be no sinecure, his fellow citizens being a demanding lot, but it did bring Necker into close contact with the King, Louis XV. It also enabled him to establish close links with the powerful chief minister, Choiseul, not least because the Vernet bank was giving interest-free credit to the royal treasury. Necker must have impressed him because in the following year he was appointed to the directorship of the French East India Company, the *Compagnie des Indes*.

Madame Necker, with a splendid house, a great deal of money and a husband whose power and influence was growing apace, was now keener than ever to enlarge her small gatherings of intellectuals into a proper salon. Her reasons were neither frivolous – frivolity was not in her nature – nor snobbish, though snob she was, but eminently practical. Her prime objective then and to the end of her days was to promote and glorify her husband, whom she believed in as a being apart. In this, if in nothing else, she would remain entirely at one with her daughter.

The Paris salon exercised an enormous influence on French thought and culture throughout the eighteenth century. In the early 1700s the salons refined and preserved the aristocratic ideals of the previous century, the *Grand Siècle*; those of *bon ton*, or good taste, cultivating the French *esprit*, and deliberately preserving a dilettante attitude to literature, politics and philosophy. Conversation was cultivated; wit and brilliance were considered as important as wisdom and knowledge; and formal manners were imposed and practised, but without the stultifying boredom and rigid protocol of the court. Conversation apart, those attending were also expected to practise the arts, compose, perform and generally excel in poetry, music and dancing. Salon life was highly competitive. The literary power of the salons was enormous at a time when the press was scarcely in existence. By the middle of the century it was the salons rather than the court – by then quite out of touch – which were the focus and seed beds of public opinion. Far from being mere social gatherings, they had become the think tanks and the social melting pots of the time, where middle-class intellectuals, self-made men and self-educated writers and philosophers mingled with the aristocracy. Here, established aristocratic power met new ideas, cross-fertilizing and revitalizing society. By educating the aristocracy, they opened their minds to new ideas, undermined their self-confidence and their belief in the established order, paving the way for change.

Following the appearance of Voltaire's *Lettres philosophiques* in 1734, in which the author popularized Newtonian mathematics, the publication of major works by some of the thinkers who came to be known as the *philosophes* expressed revolutionary new ideas on religion, science, society and history. By the end of the 1750s, however, with the publication of the seventh volume of the *Encyclopaedia*,[8] attitudes towards the Enlightenment began to harden.

The end of the Seven Years War, marked by the Treaty of Paris in 1763, left France defeated and humiliated, with most of her colonial possessions lost to England. The *philosophes*' admiration for English institutions and English liberty made the monarchy wary of a movement which might at any moment question the legitimacy of absolute power, while the humanistic philosophy they preached encouraged social awareness and questioned the justice of war and colonialism and other social ills, such as the slave trade and the harsh penal system. While the *philosophes* did not attack religion directly, they did attack superstition, encouraged scepticism and promoted science and technology. From the outset the Church had recognized them as a formidable foe and now denounced the *Encyclopaedia* from the pulpits as the work of atheists who sought to destroy the very foundations of faith. The *Encyclopaedia* was banned, but Diderot decided to publish the remaining ten volumes in one edition and although he ran into difficulties in France, its influence had already spread far and wide in Europe. From the outset, the salons had acted as the incubators and the propagators of these new ideas.

It was no wonder that the ambitious young Madame Necker aspired to having her own salon for they gave extraordinary power to intelligent women, who, while they were treated with formal gallantry, were the undisputed mistresses of their establishments, choosing or wooing the most important literary lions, establishing the rules of the game, competing with one another. The Duchesse de Choiseul, and even more the Maréchale de Luxembourg, set the tone of polite behaviour and social manners in their salons. But the two greatest *salonières* of the eighteenth century, and bitter rivals, were Madame du Deffand and Madame Geoffrin.

Madame du Deffand, once the Regent's mistress but now old and blind, ruled over her intellectual empire from her yellow salon in the Saint-Joseph convent in the rue Saint-Dominique. Encased in her famous *tonneau*, a high-backed curved chair, with her nasty little dog Tonton snapping at all comers, she entertained d'Alembert and Montesquieu, Hume, Gibbon, Gray, Chesterfield and, most famously, Horace Walpole. A curious and touching love grew between the old hostess and the strange Epicurean of Strawberry Hill, twenty years her junior. Madame du Deffand's salon definitely belonged to the old aristocratic world, although her acute intelligence, terror of boredom, great admiration for the English and a lifelong friendship and correspondence with Voltaire, made inevitable the company of some of the *philosophes*. She loved and admired Voltaire the writer, but clashed with Voltaire the political thinker and polemicist. He gave as good as he got. 'It is not enough to hate bad taste, you must detest hypocrites and oppressors,' he wrote to her sternly in 1769.

Her great rival, Madame Geoffrin, though of humble origins and almost uneducated, reigned over her salon in the rue St Honoré, where, with the help of her natural good taste, her famous chef and her elderly husband's money, she received artists such as Latour, Vernet, Chardin and Van Loo at her Monday dinners and all the Encyclopaedists at her 'Wednesdays'.[9] She was a famous scold with a bossy nature and strong character, yet eminent foreigners, such as Benjamin Franklin and David Hume, who was a constant guest, crowded to Madame Geoffrin's salon as – more surprisingly since she had never been presented at court – did visiting royals, among them King Gustav III of Sweden and the Emperor Joseph II of Austria. She corresponded with the Empress Catherine of Russia and with Empress Maria Theresa of Austria and travelled to Poland to visit her protégé Stanislaus Augustus, son of her friend Stanislaus Poniatowski, after the former had been imposed on Poland as King Stanislaus II by Catherine the Great of Russia.

If Necker did not enjoy salon life himself, he was perfectly happy to encourage his wife's ambitions. He was well aware of the importance of the salons, describing them as 'the invisible power which, without finances, without troops, without an army, imposes its laws upon the town, on the Court and even on the King himself'. The appearances of the short, stocky and rather pompous Necker were usually brief. He would sit in silence, benevolent and self-important – a man apart. If Madame Necker confided, with some irritation, in her journal that her husband neither talked nor listened but sat there sucking his thumbs, to her guests she would always laughingly pass off his silences as the lofty preoccupation of a genius.

Ever anxious to do the right thing, Madame Necker took advice from her friends before choosing her 'evening'. Madame Geoffrin's

Mondays and Wednesdays, Holbach's Thursdays and Sundays and Helvétius's Tuesdays, left her no choice but to hold her salon on Fridays when she entertained the *philosophes*. Another day was set aside for more relaxed entertaining.

And so, richly dressed in the pale satins so suited to her colouring, Madame Necker at last presided over her salon. Her first Friday, at which she made sure to serve fish for those who wished to fast, was attended by the Abbé Morellet, Suard and Marmontel, but the little group soon grew to include most of the *philosophes* as well as influential financiers, politicians, foreign visitors of note and members of the aristocracy.

'There is here one Madame Necker, a pretty woman and a wit, who is mad for me. She has been positively persecuting me to have me at her house. She is a penniless *Genevoise*, whom the banker, Necker, has set up in great style', Diderot wrote to his mistress, Sophie Volland.[10] None the less, together with Grimm[11] and d'Alembert he too was to become one of the habitués of Madame Necker's salon. By 1770, according to Grimm, seventeen venerable philosophers had gathered at Madame Necker's where they had decided unanimously to erect a statue to Voltaire. As the moving spirit behind the idea, Madame Necker was elected secretary to the subscriptions committee, a task she carried out with her customary thoroughness. The result, a statue by Pigalle, led to a prolonged correspondence with Voltaire, which lent enormous lustre to her salon, as Madame Necker well knew it would.

It might seem strange, in the light of Madame Necker's religious concerns, that she should have been prepared to receive Catholic abbots and declared atheists such as Diderot, Holbach and Helvétius, but in spite of her fervent Calvinism and sincere faith, she believed no less sincerely in toleration. She also worshipped talent, two traits she passed on strongly to her daughter. When reproached for harbouring atheists in her salon, Madame Necker once replied: 'I do have atheist friends. Why not? They are my unhappy friends.'[12] Madame Necker's salon never achieved the importance of those of Madame du Deffand or Madame Geoffrin, which perhaps explains why her relations with them were on the whole very cordial, though she was often scolded by Madame Geoffrin: 'Do you know my very dear lady, that your excessive compliments puzzle rather than touch or flatter me,' she wrote severely in response to a fulsome note from Madame Necker.

But she continued to lend her anxious young friend her invaluable support, while stuffing young Minette with sweets.

Far from following Rousseau's precepts in *Émile* that a child should be brought up in the country, with plenty of fresh air, and left uneducated until the age of twelve so as to affect his nature as little as possible, Madame Necker believed that young heads should be stuffed with ideas and that intelligence would lapse into laziness if not constantly stimulated and stretched. She therefore force-fed her daughter's mind from the age of two. Fortunately the child was exceptionally clever. Mathematics and geography, science and languages, as well as theology and religion were taught by her mother; dance, acting and declamation by the celebrated actress Mademoiselle Clairon, whose fate was to be strangely linked to the future Madame de Staël. Minette was regularly taken to the Comédie, sharing her mother's lifelong passion for the theatre both as an actress and a spectator. As a child she would make kings and queens and other characters out of paper and have them perform plays, a pastime which Madame Necker discouraged. Although her mother's strict, dutiful and unbending nature cramped the child's spirit and left her longing for affection, making for a difficult future relationship between mother and daughter, Madame de Staël seems later to have endorsed her mother's views on education, educating her own children herself and writing years later in *De l'Allemagne*: 'A child, who, according to Rousseau's theories, has learnt nothing until the age of twelve would have lost six precious years of its life. The brain can never acquire the flexibility which exercising it from earliest childhood alone gives it.'[13]

Beside the supervision of her daughter's education, Madame Necker continued to pour much of her energy, her ambition and perhaps some of her own frustration into promoting her husband's inexorable rise. Necker, who was increasingly occupied with official duties, did not hesitate to leave all the management of their affairs in his wife's capable hands. To a friend she confessed that since her husband's departure from the bank, she had 'bought, sold, confirmed, built, and disposed of everything as I saw fit', almost not daring to talk to him about their financial affairs, since 'at the first word about them he would show either bad humour or signs of the most profound boredom'.[14]

Nevertheless she minded his absences, and was jealous of whatever took him away from her, longing for perfect, exclusive love. Passionate, insecure and touchy she longed for his constant attention and made, as she herself recognized, endless demands. Writing in her journal, she confessed: 'He is bored with me. Instead of complaining to him let me try to amuse him. He does not think of what might please me, never mind, work on my own happiness and try and do for him what he fails to do for me. He is cross with me; let me ignore it and try to soften his mood. He wants things which I dislike, let me give in . . . His imagination easily wounds me, he sees faults in me which I do not have . . . let me see myself as a being who expects happiness only from God: let me do everything that is honest for my husband, without asking for anything in return.'[15] Indeed she wrote constantly: letters, diaries, reflections, imprecations to herself, passionate prayers to the Almighty. She had also embarked on a eulogy to the famous prelate, Fénelon. Most probably this was an escape for a talented and intelligent woman or perhaps she sometimes wished to punish Necker for a lack of attention; at any rate he saw her writing as a direct threat to his own comfort. Later, when Necker became equally determined to discourage his daughter from writing, he explained his reason, as Madame de Staël recalled. 'Imagine my anxiety', he would often tell me. 'I dared not enter her room for fear of tearing her away from an occupation which was more agreeable to her than my presence. I could see her following some train of thought while I held her in my arms.'[16] Perhaps he also wished her to be a little less self-analytical. In any case, he begged her to give up this pastime so ill suited to women, as he saw it. Though they lived in the same house and were never parted, Madame Necker naturally replied in writing. She would prefer to live and breathe through him: 'you or nothing is my motto on earth' she cried, explaining that her writing was nothing more than the remnants of a former habit which helped to fill the emptiness caused by his absence. But there was a catch! 'As soon as you give up the direction of the *Compagnie des Indes*, I will give up Fénelon if you demand it. I would not wish you to make a sacrifice greater than the one you ask of me.' But she ended, 'I have no soul other than yours. I must love you or die.'[17] That, M. Necker must have thought, was much more like it.

In 1770, having previously rented the Château de Madrid for a country retreat, the Neckers bought a lovely country house at Saint-Ouen, on the banks of the Seine. Madame Necker's Paris salon would move here in the summer, their discussions continuing on the terraces shaded by old trees which overlooked the river. For those who did not wish to stay, it was near enough to Paris to permit visitors to return home at night. It was here that Madame Necker at last made the acquaintance of Madame du Deffand: 'I am going to a supper tomorrow, where I would gladly send someone in my place,' wrote Madame du Deffand to Horace Walpole. 'It is to Saint-Ouen to M. & Mme Necker. They wish to know me because I have the reputation of a wit who does not like wits. They think this a rarity worthy of their curiosity. I was stupid enough to agree to this meeting. When I ask myself why, I blush to discover that it is out of fear of boredom, and that often I am as idiotic as Gribouille, [her dog] who throws himself in the water because he is afraid of rain.'[18] In spite of her well-known dislike of people outside her world, Madame du Deffand gave Madame Necker a grudging sort of approval: she was neither silly nor insipid, and more fitted to society than many great ladies, she wrote to the Duchesse de Choiseul.

In 1773 Necker published his *Éloge de Colbert*, in praise of Louis XIV's reforming minister. Necker used the study of Colbert as an opportunity to air his own views, denouncing slavery and the injustice of the *corvée*,[19] and setting out a veritable treatise on public administration for which he won general plaudits and the approval of Voltaire, as well as the French Academy's first prize. Two years later he published his *Traité sur la législation et le commerce des grains*, an important economic treatise on the laws governing trade in cereals, then of utmost importance, in which, although himself a man of property, a lover of order, and indeed a recent speculator in grain, he expressed almost revolutionary views on property, as well as a startling new view of society. His thesis was that the social order had changed. It was no longer made up of the three orders of nobility, clergy and the Third Estate, but of property owners and wage earners. Speaking out against the injustice of property laws, he wrote: 'Having created laws governing property, justice and liberty, we have done almost nothing for the class which represents the majority of our citizens. "What do we care for your property laws?" they might say, "we own nothing." "Your laws on justice?" "We have nothing to defend." "Your laws on liberty?" "If we have no work tomorrow, we die".'[20] His proposed remedy, however, was not revolution but an enlightened monarchy. As for cereals, Necker was against the free circulation or the export of grain precisely so that the government should have the necessary reserves available in times of shortage.

The Enlightenment had made the pressure for practical reforms impossible to ignore. The physiocratic school of thought, founded by Quesnay, the royal physician, had greatly influenced ideas in the second half of the eighteenth century. Its basic tenet was that land was the source of all wealth, that all land, therefore, regardless of whom it belonged to, should be taxed. Needless to say, this pleased neither the nobility, the Church nor the newly landed bourgeoisie, who were largely exempt from such taxes. The physiocrats, however, were against all trade barriers, believing that customs barriers were injurious to the nation's wealth. They too wished the reforms to be carried out by the King.

Louis XV died in 1774. Determined to be a new broom, his successor, Louis XVI, had appointed Turgot Controller General of Finance. Turgot, very much of the physiocratic school of thought, believed in a reformed absolutism. He had attempted to bring order into government finances which had been greatly destabilized by the Seven Years War. He introduced taxes that removed some of the fiscal advantages from the nobility. He believed in restoring free trade, at least inside France. The harvest of 1774 had been particularly bad. Wheat shortages had been followed by bread riots, which were blamed on him – the very riots which had supposedly provoked Marie-Antoinette's famous suggestion: 'Let them eat cake'. Turgot believed that Necker, whose treatise on grain contradicted his own views on free trade, was plotting against him and wrote to tell him so. Necker replied that he believed in free trade too, but that in periods of crisis the government had a responsibility to ensure supplies.

In April 1776, the Neckers and their ten-year-old daughter left for a visit to England, perhaps wishing to avoid any blame for Turgot's downfall, which Necker believed to be inevitable. In May 1776, while they were abroad, Turgot indeed fell and was replaced by the ineffectual Ogier de Clugny. A fortnight after his appointment, the King confided, 'I think we have once again made a mistake.' When Clugny died suddenly in October, Maurepas, the King's elderly chief minister, suggested Necker as a replacement. Well known to the court, with a justified reputation as a serious thinker and a successful businessman, trusted by the bankers and financiers, Necker proved an ideal choice. As 'Director of the Royal Treasury', he was now de facto Controller General, but Taboureau des Réaux was given the nominal position of Controller General since it was still impossible for a Protestant, a bourgeois, and a foreigner to become a minister. A letter from Grimm, then in Russia, to Madame Necker shows that even the great Catherine approved: 'The Empress, Madame, has just informed me of the choice of M. Necker for the administration of one of the most important branches of finance, made by the King. As she has been involved for some time in this business, and says that she has admired M. Necker's talents long since, she has on this occasion heaped praise on a young King who is wise enough to make such a choice.'[21]

The Neckers loved England. Jacques had friends in the City and they had many introductions and recommendations from Lord Stormont, British Ambassador to France. Necker's admiration for England's political liberties and institutions marked his daughter profoundly and for life. Gibbon, newly famous as the author of the *The History of the Decline and Fall of the Roman Empire*, the first volume of which had just been published, and now fully reconciled with his former fiancée, often entertained them at his 'hovel' in Suffolk Street, or accompanied them to the Houses of Parliament, where the ten-year-old Minette saw the King, George III. Noticing how much her parents enjoyed Gibbon's conversation, Minette offered to marry him, so that they should never be deprived of it![22]

Madame Necker had taken her daughter to see David Garrick at the theatre eleven times. They had also visited Walpole at Strawberry Hill, to whom they had been gruffly recommended by Madame du Deffand. 'I will be obliged to you for your attentions towards them. They are decent people. The husband is very intelligent and straightforward, the wife is stiff and cold and full of self-importance, but an honest person,' she wrote.[23]

The Neckers returned from England to stay only briefly at the new house they had built in the Chaussée d'Antin, before moving, after the resignation of Taboureau des Réaux in June 1777, into the residence of the Controller General, where Necker was officially appointed Director General of Finance.

Minette's father was now the most powerful man in France after the King. Gibbon, who visited Paris between May and November 1777, gratified 'by the pressing invitation of M. & Mme Necker', found them 'in the first bloom of power and popularity. His private fortune enabled him to support a liberal establishment and his wife, whose talents and virtues I had long admired, was admirably qualified to preside in the conversation of her table and drawing-room. As their friend I was introduced to the best company of both sexes; to the foreign ministers of both nations; and to the first names and characters of France, who distinguished me by such marks of civility and kindness as gratitude will not suffer me to forget and modesty will not allow me to enumerate. The fashionable suppers often broke into the morning hours.'[24] Madame Necker was equally gratified to have the now famous Gibbon at her feet, especially after the way he had treated her, as she admitted to a friend.

Left occasionally at Saint-Ouen with her governess when her parents were busy, from an early age Minette had a horror of being alone. Her letters to her mother, written when she was twelve, show a lifelong tendency to self-dramatization but also a deep longing for affection. 'My dearest mama, I need to write to you; my heart is heavy; I am sad, and this huge house which until very recently contained everything dear to me, my whole universe and my future, now seems a desert. I saw that this great space was too big for me, and I ran to my little room to try and contain the void that surrounds me.' In another letter she expressed her longing for her mother's return and begged her to come back soon. Her mother's replies, while affectionate, were always preachy: 'I was hoping to be able to come and see you today my dear child, but as I know that you care about my health, you would not wish me to go out when the air is so unhealthy; I am therefore obliged to stay in for three days . . . Do not exaggerate so when you wish to praise me or caress me. It shows a want of taste not uncommon at your age. When one is older one realizes that to really please and interest people, one must describe one's thoughts exactly, without affectation or display. Your letter to your father,' she ends, 'was simple and good.'[25]

Her father adored her and would frequently escape from the burdens of office to see her, revelling in her unconditional affection, entertained by her childish ways, proud of her quick mind. She quickly realized that he needed her to distract him. However happy their marriage, Madame Necker was not easy to live with. Frequently subject to nervous prostration, inevitably right about everything, her possessiveness and perfectionism must have been a burden. She undoubtedly exacted a price for subsuming her own talents and her will. Many years later, after her death, Necker admitted that the only thing Madame Necker lacked in order to be considered perfectly amiable was occasionally to have done something which might require forgiveness.[26] Minette's amazing intellectual faculties and the praise heaped on her by all around them was a constant source of pride to him, but it was their shared sense of humour and fun which gave him such joy. 'Let's go and see Minette!' became a frequent cry when the cares of office weighed on him. On one unforgettable occasion, vividly recalled by Catherine Huber, the daughter of Madame Necker's childhood friend, Madame Necker, having left the room for a moment, returned to the dining room to find her husband and daughter, their napkins tied into turbans on their heads, dancing around the table and shouting with laughter. Their merriment died quickly at the sight of her shocked expression, and both returned meekly to their places. In many ways Madame Necker remained the stern Swiss governess.

Minette made endless efforts to please her mother, but her standards were so impossibly high that even a child for whom learning presented no difficulties could write falteringly: 'I am resolved but with difficulty to write to you. If I felt worthy of you, worthy of your teaching, I would be thrilled to pay you the tribute of my progress and I would thank you daily; but when I can only offer you the shame and confusion of constantly falling into the same errors, my pen falls from my hand, and I am discouraged and sad.'[27] Her mother's arid recommendation was to 'tell me that you are fond of me and prove it by perfecting your heart and your mind, by constantly sacrificing yourself and lifting up your soul through religion'.[28]

Voltaire arrived in Paris on 14 February 1778, to be mobbed and acclaimed wherever he went. The Swiss writer, Henri Meister, writing to Paul Moultou, Madame Necker's old and faithful friend, compared it to the second coming.[29] In April of that year Madame Necker took her daughter to visit the celebrated eighty-year-old, who was to die at the end of May. Little over a month later, on 2 July, Jean-Jacques Rousseau, too, was dead.

Her husband's new position only increased Madame Necker's wish to produce a perfect being in her daughter, whom she thought of as her possession and who she hoped would be her masterpiece. From a very early age Minette was allowed to attend her mother's salon. Catherine Huber, a Swiss Protestant, was the only friend Madame Necker allowed her daughter – 'here is a friend I am giving you' is how she had introduced Catherine – and Minette had been thrilled and grateful. In a vivid pen-portrait of the young Minette, then only eleven years old, we see her surrounded by the cream of the Enlightenment. 'We slid behind our mothers' armchairs. Next to Madame Necker's chair there was a small wooden footstool, where her daughter always sat, obliged to keep her back straight. No sooner had she taken her place than five or six gentlemen came up to her and addressed her with the greatest interest. One, who wore a small round wig, took her hands in his and held them for a long time while he conversed with her as if she were twenty-five. It was the abbé Raynal, the others were Thomas, Marmontel and de Pezay. Mlle Necker was most anxious to present me to her friends, who from then on were mine too . . . During dinner it may be imagined that we said nothing. We listened, but how Mlle Necker listened! Her eyes followed the movements of those who were speaking and seemed to anticipate their thoughts . . . She was aware of everything, caught everything, understood everything, even political subjects which in those days were already a major subject of conversation . . . Each person who greeted Madame Necker had a word for her daughter, a compliment or a joke . . . she answered them all with ease and grace; they liked to attack her, to embarrass her, to excite her young imagination which was already showing such brilliance. The most notable wits were the ones trying hardest to make her speak.'[30]

Not everyone approved. Madame de Genlis[31] wrote witheringly that Madame Necker had brought up her daughter very badly in allowing her to spend three quarters of her time surrounded by the wits of the day, who would cluster around Mademoiselle Necker discussing such things as love and the passions while her mother was busy with others, especially the ladies who called on her. She would have done better with the solitude of her room and a few good books.[32]

But before long the relentless pressure of Madame Necker's rigid system of education on top of her own approaching adolescence began to tell on the girl. Early in 1778 she suffered a kind of manic-depressive breakdown during which periods of inertia were followed by over-elation. Called in by her anxious parents, Dr Tronchin at once prescribed rest in the country, no mental effort, as much freedom as possible and the company of friends of her own age. Every Friday

Catherine Huber would be taken to see her at Saint-Ouen, to be greeted ecstatically by her friend. Even in play, Minette's interests were intellectual. Poetry, and the writing and performing of plays, were her chief pleasures. Like her mother she disliked the country. She hated walks of any sort and could not tell one flower from another. Instead the two friends, dressed as nymphs or muses after a ballet of a play they had just seen, would practise archery in the park. Catherine recalled one occasion which perfectly illustrates Minette's state of mind, as well as her mother's over protectiveness: 'I can never forget her intense joy when . . . my mother during a visit to Madame Necker, suggested that she might take her daughter and me for an evening ride in her carriage in the Bois de Boulogne. Madame Necker to whom no one had ever dared to make such a suggestion was astonished . . . Madame Necker struggled with herself in silence while her poor child, trembling and faint with expectation, waited for her mother's decision. Finally amid general silence the great concession was made . . . Her mother made every possible recommendation to mine: on the doors of her carriage, on how to descend from it, on the horses and carriages which one might meet in the Bois de Boulogne, assuring us that her daughter's extremely excitable nature required all these precautions, and that it would be the first time that she was going out without her. There is no doubt that this outing, a taste of freedom, was a milestone in Mademoiselle Necker's childhood; but as she took nothing lightly, the very idea of going out alone with me and my mother had gone to her head so much that she had been quite unable to eat and was in a sort of fever when we arrived . . . Her heart beat almost visibly as she climbed into the carriage; she could hardly speak so great was her emotion; she could only repeatedly kiss my mother's hands and throw herself on her neck. She calmed down after a while, but looked at neither the road nor the park, nor the other carriages, nor at the people promenading; she could only see her own happiness and was entirely occupied with it.'[33]

Madame Necker took her daughter's breakdown as a personal affront. Minette's removal from her total control marked a rift between them that was never to be bridged. Worse even than the manifest failure of her pedagogical dreams, her husband seemed to be growing ever closer to his daughter, sometimes openly siding with her. Distraught, disappointed and increasingly jealous, Madame Necker addressed one of her long missives to him, full of subtle digs:

Your reproaches, my dear friend, have obliged me to look into myself seriously and since I know that you are not indifferent to my happiness, I beg you to give a moment of your time to this letter, and to read it to the end. My pride has never allowed me to solicit a single hour of your time, even if your will and my heart have made you the centre and the chief focus of my ambition, so I insist today that you comply; this is a matter of the utmost importance to me.

It was perfectly clear from what you said that you disapprove of my feelings and my behaviour towards your daughter; and that you did not think them truly virtuous or worthy of my principles. If you would enlighten my conscience, you need do no more than dictate what I should do. I hope I can even get over your attack (was it really necessary to humiliate me in front of her; to enforce) . . . If in my earliest years when my passions were alive I never resisted the idea of duty or virtue for a single instant, I am unlikely to begin to behave differently now that I am close to the end of my days, when the few remaining years of life left to me will remain empty.

I had to make serious efforts to enable my frail body to breastfeed, and I will suppress the details which required all the courage of maternal tenderness, painful trials of which I still bear the marks, and which went on for the four months of painful feeding, but all my sufferings were rewarded by maternal instinct. I will always remember those moments full of charm, when the child to whom we gave life was brought to my bed, when her blue eyes seemed to turn to me and with a colour as pure as the heavens, assured me of the happiness which I could expect. I will quickly enumerate the continuous care which I gave my daughter, wet nurse changed, weaning, inoculations, diet, continuous attention day and night; her height, her teeth, her hair, all her parts were looked after, trained or perfected: her health is the proof of it. Delightful memories, delightful and cruel, more cruel at present than the agonies of childbirth. For thirteen years, I never lost sight of her. I cultivated her memory and her mind. For thirteen of the best years of my life, in the midst of many other essential preoccupations, I hardly lost sight of her. I taught her languages, especially to speak her own easily; I cultivated her memory and her mind with the best books. I used to take her alone with me on journeys to Versailles and Fontainebleau; I would walk with her, read with her, pray with her. Her health suffered; my anguish, my solicitude, gave new zeal to her doctor. I cultivated, I ceaselessly embellished all the gifts she had received from nature, believing that it was for the good of her soul, and my own self was subsumed in hers.[34]

Although Madame Necker does not scruple to employ all her manipulative talents, to blackmail her husband and her daughter emotionally, she also inspires pity. To her rigid mind and troubled spirit anything less than total capitulation seemed like disloyalty and ingratitude. The slightest disagreement was a personal affront and a rejection. Longing for perfect love, yet incapable of giving it, she was also unable to understand her daughter's growing need for a life of her own, and unwilling to recognize her right to be herself rather than a copy of her mother. While Germaine had inherited much from Madame Necker – her passionate and highly strung nature, a love of grandeur, beauty and talent, strong intellectual tastes – she was also in crucial ways her polar opposite. Warm, generous, vivacious, spontaneous, effortlessly brilliant yet never pedantic, although she quite lacked her mother's beauty, she attracted all who saw her. Madame Necker might have been better able to accept all this if it had not become more and more obvious that her beloved husband was turning increasingly to his daughter, and that he loved her precisely for the qualities so markedly absent in his wife. It was the beginning of a contest to the death between them for Necker's love.

'Having understood her character,' she wrote to a friend bitterly, 'I realize that to live with her without making myself unhappy, I must forget absolutely that she should be contributing to my happiness; therefore I must demand nothing of her, even tolerate a great deal, correct her only by example; and if she has offended me too much, that my reproaches to her should be without exaggeration and so sweet and reasonable that I might make them in front of her father. I must close my eyes to all the contradictions that she makes me feel; and to think that unity between us makes her father happy, and accept that I alone must pay the price.'[35]

Madame de Staël's sweetness of nature, wrote her cousin much later, was never clearer than in her attitude towards her mother, about whom she never allowed a bad word to be spoken. Even when young, to a chance remark that her father seemed to love her more than her mother, she quickly replied: 'My father thinks more of my present, my mother of my future happiness.'[36]

Taciturn and constrained with others, Necker allowed his natural sense of fun full rein with his daughter. Their relationship was more that of friends than of parent and child, which perhaps explains the tenderness of their feelings for one another, wrote Catherine Huber. Albertine Necker-de Saussure, who was to marry Necker's nephew, and who became Madame de Staël's closest friend as well as her first biographer, noticed how alike father and daughter were, writing after Madame de Staël's death: 'He had the same luminous insights, the same penetrating eye, the same fine capacity for observation and the same gaiety founded on melancholy. He struggled against a strong imagination, and had a warmth of soul, a sensitivity which was all the more touching. Nothing was more moving than his demonstrations of affection. His rather reserved expression, his inevitably lively but gentle look, went straight to the heart.'[37] Although often strict with Minette, he would correct her fondly, by teasing her. 'I owe the frankness of my character and the naturalness of my mind to my father's incredibly penetrating understanding. He would see through all affectation, and I got used to believing that one could see clearly into my heart,' she told her cousin.[38]

Minette had been writing since early adolescence. In 1778 her play, *Les inconvénients de la vie à Paris*, had reduced Marmontel to tears when it was performed to a small group of friends and family at Saint-Ouen. Her father frowned on this, nicknaming her Monsieur de Saint-Écritoire, or Mr Holy Desk. The use of 'monsieur' was an early indication that writing was considered unfeminine, a charge levelled at her not only in her own lifetime but for a long time afterwards. Necker, who in his youth had been prevented from fulfilling literary ambitions, must have understood the problems of literary frustration, but clearly felt her writing to be as challenging to his comfort as Madame Necker's. Germaine, always anxious to please her papa, wrote earnestly and penetratingly: 'My father is right. Women are not made to follow the same career as men! To struggle against them is to excite in them feelings of jealousy, so different from those inspired by love. A woman must have nothing of her own, and find all her pleasures in the one she loves.'[39] Fortunately, one of the greatest women writers of her time would not be able to deny her own exceptional talents for long, even to please her beloved father, any more than she would be able to deny her nature, which would undoubtedly have pleased her mother.

Chapter 3

~

Monsieur Necker's Daughter

'Ah! I have a different destiny. I am the daughter of M. Necker.'
Germaine Necker in her journal.

SURROUNDED FROM HER earliest years by an intellectual elite that treated her father with reverent awe, an attitude that was promoted and amplified in Madame Necker's salon, and aware that in the atmosphere of impending war (that France would soon join on the side of the new United States) the entire country looked to him for its security, Minette readily and willingly believed him to be a superior being. In France, Necker was more than ever considered not only a financial genius, but as the national saviour. Minette not only loved him tenderly, but worshipped him as a hero, and her emotional dependence on him was to grow and endure to the end of her days.

No sooner had Necker taken up his post as Director General of Finance than he set about reforming the administration so as to put public finance on a healthier footing. His personal fortune had made it possible for him to refuse his salary, a useful gesture when he was about to cut those of others, although it made him enemies among people who saw it as possibly setting a worrying precedent, and as another example of his arrogance. He also deposited 2.4 million livres of his own money at only 5 per cent interest, at the royal treasury, as a personal guarantee of his management of the country's finances. It would be almost thirty years before his family got it back.

His reforms made him enemies almost at once. He abolished the offices of the corrupt Receivers General, hitherto responsible for receiving direct taxes, and replaced them with officials accountable to his own Ministry. Aware that indirect rather than direct taxes had become a far greater source of revenue, he even took on the powerful *Fermes* (the *Fermes* or Farmers-General were customs areas – part of the antiquated and venal system of indirect tax collection), abolished *mainmorte*, a feudal law which was as harmful to agriculture as to the peasants, and introduced the *régies* – new management systems to run the royal domains, the post and taxes on wines and spirits.

He took measures to improve the disgraceful state of hospitals, an area in which Madame Necker, who had founded a model hospital in the rue de Sèvres, was particularly interested. He also made efforts to improve the state of the prisons. The routine administration of the *question préparatoire* (torture inflicted on the accused to get a confession), and the *question préalable* (torture of convicted criminals before execution as a way of forcing the names of their accomplices) was abolished. Nor was the bloated royal household spared. He abolished some 400 ceremonial appointments such as cup-bearers and candle-snuffers, which all carried a pension, making it clear to all the hangers-on at court that the royal treasury was not a common pot into which they might dip at will. To one indignant lady who, when refused a pension, exclaimed 'but what is a thousand ecus to the King?', Necker replied coldly that it represented the *taille* of an entire village.[1] He even refused money to Marie-Antoinette, who took it with a good grace, making sure, however, that he did not always get his way. When the Duc de Guines, one of Marie-Antoinette's closest friends, managed with the Queen's assistance to secure a huge dowry for his daughter, and slyly wrote to thank Necker, knowing full well that he had opposed it, Necker replied drily: '*Monsieur le duc*, while I attach a great deal of importance to your gratitude, I cannot, in all truth, accept what is not due to me. Each time that the Queen did me the honour of discussing your business, as a loyal administrator of finance, I made all the points against, which I felt it incumbent on me to do. But when the Queen declared it to be the King's wish, I felt unable to do otherwise than to demonstrate my respect and obedience. You will see, therefore, *Monsieur le Duc*, that since the King commands it, you owe me nothing.'[2]

But Necker's major achievement, and the reason for his enormous popularity in the country, was that he avoided imposing any new taxes or raising existing ones. He was able to do this because of his extraordinary success at raising loans.

In February 1778 France entered the war against England alongside the new United States. Memories of the Seven Years War, as well as the new ideas of the Enlightenment, played their part in France's desire to come to the help of the rebellious colonies. Benjamin Franklin, the American envoy to France, dressed in his modest brown suit, was the darling of the salons.

Necker was against the war, which could only further damage France's finances. He was even suspected of connivance with England, with his admiration for English institutions, his many friends there and his connections in the City, but his reputation as a reforming minister who could even finance a war without new taxation continued to grow. However he was obliged to raise further loans. Maurepas, the King's Chief Minister, and Vergennes, the Foreign Minister, who was jealous of Necker's extraordinary popularity, now encouraged a defamatory campaign against him. Incensed by one particularly vicious pamphlet which had fallen into her hands – she had immediately sent out to buy up all the copies – Madame Necker naively wrote to Maurepas (unaware that he was behind them), asking him to take the necessary steps to stop the anonymous pamphleteers. Necker, as his daughter wrote later, had been angry with her for revealing how much they were concerned by this vilification, though he was also touched.[3] The adverse publicity didn't worry him personally but he was well aware that it would worry the bankers.

To allay their fears and strengthen his own position with the public, he sought the King's permission to publish his *Compte rendu au Roi*, an unprecedented public account of the country's budget. It came out on 19 February 1781. In it he pointed out that the country's finances were in excellent shape, which he did not hesitate to attribute to his own management (indeed he even gave credit to Madame Necker). He had been blamed then and since for failing to mention that the treasury was indebted as never before. His aim now was to show that so long as the ordinary peacetime obligations of the Crown could be met from normal revenue, exceptional needs such as war could be financed by the hitherto unused recourse to loans.

Thirty thousand copies of the *Compte rendu* were sold in a fortnight. The book was translated into all the main European languages. Total sales were more than 100,000 copies, a figure never attained by any book at the time, except for the Bible. It became the main topic of conversation. Letters of congratulation poured in, which Necker stolidly received as his due. One highly laudatory but anonymous letter gave Necker particular joy: he had recognized his fifteen-year-old daughter's handwriting.[4]

Nevertheless furious attacks from his enemies were beginning to frighten the money men. Necker feared that further loans, essential in the absence of taxation, might not be forthcoming. In this atmosphere he upped the stakes, not only asking the King that the Ministries of War and Marine should be brought under the control of his own Ministry, but also demanding a seat in the *Conseil d'en haut*, the Higher Council, which decided on foreign policy. Maurepas now presented the King with an ultimatum; either he must sack Necker or he and Vergennes would resign. On 19 May 1781, Necker offered his resignation to the King. It was accepted. 'The only consolation for us in this world, if such there could be, is that the Queen shares our patriotism: she cried all day on Saturday,' wrote Madame Necker.[5]

The day after his resignation, the Neckers left the residence of the Controller General for their country house at Saint-Ouen. As news of Necker's dismissal spread it brought an avalanche of letters from all classes. 'All of France came to see him: great lords, the clergy, magistrates, shopkeepers, intellectuals,' his daughter recalled.[6] From St Petersburg the Empress Catherine wrote to Grimm: 'M. Necker no longer has his post. It was a beautiful dream for France and must make her enemies happy.' Offers of posts equivalent to the one he had lost came from Catherine herself, as well as from the King of Naples and the Emperor Joseph II of Austria, but as Madame de Staël was to write later: 'his heart was too French for him to be able to accept such a recompense . . . M. Necker's retirement caused consternation in France and in Europe: his virtue and his abilities made him worthy of these tributes.'

To the especial delight of his daughter, Necker was now free to spend more time with his family. 'I was still too much a child not to be thrilled by the change in the situation. However when I saw at dinner the secretaries and officials of the ministry all looking really miserable, I began to think that my joy had been ill founded.'[7] Soon after, Necker fell seriously ill – the result of thwarted ambition, cried malevolent wits.

Meanwhile, his successor, Joly de Fleury, sought to undo his reforms. By the end of July, however, Necker had recovered sufficiently for his wife to be able to explain to Gibbon: 'M. Necker had been ill for a long time not because he had regretted offering his resignation, but from the pain of having had to do so . . . We are at Saint-Ouen, but far from living a normal life . . . We have been followed here not only by people who we believed were naturally attached to us . . . but also by an untold crowd of citizens from all ranks, concerned only with the public good. M. Necker has been soaked in tears, overwhelmed with praise and benedictions . . . my esteem for public opinion is now much higher.'[8]

The Neckers stayed at Saint-Ouen until the autumn when they returned to Paris, renting a house in the rue Bergère because their own house in the Chaussée d'Antin was let. At the end of that year, 1781, the old Minister Maurepas died. Some have thought since that had he died sooner Necker would not have needed to resign and the whole history of France might have been different.

Madame Necker's salon reassembled. The *philosophes* were now joined by disgruntled politicians, as it became the true seat of opposition. Minette, for a time called Louise, now became Germaine (except to her father, whose *chère Minette* she remained to the end of his days). Ransacking her father's library she read voraciously. She had studied Greek and Latin authors with her mother, and was thoroughly familiar with French literature and with all the major works of European literature and philosophy. Goethe's *The Sorrows of Young Werther*, published in 1777 in translation, marked a turning point in her life, 'as a personal event'. She later described the abduction of Richardson's *Clarissa* too, as one of the most important events of her girlhood. In her childhood Germaine had been reluctant to learn music. But as ever, once her mind was captured she made extraordinary progress. Discussions about Glück's music made her want to hear his opera *Armide*. Charmed by the words and the music she applied herself to learning to play the harpsichord, which, by 1778, she played extremely well, as her friend Catherine Huber remembered.[9]

Germaine read English easily and spoke it moderately well. Many English, particularly Gibbon, Hume and Walpole, were frequent visitors at Madame Necker's salon in Paris. Another was William Beckford, an extremely rich young man, a great traveller and collector who would soon become one of the chief exponents of the Gothic novel then becoming fashionable, following on the success of Walpole's *The Castle of Otranto*. Only six years older than Germaine, he had lent her a private copy of his *Dreams, Waking Thoughts and Incidents*, a travel book whose publication he had suppressed. They were also fond of singing together and Beckford left an amusing account of the first evening in which he first danced a gavotte and then a minuet with the seventeen-year-old Germaine. They had each sung an air, Germaine singing the main aria from *Didon* by Piccini – out of tune, he recalled – at which point the doors of the main drawing room opened, revealing 'a synod of pale *literati*, in court dress, and a whole row of dowagers, with their long bodices of pink and yellow, all sitting on chairs covered with the stiffest tapestry, taking snuff at intervals', who subjected him to a lengthy interrogation. At dinner, in the presence of Buffon, Lalande and other sages, they discussed 'zoology, geology, meteorology and especially tautology', Beckford added naughtily. He thought Necker very clever and good, but very pleased with himself. After spilling a glass of water over Madame Necker's skirts, he took his leave in spite of being pressed to stay by Necker, Germaine and Marmontel.

Brilliant, charming and well educated though she was, Germaine was not beautiful. Even Madame Necker admitted to Gibbon that her daughter was agreeable without being beautiful, while Necker himself had told her that as she was not beautiful she would have to please by cultivating her other talents. Some of her contemporaries at this time were less severe. Beckford thought her well made, 'very symmetrical', and declared that she could have served as a model for a sculpture,[10] while Baroness d'Oberkirch, who had been so unkind about her parents, although not kind about her looks wrote of the seventeen-year-old Germaine: 'Mademoiselle Necker seemed to me to be quite different from her parents . . . . Her eyes are admirable, otherwise she is ugly. She has a good figure, a good skin and something particularly intelligent in her look. She is a flame!'[11] Like many a young woman unsure of her looks, as she confided to her journal, Germaine often glanced in the mirror, not out of vanity but out of a need for reassurance.[12] Paintings of her at that time show a dark-haired young woman with a bosomy, rounded figure, strong features, an olive complexion, and magnificent, large dark eyes – the very opposite to the rosebud complexion and angelic fairness then in vogue. The feeling of being ugly never left her: 'Madame de Staël would have given all her intelligence for the pleasure of being beautiful,' Madame de La Tour du Pin remarked later.[13]

Brought up among adults and used to holding her own with the most distinguished intellectuals from an early age, she was, at the age of nineteen, very self assured. Madame de Boufflers, a family friend, thought her self-confidence unseemly, while Gibbon described her as 'wild, vain but good-natured'. She was lively, warm-hearted, impetuous and quite outside the common run. But she had inherited her mother's depressive nature, hidden under a gaiety inherited from her father. Unlike her mother, who had spent a lifetime trying to dominate everything around her, and had imprisoned her own passionate nature in a straitjacket of respectability, Germaine was dominant but unrestrained. The emotional outbursts and quick tears of childhood remained and sometimes displeased her older contemporaries. Madame de Genlis recalled an occasion when she was reading one of her works: 'Germaine astonished but did not please me, she exclaimed at every page, constantly kissed my hands and embarrassed me very much.'[14]

Another contemporary pen-portrait speaks of her intelligence without equal – a quick wit, wonderful memory, talent for analysis, extraordinary articulacy, all embellished by a natural charm and warmth. 'Too much vivacity constantly gets her into trouble. When excited she speaks with more heat than is acceptable, but experience will teach her to moderate her expression, meanwhile her lack of measure is simply due to the impetuosity and drive of youth; the fire and flames of genius.'[15]

She was already a master of the highly prized art of conversation. Everyone who knew her throughout her life remarked on this talent and was immediately fascinated. 'Beautiful, ugly, I don't know, I think I never saw anything but her eyes and her mouth' said Mme de Tessé, adding that if she were Queen she would command Mme de Staël to talk all the time.[16]

The time had come for Germaine to be married. With a dowry of 650,000 livres, she was one of the great heiresses of Europe, and as such had been the target of fortune-hunters for some time. Madame Necker had no wish to see her daughter married to a Catholic so the choice was restricted: their native land presented no candidates grand enough. Madame Necker, meanwhile had higher ambitions. She was determined that her future son-in-law should be worthy of and, if possible, useful to her husband. Protestant princes and noblemen being thin on the ground in France, the Neckers were obliged to look further afield, to Northern Europe.

In the autumn of 1783, when at Fontainebleau with the court, they met William Pitt, son of the Earl of Chatham, who was travelling in France with his friend William Wilberforce. Barely twenty-three, the brilliant and well-born Pitt had already served as Chancellor of the Exchequer. Madame Necker saw the possibilities at once. Here was the very thing – a young man who united everything she could wish for, and who by all accounts was certain to become Prime Minister of England. Necker's position in France could only be enhanced by such an alliance. There is no clear record of what Pitt thought of the idea of marriage to Germaine Necker. He is held to have replied that he was already wedded to England.[17] Whatever Pitt's sentiments, to her mother's bewilderment and unrelenting fury, Germaine flatly refused to consider such a marriage. She had nothing against William Pitt; indeed she admired him, but if she married him she would have to live in England, away from her two great loves: Paris and her papa. 'Ah! I have a different destiny. I am the daughter of M. Necker, I am attached to him, that is my real name,' she confided to her journal, adding later, 'Why is it that this wretched England should have been the cause of my mother's implacable coldness towards me? Accursed island, source of all my present fears and of my future regrets. Ah! It's all over I cannot go to England.'[18]

In the spring of 1784 the Neckers travelled to Switzerland where they had stayed briefly the previous autumn. Unlike his wife, Necker always had an affection for his native land and was happy to distance himself from Paris for the time being. He wished to be in Lausanne also so that Madame Necker might consult the famous Dr Tissot. For some time, she had been suffering from a nervous agitation. She was quite unable to sit down and always stood, even in company; she also suffered from chronic insomnia. For his own part, Necker wanted to supervise the publication of his book on French finance and also to buy a house in Switzerland. In May 1784, the Neckers bought the Château of Coppet from the Théllussons. The château, on the shores of Lake Geneva, was in very poor condition. While it was being restored the Neckers spent an enjoyable summer in the Château de Beaulieu, near Lausanne, scene of Madame Necker's youth. A number of friends gathered around them, including the faithful Moultou and his wife, and Gibbon, who had returned to live in Lausanne, where he was to remain for ten years with his friend M. Deyverdun.

But Germaine's stubborn refusal of Pitt still rankled with her mother, who had not given up her dream and hoped she might yet change her mind. During one serious bout of illness, convinced that she was dying, Madame Necker penned a long, final list of instructions to her husband and daughter, which began characteristically: 'Listen with attention my child, to the last advice and the final orders of your mother. Think of them as being of an almost sacred nature. You may perhaps reproach yourself for your behaviour towards me, if you consider the satisfaction you might have given me, but if I wish to awaken some sensitivity, some remorse in your soul, it is to help you find a remedy.'[19]

Madame Necker's deteriorating health was a constant source of worry to her husband and letters between them at this time bear witness to the depth of their love. However tiresome she may have been at times, Necker undoubtedly saw her as his life's companion. For a man so outwardly reserved, he was capable of an extraordinary tenderness. His wife was much occupied at this time in planning her own burial in meticulous detail, and later his. Mortally afraid of being buried alive, she consulted several doctors and scientists on the best methods of preserving her body and finally settled on a vat of spirits. After one such conversation about her imminent death, Necker wrote to her: 'Ah my angel! What a state you have put me in! Having shed torrents of tears and feeling myself almost lifeless, I am going to write to you, for I know that such conversations are almost more than we can bear. The love I bear you is beyond expression. It is my blood that flows in your veins, as yours flows in mine, and the thought of a separation makes me feel that that the world is crumbling around me.'[20]

Germaine, too, although she loved her father far more, continued to worry about her mother's deteriorating health, as she wrote in her journal of 12 August: 'I was greatly saddened yesterday; maman has had several very bad nights . . . I tried to reassure her in every way that the truth and my affection for her could suggest.'[21]

On 1 September, Baron and Baroness Necker – Coppet carried a feudal barony which Necker was keen to preserve – took up residence at their new country house. Their carriages were met with applause and salvos of cannon fire. The old feudal village of Coppet, with its narrow streets and red-tiled roofs clustering around the château, still looks lovely today in the sunshine of an Indian summer. The visitor arrives at the gates through a long avenue of trees. A wide courtyard is enclosed on three sides by a two-storey manor house, surrounded by its park, beyond which lie vineyards and orchards. A handsome, wide entrance hall leads to a sunny library across the width of the main house, from where double doors give on to the terrace and the lakeshore garden. The house is light, airy and welcoming, with an elegant staircase leading to the upstairs drawing rooms from where there is a fine view of the lake and the distant peaks of the Alps and the Jura mountains rising to the east and west. Two basin-shaped fountains playing in the courtyard add to the general sense of tranquillity.

Perhaps it was this very tranquillity, so uncongenial to a lively girl of eighteen, that put Germaine off Coppet. She always returned to it with reluctance. She was in any case essentially urban, with little feeling for the beauties of nature beyond the conventional. To her horror, she saw that her father was happy there and feared that he might decide to stay forever. 'I was mortally afraid that he might wish to spend the rest of his life on his estate. May he forgive me but I have not yet acquired enough memories to be able to live off them for the rest of my life. It isn't illusion or the thought of pleasure which holds me back, but my heart which adores him would nevertheless tremble, if the door was to close forever on us three,' she wrote earnestly in her journal.[22]

Fortunately for Germaine, her cousin Jacques Necker, son of her uncle and godfather Louis, had just become engaged to Albertine, daughter of the naturalist Horace Benedict de Saussure. Almost as clever as Germaine, the charming, lively Albertine became a fast friend, remaining close to the end of Germaine's life. Her new cousin, a future writer herself, was to be Germaine's first biographer. Germaine said of Albertine that she had all the intelligence attributed to herself together with many virtues which she lacked.

The Neckers were soon on the move again. Avignon, which they reached in mid-October, did not at first please Germaine or her mother, but after a splendid ball given by the papal nuncio, where Germaine danced half the night with the young Duke of Cumberland, brother of King George III, she was able to write cheerfully to her friend, d'Albaret. Since her mother's health was still showing no improvement – she seemed to have had problems with involuntary movements – they would be leaving in a week to winter in Montpellier in order to be near Dr Lamure, in whom her mother had confidence.[23]

Necker's book, *De l'Administration des finances de la France*, had meanwhile been published and letters poured in from Paris; even the

King was said to have read and reread it. Necker was now spoken of as the successor of the present Controller General, Calonne. Germaine was overwhelmed with admiration: 'How delightful it is, allow me to say it, how delightful, to be connected to the writer of this work!' she wrote ecstatically to d'Albaret.[24]

Germaine enjoyed a very lively season in Montpellier, with a succession of parties and the amateur theatricals at which she excelled. Much courted, she nevetheless saw clearly that most of her admirers 'were only dreaming of my dowry', adding wittily that she could only believe in the compliments of the knights of Malta since they were unable to marry her. Her mother's health continued to worry them and Germaine wanted her to try magnetism (as hypnotism, then newly invented by Mesmer, was known). They decided to rent a property at Marolles, not far from Paris, where they remained until their return to Saint-Ouen in mid-September. Here they could see some of their Paris friends, while Necker worked on a new treatise. 'We went out for a walk towards evening, my father and I. The sun was about to set; nature was so lovely. Ah! How much better placed is a great man among the great wonders of creation than in a crowd of men . . . We talked of the new work which he was writing. I thought he might call it "Of the Existence of God" but it is to be called "On the importance of religious ideas" (*Sur l'Importance des opinions religieuses*).'[25]

Her closeness to her father had grown even more intense throughout that summer of Madame Necker's illness. It was then that Germaine wrote a startling entry in her diary, on the obverse of which she had written 'Turn the page if you dare papa!': 'I did not write yesterday. I was still in bed when my father came to see me and I gave him the hour I reserve for my diary. We spoke of nothing in particular, but every instant was filled with gaiety and feeling. What grace, what charm he can display when he cares to! I shall try one day to write his portrait . . . How is it possible that we are not always in harmony, that sometimes there is passion and sometimes coldness? Why do I sometimes see faults in him, inimical to the gentle intimacy of our lives? Is it because he wants me to love him like a lover while he speaks to me like a father; because I wish him to love me like a lover while I act like a daughter? It is this struggle between my passionate love for him and the natural inclinations of my age, which he wants me to sacrifice completely, which make me unhappy. This very same struggle is what makes him impatient. We do not always love each other to excess, but we come so close to it that I cannot bear the idea of anything which reminds me that we have not reached it yet. Of all the men on earth it is him whom I would have wished for a lover.'[26]

In spite of Necker's dislike of women writers, his wife and daughter were both planning, in the fashion of the times, a pen-portrait of him of which he was to be the judge. In an uninhibited paean of love and boundless admiration in which she lists all her father's virtues, Germaine also addresses her mother: 'How sweet it must be for you, oh my mother! To enjoy the private charms of this man who is endowed with such public qualities . . . How wonderful to be responsible for his life's happiness and thereby to pay a debt to a great nation! How good it must be to be able to say: "I have the greatest and most intimate part of this mind which through its actions and writings has embraced all peoples!" ' The final paragraph of her pen-portrait is addressed to her father: 'Oh you, the first sentiment of my childhood, the first passion of my youth, you whom I would have loved under all possible titles, I was taught by you, I have turned all the faculties of my spirit towards you: I exist through you twice over, I have slowed down my steps to join you in the course of my life, and soon I will abandon the illusions of youth to be yours alone. Doubtless I have some regrets, but is there an unmixed happiness? I regret those years which nature forced you to live without me, but my age no longer frightens me and my heart will guarantee that my days depend on yours. I have also regretted that I did not find a being like you, in whose life I might come first, who might love me in every way one loves someone sensitive. I would have dispensed with greatness. Forgive me: I wanted to be unfaithful to you, but in vain; two men like you cannot be part of the destiny of one life. Ah take me then forever, take all I have of life; happy if your heart pours out into mine, if I might always receive the noble confidence of the noble sentiments of your great soul. If I can console you for just one pain, if you believe that I embellish your future life, I shall be happy when death takes me from you, that they engrave on my tomb: *she adored him, he mourned her*.'[27]

Madame Necker's portrait, equally flattering, dwelt much more on her husband's public virtues. Later Germaine was to say while he preferred his wife's version, hers had flattered him more. No wonder then that Madame Necker was jealous of her daughter! But she was not the only possessive member of the family. Necker himself wanted the constant adoration and the undivided attention of both women. None the less, throughout the summer of 1785, he was taken up with negotiations for Germaine's hand.

Several proposals to his daughter from gentlemen whose main interest, only too apparently, was her dowry, were rejected without difficulty. Prince George-August of Mecklenbourg, then forty years old, brother of the reigning Grand-Duke and of the Queen of England, conscious of the honour he was conferring, was perfectly frank. 'The reasons which make me desirous of an alliance with M. Necker, by virtue of his daughter's hand are: that I am a younger son and twenty years in the Imperial service being very expensive, my financial affairs are very much affected, forcing me to enter into considerable debt, especially after the 1778 campaign,' he wrote to his marriage broker, adding that as he believed that money alone would not ensure his happiness, he had made enquiries about Mademoiselle Necker and had received very good reports about her. That, together with M. Necker's reputation as Minister, was enough to make him wish for an alliance with so estimable a family.

Although a marriage to the Prince would have made his Minette the King of England's sister-in-law, it would have also taken her to live abroad. While he was sensible of the great honour and most humbly grateful, Necker replied, he was obliged to refuse. Lord Malden and several other candidates for Germaine's hand and money were similarly dispatched.[28]

In August, Madame Necker announced to Moultou that they were moving nearer to Paris. 'It is time to make a decision about that young life, which is a part of ours. While nothing is decided yet, it seems that my wishes are not to be considered. I accept what I cannot change with a good grace, but inside, I bitterly regret the only son-in-law [Pitt] who seemed made for us.'[29] The subject of Necker's negotiations and Madame Necker's reluctance was Eric Magnus de Staël Holstein.

Eric Magnus, born in Sweden on 25 October 1749, was the seventh son of Mathias Gustav, a cavalry officer in the Upland regiment of the Swedish army, a member of an ancient family which had originated in Holstein but had become Swedish in the reign of Queen Christina. His mother, Elizabeth Ulfsparre, was descended from Charles VIII, son of Margaret Sparre, the grandmother of many Swedish kings. In common with many young noblemen, Eric Magnus joined the army at an early age and, although poor, he had had the good fortune of being attached to the court, where as a young soldier he distinguished himself for bravery during the *coup d'état* in 1772 and thus came to the notice of the King, Gustavus III. In 1776 he was made a Knight of the Order of the Sword and Chamberlain to the Queen. Before long he was sent to the Swedish embassy in Paris, where his abilities and charm impressed the ambassador, M. de Creütz. His good looks and elegance soon won him the favour of several important ladies at court, such as the Comtesse de Polignac, a great friend of the Queen and most importantly, Marie-Antoinette herself, who was then in love with the Swedish Count Axel Fersen and therefore perhaps, particularly well disposed towards Swedes. Creütz wrote to the King: 'M. de Staël is very busy; he is very well received at court, and all the young ladies here would tear out my eyes if I did not take an interest in his affairs. Mme de La Mark and Mme de Luxembourg would exterminate me.'[30]

The penniless young baron (a courtesy title), who added gambling to his expensive tastes, found himself in serious debt. 'Poor Staël is in a pitiful situation, in dire straits and without a penny,' wrote his ambassador Creütz to the King. An advantageous marriage was essential and none could be more so than to Germaine Necker, with a dowry of 650,000 livres. The Swedish King approved, and the Queen, Marie-Antoinette, declared herself in favour of the match. Madame de Boufflers, a friend of both the King of Sweden and the Neckers, agreed to act as go-between. The prospective bride was twelve at the time but Madame de Boufflers was keen to get Staël's bid in early.

The Neckers had been in no hurry. Germaine was young and her mother intended, and could reasonably hope, to do much better. Mme de Boufflers did her best to push her protégé's cause. M. de Staël, a favourite of the King, might in due course become ambassador, their daughter would continue to live in Paris, with an entrée to the court and the Queen's favour, she pointed out to the Neckers. The Neckers promised to consider the matter, laying down certain conditions. However, the Swedish King, annoyed by Necker's pretensions, refused. Time passed. Staël's financial sitation became ever more desperate and Necker more obdurate. In the previous year, the Swedish Ambassador Creütz had been obliged to point out to his sovereign that the marriage, so much desired by the Queen, would cement Franco-Swedish relations, but that the opposite would be true if the King wouldn't consider some compromise, or withdrew Staël from Paris, as he was crossly threatening to do. Marie-Antoinette herself wrote to Gustavus reinforcing this view. The King, who needed French subsidies, reluctantly agreed to make M. de Staël ambassador when he married Mlle Necker. Necker would only agree to his daughter's marriage if Staël was ambassador for life. Five years of negotiations came to a head in the summer of 1785, as Necker made his position quite clear, via the indefatigable Madame de Boufflers.

His future son-in-law was to have life tenure of the Paris embassy and must guarantee that he would never seek to take his wife to Sweden against her will, other than for a brief visit. This was hardly flattering to the King of Sweden. A pension of 25,000 livres per annum was to be paid by Sweden to M. de Staël should he lose his embassy for any reason. Necker also asked for the title of Count and the Order of the Polar Star for his future-son-in-law, and finally that the marriage contract should be signed and approved by the Queen, Marie-Antoinette. The King agreed to make Staël chargé for the time being, in the absence of Creütz, but Staël would succeed him as ambassador for twelve years, without prejudice to further extension if the King were satisfied with him. He would receive a pension of 20,000 livres. The title of Count was refused; the Polar Star granted. Before making Staël ambassador, however, the King had one more demand up his sleeve. The British government had recognized the independence of the American colonies, following which a peace between Britain and France was signed at Versailles in 1783. A trade in West Indian and West African islands had been part of the complicated colonial share-out of the treaty. Here was a good test for the would-be ambassador. He was to ask for the island of Tobago for Sweden, which of course did not belong to Necker but to France. The French government not unnaturally declined to give up Tobago, but in the face of the Queen's support of M. de Staël's by now desperate pleas as he sank ever deeper into debt, one of the lesser Antilles, the island of Saint-Barthélemy, was ceded to the Swedish Crown instead, by virtue of an agreement signed at Versailles on the 1 July 1784 by Gustavus III himself. With that odd twist to the five-year negotiations, M. de Staël was at last, 'Ambassador of His Majesty the King of Sweden to His Most Christian Majesty'.

There were no further obstacles to the marriage. The time had come for Germaine to meet her prospective fiancé. Her parents had no wish to force the marriage. Seventeen years her senior, M. de Staël was good-looking, charming and well connected. Above all, he would enable her to remain in Paris. As the wife of an ambassador, she would have close contacts at court and the support of the Queen. Germaine was tired of her battles with her mother, knew that she could not marry her father, saw that marriage was the only way to freedom. She had nothing against M. de Staël: 'He is the only match which suits me,' she confided to her journal, adding with desperate clarity: 'Monsieur de Staël is a perfectly decent man, incapable of saying or doing anything stupid, but he is sterile and has no spirit: he won't make me unhappy because he is incapable of adding to my happiness rather than because he might trouble it . . . I regret that I have not joined my fate to that of a great man, it is the only possible glory for a woman.' It was obvious which great man was in her thoughts: 'There is one scene which will long remain in my thoughts . . . My father asked him to dance with me and began to hum a tune with that charming gaiety of his. M.de Stäel, with his attractive face and his knowledge of the art of dancing, danced well, but there was no passion in his movements; his eyes fixed on me were enlivened neither by mind or heart. His hand, which held mine seemed made of white marble; freezing me as it held me close. My father suddenly said to him; "Look Monsieur, this is how one dances with a young lady with whom one is in love". Then, in spite of his portly figure, in spite of his years, his eyes, his charming eyes, his animated movements expressed tenderness with such grace, and energy. God! How can I describe what my heart felt, what a rending comparison! I could not continue, I hid in a corner of the room and burst into tears. My father saw me, ran to me and held me to him: "my daughter, my charming daughter", he said, "that was the most beautiful step that I ever saw in my life".'[31]

Much has been made of the dubious, perhaps incestuous nature of Germaine's love for her father. There is no doubt that he was the true love of her life, as she was of his. But what she felt above all was a spiritual union, a meeting of minds and souls, with one she both utterly trusted and passionately admired; someone she celebrated, and had been taught to worship from her earliest days as a great and unique genius. Their relationship remained unaltered all her life, partly because, brilliant as she was, she never grew up emotionally. The natural bond between them was heightened at the time by the hothouse atmosphere of the Necker household. Life cannot have been easy for any of them. They were constantly on the move, Necker was still mourning the loss of power and glory, Madame Necker when she wasn't prostrated by her nervous diseases was railing at her daughter for her stubborn refusal to provide her with the son-in-law she wanted. Germaine, young, romantic, and quite innocent, with a nature to which all forms of restraint were foreign, unsure of her own attractions but only too aware of those of her dowry, had very little idea of physical love, writing in her journal 'I do not know yet what it is this fault which a woman can commit, but they are bound to tell me before my marriage vows'.[32]

Her imminent departure from the parental home into a loveless marriage sharpened her despair and longing. With Madame Necker ill most of the time, father and daughter were drawn more than ever together. Withdrawn and aloof with others, he could be himself, showing a different, sensitive tenderness to his brilliant, warm-hearted daughter. She longed for a perfect love, with someone as like her father as possible, with whom she could re-create her parents' 'perfect' marriage and enjoy the reflected glory which had been her mother's; a woman's only chance of fame and glory as she had been taught to believe. What she wanted was not so much her father for a husband, but a husband who was a father, as much like her father as possible. Anything less would never be good enough.

Once decided, the Neckers, as always, put a good face on the marriage. To her dear friend, Moultou, Madame Necker admitted that perhaps she had been a little unfair 'to the gallant man whom she is to marry; he is gentle, likeable, honest and sensitive. All we wish is for him to have a title; does not M. Necker's son-in-law deserve that?'[33] A few weeks later, Necker himself wrote to Moultou, explaining that the marriage was to be delayed. Germaine had been laid low with a 'bilious fever' for a whole month, from which, although much weakened, she was now recovering. 'My daughter's and her mother's taste for Paris, my own desire and need to be near to these objects of my love have forced our hand with regard to the marriage of my daughter, and perhaps, if one puts aside the pictures of perfection which we all imagine so easily and find so rarely, we will have reason to be pleased. The man is gentle and honest, nice looking and of reasonable age. He has an honourable position in this country, and his salary together with what we will give our daughter will put her in a position to enjoy early, those pleasures, which as a rule, we attain later in life.'[34]

The engagement that had been known to everyone for some time was at last announced officially in December 1785 after the bride-to-be had recovered from her illness. Even the Empress Catherine had her word, writing to Grimm that 'everyone thinks that M. Necker's daughter has made a very poor match'.[35]

It is hard not to agree with her. Why did Necker accept the marriage of his daughter to a penniless, indeed heavily indebted foreigner, of no particular distinction and seventeen years her senior? Germaine, although of marriageable age was still not twenty, she was a great heiress and though not beautiful, by common consent brilliant, charming and attractive to men. Why had Madame Necker, who had been so against it, now changed her mind? Clearly Staël was of good birth and reasonably attractive, but Germaine was not in the least in love with him. The only possible reason, apart from the wish of both Germaine and her father that she remain in Paris, must have been that Staël was strongly promoted by both Marie-Antoinette and the King of Sweden. The Neckers, for all their fame and money, were bourgeois foreign Protestants in France. Necker had imposed conditions, bargained for years with the King of Sweden, even forced the French government to trade in West Indian islands so that his future son-in-law might have a title and an embassy. Perhaps he did not believe that these conditions would be met. Once they were, it would have been difficult, indeed almost impossible, for him to back down without seriously annoying the Queen and thus the King. His own future at the centre of affairs in France was not played out yet. He was not selling his daughter against her will. She too loved power, loved Paris, loved her father. Her continued enjoyment of all three would be secured by this marriage. The only one she did not love was M. de Staël. Indeed she had said that of all the men she could never love, he was the one she could marry.

Madame de Boufflers, her task accomplished at last, now wrote to the King that she believed the marriage would be good for Sweden, adding: 'I hope that M. de Stäel will be happy, though I doubt it'.[36] Monsieur de Staël's creditors were certainly happy. His wife was to write later that a third of her dowry had gone at once to settle his debts. He could not have expected any other kind of happiness from the tone of the letters Germaine wrote in the late autumn of 1785, to the man she was about to marry. There is not a trace of warmth in them, indeed, some are only just polite. One letter, soon after the last problems of the settlement had been agreed with her father, seems to sum up her whole attitude to this marriage: 'Thank you Monsieur, for your kind attention [a letter from him]. I very much hope however that your health will permit you to visit us soon. My father was pleased with his conversation with you. I attach great importance to his opinion of you. I like to see him thinking as I do: my happiness depends on that. Maman's health is as poor as ever. Do not expect me be cheerful. But you certainly deserve that I should be satisfied.'[37]

The signing of the marriage contract took place at Versailles on 6 January 1786, in the presence of the King, Louis XVI, the Queen Marie-Antoinette and the Princes of the Blood. On the following Saturday, 14 January, in the chapel of the Swedish embassy, Pastor Gambs celebrated the marriage of His Excellency Eric Magnus Baron de Staël de Holstein, Knight of the Order of the Sword, Chamberlain to her Majesty the Queen of Sweden and Ambassador extraordinary of His Swedish Majesty to the French Court . . . with Damoiselle Anne Louise Germaine, native of Paris, legitimate daughter of Messire Jacques Necker, former Director General of Finance of France and the noble lady Louise Curchodi Nass, his legitimate spouse. It was said that while Monsieur de Staël had married Necker's millions, Germaine had married Paris.[38]

PART TWO

Paris, Power and Love

'True pleasure for me can be found only in love, Paris or power.'
Madame de Staël to Jacques Necker

Chapter 4

~

Marriage

'Happiness will come later, will come at times, will never come.'
Mme de Staël to her mother[1]

IN ACCORDANCE WITH the French custom of the time, the newly married couple spent the first few nights of their marriage under her parents' roof. Before she left home, Germaine wrote a letter to her mother. It was an attempt, the last one she would make, to bring some warmth into their relationship, to express the ideal image of her mother, which she was still young enough to cherish; a cry from the heart at the severance of her childhood links and a genuine expression of gratitude at this solemn moment in her life – a future with a man who could never make her happy:

My dear Mama,

I shall not be returning to your house tonight. This is the last day that I shall spend as I've spent all the days of my life. How hard it is to bear such a change! I don't know whether there are other ways of living; I have never tried them, and [fear of] the unknown adds to my sorrow. Ah! I know that I have perhaps treated you badly, Mama. At this moment, as at the hour of death, all my actions stand before me and I fear that I will not be leaving in your soul that regret which I need . . . I feel at the moment all the depth of my love which has remained unaltered. It is a part of my life, and I feel completely shattered and overwhelmed at this moment of parting from you. I shall be back tomorrow morning, but tonight I shall sleep under a new roof. In my new house, I will no longer have a guardian angel to protect me from thunderbolts or fire. I will no longer be with one who would protect me at the hour of death and shield me before God with the radiance of her noble soul. I will no longer be aware of the state of your health at any

> moment. I see only constant regret ahead. I can hardly tell you, Mama, to what extent my love for you grows in my heart. Yours is so pure that all the feelings I address towards it must pass first through the heavens. I raise them to God Whom I will ask to make me worthy of you. Happiness will come later, will come at times, will never come; the end of life puts an end to everything, and you are so sure of another life, that my heart cannot doubt it.
>
> I cannot end: my feelings can only be expressed over an entire lifetime. You have Mama, my dear Mama, my profound respect and my boundless love. M. de Staël will bring you this letter. He has not seen it. It would have inhibited me and forcibly demonstrated to him, against my will, which are the most ardent sentiments of my life.[2]

Soon after her wedding, on 31 January 1786, the new ambassadress was presented at court. Marie-Antoinette's own dressmaker, Mademoiselle Rose Bertin, had made the presentation gown. One of the most influential women in Paris, she had encouraged the Queen to give up the stiff, hooped, paniered court dresses in favour of the softer muslins and satins, clinging to the body, as seen in the portraits of Madame Vigée-Lebrun. Art and fashion had begun to reflect the new age of sensibility and Mademoiselle Bertin was a true artist. Her shop in the rue Saint-Honoré was famous throughout Europe. From here, the *poupée de la rue Saint-Honoré*, a doll dressed in the very latest fashion, would be dispatched periodically to all the European capitals and courts to be copied at once.[3] Hairstyles were changing too. The stiffly powdered, wig-like coiffures were all but gone, except on ceremonial occasions. Hair, dressed with fresh flowers rather than jewels, was encouraged to fall in natural curls on the shoulders. That year the fashion was for symbolic dress and hairstyles. Mademoiselle Bertin wanted young Madame de Staël's gown to represent the genius of the father, the virtue of the mother and the candour of the daughter. 'No easy task!' The gown had caused endless trouble, wrote the old Duchesse d'Enville to her friend Moultou.[4]

Dressed in as near a version of 'genius, virtue and candour' as could be represented in the satin and lace of court dress, the new ambassadress arrived late – a bad start. Custom decreed that on being presented to the Queen, a lady must sink into three consecutive curtsies, lifting the hem of the royal dress to her lips in a symbolic kiss as she rose from the third; a difficult manoeuvre at the best of times. Undoubtedly nervous, and to her evident misery, Germaine stepped on her train, detaching some of the decorations.

The King, seeing the young woman's confusion, and no doubt meaning it kindly, said: 'If you cannot feel at ease with us, you will not feel at ease with anyone.'[5] Marie-Antoinette had taken her off to her own boudoir to have the damage repaired there and then by her own seamstress so that Madame de Staël need not attend the dinner, to be held immediately afterwards in her honour, in a torn dress.

News of her mishap flashed around Versailles and the Paris salons. Quatrains written by Necker's friends celebrated Germaine's modesty, while vicious epigrams were written about her clumsiness to the delight of his enemies. Her looks, her taste, her manners, were all dissected. Even those ladies of the '*ton*', well disposed towards the Neckers, were shocked by young Madame de Staël's decided views and unconventional behaviour. The snobbish Baroness d'Oberkirch wrote in her journal: 'She has had little success. Everyone thought her ugly, gauche and particularly awkward. She didn't know what to do with herself, and obviously felt very out of place amid the elegance of Versailles. M. de Staël is on the contrary perfectly handsome and the best of company. He has quite beautiful manners, and is not set off to advantage by Madame his wife. Since her marriage, Madame de Staël has made herself ridiculous with her prudishness; she puts on the pinched and pretentious airs of Geneva, and the impertinent airs of the parvenue, which she takes for the manners of a grande dame . . . the Genevan is all too visible beneath the airs of a superior woman, particularly beneath the ambassadress.'[6]

The fact was that Monsieur de Staël had all the emollient charm, the looks and the polish required of a courtier-diplomat. The wife of John Adams, the American Minister, who dined with him at the rue du Bac, described him and his residence in letters home: 'Did you ever see . . . a person in real life – such as your imagination formed of Sir Charles Grandison?[7] The Baron de Staël, the Swedish ambassador, comes nearest to that character, in his manners and personal appearance, of any gentleman I ever saw. The first time I saw him I was prejudiced in his favour, for his countenance commands your good opinion; it is animated, intelligent, sensible, affable and, without being perfectly beautiful, is perfectly agreeable; add to this a fine figure and who can fail in being charmed with the Baron de Staël? . . . He lives in a grand house and his apartments, his furniture and his table are the most elegant that I have ever seen.' She continued to describe the double row of footmen on either side of the corridor, between which the guests entered the drawing room, whose silk-covered walls were embroidered with gold; the furniture to match; marble columns garlanded with gilded flowers, Gobelin tapestries in the dining room, statues of Venus flanking the chimney-piece and the table service, a present from Gustavus III, which 'shone with a royal splendour'.[8]

Another well-disposed contemporary noted that Staël had good sense, good taste, a very kind heart; he entertained lavishly and cut a very fine figure as ambassador. Although he was also a compulsive gambler, with no idea of managing money, this was perfectly acceptable in his time, indeed, it was the mark of a gentleman. He was, in short, an estimable man by the standards of the age, but a cardboard cut-out compared with the intellectual pyrotechnics and the vibrant personality of his wife: 'he was the shadow in the painting in which she was the light and very soon everything, that increased the brightness of one, cast the other further into the shade'.[9]

Germaine was in every way unsuited to the role of ambassador's wife. In fact she was unsuited to the role of wife. Young and outspoken, she had no sense at all of what was expected of her, nor did she give it much thought. She was the adored daughter of a rich and famous man, and his confidant. For most of her life she had been on equal terms with the greatest wits of the age. Brought up from the cradle among the *philosophes*, she believed in the spirit of free inquiry and in the supremacy of reason. Argument, the discussion of new ideas, the possibilities of changing life for the better, gave her intense joy. She was by nature, generous, independent, original, direct and brilliant. She was profoundly affected by the works of Jean-Jacques Rousseau as were all her generation. His novel *La Nouvelle Héloïse*, in which the heroine Julie and her lover Saint-Preux pointed the way to a new sensibility, might have been written for her, so deeply had it affected her. Rousseau preached spontaneity, passion, hostility to the conventions; a full-blown emotional response to life – the very opposite to Madame Necker's teaching. Germaine de Staël's own nature, highly emotional and deliberately unrestrained, was in a lifelong conflict with her acute, rational, analytical mind. Poised between the French Enlightenment and the German Romantic movement, and embodying both through her ancestry, she was destined through her writings to be a bridge between them. Ahead of her time, she was to defy public opinion. Although fully aware of the limits on a woman's role, she was never able to set any on her own.

Some of her father's friends, afraid that Germaine's unconventional behaviour might do harm to herself and indeed to Necker, mobilized friendly advisers, among them Mme de la Ferté-Imbault (daughter of Madame Geoffrin), who hardly knew her. When Germaine paid her a visit soon after her marriage however, the old lady (she was then seventy-one) was immediately conquered. Germaine de Staël was a *folle* she declared, comparing her to other prominent women like the Princesse de Talmont, Madame de Luxembourg and the Marquise du Châtelet: 'like them, she will always be in the public eye, but she has a charming gaiety, candour, simplicity and goodness of nature which the others never had for in place of her good qualities they had vices', adding that her father's true friends should not find it difficult to give her the public support she would need.[10]

Madame de Boufflers, who had brokered her marriage and would now bow out of her life, sighed over M. de Staël's slender hopes of future happiness with such a wife: 'his wife has been raised according to principles of honesty and virtue, but she has no idea of the world or of the proprieties and is so entirely spoilt by the high opinion in which her intelligence is held that it will be difficult to make her perceive her shortcomings. She is imperious and has excessively decided views; she has a self-assurance such as I have never seen in anyone of any age or rank. She argues about everything without rhyme or reason and while she has a very quick wit, one can find twenty things out of place for the one good point in what she says. The ambassador dares not correct her for fear of estranging her . . . Were she not so spoilt by all the incense burnt to her, I would venture to give her some advice.'[11]

Alas for M. de Staël! There was never even a faint hope that he might be able to control his wife, although she did try and listen to the Queen's advice in the early days of her marriage. Marie-Antoinette, who had been a party to the marriage negotiations, knew about their financial arrangements and, noticing the lavish receptions at the Swedish embassy, sent a message to Necker, suggesting that he should warn the young couple against undue extravagance. 'My father took this opportunity to lecture me; as he had been very struck by the warning and particularly touched by the Queen's kindness,' Germaine wrote to her husband, reminding him to order the dinner at Versailles (where the King received ambassadors on Tuesdays): 'Sixteen entrées should be quite enough. I am mindful of the Queen's lessons, as you see.'[12]

Soon after her marriage, Madame de Staël began to correspond with the King of Sweden. On 15 March 1786 a very respectful letter to Gustavus III thanks him for the letter he has 'deigned to write to her, which touched and thrilled her'. She promised to send him regular bulletins about Paris life. The King may have been surprised and amused by her artless offer, but after the first bulletin he must have realized that he had an extraordinary addition to his embassy. Her bulletins in no way reproduced her husband's official diplomatic reports (which many believed she wrote anyway), but were a journal of current events, political and social gossip and analysis. She missed nothing, writing with a rapid naturalness which still brings the Paris of her time vividly to life. After a run-through of political, military and artistic events, she ended her first bulletin with a description of her presentation at court, well aware of the King's interest in the reception given to his new ambassador's wife. 'The Queen received me with kindness, as did the King. She told me that she had wanted to meet me for some time and in this way she seems to honour everything that is Swedish. The dinner afterwards was the most magnificent ever given for any ambassadress. Eight days later I dined at M. de Vergenne's with the Spanish ambassadress. He took us both by the hand and led us in together. I am aware of this sort of politeness now, since when I am so honoured, I know it has nothing to do with me personally.' 'The Queen's balls have been truly brilliant this year,' she continues, 'the ballroom had been turned into a fairy palace, with representations of the Trianon gardens with fountains playing constantly. These pastoral themes, the dreaminess of summer in the country, were as it were, superimposed on all the glamour and luxury; on all the frenzied pleasures of the court.'[13]

Although she now had her own salon at the Swedish embassy, Madame de Staël continued to attend her mother's. But Madame Necker's salon had changed. Diderot and d'Alembert had followed Voltaire and Rousseau to the grave. After them went lesser luminaries like her friends and admirers, Thomas and Buffon. The age of the *philosophes* was now all but dead. On the eve of the French Revolution, the salons, which had started as a school of manners and progressed to intellectual fora, now underwent a further transformation. Henceforth, they would be concerned predominantly with social and constitutional reform, in short with politics.

Judging from an account by Albertine Necker-de Saussure, newly married to Madame de Staël's cousin, Jacques Necker, who spent the winter of 1786–7 in Paris with her husband, Madame de Staël's lively spirit was much needed there. 'One dared not speak. Madame Necker intimidated the bravest. After dinner, the guests crowded uneasily around the fire . . . Madame Necker tried to put forward some high-minded topic for discussion. She seems to have imposed some great role on herself which she can never leave off. She talked of virtue, decency and sentiment, not with the feelings of her own heart, but because she believed it to be the right thing to do. I don't believe that she knows her own character at all, or that she has ever allowed herself, even with her husband, a single unguarded moment . . . He is naturally very cheerful, but his wife, I think, does not consider it polite to laugh heartily in her house.'[14]

Greatly impressed by her cousin, Albertine Necker-de Saussure had congratulated Madame Necker on her daughter's brilliance. 'She is nothing, absolutely nothing, compared with what I had hoped to make of her,' was the grim reply.[15] Madame Necker could only love what she possessed and controlled. Young Madame de Staël was already one of the most brilliant and beguiling conversationalists of her time, a time which prized the art of conversation as much as our age prizes communication skills. Albertine recalled her cousin in those early days of her marriage: 'She was too well intentioned herself to guess that she might be hated, too much a friend of other people's talent to suspect envy. She celebrated genius, enthusiasm, inspiration and was herself a proof of their power. Love of glory and of freedom, the natural beauty of virtue, the charm of tender feelings, were all in their turn the subjects of her eloquence. No one should think that she lived only on this exalted plane. She always kept her feet on the ground and did not get carried away. In a country where mockery was perfectly terrifying, she was impossible to ridicule; she rose above it. No ill will could hold up against her goodness; and she always had an extraordinary sensitivity and was able to guess what answer to give to any unexpressed resentment. In full conversational flight, she would identify her adversaries at a glance, and disarm, captivate or floor them as she went along. She was never heavy-handed, never bitter, and if conversation became too serious, she would turn it into a joke and with some happy phrase, unite all opinions.'[16]

Madame de Staël's own growing circle of friends and admirers now gathered at the rue du Bac not only at her 'Thursdays' but also at a daily levée, crowding her dressing room. She often received her visitors in bed or while dressing, as was the custom of the *ancien régime*, talking animatedly, while her poor maid, vainly tried to hold on to her hair, which she was attempting to dress. Among the members of the French liberal aristocracy, who gathered there regularly, was the fascinating, much older, Comte de Guibert.

Jacques-Antoine-Hyppolyte, Comte de Guibert, twenty-three years her senior, was a friend of her parents and she had known him all her life. He became one of her closest friends after her marriage. A brilliant officer and an intellectual star, he had made his reputation as a military expert in 1772 with his *Essai sur la Tactique*, a groundbreaking treatise on the arts of war.[17] The southern good looks, so attractive to women and which had inspired the love of Julie de Lespinasse, niece of Madame du Deffand,[18] were only a little faded, while his erudition and brilliance in conversation were equalled by his vanity, ambition and love of glory. In some ways he was not unlike Necker. While gossips, and indeed Madame de Staël's husband, believed him to be her lover, he was almost certainly merely a soulmate, a figure in whom she saw something of her father, an older friend in whom she could confide her sorrows and disappointments, someone with whom she could share her intellectual and political interests, as she could not with her husband. Guibert was perhaps the first man, but certainly not the last, to appreciate Germaine de Staël's own extraordinary powers of seduction, not on the strength of her looks, but of her mind, her personality, her wit. It was at this time that he wrote a pen-portrait of Madame de Staël, disguised as a translation from the Greek, which made a deep and lasting impression on her imagination and her sense of herself, producing an image that was to appear later in her novel *Corinne*:

> Zulmé is but twenty, she is the most famous priestess of Apollo, she is the God's favourite, . . . Her great, dark eyes sparkle with genius; her hair of ebony tumbles over her shoulders in waving curls; her features are strong, not delicate. They speak of something higher than the destiny of her sex . . . I listen to her, I am transported when I look at

> her, I see in her charms well beyond beauty. How full of variety and fire is her face! How subtle are the accents of her voice! What perfect accord between her thoughts and her expressions! She speaks, and even when her words are out of my hearing, their inflection, her gestures, her look are enough. She is silent for a moment, while her last words echo in my heart; I question her silence and see in her eyes what she has not yet expressed. When she puts down her lyre, inclining her head modestly as the applause rings out, her long black eyelids cover her eyes of fire, and the sun seems clouded over.[19]

All this began to annoy M. de Staël. He may have made a marriage of convenience, but he had clear expectations of what was due to him from his wife. Conventional and rigid, he had little taste for his wife's circle and was more than a little jealous of her social success. Before his marriage he had enjoyed his own success in the salons. Now he was quite simply eclipsed. In the spring of 1786, two or three months after their marriage, a letter from her makes clear that there had been a scene for which he had felt the need to apologize. 'Your letter is very kind, my friend, so I will not enter into recriminations about a scene which lacked all sensitivity; all this is quite new to me,' she replied. He had clearly criticized her choice of friends. She was willing to forgive him but had no intention of sacrificing her friends or her tastes to her husband: 'If you love me as a lover,' she begged, a plea to be constantly repeated over the next few years, 'please put aside those airs of a husband, which stifle love and harm friendship.'[20]

In that first summer of her marriage Madame de Staël accompanied her parents to Saint-Ouen as was their custom. She would return to Paris on Tuesday nights to see her husband when he came back from the weekly court at Versailles. He in turn often joined them at Saint-Ouen at weekends. She probably chose Tuesdays for her weekly return so as to get the most up-to-date news from Versailles, which would have been of great interest to Necker, rather than from a pressing need to see her husband. When apart they kept up a constant correspondence which does point to some affection between them. She tried to please him and still idealized love within marriage. Soon after her marriage she began to learn Swedish, taking lessons from the embassy attaché, d'Asp.

In September she accompanied her parents to Plombières, where Madame Necker was again seeking a cure. She was away for the better part of the month but wrote regularly to Staël. There she also worked on her verse play, *Jane Grey*. In the early years of her marriage she wrote a number of novellas – *Mirza* and *Histoire de Pauline*, stories about ill-fated heroines – and *Sophie*, another play in verse. More importantly she had begun work on her *Lettres sur les Écrits et le Caractère de Jean-Jacques Rousseau*, which heralded her career as a serious writer. Published at the end of 1788, it was the most important study of Rousseau in that period. This, her first work of literary criticism, contained the germ of all her future writing. She was well aware of the magnitude of the task. 'Perhaps those kind enough to see some talent in me will reproach me for rushing in to treat a subject above my present abilities or even those I may hope for one day,' writes the twenty-two-year-old author, adding blithely, 'but who is to say that time does not take away as much as it gives us? . . . Is it not in youth that we owe the greatest depth of gratitude to Jean-Jacques Rousseau? He who has made virtue into passion, who has sought to persuade through enthusiasm, has used the very qualities and faults of youth and made himself their master.'[21]

She is particularly self-revealing in this essay when analysing Rousseau's novel, *La Nouvelle Héloïse*. A quarter of a century later, in the preface to the edition of 1814, and after a lifetime of intellectual activity in which her writing had brought her universal acclaim but also constant vilification, ridicule and even exile, she was clear about having no regrets, making a strong plea for the education of women:

> It has hardly ever been denied that a taste for, and the study of, literature are of great advantage to men, but there is no agreement as to the effect such studies may have on the lives of women. If domestic slavery is to be their lot, improving their intelligence might be worrying for fear that they rebel against such a fate. It is often the case however, that highly intelligent women are at the same time passionate and emotional. Study attenuates the dangers for such characters rather than increasing them; the pleasures of the mind are made to calm the tempests of the heart.

No doubt thinking of her parents' marriage, she adds: 'The most touching examples of married love have been given by women able to understand their husbands and share their fate, and marriage in all its beauty can be founded only on mutual respect and admiration.'[22]

Madame de Staël was to be beset by the 'tempests of the heart' throughout her life, but she never ceased to believe that married love was purest and best.

Defending Rousseau against contemporary charges of immorality in *La Nouvelle Héloïse*, in which his heroine, Julie, marries Wolmar although she is in love with Saint-Preux, she writes:

> Woe to the girl who imagines she can resist her father! His rights, his wishes may perhaps be forgotten when he is far away – the passion of the moment may erase all thought; but a father on his knees, pleading his own cause, his power increased by his voluntary dependence on one's will, his unhappiness in conflict with one's own! His entreaties when one expects compulsion! What a sight that is! It suspends love itself. A father who speaks like a friend, who appeals at once to nature and to the heart, is sovereign of our soul, and can obtain anything from us.[23]

Late that autumn, Madame de Staël discovered that she was pregnant. She took the pregnancy in her stride, with no intention of allowing it to get in the way of her life. She dismissed the idea of breast-feeding, as we know from a letter from her cousin Albertine to her own mother: 'Germaine is expecting a baby, which she is utterly resolved, in spite of her worship of Jean-Jacques [Rousseau], not to feed herself.'[24] Perhaps her mother's experience had put her off. More likely, she did not wish her movements to be hampered.

Her husband was becoming increasingly jealous. Finding her entertaining – perfectly innocently as it happened – the Comte de Jaucourt, he made a scene. In a note begging him to come that evening to Saint-Ouen, she asks: 'Are you going to poison the happiness we should be enjoying together with all this completely unfounded jealousy? . . . Couldn't you forgive to my youth the vain desire of wishing to please? Listen to the language of reason my friend.' She begs him, 'I am pure and I love you. What do my faults matter after that? Respect and liberty; that is what you owe to my heart. However, I can't bear your unhappiness, if you insist I will make any sacrifice. But bear in mind that you are not less loved when you leave me to my own devices.'[25] Madame de Staël certainly made efforts to be as considerate as possible to her husband, perhaps even – romantic idealist that she was – to love him in the first year of her marriage, but he never came close to representing the grand passion to fill 'the emptiness of my heart' which she so often felt and which she had so passionately longed to find within marriage. For the present, neither marriage nor pregnancy could compete with her other great love – politics.

In 1786 France was on the edge of bankruptcy. In the five years since Necker's dismissal, the royal government had continued to cover its deficits by borrowing. The Paris *parlement* – the most important of France's thirteen Courts of Appeal that legalized royal decrees – made clear that further loans were inappropriate. Instead, the *parlement* declared, expenditure ought to be cut; a view supported by public opinion, which held the court to be guilty of lavish spending. The Controller General, Calonne, an able man though notorious for his personal extravagance, believed that France's involvement in the American War of Independence rather than the court's extravagance was at the root of the country's financial problems. He argued that the time had come to raise further revenues through taxation and asked the King to convene an Assembly of Notables to whom he would explain the need to give up their exemptions and pay their fair share of tax. The Assembly, which consisted of 144 members drawn from the aristocracy, the Church and the Government, appointed by the King, met on 22 February 1787. In his opening speech, Calonne blamed Necker for some of the problems and questioned the veracity of his *Compte Rendu*. The Assembly agreed to Calonne's proposals subject to important revisions, including more equitable taxation, but they demanded that they be shown the relevant financial records. Times had changed. Necker's *Compte Rendu*, the first published budget, had set a precedent. Necker, in response to Calonne's attack, sent the King a memorandum in which he justified his former actions and statements, but the King refused to allow him to publish it. When in April Calonne's statement was made public, Necker, feeling his honour to be impugned, went ahead and published anyway. The King dismissed Calonne and two days later, on 9 April 1787, exiled Necker. Madame de Staël could still recall the pain of that day many years later: 'When the King heard that M. Necker's reply to M. de Calonne's speech was published, he exiled him to forty leagues from Paris by means of a *lettre de cachet*, (a sealed, arbitrary detention order from the King, to be carried out immediately and without possibility of recourse to the law). I was very young then; a *lettre de cachet* and exile seemed to me as terrible an act of cruelty as could be imagined; I cried out in despair when I heard it; I could not imagine a worse calamity.'[26]

After receiving many visits from well-wishers the Neckers left Paris for Orléans, but stopped at Marolles because of Madame Necker's health. This moved the King to commute their exile to within ten leagues of Paris. In May, they settled at La Rivière, a small house near Fontainebleau, where Madame de Staël joined them. As always her friends thronged to see her. In a long and friendly letter to her husband, she begged him not to come on the same day as Guibert because there was very little room in their small house, and since Guibert was only coming for the day, they would all be very much occupied with him. She included four sealed letters to deliver to various friends, of which one was for Guibert. Jealous of everyone, but particularly of Guibert, this was too much for Staël. Two days later, an icy letter from his wife makes clear what she thought of him for opening her letter to Guibert. As chance would have it, she had written to Guibert that she wished she had married Mr Pitt (only because her father had let slip that had she done so, he might have been treated differently by the King), which enraged her husband.

She repeated that it was her parents' wish that he did not to come on the same day as Guibert. 'M. de Guibert is certainly one of the men that I love and respect most,' she explained. 'He is certainly one to whom I owe most for his profound attachment to me at all times. I don't know exactly where his feelings for me begin and end. But I am certain of the perfection of his behaviour towards me . . . I repeat once again that I do not believe M. de Guibert to be in love with me . . . what is certain is that all I have for him are feelings of the most tender friendship . . . Give me back that calm which I need so much! Persuade me that you deserve to be loved, and that this vile mistrust is foreign to your nature!' Then a true *cri de coeur* – 'Ah! Make me love you: you don't know how much I would be in your debt! I was born sensitive, deeply sensitive. Often when I am alone, the emptiness in my heart fills my eyes with tears.'[27] Their correspondence about this unfortunate incident and Guibert continued back and forth for the rest of the month, but Staël must have been properly penitent for the tone of his wife's letters becomes more and more conciliatory.

The Neckers' plan was to return to Paris for the birth of their grandchild, due in early July, after which they intended to return to

Fontainebleau to complete Necker's four months of exile. Madame de Staël left, most reluctantly, a little before them in mid-June, in time for the birth, but she had obviously got her dates wrong. Her baby, a girl named Gustavine in honour of the King, was born on 22 July, probably at her parents' house at Saint-Ouen. Afterwards, she was confined to bed for a fortnight as was the medical practice at the time. The King and Queen of Sweden stood as godparents to the little girl.

France now began the inexorable slide towards revolution, as concessions were wrung from the reluctant King, to be followed by still greater demands. Following Calonne's dismissal, the King, under pressure from the Queen, appointed the Archbishop of Toulouse, Loménie de Brienne, to the revived post of Principal Minister with a Controller General under him. Brienne was an enlightened and able administrator who went ahead with Necker's reforms. He persuaded the King to allow the Assembly of Notables to see the financial records for which they had been clamouring. Now, however, the Assembly demanded that a permanent, supervisory commission of finance, independent of the royal government, be established. Refusing to countenance such a loss of royal power Louis XVI dismissed the Assembly on 26 May 1787. Brienne next put the tax measures before the *parlement* of Paris. In July it rejected them, declaring that only the Estates General, France's national parliament (which had not met since 1614), had the right to approve such measures. Public demand for the recall of the Estates General grew. The Paris *parlement*, joined by the provincial *parlements*, continued to agitate until May 1788, when the King deprived them of their powers, substituting them with courts appointed by himself. Backed by the nobility and the Church, the *parlementaires* began to stir up violence, serious in some provinces, particularly in Brittany and the Dauphiné. On 8 August 1788, with the government facing imminent bankruptcy, a serious crop failure and the country in uproar, the King was obliged to promise to recall the Estates General no later than 1 May of the following year. A week later, when the government proved unable to repay the interest on some of the loans, Brienne resigned.

Once again, the King turned to Necker to lead the country out of the crisis. Madame de Staël remembered that, as she crossed the Bois de Boulogne at night on her way to Versailles, she was seized with a superstitious fear of being attacked by robbers, because she felt that she was too happy and something awful must surely happen to her as a result. She then rushed to Saint-Ouen delighted at the news of Necker's return to power, but her father, only too aware that he was being handed a poisoned chalice, had exclaimed: 'Ah! if only they had given me those fifteen months of the Archbishop of Sens. [Brienne was by then Archbishop of Sens.] It is too late now!' As he pointed out sternly to his jubilant daughter: 'The daughter of a Minister only has the pleasure, she enjoys her father's reflected glory; but power itself, especially at the present time, is a terrible responsibility.'[28]

But Madame de Staël was not alone in her pleasure. Necker's second ministry on 26 August 1788 began in an atmosphere of such public rejoicing that it was accompanied by firework displays and popular demonstrations as well as an impressive rise on the stock exchange. This time he insisted on the rank of Director General of Finance and Minister of State (the laws against Protestants had been abolished). His first priority was to fill the treasury's empty coffers which he was able to do by raising loans which were immediately forthcoming, as his presence re-established confidence among the financiers. It also re-established confidence among the privileged classes who remembered that Necker had solved the previous financial crisis without recourse to taxation. The *parlements* were duly recalled. On 23 September, the *parlement* of Paris returned to the city in triumph. Two days later, its first act was to register the convocation of the Estates General.

On 4 September a more sober Madame de Staël wrote a short note to the King of Sweden: 'Sire, In other circumstances I would have had great pleasure in announcing my father's nomination to your Majesty, but he has been given a vessel so close to shipwreck that all my admiration for him is barely enough to inspire me with confidence.'[29]

Gustavine's birth had failed to unite the Staëls and both were bitterly disappointed in the marriage. He had married his wife's fortune, but now wanted her devotion. She had dreamed of uniting her life to an extraordinary man, but her husband was all too ordinary. She had cherished the ideal of an all-consuming passion and a union of minds: he was too cold and too conventional to inspire any such feelings in her or to respond to her with anything more than formal gallantry. He was unfaithful but jealous and inclined to long sulks, while his gambling and extravagance put him permanently in debt. In spite of the generous marriage settlement the couple lived beyond their means, obliging Madame de Staël to apply to her mother for more money, Madame Necker having long since taken over the management of the Neckers' private fortune. She did not relish the humiliation.

At times her husband's perpetual displeasure and unpleasantness to her annoyed her beyond bearing, as we see from a terse note to him in the autumn of 1788: 'I was not pleased with my reception this evening, my friend. My dressing room seemed more flowered than your face and your speech. For the sake of your own happiness and of mine could you not revert to your good manners on Saturday? By the way, everyone says that you have a mistress, and given the time you come home one might well assume it [to be true]. I must warn you that I think it every bit as bad as having a lover.'[30] By this time she no longer cared. Louis de Narbonne, who was to dominate her life for the next five years, had entered the scene.

Meanwhile, in the following spring the Staëls were temporarily united by their anxiety over the illness of their twenty-month-old daughter. At first Madame de Staël took her to Versailles where she was spending a good part of the week with her father. There the child was put in the care of the royal physician, who was also looking after the young Dauphin, sick with tuberculosis and not to survive for long. At the beginning of April Gustavine was taken back to Paris and put in the care of a well-respected English doctor. Madame de Staël, who had briefly gone to Versailles, begged her husband to ensure that the doctor did not leave the child's side for a moment: 'He could have anything from us if he manages to save her.' Her note is tender and full of gratitude to her husband for being with their child. At the beginning of April she wrote that the child was digesting her food a little better; however, by then, hope was dwindling: 'Can I tell you that she is better? I will treat you as I do myself. I dare not say so. If it is any consolation to you to be sure that your grief doubles mine, that your sensibility attaches me to you more than ever and that unhappiness will be a link between us where happiness no longer is, then believe it; believe it from the bottom of my heart.'[31]

In spite of their efforts, Gustavine died between 7 and 8 April 1789. Her child's death caused Madame de Staël genuine pain, which she would allude to later in her novel *Delphine*, but her youth, her political interests, and growing private happiness with Narbonne helped her to recover. Her relationship with her husband was very unhappy. The almost daily letters she wrote to him often refer to rows, jealous scenes, recriminations and demands for her love on his part. Unable to love him, often exasperated, she was never indifferent to his suffering and constantly attempted to re-establish their marriage more on lines of friendship and mutual tolerance to suit them both.

Chapter 5

~

A Salon in the Rue du Bac

'She is a woman of wonderful wit and above vulgar prejudice of every kind.'

Gouverneur Morris

WHILE NECKER HAD managed to deal with the immediate financial crisis in the autumn of 1788, he was unable to do much about the escalating and rapidly changing political crisis. A reformer rather than a radical, he had absolutely no wish to destroy the monarchy but, sensitive to public opinion, he saw that the time had come for real change and tried, with some success, to steer the King into granting reforms which would otherwise be imposed on him. He was blamed bitterly for this subsequently. As his daughter later recorded, he had done everything possible to associate the King's name with such reforms as the abolition of the *lettres de cachet*, the freedom of the press and the periodic convocation of the Estates General for the revision of finance. 'He tried to pre-empt the good that future deputies hoped to do, in order to draw the people's love towards the King.'[1]

That winter, Necker managed, by raising loans and importing wheat, to avert the famine which would have naturally followed one of the worst harvests in memory. Like everyone else he could now only wait and see what would come out of the meeting of the Estates General in the spring. What he hoped for was the transformation of an absolute monarchy into one more on the English model, in other words a limited monarchy in which a national parliament shared legislative power with the King, who would retain executive power.

Madame de Staël and her friends had no wish to destroy the monarchy either, but they yearned for liberty. They wanted individual freedom and civil rights for everyone, equality before the law, the right to public trial with proper legal defence; they wanted elections, freedom of information, freedom of worship, separation of the executive and the legislature, and the abolition of torture.

The political debate had intensified in the six weeks after the return of the *parlement* to Paris. Pamphlets attacking the privileged orders were appearing at the rate of several dozen a week. The main concern was the representation of the Third Estate at the meeting of the Estates General scheduled for May 1789. The First and Second Estates – the clergy and nobility – wished to follow the precedent of the last meeting (in 1614) of this antiquated assembly which, provided they voted together, would enable them to block initiatives for reform from the Third Estate. Leaders of the Third Estate and all liberals wished to see the representation of the Third Estate doubled from 300 to 600 deputies to balance the 300 deputies representing each of the other two Estates. This matter had to be settled before elections for the representatives could take place. When the Royal Council met on 27 December 1788 to decide on this, Necker voted for doubling the number of representatives for the Third Estate and the King gave in.

In January 1789, Sieyès, a radical priest from a modest bourgeois family in Fréjus, published a famous pamphlet: *Qu'est-ce que c'est Le Tiers-Etat*? (What is the Third Estate?), in which he challenged the dominance of the nobility in France.

> What is the Third Estate? – Everything.
> What has it represented in the political order until now? – Nothing.
> What is it asking for? – To become something.

Sieyès's pamphlet, the third and most famous of three revolutionary tracts was aimed at the working and educated bourgeoisie who would provide the leadership for the Third Estate. The common people, he argued, represented twenty-five million people – the vast majority of the people of France. The other two estates combined represented only half a million. Why should they run the nation? Many members of the Third Estate, the up-and-coming bourgeoisie, had demonstrated competence in running their own affairs. If the Third Estate was given power, it would be able to rebuild the nation: 'Nothing can go well without it; everything would be infinitely better without the others.'[2]

On the eve of the Revolution in spite of the Enlightenment which affected the thinking of a tiny minority, the First Estate, the Church, continued to enjoy immense spiritual, social and economic power in France. It still owned, tax free, a third of French property, although it did negotiate a free gift to the crown every five years, paid out of internal, clerical taxes. But the First Estate was divided between the parish clergy who were close to the people and the bishops and cardinals, their often aristocratic superiors, as well as the religious orders which were aloof from the people. The *curés*, or parish clergy who chose the majority of clerical deputies, in common with the liberal aristocracy and the Third Estate, welcomed the summoning of the Estates General, and hoped for reform.

The Second Estate, the nobility, was no less divided. They enjoyed many rights and privileges including exemption from personal taxation on the ancient grounds that they were a military caste. Throughout the eighteenth century, this original *noblesse d'epée* (the nobility of the sword), had been swollen by the rich bourgeoisie, who often bought their way into offices which went with a title, and also by the judicial office holders, *noblesse de robe* (the nobility of the robe), so called after the black robes worn by court officials. There were great differences, too, between the very rich landowners who mostly lived at Versailles and the much poorer provincial nobility, some of them almost indistinguishable from the peasants, who tended to cling to the old ways. The rich nobles were much better educated and more affected by the new ideas of the Enlightenment; some of their *cahiers de doléances* (collective statements of grievances, presented to the King at every meeting of the Estates General since the fifteenth century) revealed surprisingly liberal views, often against their own interest. Leading liberals, mainly aristocrats who met at Madame de Staël's and who were also members of a group called the Society of Thirty – among them Talleyrand, La Fayette, Condorcet, La Rochefoucauld-Liancourt – all backed the so-called Patriots, the leaders of the Third Estate. A number of liberal nobles, men like La Fayette, Mirabeau and the Noailles, were to go along with the radical demands of the Third Estate, never dreaming that they themselves would be swept away as a result.

The Patriots, themselves a small minority of the Third Estate, were professional people – lawyers, doctors and townsmen of the guilds, as well as a few landowning farmers. The rest were the most downtrodden and wretched people in France – the peasants. Arthur Young, the English agronomist and writer, who was touring France in the years 1789–92, was shocked by the backwardness of farming methods due to absentee landlords, sharecropping, taxes and lack of investment. The poverty of the people, particularly of women, horrified him: 'An Englishman who has not travelled cannot imagine the figure made by infinitely the greater part of the countrywomen in France; it speaks at the first sight of hard and severe labour.'[3]

Gouverneur Morris, Washington's agent in Paris and later American Minister who arrived in France in January 1789, was very much in sympathy with the liberals. Reporting to George Washington on 29 April on La Fayette's[4] election as the representative of the nobility of Riom to the Estates General, he shared the prevailing Anglo-Saxon prejudice that the French were incapable of revolution, because they were basically corrupt: 'There is one fatal principle which pervades all ranks. It is the perfect indifference to the violation of all engagements. Inconstancy is so mingled in the blood, marrow and very essence of this people . . . constancy is the phenomenon . . . The great mass of the people have no religion but their priests, no law but their superiors, no morals but their interests. These are the creatures who, led by drunken curates, are now on the high road *à la liberté*, and the first use they make of it is drunken insurrections everywhere for the want of bread.'[5]

Morris met Madame de Staël at the end of March when he had been taken to dine with the Neckers. His first impression was not greatly flattering. 'In the salon we find Madame de Staël. She seems to be a woman of sense and somewhat masculine in her character, but has very much the appearance of a chambermaid. A little before dinner M. Necker enters. He has the look and manner of the counting-house, and being dressed in embroidered velvet, he contrasts strongly with his habiliments. His bow, his address, etc, say "I am the man".'[6]

In that spring of 1789, before the opening of the Estates General, Paris had filled with beggars driven by hunger and the fear of famine. Twenty thousand prowled around the palace and the Hôtel de Ville. The government arranged for 12,000 of them to be kept employed digging on the hills at Montmartre. For this, they were paid twenty sous a day. Bread was scarce; all the bakeries were surrounded by sullen, angry crowds. There were sporadic outbreaks of mob violence. One such riot, at the end of April, in which a rich wallpaper manufacturer, Réveillon, suspected of urging wage cuts, was attacked, was reported by a nobleman from Poitiers, the Marquis de Ferrières, in a letter to his wife: 'Five or six hundred working men . . . armed with cudgels, launched themselves like furies on the house of Réveillon . . . They looted everything they could find . . . The rioting lasted until four in the morning . . . The French Guard charged, firing and killing many. There were as many as seven or eight hundred dead.'[7]

On 4 May 1789, a perfect summer's day, Madame de Staël watched excitedly as the 1,200 deputies walked in solemn procession to a High Mass at the Church of Saint-Louis in Versailles on the eve of the opening of the Estates General. Behind them, heralds dressed in purple velvet embroidered with gold fleur-de-lys and mounted on white chargers blew silver trumpets to announce the royal procession led by the King and Queen and the Princes of the Blood. They were followed by the Swiss Guard and the mounted royal falconers, each with a hooded falcon attached to his wrist. Only the duc d'Orléans,[8] cousin and bitter opponent of the King and deputy for the nobles, marched with the Third Estate. It had been decided that the etiquette observed at the last opening of the Estates General some 163 years earlier would be meticulously observed. The King, waddling in his glittering, diamond-encrusted suit of cloth-of-gold, looked displeased although cries of '*Vive le roi*' rang out as the royal procession passed through the streets lined with spectators, every window crammed with more. No one cheered the Queen, beautiful in a silver court dress with diamonds in her hair. 'She looks with contempt on the scene in which she acts a part and seems to say: "For the present I submit, but I shall have my time",' Morris reported, although he was told that the King had been very annoyed and the Queen hurt that she had received no mark of public satisfaction.[9]

From her vantage point at an upstairs window Madame de Staël had been particularly struck by the sight of the 600 members of the Third Estate dressed in black from head to foot, dramatically sober alongside the purple and scarlet of the Church hierarchy and the satin, gold lace and plumed hats of the nobility. The proud expressions on the faces of members of the Third Estate, many of whom were lawyers, as well as men of letters and merchants, bore witness, she thought, to their rising power and confidence. Full of hope, she watched this procession of the representatives of the French people, but in contrast to most of her contemporaries she was excited less by the splendid ceremonial – the last grand parade of the old monarchy as it turned out – than by what this occasion represented. 'I will never forget the moment when we watched the procession of the twelve hundred deputies of France, on their way to Church to hear mass, on the eve of the opening of the Estates General. It was a truly imposing sight and quite new to the French. All the inhabitants of the town of Versailles as well as many curious Parisians had come together to witness it. This new kind of authority within the state, whose nature or strength was as yet unknown to us, astonished most of those present who had not thought much about the rights of nations.'[10]

Madame de Staël recalled that Madame de Montmorin, the foreign minister's wife who had been standing next to her at the window, had admonished her, saying she was wrong to celebrate and that this would lead to great disasters for them and for France. 'It was as if she had had a premonition of it all. The unfortunate woman perished on the scaffold with one of her sons; another drowned himself; her husband was one of those massacred on 2 September [1792], her eldest daughter died in a prison hospital, while the youngest, Madame de Beaumont, an intelligent and generous woman, died crushed by the weight of her sorrows before she was thirty.'[11]

Among the few nobles who had managed to be nominated as deputies of the Third Estate, she noticed Mirabeau. 'It was difficult not to stare at him once one had noticed him. His immense head of hair stood out; one might have thought that his strength depended on it, like Samson.'[12]

The historic opening of the Estates General took place at the newly built Salle des Menus Plaisirs the following day. The King sat on a magnificent throne of purple velvet, decorated with gold fleur-de-lys, on a dais, the Queen's smaller throne was two steps below his to his left, with other members of the royal family sitting below them. The Third Estate, flanked by the other two, sat facing the royal family. The King wore the ceremonial robes of the Order of the Holy Ghost – made of cloth of gold, richly embroidered and encrusted with diamonds. On his head he wore the 'Henri IV', a white plumed beaver hat with its great diamond, which was to give rise to the first signs of trouble at the end of that day. The Queen, in white satin with a cloak of purple velvet, and diamonds in her hair, looked unwell and agitated, 'as was plain from the almost convulsive way she used her fan'. She often looked towards the Third Estate, 'as if trying to seek out a face in the mass of men among whom she already had so many enemies' wrote Madame de La Tour du Pin, one of the ladies of the Queen's household.[13] Morris thought also that the Queen was weeping, 'but not one voice is heard to wish her well'. Although he was a representative of a republic, he longed to cheer her and tried to encourage those around him to do so.[14]

It had been decided earlier that the Third Estate would not kneel as the King entered; an all too rare concession to the times. A loud murmur like a hiss throughout the assembly had greeted Mirabeau's entrance as, smiling contemptuously, he took his seat. Necker had been feverishly applauded when he entered, but as the King took his place Madame de Staël had felt a strong sense of foreboding. From the benches reserved for members of the diplomatic service she too noticed that the Queen, whose colour was altered, looked very upset, and that she had arrived late.[15] Hated by the French, the scapegoat for the growing unpopularity of the royal family, Marie-Antoinette was lost in her own, private grief. She had just left the bedside of her son, the eight-year-old Dauphin, who was to die a month later of tuberculosis.

As the King finished his inaugural address, he doffed the famous Henri IV hat, replacing it on his head, a traditional signal to the nobility to replace their own hats first, as a sign of their superiority. Suddenly some members of the Third Estate, whether from ignorance or design, began to replace their hats too. Seeing this, the King took off his hat once more and repeated the procedure again, watched by the Queen, who whispered something angrily to him. They were 'like troops that are not yet properly drilled', Morris noted in his diary.[16] At length Necker stood up to make his speech on the country's finances. After the first hour his voice gave out, requiring someone else to read it for two more interminable hours. As she listened Madame de Staël was herself being observed by the Marquis de Ferrières: 'I was sitting in front of Madame de Staël . . . the pleasure of observing, the natural interest of a daughter for the dear author of her days, the anxieties and warnings for his success, the injustices against this man, everything made this a critical and embarrassing moment for Madame de Staël. I followed the expression of her eyes; and I could read in turn fear and hope. One part was wildly applauded: I said to her

"Madame you must be happy". She looked at me with gratitude and her eyes filled with tears.'[17]

Necker's speech, all about tax and administrative reform, hardly touched on constitutional questions. He merely urged caution, advising the Assembly to 'never be jealous of time', an expression, his daughter wrote later, which was to become a proverb after that occasion. But a majority of the Third Estate, together with more radical members of the nobility and the clergy, angry that Necker had treated them like a provincial administration, were unwilling to take his advice. If Necker's speech had disappointed them, it had infuriated many members of the nobility who, when they realized that he was proposing new taxes, blamed him for encouraging the King to convene the Estates General in the first place. 'They had forgotten apparently, that the promise to recall the Estates General had been made before his recall to power,' wrote Madame de Staël.[18]

Six weeks later, while the coffee houses of the Palais Royal seethed with revolutionary talk and seditious pamphlets were being published by the dozen, the Estates General was still in deadlock over how they should meet and vote: 'All enlightened men wanted to break with the tradition of voting separately, by order, with a power of veto over each other, for, quite apart from its fundamental injustice, it was impossible to get on with any business.'[19] On 10 June, the Third Estate issued a final invitation to the other two estates to meet them in a general session. When this was refused, they declared on 17 June 1789 that henceforth they would be known as the National Assembly. Necker advised the King to rally men around the throne by calling a *séance royale or* plenary session and proposed a series of reforms which he hoped would isolate the extremists on both sides. The King agreed, but backtracked by declaring that until the *séance royale* was convened, all sessions of the Estates General were suspended. Barred from their assembly rooms by guards and fearing some sort of royal coup, the deputies of the National Assembly met at a nearby tennis court where, on 20 June, they swore the famous Tennis Court Oath: that they would not leave until there was agreement on a new constitution. When the *séance royale* met on 23 June, the King was obliged to make all the concessions Necker had wished for. In a statement prepared by Necker, but weakened by his opponents, who were supported by the King's brother, the Comte d'Artois, and Marie-Antoinette, he promised the abolition of the *lettres de cachet*, a new legal system, freedom of the individual and of the press and also that the Crown would in future govern with an elected assembly. However the King insisted on maintaining the division into orders, automatically making the National Assembly, as established on 17 June, illegal, and ensuring that the first two orders, by voting together, would be able to block the reform proposals of the Third Estate. They were back to square one. As the King left, followed by the majority of the First and Second Estates, his master of ceremonies, the young Marquis de Dreux-Brézé, invited the leaders of the Third Estate to leave too. Their replies heralded the Revolution: 'The assembled Nation cannot take orders,' Bailly replied; 'You are today, what you were yesterday,' added Sieyès; while Mirabeau spoke for them all: 'We are here by the will of the people and will leave only at the point of a bayonet.'

On 27 June the King caved in, requesting that the other two orders join the Third Estate. The National Assembly had now changed into the Constituent Assembly. During the next fortnight, more and more deputies from the other two estates joined the National Assembly, which began drafting a new constitution. Meanwhile the King, again influenced by the Queen and some of the diehards at court, backtracked once more, ordering up a considerable body of troops, among them a number of Swiss and German regiments. As they began to gather around Versailles it was clear that some sort of confrontation was inevitable.

On 8 July Mirabeau, who still hoped to reform the monarchy rather than get rid of it, attempted to persuade the King to order the troops, which were clearly threatening the National Assembly, to withdraw. But his words fell on deaf ears. Necker, who remained very popular with the public, was also urging restraint on the King, but he had some bitter enemies at court, the Queen now chief among them. Madame de Staël remembered the hostility of the royal circle towards her father: 'M. Necker continued to visit the King every day, but he was told nothing of any importance. This silence towards the principal minister was very disturbing at a time when foreign troops were seen arriving from all parts and were stationed around Paris and Versailles. My father told us privately every night that he expected to be arrested the next day, but that the dangers to the King were so great that he made it a rule to appear unconcerned.'[20]

Influenced by those who wanted to crush the revolt by force, the King now made a major blunder. He dismissed Necker. 'On 11 July, just as my father was going to table with a fairly large group of people, the Minister for the Navy arrived, took him aside and gave him the King's letter in which he was ordered to resign and to leave France at once, in the utmost secrecy.'[21]

In that tense atmosphere, the King's ministers were afraid, rightly, that if his dismissal became known there would be a riot. Someone suggested that Necker be arrested but the King replied that he was sure his Minister would obey his orders. He had not misjudged him. Obedient to the King's wishes, Necker wrote him a brief letter: 'Sire, Your Majesty is losing his most tenderly devoted and honest servant. I hope you will remember me kindly and allow me to justify myself if you harbour any doubts. I have never feared slander . . . I am leaving alone, without passing through Paris or talking to anyone. I ask similar discretion of your Majesty.'[22]

True to his word, telling no one, Necker and his wife left the dinner and, in the clothes they were dressed in, set off at once for Brussels without baggage or passports to avoid any suspicion. Only on the next day did Madame de Staël hear of his departure from her father. Afraid that she might become the object of demonstrations of public support because of him, Necker ordered her to the country. He was right, for all morning deputations from all parts of the city called on her at the Swedish embassy, praising her father in the most extravagant terms and putting forward their views on what must be done to ensure his return. Although she longed to stay, she obeyed her father and left Paris, probably for Saint-Ouen, where she had another letter from him informing her of their whereabouts. She left to join her parents the very next day, on 13 July. When she had tracked them down at an inn in Belgium, finding them still dressed in the clothes they had left in, Madame de Staël was so overcome with love and admiration for her father that, in a characteristically emotional gesture, she prostrated herself at his feet.

In Paris, when Necker's 'resignation' was made public, all the theatres closed as if there had been a national calamity. Green cockades, the colour of his livery, began to appear on people's clothes and hats. Two hundred thousand armed men marched through the streets of Paris, calling his name and even medals bearing his likeness were struck.[23]

The next day, 14 July 1789, and as a direct result of the unrest caused by Necker's dismissal, the Bastille, the great fortress which had been used throughout the century as a prison and which had become the very symbol of an absolutist regime, was stormed by the mob and razed to the ground. Altogether about a hundred people were killed in the fighting. The prison governor, de Launey, was summarily tried and executed, as were two others, their severed heads paraded on pikes through the streets. Two days earlier, when the liberal Duc de Liancourt had come to Versailles to report on the disturbances in Paris, the King had asked him: 'Is this a revolt?' 'No Sire, this is a revolution,' was the duke's answer.

On 16 July 1789, the British Ambassador in Paris, Lord Dorset, sent a dispatch to the Foreign Office: 'I wrote to your Grace on the 12th inst. by a messenger extraordinary to inform you of the removal of M. Necker from His Majesty's councils. I have now to lay before Your Grace an account of the General revolt of 14th July with the extraordinary circumstances attending it, that has been the immediate consequence of that step.' After a detailed description of the insurrection in the capital and the sacking of the Bastille, the Ambassador concludes: 'Thus my lord, the greatest Revolution that we know anything of has been effected with, comparatively speaking – if the magnitude of the event is considered – the loss of very few lives: from this moment we may consider France as a free country, the King a very limited monarch, and the nobility, as reduced to a level with the rest of the nation.'[24]

After two days' rest in Brussels, Necker and Staël, who against his better judgement had accompanied his wife to Brussels, left for Basel via Germany, while Madame de Staël and her mother followed at a slightly slower pace. At Frankfurt, where the ladies stopped for the night, they were met by a special messenger with letters from the King and from the National Assembly, recalling Necker to his post. Madame Necker, far from being pleased, was against her husband's return. Madame de Staël, longing to get back to the action and unwilling to see her father risk the loss of power, felt quite differently, as she wrote to her husband. The warmth of her letter was a measure of her relief and her gratitude to Staël for escorting her father: 'If you are still in Basel my friend, I send you a thousand caresses, a thousand thanks. You have looked after my treasure and my life [her father], it is I now, who owe you everything . . . Wait for me: we arrive tomorrow evening or on Thursday morning . . . Goodbye, goodbye. Tell my father, that the whole of France does not love and admire him as much as I do on any one day. Goodbye my good friend. You do not need me to tell you that I love you, you must be sure of it.' Staël had never been less sure of anything. 'My mother does not wish my father to accept,' she continued. 'This seems so irrational to me, so harmful to his glory, to his honour and to France, that I cannot understand it. However even madness is understandable, when it is a question of the people we love. Goodbye.'[25]

Such was Necker's power, and Madame de Staël's confidence, that she did not hesitate to order her husband, who was after all the Swedish Ambassador, to abandon his post at such a time and accompany her father to Switzerland. She felt no qualms in explaining her action directly to the King of Sweden herself later that summer. But her father did not share her confidence, making his own apprehensions quite clear in a letter to his brother Louis. He had received 'a letter from the King and from the Estates General, inviting me, indeed pressing me, to return to Versailles, to my post. This makes me unhappy. I had almost reached harbour. I am therefore returning to France, but as a victim of the esteem with which I am honoured . . . I feel that I am tumbling into the abyss.'[26]

Necker knew that France was in a state of near anarchy. What came to be known as the Great Fear (predominantly of famine) erupted into peasant uprisings all over France that summer. However both Necker and his wife realized that if he did not return, they would forever reproach themselves for a failure of courage.

While her parents were anxious, Madame de Staël was elated when on 25 July Necker, accompanied by his family, set out on his triumphant return to France. Still young enough to believe in her father's superhuman capacities, intoxicated by the atmosphere, she gloried in the fact that the whole world seemed to share her belief. 'I do not believe that anything like it had ever happened to a man who was not the sovereign of his country,' she wrote of their royal progress through France, where Necker's return was greeted with a delirium of joy. Women fell to their knees in the fields at the sight of their carriage. Local notables acted as postilions, and in each town they passed citizens would unhitch his carriage and pull it themselves. Sometimes his progress was interrupted by radicals of the new order whom he attempted to calm, urging respect for property, the Church and the aristocracy, as well as love for the King. He also issued passports to several nobles leaving France.[27] At last, on 28 July 1789, they were back at Versailles. The following day Necker attended a session of the National Assembly where his return was greeted with rapturous applause. On 30 July, the Neckers, with M. and Madame de Staël, accompanied by a guard of honour and military bands, set out on a triumphal return to Paris, to the Hôtel de Ville: 'I should like to linger once again at [the memory of] that day, the last of perfect happiness in a life which was still unfolding before me. The entire population of Paris was lining the streets. Men and women at the windows and perched on rooftops, shouted "Vive Monsieur Necker!" As we got closer to the town hall, the acclamations multiplied; the whole great square was packed with a multitude all animated by a single sentiment, all pressing on the footsteps of a single man and that man was my father.'[28]

As her father replied to the speech of welcome, asking for peace and reconciliation between all parties, Madame de Staël's joy was so intense that she fainted. Necker, too, recalled that day with simple feeling; 'Ah! How happy I was that day . . . how happy when I returned to Versailles!'[29] But his appearance on the balcony of the Hôtel de Ville that day did in fact mark his apogee; from then on his power and his popularity could only go down and the decline was to be swift and dramatic.

Still only twenty-three, and already famous for her 'letters on the work of Jean-Jacques Rousseau', Madame de Staël often replaced the ailing Madame Necker as her father's hostess and deputy at Versailles, where she also received visitors and delegations on his behalf. Most weeks she saw her husband only on Tuesdays, when the King received foreign ambassadors. After Necker's return from Basel, she attended almost every session of the National Assembly. Necker's interests and her own fascination with politics put her husband further into the background, although her brief but frequent letters to him throughout August still echo with her gratitude. As a woman she could not be involved in politics directly, but she was far too happy with her father's restored power to care. In this period almost everything she wrote refers to him and to the unfolding political drama. She was meeting a vast range of people, watching the last death throes of the old order and the birth of a new one and acquiring extraordinary political experience for one so young.

By 16 August, when Madame de Staël penned a long letter to the

King of Sweden, even more radical changes had taken place in France. On 11 August the National Assembly ratified the decisions taken a few days earlier to abolish all feudal rights, but still proclaimed the King as 'restorer of French Liberty'. Justifying Necker's attempts to effect change while trying to strengthen the King's position, the young ambassadress ends: 'I must now give your Majesty an account of my own behaviour. I obliged, I insisted, that M. de Staël absent himself for ten days to accompany my father, at a time when perhaps his life, but at the very least his freedom were in danger . . . I dared to believe that Your Majesty would approve. It is with great respect and some anxiety that I put M. de Staël's conduct before you. I beg your Majesty to continue to treat him with kindness.'[30]

This was not well received. The Swedish King had had enough of the Neckers' presumption. He sided naturally with Louis and Marie-Antoinette, was unhappy with the Neckers' liberal views and annoyed and dismayed by the influence which they clearly exercised over his ambassador, whom he would henceforth cease to trust. It was widely believed that Madame de Staël was writing her husband's dispatches. While this may not have been true, there is no doubt that Staël's information came from his wife's and his mother-in-law's salons. The unhappy ambassador was too much in his father-in-law's debt to be able to do more than reassure the King, feebly, that he was his own man. Nobody, least of all the King, believed him.

On 26 August, the National Assembly passed the Declaration of the Rights of Man. The political manifesto of the Revolution, it spelled out its aim to establish a government based on the rights of individuals and on political equality and liberty, while justifying the destruction of one based on absolutism and privilege. The King once again demonstrated his unerring instinct for making the wrong choice by refusing to endorse it, only to be obliged to do so later, during the October 'days'.

On 5 October, Madame de Staël, who had returned to Paris for a few days, was at home at the rue du Bac when she heard that some 200,000 people were preparing to march on Versailles to bring the King and the National Assembly to Paris. Anxious for her parents, she set off at once for Versailles, taking a little used road. As she approached in the early afternoon, she saw the King returning from hunting. Marie-Antoinette too had been called back from the Petit Trianon. The atmosphere at Versailles was tense and anxious as the royal family debated whether to stay or to take refuge at Rambouillet, which was further from Paris.

In Paris that morning a great crowd, mostly of women, hungry and driven to fury by the high price of bread in spite of a good harvest, gathered outside the Hôtel de Ville. A report in a revolutionary newspaper that, a few days before at a banquet for the royal bodyguard, the revolutionary cockade had been trampled and substituted by the white cockade of the Bourbons, brought all the latent fears of a royal counter coup to the surface. Breaking into the town hall, they seized weapons and powder and at ten o'clock set off on the twelve-mile march to Versailles. They were followed by La Fayette with a contingent of the new National Guard, and by a huge armed mob, almost certainly incited by the Duc d'Orléans, who, it was known, wished to overthrow the King and rule himself.

On arrival in their apartments at Versailles, Madame de Staël found her mother ill but nevertheless preparing to follow Necker to the palace where a council had been hastily assembled. In the ante-room to the council chamber they joined a great many other anxious courtiers. At length, the President of the National Assembly, Mounier, appeared. He had come reluctantly to urge the King to accept the Declaration of the Rights of Man. Necker too had urged him to accept the constitution. Milling around in the ante-rooms, everyone wondered if and when the King would appear and what he would do. 'Night approached,' Madame de Staël recalled, 'and our fears grew with the darkness when we saw M. de Chinon, who later, as the duc de Richelieu, has so rightly won great respect, arriving at the palace. He was pale, exhausted, and dressed almost as a common man. It was the first time that such a dress was seen in the residence of kings and that so great a gentleman as M. de Chinon had been reduced to wearing it. He had been marching with the crowd for some time from Paris to Versailles in order to hear what was being said and had left them halfway in order to warn the royal family. And what a story he had to tell! Women and children armed with pikes and scythes gathered from all parts. The dregs of the people more stupefied by drink than fury. In the midst of this infernal band, men boasted of being cut-throats and were determined to deserve the title.'[31]

After a six-hour march in pouring rain, the bedraggled and exhausted crowd reached Versailles at four o'clock in the afternoon, going first to the National Assembly where they harangued the deputies and occupied the President's chair. Before long they began to congregate outside the barred gates of the palace. It had been so long since the gates of Versailles had been shut that they had rusted in their open position and it had taken several hours and much effort to close them. While a deputation of market-women was allowed in to the Oeil-de-Boeuf ante-chamber to see the King, the constantly swelling mob, encouraged by the fiery revolutionary Théroigne de Méricourt,[32] waited outside. Carlyle, in his extravagant account of the French Revolution, had placed the lovely Liègeoise riding romantically in on a cannon, 'with pike and helmet'.[33] By her own, more prosaic account, she was already at Versailles, where she had been following the discussions at the National Assembly, and was merely mingling with the crowd.[34]

At length La Fayette arrived with a contingent of the National Guard. Greatly reassured by his presence everyone retired to bed shortly after midnight, believing the crisis to be a one-day wonder. Early the next morning, Madame de Staël was surprised in her apartment by an elderly lady whom she did not know personally, the mother to the comte de Choiseul-Goufflier, who had come to seek refuge. From her the Neckers heard of the murder of some of the royal bodyguard in the early hours of the morning, cut down in the very ante-chamber to the Queen's apartments. Marie-Antoinette herself had barely had time to escape to the King's apartments via a secret staircase.

Necker set off at once to see the King. His wife and daughter, who had dressed hastily, again followed him, both fearing for his life. On their way down the long passages between their quarters at the Contrôle Général and the palace, they passed the bloodstains where the Queen's bodyguards had been murdered. Madame de La Tour du Pin, who was also at Versailles where her father-in-law was Minister for War and her husband a serving officer, recounted how her maid had seen someone hacking off the head of one of the guardsmen. She had also seen the arrival of the Duc d'Orléans and heard the murderers acclaim him with 'Long live our King d'Orléans!'[35]

Outside the mob was clamouring for the royal family's removal to Paris. When the King's assent was announced, shots rang out and a great roar of approval replaced the chants of 'To Paris! To Paris!' A call went out for the Queen who bravely went out on to the balcony. The sight of her with her children changed the mood of the crowd yet again and she was cheered with great enthusiasm. When she came in, the Queen, stifling her sobs, said to Madame Necker: 'The King and I are to be forced to go to Paris, with the heads of our bodyguards carried before us on pikes.'[36] This proved no idle threat, as the royal family set off on their terrifying, seven-hour journey to Paris, surrounded by the baying mob, with the decapitated heads of their familiar bodyguards, swaying on pikes in front of their carriage.

A few hours after the King entered his carriage that afternoon, Madame de La Tour du Pin recalled 'The only sound to be heard in the château was the fastening of doors and shutters which had not been closed since the time of Louis XIV.'[37] The glory days of Versailles were over. No French king would live there again.

Chapter 6

Hopes of Boundless Happiness

'The nation was seized with hopes of boundless happiness.'

Madame de Staël[1]

IN THE RAMSHACKLE Tuileries Palace, to which they had been transported by force, the King and Queen were virtual prisoners. Deprived of the hunting which had been his chief and daily pleasure, the King was left to pace the rooms, but before long, with their furniture brought in from Versailles and some of the daily habits of the court re-established, life began to take on some semblance of normality. The National Assembly had followed the King to Paris and was now housed in the former riding school of the Tuileries. The Assembly too had lost some of its independence. As the balance of power shifted from the moderate liberals to the *enragés* or radicals, who had the support of the people, so the aims of the Assembly had changed from liberty to equality. After the October days, as Madame de Staël wrote, it was no longer the Assembly which was in charge of the fate of France, but popular force.[2]

Political debate raged in Paris as never before. In the absence of political parties, the clubs were the centres of the activities and organization of the Revolution. The Jacobins, Feuillants and Cordeliers were not just clubs or places for discussion, however; they were, above all, the centres of decision-making. Questions such as what was to be debated in the Assembly and which candidates would be chosen were decided there. To begin with, the Jacobins were the preserve of the liberal aristocrats, most of them Madame de Staël's friends; men like Alexandre de Lameth, one of their leading lights, and a follower of the constitutional monarchist line. Only later did they become more radical.

With her parents now back in Paris, Germaine de Staël continued to attend all the sessions of the Assembly, where, from her front-row seat, she would often send up notes of congratulation to the deputies, or invitations to her salon. She was known to have considerable influence through her father, in the making of government appointments, a fact which caused deep resentment in some quarters.

The salons were more influential than ever: none more so than Madame de Staël's at the Swedish Embassy in the rue du Bac. Gouverneur Morris described it after his first visit in the autumn of 1789: 'Quite the first salon of Paris at this time was that over which Madame de Staël presided. Her regular Tuesday evening supper, when not more than a dozen or fifteen covers were laid and her chosen friends were admitted into the little salon, the "*chambre ardente*", was the great feature of the week. Here, with the candles extinguished to heighten the effect, the Abbé Delille declaimed his "Catacombs de Rome", and here Clermont-Tonnerre submitted to the criticism of his friends his discourse before delivering it in public. Near the chimney Necker stood, entertaining the Bishop of Autun [Talleyrand], who smiled but avoided talking. Here was to be found the Duchesse de Lauzun, of all women the most gentle and timid; and in the midst stood the hostess, in her favourite attitude before the fire, with her hands behind her back, a large, leonine woman, with few beauties and no grace of gesture. She nevertheless animated the salon by her masculine attitude and powerful conversation.' Morris, who must have felt intimidated by this first visit, noted the presence of Narbonne, 'who is of course with Madame de Staël this evening', as well as several others, concluding: 'I feel very stupid in this group, which by degrees goes off leaving Madame, three gentlemen and myself.'[3]

Perhaps the most interesting and influential member of Madame de Staël's salon was Talleyrand, then Bishop of Autun. Born in 1754, Charles Maurice de Talleyrand-Périgord had forfeited his rights of primogeniture as a result of a fall in infancy which had left his feet permanently crippled, and had entered the church. Embittered and amoral, noted for his sarcastic wit, his exquisite tact and his languid inactivity, Talleyrand was as notorious for his love affairs as he was famous as a brilliant speaker. Benjamin Constant, who knew him well, said of him that his character had been determined by his feet. Elected to the Estates General, he waited to see whether the royalists would win before throwing in his lot with the revolutionaries. Like Madame de Staël, Talleyrand combined an acute, masculine intelligence with a feminine sensibility. They also shared a unique talent for conversation, but there all resemblance ended. Where she was passionate, direct, tactless and utterly loyal, he was delicate, oblique, diplomatic and unscrupulous. Talleyrand was probably Madame de Staël's first lover; although he was the only one of the men she had loved with whom she did not maintain a lifelong friendship. Gouverneur Morris, himself in love with Talleyrand's mistress Madame de Flahaut, reported that during a dinner at Madame de Staël's someone had pointed out to him that Madame the Ambassadress was making eyes at Monsieur the Bishop; 'which I had already observed, and also that he was afraid that I would see too much'.[4]

Miss Mary Berry, a correspondent of Horace Walpole's in Paris in the autumn of 1791, wrote: 'We found her, the Swedish Ambassadress, in the rue du Bac at the height of her passion for Talleyrand.'[5] Miss Berry, who was annoyed to be ignored by Madame de Staël, was reporting stale gossip, however, since by then Madame de Staël had become fully involved with Narbonne, one of Talleyrand's closest friends, by whom she had had a child. Madame de Staël could never resist masculine attention. Whether or not the attraction between Madame de Staël and Talleyrand had developed into a full love affair – she herself denied it – it is possible that she had a fling with him in the winter of 1788–9. She adored his company and was grateful to him for his support of her father's policies. When recalling her youth many years later, Madame de Staël wrote to a friend that 'the three men that I have loved most, that I loved since I was nineteen or twenty were Narbonne, Talleyrand and Montmorency'.[6]

A year her junior, Mathieu de Montmorency-Laval, vicomte, later duc de Montmorency was a member of one of the greatest aristocratic families of France. Tall, slender and fair, the gentle and poetic Mathieu was at that time a convinced and disinterested liberal. Elected to the Estates General, it was his motion in August which had swept away feudal rights. Madame de Staël may well have been in love with him from their first meeting, but at the time he was in love with his cousin, the widow of the Marquis de Laval. When she died as a result of a chill caught on the rainy 14 July 1790, during the Fête de la Fédération, his despair and Madame de Staël's staunch support was the true beginning of a friendship which, in spite of his switching of political loyalties – he became an ardent royalist after the Revolution – nothing could break. It remained a source of happiness and comfort to them both for the rest of her life.[7]

Germaine de Staël was always very uncertain about her personal charms. Used to being the centre of attention, courted for her money, her connections and her brilliant mind, she longed for personal reassurance and seems to have been susceptible to anyone who would pay court to her, even encouraging them to do so. Madame de La Tour du Pin, a slightly younger contemporary and a beauty in her day, confirmed this in her diary, long after Madame de Staël was dead: 'I knew Madame de Staël intimately, but not to the point of exchanging confidences with her . . . Madame de Staël could not understand why I was not enthusiastic about my looks, my colouring, my figure and when I admitted that I did not attach much importance to them . . . she exclaimed naively, that if she had them, she would have wanted to rouse the world.' Madame de Staël was an odd mixture of virtue and vice, Madame de La Tour du Pin thought: 'Vice is too strong a word. Her great qualities were no more than tarnished by the passions to which she abandoned herself the more easily because she felt pleasantly surprised whenever a man sought from her pleasures from which her unfortunate looks seemed to have excluded her forever. Indeed I have every reason to believe that she surrendered without the slightest struggle to any man who showed himself more aware of the beauty of her body than of the charms of her mind.' Yet, she concludes, 'she has shown herself capable of passions that were very deep and devoted while they lasted. For instance she deeply loved M. de Narbonne, who deserted her, so far as I can remember, in a most shameful manner.'[8]

Madame de Boigne who knew her well in middle age, confirmed in 1808, that 'her ugliness had always caused her great distress . . . She could never bring herself to say that such and such a woman was ugly or beautiful. Such a woman would be, in her words, either "deprived or gifted by external advantages". These were the expressions she used. One couldn't describe a person as ugly to her without creating a bad impression.'[9]

Madame de Staël may well have met Louis de Narbonne as early as 1782 at her mother's salon, to which he had been introduced by his friend Talleyrand. She probably began an affair with him in the autumn of 1788, soon after Necker's recall to the Ministry of Finance. Born in 1755, Louis de Narbonne-Lara was believed to be the illegitimate son of Louis XV and the Duchesse de Narbonne-Lara, lady-in-waiting to Madame Adelaïde, Louis XV's daughter. Some even whispered that he was the fruit of an incestuous relationship between Louis XV and his daughter, which the duchess had covered up, but he looked sufficiently like his mother for this to be unlikely. Brought up at court with the Dauphin, he had followed a military career. Handsome, elegant and witty, a gamester and a libertine with a string of love affairs behind him, he was every inch the *grand seigneur*. In 1782 he had married a fourteen-year-old heiress, by whom he had two children, but they had separated when her fortune had proved unequal to his debts. He had another daughter, too, from a more recent liaison with an actress, Louise Contat. Madame Necker had warned her daughter about such men, and had forbidden her to receive him, but Narbonne's mysterious parentage and racy reputation made him all the more irresistible to Madame de Staël.[10] Although a royalist by upbringing, Narbonne joined the liberal wing of the aristocracy soon after meeting Madame de Staël.

A year later, during one of Narbonne's frequent absences with the army – he was made Colonel-in-chief of the Piedmont regiment stationed in Besançon in 1786, and later Commander-in-chief of the National Guard – when she was being courted by the Comte de Clermont-Tonnerre, Madame de Staël wrote to him, admitting her liaison with Narbonne. She must have been tempted by Clermont-Tonnerre, whom she later described as 'an orator as brilliant as he was serious', and whom Madame de La Tour du Pin remembered as 'a young man as distinguished by his charming appearance and his eloquence as by his rare qualities of intelligence and the strength of his character',[11] and was unwilling to put him off entirely: 'I greatly loved, I still love Count Louis [Narbonne] tenderly. As soon as he saw me he changed his destiny for me, his former ties were cut and he dedicated his life to me; he convinced me that he could love me enough to be able to respect my duties, and to think himself still lucky to possess my heart, but were he to lose that irrevocably, he would not survive . . . I owe it to you to allow you to read my heart. I await your reply in fear and trembling. I must fear that you will no longer wish to please me . . . that you will wish to give me up. Your reply will seem like an edict which will decide my fate.'[12]

Staël, although unfaithful himself, was furiously jealous of all the men paying court to his wife, and was often, indeed mostly, agitated and aggressive when with her. She was bored and irritated by him, yet not indifferent to his suffering, trying yet again to establish a friendship between them which, she knew, was all she could ever offer him: 'I promised to write to you but I am impeded by the impossibility of calming a spirit like yours. What have I not tried, what will I not yet try to succeed? But the demon of jealousy, of injured pride and love agitates you ceaselessly. Sometimes you have reason to blame the apparent carelessness of my conduct. At other times, such as yesterday for instance, for no reason at all you get carried away and wound me with expressions as mad as they are hurtful. Think for a moment about me. Think how I feel in the centre of this continuous storm which upsets my life . . . Where is the heart that can bear such perpetual torment? The most passionate lovers end in separation when they make each other unhappy, and yet you expect a tender and sincere friendship to survive such storms, strong enough to uproot oaks? I am too honest to pretend to feelings I don't have. I am happy when I make you happy and when you do not trouble my happiness. But to find oneself in the arms of a man who in turn points a dagger at one's heart or his own, who overwhelms one with threats or complaints, that may be devotion but it is no pleasure.'[13]

Staël proved quite unequal to the sort of relationship his wife wanted, far from uncommon at that time when so many marriages were arranged. At a dinner at her parents' house, on 8 November 1789, Madame de Staël was seated next to Morris. As their conversation grew more animated, Madame de Staël begged him to speak English, which her husband did not understand. Observing 'much emotion' in de Staël, Morris remarked that her husband loved her to distraction. She replied that she knew, and that it made her miserable. He consoled her for Narbonne's absence and they spoke of Talleyrand: 'She tells me she rather invites than repels those who incline to be attentive, and some time after says that perhaps I may become an admirer. I tell her that it is not impossible; but as a previous condition she must agree not to repel me, which she promises.' After dinner Morris spoke to Staël who 'inveighs bitterly against the manners of this country, and the cruelty of alienating a wife's affections. He says that women here are more corrupt in their minds and hearts than in any other way.' Morris, whose vanity may have read too much into some light-hearted banter, added that he did not intend to make M. de Staël uncomfortable.[14]

The poor ambassador had other problems too. Gustavus III had by now lost all confidence in him, convinced that he was a mere tool of the Neckers'. He had asked the new embassy secretary, Silfersparre, to report separately and in detail on all that was going on in Paris. He even sent the Baron Taube as a special envoy to Paris to reassure the King and Marie-Antoinette that he put no faith in Staël's reports which were prejudiced in favour of the Revolution, but that he was pretending otherwise in order to learn more about the activities of the liberals. Taube made it clear that the Queen would be delighted to see Staël replaced by Fersen, her Swedish admirer. Staël knew that the King was also getting reports from the extreme royalists and was afraid that he might be withdrawn at any time. He was afraid to absent himself even for a day for fear that he might find himself without a job. At about this time the unhappy Staël also began to dabble in mysticism, introduced to the Illuminists by Baron Reuterholm, a friend of the King's brother, the Duke of Sudermania, Grandmaster of the Swedish Masons who had come to France to visit the French lodges. Staël had helped him organize initiation ceremonies in Avignon; they had taken part together in bizarre occult practices in which saints appeared in mirrors. They had also consulted a prophetess who preached the end of the world and a return to the golden age through the Revolution. His new-found religious faith made him feel guilty about the irregularities of his own life. Miserably, he wrote to Reuterholm: 'My tender friend, I have lived through bitter hours since your departure . . . My heart is heavy and I am flooded in tears. Pray, ah! pray that my troubles might serve to instruct me. Pray for my wife! May she never know the anguish I am suffering!'[15]

Probably longing for the maternal tenderness so lacking in his wife, Staël had become involved with an elderly actress – she was then almost seventy – who by a bizarre quirk of chance was none other than Mlle Clairon, Germaine de Staël's former drama teacher. Here, too, he showed very poor judgement. Mlle Clairon turned out to be a very canny old bird. She soon persuaded the hapless ambassador to sign over large amounts of money to her, even suing him later for more.

Uninterested in the occult herself, Madame de Staël was not displeased that her husband was occupied. Her affair with Narbonne, known to most of their friends, was now the centre of her emotional life and, together with politics, took up all her time. She was the main inspiration of the constitutional monarchists. By the end of the year she was also, once again, pregnant.

The year 1790 was, as his daughter wrote, 'the most difficult of all' for Necker.[16] It began with a serious attack of bilious fever, which his family believed was a result of the anxieties he had suffered from lack of support and a fall in his popularity. Madame de Staël described his dilemma: 'The court, seeing his popularity decline paid less attention to his advice; while the popular party, knowing that his credit at court was diminished, no longer feared his influence. His strength at court was his popularity, and he was losing it by defending the court. His credit at court would have given him influence over the popular party, but it was not forthcoming because he had supported the popular party at court.'[17]

Morris described the situation in Paris to George Washington in January 1790. The King was, in effect, a prisoner, the aristocracy divided and rudderless, the liberals, 'who mean well but have unfortunately acquired their ideas of government from books', unfocused. His respect for Madame de Staël had grown however. He described her as 'a woman of wonderful wit and above vulgar prejudice of every kind' and her house as 'a kind of temple of Apollo, where the men of wit and fashion are collected twice a week at supper and once at dinner, and sometimes more frequently'.[18]

Madame de Staël hoped that by bringing together royalists, liberals and radicals in her salon that they would come to some compromise. Liberal to the core, although she was more impatient for change than Necker, support of her father and his policies remained her main concern. Many of the reforms advocated in her salon became law. In spite of difficulties, the Constituent Assembly was hugely popular. Careers were now open to talent, the press was free, individual and civil rights established. Madame de Staël would always look back on those early years of the Revolution from 1788 to the end of 1791 with affection and pride. 'One breathed more freely, there was more air in one's lungs, and the nation was seized with hopes of boundless happiness, just as people are in their youth, improvidently and full of illusion.'

Writing about Parisian society in those years in her *Considerations on the French Revolution*, she believed that never had a society been as brilliant and as serious at the same time. Politics was still in the hands of the liberal aristocracy: 'all the vigour of liberty and all the former grace was to be found in the same person. Men of the Third Estate, those who were distinguished by their own learning and talents, were prouder of their merit than of their group privileges . . . At no time and in no other country was the art of speaking in all its forms as remarkable as in the early years of the Revolution.'[19]

For all the excitement of politics, a severe blow in the spring of 1790 – the death of the Comte de Guibert – caused Madame de Staël great grief. To ease her pain she began at once to write her *Éloge de M. de Guibert*, which she finished that summer. 'His conversation was the most varied, the most animated, the most fruitful of any I have ever known . . . he had original thoughts on every subject and an abiding interest in everything . . . Who will give me back those long conversations, where I watched him develop so many ideas with so much imagination! . . . He did not offer consolation by weeping with you; but no one was better able to soften your sorrow by talking about it, making you see all sides of a question . . . He was not a daily presence, not the friend of every moment . . . but when he returned, in an hour you had recaptured the thread of all his feelings, of all his thoughts. He would give you his entire soul as he talked to you.'[20]

Necker's enemies now launched attacks on his daughter as well. The personal price of press freedom did not put her off: she continued to defend the freedom of expression in all its forms to the end of her life. Pamphleteers and journalists from both extremes, royalist and radical, resentful of her power, portrayed her as lewd and immoral. In one pamphlet entitled *King Necker*, the writer declared that 'Germaine spares no effort to make men for her father, and her father refuses nothing to the men she has made for him.' The royalist satirist, Rivarol, in a spoof dedication to her in his *Petit Dictionaire des Grands Hommes de la Révolution*, writes: 'Ah! Madame, without doubt you possess too many advantages for a mortal to be able to love you for yourself alone; he would have to decide between your mind and your charms; he would have to constantly leave aside your works for your eyes; the weight of so much talent is beyond human strength. All good Frenchmen have therefore been reduced to desiring in you only the public good, and to sacrifice themselves for it in your arms. It has been written, Madame, that everything would be free in France including your lovers, and you have confirmed that great destiny, as no one else could.'[21]

She was called 'the Bacchante of the Revolution', accused in plays and poems of entertaining the political troops. 'Girondins for dinner, Jacobins for supper and at night everyone.' Nor was she spared jokes about her appearance, which must have been particularly wounding, as for example 'that she was the only one able to deceive the public as to her sex'. It was an early taste of the sort of vilification that accompanied her to the grave.

In May 1790 it was decided that the anniversary of the fall of Bastille should be celebrated in Paris. The Fête de la Fédération on the 14 July was also to celebrate the new Constitution which, although still incomplete, had won almost universal assent. *Fédérés*, or National Guardsmen from each of the new eighty-three departments of France, were to attend a national celebration on the Champ de Mars, in a huge amphitheatre which was to be excavated opposite the École Militaire. The idea was so popular that when it became obvious that work on the amphitheatre could not be completed in time, Parisians from all walks of life took part in the work. 'Such an extraordinary spectacle will never be seen again,' wrote Madame de La Tour du Pin, whose husband and father-in-law were directly involved in the preparations. 'Thousands of barrows were pushed by people of every quality; . . . Capuchin monks and friars pulling besides ladies of the town, laundresses and knights of St Louis worked side by side in that great gathering of all the people . . . Everyone was moved by the same impulse: fellowship. Everyone who owned a carriage horse sent it for a few hours every day to pull earth. There was not a single shop boy in Paris who was not busy on the Champ de Mars.'[22]

On the day itself, Madame de Staël, now heavily pregnant, attended the festival with her parents. Squalls of heavy rain swept the new amphitheatre around which eighty-three poles bearing the banners of the departments had been placed. The troops, in a dazzling variety of uniforms, with the National Guard at their centre led by La Fayette, their Commander-in-chief, having paraded through Paris, entered the ground through a triumphal arch, forming up around an altar which had been placed in the centre. Here Talleyrand, as Bishop of Autun, celebrated Mass, watched by the royal family from an ornate stand which had been specially erected. The enthusiastic public, not at all put off by the weather, crowded on the banks all around the amphitheatre, huddled under a canopy of multicoloured umbrellas. As La

Fayette approached the altar to swear allegiance to the nation, the King and the law, a roar of approval went up from the delirious crowd. Madame de Staël believed as she witnessed 'this last movement of a truly national enthusiasm' that the French people had always desired a limited monarchy, and were happy because for the first time they saw monarchy and liberty reconciled. Madame de La Tour du Pin on the other hand, who knew the Queen well, noticed that she was making a tremendous effort to hide her ill-humour: 'but she was not succeeding sufficiently well for her own good or the King's'.[23] La Fayette was the hero of the hour. But Necker's face registered deep disquiet. He knew that the country was all but bankrupt.[24]

Necker's popularity declined steadily during 1790. He opposed the National Assembly on two issues. The first serious clash was over the Assembly's proposal to publish the *Livre Rouge* or red book, showing how much money had gone into the pockets of the royal family and their favourites. Necker refused at first to provide the Assembly with the necessary figures, but had to give in. The second issue was over the so-called *assignats*.

At the end of 1789, the National Assembly had appropriated the Church's vast land holdings, which amounted to almost 10 per cent of France's total land surface. Needing money urgently, the Assembly decided to sell this land and to assign the proceeds to issuing interest-bearing bonds or *assignats*, which would be sold to the public. When, by the spring of 1790, the government found that it had been unable to sell most of the *assignats*, these were converted into money and issued like banknotes. Necker had opposed this idea not only because he disapproved of the confiscation of church property, but also because he foresaw all the problems which would arise as a result of speculation and depreciation. By September 1790, final steps were taken to convert the *assignats* into a paper currency and 800 million livres' worth was put into circulation. Two years later more than 3 billion livres of paper currency had been printed, leading to runaway inflation and with it a social and political crisis. Seven years later the *assignats* were not worth the paper they were printed on. When defeated on the confiscation of church property, Necker had not merely contented himself with opposing the printing of vast amounts of paper money, he had also proposed the creation of a bank into which a proportion of the church's money would have been placed as a guarantee, putting the state's finances in a comfortable situation. Then he had asked that, in view of the fact that as the minister he was not allowed to attend the Assembly's sessions, and all too often his carefully prepared memoranda were returned unread, members of his treasury team be admitted instead during debates on financial matters. Both these requests were refused.

Undermined continuously by Mirabeau, attacked on all sides by pamphleteers, and finding no support from the King, Necker realized that he could do nothing more. On 3 September 1790, he resigned. His resignation letter, read to the deputies by the Baron de Jessé, president of the National Assembly, passed without comment, indeed it was hardly noticed.

Madame Necker had feared for her husband's life as attacks on him became ever more virulent and his life as well as their house in Paris were threatened. Her fragile state of health and Necker's own conviction that all his chances of useful service had been undermined decided him to leave the country. Packing hastily, the Neckers left Paris with great sadness on the evening of 8 September 1790. The Marquis de Nicolaï, who was an eyewitness, expressed his astonishment in a letter to his friend, the young comte de Buffon, at the contrast between Necker's return a year before and his departure: 'Never had a minister left so *incognito*. The general silence on the subject, the complete indifference of the French (of Parisians), is one of the most astonishing things I have ever witnessed. Neither satires, nor eulogies were published; nothing: not a word. A chair falling in the Tuileries makes more noise than the departure of a man who was adored fifteen months ago, and whose disgrace then had provoked such momentous events . . .'[25]

In spite of his conviction that printing large amounts of paper money would ruin the state, Necker left the 2 million francs he had deposited earlier in the state treasury as a gesture of confidence and commitment. As Minister of Finance, and with a bond signed by the King allowing him to withdraw it whenever he liked, it would have been perfectly easy for him to take his money and run. Since this represented more than half his personal fortune, it was a noble gesture. His daughter, and even his grandson, were to have a great deal of trouble in recovering the money.

Four days before her father's resignation, on 31 August 1790, Madame de Staël gave birth to a son, Louis Auguste. Staël acknowledged him as his own and indeed believed him to be so, but in fact he was Narbonne's child. Still recovering from the birth, Madame de Staël was now obliged to part with her father as M. and Madame Necker left Paris – scene of so many achievements, so many triumphs – for the last time on 8 September. The very next day they were arrested by the municipal authorities of Arcis-sur-Aube. Their passports, issued by the municipality of Paris and by the King, had proved insufficient to protect them. Worried by Madame Necker's failing health, and suffering from the same trouble which had laid him low at the beginning of the year, Necker wrote at once to the National Assembly as well as to his daughter. As soon as his letter reached her, although she was still recovering from the birth of her son, Madame de Staël sent a short letter to the Baron de Jessé, president of the National Assembly that month (a different President of the National Assembly was chosen each month), in which she only just managed to choke back her indignation and fury at the injustice done to her father: 'I beg you as a favour, Monsieur, to kindly put the matter of my father's arrest before the Assembly this morning. It is essential to his health that there are no delays. This is the only consideration I put before you. I address myself to you personally, Monsieur. Your reputation gives me confidence. Permit me to assure you that I would not mention my father's name to anyone not worthy of hearing it. I have the honour Sir, to be your very humble and obedient servant.'[26]

That very day a letter went out from the National Assembly to Arcis-sur-Aube, asking the municipal authorities to free the Neckers at once. They were to be stopped once more – and even their lives threatened – at Vesoul, but at the beginning of October the couple were at their estate of Coppet in Switzerland.

Madame de Staël left Paris on 5 October, as soon as she could after the birth of her son. She left the six-week-old Auguste in Paris with his wet nurse and his nanny, the excellent Mlle Bernault, an agreeable and intelligent Swiss Protestant, who had brought up Madame de Staël herself. Staël dared not leave Paris this time. His wife was escorted to Geneva by a friend, the Comte de Gouvernet, later Marquis de La Tour du Pin de Gouvernet, who was travelling to Switzerland to bring back his own wife. It may seem odd to have left her new-born baby behind but Madame de Staël was not in fact lacking in maternal instinct. It was not at all uncommon at the time for children to be brought up by servants. She left her son in the safe and loving hands of her own nurse with whom she corresponded constantly. Later she took a great interest in her children's upbringing and education and was much loved by them all. But her father's need of her now sent her rushing to Switzerland and kept her there until the new year in spite of the boredom of Coppet and Geneva, her mother's hostility and the fear of losing her lover, Narbonne.

Necker dealt with his enforced retirement by beginning work at once on an apologia of his administration. In one of her almost daily letters to her husband, Madame de Staël wrote: 'My father is far from happy in his retirement. But you can imagine that I am entirely devoted to him. In the mornings we walk, in the evenings we play piquet. I never go out, we receive no one – I am more devoted to him than I ever was as a girl.'[27]

As Madame Necker's health deteriorated she became more embittered and more demanding of her husband. 'Women in old age, are only bearable in this world if they take up no space, make no noise, ask for nothing, give to all those who depend on them and live only for the happiness of others,'[28] she wrote bitterly. Her daughter's liaison with Narbonne and her well-founded suspicions of her grandson's paternity offended her high moral principles. She was deeply disapproving of her daughter and, perhaps above all, increasingly jealous of her closeness to Necker. She not only treated her daughter coldly but started to make life as difficult as possible for her by refusing her horses, servants, everything apart from food and drink. In addition there were constant complaints about M. de Staël's extravagance, and her own. Not surprisingly, Madame de Staël found her mother intolerable, although she could still excuse her behaviour because of her illness. Madame de Staël wrote to her husband soon after her arrival: 'she is afraid that my absence or my presence might make a difference to him. This feeling which is constantly present, makes my stay difficult sometimes and I must admit that it would make me happy if you were able to come and fetch me in early January.'[29]

Necker, too, for all his love for his wife, clung to his daughter. 'My father is definitely in better spirits since my arrival,' Germaine wrote to her husband. 'You can't imagine what lengths I don't go to, to represent an entire National Assembly in my person. I make every effort to be gay, not to give way to low spirits which I easily could, were I to reflect on his sad situation and on mine, the horrible ingratitude he has to bear, the difficulty of living in Paris; the boredom of living here, my mother's character, impossible to bear, even for him in his solitude.'[30]

While Narbonne was so busy with his own affairs that he hardly wrote to her, Germaine's husband, believing a rumour that he had spent several days at Coppet, threw another jealous scene. His wife wrote to reassure him that Narbonne would never have been allowed to stay by Madame Necker: 'He has completely neglected me. I know that he is in Paris and due to return to Toul in a week, but I know this indirectly for he has not deigned to write to me since his return [to Paris].'[31]

Nevertheless she longed for Paris, for Narbonne, for her friends. Her correspondence with the Comte de Gouvernet throughout the month of November shows how closely she followed events in Paris and how much her advice was sought. To Gouvernet, who had not wished to succeed his father as Minister of War, she wrote: 'As it's not to be you, it may as well be someone[a Jacobin candidate] who would be finished if there was the shadow of an insurrection, and whose behaviour would finally make it clear to us all what the Jacobins are up to – perhaps even discredit them because of the efforts they would be obliged to make to support this person.' As for the aristocrats, who were emigrating in great numbers to Turin, 'You will have some idea of what they are like, when I tell you that I would prefer the Jacobins.'[32]

The Neckers left for Geneva at the beginning of December. In spite of the solitude and boredom of Coppet, Madame de Staël was not keen to exchange it for the balls, assemblies and suppers of Geneva, much preferring the work she was engaged on. She was now writing a play, *Montmorency*. Her cousins Madame Necker-de Saussure and Madame Rilliet-Necker tried to amuse her, each giving a ball in her honour. She was grateful, but wrote to her husband: 'If you promise to keep it secret I will admit to you that the society of the *Genevois* is almost unbearable to me. Their love of equality is no more than a wish to bring everyone down; their love of liberty is mere insolence; and their high minded morality – boredom.'[33] By the end of that month she was quite resolved to return to Paris. She needed to do so to see to Necker's financial affairs, which M. de Staël was incapable of managing. She was looking forward to seeing her baby son, writing to her husband that it would be a sweet moment for her when she saw them both again and to expect her arrival on 10 January.[34]

The first days of the New Year found her in Lausanne, much more agreeable than Geneva, where she stayed with the Cazenove d'Arlens. Here she was much admired and a splendid ball was given in her honour. After hearing her read extracts from her *Sophie ou les Sentiments Secrets* at a soirée, the crotchety Rosalie Constant, spinster cousin of Benjamin, was thoroughly won over and wrote to a friend that Madame de Staël was like no other woman: 'Such words as sweetness, grace, modesty, a wish to please, conformity to custom and manners, cannot be used in relation to her, but one is swept along, subjugated by the force of her genius. It follows a new path; it is a fire which lights the way, which sometimes blinds you but which cannot leave you cold or indifferent. Her mind is too superior for others to shine or be able to argue with her. Wherever she is, most people become mere spectators.' And yet, she added, Madame de Staël had a kind of childlike good humour which saved her from any charge of pedantry.[35] In spite of the pleasures of Lausanne and the anticipated joy of returning to Paris, the fast approaching separation from her father weighed heavily on her. On New Year's Day, 1791, wishing him a happy New Year, which she hoped would be less horrible than the previous one, Madame de Staël wrote to her husband announcing that she would not be going back to Geneva to take leave of her father as planned, but would be returning directly to avoid the pain of parting with him.[36] On 8 January 1791, a teasing note to Staël announced her arrival. She was at Nogent, near Paris, and would be home that night, sooner than he might have expected – 'in spite of the reasonable hope you might have had that I would break my neck!'[37]

Chapter 7

~

From Constitution to Revolution

'At Madame de Staël's this evening I meet the world'
Gouverneur Morris[1]

THE FRANCE TO which Madame de Staël returned in January 1791 was in a dangerous state of near anarchy, as the troubles caused by a complete upset in all the institutions, coupled with a growing struggle between the partisans of the old and new regimes, erupted all over the country. This and the Constitution which was still being drafted were the focus of the salon which she reopened. Sieyès was one of its central figures. Madame de Staël believed that his writings and opinions would herald a new era – 'that they would be to politics what Newton's were to physics'.[2] Believing more than ever that a constitutional monarchy on the English model was the only way to save France from anarchy, Madame de Staël and the liberals would now be fighting a war on two fronts; against the diehard royalists and, on the other side, against the increasingly radical and powerful Jacobins. The moderate, centrist position of the constitutionalists brought them crossfire from both the right- and left-wing press.

The Constituent Assembly had not intended to destroy the Roman Catholic Church in France. It had merely wished to reorganize society. However the Civil Constitution of the Clergy, a decree passed in the Assembly the previous July 1790, followed by the nationalization of church property, became more radical still with a further decree in December 1790, imposing an oath of loyalty to the state on all priests (those refusing to swear were forbidden to exercise their priestly functions). It was reluctantly sanctioned by the King, who bitterly regretted doing so for the rest of his days. It severely restricted the church's power, thus creating a serious schism in the French Catholic Church between 'jurors' and 'non-jurors'. Church and state were henceforth separated. The effects of the resulting conflict, circumstantial rather than intended, last to this day. The army too was polarized, as royalist officers resigned, accusing those who remained of treason. 'The executive power *played dead* . . . believing wrongly, that good might come out of yet more ill. Ministers waited on the Assembly to give the government more power to deal with matters, while the Assembly concentrated on administration, instead of getting on with legislation – the only constitutional decrees passed were designed to remove the King's power to appoint any members of the government,' wrote Madame de Staël later.[3]

Added impetus for those who sided with the diehard monarchists in November 1790 had come with the publication of Edmund Burke's *Reflections on the Revolution in France*. A leading member of the Whig opposition in England, who had supported the American colonists and the cause of liberty, to the shock and dismay of many of his liberal friends, Burke had written a bitter invective against the aspirations of the French to rid themselves of a corrupt and incompetent system. Translated into French, his book had required ten reprints and was to become the bible of the counter-revolutionaries, although Madame de Staël later noted: 'those who quote Burke today as the enemy of the Revolution perhaps ignore the fact that on every page he reproaches the French with not having adopted the principles of the British constitution'.[4] Burke's thesis was that society was a slow-growing and organic thing and any sudden innovation was dangerous. Liberty should never be confused with licence. To a man of his conservative temperament, the constitutional monarchists were as bad as the Jacobins. By 1791 he would be strongly urging England to go to war.

By the end of 1790 the King himself had given up any idea of co-existence with the Constitution, if indeed he had ever entertained one. The decree which – much against his will and conscience – he had signed in December, and which obliged priests to swear loyalty to the Constitution, was the last straw. A letter from the Pope expressing dismay, together with pressure from his brother-in-law Leopold II of Austria, helped make up Louis's mind that he must now escape from Paris and attempt to re-establish royal authority from the outside.

Early in the new year, the King's aunts, Mesdames Victoire and Adélaïde, unwilling to hear Mass from juror priests, decided to emigrate to Rome. They left Paris on 19 February 1791, accompanied by Narbonne, who had been brought up at Madame Adélaïde's knee and was her equerry. They were stopped at Arnay-le-Duc. Narbonne was obliged to hurry back to Paris and get a pass from the National Assembly to ensure their safe departure. At length the Princesses reached Rome, where Narbonne also left his mother, his wife and his eldest daughter.

The royalist press meanwhile, redoubled its attacks on Madame de Staël. She was blamed for the whole affair, supposedly because she had wished to prevent the departure of her lover, Narbonne. The many attacks from both sides on Madame de Staël, as indeed on Marie-Antoinette, were not merely political but sexual, varying from innuendo to the downright pornographic. Both were portrayed as immoral and promiscuous. A three-act play entitled *On the Intrigues of Madame de Staël on the occasion of the departure of Mesdames de France* linked her publicly with Narbonne, depicting her as a modern Circe, and her husband as a cuckold and a fool.[5] The play, while not performed was widely circulated, increased Staël's seething resentment against his wife, prompting him to new accusations and questions in his letters as to how often, for how long and where she saw Narbonne. Madame de Staël replied indignantly that she had merely seen Narbonne to say goodbye to him at her friend Madame de Castellane's,[6] and only because M. de Staël had forbidden him the house.[7] Her protestations that he was just a friend, that she had been at her milliner's, and all the other excuses which serve at such times, were sounding more and more hollow. The truth was that she was now deeply involved with Narbonne, whom, as a leading moderate, she wished to see take her father's place at the helm of public affairs. For the moment, she concentrated on promoting his military career. Her friend, the Comte de Gouvernet, who was about to be appointed ambassador to the Hague, was still in the army. Through him, she managed to get Narbonne's regiment transferred from Besançon to near Alsace.[8]

Mirabeau had been as convinced as Necker that the King was the best defence against both popular anarchy and a counter coup by the diehard royalists. Although he liked to play a more radical hand in the Assembly, he had entered into secret negotiations with Louis, urging him to accept a moderate constitution. 'I have in my hands a letter from Mirabeau, written to the King,' Madame de Staël wrote, 'in which he offers every chance to give France a strong and worthy monarchy, but a limited one. In it he uses a remarkable expression: *I would not wish my work to have been merely one of a vast destruction.*'[9]

Mirabeau's death on 2 April came as a shock to Madame de Staël as to all the political world. She thought it a great disaster: 'On the day after his death, no one in the Constituent Assembly could look at the place where Mirabeau usually sat without sorrow. The great oak had fallen, the rest was barely noticeable.'[10] Distrusted by both sides, Mirabeau was nevertheless given a state funeral, although his reputation with the radicals was to suffer an irreparable blow when, after his death, they learned of his secret correspondence with the King. For all his notorious vices, Madame de Staël, who contributed to the funeral speech made by Talleyrand, mourned him also as a rare mind whose like they would not see again.

Necker's resignation and Mirabeau's death marked the end of the early stage of the Revolution when a limited monarchy might still have been possible. Their places would soon be taken by radical left-wing activists like Marat, Danton, Brissot and Robespierre – all convinced republicans.

On 17 April, not wishing to receive the Easter Sacraments from a juror priest, which they would certainly have been obliged to do had they remained in Paris, the royal family left the Tuileries for Saint-Cloud. It was soon clear that La Fayette could no longer guarantee their safety when they were stopped by the mob, but more importantly, by the National Guard who had refused to obey their general, La Fayette. Embittered by the petty restrictions on his power and on his freedom of movement, the King fell into a deep depression. Deciding that he was in effect a prisoner in Paris, he believed that the time had come to escape to the provinces on the eastern border where, defended by royalist troops and foreign forces, he might be in a better position to force the revolutionaries to accept compromises. The actual plan of escape was left to the much more resolute Queen, with the help of her admirer, the Swedish Count Fersen.

At the end of April, Madame de Staël set off once more for Switzerland where she remained until mid-August. On the way she stopped in Besançon, where Narbonne's regiment was still stationed. Although she had again left Auguste behind, her letters to Staël, to Auguste's nurse and to Madame Rilliet-Huber, her childhood friend, who was obviously keeping an eye on him, reflect her growing attachment to her child.

A week before her departure she had published her first political article in the *Indépendants*, the paper of her friend Suard. It was unsigned and entitled '*How can the opinion of the majority of the nation be recognized?*' (*À quels signes peut on connaître quelle est l'opinion de la majorité de la Nation?*) In it Madame de Staël argued for a limited monarchy and a strong legislature, but for the first time she also declared that if the country preferred a republic she would accept it.[11]

The question of universal male suffrage was an important part of the civil liberties desired by those who had begun the Revolution. The rights of women, still legally minors with no economic rights, was also on the agenda. The bid for equality had been championed by Madame de Staël's friend, the Marquis de Condorcet,[12] who had in the previous year published a plea for women's suffrage, *Sur l'admission des femmes au droit de cité*, as well as by the playwright, Olympe de Gouges, who in that year had published her manifesto, *The Rights of Women*, based on the *Declaration of the Rights of Man*. Madame de Staël may have often disregarded at least the social limitations on women, but she had also suffered enough ridicule, calumny and vilification from all sides, particularly from other women, to make her believe that for the vast majority of women there might be too high a price to pay if they became politically active on their own behalf. While she fully recognized the power of her mind and her own talents, and interested as she was in power, she was content to exercise it through and for the men she loved. Her views would change later. Her two influential novels, *Delphine* and *Corinne* were to tackle the problem of women's rights and their role in society head on. Her contribution to the cause of women's rights would be made not through politics but through her writing; through her powerful denunciation of the social order and her declared conviction that the way in which societies treated women was a measure of their level of civilization. Her literary, political and social writing emphasized women's inferior role in society, their 'deplorable fate', and championed their education.

'The first, the dearest interest in my life' was still her father, whose political apologia, *Sur l'administration de M. Necker, par lui-même*, which he had been working on since his enforced retirement, was published in Paris on 10 May 1791. A letter from Geneva to her husband, dated 8 May, begs him to report on its reception.[13]

She spent the next six weeks promoting Necker's book as best she could while recovering from scarlet fever and a bad attack of toothache. Neither were as difficult to bear as her mother. Her letters to her husband make it clear that as always, she couldn't wait to get away from Coppet, although she was reluctant to leave her father. 'We are absolutely alone here and it's great proof of my feelings for my father, that I am able to put up, night and day, with my mother's character, who treats me in a way which might make you pity me, if you still loved me.'[14]

Staël had his own worries. He was seriously concerned about the possibility of losing his post. Determined to intervene to strengthen the French King's position, Gustavus was threatening to break off relations with the French government. Staël knew that since he was Ambassador to the King of France, if the King went, so would he.

On 21 June news of the attempted flight of the royal family, and their arrest at Varennes, sent shock waves through Paris, sealing the King's fate. The Jacobin press had already pointed to unusual movements of troops at the frontier. The declaration, which the King left behind in the Tuileries, showed only too clearly how far Louis XVI was from understanding the popular support enjoyed by the Revolution. His flight, followed by the royal family's return two days later in their outsize *berline* (the all too noticeable carriage which had been specially commissioned by Fersen because the King refused to travel separately from the rest of his family) to be greeted by silent, hostile crowds, removed once and for all any possibility of a constitutional monarchy in France. On 24 June a huge crowd marched on the National Assembly to call for a republic, but were turned back by the National Guard. As news of the attempted escape spread through Paris, furious crowds smashed windows while the radical press, especially Marat's *L'Ami du Peuple*, called for popular action to depose the King. Even moderates like Condorcet converted to republicanism. The Queen was the target of particular fury. Had she not connived with foreign powers?

'Sire, All is lost' wrote Fersen to the King of Sweden, who now determined to put together a coalition to save the French monarchy. At Aachen in Germany, where he had arrived on 16 June, he began to gather together the forces of the counter-revolution. 'All of Paris believes that your Majesty will attack France at the head of an army of 30,000 men on behalf of the counter-revolution,' Staël wrote to

Gustavus on 24 June. Accused of supplying passports for the royal family, and afraid for his life, he explained to the King that he had been lucky because although on 19 June he had gone to see Fersen, the latter had refused to receive him, proof that he had not taken part in the plot. However this might not be enough to save him. If the King wished to recall him, might he not do so now before hostilities began?[15]

The royal family's flight provoked a final split between the moderates and the radicals at the Assembly. Deserting the Jacobins, the triumvirate of Barnave, Adrien Duport and Alexandre de Lameth, as well as many other friends of Madame de Staël, among them Sieyès and Talleyrand, left to form the Feuillant Club[16] where they were joined by a majority of deputies. Robespierre, who had been elected president of the Jacobin Club in 1790, would now set its agenda. Barnave tried to persuade the Assembly that what mattered was the new Constitution which they had worked on all this time, and which was much more important than the personal qualities or faults of the monarch. The deposition of the King, he pointed out, carried a risk of war with European powers (and indeed the Pillnitz declaration of 27 August 1791, signed by Leopold of Austria and Frederick William of Prussia, threatened armed intervention against France on behalf of Louis XVI).

Barnave's increasingly friendly relations with the Queen allowed him to hope that he could reconcile the royal family and the public. The public, however, was now much more radical and calls for the King to be punished, and for a republic, grew more insistent.

On 16 July 1791, the Assembly voted not to depose the King. Instantly the Cordeliers club drew up a petition declaring the Assembly's decision contrary to the will of the people. The next day, a huge crowd gathered to sign the petition on the Champ de Mars, the very place where only a year before France had celebrated national unity at the Fête de la Fédération. The volatile crowd, mistaking two men found hiding under the steps of the platform on which the petition was to be signed for spies, hanged them. As Commander of the National Guard and responsible for security, La Fayette marched to disperse the crowd. In the scuffles that followed, he gave the order for the National Guard to fire on the unarmed crowd. Fifty people were killed. 'The massacre of the Champs de Mars', which marked the first time that the National Guard – a product of the Revolution – had turned on the people on behalf of the King, was also the beginning of a clamp-down on popular political demonstrations, and the banning of radical newspapers.

News of the flight had reached Madame de Staël on 28 June together with a miserable letter from her husband about the probable loss of his embassy. Heavily in debt, friendless and fearing for his life, his post and ultimately his marriage, Staël could only turn to his wife for reassurance. Rallying him by return of post, she begged him to entrust Auguste, 'our chief interest', to her friend Mme Rilliet, should Staël have to leave Paris suddenly. She also reminded him that Gustavus had promised him a pension of 20,000 livres should he be removed from Paris. If he kept his promise, together with what she had, they would have enough to live on. She hoped that her father's assistance, and the sale of part of their silver, would clear their debts, but the probable loss of her father's own fortune (the two million left in France, which they were now unable to recover) made it difficult for her to make her husband any firm promises. If they lived five months in Switzerland and seven in Paris, they would get by. The royal camp[17] and her mother's house were equally odious to her. She begged him to give her at least ten days' warning should he intend to leave Paris, to give her time to get there. On no account must Auguste be left without one or other of his parents. While her husband agonized and floundered, Madame de Staël began to make contingency plans for their financial recovery, the sale of their silver, and their future life together.[18]

Staël, meanwhile, had been expressly forbidden by Gustavus III to have any dealings with the Foreign Minister or the National Assembly. Perhaps he should ask the King for some leave? he wrote to his wife. 'Leave and recall would be one and the same at such a time,' she replied. She urged him to stay and to consult Talleyrand who 'will develop further the ideas I believe to be right', which were broadly that it was nonsensical of the King of Sweden to think of attacking France. Gustavus III should certainly make no move until the end of the current parliament and the presentation of the Constitutional Act to the King. Necker had endorsed this view.[19]

Worried about her husband's position as ambassador, though not yet about the political situation, Madame de Staël decided to cut short her stay by a fortnight and return to Paris. Although Staël needed her help, this was not what he wanted. Her absence simplified his relations with the Swedish King and made his personal life easier. He offered to send Auguste to her in Switzerland in the hope of keeping her there, even writing to the Neckers to this effect. But Madame de Staël was determined to return to Paris for the final stages of the drafting of the new Constitution. If the situation demanded it, she wrote, she would come back to Coppet, taking Auguste with her. Meanwhile, the child was safe in the country with Madame Rilliet, separation from his nanny would be cruel and Madame de Staël was loath to ask her mother for any favours.[20]

She was back in Paris on 21 August. The first salvoes from the royalist press were fired even before her return, mocking the 'Suissesse' who would have to sleep in the street on her return, 'since her husband had been forbidden to communicate in any way with the National Assembly, he would be exposed to the risk of finding many of its members in his bed, if he allowed his wife back to his house'. The King of Sweden had indeed commanded his ambassador that his house must reflect 'mourning and sorrow'.[21]

'Madame de Staël is returned to Paris; her husband announced his King's commands of affecting *tristesse: elle s'en est moquée* (sorrow: but she ignored it) and sees everybody,' wrote Horace Walpole to the Misses Berry.[22] No wonder the sorely tried ambassador had wished her to stay away. Soon after her return she wrote once again to the King of Sweden, justifying her own and her father's position. It was to be her last letter to him – Gustavus III put an end to their correspondence. As far as the King was concerned Madame de Staël was siding with the enemy.[23]

On 14 September 1791, although privately both he and the Queen thought it unworkable, Louis XVI solemnly signed the new Constitution, because, as Madame de Staël pointed out, it would end his captivity. The members of the Constituent Assembly, which was to be formally dissolved on 30 September, had taken the fatal step of disqualifying themselves from membership of its successor – the Legislative Assembly – which was to meet on 1 October. This measure, which eliminated all the moderates from the Legislative Assembly, had been proposed by Robespierre, but had only been passed with the help of the extreme right, who hated the constitutionalists and were ready to destroy them even though it should prove fatal to themselves and to the monarchy.

Marie-Antoinette's opinion of it was only too clear from a letter she wrote to Fersen: 'There is nothing to be done with this assembly, it is a gathering of scoundrels, madmen and fools. The few members, less ill-intentioned than the rest who want order, are not heard and dare not speak. It is discredited even by the people . . . who in any case, are only interested in the high cost of bread.'[24]

Madame de Staël herself knew that the Constitution was no more than the appearance of what they had wished for. Civil liberties had been established, but they were unprotected by corresponding political safeguards. One of its glaring defects in her eyes was the absence of a two-chamber legislature, which had been rejected on the grounds that an upper house on the English model would have become a bastion of aristocratic power. Another deficiency was the right of the 'suspensive veto' granted to the King, which enabled him to suspend legislation for up to five years. He was to use it on 9 November, against the law declaring all émigrés traitors unless they returned by the end of the year, and again on 29 November when he vetoed a decree against the 'refractory clergy' (those who had refused to swear the oath, and in some cases, who had condemned the Revolution outright).

None the less, the new Constitution was celebrated 'as if we believed ourselves happy', with splendid illuminations from the palace of the Tuileries all the way up the Champs-Élysées, which was garlanded with lights. When the King and Queen arrived at the opera they were sincerely applauded by everyone, Madame de Staël recalled. The ballet *Psyché* was being performed that night. In one scene, when the furies dance by torchlight, 'I saw the faces of the King and Queen lit by the pale light of this imitation of hell, and was seized by a fateful foreboding for the future.' The Queen smiled obligingly but Madame de Staël saw a deep sadness behind the smile. Later, walking down the Champs-Élysées, she met several members of the Constituent Assembly. Their task was over and they looked anxious about their successors. 'It seemed that the Revolution had been completed and liberty established. None the less, we all looked at each other, as if trying to find in our neighbour, that sense of security which we could not find in ourselves.'[25]

In her account of the French Revolution, written towards the end of her life (but published by her son Auguste in 1818, a year after her death), when time and the horrors of the Terror had altered some of her judgements, Madame de Staël still did not retract her belief in the ideals of the Revolution, nor alter her view that the aristocracy bore the blame for delivering the country up to extremists. The injustices of the French political system had created such a rift between the aristocracy and the people that there were in effect 'two nations' in France, she wrote, well before Disraeli used the term to describe the gulf between the rich and the poor in England (in *Sybil*, published in 1845). When the aristocracy proved unable to fight the whole nation, they emigrated en masse and went off to join foreigners.[26] Madame de Staël made a clear distinction between the early, voluntary pre-1792 emigration of aristocrats and those who were obliged to flee for their lives later. The former, she believed, identified more with the European aristocracy rather than with their fellow citizens. Had they not abandoned the King, they might have saved the monarchy.

Gouverneur Morris summed up the situation admirably to Washington: 'The King has accepted the new Constitution, and been in consequence liberated from his arrest. It is a general and almost universal conviction that this Constitution is inexecutable; the makers to a man condemn it. The King's present business is to make himself popular, and indeed his life and his crown depend upon it . . . but his advisers have neither the sense nor spirit which the occasion calls for. The new Assembly, as far as can at present be determined, is deeply imbued with republican, or rather democratical principles. . . . The aristocrats, who are gone and going in great numbers to join the refugee princes, believe sincerely in a coalition of the powers of Europe to reinstate their sovereign in his ancient authorities, but I believe that they are very much mistaken.'[27]

Throughout those last months of 1791, marked by renewed attacks from the revolutionaries on the supporters of the *ancien régime*, Madame de Staël's main objective was to help to consolidate the gains of the Revolution by supporting the new Constitution, however inadequate. France, she believed, must above all be prevented from falling into the hands of fanatics. The Constitution was the best safeguard against either a return to absolutism or to mob rule. 'We are more in a state of revolution than ever,' she wrote to the Comte de Gouvernet, then ambassador to the Hague; 'All the more reason to rally to the Constitution. We can change it later, but it must triumph first.'

To this end, she continued to receive at her salon all shades of moderate opinion, believing that rational solutions were possible if men of good will and intelligence were in control, no matter how much they disagreed on specific points. She hoped that Narbonne would be one of them. With her father now gone from the political scene, Madame de Staël wished to see Narbonne in power because, as a constitutional monarchist, he was eminently capable of rallying the centre. An able and active man, Narbonne was worthy of the post. His appointment would also enable her to participate in politics, for the good of France, she believed. When at the end of September Montmorin resigned she tried hard to have Narbonne made Foreign Minister in his place. However, the King and particularly the Queen, who detested the Constitutionalists as much as they hated Madame de Staël, opposed his nomination. Montmorin had admitted to Morris that the King objected to appointing Narbonne to the Ministry of Foreign Affairs precisely because of his connection with Madame de Staël.[28]

As a result of intense lobbying by Madame de Staël, who had enlisted Barnave to plead Narbonne's cause with the Queen, and Montmorin with the King, Narbonne was nevertheless appointed Minister for War on 6 December. The next day he addressed the Legislative Assembly in his new capacity, affirming the principles for which he (and Madame de Staël) stood. Liberty and equality for all – these were non-negotiable – but also the establishment of order and justice and loyalty to the Constitution. From the diplomatic benches a radiant Madame de Staël joined in the enthusiastic applause. She had every reason to be pleased with her success. With war imminent and the army in total disarray as a result of the massive emigration of officers and the subsequent breakdown in discipline, this was a post as important as the foreign ministry. Madame de Staël now prepared to give her lover the support which she had formerly given to her father.

In spite of his misgivings, Louis had accepted Narbonne because Narbonne believed that a short and limited war would help to restore discipline and order, benefiting the new Constitution and the monarchy. The King also wanted war as a means to restore himself to his former position, so for the time being, however different their motives, they were on the same track. The Queen bowed to the inevitable, explaining their position acidly to Fersen: 'At last, since yesterday, Count Louis de Narbonne is Minister for War. What a triumph for Madame de Staël and what a pleasure to have all the army at her disposal. He might be useful if he chooses to be, since he is clever enough to rally the Constitutionals and just what is needed to speak to the army of today. What a happiness it would be if one day I might be powerful enough again to prove to all these rogues that I was not their dupe.'[29]

The royalist press meanwhile renewed its attacks on 'the machinations of the Genevan she-wolf', who 'is to be seen rushing around from nine o'clock in the morning, in a short petticoat and stays to all the journalists to give them the official papers; the letters and reports which she herself has dictated to her darling lover'.[30] Madame de Staël's own letters confirm the general view that she was at least as important as Narbonne and that she was behind ministerial and ambassadorial appointments. To her friend, the Comte de Gouvernet, who was French Ambassador to Holland, she wrote: 'We have decided in our Council, my dear Gouvernet, that we cannot do better for the moment than to leave you where you are.' After a run-through of the various still vacant posts, among them Naples and Spain, which 'do not exist until such time as these kingdoms have accepted our Constitution', she describes the present situation in France. She is under no illusion as to the difficulties ahead. Could Gouvernet perhaps try and find out what Prussia intended? Above all she entreats him to support Narbonne as he prepares for war. Narbonne believed that there could be no peace in France unless the émigré faction was dispersed. 'We are to go to war without money or officers . . . Adieu! . . . If only you were here! But you must remain where you are. M. de Staël will be recalled in the next three or four days. Everything around me is being destroyed. I place my hope in M. de Narbonne's talents and courage. If he manages to save this country it will be through a miracle rather than genius.'[31]

Chapter 8

~

War

'We are terrified of the precipice opening up before us.'
Madame de Staël to the Comte de Gouvernet[1]

WAR NOW SEEMED inevitable. In the Assembly the left-wing group soon to be known as the Girondins (so called because its leading members came from the Gironde province of France), led by Brissot, Isnard and Vergniaud, called for war as a way of repelling the 4,000 or so émigré troops assembled under Condé and Artois at Coblenz. They hoped, too, to spread the revolution to the rest of Europe. Narbonne, as has been seen, and the other Feuillants[2] saw some possible advantages in a brief campaign which, if they were victorious, would help to re-establish law and order. The royal family hoped to be saved by it and looked to Marie-Antoinette's brother Leopold of Austria, while the émigrés hoped, as Morris put it, 'to be able to return victorious and re-establish that species of despotism most suited to their own cupidity'.[3] Only Robespierre, who saw that it might play into the hands of the King, opposed it, declaring in the Assembly: 'Crush our internal enemies first, then march against foreign ones . . . the immediate threat to the revolution is entirely within France.'[4]

Narbonne now had the task of reorganizing the army, which was in a wretched state. Determined that the constitutional monarchy should be adequately defended, he persuaded the Assembly to vote 20 million livres for the army, while he set off on a tour of inspection, accompanied by Mathieu de Montmorency. Within two months, some sort of miracle was achieved: garrisons had been reformed, fortifications renewed, and an army of 150,000 men stood ready to repel France's enemies from her borders, even if the Generals La Fayette, Luckner and Rochambeau, who shared the command of the army, did not believe their forces were prepared for war. A plan which eventually came to nought – to offer the supreme military command of French forces to the liberal Duke of Brunswick, nephew of Frederick the Great and strategist of the Seven Years War – was seriously negotiated throughout January. It was hoped that this would have the double advantage of depriving the émigrés of his leadership and uniting the bitterly divided French generals by imposing an outsider on them. Talleyrand meanwhile was dispatched to London to secure a promise of English neutrality in case of war. In spite of the tremendous impact which Burke's *Reflections on the Revolution in France* had had on public opinion, Talleyrand achieved his objective only because William Pitt had no wish to support the European counter-revolutionary crusade. A similar mission was sent to Berlin, but too late – Prussia and Austria had signed a defensive alliance on 7 February 1792.

The rulers of Austria, Sweden, Prussia, Saxony and Spain were all in favour of active intervention, strongly encouraged by Catherine II of Russia. Fersen, through whom Marie-Antoinette was able to send out secret information about French military plans, had been put in charge of secret negotiations with the King of France about allied plans to save him. On 12 January 1792, Gustavus III of Sweden instructed Staël to leave Paris within a fortnight, but to announce that he was going on extended leave at his own request. In a later instruction, Staël was also forbidden to return to Sweden, but this was sent too late and Staël had already left for Stockholm. Bad weather prevented him from reaching Stockholm until the end of March, just two days after Gustavus had been shot dead at a masked ball.[5] As chance would have it, one of the three principal conspirators of the King's assassination was the handsome Count Ribbing, who was to be closely involved with Madame de Staël in the future. Gustavus III was succeeded by his young son, Gustavus Adolphus, with his brother, the Duke of Sudermania, a mystic and a friend of Staël's, as regent – a stroke of luck for Staël.

Before Staël's departure from Paris, Necker had offered him refuge at Coppet. Evidently touched by this gesture from his father-in-law at a time when he was estranged from his wife, Staël replied gratefully that while he could think of nothing better than to spend the rest of his life beside a great man, he was obliged to return to his own country. He urged Necker to persuade his daughter to leave Paris. Unable to resist pointing the finger of blame for his troubles where it lay, he added: 'You cannot be unaware Monsieur, that the King [of Sweden] was unlikely to view with favour a man whose wife has the reputation of governing ministers whom he regards as rebels against their legitimate master.'[6]

From Coppet Necker was indeed imploring his daughter by every post to join them, with her son Auguste.[7] Edward Gibbon, who had spent a month staying with the Neckers, bore witness to this, when he wrote some months later: 'Her husband is in Sweden, her lover is no longer minister for war, and her father's house must be the only place where she can reside with the least degree of prudence and decorum.'[8]

Prudence and decorum were not Madame de Staël's forte, however. She sent Auguste to Coppet with his nurse, but remained in Paris. While Narbonne threw himself into his new task of saving the country, Madame de Staël was doing her utmost to save Narbonne. In the early months of 1792, she had to find 100,000 livres, a huge sum, to pay off her lover's most pressing debts.[9] The rich plantation of Limonade in Santo Domingo, which had been part of his wife's dowry, had been burnt to the ground during a black revolt. Thanks to Madame de Staël, Narbonne managed to pay his debts, but the King, and indeed those like Morris, who did not know this, suspected him of dipping into ministry funds.[10]

Narbonne's position as Minister of War and Madame de Staël's moment of power and influence were short-lived. Unable to carry through measures which he believed necessary, his moderate policies under attack by both royalists and republicans, and distrusted by the King whom he had begged to abandon the royalists and side with the Constitutionalists, Narbonne offered his resignation on 3 March. Orchestrated by Madame de Staël, the three commanders of the army threatened to go if Narbonne was dismissed. In a direct appeal to the public, and with Narbonne's approval, Madame de Staël had the almost identical texts of their resignations – which were generally believed to have been drafted by her – published in the *Journal de Paris* on 9 March 1792. This was too much for the King's advisers. In a note as curt as it was to the point, the King dismissed Narbonne: 'This is to inform you Monsieur, that I have just nominated M. de Grave to the Ministry of War. You will let him have your portfolio.'

Narbonne set off at once to join the army on the northern border, under the command of La Fayette. Fersen was informed that Madame de Staël had gone to join her lover at Arras, armed with opium which she proposed to drink if any harm befell him, and that on the return journey her carriage had overturned.[11] Narbonne's departure signalled the end of the moderate ministry of the Feuillants. Within two weeks the Girondins had seized power. General Dumouriez, a clever and ambitious professional soldier of bourgeois origin, promoted by Brissot and the Girondins, now became Prime Minister. Dumouriez was able to persuade the King and Queen that war should be declared on Austria if the new Emperor Francis II (who had succeeded his father Leopold II of Austria and Hungary in March) did not remove the émigré forces massed along the Rhine, which were threatening France. Gambling on a French defeat, on 20 April 1792 the King duly proposed a declaration of war on Austria to the Legislative Assembly. Madame de Staël who was present, recalled how 'On entering the Assembly, he peered to the right and left with a kind of vague curiosity that one finds in people so short-sighted that they can hardly see. He proposed war with the same tone of voice which he might have used to propose a matter of utter indifference.' The deputies who doffed their hats and cheered were in fact pronouncing their own death sentence that day – 'the first in a bloody conflict which would tear Europe apart for the next twenty-three years'.[12]

The ill-prepared French forces were soon routed. The advance against Tournai, in the Austrian Netherlands, ended with a panicky retreat to Lille, where they murdered their commander, General Dillon, as well as some Austrian prisoners. The Girondin ministry now had to deal not only with a military disaster but also with a deteriorating economic situation and food riots. It suited them to divert public anger by stirring up anti-monarchist feeling. This was not difficult because it was widely known that the King had supported war on Austria for his own salvation and that Marie-Antoinette had secretly passed military information to the enemy. Strongly influenced by his implacably republican wife, Roland, the Minister of the Interior, proposed a measure to establish a permanent military camp just outside Paris for the 20,000 *fédérés* or National Guardsmen, who were in any case converging on the capital for the celebration on 14 July, but who would now be useful in defending the city from the approaching allied armies. The King vetoed it. For good measure he also vetoed a decree proposing to banish non-juror priests. The response was a threatening letter to the King on 10 June, drafted by Madame Roland but signed by her husband. Outraged, Louis dismissed Roland and the other Girondin ministers in a curt note, replacing them with some little-known Feuillants. Fanned by daily denunciations from Marat in his *Ami du Peuple*, and by other revolutionary sheets, popular unrest grew more threatening by the day.

On 20 June 1792, the anniversary of both the Tennis Court Oath and the flight to Varennes, an armed mob was admitted to the Assembly where they sang revolutionary songs for an hour, afterwards moving on to the Tuileries where, unopposed by members of the National Guard, they smashed their way into the royal apartments with hatchets and pikes. For two hours they demonstrated in front of the King and the terrified royal family, jeering, threatening and shouting 'down with the veto'. The King was forced to wear the *bonnet rouge*, the red 'cap of liberty',[13] and to drink to the country's health, which he did with good grace and immense courage while the Queen held her terrified children close to her. Perhaps it was their bravery that prevented any further outrages, or perhaps the mob dispersed only when bidden to do so by the Girondin deputy, Vergniaud. 'You will soon hear all the details of the insult offered to the king,' Narbonne wrote to his friend and former chief of staff General d'Arblay. 'It is no longer possible for a man of honour to stay, unless the whole of France refutes and avenges this act.'[14]

The Girondins had hoped that by intimidating the King they would induce him to restore Roland and the other ministers. Vergniaud, the most brilliant orator in the Assembly, indicted the King on whose behalf foreign armies were descending on France. But they had overplayed their hand. In doing so they handed France over to fanatical extremists far more dangerous than themselves.

Narbonne, La Fayette and Madame de Staël herself were outraged by the attempt to bully the King into submission. Furious at the insult to the King, La Fayette left his troops on the northern border to come and seek justice from the Assembly. In his own name and on behalf of the army, he demanded that those who had taken part in the insurrection be punished, as Madame de Staël, who had been present at the Assembly when La Fayette made his speech, recounted at a dinner she attended at the British Embassy on 28 June. Narbonne too, while continuing to be a convinced liberal, was close to the royal family and felt a soldier's loyalty to the monarchy. His sense of personal honour now made it a priority to save the King and his family. Madame de Staël, under no illusion that the days of the monarchy were now all but over, and in spite of the Queen's hatred of her, also wanted to save the royal family from a situation which grew daily more unpredictable. At the beginning of July she asked Malouet, a deputy on the right wing of the Constitutional monarchists, who had been her father's friend and supporter, to act as her go-between with the King and Queen. Together with Narbonne she put forward a daring plan of escape to the royal family. Madame de Staël would buy an estate in Normandy. She would travel there several times on the business of buying it, accompanied by three people as like as possible to the King, the Queen and the Dauphin, so as to make them seem familiar to the post-houses and postilions on the way. On the appointed day, the three royals dressed as servants would take their place. Once in Normandy they would sail to England. Malouet thought it an excellent plan, but the King and Queen turned it down. It may have been that they did not believe that the plan would work, but the most likely explanation is that Marie-Antoinette hated Madame de Staël and the Constitutionalists as much and more than she hated the Jacobins and preferred to stake everything on the probability, as she saw it, of their imminent rescue by the advancing allied armies. A polite refusal was sent to Madame de Staël. La Fayette's alternative plan to spirit them away to safety and hide them in the midst of the army at Compiègne was also rejected. The King, as Madame de Staël wrote in her account of the Revolution, 'put himself at terrible risk waiting in Paris for the German troops to arrive'.[15]

In spite of the King's veto, the *fédérés* or National Guardsmen were already marching on Paris from all over the country. Rumours flew that the most fierce revolutionaries were to be sent to Paris to massacre the royal family, while the King and Queen were denounced in the press, particularly by Marat and by Camille Desmoulins. On 14 July Madame de Staël was present on the Champ de Mars at the anniversary celebration of the fall of the Bastille. She was never to forget the expression on the Queen's face, her eyes blinded by tears. Although Marie-Antoinette was splendidly dressed and conducted herself with dignity, only a few Guardsmen separated her from the people: armed men who looked for the most part as if they had come for a fight not a celebration. The King then once again swore to abide by the Constitution: 'I followed his powdered head among the many dark ones from a distance; his coat, embroidered as in the past, stood out among the clothes of the common people who pressed around him. When he climbed up the steps of the altar he looked like a saintly victim offering himself up for sacrifice. He came down . . . and took his place next to the Queen and his children. From that day on, the people were not to see him again except on the scaffold.'[16]

Into this already explosive situation, on 25 July, fell the spark of the Brunswick manifesto, which threatened Paris with total military occupation if any harm came to the royal family. It was issued in the name of the Duke of Brunswick but against his better judgement; he was now in command of the allied forces, which were already at Longwy, a town on the French border.

In a speech to the Jacobin Club on 29 July, Robespierre called for a complete political renewal with the setting up of a National Convention, based on universal suffrage. The next day, the *fédérés* from Marseilles, the most renowned of the provincial contingents of the National Guard, entered Paris to the strains of the war song of the Army of the Rhine, known thereafter as the 'La Marseillaise'. Nobody slept in that week of hot, sultry weather with news of daily murders and attacks on property. On 5 August, Morris, recently appointed as America's Minister Plenipotentiary to the court of France noted: 'Go to Court this morning. Nothing remarkable, only that we were up all night, expecting to be murdered.'[17] Everyone was on tenterhooks: Narbonne, who had been pronounced a traitor in the Jacobin Club, was in hiding in Paris, determined at all costs to defend the King. Together with other liberal aristocrats, among them Lally-Tollendal, Castellane, Montmorency and La Tour du Pin Gouvernet, he had begged for permission to enter the Tuileries to help defend the royal family, but had been refused by the King's advisers. In spite of this, as Madame de Staël put it, 'they prowled around the palace, exposing themselves to massacre to console themselves for not being able to fight'.[18]

On 9 August, the Legislative Assembly rejected an ultimatum for the King's deposition. The Paris Commune had been replaced by an Insurrectionary Commune, led by Robespierre and Danton, and was now far more powerful. Madame de Staël never forgot that stifling August night when, with a few friends, she had kept a sleepless vigil at the window as they waited for news of the volunteers' patrol, led by Narbonne, who had gone to defend the King at the palace. Somehow news of them had got through to her every quarter of an hour: 'before midnight the forty-eight tocsins, the bells of the different sections of Paris began to toll, and all night this monotonous, dismal, insistent, sound did not cease for an instant'.[19] Nobody had any idea of what might happen the following day or whether they would still be alive. Early in the morning of 10 August, the storm broke when the Insurrectionary Commune unleashed the National Guard in an attack on the Tuileries. As the King and the royal family fled to the Legislative Assembly, eight hundred men including the *Cent Suisses* (the King's Swiss Guard) were butchered, literally hacked to pieces in scenes of violent carnage. Half as many of the insurgents died, some of the most militant among them, the *fédérés* from Brest, killed by their own side because they had been wearing red coats, similar to those of the Swiss Guard.[20]

It was now that Madame de Staël showed what she was made of. In the bloody chaos of revolutionary Paris, with the capital torn apart from within, and the allied armies on the doorstep, she exhibited the high courage, the resourcefulness and the generosity so characteristic throughout her life. Although she had permits which would have enabled her to leave for Switzerland immediately, this twenty-six-year-old young woman, who was six months pregnant with her second child by Narbonne, decided without hesitation to remain in Paris. Over the next three weeks she contrived to save not only her lover, but other friends who had been caught in the noose. Using her formidable wits, her charm, her authority and her money, she arranged for them to be smuggled out of the country. In her own account of the events of 10 August she recorded that news reached her that afternoon that all her friends had been massacred outside the palace. 'I left at once to find out what had happened. The coachman who was taking me was stopped on the bridge by men who barred our way, with silent gestures indicating that throats were being cut on the other side. After two hours of pointless effort to try and get through, I learnt that all those who interested me vitally were still alive, but had gone into hiding'.[21] Setting out on foot that evening to the various houses sheltering her friends, she came across armed men sprawled in front of the doors in a drunken stupor, who half roused themselves only to swear foully. She was particularly appalled at the women whose cursing seemed even more terrible.

The Assembly was invaded soon after the massacre at the Tuileries. The terrified deputies were forced to depose the King and to prepare for the election of a new republican assembly, known as the Convention, which would draw up a new Constitution and whose Council of Ministers included Roland and Danton. The fall of the monarchy left France with a divided government. On the one hand was the Convention, on the other the radical and more powerful Paris Commune, where Robespierre and Marat set up a Jacobin stronghold. After a night sheltering in the convent of the Feuillants, the headquarters of the Constitutional monarchists, the King and his family were transferred to the tower of the Temple, not far from the Bastille.

New arrests, authorized by the Commune, took place every day during August, with house-to-house searches for fugitives. The prisons were overflowing. On the Place du Carrousel, a new machine for swift and humane decapitation, the guillotine, was now in regular use. Narbonne, Montmorency, Lally-Tollendal and Jaucourt were in danger of their lives – all of them in hiding in various bourgeois houses, but obliged to move on every day because people were afraid to shelter them for longer. Narbonne had been unwilling to hide in Madame de Staël's house at first, as it was the obvious place to look for him, but in the end there was no choice. They could only hope that the Swedish embassy would continue to enjoy some sort of immunity. When Narbonne arrived, pale but still elegant, Madame de Staël hid him and another, probably Montmorency, in a little-used room, taking only one trusted servant into her confidence. She spent the following night awake, terrified that she would receive one of the house visits which were intended to flush out wanted men. 'One morning, one of my servants whom I did not trust, told me that there was a poster on the corner of our street denouncing Narbonne.' Thinking that he was trying to trick her, she said nothing, but soon realized that he was simply stating a fact. She persuaded Pastor Gambs, the chaplain of the Swedish embassy and the man who had officiated at her wedding, to hide Narbonne behind the altar of the embassy chapel. 'A little later the frightening house-to-house search party arrived. I knew that M. de Narbonne, having been outlawed, would perish that very day if found, and I knew . . . that if the search went ahead he would be found. The search had to be prevented at all costs.'

Pulling herself together in spite of her fear, and realizing at a glance that the men in front of her were simple policemen, she decided on attack as the best means of defence. Summoning up all her hauteur, she informed them that they were committing a serious breach of international law in entering the house of an ambassador. Realizing that they were ignorant men who knew very little of geography, she convinced them for good measure that Sweden lay on the very borders of France and could attack at any moment.[22] Having thoroughly intimidated them, Madame de Staël turned on the charm. Softening her tone, and addressing them as equals, though 'with death in my heart', she joked with them about the absurdity of their suspicions. Her tactics worked. As she led them to the door, she could only thank God for the strength he had given her.[23]

It was clear though that Narbonne would have to be moved at once. Pastor Gambs knew of a young Hanoverian doctor, Erich Bollmann, who might be able to help. Like many young men from all over Europe, he had come to revolutionary Paris in search of adventure. No sooner had he met Madame de Staël than he was conquered by her and by the romance of it all, as is clear from letters he wrote to his father soon afterwards: 'Madame de Staël has a friend, and this friend is Narbonne, ex-Minister of War. They are inseparable. Narbonne is one of the most agreeable men I have ever met. To a very wide understanding of people, of the world and of literature, to an endless capacity for fun and gaiety, to an intelligence which sparkles constantly in everything he does or says . . . he adds complete self-effacement and modesty . . . as well as the chivalrous frankness of the *ancien régime* . . . he is a postive miracle! . . . it's no wonder that Madame de Staël should be so attached to this friend, all the more so, as she was saddled with a husband incapable of inventing a dish of potatoes, never mind gunpowder! You can imagine the state in which I found Madame de Staël in the morning of 14 August, when I entered her room. A woman about to give birth, lamenting the fate of her lover made a great impression on my imagination. Narbonne was with her. We all realized that only I was capable of saving him.'[24]

The young man was as good as his word but first a passport had to be found for Narbonne. 'For three whole days I ran between all the Englishmen and foreigners of my acquaintance.' At last he found a German friend who was happy to pose as a Hanoverian, and therefore to obtain a British passport (the King of England was still Elector of Hanover). Narbonne left Madame de Staël on 19 August, at nine o'clock in the evening. He spent his last night in Paris with Bollmann. Disguised as Englishmen, they left early the next morning. At the various guard posts, Narbonne pretended to be half-asleep while the others discussed the Revolution 'in the manner of the English', thus fooling the guards. At last, four days later, after a rough crossing during which Narbonne had been violently ill, they arrived in London and went to Madame de La Châtre's house in Kensington Square.

The adventure had done the young man much good. Narbonne, 'whom I appreciate and like more the more I know him', had given him fifty guineas a year and had presented him to friends in Hanover who would help him, but 'nothing gratified me as much as Madame de Staël's joy. A few days ago, she wrote the following to me . . . You can imagine, my dear father, how much this note delighted me! "You have saved my life and more than my life. Please attach some importance to the sentiment which is anchored in my heart and inseparable from my existence, and remember at all times in your life, that it gives you the rights of a friend, of a brother, of a benefactor!"' Madame de Staël had written the moment news of their safe arrival had reached her.[25]

To Narbonne, she wrote on the same day, 25 August 1792, 'Ah! My friend, what can I say of my sentiments this morning, which have eased my anguish. I can only give thanks to the Supreme Being who has so delightfully saved my life! After four months in which I have carried poison at all times, I may at last hope that I no longer need it, that your child will be born, and that so long as I live I will clasp to my heart his adored father, his father who is the object of such tender and passionate worship . . . You are safe, that is my only sentiment, my only opinion, my only existence.' The rest of her letter is full of the latest political news, news of the fate of their friends and a report of the practical measures she has taken on his behalf. She had found time to pay off his staff, had busied herself about his estates in Santo Domingo and sent his trusted personal servants to England to join him. She ends with the cryptic message: 'I have hopes of being able to serve you in another way which I cannot disclose at present. It is not impossible that you will soon see the arrival of the bish[op], [Talleyrand] in company.'[26]

Narbonne was extremely lucky to have got away. On the day after his departure Morris reported that some Englishmen were turned back. On 22 August, Morris wrote to Thomas Jefferson, then American Secretary of State: 'The different ambassadors are all taking flight, and if I stay I shall be alone', adding, 'I mean, however, to stay, unless circumstances should summon me away.'[27]

With Narbonne now safe, Madame de Staël could leave at last;

indeed Gibbon had reported to a friend that her father was in such a state of agitation and affliction as could hardly be imagined. Necker had told Gibbon that he believed his daughter was terrified by the situation in Paris since her letters to him were guarded and cautious: 'she who is afraid of nothing and never expresses herself cautiously'.[28] Torn between her father's desperate anxiety and her own wish to leave she wrote: 'It was so sad to see to one's own safety, when one was leaving so many friends still in danger, that I postponed my departure from day to day, to try and find out what had become of each one of them.' On 27 August her informers told her that 'M. de Jaucourt; a deputy at the Legislative Assembly, and M. de Lally-Tollendal had both been imprisoned in the *Abbaye*, and it was already well known that only those who were to be delivered to the assassins were put in this prison.'[29]

Lally-Tollendal, unlike Jaucourt, had several important protectors, among them Condorcet and the British Ambassador, and had already been freed at Condorcet's request. Madame de Staël, who knew the members of the Commune, then masters of the capital, only by their terrible reputation, got hold of a list of their names, wondering how to choose one among them to whom she could appeal for Jaucourt's life: 'I suddenly remembered that one of them, [the public prosecutor] Manuel, who dabbled in literature, had just published Mirabeau's letters with a preface which he had written, rather poor it is true but in which none the less, one could discern the laudable desire to demonstrate some wit,' she recalled.[30] Shrewdly, she decided that Manuel's evident desire for admiration made him susceptible. She wrote at once to ask for an audience. Flattered by the attention of such a well-known person, he granted one for the following morning, 28 August – 'at seven o'clock – a rather democratic time of day, but I was there on time', she wrote.

While she waited in his study, she noticed a large portrait of Manuel on his desk, which confirmed her intuition that his vanity might be his weak spot. Madame de Staël begged Manuel to secure Jaucourt's freedom, a good deed which in six months he might not have the power to do. But before the six months were up he was himself executed for defending the King at his trial, Madame de Staël recorded later.[31]

That same day, 28 August 1792, she wrote to Narbonne to tell him that she had managed to secure Jaucourt's release. She had been tempted to join him in London, but a sacred duty, which might influence their whole future, had prevented her. She must have been referring to the fact that she could not decently have her baby in her lover's company. She would go to her parents' house in Switzerland and join him as soon as she could. 'Look after yourself,' she concludes: 'in the meantime I can only adore you, miss you and give birth to your child.'[32] Afraid for her safety, Narbonne had warned her that he would return to Paris if she remained there. On 1 September, acknowledging his letter, she writes: 'All would be well if you had not had the *atrocity* of telling me that you would return if I stayed. Those words have driven me mad. You would kill me to make me leave! . . .'[33]

The next morning news of the attack on Verdun by the allied troops reached Paris. Panic-stricken, the Commune issued the proclamation: 'To arms! The enemy is at the gate!' In the Convention, Danton, now the Minister of Justice, called for 'daring, more daring and again daring'. Marat now called for the massacre of all those lately imprisoned who, it was put about, were counter-revolutionaries waiting to escape and help the approaching Prussians: the tocsin was to be a signal for the conspirators to be killed. Over the next five days, which became known as the September massacres, armed bands of cut-throats entered the overflowing prisons, massacring men and women on the slightest pretext. All Madame de Staël's friends, whom she had just helped to escape, would have surely perished. Among those murdered was Marie-Antoinette's dearest friend, the Princesse de Lamballe, whose decapitated head and entrails were mounted on pikes and paraded in front of the Queen's windows. A young woman, Marie Grosholz, an apprentice sculptor in wax, had been forced, with trembling hands, to make a cast of Madame de Lamballe's head, whom she had known. In the future she would be better known as Madame Tussaud.[34]

At the Swedish Embassy, Madame de Staël was preparing to leave Paris, having promised to take with her the abbé de Montesquiou, Narbonne's cousin. Montesquiou, also on the wanted list, was in imminent danger of arrest. It had been decided that he would meet her just outside the city and travel with her, using the papers of one of her servants. From all parts of Paris she could hear the terrifying sound of the 'tocsin' summoning people to the defence of the Revolution. Her people wanted to stop her from leaving, 'but how could I compromise the safety of a man [Montesquiou] who had trusted in me?' She decided to leave in the embassy coach, pulled by six horses, with her servants in livery, thinking that when people saw her travelling openly they would realize that she had permission to go. It was to be her sole mistake. As soon as her coach left the embassy courtyard it was surrounded by a 'swarm of old hags from hell', who fell on her horses, screaming that she must be stopped, that she was carrying away the nation's gold and going to join the enemy. The women were quickly joined by a fierce mob, with murderous faces, who seized her postilions and ordered them to drive to the assembly rooms of her local section – the Faubourg Saint-Germain. Descending from her coach, she barely had time to whisper to one of Montesquiou's servants to go and warn his master of what had happened. The officials who examined her papers noticed that one of her servants was missing. This was serious enough to require a re-examination of her papers at the town hall, to which she was to be escorted by a gendarme. She was now in serious danger.

'It took three hours to get here,' she recalled. 'I was driven at walking pace through a huge crowd who howled death threats.' There was no personal enmity in this. Her mistake was not to realize that anyone in a luxurious coach aroused violent hostility. Her pregnant state and her appeals to passing gendarmes only infuriated people further. At length they arrived at the Place de Grève, opposite the Hôtel de Ville, the town hall. Stepping down from her carriage, she was surrounded by a baying, armed mob. Escorted by her gendarme, who bravely defended her, they made their way through an arch of pikes. She recalled: 'As I began to climb the staircase, bristling with pikes, a man pointed his pike at me, which the gendarme fended off with his sabre. Had I stumbled at that moment it would have been the end of me. And so I arrived at this commune, presided over by Robespierre! . . . The room was full of people, women, children and men all screaming "*Vive la Nation*".' Half-fainting, Madame de Staël was given a chair beside a man who, although a slight acquaintance, refused to acknowledge her. Her anger gave her new strength. She rose to explain her diplomatic status and the fact that she had permission to leave.

At this moment, most providentially, Manuel arrived: 'He was deeply shocked to see me there, and answering for me to the Commune, he took me to his study where he locked me in with my maid.' Hungry, thirsty and terrified, they waited there for six hours. The windows of Manuel's rooms looked out on to the Place de Grève, and they could see the cut-throats returning from the prisons with blood-curdling screams, their bare arms soaked in blood. At the same time Madame de Staël noticed that a tall National Guardsman had climbed up to the coachman's seat of her carriage, from which vantage point he defended it for two hours from would-be looters. Why he should have done this was beyond her comprehension. Later he came with Manuel to the room where she was detained. It turned out that he was the infamous Santerre who had led the column of National Guardsmen from the St Antoine district, which had attacked the Tuileries on 10 August. He had been a brewer in charge of distributing wheat which Necker had procured at the time of acute shortages. Now he wished to show his gratitude to Necker's daughter.

Manuel came late that night to escort her home. He had not dared to come earlier and did not wish to be seen with her in daylight. She remembered that there was no street lighting, but that the light from the torches carried by passing groups of men had been even more terrifying than the darkness. At last they were back at the embassy. Manuel told her that she would be allowed to leave the next day, with new papers, taking her maid only. She was to be escorted to the frontier by a gendarme.

The following morning, 3 September, with the streets running with blood and full of wild men, she left Paris accompanied by a man sent by the Commune. That man was Tallien, 'who would deliver France from Robespierre twenty months later on 9 Thermidor'. There had been several suspected people in her room when Tallien entered. She had begged him not to reveal them. He had promised not to and had been as good as his word. They had been unable to speak in her coach. 'Events froze the words on our lips.'

As they got further away from Paris, 'the violence of the tempest seemed to abate'. In the Jura mountains there was nothing to recall the horrors going on in Paris. There were exhortations on all sides, however, for the French to repel the foreign enemy. At that moment, Madame de Staël confessed: 'I could see no enemy other than the murderers to whose mercy I had left my friends, the royal family and all decent Frenchmen.'[35] On 7 September, exhausted but safe, she was once again reunited with her parents and her two-year-old son Auguste at Coppet.

PART THREE

Tempests and Pleasures

'The pleasures of the mind are made to calm the tempests of the heart.'

Madame de Staël

Chapter 9

~

Burning Letters

'Burning letters for burning – a fine moral lesson too.'
Fanny Burney[1]

DISTRAUGHT TO FIND no letter from Narbonne, Madame de Staël was at her desk, writing to him feverishly, within an hour of her arrival at Coppet: 'My friend, my angel, you know that I live only through you, that the child I carry is subject to your will. Do not kill me with your silence . . . Write to me constantly and don't forget one whose soul, whose heart and whose thoughts are entirely yours.'[2] Still haunted by the agony of their parting, she hoped that he might be able to join her in Switzerland: 'It was believed in Geneva, as it had been in my *quartier* in Paris, that I had been massacred with my maid on the steps of the Hôtel de Ville, and as nothing could have been closer to the truth, I was received by all Geneva with an interest which makes me believe that if you wished it we would find a very sweet refuge here.' Their two-year-old son, Auguste, is very interesting, she adds, and she feels 'the new gage of their love stirring in her breast'.[3]

Her father had received her tenderly, but had not disguised his disapproval, nor his hope that this parting with Narbonne would be the end of the affair. He warned her that Narbonne's name was never to be mentioned in front of her mother, to whom Madame de Staël's all too obvious pregnancy was a constant affront. It was impossible to pretend this time that the child was Staël's. Madame Necker was utterly unable to accept the irregularities of her daughter's life and, as ever, she blamed her husband for his forbearing attitude. Caught between his wife's implacable morality, a well-founded fear that his Minette was hurtling towards emotional, social and financial ruin, and his love and pity for this haunted young woman who had so narrowly escaped death and whose anguished face wrung his heart,

Necker was nevertheless not quite as indulgent as his wife believed. Madame de Staël felt a rift opening up between them for the first time in her life. 'He does not cease, when speaking of my pregnancy and my passion for you, to use the most contemptuous expressions,' she wrote to Narbonne. 'My mother, bible in hand, reproaches him with what she calls his indulgence to me, while he believes that he is acquitting himself before God by talking endlessly to me of vice and shame. Sometimes I am revolted to the bottom of my being. This is followed by animadversions on your character, on the probability of your inconstancy and your ingratitude. Absurd as this may be, he knows that these dire warnings always hurt.'[4]

Madame Necker, who privately was barely on speaking terms with her daughter, put as good a face as she could on the situation in public. 'In the midst of all these misfortunes [for France], the ambassadress's arrival has taken a terrible weight off our minds,' she wrote to Gibbon who, since their return to Coppet, had become a constant visitor and a confidant. 'Our consciousness of the dangers to which she has been exposed enables us to ignore the thoughtlessness which led to them in the first place. In spite of her pregnancy and the terrors she has lived through, she is not as attracted as you might suppose by the rest which we are imposing on her. She is like those ephemeral butterflies, so well described by your poet Gray, who live only for the day.'[5]

In fact, Madame de Staël lived only for the post. Every day without a letter from her lover triggered an anguished missive from her. Her only thought now was how soon she would be able to join him in England. Her pregnancy made it unlikely that they would see each other for five months. The slowness of the post – letters took between ten days and a fortnight – and the fact that Narbonne wrote infrequently, drove her almost mad. Her daily letters to him over the next four months were written in the heat of her all-consuming passion. She was as demanding as she was unguarded; as careless of her own pride as of any need for tact in her dealings with him. Her letters betray a terrified insecurity. In her passionate wish to bind him to her forever she does not scruple to use emotional blackmail, reminding him of what he owed her, threatening suicide, wallowing in self-pity. Unbalanced no doubt by all she had been through, suffering the inevitable sense of anti-climax after the terrifying events in Paris, pregnant and closeted at Coppet with only her unhappy and anxious father and her sour-faced mother for company, she longed for

Narbonne and her friends. She felt isolated and abandoned – 'wiped off from among the living'. Without his presence she was unsure about Narbonne's love for her, and unsure about their future together. A further anxiety was that her husband might appear on the scene at any time. Only her exceptionally bright little boy gave her any pleasure: 'I am teaching Auguste to read,' she wrote on 18 September 1792. 'In six weeks, another child, born in sorrow, will tighten the links between us; and still I can be anxious about Madame de Fleury, and still you do not write. Ah! Why live? Tell me if there is room for me at the country house you have taken. Adieu.'[6] (The beautiful Madame de Fleury was a rather racy lady, then in London, who had caught Narbonne's eye.)

Four letters had arrived from Mathieu de Montmorency, but not one from Narbonne. It was from Mathieu that she garnered some idea of Narbonne's life in England. Following the September massacres, most of the members of Madame de Staël's Paris circle had taken refuge there. Talleyrand was also in England, not yet a refugee, although he was soon to find himself on the proscribed list as well. The gatherings at Madame de La Châtre's house in Kensington Square, where sometimes as many as eighteen French refugees dined together, had become ever more animated and brilliant.

'I take up my pen once again to beg you to write and explain your inconceivable silence,' she wrote to Narbonne in despair. 'If you are tired of my life, at least wait until I have given birth. I am desperate, all alone and unable to talk to anyone here. I have been crying all night and all day. My God, who would have thought that after saving his life on 20 August, it would be he who condemns me to death?' she added in one of her rhetorical asides. 'I am resolved: I have suffered for too long. If I have no news from you I will end my life. You are the most cruel, the most ungrateful, the most barbarous of men.' Pausing to consider that it might not be his fault, she begs: 'Please write to me, let me come to London. I am only twenty-five years old [she was, in fact, twenty-six]. Grant me one more year of life. Could you not be tempted to give me a little happiness? It is to me that you are so ungrateful; to me! What is there left to believe in; why live?'[7]

That evening, the first longed-for letter arrived at last: 'I am on my knees in front of my desk, to beg pardon of my friend for all the stupidities I wrote in my last letter, but he may not yet realize what he means to me. I cannot – I feel this more every day – exist without him; my blood runs cold when there is a missed post, and perhaps your heart too might have been touched by the magical effect which your letter had on me. I was literally dying, I could no longer speak; I was about to go mad and was already preparing for death. Your letter arrived. I trembled when I recognized the beloved handwriting; ten times I re-read the sweet words in it, and all the shadows over the future disappeared. Ah! make frequent use of that power and forgive your friend the faults of a grand passion. She will prove to you that she has qualities . . . that she would be happy with you at the ends of the earth, unable to enjoy any pleasure without you, more drunk with love for you than ever before.'[8]

In France the National Convention, the new assembly nominally elected by universal manhood suffrage, had replaced the Legislative Assembly on 21 September 1792. In practice, since much of the voting had taken place openly in the Jacobin clubs, only militant revolutionaries had dared to vote. Fear had begun to drive out people's genuine participation in public affairs. At the same session, the monarchy was formally abolished and the Republic proclaimed. On the previous day, at Valmy, the combined revolutionary French armies under Generals Dumouriez and Kellerman had halted the advance on Paris by the Prussian army under Brunswick's command. For the first time, almost half of the French troops were 'national volunteers', many of them raw recruits who fought alongside professional soldiers, going into battle to the tune of the revolutionary song 'Ça ira'. The battle of Valmy saved the Revolution. It also demonstrated that the French army had not only recovered from its losses and internal divisions, but that it now marched to a different tune – that of revolutionary ideology. Goethe, who was travelling with the Prussian forces and had witnessed the battle, believed that it marked 'the beginning of a new epoch'. On the same day republican troops of the Armée du Midi under General Montesquiou entered Savoy. Geneva filled with refugees while the city fathers, fearing invasion and sack, turned to neighbouring Berne and Zurich for help.

In England, the deposition and the arrest of Louis XVI, followed by a wave of arrests and then by the September massacres, had horrified public opinion. While clubs and societies in Scotland and Ireland openly called for conventions, and meetings demanding constitutional reform were held all over the country, the influx of French émigré aristocrats concentrated the minds of the English peerage, Whig as well as Tory, on what they stood to lose. Events in France would undoubtedly encourage radical minorities, but initially they brought a strongly conservative swing in both religion and politics. King George III, who only recently had bowed to a tree in Windsor Great Park and engaged it in conversation under the impression that it was the King of Prussia, was now happily restored to sanity and seemed a model of stability when set against the murderous anarchy in France. Many of those who had greeted the Revolution as the dawn of a new age, and had bought Thomas Paine's *The Rights of Man*[9] by the thousand, suddenly became more conservative and more royalist.

Even before the September massacres, Horace Walpole had summed up the prevailing view of the Revolution as well as traditional Anglo-Saxon prejudice, in his satirical parody of the Creed: 'I believe in the French, the makers of fashions. I acknowledge their superiority in conversation, and their supremacy in dancing. I believe in their fanaticism for what is new, not in their enthusiasm for what is great, and I expect neither consistency in their plans nor constancy in their sentiments. I believe in the King, the weakest and most injured of mortals, and in the Queen, as equal to him in sufferings and surpassing him in understanding; and in the Dauphin, whose kingdom will never come. I believe equally in the folly of the Princes, the baseness of their counsellors, and the cruelty and madness of their enemies. I expect neither the resurrection of order, nor the regeneration of morals, and I look neither for the coming of liberty, nor the permanence of their constitution. Amen!'[10]

In England, Narbonne and his friends had at first been warmly welcomed by the patrician Whigs, while the Tory government, egged on by the royalist émigrés, who spared no effort to attack the constitutionalists, regarded all the liberal aristocrats with suspicion as dangerous subversives and blamed them for the recent events in France. As the political situation worsened in France and concerns about the fate of the King increased, it became advisable for the constitutionalists to withdraw from public view. This and their precarious financial situation decided most of them to leave London. Narbonne was enabled by Madame de Staël's regular transfers of money to 'Sir John Glayre', his assumed name, to survive and to pay the rent on Juniper Hall, a house he had found near Dorking in Surrey. There he was joined by Montmorency, d'Arblay, Charles de Lameth,

Beaumetz, Malouet, Madame de La Châtre and her lover, François de Jaucourt.[11]

Once an inn, Juniper Hall had been enlarged and decorated in the Adam style in the middle of the eighteenth century. The large and handsome house with its arched windows looked out over lawns across the Surrey countryside towards Box Hill. An elegant drawing room, with a tall, grey and white marble chimney piece at one end, was painted in pastels and decorated in gold and white in the classical style. A handsome painted ceiling and panels depicting classical scenes, swagged with garlands of fruit and flowers, added to its distinction.

Finding themselves in much more luxurious surroundings than they could have hoped for, the little band of French refugees settled down to English country life, some of them making great efforts to learn or to perfect their English. They were fortunate in their English neighbours, to whom their arrival was the object of the liveliest curiosity and interest. Grandest among them was William Lock of Norbury Park. Rich and cultivated, with a beautiful Swiss-French wife and several lovely daughters, Lock was part of a circle which included many of the leading artistic and intellectual figures of the day. Liberal, generous and with wide interests Lock had travelled extensively on the continent and was an enthusiastic collector of art.

In the village of Mickleham, at the end of the Park, lived the charming and warm-hearted Mrs Susanna Phillips with her husband, Captain Molesworth Phillips, a naval officer who had taken part in Captain Cook's last expedition. An accomplished musician, Susanna spoke excellent French, having lived in Paris as a girl. The daughter of the famous musicologist, Dr Charles Burney, and sister to the novelist Fanny Burney, she was an enthusiastic and lively correspondent. Fanny was immensely curious about the new arrivals and letters between the two sisters flew back and forth. 'We shall shortly, I believe, have a little colony of unfortunate (or rather fortunate, since they are safe) French noblesse in our neighbourhood,' Susanna wrote to Fanny. 'Two or three families have joined to take Jenkinson's house, Juniper Hall, and another family has taken a small house at Westhumble, which the people very reluctantly let, upon the Christian-like supposition that, being nothing but French papishes, they would never pay.'[12]

The 'papishes' in question, whose rent Mr Lock at once offered to pay, were the Princesse de Broglie, who, following the disgrace of her husband General Victor Broglie, had escaped to England, enduring fourteen hours at sea in an open boat with her young son (later to be Madame de Staël's son-in-law when he married her as yet unborn daughter Albertine). The cottage, which she shared with friends, was far too tiny for the several adults and three children and on most days the group made their way to Juniper Hall for dinner.

Unlike Fanny Burney and her father, who were staunch Tories, the liberal Phillipses were more in sympathy with the French Constitutionalists. Susanna Phillips, having at last made the acquaintance of their 'amiable and charming neighbours', reported to her sister Fanny: 'Mrs Lock had been so kind as to pave the way for my introduction to Madame de La Châtre and carried me on Friday, to Juniper Hall.' Madame de La Châtre had received them with great politeness. She was about thirty-three, 'an elegant figure, not pretty but with an animated and expressive countenance'. M. d'Arblay was with her. 'M. de Narbonne now came in. He seems forty, rather fat, but would be handsome were it not for a slight cast of one eye. He was that morning in great spirits. Poor man! It was the only time I have ever seen him so.'[13]

If, as Susanna Phillips implied, Narbonne was mostly depressed at Juniper Hall, at Coppet Madame de Staël was in a state of almost constant hysterics, threatening to leave for England though her baby was due in six weeks. Her parents were at their wits' end. A friend of the family, Charles-Victor de Bonstetten, recollected how one day he had arrived at Coppet to find both Neckers in absolute despair. They had been trying in vain to persuade their besotted daughter that it would be foolish in the extreme to set off for England. Promising to bring her to her senses, Bonstetten went up to her apartments to reason with her. He found her miserable and in tears. Hoping to lift her spirits, he reminded her of her reputation and of her glorious future, whereupon she interrupted him, describing her love with such ardour and passion, depicting the union of the two lovers so delightfully, that much moved, Bonstetten forgot all about his mission and offered to lend her the money which she needed to travel to England. It was only on leaving her room that he realized that he had allowed himself to be carried away. When Necker, waiting anxiously below, asked him what success he had had, he was obliged to confess ruefully that she had been so miserable that he had lent her three hundred louis for her journey![14]

As Coppet was but five kilometres from the French border, Madame Necker lived in constant fear of danger from advancing revolutionary troops. 'The whole of Savoy has been occupied and is sporting the cockade with delight,' Madame de Staël wrote to Narbonne. 'My mother wishes us to leave Coppet. My God! How tempted I am to escape and join you. Shall I confess what holds me back? It is your debts. Very sad but true.'[15] By the end of September, when Vaudois troops were seen assembling in the fields around the château, Madame Necker could bear it no longer. On 4 October the family moved to Rolle, some twenty kilometres away, where they were to remain for six months.

In spite of the agonies of love and her stormy relations with her parents, Madame de Staël continued in all other ways to be her eminently rational self and to take her usual lively interest in politics while dealing at the same time with the financial affairs of Narbonne and her husband. Practical letters to her man of business in Paris with detailed accounts and instructions, as well as perfectly normal ones to her friends and her husband, were frequently written on the same days as her passionate and desperate letters to Narbonnne. She was much occupied with finding ways of paying both Narbonne's and Staël's debts, juggling the available money to pay off their most pressing creditors. Narbonne, like Staël, was an inveterate gambler, with extravagant tastes and a lordly attitude to money. At the beginning of October she was able to reassure Narbonne that she did not, after all, need the money she had asked him for, because Staël had been reappointed Ambassador to the French Republic, at least until 1796. Her husband's new salary would enable him to pay some of his own debts for the moment, thus making it possible for Madame de Staël to pay Narbonne's. Meanwhile Staël had written to Madame Necker, proposing to join them in Switzerland while awaiting his posting to Paris. In the same letter he proclaimed his adoration for his charming little Auguste and his admiration for Madame Necker's religious virtues. This delighted Madame Necker who, praising Staël's cleverness and virtue, announced that she had excellent news as she handed the letter to her daughter.

An almighty row followed. After her mother had left the room in a rage, Madame de Staël informed her father that she was off to England at once, that she couldn't bear the thought of Staël calling Auguste his son, that the new baby would be born at a time which would be most embarrassing for Staël (ten months since they were last together). Moreover she had no intention of living with him ever again. There were only two possible journeys for her now: either to England or to the bottom of the lake! She proposed to leave for London, via Paris, at four o'clock the next morning. Wearily, Necker could only reply that for the moment her pregnancy must come first, that she should beware of throwing away the advantages of being married, and that if in three months' time her feelings for Narbonne were unaltered, no one would be able to insist that she live with someone she hated. Perhaps then she might seek a separation from her husband and live in a way which would put an end to these arguments which he could bear no longer.[16]

After several months of freedom in Paris, alone with Narbonne, where they had lived through heroic times, the idea of returning meekly to Staël revolted her whole being. As part of the new order, divorce had just been made legal in France. She hoped – but was far from sure – that Narbonne might one day marry her, or if not that they might live together somewhere with their children – Italy perhaps, or the United States?[17] In several tormented and tormenting letters, she begged Narbonne to find out about the divorce laws in Sweden, suggesting that he consult an English lawyer. Aware that for the moment their lives and interests were as wide apart as they could be, she tried desperately to interest him in their child in the hope of binding him closer to her. 'I beg you to give me details about your childhood,' she wrote. 'I want to see if Auguste is like you. He is mad about his nanny to a degree that makes me jealous, but he is very lively and remarkably good humoured. My mother preaches to him with a gravity which the child's boredom makes comical. I asked my father the other day how it was that his love for this child could not allow him to forgive the author of his life. He answered drily that he only wished to think of the mother.'[18] Her mother had already started to give Auguste religious instruction: 'He responds by insisting that he be allowed to leave. My mother forgives him this year, as he is only two . . . What is true is that he is remarkably intelligent, and if you are not unnatural you will love him, but there is some doubt about that.'[19]

Narbonne, meanwhile, preoccupied with the King's fate, had other things on his mind. His infrequent letters continued to provoke a hopeless pattern of suicidal, jealous, angry and threatening letters from Madame de Staël, followed by penitent grovelling and passionate declarations of love. It must have put a severe strain on his love and patience. In the grip of her first real love affair, Madame de Staël's formidable mind was powerless against the ardent wishes of her heart. Exasperating, but pitiful too, like the spoiled child that she was, she could never be anything but entirely natural. She was heedless of all those around her, believing that a great passion had its own laws, that an extraordinary person need not behave like other people. From the time of her arrival at Coppet, she had embarked on a work in which she would write about love and human passions, personal and political, with unparalleled lucidity. She wrote, as she put it, 'to calm the tempests of her heart' and also because throughout her life she needed to put her own experience on paper. Her *De l'influence des Passions sur le Bonheur des Individus et des Nations* (On the Influence of the Passions upon the Happiness of Individuals and of Nations), not to be published for four years, was written during the years of her wanderings from Coppet to England, to Paris and finally back to Coppet.

Never one to remain inactive, even before the birth of her child in October 1792 she began to think of ways in which she could set up a refuge in Switzerland for all her friends on the proscribed list in France. It was understandable that she should wish to provide a refuge for her lover and her closest friends, but her interest was to extend much further afield. Geneva, with its Jacobin sympathies and constant risk of an invasion by the French, was far too dangerous. She decided that Lausanne in the Canton of Vaud would be most suitable. To this end she contacted all the important people she knew, among them Gibbon, who was a friend of Gabriel-Albert d'Erlach, the bailiff of Lausanne, to whom she wrote countless letters, sparing no effort to achieve her goal.

Throughout that autumn, the French revolutionary armies went from victory to victory. By the end of October 1792, General de Custine had occupied the Rhineland. The occupation of Nice had followed that of Savoy. At the beginning of November General Dumouriez, the victor of Valmy, had led his troops to a decisive victory at Jemappes, overrunning the Austrian Netherlands (Belgium) and entering Brussels.

In the same month, Necker addressed a written defence of the King to the National Convention. Uncharacteristically, Madame de Staël did not entirely approve her father's efforts. Necker's money was blocked in France and this démarche would threaten any possibility of its recovery and thus prejudice her future with Narbonne. In her later account of the French Revolution, however, she would see things differently: 'In October 1792, before the horrible trial of the King, before Louis XVI had named his defenders, M. Necker presented himself for this noble and perilous task. He published a memoir which posterity will consider one of the truest and most disinterested witnesses on behalf of that virtuous, imprisoned monarch.'[20]

On 22 November, Madame de Staël was able at last to inform Narbonne of the birth, two days before at Rolle, of another son, 'dark and handsome' like him. On 27 November the child was christened Matthias Albert by the Neckers, who presented him as the son of Eric-Magnus, Baron de Staël-Holstein. His first name, Matthias, was that of M. de Staël's father and grandfather.[21] 'Behold me mother of the Gracchi. I hope my sons will help to restore liberty in France.'[22] Madame de Stael wrote to Gibbon a week later.

Narbonne must by now have had serious doubts about his demanding mistress's threatened arrival. His own thoughts were far more with the King, who was not only his godfather but perhaps even his half-brother. He had spent his entire childhood in royal circles; they were his family. He had been sincere in his wish to reform the monarchy, never dreaming that he would witness its destruction. When the King had come under serious threat in July, Narbonne had been prepared to risk his life to help him escape in spite of the distrust in which he was held by then by the royal family. Safe in England, he was filled with guilt and remorse, acutely aware that the royalist émigrés and many of his English acquaintances blamed him and his friends for the King's present predicament. He did everything in his power to muster support for the King, trying to persuade Fox and Erskine to intervene if not directly on behalf of the King, then at least in the name of liberty and justice. He even managed to get an interview with William Pitt. But the Prime Minister remained obdurate – 'under no conceivable circumstances could England ever expose herself to intercede in vain on such a matter and before such men', was his stony reply. Pitt had been determined to distance Britain from the affairs of the continent, but France's recent victories and the Convention's disregard of Dutch rights over the Scheldt estuary were now threatening Britain's interests. Relations with France were increasingly strained.

The King's trial had been uppermost on the Convention's agenda for the past month. Since by the terms of the Constitution of 1791 no court in the land had jurisdiction over the King, the problem had rested on whether the King of France could be tried at all. In his maiden speech on 13 November, the twenty-five-year-old Saint-Just, the youngest deputy in the Convention, argued against the need for a trial at all, since any king was by definition a tyrant. To try the King was to presuppose his innocence, Saint-Just cried, but 'one cannot reign innocently'. The Republic could only live if the King died. A few days later, Robespierre too argued that the King could be condemned unheard, but in the end his proposal was rejected and on 3 December the National Convention decreed that the King must face trial and that the Convention was the only tribunal capable of trying him. Louis 'Capet's' trial, was to begin on 11 December 1792. As the King, who was a Bourbon, pointed out, Capet was not even his name, but that of the dynasty that had ruled France until 1328.

His efforts in England having proved useless, Narbonne had written to Grégoire, President of the National Convention, demanding his right as a former Minister of War to give evidence on behalf of the King. When news of his démarche to the Convention to testify on behalf of the King reached Madame de Staël, who had barely recovered from the birth of their son, she could hardly believe that he was preparing to put his life at risk without consulting her. In three separate letters, dated 2 December, sent by three different routes (presumably to ensure that one of them reached him) Madame de Staël gave full vent to her fear, her sense of betrayal, her incredulous rage and her bitter disappointment: 'If you put a foot in France I will instantly blow out my brains.' Then in a longer letter, she remonstrated: 'You have given me a mortal blow, M. de Narbonne. I believed that my life was of more value to you than this, the maddest, the most pointless and the most dangerous of actions, for the King as much as for you. I will be with you in a fortnight. Ah, my God! Am I in time or have you already killed me? Barbarian! What have I done to you that you make my life a constant torture?'[23] That she was equally dismissive of her father's attempts to help the King when it might threaten her future with Narbonne is a measure of how unbalanced and self-absorbed she was at this time. Anxious that her husband's arrival in Switzerland might prevent her departure, at loggerheads with her parents, terrified for Narbonne's safety if he went to France, she felt betrayed that he had put the King's interest before hers and their children's. She knew that all this was folly, but her nerves were in tatters.

Deaf to her parent's exhortations, threats and pleas, Madame de Staël made preparations to leave. She was as exhausted by the struggle between them as they were. Madame Necker had not only threatened to cut off her allowance but had mobilized her uncle and her cousins to warn her that she was about to become a woman lost. Madame de Staël wanted to leave her children with her parents, intending to return within four months, 'but to them, I am "abandoning" them, and Heaven will punish me'. Her father had used every possible argument to prevent her departure: 'I will be stopped, assassinated on the way, . . . I don't know what else. I was on the point of killing myself after the last scene with my father.'[24]

On Christmas Day, the news that Madame de La Châtre, Madame de Broglie, Jaucourt and Mathieu de Montmorency were proposing to return to France rather than risk perpetual banishment and the loss of all their possessions – as proposed under the terms of a new law in France – further upset Madame de Staël's plans. To be at Juniper Hall without the face-saving presence of female friends would be even more compromising. Narbonne had also written to tell her that in a climate of impending war with France the British Parliament had passed an 'Aliens Bill', which required all French citizens to register with the authorities and authorized their immediate expulsion were it considered necessary. This would obviously make all their positions much less secure, particularly as Madame de Staël, more than most, had bitter enemies among the many royalist émigrés in England who were pouring poison in whatever ear they might. Her mind fixed on one thing only – how to rejoin her lover – Madame de Staël could only suppose that he did not want her. 'In your letter which delays my departure, you seem not to want me to come to London. Do you not love me any more? Are your feelings such that you are afraid to tell me?' she begs him anxiously. Her father had warned her that if her arrival in London was a source of further trouble, Narbonne would love her less: 'You are so cold in your letters and I am so passionate. You seem to have so little wish to see me again that my heart is withered by fear and open to every kind of pain.'

To prevent her leaving, her parents, afraid for her safety and aware that their presence would lend their daughter some respectability, were now willing to receive Narbonne in Switzerland. Her mother herself came to tell her so, and this, as Madame de Staël wrote to Narbonne, 'meant a great deal from her'. But she would wait to hear what he preferred. Her papers were ready. 'Ah! If you love me I will leave at once!'[25]

Terrified that political and military developments might put an end to her plans, Madame de Staël now persuaded her parents that a short trip to Geneva would do her nerves good. 'The earth trembles on all sides,' she wrote to Gibbon, 'and I think that if I do not make haste to leave, an abyss will open up between my friend and myself.'[26] A few days later, Madame Necker announced her daughter's departure to Gibbon herself. They had done everything in their power to prevent her from leaving but she had taken matters in her own hands.[27]

Free at last, Madame de Staël sped to Paris where she arrived in the middle of January 1793, staying with the Gouvernets at Passy. Nothing is known about what can only have been a very dangerous journey. Paris was hushed, waiting for the verdict on the King. Escorted by Mathieu de Montmorency to Boulogne, whose mayor was favourable to the Constitutionalists, and where she was briefly reunited with Madame de La Châtre, Jaucourt and Madame de Broglie, Madame de Staël arrived at Dover on 20 January.

That very day in Paris, the National Convention had found 'Louis Capet, last King of the French, guilty of conspiracy against national liberty and of assault against national security'. After a vote, Louis XVI was formally condemned to death. Among the seventy or so deputies voting for imprisonment and banishment instead was Thomas Paine. The next day, 21 January 1793, at ten o'clock in the morning, the King was guillotined in the former Place Louis XV, renamed the Place de la République (today, the Place de la Concorde).

'The late King of this country has been publicly executed,' wrote Gouverneur Morris to the American Secretary of State, Thomas Jefferson. 'He died in a manner becoming his dignity. Mounting the scaffold he expressed anew his forgiveness of those who persecuted him, and a prayer that his deluded people might be benefited by his death. On the scaffold he attempted to speak, but the commanding officer, Santerre,[28] ordered the drums to beat . . . The greatest care was taken to prevent a concourse of people. This proves a conviction that the majority was not favourable to that severe measure. I consider a war between France and England as inevitable.'[29]

Madame de Gouvernet, with whom Madame de Staël had just been staying, had stood with her husband at their window that morning when 'the gates of Paris were closed and orders were given that no reply should be made to those outside who asked the reason why. We stood there in shocked silence, hardly daring to say a word to one another . . . Alas! The deepest silence lay like a pall over the regicide city. At half-past ten, the gates were opened and the life of the city resumed its course, unchanged. A great nation had that day soiled its history with a crime for which the future would hold it guilty. Yet not the smallest detail of the daily round had changed.'[30]

Chapter 10

~

Juniper Hall

'Four months of happiness salvaged from the shipwreck of life.'
Madame de Staël[1]

MADAME DE STAËL's ardently longed-for reunion with Narbonne had been completely overshadowed by the execution of the King. The news had reached them in Richmond, at the house of the beautiful Princesse d'Hénin which she shared with her lover, the Marquis de Lally-Tollendal, where Madame de Staël had spent her first few days in England. Madame de Staël had wept bitterly for the King, but perhaps even more for her guilt-ridden and devastated lover. 'Narbonne and d'Arblay have been almost annihilated: they are forever repining that they are French and, though two of the most accomplished and elegant men I ever saw, they break our hearts with the humiliation they feel for their guiltless birth in that guilty country!' Fanny Burney wrote to her father.[2]

Perhaps to avoid gossip, Narbonne had back gone to Juniper Hall ahead of Madame de Staël, who remained at Richmond for a few days in order to make some necessary calls in London. From Richmond she wrote to him: 'Alas! More than anything else, the pain which you have suffered has wrung my heart. The expression on your face, the efforts you were making to master your feelings, all echoed painfully in my soul. Forgive me for loving you so passionately that I see pain like happiness in you and you alone.' Ever practical, she adds, 'it would be prudent to cover oneself diplomatically' and encloses a letter of recommendation from Lally-Tollendal, and one from herself, addressed to Lord Grenville, which she asked Narbonne to deliver personally. (William Wyndham, Baron Grenville (1759–1834), a cousin of William Pitt, was then Secretary of State for Foreign Affairs.) Madame de Staël also urged Narbonne to speak to William Pitt and to

John Villiers, Member of Parliament for Dartmouth and an old friend of Narbonne's: 'not out of concern for the [Aliens] Bill, but out of fear *of the malice of the aristocrats* [the royalist émigrés] *about Necker's daughter*. Those words are essential,' she stresses.

To Grenville, she wrote: 'The horror which France inspires at this the most disgraceful moment in the history of man makes it impossible for me to remain in a land forever dishonoured. Unable to await M. de Staël's arrival, I made haste to seek asylum in this glorious country, whose virtues alone still enable one to believe in the benefits of true liberty. M. de Staël's diplomatic status requires that I inform you of my sojourn at the country retreat of Juniper Hall.'[3] She had every reason to be worried as Chauvelin, the Convention's representative in England, had been ordered to leave the country that very day. Two days later, on 26 January 1793, *The Times* thundered: 'The present moment is of all others the most favourable for declaring war against France. It has been perhaps a matter of sound policy to delay this declaration to the present moment; and we will venture to say, that no war was ever undertaken with the more general concurrence of the people, than that in which we are about to engage.' But in the end it was the Convention that declared war on Britain (and the Netherlands) first, on 1 February 1793.

Madame de Staël's arrival at Juniper Hall greatly lightened the atmosphere of gloom and despondency and drew all her friends there. Talleyrand frequently left his London house for long visits. Madame de Staël's experiences in Paris, and her unrivalled ability to recount them, left Fanny Burney, who was staying at nearby Norbury Park with the Locks, breathless with admiration. 'Madame de Staël, daughter of M. Necker, is now at the head of the colony of French noblesse . . .' she wrote to her father in early February. 'She is one of the first women I have ever met with for abilities and extraordinary intellect.'

Madame de Staël had just received a letter from Paris describing the King's last moments with his family: the desperate cries of the women, the Dauphin's last pleas for his father, Louis's dignified courage on mounting the scaffold and his attempt to address his people – an attempt which Santerre had silenced by a roll of drums – and his confessor's last words: '*Fils de Saint Louis, montez au ciel*' ('Son of Saint Louis, go up to heaven'). Narbonne, sickened by the news, as was d'Arblay, had been a little comforted by a letter from old M. de Malesherbes, who had acted on behalf of the King at his trial, and had written to tell them how touched Louis had been by Narbonne's letter on his behalf. Fanny, who had disapproved of the progressive politics of the little French colony before she met them, now adored all the Juniperians, declaring that they had become 'bosom friends'.[4]

The author of *Evelina* (1778), her much acclaimed first novel, and *Cecilia* (1782), Fanny Burney had only recently left her position as Second Keeper of the Robes to Queen Charlotte, where she had been a witness to the King's descent into madness and where her talents had been dissipated and her nerves put under severe strain by the boring routines and petty rivalries of the court. A pension of £100 a year, her reward for five years of loyal service to the Queen, to whom Fanny remained devoted, now gave the forty-year-old spinster a measure of independence. Small, neat and timid, Fanny Burney had suffered her own disappointments in love. Madame de Staël admired Fanny's talent as a novelist. The two women, although temperamentally polar opposites, instantly took to each other, offering to teach the other their native languages. Madame de Staël had learned to read English from her mother, who characteristically had started with Milton. Begging Miss Burney 'to correct the words but to preserve the sense of the card', her new friend plunged into her first letter written in English with her customary lack of caution, after which she declared 'nothing can affright me'. Nothing did. In her next letter to Fanny, Madame de Staël confessed that she had not consulted her teacher, Mr Clarke, before writing to her: 'What may be the perfect grammar of Mr Clarke, it cannot establish any sort of equality between you and J [sic] then I will trust with my heart alone to supply the deficiency. Let us speak upon a grave subject: do J see you this morning? What news from captain phillip? When do you come to spend a large week in that house? every question requires an exact answer; a good also. My happiness depends on it, and J have for pledge your honour. Good morrow and farewell. Pray Madame phillips, recollecting all her knowledge in french, to explain that card to you.'[5]

After her years of stultifying boredom at court and the modest propriety of her life at home with a disagreeable step-mother and a much younger sister, it was no wonder that Fanny Burney, who lacked neither imagination, wit nor humour, should have been utterly bewitched by her new French friends, particularly by Madame de Staël's warmth and brilliance, but very soon also by M. d'Arblay's quieter charms. At the end of February 1793 she wrote to her father that she had remained longer than she had intended because of Madame de Staël, who was 'of the first abilities'. Her current work – *De L'influence des passions . . .* – from which Madame de Staël had read extracts, was 'truly wonderful for power both of thinking and expression'. In short, Madame de Staël had been impossible to resist. Fanny was proposing to spend a week with her. Narbonne bore 'the highest character for goodness, parts, sweetness of manners and ready wit. You could not keep your heart from him if you saw him for only half an hour'. D'Arblay was sincere, frank and open and a wonderful judge of literature, and even Talleyrand, against whom Fanny Burney had been deeply prejudiced, turned out to be 'a man of admirable conversation, quick, terse, *fin*, and yet deep, to the extreme of these four words'.[6] What Fanny did not tell her father was that she was also falling in love with d'Arblay.

Fanny's letter had filled Dr Burney with alarm. Rumours of Madame de Staël's moral character and her relations with Narbonne had reached him and been confirmed by the Burkes and his old friend, James Hutton, who had written begging that Fanny should avoid any connection with the 'adulterous demoniac'. Fanny could not be too careful, particularly as she was financially dependent on her pension from the Queen, who was extremely strait-laced. While he could understand the fascination of her new friend, Dr Burney cautioned his daughter to have as little to do with Madame de Staël as possible and on no account to accept an invitation to stay at Juniper Hall.

Intoxicated by her new-found happiness and the pleasures of congenial company, Fanny had no doubt that the calumnies against her new friends had been put about by Jacobins or the ultra-royalists. Utterly unworldly herself, she could not believe, as she explained to her father, that the relations between Madame de Staël and Narbonne were in any way improper. 'M. de Narbonne was of her society, which contained ten or twelve of the first people in Paris, and occasionally, almost all Paris; she loves him even tenderly but so unaffectedly, and with such utter freedom of all coquetry, that, if they were two men, or two women, the affection could not, I think, be more obviously undesigning.' She went on, 'She is very plain, he is very handsome; her intellectual endowments must be with him her sole attraction.'[7]

For all her spirited defence of her friends, the prudish and cautious Fanny none the less refused Madame de Staël's invitation, for which a sore throat provided a timely excuse. On 1 March, Fanny returned home to Chelsea College with a heavy heart.

Madame de Staël was not fooled by Fanny's excuses. Aware that she was the subject of the most vicious calumny, aware too of the growing love between Fanny and d'Arblay, she decided to go to London: 'My dear Miss,' she wrote from Juniper Hall on 8 March, 'this time you will permit me to write to you in French; I want to make plans to see you and I do not want to risk any misunderstandings in this important matter. On Tuesday, I shall be at Chelsea's College [sic] with your French tutor [d'Arblay] and Mr Clarke; they will chat together and you – you will talk to me. I know that you are full of kindness for me, and that you have bravely stood up to certain examples of French spite to which one must become accustomed in times of civil war. All I ask is that you continue to love me even if you must wait for other times to say so.'[8] Refuting some of the lies about her – that she was a republican (when she and her friends had barely escaped with their lives from the Jacobins); that she was fond of meddling in public affairs (if that were so she would have been back in Paris where her husband was urging her to return and where she would be involved in affairs of the utmost importance; this was for Fanny's ears only) – Madame de Staël looked forward to seeing Fanny and to resuming their friendship.

Before she left, Fanny had confided her growing anxieties about Madame de Staël to d'Arblay, with whom she had embarked on an epistolary courtship: 'Everyone says that she is neither an émigré, nor banished, but that it is M. de Narbonne who has seduced her away from her husband and children. In vain do I speak of the different customs of her country. "She is a wife and a mother" is the only reply.'[9] Abandoning any attempt to write to Fanny in English – they too had been teaching each other their native languages – d'Arblay wrote in French, and from the heart: 'What have people been saying to you about Madame de Staël?' he cried indignantly. 'They wrong her if they fail to do justice to her extraordinary qualities of mind and heart. Her kindness, her humanity, her benevolence as well as her need to exercise them are matchless.' Madame de Staël's marriage, like many other marriages of convenience among the French aristocracy, had not been happy and it would be wrong, indeed barbarous, to blame her for that or judge her by the standards that applied in England. Whatever their previous relations might have been, d'Arblay could swear on his honour that Madame de Staël was now living on terms of the purest friendship with Narbonne and he would be happy to recommend her company to his mother or to his sister.[10] Devoted to Narbonne, but never less than honest and sincere, d'Arblay must have believed what he was saying. Fanny herself had seen nothing to arouse her suspicions yet she was thrown into complete turmoil by the prospect of Madame de Staël's visit. Unable to face her, she had gone to spend the day with her married sister, Charlotte Francis, when Madame de Staël turned up at Chelsea College as promised. Undeterred by Fanny's absence, Madame de Staël decided that this was an excellent opportunity to meet her family. She was courteously received by Mrs Burney, with whom she spent a quarter of an hour, when, as ill luck would have it, Mrs Orde, a bluestocking friend of theirs, arrived. Undaunted by her coldness, Madame de Staël launched a serious charm offensive but this time to no avail. Redirected to Fanny's sister's house, the starchy Mrs Orde was greatly put out when she arrived, to find that Madame de Staël's coach had preceded her. In spite of Fanny's efforts to appease her she had refused to come in. 'Nothing could happen more perversely than the events of this day,' Fanny wrote wearily to Susanna later that evening. Madame de Staël, 'so charming, so open, so delightful', had as always, utterly won her over so that 'while she was with me, I forgot all the mischiefs that might follow'.

Madame de Staël, Narbonne and d'Arblay spent a fortnight in London, scarcely enough time to see all their French friends as well as their English ones. There was Talleyrand in his little house in Woodstock Street, and his former mistress, Madame de Flahaut, who lived with their son in miserable lodgings above a grocer's shop in Half Moon Street. She had been reduced to making the chip straw bonnets then in fashion but had recently taken to writing to supplement her meagre earnings. Her novel, *Adèle de Sénange* – the proofs were then being corrected by Talleyrand – was to be unexpectedly successful. She had received her English and French guests, specially invited to meet Madame de Staël, exactly as she used to receive in her apartments at the Louvre. Led by Madame de Staël, their conversation was as gay and brilliant as in the Paris salons. It had lasted till two in the morning.[11]

Most of the émigrés were living in pitifully reduced circumstances. It was the women who began to earn money first, by using skills such as lace-making and dress-making. The men, initially lost, were employed before long teaching French and working in restaurants and shops. In order to be able to continue to enjoy the social gatherings which had been such an indispensable part of their former lives, everyone now brought a cooked dish or some sugar as their contribution to the feast. It was considered gallant to bring a candle and offer it to the mistress of the house, placing it, already lit on the chimney piece.[12]

England had been most generous to the French émigrés of all political persuasions. Whatever their private views the English throughout the twenty-five years of war and revolution would continue to extend the surest welcome and the most generous hospitality. Charitable trusts bearing some of England's grandest names helped to alleviate the misery of the French émigrés. Somewhat more eccentrically, Lord Bridgewater sheltered a large number of monks from different orders on his estate, his only request being that when he was entertaining guests, they should all wonder around the grounds in their different habits – much more picturesque than sheep or deer, he liked to say![13]

While in London, Madame de Staël also took the opportunity to see Erich Bollmann the young Hanoverian doctor who had saved Narbonne. However Bollmann's initial hero-worship of Narbonne had turned to rancorous disappointment after Narbonne had offered him a pension, which he refused. Summoned by Madame de Staël, he had arrived at her house as she was about to go out. They needed to talk, so he must come with her, she declared. Noticing the Minister of Geneva, Jean-Armand Tronchin, who had come to call, she bundled him into her carriage as well, granting him an interview 'en route'. When they reached her destination she dismissed Tronchin and asked Bollmann to wait while she paid her call. Half an hour later she came out with the friend she had called on and, after depositing her at another address, returned home with the thoroughly bemused Bollmann.

'She was dressed in morning clothes, and when we arrived at her house she called her maid to undress her. It was only then that we were alone, for servants don't count according to French customs . . . I stood on one side of the fireplace, dressed in black from head to foot, my hat in my hands, she was on the other side, in her petticoat and a simple gown, rolling a little piece of paper in her fingers as she always does.'[14] Madame de Staël then launched into an eloquent defence of Narbonne's actions. Taken aback, Bollmann stammered that he had not wished to offend anyone but he had been upset by the offer of money from a man who was not a close friend. 'You are a little like Jean-Jacques Rousseau,' she teased him flatteringly about his susceptibilities. Soon after his departure she then dashed off a note to him: 'I am very fond of you and will prove it to you in order to have the right to talk to you of gratitude.' Thoroughly mollified Bollmann was invited to spend a few days at Juniper Hall, where Madame de Staël had no difficulty in making peace between him and Narbonne.[15]

Madame de Staël was 'an extraordinary, eccentric genius', who only needed a few hours of sleep and who was otherwise constantly busy, Bollmann declared in a letter to a friend, in which he also compared Narbonne and Talleyrand with some perceptiveness: 'Narbonne is quite a tall man, a little heavy but vigorous, with something striking and superior about his features. He has great wit, an endless fund of ideas and he possesses all the social graces to the highest possible degree. He is irresistibly attractive and when he chooses he can intoxicate a person or even a roomful of people. There was only one person in France to be compared with him and who, in my opinion, far surpasses him and that is his friend Talleyrand, former bishop of Autun. Narbonne pleases but is ultimately boring; whereas, on the contrary, one might listen to Talleyrand for years . . . Narbonne's conversation is more brilliant; Talleyrand's more graceful, more subtle, more beguiling. Narbonne is not for everyone; people of sensibility can't bear him – he has no hold over them. Talleyrand while no less morally corrupt, can move to tears even those who despise him.'[16]

Madame de Staël and Narbonne had several other friends among the English. Lord Sheffield, a close friend of Gibbon's, wrote to him describing Madame de Stael's visit. He had first escorted them to the Tower of London and then hosted a dinner, to which he had also invited their friends Malouet, the Prince de Poix, Lally-Tollendal, the Princesse d'Hénin and others. After dinner they had all gone on to call on Lady Katharine Douglas where Lord Loughborough, the new Lord Chancellor, was her guest of honour. Used to the reserve of Englishwomen he was visibly taken aback and none too pleased when Madame de Staël immediately engaged him in a serious discussion on the principles of government and politics. 'There is much prejudice against her,' the exhausted Sheffield admitted to Gibbon after the visit was over: 'She is considered to be the worst type of intriguing democrat [the term usually used for republicans in the language of the time], capable of setting the Thames on fire. I've had the greatest trouble convincing people that she is eminently lively, agreeable and blessed with extraordinary intellectual gifts, although she can at times make herself ridiculous.'[17]

Refreshed by their visit to London, where in addition to her social calls Madame de Staël had fitted in several visits to the theatre, they returned to Juniper Hall at the end of March. As always she drew people like a magnet. Susanna Phillips, however, noticed that Narbonne, with his exquisite manners and his sad look – 'as delicate as a truly feminine woman' – was often embarrassed by Madame de Staël's robust self-confidence and utter disregard for convention. It was with Talleyrand that she seemed to have the easiest relationship. With a shared joy in brilliant conversation and their close familiarity, they sparked each other off: 'Madame de Staël was very gay, and M. de Talleyrand very *comique*, this evening; he criticized, amongst other things, her reading of prose, with great *sang-froid*,' Susanna wrote to Fanny in her regular reports. 'You read prose very badly,' Talleyrand had told Madame de Staël, 'you have a sing-song way of reading which is no good at all; listening to you one thinks one is hearing poetry!' They had then gossiped about their many friends and acquaintances 'with the utmost unreserve, and sometimes with the most comic humour imaginable'.[18]

For all the pleasures of each other's company, life was not easy for the little colony at Juniper Hall. Money was a constant worry as they began to sell off whatever they could: Talleyrand's splendid library was sold at Sotheby's in the second week of April. Narbonne sold his bronzes, which Madame de Staël had managed to save before she left Paris, to Mr Lock. Madame de Staël, meanwhile, continued to depend on her father for money. On 1 April 1793 they had had a disagreeable visit from Mr Jenkinson, who had come to raise the rent on Juniper Hall. He was accompanied by his attorney – 'a man whose figure strongly resembles some of Hogarth's most ill-looking personages, and who appeared to me to have been brought in as a kind of spy,' wrote Susanna Phillips to Fanny Burney. Narbonne had been angry, while Madame de Staël tried to charm him in her imperfect English with earnest interjections of ' "What will you, Mr Jenkinson? Tell to me, what will you?" '[19]

Staël, meanwhile, had taken up his post in Paris on 1 March and immediately set about negotiating a Franco–Swedish pact with the new Committee of Public Safety. Madame de Staël wrote to him frequently throughout April. Her tone was now much more conciliatory. She was at Juniper Hall with Madame d'Hénin, she wrote, and hoped that he would come and escort her home to Switzerland. Her letters to Staël, in which she even proposes returning to Paris if he wants her there, suggest that she was beginning to see the wisdom of preserving her marriage as her father had wished. She may have already sensed that Narbonne's lukewarm affections were not all that she had hoped for, although she was not yet ready to give up her dream. It was, in any case, time for her to return to her father and to her children. She hoped and planned that Narbonne and her inner circle of friends would join her in Switzerland as soon as they could. Meanwhile she needed her husband's help with passports, escort and transport to cross France.[20]

However much they liked England, real life, for the little French colony, remained across the Channel. At the end of February 1793 the Convention had mobilized 300,000 men into the army. This, coupled with economic distress and continuing resentment of the treatment of non-juror priests, had led to uprisings and confrontations in the provinces, particularly in the Vendée. In mid-March, General Dumouriez, the hero of Valmy and Jemappes, was defeated at Neerwinden in Holland and opened negotiations with the enemy. So it was that when Talleyrand had arrived at Juniper Hall on 8 April Madame de Staël, wrote Susanna Phillips, 'in a state of the most vehement impatience for news', hardly gave him time to breathe as she fired question after question at him. Reports had just come in that General Dumouriez had seized the Minister of War, Beurnonville, as well as the two members sent by the Convention to investigate his activities, proclaiming to the *département du Nord* that he would not hesitate to march on Paris 'to put an end to the bloody anarchy which reigned there'.[21] On the same day, he appealed to the French army that France must return to the Constitution: 'It is time that the army declare its wish to purge France of assassins and agitators.' This was followed by a third proclamation to the people of France.[22]

Did Talleyrand think Dumouriez would be successful? Might they now hope for peace, security and happiness? Madame de Staël asked. Outwardly his usual urbane and imperturbable self, Talleyrand was very excited and longing to return to the fray. Only Narbonne urged caution, they should wait at least a week before making any plans. One thing was certain: they all needed to understand the situation more clearly. Madame de Staël and Narbonne therefore left for London two days later to see what they might find out.

Learning in London that the Prince of Saxe-Coburg, commander of the Austrian forces, was prepared to co-operate with Dumouriez in order to restore the Constitution and the monarchy with no thought of invading French territory, Narbonne and d'Arblay at once drafted a letter offering to support him, but they were overtaken by events as news reached them that Dumouriez had failed to carry the army and had defected to the Austrians on 5 April. The letter was never sent. Narbonne remained adamant that he would not join an expedition led by foreigners and royalist émigrés.

Madame de Staël was now desperate to find the solution to her future, which she hoped would be with Narbonne in Switzerland until such time as they could all return to France. In England against a background of government repression and virulently anti-French and pro-war public opinion their life grew ever more difficult. Only Charles James Fox, with a small band of supporters, continued to defend political rights and press for peace, accusing the government of grossly exaggerating the potential for revolutionary activity in the country and severely restricting rights of free speech and assembly.[23] Madame de Staël was to pay a special tribute to Fox when comparing him with Pitt in her account of the French Revolution written at the end of her life. 'It might well have been in England's favour that Mr Pitt was head of government during the most dangerous crisis that that country had ever been in; but it was no less important that a mind as great as Mr Fox's should continue to uphold his principles in spite of the circumstances, and that he was able to defend the household gods of liberty amidst the conflagration.'[24]

To Gibbon Madame de Staël admitted that, much as she admired the British parliamentary system, she felt that the present situation, in which the ruling Tories enjoyed complete support and where all argument was stifled, made London the most boring place on earth. She had done her best to keep the lowest of profiles, avoided all the most controversial company and had hardly been mentioned by the press, but 'I feel choked by my good behaviour, and I have paid heavily for the brilliant triumph of not being talked about.'[25]

Unwilling to leave, Madame de Staël nevertheless realized that her reputation made the situation of her friends more difficult, and that she must return to Switzerland, as her father was repeatedly urging her to do. Indignant that her husband had suggested that she travel through Germany alone, she pointed out the possible dangers of such a journey and asked him to fetch her at Ostend and escort her himself.[26] But Staël had his own problems. He was still engaged in negotiating a Franco–Swedish pact, only to find that the Swedish Regent now opposed it. Soon after Dumouriez's defection, the Regent gave orders that all dealings with the Convention were to be suspended at once and ordered Staël to leave France as quickly as possible. Fersen was appointed in his place.

At Juniper Hall, Madame de Staël continued to work on her book on the influence of the passions, which d'Arblay was copying out as fast as he could. She had been hurt by Fanny Burney's attitude, though they had met by accident during Madame de Staël's farewell visit to the Locks in London in the first week of May. They had parted amicably but Fanny was doubly determined afterwards not to go down to Surrey while Madame de Staël was still there. Fanny's excuse that she was unable to come down because her father needed her provoked Madame de Staël to ask of Susanna Phillips: 'But is a woman under guardianship all her life in this country? It appears to me that your sister is like a girl of fourteen.'[27] Fanny, who now intended to marry the penniless d'Arblay, had good reason to avoid Madame de Staël, although she was ashamed of having to do so. Her future depended entirely on her pension from the Queen, and she dared not offend her. After Madame de Staël's departure, Fanny nevertheless expressed regret and annoyance at their curtailed friendship. She wished that the world had minded its own business: 'I am vexed, very much vexed by the whole business' she admitted to her friend, Mrs Lock.[28]

On 20 May Madame de Staël had been visibly upset by a letter delivered to her during dinner, wrote Susanna Phillips to her sister. It was from her husband's secretary, Pierre Signeul, who was at Ostend waiting to escort her to Switzerland. The next evening, after a distraught Madame de Staël had spent her final day at Norbury Park, Susanna was 'truly concerned' at her evident misery. Begging Susanna to watch over her friends, Madame de Staël had also asked her to 'please tell Miss Burney that I do not hold anything against her – that I leave this country sincerely attached to her and bearing her no ill will.'[29] Narbonne then escorted Madame de Staël to Dover from London where they had spent her last two days with Talleyrand and Lally-Tollendal. They parted with great emotion, Narbonne repeatedly promising that he would come to Switzerland as soon as she sent for him.

Later that summer, Madame de Staël expressed her love and admiration for England and the English in a brief essay, 'On Norbury Park', which she sent to Susanna Phillips. 'Sweet image of Norbury, come and remind me that a pure and vivid happiness can exist on this earth! . . . In that retreat . . . I found for a while, shelter far from the crimes of France, and from the prejudice which the horror they must cause, inspire in everyone . . . The respect and enthusiasm which fills my soul when I contemplate the moral and political virtues which constitute England; the admiration at such a spectacle, the heavenly peace which I enjoyed; these sentiments, so sweet and so necessary after the torments of three years of revolution, unite in my memory with the worthy friends and the delightful retreat where I experienced them. I thank them for four months of happiness, salvaged from the shipwreck of life. I thank them for having loved me.'[30]

Chapter 11

Scarlet Woman and Scarlet Pimpernel

'There is, in the short span of existence, no greater chance of happiness than to save the life of an innocent man.'

Mme de Staël[1]

LOOKING BACK MANY years later, Madame de Staël would compare the months when the Terror raged in France to Dante's descent through succeeding circles into the depths of hell.[2] The Revolutionary Tribunal of Paris which had been set up to deal with counter-revolutionaries on 10 March 1793 was fed an endless supply of suspects by the *comités de surveillance*, leading to an ever increasing number of executions. Popular newssheets like Hébert's *Le Père Duchesne*[3] denounced the Girondins as no better than the royalists and called on the Paris radicals, the so-called *sans-culottes*, to oppose them. The expulsion and arrest of the Girondin deputies from the Convention in May led to a deluge of protests to the Committee of Public Safety from all over France, and the cities of Lyon, Bordeaux, Marseilles and then Toulon rose in revolt. France was in a state of civil war. In Toulon the rebels signed a treaty with the British, allowing them to occupy the port. In August, the Convention decreed mass conscription to combat the counter-revolution both within and outside France. Rebellions in provincial France were put down with maximum brutality, while a policy of de-Christianization – the closure of many churches and the stripping of religious decorations in those that remained – gathered momentum. After the fall of Lyon to the revolutionaries in October, there followed a slaughter of some 1,800 people, ordered by Fouché and Collot-d'Herbois. 'Lyon made war on liberty, Lyon no longer exists' read the proclamation from the Convention. Prisoners were packed into old boats on the river and drowned. Many more were mown down by grapeshot in mass *mitraillades*. Toulon held out until December, when it was recaptured for the Republic by troops under the leadership of a young artillery officer, who was at once promoted to major-general. His name was Napoleon Bonaparte.

Despite *sans-culottes* anarchy in France, the army, swollen by mass conscription, stood at some 650,000 men in July 1793, far bigger than any of the forces opposing it and inspired by revolutionary ardour and patriotism. By the end of the year a series of victories had pushed back the armies of the first coalition (Great Britain, Holland, Russia, Piedmont, Spain, Naples, Prussia, Austria and Portugal) and enabled the Committee of Public Safety to re-establish control. The royalist uprising in the Vendée was put down with great ferocity. 'The people were inspired by a fury which was as fatal within [France] as it was invincible abroad,'[4] wrote Madame de Stael in an effort to explain the amazing success of the French revolutionary armies in 1793 and in the following year.

Madame de Staël's journey home had been 'boringly easy', she confessed to Narbonne, but her thoughts were all in England. The Rhine had reminded her of the Thames and made her cry. She dreaded her reunion with her husband, who was once again heavily in debt. 'This man adds an unimaginable degree of extravagance and disorder to all his faults. He is brought to ruin not by generosity, but by weakness and by a love of ostentation. He must have his own travelling bed, the most beautiful horses, a pack of hounds, three valets and with all that he is as democratic as Robespierre!' she wrote contemptuously to Narbonne.[5] In the event, her reunion with Staël in Berne on 10 June was cordial. It was in both their interests to get on. She needed him not only to give her a cloak of respectability but also because she intended to help all her friends, and for this Staël's diplomatic status would be an indispensable advantage. He, of course, needed her money. A regular pension prised out of him by the elderly but wily actress Mlle Clairon added to the debts run up by his lavish tastes and his gambling. He proved most accommodating, even agreeing to share a house with Madame de Staël's friends, including Narbonne.

But two days later a letter from the Swedish Regent to Staël led to another change of plan. As a result of France's agreement to pay Sweden 10,000 livres per annum in subsidies, the Regent, who had made his ambassador's life extremely difficult, was now urging him to return to France to conclude the agreement.[6]

Delighted by this turn of events, which at one stroke vindicated her husband's judgement, restored his salary and got rid of him, Madame de Staël wrote to inform Narbonne that Staël spoke of returning to France within a fortnight and to Sweden in October. He had seemed as much in love with her as ever, she added, and she believed she could persuade him to do her bidding. She may have been right about the power of her influence, but it was precisely because he was no longer in love with her that he could now become what she had always wanted him to be – a malleable friend.

Madame de Staël's active and fertile brain was already engaged in plotting not only a life with Narbonne but also his political future. Conditions in France seemed to her to offer an opportunity for Narbonne to fill a gap as a political leader of moderate opinion. She tried to galvanize him into action, sketching out rather high-handedly a political statement she urged him to write, without further delay: 'The introduction . . . would state that you are only referring to the situation between the acceptance of the Constitution by the King and 10 August.' She followed this with a brief outline in four parts: an analysis of the history of the constitution; suggestions as to what could and should have been done differently at the time; what measures might be taken now; and a brief statement in conclusion about the pain of exile. 'Start writing at once,' she urged, 'and get d'Arblay to compile the material. For my part, I will write something, but such is your laziness that if you don't write your own version first, you would use everything I send you instead of selecting from it. You will get the first part within a fortnight of this letter. Make sure that you have written yours by then.'[7]

A week later Madame de Staël was once again reunited with her children and her parents at Coppet. 'The mother of the Gracchi is here, with her beautiful children and with her husband whom I hold in great affection,' Madame Necker wrote to Gibbon. The seven-month-old Albert, whom his mother had left behind as a five-week-old baby, was 'sweet, beautiful and dark-haired' and, Madame de Staël reported to Narbonne, Auguste at three was 'intelligent, independent, and cheerful'. But not all the news was good. She had been right to worry about her father's letter in defence of the King. As a result, his possessions in France, the two million livres he had deposited at the Treasury, his houses in Paris and Saint-Ouen, had all been sequestered and his name put on the list of proscribed émigrés.

Moreover, Madame de Staël was back again on the agonizing emotional see-saw of watching the post, urging Narbonne to start planning his journey at once, so as to arrive at the beginning of September before her husband's departure later that month, or they would lose 'the advantage for the world and my parents of Narbonne having been established here in his presence'. Everyone was now prepared to receive him, even Madame Necker, who in spite of her deteriorating health was grimly engaged in writing an essay against divorce (published the following year in Lausanne), supposedly in answer to the recent legislation by the National Convention, but really to punish her wayward daughter.[8]

When three letters from Narbonne arrived together, making Madame de Staël 'happier than the angels in heaven', she began at once to search for a house in the canton of Geneva. Ten days later she teasingly mentions for the first time to Narbonne 'a count Ribbing, the famous, accomplice of Anckarström, who is here under an assumed name', who was very handsome and had shown some inclination to fall in love with her.[9] From England, Talleyrand wrote that Narbonne was sunk in depression which left him listless and passive. He had sent his linen out to Switzerland but for the moment there was no sign of his own arrival. One piece of happy news was that of Fanny Burney's marriage to d'Arblay. Delighted, Madame de Staël wrote at once to congratulate her – 'Now that you are in some way a part of my family, I hope that if I come back to England I will be able to see you as much as I like, that is all the time.'[10]

Madame de Staël's attention was, as always, focused on events in France. Her torments of unrequited love were as nothing to the torments France was experiencing as the country slid further into the grip of terror. Head after head tumbled into the baskets beneath the guillotines, as the Convention tried to save the Revolution and eradicate all enemies of the new France. France's very history was to be erased with the introduction of a new, republican calendar, dating the year I from the previous September 1792 with months newly named for the seasons and divided into *decades* (ten-day periods) and the last day, *decadi*, taking the place of Sunday. Popular events were organized in an effort to distract the people and create favourable public opinion. Designed and choreographed by the painter Jacques-

Louis David, these grandiose spectacles relied heavily on allegorical instead of religious symbolism. To celebrate the revolution of 10 August one such pageant lasted from seven in the morning to eleven at night, complete with floats carrying plaster statues symbolizing republican virtues, with processions of young men carrying oak leaves and young women with baskets of roses. This was followed, on 10 November 1793, with a festival of Reason to celebrate de-Christianization. It was held in Notre-Dame, where a temple to Philosophy had been hastily erected in the choir on top of an artificial mountain crowned with the flame of liberty and flanked by statues of the fathers of the Revolution. Two rows of very young girls dressed in white and crowned with oak leaves attended a young woman, also in white, with an azure blue cloak representing Reason. Three days later all the churches in Paris were closed by the Commune.[11]

Marie-Antoinette's unhappy existence was now also nearing its end as the Convention prepared her trial. Since July 1793 the luckless Queen had had to face the agony of separation from her eight-year-old son, who had been forcibly removed from her to be re-educated. Before long she was moved from the Temple to the Conciergerie, from where, it was now all too obvious, she would follow her husband to the guillotine. More than ever the focus of anti-royalist hatred, the 'Austrian she-wolf' had not only been accused of treason, but also of lesbianism and even incest with her young son.

Madame de Staël, whom Marie-Antoinette had detested but who was incapable of bearing a grudge, now threw all her energies into composing a defence of the Queen. She had been against her father's and Narbonne's efforts to defend the King, but consistency was for lesser mortals and her *Réflexions sur le procès de la Reine* was published in August that year. The pamphlet was seized and destroyed in France but was published in Switzerland and in England – in the latter case under Talleyrand's supervision, as is clear from his letters to her. She had never admired the Queen but Marie-Antoinette's appalling predicament touched her heart. She could easily identify with her, both as a woman who was subjected to the crudest sexual slander and as a foreigner – the eternal scapegoat. Appealing directly to the emotions of 'women of all countries, of all social ranks', she drew a heartrending contrast between the rapturous reception for 'Maria Theresa's daughter' when she had first arrived in France, 'young, beautiful, combining grace and dignity', with her present state as a bereaved wife and mother, hated and defenceless. Calling on the women of France as wives and mothers themselves, to stand up for her, she begged them to defend the Queen and the young King, now torn from his mother, 'with all the weapons nature has given you. Seek out that child, who will surely perish if he must lose one who has loved him so much!'[12] Although the pamphlet was published anonymously, there was no doubt as to its author.

Madame de Staël's defence did no more for the Queen than her father's and Narbonne's had done for the King, but it was a brave act for all that. She had nothing to gain and much to lose. It would make her return to Paris difficult, reduce her chances of saving her father's fortune, and cause difficulties for her husband. Staël himself had written to Marie-Antoinette's lover Fersen: 'In spite of your injustice towards me . . . I could not but tell you of the sympathy which I myself and mine have never ceased to feel for one who is being so cruelly persecuted today.'[13] As a result of Madame de Staël's defence of the Queen, on 21 August the commissioners of two of the revolutionary sections of Paris, accompanied by an armed force, descended on the Swedish embassy, where, in spite of his diplomatic immunity, they impounded her husband's papers, confiscated Madame de Staël's papers and Pastor Gambs's correspondence, and arrested her footman and Staël's private secretary. It was only thanks to Gambs's determined and prolonged complaints to the foreign ministry that order was restored.

On 16 October 1793, Marie-Antoinette, by now a gaunt and tragic figure in her plain white shift, her hair cut short in preparation for the blade, her hands tied behind her back, was sketched on her last journey to the guillotine by Jacques-Louis David. She was soon followed by Madame Elizabeth, the King's sister, who had shared her imprisonment. Among the better known of the twenty or so people a day who went to the scaffold in the days and weeks after Marie-Antoinette's execution were the former Duc d'Orléans, Philippe Égalité as he was now known, and twenty-one Girondins, among them Madame Roland (Roland, like Condorcet and Pétion, had committed suicide).

In late August, the Staëls rented a house near Nyon, close to Coppet, from a Mr Trachsel, dubbed Trachsenhouse by Madame de Staël. She hoped that she would soon be joined in this refuge by Narbonne as well as by Mathieu de Montmorency and Talleyrand. A month later, when the Staëls moved in, it was all too clear that Narbonne had still made no plans to join her. His excuse was that his interests on the island of Saint Domingue, which was about to be invaded by the British, made his presence in England essential. By then she knew in her heart that Narbonne could only disappoint her dream of perfect reciprocal love and her hopes of sharing in his political glory. If she still begged him to come, it was perhaps because she was as yet unwilling to give up the hopes she had cherished over five years – hopes which had given her two children, on which she had risked her reputation and which had strained her relationship with her father. Perhaps, too, she needed to save face. Her family had never believed in Narbonne and were now openly telling her that he had grown tired of her. She had gone to tremendous trouble to make it possible for him to live in Switzerland, petitioning friends and officials and even moving house. People were slyly asking when she expected him. If he didn't come now, she would be a laughing stock. Her husband alone had showed some sympathy for her humiliating predicament. As she had come round from a fainting fit, she wrote to Narbonne that her husband had said: 'I can see my dear friend that M. de Narbonne has no wish to come here. For some time your father and I have known that at the last moment he would invent excuses, and since he refuses all your appeals, it is clear that he wishes you to either give him up or to go and fetch him. This struggle is killing you, and since I cannot make you happy I must not kill you. Write to M. de N. therefore and tell him that if he persists in offering such miserable excuses, unworthy of you and of him, next month, as soon as you have had an answer to this letter, I will personally escort you to Frankfurt, from where you will leave for England. I know that in doing so I will lose credit in France and thereby in Sweden, but your life is more precious to me than anything and I can see that you are dying.'[14]

Madame de Staël threatened Narbonne that if he had not joined her within a month she would take up this kind offer. Would he look for a small house in Mickleham? She ends: 'Do not abandon me, do not leave for America, or take me with you. I am dying of fear. I cannot bear it any longer. May my cries, my terrible despair, soften your heart. I am ashamed that I have not yet put an end to my miserable existence, but how can one die if there is a hope of seeing you again? And your children! Have pity on them and on me. Save me, save me!'[15]

While Madame de Staël was engaged in her highly charged emotional exchanges with Narbonne, she was also, from the moment of her arrival, engaged in an extraordinary 'scarlet Pimpernel' type operation. 'With difficulties almost incredible, Madame de Staël has contrived a second time, to save the lives of M. de Jaucourt and M. de Montmorenci, who are just arrived in Switzerland,' Fanny, now Madame d'Arblay, wrote to Dr Burney at the end of October.[16]

Her two old friends were the first to be saved by a remarkable network which was organized, operated and financed by Madame de Staël and which she used to rescue more than twenty people during the Terror, among them Jaucourt's mistress, Madame de La Châtre; Narbonne's former mistress who was Mathieu's mother, Madame de Laval; her father's old friend Malouet, together with several members of his family; the Marquise de Simiane; the Princesse de Noailles; the Duchesse de Broglie; the Princesse de Poix; the Maréchale de Beauveau; the Abbé Damas; the Marquise Laborde; Théodore de Lameth; and Achille du Chayla.

Her method was very simple, she explained in a letter to Madame d'Hénin, and it worked every time. A Swiss passport holder, chosen to look as much as possible like the person to be rescued, would travel to Paris, supposedly on business, their passport having been stamped at the frontier. Once in Paris, having got the necessary exit papers which enabled them to return to Switzerland, they would hand over their passport and papers to the person to be rescued. The endangered Frenchman or Frenchwoman would then cross back into Switzerland by a different frontier post on genuine Swiss documents, stamped with the necessary French visas, while the Swiss courier would return to the same frontier post from which he or she had set out, claiming that they had lost their papers. Madame de Staël retained a local magistrate who would confirm their identity as genuine Swiss citizens if necessary. Since they came and went often, they were mostly recognized by the border police and had no trouble.[17] Some of her agents were volunteers but most worked for money. Mathieu and Jaucourt were now safe with Madame de Staël at Trachsenhouse, living there disguised as Swedes to avoid embarrassing the Swiss authorities: 'I fished them out of that abyss of horror and Treboux, the sublime Treboux (one of her couriers), brought them to me across the mountains,' she wrote to Narbonne.[18]

Things did not always go smoothly, however. Recollecting the fate of those 'friends of liberty' during that dreadful time, Madame de Staël recalled one particular case, that of the young Achille du Chayla, Jaucourt's nephew, who had travelled through France on a Swiss passport, under a false name. 'At Moret, a frontier town at the foot of the Jura mountains, M. du Chayla was suspected of not being the person indicated on his passport and was arrested by the border police who declared that they would hold him until the bailiff of Nyon confirmed his Swiss nationality. M. de Jaucourt was then living with me under one of those Swedish names which we had invented. When he heard of his nephew's arrest, he fell into extreme despair since the young man, then a conscript, was carrying a false passport and moreover, was the son of one of the leaders of Condé's army. He would have been shot on the spot had his identity been discovered. There was only one hope; to convince M. Reverdil, bailiff of Nyon, to pronounce M. du Chayla a true native of Vaud. I went to see M. Reverdil to beg him for this favour. He was an old friend of my parents and one of the most enlightened and respected men in French Switzerland. At first and for perfectly good reasons, he refused. He was unwilling to bend the truth for any reason whatsoever, and furthermore, as a magistrate, he was afraid that he would compromise his country by being party to a falsehood. "If the truth is discovered," he told me, "we will forfeit the right to claim our own compatriots who might be arrested in France and so I would be damaging the interest of those for whom I am responsible, to save a man to whom I owe nothing." '[19]

While she was perfectly aware of the force of his arguments, Madame de Staël had none the less stayed with M. Reverdil for two hours: 'trying to conquer his conscience through his humanity. He had resisted for a long time but when I had repeated to him several times, "If you say no, an only son, a blameless man, will be assassinated within twenty-four hours and your simple word will have killed him" my feelings, or rather his, triumphed over all other considerations and the young du Chayla was saved.' It may be that M. Reverdil's wish to be rid of his persistent young friend was as great as his humanity. At the end of her extraordinary life Madame de Staël was to recall this incident with the observation: 'There is, in the short span of existence, no greater chance of happiness than to save the life of an innocent man.'[20] Saving her friends was one problem. Madame de Staël then had to face endless difficulties with the Bernese authorities with whom she was obliged to negotiate constantly to enable them to stay.

Engaged in her rescue mission, Madame de Staël still longed for Narbonne and Talleyrand to join her household, expecting to hear at any time that they were on their way. Instead, a letter from Talleyrand announced that they were proposing to go to Toulon, which had fallen to the English again that August and where Admiral Hood was now proposing support for a constitutional monarchy in France and recognizing the ten-year-old Dauphin as Louis XVII. Narbonne, Talleyrand and d'Arblay had felt honour bound to support the Dauphin and hoped that they might be on the way to a successful counter-revolution backed by Britain and the allied powers. A day or so later their intentions were confirmed by Narbonne himself. Madame de Staël was beside herself. 'I swear that if you go to Toulon, I will leave at once for Paris, I will assassinate Robespierre, and help you by dying'.[21] The fall of Lyons in October 1793 put an end to any such plans.

In the late autumn the Neckers left Coppet, renting once again the Château de Beaulieu, near Lausanne, so that Madame Necker could be near Dr Tissot. She was more obsessed than ever with the fear of being buried alive and spent most of her remaining months designing a mausoleum in which a double stone coffin would hold her body preserved in spirit, until Necker himself came to join her.

While Madame de Staël bombarded her lover almost daily with passionate reproaches she continued to expand her underground rescue networks. Towards the end of November, Narbonne at last announced his departure from England. A month later, with no idea of his whereabouts, Madame de Staël had worked herself up into a state of utter terror for his safety. When his next letter announced that he had been unable to leave after all, her relief that he was safe soon turned to fury. His letter had filled her with the deepest contempt, his ingratitude was of the blackest and vilest sort, she wrote: 'I will remain in Switzerland; I will not leave. And rest assured that I will die from the despair of having known you; of having loved the most base of men. You have played with my feelings so often, if you were capable of pity you would come to receive from my hands what I wish to put in your care. You are quite detestable, but to refuse a son from the hands of a mother whom you have killed, is perhaps too much even for you.'[22] This was too much for Narbonne, who now retired into offended silence for more than a month.

Madame de Staël was justified in believing that Narbonne's ardour, never very strong and sorely tried by hers, was waning, but she was being less than honest about her own feelings. At the time she was already engaged in a flirtatious correspondence with Count Ribbing, a correspondence which was soon to turn into a love affair. Throughout the next six months, her letters to Narbonne, her much warmer letters to her husband, whom she was now addressing as the father of her sons, and her letters to Ribbing, made up an epistolary troika which Madame de Staël seemed able to drive with no trouble at all.

Staël's departure had paved the way for the closer attentions of the young Swedish nobleman Ribbing, who was living in Switzerland under the assumed name of Bing. Adolphe-Ludvig, Count Ribbing, was a member of one of Sweden's oldest noble families. His father Frederick, Count Ribbing of Koburg, had been Grand Marshal at the court of the formidable Queen Mother, Louisa-Ulrika, sister of Frederick II of Prussia, who had detested her effeminate and homosexual son, King Gustavus III. Adolphe Ribbing had been brought up at court as part of the anti-Gustavian faction. In 1788 his antipathy for the King had been reinforced when Gustavus had ruined Ribbing's hopes of marriage to a rich heiress, arranging instead for her to be married to one of his favourites. Ribbing's duel with his rival resulted in banishment to a lonely fortress. His disenchantment with the King's foreign policy after the French Revolution – Sweden's involvement in war with Russia and then Gustavus's attempts to lead a crusade against revolutionary France – brought him into contact with a group of plotters. On 16 March at a masked ball, while a pack of revellers wearing dominos surrounded the King, the chief plotter, Anckaström, shot him at point-blank range. They were soon caught. Anckaström was executed immediately. The remaining four were condemned to be beheaded, their right hands to be cut off and their bodies broken on the wheel. As a result of a series of appeals launched by Ribbing's mother, to whom he was very close, Ribbing's sentence and that of his fellow conspirators was commuted to perpetual exile. After a few months in Paris, where he had previously spent several years and where he had many friends, Ribbing had come to Switzerland.

Twenty-nine years old when he met Madame de Staël, Ribbing was handsome with a quantity of beautiful hair and magnificent, expressive dark eyes. Soon after their meeting, he had been obliged to leave the canton of Berne following a violent dispute with another young man. His plan was to travel to Denmark, but Madame de Staël, already quite smitten, persuaded him to go to Geneva instead. Her letter of 19 November, promising him his passport, is positively encouraging: 'M. de Staël is now well so he will be leaving soon,' she writes, 'and so I will see you; and so at all times of day I will be happy if you find yourself happier here than in Denmark. Adieu, adieu.'[23]

A day later Madame de Staël discovered that Ribbing's dispute had been over her. She was ecstatic. 'I know now the subject of my glory and my misfortune,' she wrote, 'I know the subject of your conversation with Madame Archer's brother. And you sought to hide it from me!' Ribbing's noble behaviour in defending her, and his refusal to tell her about it, made a profound impression. 'Every day I am more attached to you; your character is a treasure store of goodness, pride, nobility which becomes ever more apparent with each day,' she wrote.[24] Perhaps a little afraid of Madame de Staël's élan, Ribbing answered her letter but declared that 'his heart was for ever closed to love' – a declaration she ignored. Their correspondence and their meetings continued.

On 13 December 1793, after a brief visit to take leave of the Neckers, Staël left for Sweden. He may have been surprised by the tone of his wife's letter: 'I need to tell you, my dear friend, with what bitter pain I parted from you. I did not know how much I needed you.' She urged him to look after himself and consider how much his life was worth to 'your wife and to your sons'.[25] Confused by her new tenderness, but finding no letter from her when he arrived in Zurich, Staël wrote that he was afraid that she would never make him happy. She replied that after all they had been through, nothing could separate them. He had been very good about Narbonne and he was not to worry about Ribbing, whose character and mind were agreeable to her. Nobody had seen him at her house, she added.[26]

If Madame de Staël was less than frank with her husband, her lover, and the new man in her life, they too were less than fully committed to her. She had decided to mend her marriage: her husband had been understanding and considerate, apparently willing to accept life entirely on her terms; she was grateful for his kindness, grateful for his acceptance of her sons and her longing to escape from Switzerland, for which she needed his diplomatic status. Irritated by the constant obstacles to her rescue plans thrown up by the cantonal authorities and bored to death with living in the country, she wrote to him: 'I hold the whole of Switzerland in magnificent horror. Sometimes I think that if only we were in Paris with a title [i.e. his diplomatic status] that they [the Jacobins] were obliged to respect, we could help a great many people and that hope makes me bear everything. I realize a little sadly that what I like least in the world is country life. I've got rid of my horses to economize . . . I hope you realize that I have condemned myself to this prison to please you, and that I would rather be in England. Be sure therefore, that I am resolved in heart and mind and that my life is joined to yours for as long as you attach any value to it, for as long as you remain that friend whose company I so enjoyed here for six months. Our children are well. Auguste grows stronger, my maternal love, at least as much. Adieu, adieu, very tenderly.'[27]

Several letters passed between husband and wife while Staël was in Zurich, where he remained for some weeks. During this time he met Barthélemy, the French envoy, who was negotiating a peace with Prussia in which Sweden and Denmark were to act as mediators. Here too he renewed his friendship with Lavater, the famous Swiss pastor and mystic, who was a theosophist and a theoretician of physiognomy and who, Staël hoped, might help to convert his wife. Madame de Staël corresponded with Lavater, but while she was always religious, she was absolutely not given to mysticism. At the end of January 1794, in a letter announcing Gibbon's death, she begged her husband to allow her to go to England in April. But it was soon clear that any such plans would have to be shelved for the time being because her mother was dangerously ill. Instead she left Nyon at once for Lausanne to be with her father.

Madame de Staël's letters to Narbonne continued unchanged over the next three months. Angry and bitter at his continued absence and the month-long pauses between his letters, she used anything and everything as ammunition against him. News that Talleyrand, who had been expelled from England under the Aliens Bill, was not to be given asylum in Switzerland was a great setback. An appeal to Pitt by Talleyrand and Narbonne had merely given three weeks' grace for Talleyrand to wind up his business before he left for America with his loyal friend Beaumetz. To Narbonne she wrote: 'It is therefore true that the bishop [Talleyrand] has left for America? Ah! what pain this terrible news has given me! I can hardly write to you my eyes are suffused with tears. And not a word from you on the day of such a terrible blow!'[28] Talleyrand had set sail on 2 March 1794. 'At the age of thirty-nine I am starting a new life, for it is life that I want. I love my friends too much to have other ideas . . . and I wish to show how much I have loved liberty and how much I still love it,' he had written to Madame de Staël before his departure.[29]

By the middle of March, Madame de Staël's little colony of refugees at Trachsenhouse had scattered. Her six-month lease on the house was up and the Bernese Government was unwilling to allow any refugees below the age of forty to remain. Madame de Staël was anxious for her friends, and for Ribbing, and hoped to install them all in Zurich.

She herself was obliged to go to Lausanne to be with her parents. Madame Necker had at first refused to see her. Now terminally ill – she had almost died in the night of 22 March – she had sent for her daughter the following morning. With a final twist of the knife, she took leave of her: 'My daughter, I am dying of the pain which your guilty and public attachment has caused me. You have been punished by the attitude of its object towards you. It puts an end to what my prayers could not make you abandon. It is through your care for your father that you will obtain my forgiveness in heaven. Say nothing. Leave now. I have no strength to argue at the moment.'[30] Madame de Staël's relations with her mother had deteriorated to such an extent that her only real concern was for her father. In April, when her mother rallied temporarily, Madame de Staël escaped to Zurich for a couple of weeks. Her novella, *Zulma*, had just been published in Lausanne. Madame de Staël used this short tale set, in the fashion of the times, in an exotic location on the banks of the Orinoco, to exorcize her love for Narbonne. Zulma, having followed her lover Fernand, handsomest and bravest of young men, into exile when he was expelled by his tribe, saves his life. When he is recalled he ignores her. Surprising him one day at the feet of a rival, Zulma shoots him with an arrow. She is acquitted by the elders of her tribe but, unable to live without her lover, kills herself.

At the end of the month she returned to Zurich, where Ribbing was waiting for her. It was during the next three days spent together that she and Ribbing became lovers, as was evident from her next letter to him. 'Our roles have changed but treat me gently in my new enslavement.' That evening, as news from France reached her, she added a postscript. More friends had perished on the scaffold: 'Ah! what a terrible list of massacres! Madame du Châtelet, Mme de Gramont, and M. de Malesherbes!' Brave old M. de Malesherbes, who had not hesitated to defend the King at his trial, had now gone to the guillotine himself.[31]

Madame de Staël remained in Berne for an extra day to try and save Mathieu de Montmorency's parents, who were in peril of their lives in France. On 2 May she was back in Lausanne, where she moved into the Château de Mézery which she had just rented – the very same place where Gibbon had lived all those years ago when he was first courting Madame Necker, then Mademoiselle Curchod. Her mother was still alive but only just. From her deathbed, Madame Necker continued to write long tender letters to her husband, begging him to carry out her last wishes, hoping to bind him to her for all eternity. He could only watch helplessly.

'She suffered from frequent insomnia, and during the day she would sometimes fall asleep suddenly, her head on her husband's arm. I have seen him sitting immobile for hours at a time in the same position, afraid to make the slightest movement in case he woke her.' At other times, unable to find any rest, Madame Necker sought solace in music. Musicians came every evening to play in the room next to hers. One evening, when they had failed to arrive, Madame de Staël recalled: 'my father ordered me to play the piano: having played a few pieces I began to sing the aria of Oedipus at Colonna by Sacchini . . . Hearing it my father burst into a flood of tears; I had to stop. For several hours I watched him at the feet of his dying wife give way to such deep emotions, to that unrestrained feeling – the hallmark of a great man.'

Madame Necker died on 15 May 1794. A few hours after her death Madame de Staël entered her father's room. The view of the sunrise on the distant Alps was magnificent. 'Perhaps her soul is soaring over there,' he had said to his daughter, pointing to a light cloud which was passing overhead, and then fell silent. She wondered only if he would feel that way about her own death.[32]

Her mother's will, altered in January 1794, had left everything to her husband, cutting Madame de Staël and her children out completely. 'May God have pity on my soul; I declare here that my express wish is that everything that I posess, anything belonging to me in any way, pass to Monsieur Jacques Necker, my husband, and the sole object of my affection in this world. I make no exception to this whole bequest; papers, letters, jewels, linen, clothes, silver, in a word everything belongs to him to do with as he pleases. Signed in Lausanne this 5 January, 1794.'[33]

Madame Necker's death did not make her daughter unhappy. They were far too estranged for that. But years later, when writing about her beloved father when she was in despair at his death, Madame de Staël again acknowledged the Neckers' married happiness, comparing it sadly with her own loves. 'Ah! what years my mother enjoyed; whereas a love which time and age weaken, a love unconsecrated by conscience, respect, endurance, what is it beside that admirable union? A life ever pure, an identical existence, the same memories covering an entire destiny are a further guarantor of immortality . . .'[34]

In France, the Terror was now moving towards its climax. The all-pervasive atmosphere of fear and suspicion had now infected the revolutionary committees themselves. The guillotine had been working continuously in the Place de la République to such an extent that the surrounding streets and gutters were mired in blood and the guillotine had had to be moved outside the city. To raise spirits and revolutionary fervour, on 18 Floreal (7 May), Robespierre, an arch-manipulator of public opinion, persuaded the Convention to institute a new civic religion, the cult of the Supreme Being. He had always hated atheism as being destructive of morality and had been against de-Christianization.

On 22 Prairial (10 June) a law prepared by Robespierre's henchman, Georges Couthon, was passed by the Convention. This totalitarian measure removed all safeguards from revolutionary justice, denying the accused a defence counsel and the right to cross-examination, making it unnecessary to produce solid evidence. The law of 22 Prairial unleashed the 'Great Terror'. From the overflowing prisons, men and women accused of crimes against the Revolution were tried by the Revolutionary Tribunal in batches of fifty. Among those who went to the guillotine were the poet André Chénier and Mathieu de Montmorency's brother, as well as many nobles and peasants, rich and poor. In the seven weeks between 22 Prairial and the coup of 9 Thermidor (27 July 1794) which removed Robespierre, more than 1,500 people were executed. Robespierre's enemies began to wonder what need there was of the Terror. Any one of them might be next. On 9 Thermidor a coalition of right- and left-wing deputies, who agreed on nothing but the removal of Robespierre, overthrew him. He attempted to shoot himself but merely shattered his jaw which was bandaged up so that his head could be cut off. He was executed, groaning in pain, together with St Just and a hundred allies that same day. Robespierre was dead and France was in a state of anarchy.

Narbonne's arrival in Switzerland at the end of July had come too late to rescue his relationship with Madame de Staäl, even if he had wanted to save it. Instead his presence, a little awkward at first, had given her the perfect cover for her affair with Ribbing, which remained secret. Narbonne had been a little piqued at being ousted. Soon after his arrival the two men were seen leaving the château together at dawn. There had been a sharp exchange of words between them the previous evening and, after several hours of anxiety, Madame de Staël fell into hysterics convinced that they had fought a duel. Later that evening all was clear when they reappeared in high good humour carrying a basketful of fish. Both keen fishermen, they had spent an enjoyable day together on the lakeside.[35]

Madame de Staël managed to spend the rest of August in the arms of her darling Adolphe, but at the end of the month the Bernese government expelled both him and Mathieu de Montmorency. Madame de Staël accompanied her lover to Suhr, where they parted in tears. She now regretted her affair with Narbonne, which had brought her so much pain and disgrace. 'Ah my friend, how bitter a thought it is not to feel worthy of you! Will the future expiate the past?' she wrote to Ribbing.[36]

While her father remained at Beaulieu, 'watching over that wretched coffin' until such time as the mausoleum, built to Madame Necker's precise instructions, would be ready at Coppet, Madame de Staël visited him constantly, in between welcoming new arrivals saved from France, among them, after several failed efforts, Madame de Montmorency-Laval, mother of Mathieu and Narbonne's former mistress. Several friends were still unable to leave, causing her much anxiety, although she was successful in the end. She spent much of her time calling on all the houses which were sheltering her new arrivals, helping to settle them, and trying unsuccessfully to hatch a plan, involving Bollmann, to save La Fayette, who was languishing in the prison of Olmütz in Austria. Madame de Staël continued to write to Ribbing, but although she did not yet know it, the whole course of her life had already been changed by a chance meeting with a tall and gangly young man with flaming red hair.

Chapter 12

Benjamin Constant

'Love is the history of a woman's life; it is but an episode in the lives of men.'

Madame de Staël[1]

SINCE THE FALL of Savoy to the revolutionary French army under the command of General de Montesquiou in 1792, the Republic of Geneva had been in a state of preparedness for war. Unwilling to attack Geneva, Montesquiou had negotiated a treaty whereby Genevese neutrality would be respected. This was repudiated at once by the National Assembly, forcing Montesquiou – his own life now in danger – to escape to Lausanne. The National Assembly had then itself come to the conclusion that a direct confrontation with Geneva was best avoided. Instead they sent an agent, Soulavie, to Geneva with the task of undermining the oligarchy and provoking a popular rising. Throughout July and August 1794 there were serious riots in the city. Revolutionary tribunals were set up and many citizens murdered. Lausanne, in addition to sheltering many French émigrés, was now filling up with refugees from Geneva. Madame de Staël's uncle, Louis de Germany, was imprisoned but released on the payment of a large sum of money; her cousin Albertine Necker-de Saussure's father, the distinguished naturalist H. B. de Saussure, had all his property confiscated and Necker himself was condemned to a year's house arrest as well as the loss of his burghership of Geneva for three years.[2]

In mid-September 1794, on her way to join her father at Coppet for a few days, where he was about to transfer Madame Necker's remains to her new mausoleum, Madame de Staël stopped for a night at Montchoisi, just outside Lausanne, at the house of her friends the Cazenove d'Arlens. 'I found here this evening a man of great wit called Benjamin Constant. He is . . . not very handsome but exceptionally intelligent,' she wrote to Ribbing that night.[3] She had already heard of this extraordinary young man from his cousins Rosalie de Constant and her hostess Constance Cazenove d'Arlens. He too knew Madame de Staël by repute. His mistress, Madame de Charrière, had recently met her but had not been impressed. 'I was able to get some insight into all her various sillinesses,' Madame de Charrière had written to Benjamin. 'She boasted of her wits as if she had none. She boasted of her titled friends as if her husband had picked her up the day before in a milliner's shop. She boasted of the great world of Paris as if she had been a girl from the provinces who had only been there six weeks . . . What fun we shall have discussing her.'[4]

In the late afternoon of 28 September, Madame de Staël's familiar yellow carriage pulled by six horses, the postilions in their green Necker livery, had just left Coppet when a lanky, red-haired young man on horseback called at the house. Benjamin Constant had come to offer his services in the event of further troubles in Geneva. Informed by her servants that she had only just left, he wheeled his horse around and, riding hell for leather, caught up with her carriage just outside Nyon. Madame de Staël had been touched by his concern and intrigued. She invited him to join her in her carriage. Within minutes they were deep in conversation. That evening when they stopped at Rolle, where Madame de Staël was to attend a grand dinner for the whole of émigré Geneva at the house of M. Rolaz, she invited Constant to join her. During dinner she spoke indignantly about an article in a journal, the *Quinzaine*, which had slandered her father and her friends as 'constitutional mongrels'. The article she exclaimed, should be suppressed. Benjamin Constant at once rose to the challenge. The liberty of the press was sacrosanct. No true liberal should ever question it even when they suffered personally as a result. Madame de Staël listened in silence. This was fundamentally her own view. The discussion which followed was the beginning of a dialogue between them which would continue almost uninterrupted for the next fifteen years. The next day they continued their journey and their discussions in her carriage. On arrival at Mézery, where Madame de Staël's house was overflowing with her refugee friends, she invited him in.

Much has been written of Benjamin Constant's brilliant mind and his fundamental instability of character. There was nothing very surprising about the latter for he had had a most peculiar upbringing.

The son of Henriette de Chandieu de l'Isle and Baron Juste de Constant de Rebeque, fifteen years her senior, Benjamin was born at his mother's family house, the Maison Chandieu, in Lausanne on 25 October 1767. A fortnight after his birth, his twenty-six-year-old mother was dead. From her he inherited his red hair and pallid complexion. To lose a mother must be a major deprivation in the emotional development of any child. In the life of Benjamin Constant it was catastrophic, largely because of the peculiar character of his father, Juste.

In 1761, before he was married, Juste, who had been staying with his sister near Lausanne, had taken a fancy to a nine-year-old village girl, Marianne Magnin, who it was said, possessed exceptional intelligence. He began to entertain the idea of training her to become the woman of his dreams. When the time came to leave, Juste kidnapped the child and, in spite of the protests of her family and his own, took her off to Holland where he was stationed as an officer in a Swiss regiment in Dutch pay. Paying off her relations, he entrusted her to a Dutch family who gave her an excellent education. Instead of entrusting his newborn son to the hands of one of the many female relatives who were clamouring to look after him, Juste now proposed to entrust his son to this fifteen-year-old girl. Furious protests from his mother persuaded Juste to allow his son to be looked after by his grandmother, but when Benjamin was five and Marianne twenty, Juste suddenly moved Marianne back to Switzerland, made her his mistress, or perhaps married her, and placed his five-year-old son in her charge. There Benjamin remained till he was seven. Two children were born of this marriage, a fact unknown to Benjamin until he was twenty. He always disliked his stepmother but remained close to his paternal grandmother until her death when he was fifteen, and to his maternal aunt, the Comtesse de Nassau.

His relationship with his father was always difficult. A soldier, Juste cared more for discipline than affection or trust. Juste's harsh, sneering, unpredictable treatment of his brilliant eldest son turned Benjamin in on himself, inflicting lasting and serious emotional damage on the sensitive young man.

Juste also employed a German tutor to teach Benjamin, for it was soon obvious that the shy, red-haired boy was exceptionally clever. The tutor, Stroelin, alternately beat and fondled the child, who kept up easily with the Greek, Latin and maths imposed on him. When he was seven, Benjamin was suddenly removed from his stepmother's care and taken to live with his father in the Low Countries where Juste attempted to educate him himself. When this failed, Benjamin was put in the care of a series of highly unsuitable tutors, one of whom took him to live in a bordello but taught him nothing. In spite of his unorthodox upbringing, at twelve Benjamin was a musical prodigy as well as being able to read and compose poetry in Latin and Greek with ease. His letters to his grandmother at this age were so adult, that they were later believed to be forgeries. Invariably cold and sarcastic with his son, Juste was proud of his exceptional talents, and often took him out into society dressed up in a smart suit with sword and hat, where the boy was encouraged to show off.

When Benjamin was thirteen, in another sudden swoop, his father decided that the time had come for university. After two false starts at Oxford and Erlangen, Benjamin was dumped at Edinburgh. Here he lodged for a year with the family of Dr Andrew Duncan, which he later recalled as 'the most agreeable year of my whole life'. At Edinburgh, as part of an exceptionally brilliant group of students which included Sir James Mackintosh, he learned to work hard. It was here that his natural respect for the concept of liberty as an ethical principle was reinforced and remained with him for the rest of his life. Benjamin benefited greatly from his two years at Edinburgh, but was obliged to leave after trouble over his gambling debts.

In the spring of 1787, he met Madame de Charrière in Paris. Born in Holland, Belle de Zuylen had been among the cleverest women of her generation. At the time of her meeting with the nineteen-year-old Benjamin she was forty-seven. For the first time Benjamin surrendered to the delights of conversation with an intelligent woman with whom he shared a temperamental affinity. Both were egotistic, sceptical, gloomy, nihilistic and proud of a brilliance which ensured that they were forever misunderstood by the world. Intellectual compatibility and opium ensured that at her house in Colombier, near Neûchatel, where Benjamin was recovering from a bout of syphilis, he felt truly happy for the first time in his life. She wanted only to keep him near her but his father had already found him a post as 'Gentleman of the Chamber to his Serene Highness, the Duke of Brunswick'. He remained in Brunswick for a miserable five years, during which time he was married and divorced and had an affair with Countess Charlotte von Hardenburg, who would come back into his life many years later.

Back at Colombier in 1793, he read much and began to take a serious interest in politics. This was not altogether to Madame de Charrière's liking. Afraid of losing him, she criticized everything he wrote, undermining his self-confidence in the hope of maintaining her own influence. With his remarkable talent for self-analysis, Benjamin had described his state of mind to Madame de Charrière: 'I am blasé about everything, bored with everything, bitter, self-centred; endowed with a sensibility that merely tortures me; unstable to the point of seeming mad; subject to bouts of melancholy that cut short all my projects and while they last make me act as if I had given up everything; . . . how do you expect me to succeed, to please, to live?'[5] He was about to meet the very person he needed.

'I must tell you that M. Benjamin Constant, Gentleman [of the chamber] to his Excellence the Duke of Brunswick, aged twenty-six and remarkably intelligent, has fallen in love with your Minette,' Madame de Staël wrote to Ribbing from Coppet on 8 October. 'I will keep his letters for you but will hide his face, which would give only some idea of my profound indifference to him.'[6] It is true that while she was instantly seduced by his mind, Madame de Staël was at first positively repelled by her brilliant new friend's appearance. In any case, Ribbing still had her heart, while her former lover Narbonne was still living with her at Mézery. Though their relationship had cooled, Narbonne was now being difficult and trying to revive it, perhaps because he was financially dependent on her. For her part, she might have sent him packing, as she suggested to Ribbing.[7]

Thin and stooping, with a pale face, red-rimmed eyes, which he shaded with green glasses, and wild carrot-coloured hair, Benjamin Constant found that in Madame de Staël's presence his depression lifted as if by magic. A few days after their second meeting he replied to Madame de Charrière's letter about Madame de Staël in a way which cannot have pleased her. 'I feel that you have judged her too harshly, I think she is very active, very incautious, talks a great deal, but is good, trusting and acts in good faith. One proof that she is not merely a talking machine is the very lively interest she takes in all those she has known who have fallen on hard times . . . I don't think that she is proud of her intelligence . . . she is merely aware of how great it is, and has a great need to talk, to give herself up to it, to know neither boundaries nor prudence.' Putting his finger on the two aspects of her personality which would separate them many times but would always bring him back, he added: 'I am far from considering a liaison, because she is too much surrounded by people, too active, too absorbed; but this is the most interesting acquaintance which I have made for a long time.'[8] Constant himself had been so enthralled by her, that he promised there and then, to leave her all his English books in the event of his death.[9]

Madame de Charrière could not resist another attempt to squash his youthful enthusiasm, but he was more enchanted every day. In a devastating reply to the older woman, he wrote that now he could look forward with hope, he was disinclined to be mired in the past. As for Madame de Staël: 'I have seldom seen such a combination of astonishing and attractive qualities; so much brilliance together with so much truth, such expansive but also positive goodness, such immense generosity, such sweet and sustained politeness in society, so much charm and simplicity; such a total naturalness with her intimate friends. This is the second woman in my life who could be all the world to me, who could be a whole universe in herself. You know who was the first. Madame de Staël is infinitely more intelligent in her intimate conversations than in her social ones. She is a wonderful listener . . . she feels other people's intelligence with as much pleasure as her own. She brings out those she loves with an amazing and constant attention which demonstrates in her as much goodness as wit. In short, she is a being apart, a superior being such as one might come across once in a hundred years, such a one that those who are close to her, know her and call themselves her friends, need not ask for any other happiness.'[10] Madame de Charrière tried to hold on to Constant for the rest of the year. He continued to write to her, but she now bored and depressed him and their former closeness, and with it her hold over him, were gone for good.

Madame de Staël, as Benjamin Constant had said, was indeed 'surrounded by people'. The château of Mézery was overflowing with all the former Juniper Hall colony joined by François de Pange, Madame de Broglie, Bonstetten and de Bussigny. There were constant new arrivals who must be settled and whose affairs claimed her time and attention. While Madame de Staël was occupied with them and with her writing, Constant, who had taken a house nearby, now felt that his whole life depended on his vital and brilliant new friend. She had been delighted to welcome this slightly provincial young man into her circle, discovering in him the incomparable delight of an intellectual equal. Not since Talleyrand had she been able to enjoy the pleasures of conversation to such a degree, coupled this time with the joy of a perfect union of minds. Both believed passionately that, now that royal despotism and the bloody dictatorship of the people had been tried and rejected in France, their time had come. For Benjamin there was now the promise of a new and active life where his talents might at last be put to the service of humanity, made possible by Madame de Staël's life-enhancing vitality, her encouragement and her limitless generosity. He fell madly in love with his new Egeria.

Later, he gave a touching description of Madame de Staël, in the fictional person of Madame de Malbée in his novel *Cécile*:[11] 'When I first met Madame de Malbée she was in her twenty-seventh year. She was small rather than tall, and too heavy for slenderness, her features too strong and irregular, an unattractive complexion, the most beautiful eyes in the world, very beautiful arms, her hands a little too big but dazzlingly white, a superb bosom; movements which were too quick and gestures too masculine, a very sweet voice which would break most touchingly when she was moved; all these were part of a whole which at first sight struck one unfavourably, but when she talked and was animated, she became irresistibly seductive. Her intelligence, which was of a range unknown in any woman, and perhaps in any man when she was being sensitive, was perhaps a touch solemn and affected. But her gaiety had an indefinable charm, a kind of childlike goodwill which captivated the heart, establishing between her and those she was talking to a complete intimacy, which broke down all reserve, all mistrust, all those secret restrictions, those invisible barriers which nature puts up between all people, and which even friendship cannot entirely remove.'[12]

As for Madame de Staël, much as she enjoyed Constant's company, his growing and passionately proclaimed devotion left her, generally so susceptible to admiration torn between pity and exasperation. Her impressions of Constant come down to us thanks to her letters to Ribbing, with whom she was still in love. Her love for Narbonne, the father of her children, was now in much calmer waters. She was also powerfully attracted to the gentle Chevalier François de Pange, whose affections were otherwise engaged. He had started a printing press at Neuveville on the lake of Bienne with the help of Montmorency and Jaucourt. An intellectual and a passionate liberal, Pange was already suffering from the consumption which would soon kill him. There was also Mathieu, whose love for her had now changed into a constant friendship. Deeply religious he was engaged in trying to convert her to a better way of life. Mathieu and her cousin Albertine spent the rest of her life trying to protect her from herself. So, quite apart from a genuine physical aversion to Constant, she was not ready for yet another romantic entanglement, at any rate not with him. 'M. Constant, about whom I have already told you,' she wrote to Ribbing at the end of October 1794, 'is I think, entertaining such a passion for me as you cannot imagine. He is dying of it and inflicts his unhappiness on me in a way which removes his only charm – a very superior intelligence – and makes me pity him, which in turn tires me and reminds me that never, perhaps never, has my Adolphe been loved so much. If you hear that M. Constant, gentleman to His Highness the Duke of Brunswick, twenty-seven years old and red-haired like the House of Hanover itself, has killed himself in the woods of Cèry, which he has just rented so that he can spend his life in my garden and in my courtyard, do not in truth think it to be my fault. I have genuinely praised him for his work entitled *L'Esprit des religions*, in which he truly shows a talent equal to Montesquieu, but forgets that his face is an unconquerable obstacle, even for a heart were it not all yours.'[13]

But Constant, deciding to conquer all obstacles, did not give up, writing her 'five letters a day' and hoping that his invaluable collaboration would finally seduce her. Madame de Staël had met her match. Not long before, they had agreed that in order not to compromise her Constant would leave before midnight no matter how interesting their discussion. Constant noted in his diary in January: 'I took out my watch to demonstrate that the hour of my departure had not yet arrived. But the inexorable hand of the watch proved me wrong and in a thoughtless and childish moment of fury, I hurled it on the parquet . . .' Madame de Staël had smiled with amusement and obviously lifted the moratorium, for the next morning Constant noted: 'I shall not have to buy another watch.'[14] For the next three months, while they worked together amicably, he continued to lay siege to her heart. 'He bangs his head against my chimneypiece when I beg him to leave my room. He will take me to Paris, willy nilly, if you do not come. He is a hugely intelligent madman, and singularly ugly, but he is mad,' she wrote to Ribbing in March 1795.[15]

By this time, Narbonne had moved out to join his former mistress, Madame de Laval, in a nearby house. Her jealousy of Madame de Staël's relationships with Narbonne and with her son Mathieu de Montmorency had not been softened by her personal debt to Madame de Staël for saving her life, and she was forever trying to sow discord between them. Before long Constant had moved into Narbonne's rooms at Mézery. Under her roof but not yet in her bed, Constant now staged a scene in which he demonstrated that his talent and love of drama were in every way equal to Madame de Staël's.

Everyone had gone to bed when at midnight they were roused by shrieks of agony coming from Constant's room. Madame de Staël's childhood friend, Madame Rilliet-Huber, had been first on the scene. She found Constant, pale and disfigured, writhing in agony on his bed, an empty bottle of opium bedside him. All he wanted, he gasped, was to see Madame de Staël before he died. While Madame Rilliet-Huber ran off to fetch her, M. de Chateauvieux, an old friend of Necker's who had also arrived on the scene, rushed off to fetch Mathieu de Montmorency, whom he found in his dressing gown in his bedroom, calmly reading the *Confessions* of St Augustine. Chateauvieux explained what had happened to Constant. 'Throw the man out of the window. He is disturbing the peace and will cause a scandal by his suicide,' was the unsympathetic suggestion from the pious Mathieu as he followed the rest of the household to Constant's bedside where Madame de Staël had also arrived. 'Wretch! What have you done?' she cried; 'Call the doctor! call the doctor!' 'Ah it is you, it is for you that I perish,' Constant gasped. As Madame de Staël bent over him, begging him to live, he seized her arm and, covering it in kisses, murmured; 'If you command it I will try', whereupon he recovered at once. 'What a performance!' Mathieu pronounced as he left in disgust. A shaken Madame de Staël also returned to her room, accompanied by Madame Rilliet-Huber. Plunging the arm so ardently kissed by Constant into cologne-scented water, she confessed to her friend that she feared that he inspired her with an insurmountable physical revulsion.[16]

When Constant was not enacting idiotic scenes, which he admitted in his diary were childish and pointless, they worked together in perfect harmony and to great effect. The first printed edition of Madame de Staël's remarkable pamphlet, *Réflexions sur la paix adressées à M. Pitt et aux Français (Reflections on Peace addressed to Mr Pitt and to the French)* was printed by François de Pange in December 1794 at Neuveville. Corrected editions of the pamphlet came out in Paris in May 1795, at the time of her return, although she had begun to send copies to her friends in February. This manifesto of her own liberal opinions was addressed to Pitt who, had Madame Necker had her way, might have been her husband. It was Pitt, she wrote, who 'must be held to account for the destiny of Europe'. The British constitution, 'a masterpiece of reason and liberty', gave him that right. It was also intended for the new leaders in France, who, she hoped, would be able to establish a constitution which could reconcile 'the possible with the desirable'.

Calling on France to make peace, 'more important to you than to your enemies', she urged the French to go back to the spirit of 1789 and to repel both the royalists and the Jacobins. For the first time she accepted the Republic, now a *fait accompli*, urging all moderates to unite in its defence,[17] while she proclaimed her hatred of the Terror and of Robespierre. France would not give in to threats of a restoration of the *ancien régime*: 'A thousand times more people supported the Constitution of 1789, for all its faults, than the *ancien régime*.' One 'must go forward with the times'. Pitt had refused to intervene in support of the moderates when he might have helped to restore liberty and order in France. The French must now be allowed to choose their own government freely. War would ruin France and if France was ruined Europe would be too. The pamphlet was, above all, a call for peace. 'War keeps Mr. Pitt at the ministry; peace will return Mr. Fox,' she concluded: 'that is the real alternative which ought to be put before the English, that is what Mr. Pitt fears . . .'[18]

This final salvo so impressed Fox that he borrowed from Madame de Staël's pamphlet in his great anti-war speech in Parliament on 24 March 1795. In one of the outstanding speeches of his career lasting for four hours, he called for an inquiry, not only in order to answer a number of questions about the conduct of the war, but also to stress the need for morality in foreign policy.[19] Madame de Staël was very proud of his quoting from her pamphlet, as she mentions in a letter to her husband on 8 May: 'the work you mention is so much in favour of the French that M. Fox . . . quoted twice from it in the British Parliament when he was attacking M. Pitt.'[20]

Madame de Staël's experience of the Terror had also strongly influenced one of her early works of literary criticism, the *Essai sur les fictions*, which was published in the spring of 1795 and in which she also praised Benjamin Constant's *L'Esprit des religions*, which was only published thirty years later. How should the novel respond to the recent horrors of the Terror? Novels were not yet properly respected, yet they were a way to the deeper understanding of the human heart. Madame de Staël argued for greater realism. 'Great heroes' or fantastic exploits 'should be avoided. The marvellous is a deformation of nature and of the truth'. What mattered was an accurate and truthful portrayal of the human heart. Imagination was of course essential but it must be used to portray reality. Nor was the aesthetic principle enough. A work must also obey moral principles and seek to be a power for good. Nor, in the light of recent events, should novels deal only with the subject of love. All human passions, such as vanity, greed, ambition, study, gambling – to cite but a few which she would amplify in *De l'Influence des Passions* – and their consequences, should be portrayed realistically and without too much philosophizing.[21] This essay, prefiguring her great work on the influence of the passions (*De l'influence des passions sur le bonheur des individus et des nations*) which was published in the following year, so impressed Goethe that he had it translated into German.

In post Thermidorian France, to which M. de Staël had returned in January 1795 to begin negotiations with the Convention, the forces of popular radicalism were ebbing. The Terror had been followed by one of the most severe autumns and winters in memory. The English Channel froze for two miles off the French coast, while in Paris the Seine froze and wolves were heard howling on the outskirts of the city. Severe food shortages brought famine and epidemics. The abolition of the maximum price laws of December 1794 caused runaway inflation, making the *assignat* or paper money almost worthless. In these grim conditions, political activism took a back seat. Moderates replaced the ousted radicals in the Paris sections, while in the streets the *sans-culottes* had given way to a new breed of thug: young men who had managed to avoid conscription and were known as the *jeunesse dorée* or gilded youth. Also known as *muscadins* or fops, they were drawn mainly from the right-wing petite bourgeoisie. Dressed in tight breeches, square-shouldered coats and blond wigs, and carrying weighted cudgels, they brawled in streets and theatres, closing down Republican plays, attacking anyone wearing the *bonnet rouge*. Still frightened of a *sans-culotte* come-back the government let them be.

Their political value was mainly symbolic and short-lived. Their greatest success had been the closure of the Jacobin club – they were associated with opposition to Robespierre's centralized rule and the Terror. They were to be dispersed once and for all in the *coup* of Vendémaire that autumn by Napoleon Bonaparte's famous 'whiff of grapeshot'.

With her husband once more in France and her diplomatic immunity thus restored, Madame de Staël longed to return to Paris where she still hoped that Ribbing might join her. 'M. de Staël is very happy in Paris and believes that it is perfectly safe,' she wrote to Henri Meister in March 1795. 'In truth there is only the nature of things to fear; the intention of the government is good.'[22] But her private life was muddled and unsatisfactory. She was torn between her father, glued to his wife's tomb at Coppet, and her longing to be in the front line of politics in France. Constant too was anxious to begin his political career on a stage wider than a Swiss canton. They were not yet lovers, in spite of the continuous banging of his head against her chimneypiece. Madame de Staël decided to take her son Auguste with her, leaving the younger Albert with her father. After the inevitable delays, due in part to Necker having an accident – he had fallen and hurt his leg – but also to endless letters from her husband putting her off, she made arrangements to leave in May 1795. Ribbing, who was settled in a splendid new Palladian mansion near Copenhagen, bought for him by his adoring and adored mother, was doing his best to wriggle out of the promises he had made. They had discussed the possibility of her divorce and their marriage. In March he was suddenly seized with a fear of hurting Staël and of being accused of seducing his friend's wife. In April he regretted his 'indiscreet promises'. In May he promised reluctantly to come to Paris in June. Her letters to him, as those earlier missives to Narbonne, expressed her sorrow, her disappointment and sometimes her anger but they lacked the anguish of those she had written to Narbonne.

For his part Staël, busy with his new posting, could only regard the prospect of his wife's arrival with horror. Reasonably enough, he feared that Madame de Staël's presence would complicate his political dealings and trouble his peace. He tried to put off her arrival. He was at a critical stage in his negotiations with the Convention. He had been sent to France, not to recognize the new Republic but to negotiate the repayment of money which Sweden had spent on arming her navy in aid of France. When the negotiations came to nothing – the French were more interested in alliance with Russia at that point – Staël decided on his own initiative that he would recognize the Republic on behalf of Sweden. The resulting promise from France was that forty tons of gold would be repaid at once and forty more on the ratification of the treaty by the Swedish Regent. In return Sweden was to arm ten frigates secretly, and to demand that England should observe her neutrality and restore the Swedish ships held by her, failing which there would be an embargo on all English ships in the Sound. It remained to be seen how these proposals would be met.[23]

Accompanied by her maid, her manservant Eugène, her young son, Auguste, and several other servants, and escorted by Constant who was going to Paris with her, Madame de Staël left Coppet on about 13 May 1795. In Lausanne she was met by her cousin Albertine de Saussure and Mathieu de Montmorency, who accompanied her to Yverdon. Here they were joined by Narbonne, Jaucourt and Madame de La Châtre (now his wife), who had come to bid her farewell and with whom she discussed the various tasks she was to carry out for them in France. This meeting was to be used against her later.

On 15 May, the anniversary of his wife's death, Necker wrote a sad letter to his headstrong daughter while she was still at Yverdon. He said he had been alarmed by a note he had received from his brother, in which 'while he praises you greatly, he mentions the honourable and unexpected role which you may perhaps play. Alas! He was writing after a conversation with you and I fear that you may have divulged to him a secret plan to make yourself talked about. How to achieve such a project without all manner of problems! Remember all the difficulties to which you had exposed yourself last time. Calm your ambition until you are once again in a country where you may say and write what you like. Allow me here to ask M. Constant not to encourage you and to lecture you frequently on the virtues of prudence and patience . . . I will do as you ask regarding your finances. Be careful of M. de Staël's extravagance and bear in mind that I shall be spending more than my income and cannot cover the follies of others. Adieu, my dear Minette, may Heaven protect you and bring you to safety. Do not neglect your health . . .'[24]

Chapter 13

The New Republicans

'They are both quite enthralled with republican hopes and ideas.'
Necker to Henri Meister.[1]

As SWEDEN HAD been the first country to recognize the new French Republic, much was made of the presentation of her ambassador's credentials to the Convention at a solemn ceremony on 23 April 1795. Accompanied by two members of his staff and a large retinue of Swedish merchants, Staël had entered the Senate chamber in full dress uniform to be met by the assembled deputies, who awaited him in the most respectful silence. His speech, in which he paid homage to 'the natural and unalterable rights of the nation', and declared that France would 'set an example to the human race of the union of power and virtue', was greeted with rapturous applause. His speech was reported in all the papers.[2] Staël had every reason to be pleased with his moment of glory. 'Your speech was not one I would have made, but perhaps all the better for it; and it was with great emotion that I read of the great and sincere applause with which it was rewarded,' his wife wrote to Staël on 3 May.[3] To Ribbing her comments were more cutting: 'You will have realized, I hope, that M. de Staël's speech was not mine. I am less patriotic and certainly less vulgar . . .'[4]

It was hardly surprising that Staël had done his best to keep his wife away, or that he failed to counter the attacks on her which were already beginning to appear in the press. Jacobsson, his secretary and friend, recalled that when Staël heard that his wife and her party had crossed into France on 17 May, he had staggered into his room and said in a faint voice, 'Damnation! my wife is arriving!' Unable to stop her himself – he knew it was useless to try and had no wish to upset her or her father on whose money he still depended – he begged his colleague to do what he could. Two days later, after much bustling about, Jacobsson set off to try and forestall her, armed with a passport to Basel for himself as well as return documents for Madame de Staël and her party. He had obtained instructions from the Convention to Barthélemy, the French ambassador to the Swiss Cantons, not to issue her with a passport and an order to all post-houses in France to deny her fresh horses. Somewhere between Troyes and Langres, unknowingly they missed each other. She had taken a different route to Paris and, probably out of politeness, had ordered post-horses in the name of Constant. Neither of these decisions were intentionally deceptive, as Jacobsson later believed. She knew that her husband did not want her back, but had no idea of the lengths to which he had gone to prevent her return. Indeed, she had sent detailed plans of her journey to him but her letter had arrived too late. On arrival in Basel, Jacobsson rushed straight to the French envoy, who informed him that he had issued a passport to Madame de Staël and her party some days before.

While many had welcomed the fall of Robespierre and the end of the Terror, the Paris to which Madame de Staël returned with Constant on 25 May 1795, (6 Prairial) was in a state of general misery. Famine, inflation and political uncertainty had led to several popular uprisings in 1795. The abortive insurrection of 1 April 1795 was first and foremost a bread riot although crowds had marched on the Convention demanding a return to the Republican Constitution of 1793. The widespread confiscation of weapons in Paris, especially from those in any way associated with the Jacobins, soon restored order, while the deportation to French Guiana of the ring leaders and the arrest of some twenty deputies further strengthened the right. A month later, on 4 May, there took place a massacre (known as the White Terror) of former Jacobins in prisons in Lyons, Marseilles and some towns in the Rhône valley, as old scores were settled, often with the participation of returning royalists. On 20 May 1795, a more serious popular insurrection took place in Paris. As the tocsin sounded once again in the Faubourg St Antoine, a mob marched on the Convention, which tried to defend itself, resulting in the mob waving the severed head of one deputy, Féraud, on a pike. With commendable sang-froid, the President Boissy d'Anglas doffed his hat to it, but refused to suspend the session. The mob was driven out by the National Guard. Three days later the Convention crushed the rebellious sections, savagely purging former Jacobins and *sans-culottes*. Six of the deputies who had supported the insurgents were tried and sent to the guillotine.

Madame de Staël returned to the Swedish embassy in the rue du Bac, where her husband had taken to his bed with an acute stomach ache, which may not have been due entirely to dysentery. Benjamin Constant took a large suite of rooms in the rue du Colombier. Life was extraordinarily cheap for those with foreign gold. The city they entered was unrecognizable. To the new Prussian minister, Gervinus, who happened to arrive on the same day, it appeared to be in a state of siege. Three guillotines had been set up to dispense justice to the insurrectionists some of whom were seen on tumbrels on their way to the scaffold. Everywhere there were troops, armed men and cannon, while the Tuileries had been turned into a full-scale military camp.[5]

Necker's Swiss friend, the writer Henri Meister, who arrived in France later that year, was another witness to the misery. He described the appalling conditions: the cities starving, no carriages on the roads, whole quarters of Paris completely deserted; the splendid houses of the Faubourg Saint-Germain pillaged or boarded up; people bartering whatever they possessed for food; whole quarters given over to selling anything and everything so that 'the capital of the world looks like a flea market'. What had struck him as being worst of all was 'the strange air of uncertainty, of displacement; the haggard, convulsed, anxious and defiant expressions on almost all faces'.[6]

Madame de Staël later described the fifteen months or so between the fall of Robespierre on 27 July 1794 to the establishment of the Republican government under the form of a Directory after the coup of 5 October 1795 as 'a period of true anarchy in France'.[7] Although many of the institutions of the Terror were abolished after the fall of Robespierre, the leaders of the Thermidor coup, men like Tallien and Barras, were initially more concerned with their own survival than the wretched state of the country. It was a time when everything was for sale and new men prospered: the corrupt speculators, war contractors, profiteers, self-serving bureaucrats and politicians now rose to power creating a society of *nouveaux riches*. Madame de Staël recognized them as unprincipled opportunists, but at least they were moderates. For the time being anything was better than the return to the fanatical terror of the Jacobins or the violent reaction that would have surely followed any attempt to restore the Bourbons. Any hopes of a peaceful restoration of a (constitutional) monarchy were ended with the death, on 10 June 1795, of the young son of Louis XVI and Marie-Antoinette (proclaimed Louis XVII) in the Temple prison where he had been incarcerated for the past two years, and the issue by his uncle, the Comte de Provence (who succeeded him as Louis XVIII), of an uncompromising manifesto from Verona in which he swore to restore the *ancien régime* in every respect and to punish the regicides.

Soon after her return an article was published in the journal *Nouvelles Politiques*, accusing Madame de Staël of plotting against the Republic with her émigré friends. It quoted a report by the French ambassador, Barthélemy, to the Committee of Public Safety about a final meeting she had had with Narbonne, Montmorency and Jaucourt at Yverdon before her departure from Switzerland. Now that she was back with him in Paris, Staël had no choice but to defend his wife, while Madame de Staël herself sent a letter to the editors of the journal denying any wish to plot against the Republic. She realized 'that since the revolution of 9 Thermidor [27 July 1794] there were only two parties of influence; the friends of a free and just republic supported by all enlightened and patriotic Frenchmen, and that of those who promoted bloody anarchy, which everyone must reject.'[8] Her letter was reproduced in several papers but she was dogged by the suspicion of plotting against the Republic for the rest of that year.

In fact she applied herself energetically to the affairs of her exiled constitutional friends who hoped to be able to return to Paris and recover their properties. She was also looking to her own interests – the recovery of her father's two million livres which Necker had deposited in the Treasury when he left. Meanwhile she completed her pamphlet, *Réflexions sur la paix intérieure* ('Reflections on Internal Peace') with Constant, in which she reaffirmed her support for the Republic as the best guarantee of political liberties in France, a position which upset many of her former constitutional monarchist friends. 'A monarchy offered too many dangers at the present time,' she wrote, adding prophetically: 'France can remain where she is as a republic; but to become a constitutional monarchy she would first have to pass through military dictatorship.'[9] She explained her thoughts at the time in a later account of the French Revolution: 'I would certainly not have been in favour of establishing a republic in France, had there been a choice; but given that it already existed, I did not believe it should be overturned.'[10]

She was determined to do all she could to promote an alliance of moderate republicans and former constitutional monarchists. Helped by a flattering review by the influential Roederer of her newly published 'Reflections on internal peace', Madame de Staël lost no time in re-establishing her salon, which again became the foremost intellectual and political meeting place in the city. Old friends like Sieyès, former aristocrats turned republican, like the corrupt and immensely rich Barras, new men like Tallien and Cambacérès, and moderates such as Boissy d'Anglas, were members of the Commission of Eleven which had been set up charged with the task of drafting a new Constitution. Journalists and publishers, among them Suard, Roederer, La Harpe, Charles de Lacretelle and Marie-Joseph Chénier, brother of the guillotined poet André, came to discuss the draft Constitution in Madame de Staël's salon. Some thought her an intriguer, but no one had any doubt about her political experience, her acute intelligence, her liberal views, or her love of France – and few were immune to her extraordinary charm. Jacobsson recalled a gathering on 7 June 1795, attended by all the new men of power, when Madame de Staël, a turban on her head, her magnificent bosom exposed, and trailing multicoloured gauze scarves, had successfully turned her famous charm on the new rulers of France. Afterwards she had led a dozen of the more important men into a small salon where she remained closeted for almost an hour. Calling Jacobsson, she declared that, as he had told her that all these men had wished her to leave Paris, he should now hear what they had to say. One by one they were heard to stammer 'no no' until one of them spoke up: 'Since the ambassadress was already in Paris we can no longer wish her to leave us'. Feeling extremely foolish, Jacobsson stammered out an apology and the hope that she could forget the role he had played in preventing her arrival. 'Think nothing of it', Madame de Staël had replied obligingly, 'you believed that you were acting in the interests of Sweden.'[11]

If Madame de Staël was mistress of the foremost intellectual salon and the only woman who bridged both the old and the new worlds, there was strong competition socially from the mistresses and wives of the new men of power. Above them all was the lovely twenty-one-year-old Madame Tallien, nicknamed Notre-Dame de Thermidor, formerly Teresia Cabarrus and later to be the Princesse de Chimay. At her cottage, the Chaumière, Madame Tallien literally held court. Here, against the curiously mixed backdrop of Rousseauist pastoral simplicity and classical Greek and Roman interiors – a fashion for antiquity had been decreed by the terrorist artist David – her own startling beauty was fully revealed in transparent Grecian tunics, slit to the navel and split to the thigh, often first dipped in scented oil to make them cling to the body, rings on the toes of her sandalled feet and jewelled bracelets around her arms and ankles, her hair cut short and curling around her head to resemble a Roman statue. Her stunning looks, her great vitality and her undoubted originality made Thérésia Tallien the undisputed leader of fashion in Thermidorian France. The idol of the *jeunesse dorée*, she was to be seen escorted everywhere by a strutting posse of Muscadins.

Presiding over their own salons were the charming and graceful Josephine, widow of Beauharnais, now Barras's mistress and soon to be Napoleon's Empress; the beautiful and virginal eighteen-year-old Madame Récamier, always dressed in white, married to a very rich and much older banker; and the notorious Fortuné Hamelin, who was said to have walked the entire length of the Champs-Elysées with her breasts on display.

Different as they were, Madame de Staël's and Madame Tallien's salons had in common the fact that both were attempting to reconcile the moderates. Jacques Mallet du Pan, a stiff-necked Genevan journalist who had followed the Revolution day by day in the *Mercure de France*, and who became a royalist agent, was scathing in his reports of both: 'the Tallien woman who is adored as a queen, and the Swedish Ambassadress with her *sans-culottes* husband who flaunts her impudence and her immorality.'[12] The young and unsophisticated Napoleon Bonaparte, kicking his heels in Paris because of his Jacobin past, wrote to his brother Joseph: 'Women are everywhere, in the theatres, the promenades, the bookshops . . . Here, alone, of all places, they deserve to rule; all men are mad for them, think of nothing but them, live only for them. A woman needs to live in Paris for six months to know her due, to know what her empire is.'[13]

For the next five years, Paris society, desperate for gaiety and pleasure, was a never-ending carnival surrounded by ever-worsening poverty. In that first year after the end of the Terror, although the great private houses stood looted and empty, the press, active and influential, was free again; theatres were thriving as never before; dance halls and restaurants (more than 2,000) had sprung up all over the city, often belonging to former chefs of the *ancien régime*. New dishes like lobster Thermidor were added to the French *haute cuisine*, spreading the culinary fame of Paris all through Europe while many of her citizens starved. In the streets the Muscadins swaggered around in their high-collared tight jackets, their waistcoats sporting large mother-of-pearl buttons, their long curls hanging to the shoulder (known as *oreilles de chien* or dog's ears), hats drawn down to their eyes, so that their heads were almost invisible in a grisly reminder of the guillotine. With a *merveilleuse* on their arm – a scantily dressed woman in transparent muslins and bared bosom – they walked the new walk and talked the new talk, an affected form of French filleted of all 'r's. Looking at the women's fashions one wag asserted that 'the *sans-culottes* had given way to the *sans-chemises*'. Balls were held every night and at every level, the most famous and exclusive being the *bals de victimes*, when only those whose relations had perished in the Terror were admitted, at which the women wore thin red ribbons around their necks, their hair fashionably cropped in imitation of the shorn heads of those who had perished on the guillotine. Orgies were even said to have been held in the cemeteries among the tombs of the guillotined. 'The memory of the terror is no more than a nightmare here. Everyone is determined to make up for their sufferings, determined also because of the uncertain future not to miss a single pleasure of the present,' Napoleon Bonaparte wrote to Joseph.[14]

Madame de Staël herself later recalled the society of that period: 'The influence of women, the ascendancy of good society, of what were popularly known as the gilded salons, seemed unattainably formidable to those who were excluded and seduced those who were not. Every *decadi* [the tenth day of each month in the new Republican calendar week, which had replaced Sundays] for Sundays no longer existed, one could see all the elements of the old and the new regimes mingling but not yet reconciled at the soirées. There were members of the *ancien régime* whose elegant manners marked them out in spite of the simple dress they had worn since the Terror; there were the converted Jacobins who were entering society for the first time, more sensitive than anyone and keener than most on elegant manners which they longed to emulate. These men were usually surrounded by women of the *ancien régime*, who were hoping through them to obtain the return of their brothers, their sons and their husbands. The graceful flattery which they knew how to use so well, poured into those rough ears, making them more susceptible still to what we have seen since; the re-creation of the court, the revival all the old abuses, but making sure that it should now serve them.' Nothing she added, 'could have served as a more incredible school of sophism than the excuses and justifications put forward by those who had taken part in the Terror'.[15]

A draft of the new Constitution was submitted to the Convention on 23 June 1795. Madame de Staël thought it 'very reasonable' at that time and was convinced that it would establish 'order and liberty'.[16] It reflected a post-Terror fear of both democracy and dictatorship and confirmed the sharp swing to the right. Universal suffrage was abolished and elections were to be indirect; the restricted franchise was to be concentrated in the hands of the propertied classes. Political clubs were to be closed. Members of the legislature had to be over thirty. There were to be two chambers, the lower to be called the Council of 500, to be elected by primary Assemblies, while the upper chamber, the *Conseil des Anciens*, would be chosen by the entire legislative body and number 250 members. Executive and legislative powers were separated, the former being put into the hands of a Directory of five, to be selected by the *anciens* from a list of fifty names proposed by the lower chamber. The members of the expiring Convention were afraid that at a time of strongly anti-revolutionary feeling they had no hope of being re-elected and risked losing everything, so an amendment, 'the law of the two thirds', was brought to the draft Constitution on 18 August by Pierre Baudin, a member of the Eleven, under which two thirds of the outgoing Convention were to be automatically re-elected.

Madame de Staël and Constant were angered by this amendment. Later she wrote that it had been a great misfortune that France had had to place the fate of the Republic into the hands of the Convention. Some were capable men but nevertheless the old apparatchiks of the Terror 'had inevitably acquired habits which were at once servile and tyrannical'.[17] She was on good terms with the Convention in order to promote the return of her friends, but she was strongly opposed to their automatic re-election.[18] Constant, who did not wish to see the Thermidorian government perpetuated any more than did Madame de Staël, and who did not believe that it was right for a former parliament to allocate to itself two thirds of the seats in a new one, wrote an article against it in the form of three unsigned letters 'to a deputy at the Convention', which were published in Suard's journal the *Nouvelles Politiques*.[19] A tremendous row erupted. In that period of great instability, to be against the Convention was to be against the Republic. Soon, however, as a result of Madame de Staël's disclosure of his authorship in the salons, Constant, to his surprise and chagrin, found himself the darling of the intellectuals and the royalist salon hostesses while vilified as anti-Republican by the Convention. He even received an invitation to co-operate with a plan to restore the monarchy. 'This invitation gave me a jolt,' he recalled, 'and I returned home cursing salons, women, journalists and all those who were against the Republic.' Obliged to retract, in a letter to the editor of the *Républicain Français*, Constant admitted publicly that the Republic must be supported at all costs and that some continuity was necessary if civil war was to be averted. 'The Convention in 1795 . . . was a great dyke of mud and blood against the partisans of the *ancien régime*. It was a nasty dyke but it was important not to break it down.'[20] The Baudin amendment was passed on 18 August.

On the same day Madame de Staël's former butcher Legendre, who had taken part in the storming of the Bastille and was now a deputy, rose in the Convention and denounced her as the protector of émigrés and as a siren who was seducing all his colleagues at her grand dinners. 'They would do better to dine at home than attend banquets intended to corrupt them.' His speech was warmly applauded, though many deputies were seen to be grinning broadly. Staël, who was known to be sympathetic to the Republic and who was sitting in the diplomatic enclosure, was visibly upset and left the hall soon after. His treaty with the French government was at a critical stage in the negotiations and this was not helpful. The royalist Mallet du Pan reported him as saying to Legendre: 'Citizen deputy, come and dine with me, you will get a good dinner, I will give you good wines and my wife will be absent.'[21]

The next day, Legendre was blasted by Madame de Staël's friends and admirers in the press: 'He has abused the freedom of the tribune,' thundered *Les Nouvelles Politiques Nationales et Étrangères*. 'He has breached all social and political decencies in attacking a person who through an extraordinary combination of intelligence, contacts and talents, does honour to the France of her birth; whose natural goodness and the extreme openness of her character can only frighten fools, whose enemies must lack all merit; who by the nature of the public role of the foreigner to whom she is married and by virtue of the ample proof of devotion to the Republic given by them both, should find, especially at the Convention, the respect due not only to relations between countries, but also to her sex and her rare worth.'[22] On a lighter note, the *Gazette française* wrote: 'One hears about nothing but Madame de Staël's dinners. One has even noticed that as a result of those charming evenings some of the men of the day are better turned out. Madame de Staël has changed her world. M. Legendre compares her to Circe; this is a mistake: Circe transformed Ulysses's courtiers into bears [in fact pigs in Homer], whereas here Madame de Staël has almost managed to do the opposite.'[23]

Her efforts to get permission for Talleyrand to return to France undoubtedly stirred up trouble. Talleyrand, who had been in the United States for two years, was dying of boredom and had begged her to do all she could. Madame de Staël of all people could understand that to be away from Paris and politics was unbearable. In any case, she missed Talleyrand and passionately wanted all her constitutionalist friends to return to France and rally to the Republic. She spared no effort and, at some personal cost, won him the much-longed-for permission to return.[24] In spite of support in the press, Madame de Staël was upset to be linked with the royalist émigrés. She had made a point of only helping those who had left in danger of their lives at the time of the September massacres.

All this was too much for Jacobsson, who put her under renewed pressure to leave Paris and, tormented her in a thousand ways, believing that the 'little good I have been able to do for my friends was harmful to Sweden's interests'. He had urged Staël to separate from her.[25] Towards the end of August, to avoid any more controversy during the elections which had been set for the following month, she left Paris with her young son Auguste for Mathieu de Montmorency's estate at Ormesson.

She remained at Ormesson for the next six weeks, although she was unable to resist a brief return to Paris in the early days of September, when at a big dinner at the embassy, attended by all the members of the opposition, she urged them not to resort to violence. They were not to heed her advice. At Ormesson she gave refuge to several friends who felt unsafe in Paris, as always drawing a group of interesting people around her. Benjamin Constant came to stay for some of the time. He was still madly in love with her but she continued to resist him. She was still in love with Ribbing but she was lonely and perhaps because she sensed that that affair was ending, she renewed her efforts to conquer François de Pange. Pange's fine intellect, his passionate love of ideas, his courage and his consumptive fragility had always attracted her. While absolutely devoted to her, Pange had been in love with a young married cousin, Madame de Sérilly, all his life. He fended off Madame de Staël's advances as best he could. Perhaps because his natural reserve made her unaware that his affections were engaged elsewhere, Madame de Staël bombarded him with ever more encouraging letters. 'I am not surprised that Madame de Staël should continue to annoy [Pange],' wrote Madame de Sérilly (now a widow) to their mutual friend Madame de Beaumont, 'but I must admit that I would be surprised if it brought her any success, it is rather clumsy. One does not win a heart by assault. Such an openly advertised intention must, I think, inspire a wish to resist . . . rather than to surrender.'[26] That was a lesson Madame de Staël was never to learn.

While Madame de Staël was stuck at Ormesson, there was growing agitation in Paris. The new Constitution had effectively excluded any possibility of a royalist majority. At the beginning of October there was an uprising in some of the Paris Sections. Throughout the evening of 4 October, a day of torrential rain, the tocsin rang continuously as drums beat a call to arms. The next day (13 Vendémiaire), a serious coup attempted by the right – the last great revolutionary spasm – was foiled by Barras, who had been put in charge of the armed forces, and especially by his second-in command, Napoleon Bonaparte, who did not hesitate to fire on the bands of assorted anti-Republicans led by squads of Muscadins mowing them down ruthlessly. By nightfall several hundred bodies lay in the rain-soaked streets around the Tuileries. But the Convention had been saved. Napoleon's role in the suppression of the coup of Vendémiaire brought to an end his years of obscurity and poverty. As General Vendémiaire he was to be showered with money and honours.

On the day of the attempted coup, Constant and François de Pange were arrested and put in prison. Madame de Staël's intervention with her friend Marie-Joseph Chénier and her direct appeal to Barras led to their release twenty-four hours later. Ten days later, on 23 Vendémiaire (15 October), the Convention, keen to consolidate its victory over the right, accused several deputies of collusion with the royalists. Since all of them were friends of Madame de Staël, the Convention issued an order at the instigation of Legendre, expelling Madame de Staël from France within ten days. Under suspicion himself, Staël made an official protest, which sounded so half-hearted that it caused Boissy d'Anglas to remark that 'Staël would sooner sacrifice his wife than his position'. But the protest was partly successful. The order for his wife to leave France was postponed; for the time being she was merely to leave Paris. To save face she was allowed to take the waters at Forges les Eaux, a spa in Normandy, with her friends Madame de Valence and Madame de Beaumont, after which she would have to leave France. Believing that she would be safe under the new Constitution of the Year III, as it was known, Madame de Staël played for time. Staël himself now had to contend with the Swedish Regent, who was displeased with the terms imposed on Sweden by the French Republic. He had managed to negotiate new terms with no reference to England or Russia, but he did not obtain the large sums of money he had been promised and so fell into disgrace.

The Directorate was established on 12 Brumaire (3 November). Such was the disorganization that the five new Directors had found no table or chairs when they arrived at the Luxembourg palace for their first meeting. Madame de Staël was to recollect later that 'the state was no more ordered than the palace. Paper money had been reduced to almost a thousandth of its nominal value, there weren't a hundred thousand francs in cash in the state treasury; the necessities of life were so scarce that it was hard to contain the people's displeasure; the insurrection in the Vendée was still going strong, and civil strife had enabled bands of brigands, known as *chauffeurs*, who committed horrible crimes, to roam the countryside; and finally almost all the French armies were disorganized.'[27]

Madame de Staël returned to Paris towards the end of November where she was placed under surveillance, as several police reports testify. She managed to postpone her departure for another three weeks. During that time she rekindled her affair with Ribbing, who had arrived on a brief visit. He promised to join her in Switzerland in April, even giving her a bracelet made out of his hair as a love token.

Accompanied by Constant, Madame de Staël left Paris on 21 December. She was reunited with her father in Lausanne on the last day of 1795, and with her younger son Albert, who, she told Staël, was as beautiful as the day and looked like him! By taking more after her, Auguste was less beautiful alas![28] Ribbing questioned her about

Constant, who was generally disliked by Madame de Staël's Parisian friends. Her own feelings about him had not changed she assured him: 'He is man of very superior intelligence, whatever you might be told, and there are few who suit me as well when it comes to my tastes for conversation and literature. So much for his attractions. As for his qualities, he is as devoted to me as no other man on earth could be, given the conditions I impose on him. He lacks strength of character and physical attraction and I cannot think of love without one of these advantages.'[29]

Although it was not her intention, Madame de Staël was to spend the whole of 1796 in Switzerland, which made her unhappy and affected her health. But if it was miserably frustrating for her to be away from Paris, it was undoubtedly very good for her work. Alone, with only her father and Constant at Coppet, she collaborated with Constant on his pamphlet, *De la force du gouvernement actuel de la France et de la nécessité de s'y rallier* ('On the strength of the present government in France and the need to support it'), published at the end of April. In spite of the title, they both believed that the government was far from strong, and this was all the more reason to support it, because there was no going back. In spite of the horror and excesses of the Terror, which both Constant and Madame de Staël deplored and excoriated, they never reneged on the idea that the Revolution had been necessary, that it had been rooted in the ideals of liberty and equality, good and noble in themselves but also essential for a changing society, and that it had been inevitable. Like her, Constant believed the Terror had been an aberration which 'during its reign served the friends of anarchy, just as the memory of the terror today serves the friends of despotism'. It was pointless as well as stupid to try and reverse progress and the march of history and attempt to return to an old form of absolute power. The Republic must be supported therefore, since consent was essential if it was to be founded on the rule of law. Only then could peace be ensured, which was so greatly desired by all the French.[30] Madame de Staël was to repeat this general principle in one form or another in all her writings. Future generations might be able to make sense of the Terror but it was pointless to try and understand something so monstrous; indeed, any attempt to make it comprehensible was to 'put it among accepted ideas for which there were words and expressions' and therefore make it possible to justify it.[31]

At Coppet she finished part one of her first important book, *De l'Influence des passions sur le bonheur des individus et des nations*, begun there in the autumn of 1792, continued in England and then in Paris. (The second part, in which she intended to analyse constitutional arrangements throughout history, was never written.) It was published in Lausanne in September 1796. It was a work 'written on the body': clearly marked by the misery of her experiences in love with both Narbonne and Ribbing and her deep disappointment and horror at the betrayal of her generation's hopes and ideals by the events of the Terror. Written in her late twenties, as she surveyed the ruin of all she had believed in, she felt compelled to analyse the mysterious effect of the passions on human happiness, both private and public; of their destructive force on our personal freedom and sense of self-worth. It is a great work of self-analysis, remarkable for the clarity and objectivity with which she judges her own experience and that of her political generation. She hoped that it might help others because, having suffered greatly, 'a painful anxiety seizes me at the thought of other people's pain, their inevitable suffering and the torments of the imagination; the upsets of the just man and even the remorse of the guilty; the most touching wounds of the heart, and regrets which we feel keenly though they make us blush, everything which makes us shed tears, those tears which the ancients used to preserve in an urn, so mighty was human pain in their eyes.'[32] It is also an apologia, a need to explain herself, as she states in the foreword: 'I feel a need to be judged through my writings. Constantly slandered, yet believing that I am too unimportant to write about myself, I have dared to hope that by publishing this fruit of my reflections, I might give a true picture of my life's habits and of the true nature of my character.'[33]

Passion, she believed, could only lead to suffering. The longing for perfect happiness, whether personal or national, was doomed to failure. A lifelong opponent of all political fanaticism, she makes a case for tolerance and moderation as relevant today as it was in her time. Taking examples from the Stoics to Rousseau to illustrate her points, she is never moralizing or didactic, but merely aware of the dangers we all face. The depth of her scholarship, her acute intelligence and advanced views are tempered at all times with empathy and warmth, with extraordinary self-awareness and a sense of common suffering, and so she never bores. She may warn us of the dangers, but she urges us to live bravely for 'anything one has not felt for oneself, is understood by the mind but has no effect on our actions'.[34] The themes of this book were to be developed further in her great work on literature and in her two major novels, *Delphine* and *Corine*.

As always Madame de Staël's liberal views put her under suspicion from extremists on both right and left. Although she was quite unaware of it, the Directory had put her under close watch as an anti-Republican, while the government of Berne, believing her to be a Jacobin sympathizer, did the same.

At the end of the month Madame de Staël suffered a blow to her pride when her friend François de Pange wrote to announce his marriage to his cousin, Madame de Sérilly. Her first letter must have been destroyed; the second is completely characteristic of the child-like sincerity of her feelings, her complete inability to hide her despair and loneliness, her trust in her friends. 'Now that I have put my grief into some sort of order, I can explain it to you. First I believe – and this will soon become a very sweet solace – I believe that you have done well for yourself, and that you have been true to your character. This is not a passion so it is not slavery; and in some ways you will have won rather than lost your freedom. I had no right to be sad, as I said to you, and yet I will admit that I shed many tears at the news; and since I may do so again when I see you, there is no point in hiding them. I had become used to thinking of you as immune to this feeling [of love] . . . and believed you to be a being apart. When I realized that you were after all one of us, I felt that I had lost you, that you might have loved me as much as anyone else. Anyway I was hurt. I think I had a right to be . . . I have said everything. You can see that I will not love you less, but you will understand that I loved you more. It is important to me to know whether I will see as much of you as before, and whether your attitude towards me will remain unchanged.'[35]

He replied to reassure her that when 'he had capitulated to his wife' he had made it clear that nothing would be changed in the dispositions he had made for his happiness of which his friendship with Madame de Staël was a part. Trying to explain himself he wrote: 'no two ideas could be more dissimilar than the ones we have formed about happiness . . . You see it in a grand passion in the midst of great events, anxieties, pleasures and sacrifices; in a word in everything that might interest and agitate the spirit. I ask for nothing for my happiness except peace . . .'[36] Reassured by his response, there was no doubting his admiration and devotion to her. That summer she mourned his premature death with all her heart.

A second emotional blow had come when Ribbing himself confirmed the rumours that he had fallen in love with her friend, Pulchérie de Valence, daughter of Madame de Genlis. 'What a terrible blow to her sensitive heart once again!'[37] wrote Mathieu to Albertine Necker-de Saussure. Mathieu had never liked Ribbing. Some months before he had remarked that 'the handsome Swede' was still in Denmark and he hoped he would stay there. He need not have worried. Their love affair had ended, but not their friendship, which lasted to the end of her life. Her subsequent correspondence with Ribbing, who married in 1799 and had his much hoped-for son, was very friendly. In 1812, when exiled by Napoleon, Madame de Staël, then in Sweden, intervened unsuccessfully on Ribbing's behalf with Bernadotte, for the former regicide to be allowed to return to Sweden.[38]

So at last Benjamin Constant's devotion was to be rewarded. 'Benjamin, whose endless goodness to me spreads real charm through my life, is intending to go to France in two or three weeks,' she had written to François de Pange in mid-March, adding that she was intending to follow him in May.[39] It is probable that it was at about this time that they became lovers, and that a curious document, signed by him but not by her, and undated, was drawn up then too: 'We promise to dedicate our lives to each other; we declare that we see ourselves as indissolubly bound to one another; that our future destiny shall in every sense be our joint destiny, that we will never contract any other tie; and that as soon as we are able we will further strengthen the ties that bind us. I declare that I enter into this engagement from the bottom of my heart, that I know of no one else on earth as lovable as Madame de Staël; that during the four months passed in her company I have been the happiest man on earth; and that I count it as the greatest happiness in my life, to make her youth happy, to grow old gently by her side and to reach the end with a person who understands me and without whom there would be no interest and no feeling on this earth.'[40]

Constant left for Paris at the end of April. The Directory were pleased with his pamphlet, but Madame de Staël, who had helped him write it, was warned by the French Resident in Geneva that if she attempted to cross into France she would be arrested. She remained at Coppet, her relationship with her father back to its former closeness.

Necker must have known about Constant, whom he always liked, and in any case he had realized that there was nothing to be done with his beloved daughter: she would go her own way. However unorthodox her private life, Madame de Staël was still married, which allowed her to maintain a respectable front. Madame Necker was no longer there to come between them with her moralizing and her jealousy. Necker adored his grandsons as much as they loved him. As for her, much as she loved her father, she was bored to death at Coppet and longed for action, bombarding her husband with letters to obtain a revocation of the order which prevented her from entering France. In June, however, she learned that Staël had been sent on indefinite leave by the Swedish Regent, who wished to cut down the Swedish embassy in France and had appointed a chargé d'affaires in his place. Staël was obliged to return to her for the usual reason – he was up to his ears in debt.

At the beginning of August she wrote to a friend, Albert Pictet-Diodati: 'M. de Staël is arriving in the next few days, having taken no interest whatever in my affairs, and offering me only the prospect of ruin in order to pay his debts; I am not much tempted.'[41] Ignoring Jacobsson's pleas, Staël had put himself in the hands of moneylenders as he gambled more and more wildly. Jacobsson, who liked him, was nevertheless forced to admit that 'had all of Necker's fortune been poured into his wallet it could not have prevented his ruin'.[42]

Constant had returned from Paris, a few days before Staël's arrival. He too had had his problems. His pamphlet had come in for strong criticism from Bertin de Vaux, a journalist writing in the *Feuille du jour*, who had suggested that the 'little Swiss foreigner' should be sent back home with the words 'unwanted rubbish' pinned to his back. The fiery Constant at once challenged him to a duel. Bertin de Vaux was forced to retract. Although Constant had come well out of the affair, he realized that to play any part in France he would have to take French nationality (which he hoped to do on the basis that his family had originated in Artois). In order to have a French domicile for his future political activities he also bought the ruined Abbey of Hérivaux near Luzarches, some twenty miles north of Paris, with financial help from Necker. At about the same time Madame de Staël bought a small house near Angervilliers, very near Mathieu de Montmorency's family Château de Dampierre. A new law under the Directory now allowed foreigners to buy properties in France and to live there. Madame de

Staël hoped this house would reinforce her own rights until she could get back her father's properties, which were still sequestered.

Constant's dashing response to the insult and Madame de Staël's fears for his safety when she heard about the duel, had removed any final reservations. She was in love again and proclaimed it *urbi et orbi*, to the embarrassment of both families. 'Benjamin has arrived at his love's house: great joy, great happiness! God knows where all this great love will lead them,' wrote his starchy cousin Rosalie de Constant to her brother Charles.[43] Upset by Madame de Staël's free and easy ways and by her disrespectful references to her husband, offended by her and Constant's disparaging remarks about Switzerland, Rosalie wrote at the end of August that she had 'seen my cousin de Staël, and my cousin *le tondu*, (the shorn one) [Constant had returned from Paris sporting a fashionable new haircut *à la Brutus*] two or three times.' She thought that Staël, whom she declared she liked better than all Madame de Staël's lovers, had looked 'defeated, crushed and overwhelmed' while she looked at him 'haughtily and disdainfully'.[44] The truth was that the clever Rosalie disliked Madame de Staël, who always made her feel uncomfortable, as much as she admired her as a writer: 'the all too famous one must be seen from a distance if one is to like her books'. *On the influence of the Passions*, she added, was 'an admirable book', which had enthused her at first, chilled her in the middle but had finally enchanted her.[45]

Staël arrived at Coppet in early September, leaving later that month to take the waters at Aix-les-Bains. Whatever Rosalie de Constant may have thought, his visit seems to have been entirely satisfactory and he left once more under Madame de Staël's spell. A hint in one of her letters to him that they may even have resumed marital relations may be explained by the fact that as she and Constant were now lovers she needed some cover for a suspected pregnancy, confirmed later that month. They had long since established a bargain: respectability for her, money for him, but there was undoubtedly a feeling of friendship between them at this time and she wished to save his feelings and his face.

Constant returned to Paris in October to promote Madame de Staël's book on the passions. She had written to Roederer soliciting his help, begging him to make sure when writing about her book to always refer to her as a Frenchwoman, by virtue of her birth, her country of residence, property, habits and patriotism. The edict preventing Madame de Staël from returning to France had been based on an attempt to deprive her of French nationality. Roederer complied, praising the book and the 'extraordinary intelligence' of its French author. He added that the first edition of such a work would have been better edited in France, where he hoped the second edition would soon be published.

The following month brought happy news that the Swedish regent had reinstalled Staël as ambassador. Delighted, Madame de Staël prepared to join him in Paris, only for her hopes to be dashed when Staël was dismissed from his post by the new young king, Gustavus IV, who had assumed powers from the Regent. She was still forbidden to return to the Paris region, but her friendship with Barras enabled her to risk a return to France. Leaving her two boys behind with their grandfather, Madame de Staël and Constant left Coppet on 19 December, reaching his abbey at Hérivaux on Christmas day 1796.

PART FOUR

The Sword and the Spirit

'There are only two powers in the world; the sword and the spirit . . . In the long run, the sword is always beaten by the spirit.'

Napoleon to the writer Fontanes

Chapter 14

From Fructidor to Brumaire

'Madame de Staël had approved the 18th but not the 19th of Fructidor.'

Talleyrand

THE PARTING WITH her father at the end of 1796 had been very hard for Madame de Staël; it was a recurring source of grief to them both, a problem they would never solve, since he refused to leave Coppet while she needed the stimulus of the outside world. 'What a fate!' she wrote en route to France, 'Anyway, your portrait and your note – these are my talismans. You have, all this time, been superhuman in your kindness, wisdom, generosity; in all the heavenly virtues . . . As for you, know that you are my only support on earth, that all the rest is transitory. This sentiment is at the very source of my life. Adieu, Adieu. Ah! how I embrace you now.'[1]

Since Madame de Staël was in France without official permission, she wrote to the Directors as soon as she arrived at Constant's house at Hérivaux. A carriage accident 'in her state of pregnancy' had forced her to rest for two days or she would have requested permission sooner, she explained. She promised to stay in the country and 'give no pretext, not even the most frivolous' to her enemies. The press was already reporting that she had been forced to reside in the country where she could only 'intrigue from afar'.[2]

A former convent, Constant's new house at Hérivaux was unheated and miserably uncomfortable in the winter. Madame de Staël nevertheless asked her father to send Auguste to her. Necker was reluctant to send him 'in her present uncertain situation', afraid that Staël might lay some claims to him, and unhappy about the discomfort and isolation of Constant's house, as he confided to his niece Albertine.[3]

Proscribed by the authorities, and attacked in the press, Madame de

Staël felt particular gratitude to Constant who, she wrote to a friend, had been absolutely wonderful. 'First of all I owe him everything, absolutely everything, but even were I to owe him nothing I will never cease to be grateful for the way in which, from the time of my arrival in France, when he alone was in charge of me, even the shadow of his faults disappeared. His unhappiness in the early days of his passion for me was now equalled by his tenderness to me in mine.' For all their difficulties she was delighted to be back in France and would be happy to stay there forever if her father and her sons could be with her. 'I still love this country,' she declared, 'we have no security, no money, and much discomfort. But there is interest in the very air one breathes, there is movement, there is a sense of welcome from people known and unknown which one feels in one's own country; the feeling that one is at home . . . more space to live in, less narrow passions even among ordinary people; sweeter air, what can I say?'[4]

Staël did not accompany her but remained in Switzerland and waited for permission to return to Paris. Back there in early February 1797, he did not immediately make contact with his wife in spite of her letters urging him to do so and to say nothing and do nothing before he had consulted her. Madame de Staël heard indirectly that he was proposing to let the residence in the rue du Bac. She remonstrated that he had no doubt forgotten that her baby was due at the end of May and that she had planned to give birth in Paris. Did he expect her to give birth in the street? 'I am pregnant; I am exiled and chained to this spot, and you are in Paris and do not come to see me, and you are about to sell my bed without consulting me, when I have the right, I think, to insist that no decision is taken before I give birth.'[5] Wearily, Staël could only promise that he would do nothing until October.

Madame de Staël remained at Hérivaux throughout the spring, helping Constant write two important pamphlets. The publication in April 1797 of *Des réactions politiques*, on the question of law and arbitrary government, stated the liberal position and further enhanced Constant's reputation as a political writer. It was followed by *Des effets de la terreur*, a response to an article by Adrien de Lezay in which Lezay had attempted to justify Jacobin crimes. 'Nothing on earth can ever justify a crime . . . if you grant an amnesty to the past you are corrupting the future,' Constant maintained.[6]

During this time she was in constant correspondence with the Directory over her French citizenship. She was seeking permission to live in Paris by right of her French birth, while they were trying to deny her citizenship on the grounds that she was the daughter of a foreigner and had married another while still a minor, making her doubly foreign. Meanwhile she was not quite forgotten. Goethe had sent her a splendid edition of his novel, *Wilhelm Meister*, but, she confessed to Henri Meister, as it was in German she had only been able to admire the binding, 'and between ourselves Benjamin, who has read it, assures me that I am luckier than him'. Would Meister thank Goethe warmly on her behalf, she asked, throwing a veil over her ignorance while expressing her gratitude and her admiration to the author of *Werther*?[7]

Soon after the publication of Constant's pamphlets, Madame de Staël left for Mathieu de Montmorency's estate at Ormesson, where she remained until the end of May. Before she left Hérivaux, she was reunited with Talleyrand, who had returned to Paris in the previous September, thanks to her efforts. It was the first time they had seen each other since her departure from England three years earlier. He was a frequent visitor at Ormesson, which was much closer than Hérivaux to Paris. They were both unhappy. His visit had alleviated her boredom but intensified her frustration. Talleyrand was absolutely without funds and had been obliged to borrow money and horses from her. Her relations with Constant, to begin with so happy, had been strained by their enforced cohabitation at Hérivaux. While he was happy alone with her and his books, she could not live in seclusion for long. Solitude frightened her and life in the country depressed her. Only the company of the faithful Mathieu, Adrien de Mun and one or two other friends made life bearable. In a bitter mood, perhaps as a result of her departure for Ormesson, Constant wrote to his aunt, Mme de Nassau: 'I must give some happiness to somebody . . . I beg you to find me a wife. I need one to be happy.' The bond with Madame de Staël, maintained out of weakness, and perhaps a sense of duty, had made him thoroughly unhappy: 'it had kept him in chains for the past two years'. However his mood had changed by his next letter. He did not want a new wife after all, he wrote, 'or anything which might wound his friend, who has just given him new and remarkable proofs of her devotion'.[8]

The proof of her devotion, her daughter Albertine, was born on 8 June 1797, in Paris, at the rue du Bac, to which, after prolonged correspondence with the Directors, Madame de Staël had at last been able to return the previous month. Although her husband had behaved 'with sympathy and solicitude', and believed or pretended to that the child was his, Madame de Staël encouraged Constant to think that he was the father. The truth has been disputed ever since. Constant had no other children and was thought by some members of his family to be sterile, but Albertine's red hair and marked resemblance to him speak for themselves. He certainly believed that she was his child and always held her in special affection.

'Madame de Staël has at last been delivered of a girl and has not ceased for a moment to entertain fifteen people in her room,' wrote General Montesquiou to his friend Mme de Montolieu in Lausanne. 'I went to see her this afternoon. She was in bed but she was talking and holding forth in her usual way. She really is a woman like no other. I don't think you need worry about the child: there is no shortage of people to look after it and if need be, as you say, Mathieu [de Montmorency] would replace Mme Necker.'[9] The faithful Mathieu had indeed tried to check his wilful friend's behaviour. He had been obliged to be strict, he wrote to Madame Necker-de Saussures on the day after the baby's birth, in order to prevent Madame de Staël from seeing anyone for at least a couple of days after giving birth.

Overjoyed by her return to the capital after eighteen months away, Madame de Staël was not going to allow the birth of her daughter to stop her from her political activities. A week later she was sending out dinner invitations to those Deputies who were of particular interest to her. It was to be a good summer for her in spite of the fact that the May elections had brought in a royalist majority, increasing the danger of a counter-revolution. In June, with Madame de Staël's help, Constant helped to found the Constitutional circle or the Club de Salm intended to counteract the propaganda of the well-organized royalist Club de Clichy. Further cause for celebration that month was news of La Fayette's release. He had been imprisoned in Austria under harsh conditions for almost five years. Throughout that time Madame de Staël had not ceased to agitate on his behalf.[10]

That summer, Madame de Staël enjoyed another triumph which was to be of lasting importance to European politics. In July, after much effort, she convinced Barras to appoint Talleyrand as Minister for Foreign Affairs. Talleyrand, she pointed out repeatedly, was a man of rare talent. The Directory was in deep trouble and there were few people around of his calibre. According to Barras's own colourful account, after several unsuccessful démarches on Talleyrand's behalf, Madame de Staël had appeared at Barras's office one day, half-dressed and in a state of violent agitation. Before he had a chance to master his astonishment at the vision before him, she seized his hands, swearing that Talleyrand was on the point of suicide. Talleyrand had just been to see her, and flinging his last ten louis on the table, declared that when they were finished he would throw himself in the river or blow his brains out. She could bear it no longer, would Barras please do something she wept.

Torn between hysterical laughter, terror at what his impetuous visitor might do next, and alarm that she was about to have some sort of fit, Barras promised to do his best. Madame de Staël, he insinuated, had been prepared to give even more for her friend's sake, but he had resisted her advances.[11]

Barras's account is not to be trusted in detail – he was prone to exaggeration and ridiculing Madame de Staël's manner and appearance was a national pastime among her acquaintances of both sexes – but there is no doubt that Talleyrand owed his return to public life entirely to her. He would prove singularly ungrateful. Madame de La Tour du Pin, recently returned from America where she had often seen Talleyrand, corroborated the story of his supposed suicide threat. Of course nobody believed that he would do anything of the sort, she wrote, but Madame de Staël was known to love drama, and the urbane Talleyrand had staged a most uncharacteristic scene to impress her.[12] Constant recalled that when Talleyrand learned that he was to be foreign minister, he had been overjoyed. On his way to the Luxembourg palace, accompanied by Constant and by his old friend Boniface de Castellane, he could only think of the money he would make out of the appointment. 'We have the post. Now we must make an immense fortune, an immense fortune,' he had repeated. True to his word, in the process of his long and brilliant political career, in which he always put the interests of France first, he never missed an opportunity to enrich himself.

Madame de Staël was also successful in her effort to have her father's name removed from the list of émigrés, subject to ratification by the Directory. His properties – two houses in Paris and the country house at Saint-Ouen – would therefore be returned to him when this provisional act became law. The royalist press however, angered by Talleyrand's new appointment and Constant's major role at the

Constitutional club, now launched a vitriolic attack on Madame de Staël. Among the epithets they hurled at her were 'Messalina-Staël', 'a prostitute and a hermaphrodite', 'a witch', and 'the most active and miserable intriguer in Europe'.[13]

The royalists had won a majority in the Assembly in the summer of 1797 and Paris was full of returning members of the nobility. There seemed every chance of a restoration of the monarchy. Two of the Directors, Carnot and Barthélemy, were sympathetic to their cause. Peace negotiations with Britain were going on in Lille. The royalists could have won the day, if the old guard had been prepared to make some concessions. But they refused to co-operate with the constitutionalists, determined on nothing less than a return to the *ancien régime*. They seemed to be living in a fevered world of conspiracies, as Madame de La Tour du Pin recalled, some even going so far as to adopt secret signals, such as the wearing of black velvet collars, knots in their handkerchiefs and other such absurdities, to make immediate recognition possible between them.[14]

Even before the sequestration orders on her father's properties had been finally lifted, Madame de Staël had been allowed to return to Saint-Ouen, which at once became a centre of political discussion. Madame de La Tour du Pin, visiting her aunt, Madame d'Hénin, who was living in a borrowed house nearby for the summer, was astonished at the extreme lack of caution with which people discussed royalist plans and hopes, even naming émigrés who had returned with false papers. She recalled that Talleyrand, who was often there, must have been aware of every single plot that was being discussed and was laughing at them. 'I saw Madame de Staël nearly every day. Despite her more than intimate friendship with Benjamin Constant, she was working for the royalists, or rather for some form of compromise.'[15]

She was indeed working for some form of compromise. As for the royalists, she was not working for them at any time but she was in a difficult position. Many of her friends were royalists. She was absolutely loyal to them personally, but, like Talleyrand, she saw that the real danger lay with the royalists who, if they achieved a restoration of the monarchy, would attempt to reverse all the gains of the Revolution and send France hurtling back into violence and terror. She never ceased to believe in the original aims of the Revolution and was convinced that the Republic had to be saved. A Republican majority in the Councils would also avert the danger of a possible Jacobin resurgence. (A conspiracy financed by former Jacobins, sworn enemies of the Directory, had been put down in May 1796. Led by Babeuf who had advocated an early form of Communism, his followers, known as the *Equals*, numbered many former terrorists.) With Talleyrand and Constant, she had urged the Deputies throughout August to come to some agreement to ensure a Republican majority. In early September, when no such agreement had been reached, the three Republican Directors, Barras, Reubell and Larevellière-Lépeaux, realizing that the Republic was in danger of an imminent and perfectly legal royalist takeover, turned to the one man who might save them.

Napoleon Bonaparte had been in command of the army of Italy since the coup of Vendémiaire (October 1795). Not wanting to be associated with the use of armed force against the citizens of Paris, he sent his lieutenant, the rough and ready General Augereau, to the city. In the early morning of 18 Fructidor (4 September), Paris awoke to find itself under military occupation: the Tuileries, where both chambers were in a hastily convened emergency session, were surrounded by Augereau's troops. Madame de Staël undoubtedly knew of the projected *coup d'état*. She had dined with Barras, Talleyrand and Constant on the evening of 3 September and had then spent the night at Madame Condorcet's house, where they watched cannon being moved through the deserted streets to their positions around the Tuileries. It was a moment of real crisis for her, a time when, scarred by the Terror, despite her fundamental liberal beliefs and with much misgiving, she accepted the need for pre-emptive action, to save the Republic and avert a return to anarchy and bloodshed.

On the day of the coup, unable to contain their curiosity, as Madame de La Tour du Pin recalled, she and Madame de Valence – modestly dressed so as not to attract attention – had set out at noon to Madame de Staël's house to try and find out what had happened. There was an atmosphere of fear, all the shops were shut, the streets full of silent people. Many of the side streets in the short distance between their house and Madame de Staël's were barricaded by soldiers, making it necessary for them to take a roundabout route. On arrival they found their friend arguing furiously with Constant. Madame de Staël was afraid that the Deputies would be tried by a government commission. Constant replied that it was probable and that 'it would be unfortunate but perhaps necessary'. He warned

Madame de La Tour du Pin that all émigrés who had returned would be expelled again, as indeed proved to be the case.[16]

The coup was over swiftly. The next day, Madame de Staël's worst forebodings were realized when, in a savage purge, the Directors shut down newspapers, annulled elections and expelled almost 200 Deputies. The two dissenting Directors were eliminated. Carnót had managed to escape through his garden in his nightshirt, but Barthélemy was arrested and subsequently transported in an iron cage before jeering crowds to the port of Rochefort and then shipped to French Guiana. Banishment to the tropical swamps of South America, known as the dry guillotine, was tantamount to a death sentence. Altogether 163 opponents of the regime – priests, journalists and Deputies – were imprisoned without trial and either shot or deported to Cayenne.

Horrified at the suppression of liberties and at the severity of the measures taken against the right, Madame de Staël argued against them, but in vain. Talleyrand summed up her position with his customary perspicacity and wit: 'Madame de Staël had approved of the 18th Fructidor but not of the 19th'. Her misgivings about her own tacit approval of Fructidor are clear in a letter she wrote to Samuel de Constant, Benjamin's uncle. 'There has been no bloodshed during this revolution of 18 Fructidor, but there have been a number of unfortunate occurrences, the length and consequence of which are incalculable.' Always the more radical of the two, Constant had made an impassioned speech full of Republican ardour at the Club de Salm a few days later, which was wildly applauded, 'like Gracchus's in Rome', she wrote.[17] But Constant too would deeply regret his enthusiasm in later life, referring to that day as 'a day of illegality, . . . which had destroyed the confidence between the government and the governed.'[18]

Later Madame de Staël denied that she had been in favour of the actual coup. She had indeed supported the Republic, but had hoped that the Directory would adopt constitutional measures and would choose ministers who would support the government. Talleyrand had seemed the best possible choice as foreign minister. She believed his nomination, 'the only part I played in the crisis which preceded 18 Fructidor', would help to prevent a coup and that 'M. de Talleyrand's abilities would make a reconciliation between the two sides possible'.[19]

Although this was true, Madame de Staël had made a serious

misjudgement and she knew it. 'I always believed that reason would triumph given time and good will: in all the circumstances of my life, my political mistakes were due to the belief that men could always be stirred by the truth, if it was presented to them forcefully.'[20] Talleyrand believed in no such thing. He had perfectly understood which way the wind was blowing. A return to the *ancien régime* was unthinkable. The Directory was rotten and would be got rid of in good time, but that time was not yet ripe. Although a monarchist at heart – he would soon be helping Bonaparte to found a new imperial dynasty – he spent the remaining two years under the Directory securing his own position with the future master of France.

Bonaparte in the meantime, had almost completed his conquest of Italy. The grateful Directory now gave him a free hand in the peace negotiations. The Treaty of Campo Formio in October 1797 gave France the Austrian Netherlands and the left bank of the Rhine. A new Cisalpine Republic was created out of the conquests in Northern Italy. The Venetian Republic was handed over to the Austrian Emperor in exchange for certain territorial advantages, but not before it was looted of major works of art, among them the horses of St Mark. As Madame de Staël later noted, a Republican government had committed the inconceivable act of handing over a republic to an emperor.[21]

In France Bonaparte was the hero of the hour. There is no doubt that in those early days of his rise to power Madame de Staël too was breathless with admiration for him. He seemed to have all the attributes that she loved in men: genius, passion, love of glory, personal modesty and a love of liberty. His proclamations during the Italian campaign such as: 'You were divided and bent by tyranny; you were in no state to win your liberty', were widely quoted. A tone of moderation and nobility predominated in his style, in stark contrast to the revolutionary harshness emanating from the civilian authorities in France. 'The warrior spoke like a lawmaker, while the lawmakers expressed themselves in terms of warlike violence.'[22] At the time she thought him 'the best republican in France, the most liberal of Frenchmen'.[23] Her romantic imagination was further struck by the fact that Napoleon wrote, loved the arts and the sciences, and was said, like herself, to admire the poems of Ossian.[24] A friend of both Napoleon's brothers, Lucien and Joseph, Madame de Staël longed to get closer to her hero and had addressed several adulatory letters to him while he was campaigning in Italy. These letters have not survived but according to his friend and secretary, General Bourrienne, there were four or five. 'The woman's mad!' Napoleon had laughed as he read excerpts to Bourrienne, asking him what he made of such excess; they seemed almost like love letters. He had not bothered to answer them. Fulsome praise was one thing but she had apparently also suggested that he was married 'to an insignificant little Creole, quite incapable of understanding or appreciating his heroic qualities'.[25] If true, and this is open to question, this was a serious miscalculation. Bonaparte adored his wife Josephine. In any case he liked women who were beautiful, feminine and submissive; he disliked and was profoundly uneasy with intelligent women, especially if they meddled in what he considered men's business. He could bear no disagreement and never forgot a slight.

Madame de Staël remained at Ormesson until the end of October when she returned to Paris. Here, protected for the moment by her friendship with Barras and with Talleyrand, she resumed her normal life.

Bonaparte returned to Paris from Italy on 5 December 1797. He told Talleyrand that he was so exhausted, that he could barely mount his horse and felt he needed two years of rest.[26] Madame de Staël, who had been invited to meet the general when he paid an official call on Talleyrand at the Ministry for Foreign Affairs at 11 o'clock the next day, was in his salon by ten. Bonaparte was announced. Short-legged and small in stature, gaunt and pale, he did indeed look tired, but his pallor and thinness suited him, she thought. His social manner was uneasy but not timid, there was a haughtiness about him when he was reserved, although he tended to vulgarity when at ease. When she was introduced, Madame de Staël had felt strangely intimidated, almost unable to breathe. She was gratified when he told her that when crossing Switzerland he had sought out her father at Coppet, expressing regret at not having met him. Then he had turned away brusquely to talk to someone else and soon disappeared into Talleyrand's office.[27] When he came out again the reception room was full of people. He thanked them briefly. He had done his best in war and in peace and it was now up to the Directors to profit from his actions for the happiness and prosperity of the Republic. With that he was gone.

Four days later, the Directory celebrated the victor's return in a solemn ceremony in the courtyard of the Luxembourg palace. No hall was big enough to accommodate all those who wished to attend. All the surrounding windows and roofs were jammed with spectators. An orchestra played patriotic airs. On a platform at the end of the courtyard, in front of an altar draped with the colours won in the Italian campaign, stood the five Directors, magnificent in scarlet togas, surrounded by the Deputies of both chambers and by other dignitaries. Bonaparte entered the courtyard flanked by his aides-de-camp, all a head taller than him, but bent almost double with deference. His simple grey coat could not have stood out more starkly against the splendour and pomp of his surroundings. Talleyrand then presented 'the son and hero of the Revolution' to the Directors, lauding 'the liberator of Italy; the pacifier of the continent' for his dislike of luxury and show. Here was a simple soldier, a man uninterested in power, a scholar who loved the sciences and admired the poems of Ossian. Madame de Staël, who was present, recalled that handing the Treaty of Campo Formio to the Directors, Bonaparte had replied 'with a kind of affected negligence, as if he wished it to be understood that he had little liking for the regime he had been called on to serve, "Monarchy and feudalism had reigned for two thousand years – now the peace just concluded by him would herald an era of republican government"'. Barras then thanked the hero on behalf of the Directors, urging him to go forth and conquer Britain. A rather more difficult mission, Madame de Staël reflected.[28]

She saw Bonaparte several times that month. She thought him a being apart. She had no doubt about his brilliant mind but began to notice his single-minded ambition and calculating coldness, 'like an icy sword that freezes as it cuts'. Seated between him and Sieyès at dinner at Talleyrand's, she observed him carefully. When he noticed this, his face became utterly expressionless, his eyes like marble, his thoughts impenetrable. He hated that kind of attention. Sieyès had spoken very flatteringly of Necker, declaring that he was the only man who had ever united in his calculations the perfect precision of a great financier with the imagination of a poet. Bonaparte had agreed politely, even adding a few obliging remarks about Madame de Staël herself, but in a distant, half-hearted way. He was perfectly aware of her political importance and had no wish to make an enemy of her, but he was determined to keep her at arm's length. She was everything he disliked most in a woman – outstandingly intelligent, outspoken, imprudent and lacking beauty.

Bonaparte liked to humiliate women, she recalled: 'I remember him one day coming up to a Frenchwoman well known for her beauty, her mind and her vivacity [Madame de Condorcet]. Standing before her like the stiffest of German generals, he said "Madame, I do not like women who meddle in politics". "General, you are quite right," the lady replied, "but in a country where their heads are cut off, it is natural for them to want to know the reason why." ' Taken aback, he was silent.[29] He disliked what he saw as Madame de Staël's meddling and was embarrassed and a little frightened by her uninhibited advances, but he never underestimated her. The more he avoided her the more she longed to conquer the conqueror, to break down that iron reserve, to be his Egeria. She could only meet resistance with force, accosting him at every opportunity.

In early January 1798 Talleyrand gave a magnificent ball in honour of Josephine. What more subtle way to flatter the modest hero than through his adored wife? Talleyrand had sought to unite the old world and the new and had done so triumphantly. Everyone who mattered in Paris was there: nobles and *parvenus*, the *ancien régime* mingling with former terrorists. The evening was an outstanding success, the Bonapartes treated like royalty and the general well pleased – though careful to preserve his austere front – when suddenly and unexpectedly he was cornered by Madame de Staël. Unable to resist an opportunity to bring herself to his notice, she hurled questions at him. 'Which woman did he love the most,' she asked. 'Madame, I love my own' was the embarrassed reply. 'Ah how sublime!' Madame de Staël exclaimed to Lucien Bonaparte. Returning to the charge, before a now gathering crowd of people, she persisted. But who was the woman he most respected? 'The one best able to look after her household' came the unpromising reply. Flustered, Madame de Staël tried one more tactic: Who then did he think was the greatest woman in history? 'The one, Madame, who has had the greatest number of children,' replied the exasperated general as he turned on his heel.[30]

Undeterred, she too gave a ball in his honour. He refused to attend. A force of nature in her turban and shawls, she had even attempted an assault on the hero in his own house. When told by a gaping manservant, trying to bar her way, that the general was undressed, she tried to barge into his bedroom, declaring that it didn't matter for 'genius has no sex'. The warrior retreated still more.

Determined that his military glory should give the nervous Directors no cause for alarm, but not yet ready to get rid of them, Bonaparte played a long game. With Talleyrand's help, he took good care to present himself as modest, serious, retiring; interested only in becoming a member of the Institute. In his speech of acceptance, when this honour was conferred on him, he thanked the Academicians, aware, he said, that far from being their equal, he was merely their pupil. 'True conquests, the only kind that brings no regrets, are those over ignorance,' he added, knowing that he could count on Talleyrand to ensure that such high-minded modesty would be quoted all over Paris. Occasionally the mask slipped. Madame de Staël recalled an evening when, a little carried away, Bonaparte had boasted to Barras that the peoples of Italy had so admired him that they had wished to make him Duke of Milan and even king of Italy. 'You are right not to dream of any such thing in France,' Barras replied, 'for if the Directory was to send you to the Temple [prison] tomorrow, you would not find four people who opposed it.'[31] Bonaparte, sitting on a sofa next to Barras, had leaped to his feet with irritation. But he recognized the truth of that remark. Recovering quickly, he declared that all he wanted was to be put in charge of a military expedition. 'The fruit is not yet ripe. I've tried everything but they don't want me. I should overthrow them and be crowned king, but it is not yet time for that,' he confided to Bourrienne afterwards.[32]

The expedition in question was not to be to Britain, as the Directors had hoped, but to Egypt. In England, preparations for resisting an invasion had been under way for some time. While militia armies of volunteers were being trained, British ships prowled up and down the Channel, protecting her coast. After several visits of inspection to the Channel coast, Bonaparte declared that the French navy was inadequate to the task of taking on the British navy. It would be far preferable to mount an expedition to Egypt, he and Talleyrand believed. A French colony in Egypt would not only further burnish his reputation, it would also establish a base from which to attack Britain's trade and provide a foothold for a future French empire in the east. To finance the expedition Bonaparte proposed to invade Switzerland, ostensibly to liberate it, but actually to shake out the gold amassed by the Bernese government.

Terrified for her father, who was still on the list of French émigrés, and as such in danger of his life should Vaud be occupied by French troops, and unwilling to see the Swiss Cantons lose their independence, Madame de Staël managed to obtain a private meeting with Bonaparte. For almost an hour Bonaparte stuck to his role of convinced Republican and democrat. 'He pointed out to me that the Vaudois were subjugated by the Bernese aristocracy and that men could no longer be expected to live without political rights. I tried to temper his Republican ardour by pointing out that the Vaudois enjoyed perfect freedom as far as their civil rights went and that, when such liberties existed *de facto*, one should not seek to enforce them *de jure* by exposing the country to the greatest of misfortunes – that of foreign invasion.' In an ironic reversal of roles, Bonaparte had replied that none the less 'self-respect and imagination' required that people have the right to participate in their own government. Agreeing in principle, Madame de Staël countered that liberty should only be won by one's own efforts and not imposed by a necessarily dominant outside power. She tried to move him by pointing out that Switzerland had enjoyed prosperity and happiness for several centuries. 'That is doubtless true,' Bonaparte replied stubbornly, 'but men need political rights.' He kept repeating 'political rights' as if it was a lesson he had learned by heart. Then he changed the subject, talking simply about his love of solitude, of the countryside and the arts, and generally taking the trouble to present himself in a light which he supposed would appeal to her. She noted how well he could charm people when he chose to.[33]

Realizing that Bonaparte's mind was made up, Madame de Staël left France at the end January 1798 to join her father and her children at Coppet. She had been as unsuccessful in dissuading her father from staying at Coppet as she had been with Bonaparte. He was too old to be wandering around, he said. Later that month they watched the approach of the French troops from a balcony. Although it was the middle of winter the weather was lovely: 'the Alps reflected in the lake and only the beating of the drums disturbed the peaceful scene'. Her own heart was beating with terror at what might happen next, particularly to her father. She saw a French officer detach himself from the troops to ride up to their château. He had come to reassure Necker on behalf of the Directory. The officer was the future Marshall Suchet and Necker was indeed very well treated.[34] Switzerland was soon overrun and renamed the Helvetic Republic. Madame de Staël was unhappy at the annexation of Geneva to France, although as a result her father was now legally a French citizen, as indeed she was.

Although Coppet had not been sequestered, there was a question over the feudal rights from which Necker benefited. If these were abolished he would lose the main part of his income, making the regularization of his financial affairs in France imperative.

Madame de Staël remained in Switzerland until June when she left for Saint-Ouen for the summer, taking Auguste with her. Afraid for her safety, her father cautioned her: 'I am always afraid, my dear Minette, that you will talk and stir things up and that an enemy will jump on you.'[35] While in France she continued to petition the Directory to remove Necker's name from the proscribed list and to return his two million livres. Both were delighted when at long last, in July 1798, Necker's name was definitively removed from the list of émigrés. Constant spent the summer between his property at Hérivaux and at Saint-Ouen. Madame de Staël was now living apart from her husband, who had moved to new and more modest premises in the rue de Grenelle, but she corresponded with the new attaché, Brinkman, whom Staël believed had been sent by the King of Sweden to spy on him. Brinkman greatly admired Madame de Staël. Thanks to her friendship with Talleyrand, who had intervened personally with the King, Gustavus Adolphus IV, Staël had been confirmed in his post against the King's better judgement. Sweden needed France's support in the matter of the annexation of Norway and the King had been anxious to accommodate Talleyrand.

Bonaparte sailed for Egypt from Toulon in the month of Floréal (May 1798) with a large expedition duly financed by Swiss gold. Apart from the 40,000 troops, he took with him an important group of Orientalists, scientists and officials, who were to help set up the new colony. Madame de Staël wrote delightedly to her father that Bonaparte had asked for her book *De L'influence des passions sur le bonheur des individus et des nations* to be sent to him in Egypt. 'There you are in glory on the banks of the Nile,' her father replied, teasing her proudly. 'Alexander of Macedon imported philosophers and sophists from all corners of the world to listen to hear them. To save time, the Corsican Alexander, communicates only with the thoughts of Madame de Staël.'[36]

For all her lack of success with Bonaparte, Madame de Staël still saw him as a heroic figure. He was the 'intrepid warrior, the deepest thinker, the most extraordinary genius ever seen', as she wrote in a treatise which she had been working on for most of that year. *Des circonstances actuelles qui peuvent terminer la Révolution, et des principes qui doivent fonder la République en France* (On the Present Circumstances for ending the French Revolution and the Principles on which the Republic in France should be established) was to remain unpublished in her lifetime although it undoubtedly strengthened her reputation as a major political thinker. It was simply too dangerous to publish at a time when either the royalists or the Jacobins, both of whom she had attacked strongly in this work, might return.[37] It would have also have harmed Constant's political ambitions. In this important work of political theory, her main objective was to put an end to the Revolution, to stress the importance of legality, to defend the freedom of the press and of expression generally, and to oppose militarism. In short, to bring to an end the series of coups and arbitrary measures by which the Directory governed, as well as the royalist insurrections which flared up periodically in the provinces. Constant, now a French citizen, was trying, with Madame de Staël's help, to get himself elected as Deputy for Geneva. When a royalist, Boulay de la Meurthe, published a pamphlet in favour of a Bourbon restoration, extolling the virtues of the English Restoration of 1660, Constant at once replied with *Des suites de la contre-révolution de 1660 en Angleterre* (On the Consequences of the Counter-Revolution of 1660 in England), in which he pointed out that reprisals in France would be far worse than those which had followed in England.

In Egypt on 1 August 1798, the French fleet, at anchor in Aboukir Bay, was destroyed by the British fleet under Nelson's command. Undeterred that the Armée de l'Orient was now cut off, Bonaparte marched on Cairo. With his army soon decimated by hunger, thirst and plague, Bonaparte dispatched nothing but good news, which in any case took six months to reach the Directory. The ill-fated expedition to Egypt did have the undesired result, feared by the Directory, of bringing Turkey into the second coalition of 1799, as well as her ally Russia, uniting them with Great Britain and soon also with Austria.

Rocked by the threat of coups from both right and left, and with a large part of the army cut off in Egypt and part of her navy destroyed, France was once again threatened with invasion by the second coalition. At home, military defeats, economic difficulties and enforced conscription had also again raised the spectre of a Jacobin resurgence in the Council of the Five Hundred, which had been firmly Republican since the purge of Fructidor. Moderates feared a return of the Terror, while fresh royalist revolts broke out in Brittany and in the south-west. These threats were largely spent forces; the longing for stability was too great, but disgust with the corrupt and feeble Directory was widespread and many believed that the time was ripe for a dictatorship. In Egypt Bonaparte feared only one thing: that he might miss his chance. Abandoning his starving and plague-ridden army, he returned to France. By the time he disembarked at Fréjus, at the beginning of October 1799, the military defeats of the summer had been reversed. Masséna had successfully averted the threat of invasion by defeating the Russians in Switzerland at the Battle of Zurich. The immediate crisis was over.

Sieyès had replaced Reubell as Director in May 1799. For ten years he had bided his time to shape a Constitution. To Fouché, who thanks to him was now Minister of Police, he declared as he plotted to oust at least three of the Directors, that two things were needed: a head and a sword. He would be the head and as for the sword, who but Bonaparte? Bonaparte would be put in charge of interior security and would help him to consolidate power. Sieyès's great mistake was to think that Bonaparte would then quietly retire.

Madame de Staël spent the first four months of 1799 at Coppet, returning to Paris and then Saint-Ouen with Auguste at the end of April. He was now eight, an exceptionally clever and studious little boy whom, having failed to find a good tutor, she was teaching herself. Her other two children, Albert who showed no interest in his books, and the baby Albertine were left at Coppet with her father. 'My dear Minette, I parted from you with great pain, and you did not look up at the three windows to which I had gone consecutively so as to see your dear little face one more time. I am following you on your journey with the most tender affection. You said so many sweet and feeling things to me on the eve and on the day of your departure that I live for them.'[38]

Constant, who had failed to be elected for the district of Geneva in the April elections, had returned to Paris some two months earlier. Madame de Staël remained in Paris for a week in May in a fever of anxiety over Mathieu de Montmorency, who had almost died before she moved to Saint-Ouen. A fervent Catholic, Mathieu had all but starved himself to death during Lent. 'I've been here a week, unable to think because of the danger Mathieu was in,' she wrote to a friend from Saint-Ouen a month later. 'He is fine now and staying with me. But rigorous fasting might bring him to the same point every year. One can't get through to him; his opinions are as difficult to change as a physical obstacle. What a misfortune it is to love him!'[39]

Staël's financial affairs were also causing her concern. His situation was now extremely precarious. He had written to her at the end of the year to tell her that he was sure that he would be recalled: 'When one has done everything possible but fate is against one, one must accept the situation – which is what I intend to do.' He would go to Sweden, but not before his debt had been paid.[40] This was a not so subtle hint that he was once again up to his ears in debt. In April he was sent on indefinite leave by the Swedish government and Brinkman took over as chargé d'affaires. Once more Necker was obliged to provide the means for Staël's return to Sweden. Staël took the money but refused to leave Paris.

After spending the summer at Coppet with her father, Madame de Staël returned to Paris on the evening of 18 Brumaire (9 November 1799). Constant met her on the outskirts of the city. Bonaparte's name was now on everyone's lips and it was from the postilions that Madame de Staël first heard rumours of an impending coup.

Bonaparte and Talleyrand, who had nothing but contempt for Sieyès, had seen the advantage in a temporary alliance with him. They had not been idle in the five weeks since Bonaparte's return in October. With Fouché's help, rumours of a Jacobin plot had been spread far and wide and all sides were prepared for the supposed coup. When Madame de Staël arrived in Paris, Sieyès and Ducos, the two Directors in the plot, had resigned. Barras had been made an offer he couldn't refuse. Pocketing a large bribe, he agreed to go and was dispatched to his country estate, his carriage actually passing hers on his way out. The remaining two Directors who had been unwilling to co-operate were arrested. Afraid to remain in the capital in case of a Jacobin victory, Madame de Staël was none the less obliged to do so. The legislative councils had been moved to St Cloud that day, allegedly to protect the Deputies from a terrorist conspiracy, and from the Paris mob. Taking several of Madame de Staël's grooms, Constant left for St Cloud at once. They had agreed that he would send one back to her every hour with news of events as they unfolded.

Bonaparte had not acquitted himself well during his address to the Council. Unused to public speaking, he had, as Madame de Staël fancied, tried to say to the Council of Ancients: 'I am the God of War and of fortune, follow me', but had succeeded merely in sounding pompous and arrogant. What he had really wanted to say to them, thought Madame de Staël, was: 'You are miserable nonentities, and I will have you all shot if you disobey me.' Entering the chamber, flanked by four grenadiers, he harangued the Deputies. They were not yet disposed to put up with such dictatorial behaviour. Amid wild scenes and threats of physical violence, they rose up and denounced him. Unnerved by cries of '*hors la loi*' (that he be outlawed) 'down with the dictator', and 'down with Cromwell' from the Jacobin delegates, some of whom tried to attack him physically, Bonaparte fled from the chamber. He was saved by the presence of mind of his brother Lucien, who, as Chairman of the Five Hundred, kept this head, refusing to put the motion to outlaw him to the vote. Leaving the chamber briefly he sent in the grenadiers assembled outside to protect their general. Their appearance (led by Murat) in the Orangery, where the session was being held, frightened the Deputies, causing a headlong rush into the garden where they scattered, their senatorial togas flapping like so many crows. In the early hours of the next day some fifty Deputies and a few *Anciens,* who had been rounded up to give the proceedings some semblance of legality, recognized three provisional consuls: Bonaparte, Sieyès and Roger Ducos.

In Paris, Madame de Staël once again prepared to flee when it looked as if the Jacobins might gain the upper hand, as she received her hourly messages from Constant. When she heard that Bonaparte had carried the day, however, she knew that she was safe, later recalling that she had cried: 'not for liberty, it had never existed in France, but for the hope of liberty, without which this country would only suffer shame and misfortune'.[41] Perhaps she was being wise after the event, if her father's reply to her letter, dated 25 Brumaire, is accurate. 'I have received, my dear Minette your much longed for letter of the 20th [the day after the coup]. You have painted the joy of Paris and your own approval of the power and glory of your hero [Bonaparte] in bright colours. I hope and pray that the satisfaction you all share will be justified, and I think like you, that Sieyès, finding no further obstacles to his genius, will produce a faultless constitution, perhaps a perfect one as you say.'[42] On the other hand, it is also true that throughout the period of Bonaparte's rise to power, Necker, to protect his daughter, invariably wrote flattering things about Bonaparte in his letters to her, making it seem as if he was agreeing with her own opinions for good measure.

Sieyès' constitution, by removing popular sovereignty, had paved the way for Bonaparte's dictatorship. The coup of 19 Brumaire put an end to the Directory, but it also ended France's first attempt at representative government.

Chapter 15

The First Consul

'It is not a matter of what I want, but what I think.'
Madame de Staël to Joseph Bonaparte[1]

IN THE REMAINING few weeks of the year, and of the century after Brumaire, a drafting committee met daily in Bonaparte's offices to work on a new constitution. Madame de Staël, having overseen the publication of an extract from her father's latest work, *L'Examen de la constitution de l'an III*, for which she had written the preface, was in the thick of things again. Her salon in the rue de Grenelle was now the central political meeting place for the Bonapartist elite.

Drafted by Sieyès but driven by Bonaparte, the Constitution of the Year VIII was presented on Christmas day, 1799. There were to be no elections. The Constitution provided for three Consuls. There were to be four separate assemblies: the Senate, whose sixty Senators were to be nominated by the three Consuls; the Council of State, whose councillors were to be nominated by the First Consul; the Legislative Assembly; and the Tribunate, whose members were to be appointed by the Senate. It was Bonaparte who had proposed that a First Consul holding full executive powers should be appointed for ten years. He would choose the other two (thereby ensuring that they were nothing more than rubber stamps). Sieyès, believing that he would be First Consul, agreed but was quickly outmanoeuvred by Bonaparte. On that last Christmas eve of the eighteenth century, by accepting Sieyès', Constitution and Bonaparte's proposal for a First Consul, the members of the Commission made sure that henceforth executive power would be in Bonaparte's hands. 'Citizens,' Bonaparte declared even before the plebiscite confirming the new Constitution had taken place in February, 'the Revolution is finished.' And so, Sieyès, who ten years before had been one of the godfathers of the Revolution, now dug its grave. He was pensioned off with a large estate soon afterwards. It was exactly ten years since the end of the absolute monarchy, but very few suspected as yet that a dictatorship had begun. Necker, however, had no doubts. On 28 Brumaire, he wrote to his daughter: 'I have your note of the 22nd with your account of the first days. This represents a complete change of scene. There will be a simulacrum of a Republic, but all power will be in the hands of the General.'[2] What he would do with that power was so far an unknown, perhaps even to Bonaparte himself. Ironically, what made Bonaparte so acceptable to all sides was that he promised peace. Whatever Bonaparte's intentions, Necker was worried about the new arrangements and even more concerned that his letters might fall into the wrong hands. 'In any case if the Constitution depends on one person, his death would lead to any number of risks,' he wrote, urging his daughter to 'burn my letter, and take care of your papers more than ever, with this new master over your head.'[3] Unhappily for posterity, for once Madame de Staël took her father's warning seriously. The few letters that have come down to us from this momentous time are uncharacteristically reserved. Necker must have destroyed any that she wrote to him. None the less she continued to lobby for Constant's nomination to the Tribunate as well as to concern herself on behalf of her friends. Talleyrand was once more Minister for Foreign Affairs; Fouché, ex-abbot, ex-Jacobin, and ex-organizer of massacres, was Minister of Police. The journalist and publicist Roederer had just been appointed President for Internal Matters at the Council of State.

The First Consul had made it clear that he was against large assemblies and would treat any opponents as enemies of the state. The government had already decided that discussions in the Tribunate, which met for the first time on 1 January 1800, were to be subjected to a rigid time limit. Constant, fully supported by Madame de Staël, was among those who believed such arbitrary measures to be unacceptable. Together with like-minded tribunes he and his friends attempted to form an opposition on the English model.[4]

On 4 January, on the eve of his maiden speech at the Tribunate, Constant took Madame de Staël aside in her salon, packed with the ruling elite, among them Lucien Bonaparte, Roederer and Talleyrand. 'Your salon is crowded with all the people whose company you love,' he whispered. 'If I make the speech tomorrow, which will put me in the ranks of the opposition, it will be deserted; think about it.' As he well

Madame de Staël's father, Jacques Necker, at the height of his power

Her mother Suzanne Necker, who ruled over one of the last important pre-revolutionary salons in Paris

A portrait of the fourteen-year-old Germaine Necker, the future Madame de Staël, as she would have looked attending her mother's salon

The Château de Coppet, Madame de Staël's house on the shores of lake Geneva

Madame de Staël's bedroom at Coppet. A portrait of Madame Récamier hangs on the wal

Madame de Staël's eldest son, Auguste de Staël, with Coppet in the background

Her second son Albert de Staël, killed in a duel at the age of 21

Her daughter Albertine, duchesse de Broglie

Her husband, Baron Eric Magnus
Staël Holstein, Swedish ambassad
to the court of Louis XVI, and
chamberlain to the Queen of Swed

Charles Maurice de Talleyrand-Périgord

Benjamin Constant

Madame Récamier

A.W. Schlegel, friend and literary collaborator whom Madame de Staël brought with her from Germany and who remained with her until her death

The Emperor Napoleon in full Imperial splendour

Madame de Staël with her daughter Albertine

Madame de Staël as 'Corinne'

Madame de Staël's second husba
John Rocca, in Hussar uniform w
his horse Sultan

The Duke of Wellington, one of the last of Madame de Staël's friends to visit her before she died

knew and she herself admitted, love of political and social life was her great weakness: 'the spectre of boredom has pursued me all my life'. Bonaparte was aware of this too and would know how to play on it. Her father had warned her repeatedly: 'In your conduct never lose sight of the fact that your taste for Paris, very natural at your age, and for one with your mind, makes you vulnerable. It is around that truth that you must make your decisions.'[5] But, to her great credit, it was not a compromise Madame de Staël would ever be prepared to make once Bonaparte's true intentions became clear. 'One must be true to one's convictions', she whispered back to Constant.

The next day at the Tribunate, as he had warned her he would, Constant voiced his concerns at the 'exaggerated and restless impatience of the First Consul'. He accused the government of 'rushing through proposals on the wing, in the hope that we shall be unable to catch them', depriving the speakers of any chance 'to plead the people's cause'. He ended by insisting that the Tribunate be accorded 'that essential independence without which there would be nothing but servitude and silence, a silence which would be heard by the whole of Europe'. Servitude and silence was precisely what Bonaparte wanted. Nor did he care who knew it. 'The Tribunate has some twelve or fifteen metaphysicians who should be drowned,' he raged. 'Those intellectuals are like vermin in my clothes; I will shake them off.'[6]

By five o'clock that afternoon Madame de Staël had received no fewer than ten letters regretting that their senders could not attend her dinner. She realized that Constant had been right.[7] The First Consul had not bothered to hide his anger. Next day the official newspaper, *Le Moniteur*, reproved Constant for 'self-advertisement' and for courting popularity. In the days that followed, a campaign of vilification of them both was launched in both the right- and the left-wing press. Constant's nomination to the Tribunate was declared unconstitutional by the Jacobin *Journal des hommes libres*. The same newssheet, in a vicious open letter to Madame de Staël, 'on behalf of the French people', declared: 'It is not your fault that you are ugly, but it is your fault that you are an intriguer. Correct this quickly, for your reign is over. You know the way to Switzerland. Make a journey there if you wish no harm to come to you . . . and take your Benjamin. Let him practise his talents in the Swiss Senate.' The royalist press was no kinder, *L'Ange Gabriel* writing: 'She writes on metaphysics which she does not understand, on morality which she does not practise; on the virtues of her sex which she lacks.'[8]

Astonished by the bitterness of the attack, but even more deeply hurt that her friend Roederer had been involved, Madame de Staël wrote to ask him why all this fury had been unleashed against her, simply because her friend [Constant] had pronounced an independent view on a mere regulation? While this was perhaps a little disingenuous, she was genuinely puzzled that Roederer should abandon her. 'I am more astonished, more confounded than I have ever been in my life,' she wrote. 'I need to talk to you. You had my friendship in the hour of misfortune [after Fructidor when she had defended and supported Roederer who had been in danger] . . . I had counted on you to defend me and yet I learned that it was from you that Bonaparte heard what was supposedly said at my house . . . Is such intolerance really part of your character? Does it accord with your enlightened views? Wake up and come and see me. Have I ceased to be the one who cared for you and defended you over two years? Was Benjamin not the first of Sieyès' friends to bring you closer to him? Please give me an hour of your time, at my house or yours. It is only by meeting that we might understand one another.'[9]

Although she was used to vilification in the press, Madame de Staël was not yet used to betrayal by her friends. If Roederer's cowardice surprised and upset her, what really hurt her was that Talleyrand turned his back on her. He had been one of her greatest friends since her youth, perhaps even her lover, someone with whom she had shared political hopes, intellectual and social pleasures, and the bitterness of exile. Her house and her purse had always been open to him. He owed his return to France and to power to her. 'I rendered M. de Talleyrand some very important services,' she recalled later in *Ten Years of Exile*, 'but what is much more important than any service I might have done him was the most sincere friendship I had for him. For ten years he spent his life in my house. I brought him back from America and persuaded Barras to save him from his creditors by making him a minister. I have several letters from him in which he assured me that he owed me more than his existence. It was he who first showed through his conduct, that to please the First Consul, I must be avoided. Afraid of being thought my friend because of our former social relations, he spoke of me to the First Consul in a way which made a strong impression on him. He did me the honour and the wrong of representing me to Bonaparte as a woman with an all-powerful intelligence, repeating ceaselessly that I was irresistible . . . I have never seen M. de Talleyrand since that time.'[10]

As soon as the First Consul's displeasure with Madame de Staël and with Constant became known, three quarters of her salon simply vanished. Even Joseph Bonaparte, who was to remain a friend, having been publicly reproved for his friendship with her by his brother, was persuaded not to see her for three weeks. But, having shown his fist, Bonaparte was also keen to placate all opposition. He always believed that men were ruled by two things: fear and self-interest. Jobs, favours and bribes were used liberally to bring round those he needed. He knew that Madame de Staël would be a formidable opponent. With his own position still unstable, Bonaparte understood and feared her influence. While she had supported the coup of Brumaire as the lesser evil, she and Constant spoke out constantly about the need to check any dictatorial tendencies in the new government. Madame de Staël's salon, where the entire governing elite gathered, where ideas were freely discussed, where humour and wit reigned, was subversive by its very nature. Although Bonaparte had a strong personal antipathy for her, he had no wish to make her an enemy. He sent his brother Joseph as an emissary. 'My brother complains of you,' Joseph told her, 'Why does Madame de Staël not support my government? What does she want? Is it the repayment of her father's deposit? I will order it to be repaid. Is it permission to remain in Paris? I will allow it. What is it that she wants?' 'Dear God!' Madame de Staël had replied, 'It is not a question of what I want, but what I think.'[11]

In these early days of the Consulate, as she herself admitted, if Bonaparte had offered her friendship, she would have accepted it gladly. But friendship on her terms. To her this meant equality, generosity, tolerance, loyalty, liberty, mutual admiration and respect. Bonaparte certainly wanted loyalty, by which he understood obedience and silence. Madame de Staël was constitutionally incapable of either. Powerful, utterly controlling in all things, Bonaparte was also insecure, touchy and proud. To him criticism equalled treason. He demanded subservience, publicly humiliating even his close friends and family to ensure that he had it.

Soon after Constant's maiden speech, Madame de Staël was requested to call on the Minister of Police, Fouché. He told her that the First Consul believed her to have been responsible for stirring up

Benjamin Constant. Fouché was therefore advising her to leave the capital, at least for a while. 'Fouché', she wrote later, 'already knew perfectly well that there would be no question of principles under the man he wished to serve, and had made his arrangements accordingly . . . His previous conduct [during the Terror he had been in charge of the massacres in Lyon] would in any case not have suggested that he was likely to adopt a moral stance; indeed he often spoke of virtue as of an old maid's tale.' But he was an able politician who saw that it was wise to do only as much harm as was necessary to achieve his aims. He therefore sometimes chose to do good because it was sensible, where another might have followed his conscience.'[12]

Prompted by several letters of love and support from her father, who repeatedly urged her to be discreet, Madame de Staël removed herself to Saint-Ouen on 15 January 1800. There she remained for almost a month, visited only by Mathieu de Montmorency, Constant, and her women friends, while she worked on the final proofs of her book *De la littérature*. Social ostracism and Talleyrand's betrayal had deeply upset and depressed her. As always, she turned to her father. Worried about her health and sad that he was far away, he wrote at once to comfort her: 'Dear and sweet friend, the melancholy which is so clear in your letter of 12 Nivôse, which has just reached me, makes me write again today . . . My dearest Minette, I should like to make you happy with all my might. I think I know what is going on in your soul, and I regret my absence from your side as your confidant even more than the loss of the pleasures of your imagination and of your mind.'[13]

Madame de Staël knew that if she was to live in Paris she must somehow mend her bridges with Bonaparte. Convinced of the power of reason, she set about energetically to try and see him, only to be rebuffed at every turn. Hearing that Talleyrand was giving a grand ball in honour of the First Consul and his wife on 25 February, and aware that her presence there would restore her to society, Madame de Staël wrote 'in the name of their former friendship' to ask him if she might attend. 'In the name of our former friendship I beg you not to come,' Talleyrand replied. When she learned that Madame de Montesson was to give a ball in honour of the newly married Murats – Caroline Murat was Bonaparte's sister – to be attended by the First Consul and his wife, Madame de Staël begged an invitation through Mathieu. Madame de Montesson, an old friend of the Neckers, was one of the arbiters of taste. An invitation to her parties was highly prized and would help to re-establish Madame de Staël in society. Madame de Montesson agreed, perhaps because she knew that Bonaparte himself would not be there after all. 'When poor Madame de Staël appeared in Madame de Montesson's salon, in a heavy dress of slate-coloured satin, she was shunned by everyone and left alone in a corner as if she was suffering from the plague,' Madame de Chastenay recalled in her memoirs.[14]

Madame de Staël did not forget that evening either. 'Of all the people I knew there, apart from the hostess, only Madame de Custine [formerly Delphine de Sabran] curtseyed to me. Since she had braved death because of her generosity, that quality was as natural to her in little things as it was in important ones. Everyone else turned their back on me, looking at Madame Bonaparte . . . [who] seeing my situation treated me courteously, and gradually people came up to me.' Madame de Staël later used this scene in her novel *Delphine*, to whose eponymous heroine she gave Madame de Custine's name, in tribute to her sensitivity and courage.[15]

In spite of his growing, though still precarious power, Madame de Staël remained a thorn in Bonaparte's flesh. It was curious that among his many important preoccupations he should pay such close attention to her. The very thought of her irritated and offended him. Powerful he might be, but he had remained a provincial southerner, with vendetta strongly rooted in his psychology and with Latin notions of a woman's virtue and role in life. Not only was Madame de Staël intractable and, as he thought, ugly, but she lived openly with her lover according to the habits of the *ancien régime*, which made Bonaparte profoundly uneasy. In spite of his wife Josephine's adultery since her marriage to him and her racy past, or perhaps because of it, he was determined to clean up public morals and restore family values, at any rate for women. He let it be known that transparent gauze dresses and bared bosoms were out. Women needed to be brought under control. 'We need the notion of obedience, in Paris especially, where women think they have the right to do as they like,' he said, banning some of Josephine's more scandalous friends from the Tuileries where, with an eye to the future, he had already taken up residence. His civil code, the Code Napoleon, the most permanent of his accomplishments, clearly reflected his own views on women and greatly strengthened the authority of the husband and father, depriving illegitimate children of their heritage unless they had been legally recognized. 'A wife must promise obedience and fidelity in marriage' states one of the articles of the Code, under which women lost even those freedoms and property rights they had enjoyed under the *ancien régime*, although divorce was retained.

Madame de Staël who, if she had ever entertained such ideas, had long since abandoned them, now had to face, yet again, serious problems with her own husband's affairs. Soon after her return to Paris, on the eve of the Brumaire coup, Staël, supposedly returning to Sweden, came back to Paris. He had spent the money given to him by Necker for that purpose on a prolonged stay in the Hague where he had incurred further huge gambling debts. There was now no question of them living together. Staël moved out of the rue de Grenelle and took a small apartment on the Place de la Concorde, but he was jobless, penniless and in poor health. Brinkman continued as chargé until February 1800, when diplomatic relations between Sweden and France were once again broken off.

At the end of April 1800, Madame de Staël published her book, *De la littérature considérée dans ses rapports avec les institutions sociales* (On literature considered in its relations with social institutions). The timing, at the crossover from the eighteenth to the nineteenth century, could not have been more apt artistically. Deeply rooted in the values of the Enlightenment, Madame de Staël sought to establish the rules for a new literature, suited to a post-revolutionary society. In the early dawn of Romanticism, of which she was a pioneer, she also remained a child of the Enlightenment. She was never going to choose between them; to her they were the two halves, the indispensable balance, the mind and the heart of liberal idealism. This was always, and would forever remain, her great theme. Well before her journey to Germany and her contact with German Romantic philosophy, she threw the first bridge between the Enlightenment and what would soon be known as the Romantic Movement. In this original and influential work, Madame de Staël's main theme was progress and perfectibility. Looking down the centuries, she wrote in her introduction: 'There is a fundamental idea which I never lose sight of; it is the perfectibility of the human race. I do not think that this major undertaking of moral life has ever been abandoned. In times of enlightenment or in periods of darkness, the gradual march forward of the human spirit has never been interrupted.'[17]

Madame de Staël understood literature to include philosophy, history, social and political writing. Her book was therefore as much about politics as it was about literature. Stressing the intimate links between literature and society, she drew on examples from Greek and Latin, English, French, Italian, Spanish and German literature up to her own time to trace the development of philosophy from the Greeks and Romans through the barbarian invasions to the Middle Ages, which she was far from seeing as 'the dark ages' of contemporary belief. The Renaissance, she maintained, could only have been built on the foundations of the considerable intellectual progress made in the millennium which had preceded it. She discussed the effects of scientific advance on thought. Newton had triggered the Enlightenment: 'Scientific progress makes ethical progress essential, since when we increase men's power [over nature] we must also strengthen the brake which prevents them from abusing that power.'[18] Against the current of her time, she stated a preference for Latin over Greek literature, believing that it marked progress in thought. She saw Romans as much closer to her own times. This was to bring the anger of many distinguished classicists on her head.

While acknowledging her debt to Montesquieu, Rousseau, Voltaire and other Encyclopaedists, she strongly rejected the materialism of the eighteenth century. Like her parents, her belief in progress went hand in hand with a conviction that religion was an indispensable moral guide, support and source of happiness for the individual and for society. But she favoured Protestantism rather than the Roman Catholic religion, believing that of the two Protestantism was least likely to become an instrument of temporal power. She saw social and political progress in northern Europe as intimately linked with the Protestant movement.

By the same token, Madame de Staël was instinctively drawn much more to the literature of northern Europe, with its misty, melancholy, yearning Christian sensitivities than to the sunlit clarity, sensuality and love of pleasure of the pagan Mediterranean south. Her studies broke new ground in the field of comparative literature, indeed she can be said to have invented it. Like Montesquieu, she believed that the natural inclination of northerners towards melancholy made them more reflective, and therefore more apt for social and political progress. 'Melancholy poetry is closest to philosophy,' she wrote. 'Men's characters and destinies move forward much more as a result of sadness than through any other disposition of the spirit . . . The northern imagination tends towards the future, towards another world, tired of their destiny their souls look beyond the confines of their own land.'[19] Northern people have also always respected women, a concept that was unknown in the south. In northern countries they enjoyed independence, elsewhere they were condemned to slavery. This is a principal reason for the finer sensibility of northern literature.[20]

De la littérature was an immediate success, going into two or three reprints before the publication at the end of that year of a second edition, which she revised, corrected and augmented in the light of the furore that the book caused. A generation later, Saint-Beuve, who admired Madame de Staël – 'that good and cordial genius' – unreservedly gave a detailed account of the debates which followed in the press. In his view, 'there was in her writings, in her conversation, in her entire person, a salutary, improving sensibility, which was communicated to all who heard her, which is rediscovered and survives for all who read her'.[21]

If the timing of the book had been ideal in artistic terms, politically it was disastrous. Her clearly stated liberal values were bound to offend all absolutists: Jacobins and monarchists, Catholics and atheists. Underlying their various reactions was a strong and prevalent misogyny. Exhausted by the Revolution, French society as a whole was hostile to ideologies and philosophies. Those on the right believed that the fall of the monarchy and the suppression of the Catholic Church was the principal cause of all present ills. Atheists like Fauriel reproached her for supporting religion; conservative Catholics, such as the writer Fontanes, strongly attacked her for favouring Protestantism but also for her belief in perfectibility, condemning her above all as a woman who had presumed too much. Madame de Staël's wish to decouple French literature from the straitjacket of classicism, her refusal to worship Louis XIV, the great Sun King, who had presided over the golden age of the *grand siècle*, brought down the fury and ridicule of several angry conservatives on her head. Fontanes, in particular, picked her work to pieces, pointing to her occasional lapses of knowledge of the Greeks (inevitable in a work of this scope) and to her criticism of the literary style of the 'golden age', thereby winning the approval of the First Consul, who very much approved of the Sun King and was proposing to be the next one. In the second edition of *De la littérature*, published six months later, Madame de Staël made a renewed plea for freedom of style and originality. In response to Fontanes's points on classical literary style she wrote: 'These expressions so familiar to us, are like the habitués of one's house. One allows them to pass, and asks nothing of them. But there can be no writer who is both eloquent and thinking, whose style will not contain expressions which shock those reading them for the first time.' This brought out the heavy artillery: 'All good writers agree that the form of our language was fixed and determined by the great writers of the last century and the one before' thundered an article in the *Journal des Débats*.[22] But Madame de Staël was unrepentant.

The publication of her book had anticipated by a year that of Chateaubriand's *Le Génie du Christianisme* (The Genius of Christianity). Perhaps a little annoyed that she had been the first to discuss the civilizing effects of Christianity, the young Chateaubriand, in an open letter to his friend Fontanes published in the journal *Mercure de France* later that year, wrote: 'Madame de Staël has attributed to philosophy what I attribute to religion . . . You know that my particular weakness is to see Jesus Christ in everything, whereas Madame de Staël sees perfectibility. . . . Sometimes Madame de Staël seems to be a Christian, but a moment later, philosophy gets the upper hand. Sometimes, inspired by a natural sensibility, she allows her soul to escape but all at once reason awakes and contradicts the movements of the heart.'[23] He was right. While she was religious, Madame de Staël was not mystical. She was to be profoundly sceptical about German metaphysics, which was to divide her from the German Romantics. Nor was she given to looking back to some golden past. The difference between her and Chateaubriand, who was to become a friend, was that of completely dissimilar temperaments. Where he took refuge in the past and feared the future, Madame de Staël looked ahead with hope, interest and optimism.

No matter what people thought of the author, the generally accepted brilliance and the critical success of her book had brought Madame de Staël back into favour. Once again her salon overflowed with old friends, politicians and members of the diplomatic corps. Lucien and Joseph Bonaparte were frequent visitors. Much as she still hoped to placate their brother, the First Consul was not among her admirers. 'There was not a word about Bonaparte in my book on literature, while the most liberal feelings were, I think, expressed with force,' she wrote.[24] This was the trouble in a nutshell. He would have preferred to have been mentioned constantly and to hear no liberal opinions. Bonaparte had tried to read the book 'for at least a quarter of an hour' he confessed to his brother Lucien. 'The devil take me if I could make any sense of it: not the words, there were enough of those, and big words at that; but in spite of concentrating all my faculties, I failed to discover a meaning in any one of those ideas which are supposed to be so profound.'[25] The truth was that he understood them only too well. With this book Madame de Staël, who was above all a moralist and a political and social thinker, had nailed her colours to the mast. She made it unequivocally clear that for her literature was not mere art, but thought expressed in writing. Passion, enthusiasm and understanding were essential in literature because they stimulated these qualities in the reader. Thus literature became a means to a moral and social end, an instrument of perfectibility, a means of cultivating reason and feeling, a civilizing force which would free mankind from ignorance and superstition and so from wrongdoing. Such views could not but annoy and cause disquiet to a man whose ruling passion was power. He saw the book, rightly, as a declaration of war.

Her father remained anxious about her, and wrote repeatedly, begging her to return to Coppet, urging her to remain calm and keep out of trouble. In case his letters fell into the wrong hands, he took good care to praise Bonaparte, to whom he invariably refers as 'your hero' in all his letters. He had intended to write to Bonaparte himself, but hearing that he was about to leave for Italy and would be in Switzerland in early May resolved to try and see him personally to plead his daughter's case.

Madame de Staël's salon was now frequently graced by the beautiful, young Madame Récamier, who was to remain a true friend for the rest of Madame de Staël's life. Some ten years younger than her, the lovely Juliette, born in Lyons, came to Paris and was married to Récamier at the age of fifteen. Their marriage, though very happy, was unconsummated. Jacques Récamier, almost thirty years his wife's senior, always seemed to be an indulgent father to her rather than a husband. It was rumoured that Juliette was in fact his illegitimate daughter and that he had married her during the Revolution in order to be able to leave her his enormous fortune, should the guillotine have claimed him too. Madame Récamier was exceptionally close to her beautiful and socially ambitious mother, Madame Bernard, who was reputed to have a good head for business and who had ensured that her daughter was well educated. Apart from her beauty, her grace, her natural good taste and sympathetic tact, Madame Récamier had a quick intelligence and was very musical. Although all men, including the First Consul, found her irresistible, she seems to have had a genuine talent for friendship and was universally liked and admired by everyone who knew her. 'To be beloved, was the history of Madame Récamier. Beloved by all in her youth, for her astonishing beauty – beloved for her gentleness, her inexhaustible kindness, for the charm of a character which was reflected in her sweet face, beloved for the tender and sympathetic friendship which she awarded with an exquisite tact and discrimination of heart' was how one friend remembered her.[26] Brought up to consider style and dress as being of the utmost importance, Juliette's exhibitionism and narcissism seem to have been her only faults. Always dressed in white and wearing the various pearls from her magnificent collection as her only adornment, she was followed by crowds and mobbed like a modern film star.

Madame de Staël had met her the previous summer when she sold her father's house in the rue du Mont-Blanc (now the Chaussée d'Antin) to Jacques Récamier, who wanted a setting worthy of his beautiful wife and his expanding fortune. Madame Récamier described that first meeting in her memoirs: 'One day, a day that marks an epoch in my life, M. Récamier arrived at Clichy with a lady whom he did not introduce to me by name, leaving her with me in the salon . . . The lady had come about the sale of the house. She was oddly dressed. She wore a morning gown and a little dress hat, trimmed with flowers. I took her for a foreigner. I was struck by the beauty of her eyes and of her expression. I was not sure of my feelings but I believe that I was more concerned at finding out or guessing who she might be than of addressing the usual commonplaces to her, when she said that she was truly delighted to make my acquaintance, that her father, M. Necker . . . – at these words I recognized Madame de Staël.'

Madame Récamier had just been reading Madame de Staël's *Letters on Rousseau*. 'I was conscious at once of her genuineness and her superiority. For her part, she fixed her splendid eyes on me, but with a friendly scrutiny and complimented me on my appearance in a way that might have seemed too direct and exaggerated had it not seemed to have escaped her unconsciously, giving her praise an irresistible fascination . . .'[27]

Benjamin Constant, who had been in love with both women, was to write of the close friendship between them: 'Nothing could have been more charming than Madame de Staël's conversations with her young friend. The speed with which the one was able to express a thousand new thoughts, the speed with which the other was able to grasp and judge them; there was that strong male intelligence which unveiled everything, and the delicate feminine one which understood everything; all this was united in a way impossible to describe if one had not had the happiness of witnessing it for oneself.'[28]

Bonaparte had not wasted his time after Brumaire (November 1799), consolidating his position in power by a mixture of personal charisma, bribery and propaganda. He had let it be understood that he wanted everyone's support and that they would be rewarded and promoted providing they were willing to abandon their principles in his service. A new administrative structure for France was now being put in place. France was still at war with Austria, Russia, England and the United States, but in response to the ardent wish of all the French a peace offensive was launched, with personal letters from the First Consul to George III and to the Emperor of Austria. The rebels in the Vendée were pacified by a mixture of force and clemency. For all that, Bonaparte's position was still precarious. Most people still believed that his so-called republic was a temporary arrangement to be replaced by a constitutional monarchy. France's military situation at the beginning of the new century was even less promising. The army of Italy, besieged by the Austrians, was starving near Genoa, and its final collapse would be a signal to the Austrians to invade France. Bonaparte knew that a military defeat would be the end of him. 'My power depends on my glory and my glory on my victories,' he told Bourrienne. Leaving General Moreau in command of an offensive on the Rhine, Bonaparte slipped out of France and marched to Italy where he clashed with the Austrians at Marengo on 14 June 1800. By the early afternoon his army was all but routed by the much stronger Austrians. But the arrival of reinforcements under General Desaix at the last moment saved the day, and with it Bonaparte's whole career. Madame de Staël had perfectly understood that Bonaparte had gambled his future on the battle of Marengo: 'I hoped that Bonaparte would be beaten, because it was the only way to put an end to his tyranny, but I did not yet dare admit this desire.'[29] Marengo gave him back Lombardy, saving France from the threat of an Austrian invasion. General Moreau meanwhile, after beating the Austrians at Hohenlinden, advanced through Bavaria, taking Munich, and was to be at the gates of Vienna by the end of the year.

On the way to Italy Bonaparte had dined with Necker in Geneva on 8 May 1800. 'The First Consul and M. Necker had seemed very pleased with each other after their long conversation,' the *Publiciste* reported on 25 May. Bonaparte had made a good impression on her father, Madame de Staël later admitted,[30] but Necker struck Bonaparte as 'a dull and pompous pedant'.[31] He had none the less dined at Coppet the next day with Necker and his brother Louis de Germany, a member of the important Economic Society of Geneva, who had engineered the meeting. Madame de Staël left Paris with her son Albert a day after the departure of the First Consul from the city, but she was unaware of her father's meeting with Bonaparte until her return to Coppet a week or so later. She had stopped on the way to see the La Fayettes. 'Bonaparte was agreeable to my father, and even kind about me in his discussion,' she wrote.[32] In any case he had agreed that Madame de Staël should be allowed to remain in Paris.

The summer passed happily for Madame de Staël. Still a tribune, Constant had come to join her. She was reunited with her adored father and her three children. In spite of her occasional absences, Madame de Staël was a loving mother, taking a much closer interest in her children's intellectual and spiritual development than was usual for the times, terrified when they were ill and proud of their success. After her father's death she admitted to her cousin Albertine: 'I don't know why, but I express much less than I feel to Auguste. There is a kind of maternal reserve which I have always had. One needs to keep a little distance in this relationship. Have I not outlived the very best that there is on earth! Why love so greatly what death will break?' In spite of this, her cousin wrote, she had given a thousand proofs of her maternal feelings. She did not believe in theories when it came to bringing up children. Children needed to be taught and inspired by religion but they needed to live in the real world. 'I presented life as it is to my children', she said, 'and I never tried to fool them.' By the same token, Albertine Necker-de Saussure recalled, 'she never talked down to children nor adopted any affected language with them. In general she got on well with children and they liked her . . . she had a young way of talking; genius always has an element of childishness and freshness. She would observe children with tenderness and curiosity and loved their funny expressions and ideas. She expected children to fit in with the adult world and disliked making them the centre of attention. She was strict, but moderately so and while she explained her reasons to her children she nonetheless expected to be obeyed.'[33]

Her daughter Albertine, closest of Madame de Staël's children to her, wrote to Madame Necker-de Saussure after her mother's death: 'My mother attached great importance to our happiness in our childhood; she entered fully into the woes of our age group. She sometimes had conversations with me when I was twelve as with an equal, and nothing can describe the happiness we felt when we had spent half an hour alone with her. One felt renewed, one stood higher, and this gave one the strength to go forward in all our studies. Her children have always loved her passionately. From the age of five or six we used to argue about whom she loved the most, and her tête à têtes with one of us was a reward which we guarded jealously . . . The development of our minds was such a strong joy for her that no reward could have equalled witnessing the pleasure it gave her . . . She treated our characters with respect and yet we never ceased to respect her, and our respect was always mingled with a sort of fear. While she showed the greatest confidence in us, when she was teaching us, she knew how to impose her will.'[34]

Madame de Staël spent the rest of the summer at Coppet, revising the second edition of her book on literature, which was to be reissued on 14 November, and corresponding with a number of friends, among them Joseph Bonaparte. She longed to be reunited with them, begging for news of Narbonne, who had at last returned to France as a result of her démarches to Fouché. What did he think of her book? How did he and Talleyrand get on?[36] By the autumn, tired of Coppet and suffering from the depression which dogged her all her life, she wrote again to a friend, Gérando: 'You ask whether you will find me happier. I cannot promise you that, for I have come to the conclusion that pain is the usual state of mankind and I live with heartache as others do with a physical ill.'[37]

Madame de Staël was nevertheless fully occupied. That summer of 1800 she was learning German with the help of her children's new tutor, Gerlach; she taught her sons Latin, played music and embarked on a novel. By October she was making plans for her return to Paris for the winter. 'One must choose in life, between boredom and torment,' she wrote to Claude Hochet, (attached to the Council of State, he was a frequent contributor to literary journals and had written an enthusiastic review of Mme. de Staël's book in the *Journal des Débats*), referring as always to the boredom at Coppet, contrasted with the torment of parting from her father. 'But I intend to live quietly this winter, for the arrival of a cousin I love [Albertine Necker-de Saussure] will ensure that I spend all my time at concerts and theatres. I shall be frivolous, although I am making a late start at thirty [she was actually thirty-four] . . . I am continuing with my novel. It will be finished in a year I think. There will be not a word about politics in it although it takes place in the final years of the Revolution.'[38]

Chapter 16

~

The Empress of the Mind

'Advise her not to stand in my way. Or I shall break her, I shall crush her.'[1]

Napoleon to his brothers Joseph and Lucien

Bonaparte had returned to Paris immediately after Marengo, aware that his political future was still uncertain. With his keen eye for publicity, he chose to enter Paris with his battle-stained troops on 14 July 1800, a day when the streets would be full of people for the celebration of the fall of the Bastille. 'One thing which struck my husband and me very forcibly,' Madame de La Tour du Pin recalled, 'was the apathy with which the usually enthusiastic people of Paris heard the news of the battle of Marengo. On the anniversary of 14 July, we went with M. de Poix to walk on the Champs de Mars. After the review of the Garde Nationale and the garrison, a small formation of about one hundred and fifty men marched into the enclosure, all in dirty, torn uniforms, some with an arm in a sling, others with their heads bandaged, but carrying the standards and Austrian flags captured at Marengo. I expected wild and very justifiable cheering. But there was not a single shout and scarcely any sign of rejoicing. We were surprised and indignant . . . and could find no explanation for this apathy.'[2] Her account is very much at odds with Bonaparte's own memoirs and those of his entourage, who only saw and heard explosions of joy and acclamations from the people.

Austria acknowledged defeat at the end of 1800, after Moreau's victory at Hohenlinden. By the terms of the Treaty of Luneville, dictated by Bonaparte and signed in February 1801 by his brother Joseph, France kept the whole of the east bank of the Rhine. Present-day Belgium and Luxembourg, Switzerland, Piedmont, the Cisalpine Republic and Liguria all remained under French control. Most importantly, France was to have a say in the territorial redistribution within the German lands, which was to indemnify the German princes whose territories had been seized on the east bank of the Rhine.

Only Britain now remained and Britain was weakened by a political and economic crisis. Her trade was badly damaged by Napoleon's treaties of Armed Neutrality which barred her ships from the Hanseatic ports. Domestic issues following the Union with Ireland added to the difficulties which brought down Pitt and Grenville's government in March 1801, just as the King, George III, succumbed to one of his periodic bouts of madness. Bonaparte could reasonably have hoped for a Continental coalition which would help him to crush Britain once and for all, when the death 'of apoplexy' of Paul I of Russia on 11 March 1801 (the unstable Tsar had actually been murdered by a group of nobles) upset all his plans. Meanwhile, in Britain, peace with France was considered essential if she were to regain her prosperity.

The Treaty of Amiens, signed in March 1802 and brilliantly negotiated by Talleyrand, was however unaccountably advantageous to France. Bonaparte could have reasonably believed that he had achieved victory with peace if peace had been what he sought. But Madame de Staël later wrote: 'he was undoubtedly resolved on constant war, interspersed with those moments of peace which have always increased his power more than the battles themselves. His military talents would necessarily contribute to his glory, and the natural restlessness of his character, independently from his need to dominate, is such that he could not be content with a mere thirty million people to govern and make happy.' She recalled his restlessness: 'The symptoms of his constant agitation are noticeable in all his gestures, in all his habits. While his face is a mask of imperturbable coldness, he takes snuff or swallows mint pastilles constantly. His armchair at the Council needs to be changed every three months, because he cuts it to shreds with constant stabs of his penknife.'[3] Madame de Staël's description of Bonaparte's nervous habits was accurate, but she had some of her own. Although she had none of Bonaparte's coldness, they shared the dynamic energy, the high intelligence and the fertile imagination which sought an outlet in constant activity, and which was expressed in ceaseless nervous fidgeting when forced to be still. Where the First Consul wrecked the furniture, Madame de Staël was never seen without a small tube of paper or a small twig, cut for her daily by her servants, which she twiddled constantly in her fingers.

In December 1800, accompanied by her eldest son Auguste, and for part of the way by his German tutor Gerlach, a sensitive young man who fancied himself in love with her, Madame de Staël once again left for Paris. Her younger children, Albert and Albertine, remained with their grandfather.

In her absence, Constant had fallen violently in love with Anna Lindsay, even proposing marriage to her in the week before Madame de Staël's return, only to back off after her arrival. He had met Anna at the salon of a former mistress, Julie Talma, wife of the famous actor. The daughter of an Irish innkeeper, Anna had been adopted and educated by the Duchesse de Fitz-James, rather in the manner of Benjamin's father's adoption of Marianne. Turned out by the Duchess at the age of sixteen, alone and unprotected, Anna had been forced to fend for herself, even resorting to prostitution. Now the mistress of the Comte de Lamoignon, by whom she had two children, she had fallen in love with Constant and even more perhaps with the hope of married respectability. She was to be bitterly disappointed. Constant's relationship with Anna followed his usual pattern of a passionate beginning, that was soon soured by distaste. His longing for love was as great as his morbid fear of it. His love affair with Madame de Staël had degenerated into an emotionally destructive and exhausting tug of war, which was to last for more than another decade. In perfect accord politically and intellectually, their loyalty to each other was absolute but they could not live together amicably for long.

On Christmas Eve, Madame de Staël was celebrating with a group of friends when they heard several bangs to which they paid no attention, taking them for cannon fire during some military exercise. Later they learned that an attempt had been made to blow up the First Consul with an infernal machine while he was driving to the opera to hear Haydn's *Creation*. Twenty-two people had been killed and fifty-six wounded. Bonaparte had escaped unharmed, appearing pale but composed in his box at the Opera where he was wildly cheered. In spite of clear evidence produced by the Minister of Police, Fouché, that this had been the work of the *Chouannerie*, (Breton royalists led by Georges Cadoudal), the First Consul seized this opportunity to get rid instead of those Jacobins who had not come to heel. It did not matter that they had not been guilty. Dispensing with any need to try them, 'a hundred and thirty Jacobins were sent into exile in Madagascar, or perhaps to the bottom of the sea, since nothing more was heard of them', Madame de Staël recalled.[4] Cadoudal and the royalists would be dealt with later at a more convenient time.

Madame de Staël spent the winter and spring of 1801 trying to keep out of trouble. The second revised edition of her book on literature had come out in the previous November. If the first edition had provoked arguments around the question of a religious restoration, the second gave rise to furious debate on the subject of perfectibility. Her letters and articles in response to the many and varied attacks, and to the lavish praise heaped on her work, did not interrupt her work on her novel. Her father's representations to Bonaparte on her behalf at least enabled her to live in Paris for the time being. She did her best to keep out of his way.

'I was never invited by the First Consul,' she recalled, 'I never saw M. de Talleyrand. I knew that Bonaparte disliked me, but he had not yet reached the levels of tyranny of later years. Foreigners treated me with the greatest consideration; the diplomatic corps spent most of their time at my house and this European atmosphere served as a shield.'[5] Madame de La Tour du Pin confirms this in her memoirs: 'Bonaparte could not bear her, although she had made every effort to win his liking. I do not think that she visited Madame Bonaparte either. But one day, I did meet Joseph Bonaparte in her salon. She received people of all shades of opinion. You would find at her house large numbers of former émigrés side by side with former supporters of the Directorate.'[6]

She saw the First Consul on one occasion only that winter. She was invited to a ball by General Berthier, the Minister of War, who continued to see her and was one of the few men around Bonaparte brave enough to defy him. Knowing that the First Consul would be present, she admitted that she had been sufficiently intimidated to have rehearsed beforehand a number of replies to any cutting remarks he might make. In the event, his crudeness was to leave her speechless. Leaning over ostentatiously to inspect her generous décolletage, he enquired: 'No doubt you have nursed your children yourself, Madame?' When she remained silent, he turned to his brother Lucien, saying, 'You see. She refuses to say yes or no.'[7]

Her husband's affairs continued to preoccupy her. Sick, alone and destitute, Staël was drowning in debt. Necker had had a letter from one of his friends, informing him that Staël lacked the barest essentials. 'I have from my own modest means given him 1,000 francs with which he has paid for food and medicine this past month.' Necker sent money for his most pressing needs at once, adding that his own house was open to him as a refuge, Staël was free to return to his wife, and that he had asked one of his friends to look into the matter and provide for his needs.[8]

When news of Staël's condition reached Bonaparte, who continued to keep Madame de Staël under close watch, he wrote to his brother Joseph: 'M. de Staël is living in the most abject misery while his wife gives dinners and balls. If you go on seeing her, it might be a good thing to try and persuade that woman to give her husband a pension of a thousand or two thousand francs a month. Or have we reached an age in which we may trample underfoot not only morality, but even duties more sacred than those which unite mothers and children, without incurring the contempt of decent people? . . . By all means judge Madame de Staël's conduct as if she were a man, but would a man who is heir to M. Necker's fortune, who has always enjoyed the privileges attached to a distinguished name, but who left his wife to live in misery, while he lives in splendour; would such a man be someone one would wish to know?'[9]

In fact, although heavily in debt, Staël still owned valuable works of art and furniture and was living in the private house of the Marquise de Coislin in the Place de la Concorde, where he kept a good cellar. Necker and Madame de Staël were doing their best to agree a legal settlement before his uncontrollable debts swallowed her entire fortune. Later that year they succeeded. Staël was to be given a lump sum of 10,000 francs and an annual allowance of 3,600 francs. It was at this point that his mistress, the septuagenarian actress Mlle Clairon, chose to sue him for non-payment of the pension which he had contracted to pay her.

Madame de Staël was no longer interested in Bonaparte's approval but his disapproval was dangerous and she was determined that he should know the truth about their financial arrangements. 'Citizen Consul', she wrote to the Consul Lebrun, with whom she was on good terms, 'had General Bonaparte not been informed of my domestic affairs I would not have been so indiscreet as to raise them with him; but I do not wish him to look on me with disfavour . . . Two hundred thousand livres, a third of my dowry, have already gone to pay for M.

de Staël's debts. The other two thirds, bringing in an income of twenty thousand livres are in my father's name. I dispose of the income alone. I have offered M. de Staël the chance of sharing it by living with me and my children. If he were to consent I would do my best, as I have always done, to make him happy. My father has given M. de Staël twenty thousand francs in the past three years, and is willing to pay him two thousand ecus now to return to Sweden where important business has awaited him for some time. He has a pension of ten thousand livres from the court payable in Paris, or twenty thousand were he to live in Sweden, in which case his income would be precisely equal to mine. I alone have undertaken the care and education of my three children since their birth. The eldest is ten. When he is eighteen, the First Consul will be able to judge whether I have fulfilled my duties as a mother. My father has offered M. de Staël shelter at Coppet free of any charge but he has not been to see him for five years. M. de Staël, through the weakness of his character, has ruined himself with debts to such a degree that my entire fortune would not be enough to meet them . . . Among other things there are the eight thousand livres promised to Mlle Clairon . . . M. de Staël separated himself from me, never me from him. He did so in 1798. It was an ill-chosen moment. He had just been re-appointed ambassador, I had been instrumental in this [Talleyrand had requested Staël's reappointment at Madame de Staël's urging], my father was still on the list of émigrés and the revolution in Switzerland was about to ruin us. Neither I nor my father turned to the First Consul for help, but it is important that you point out to him, Citizen Consul, that we will have no secure funds until such time as our claims on the state treasury have been met.' With this brisk reminder that the state treasury still held Necker's two million, Madame de Staël begged Lebrun to be so kind as to put her letter in the hands of the First Consul.[10]

He must have done so for Madame de Staël mentions in a letter to Joseph that the First Consul had been kind enough to read her letter, and even kept it to read again at his leisure.[11] In spite of his brother's displeasure, Joseph and his wife Julie continued to be on very friendly terms with Madame de Staël and she was frequently invited to their country estate of Morfontaine, which had been bought from the Prince de Condé, one of the Princes of the Blood, and where he had created magnificent gardens. 'Joseph loved country life and would happily walk in his gardens for eight hours at a time,' Madame de

Staël recalled.[12] Here she read Chateaubriand's *Atala* and *René* out loud to the company which included many intellectuals, foreign diplomats and leaders of society, among them her old friends Mathieu de Montmorency and Jaucourt, and new ones like Madame Récamier.

Accompanied by her son Auguste and by Benjamin Constant, who had put an end to his affair with Anna Lindsay, Madame de Staël left Paris in the early summer of 1801 to spend some months with her father at Coppet. Here she worked on her novel, while her father worked on his *Dernières vues de politique et de finances* (Final Views on Politics and Finance), to be published a year later.

In France the *Code Civil*, was completed in January 1801. Founded on the social principles of 1789 – freedom of conscience, liberty of the individual, equality before the law and the secularization of the state – it spelled the end of the old feudal aristocracy, helping to establish a social hierarchy founded on wealth. However, Bonaparte was anxious to win the backing of the aristocracy and the counter-revolutionary bourgeoisie and to do this he had to come to terms with the Church. Negotiations between Bonaparte and the Vatican were concluded in July 1801, though not announced until April 1802. The Concordat reasserted papal authority over the French Church, but it also enabled Bonaparte to use the Church as an instrument of government. He even created a national holiday on 15 August, the Feast of the Assumption, which happily coincided with his own birthday.

Restoration of religion would support class divisions. 'Society cannot exist without inequality of wealth, and inequality of wealth cannot exist without religion,' he had told Roederer. 'Religion is a kind of inoculation which by satisfying our love of marvels, guarantees us against charlatans and sorcerers. The people must have a religion and that religion must be in the hands of the government.'[13]

On 1 October 1801, when the preliminaries were concluded for the peace with England, to be signed at Amiens in the following spring, Bonaparte's popularity reached new heights. Preparing to leave for Paris in mid-November, Madame de Staël delayed her return by a day or two to avoid the festivities for the peace. She could hardly bear to see the French celebrating the First Consul as the father of the nation even as he was preparing to subjugate them. Hopes of peace had fuelled yet another attempt on her part to persuade her father to come to France. His presence in Paris would not only safeguard her but would be useful in another attempt to recover their money from the state treasury, she argued. Most of all it would avoid the heartrending separations which both hated more with every year.

While Necker perfectly understood his daughter's need of Paris, not so much as a place of distraction but the proper setting for her formidable talents which he believed to be 'without limits and without equal . . . where else might one exercise such a talent? even Paris is barely enough',[14] and was tempted to go with her, something always held him back. Madame de Staël knew that he was loath to leave Madame Necker's remains, which he visited faithfully every day. He was embarrassed, too, by the indignities of age. He had grown very fat and his legs were so swollen that he could barely waddle around. His teeth were loose and he dared not talk while eating. He was afraid above all that he would find himself in an awkward situation in the new world of the consulate.[15] So once again they had to face agonizing goodbyes. Accompanied by her cousin Albertine, as well as her son Albert, Madame de Staël left Coppet on 13 November.

Madame de Staël's salon was more brilliant than ever that winter. The two Consuls Lebrun and Cambacérès and the Ministers Fouché and Berthier were frequent visitors. Lebrun, she told Joseph Bonaparte who was away from Paris, had spoken up for her to Bonaparte who had replied: 'Yes I believe you for I have heard nothing of her recently.'[16] But this happy state of affairs was not to last. On 4 January 1802, Bonaparte withdrew all the bills submitted to the Assemblies. Three days later the Council of State declared the sessions of the Assemblies at an end. The time had come for the first renewal of a fifth of the representatives, but the method of selecting outgoing members, not defined by the Constitution, was referred to the Senate. It was an easy matter for the First Consul to induce the Senate to remove all the most prominent so-called '*idéologues*' in the Tribunate. Thus, Benjamin Constant and other members of the opposition – all friends of Madame de Staël – found themselves ousted. Madame de Staël was naturally incensed and naturally unable to keep quiet. Bonaparte had called the liberal Tribunes *idéologues*: she accused him, in private, of being an *idéophobe*. In reply to a remark that the First Consul had purged the Tribunate, she replied witheringly: 'Purged, surely you mean creamed off?'[17]

Her remarks did not take long to come to Bonaparte's ears. Torn between fury and a desire not to show how much this woman bothered him, he told his brother Joseph that the whole thing smelt of Madame de Staël. 'So she wants war does she! . . . Ideophobe eh? How charming! . . . Serve notice to this woman, to her illustriousness, that I am neither a Louis XVI nor a Barras. Advise her not to block my path, no matter what it is, no matter where I choose to go, otherwise I will break her . . . I will crush her . . . but it's foolish of me to get heated . . . tell her; tell her to be quiet. That would be the most prudent thing,' he warned his brother. When the message was given to her she said proudly: 'There is a kind of pleasure in resisting an iniquitous power. Genius too is power.'[18]

Madame de Staël was dining with the British Minister, Francis Jackson, when the terms of the Treaty of Amiens, signed on 25 March 1802, arrived. As he read them out to the assembled company she was astonished at England's willingness to give up so many of her conquests.[19]

Soon after, the Concordat, concluded in the previous autumn was celebrated with every circumstance of royal pomp. 'On the day of the Concordat, Bonaparte went to Notre-Dame Cathedral, in the King's former carriages, with the same coachmen, the same footmen running beside the doors. He had followed court etiquette to the last detail,' Madame de Staël recalled. Disgusted by 'the odious spectacle', she had remained at home.[20] It was reported to her afterwards that when they had returned to the Tuileries after the ceremony, Bonaparte had turned to his generals with satisfaction and said: 'Well, now everything was just as it had been before.' 'Yes,' General Bernadotte had replied, 'except for two million men who died for liberty and who are no more.'[21]

The Peace brought a flood of English into Paris as well as many members of the European elite. Among those who crossed the Channel that spring were the d'Arblays. Madame de Staël was very anxious to see them again and to resume her friendship with Fanny d'Arblay, and she sent her a note at once: 'I hope you will let me know when you are sufficiently rested from the fatigue of your journey, so that I might have the honour of seeing you without importuning you.' But Fanny d'Arblay was too concerned by the damage that contact with Madame de Staël might do to her reputation and wrote an icy note in the third person, putting Madame de Staël off. In her diary she wrote: 'She gives, however, great assemblies at which all Paris assist, and though not solicited or esteemed by her early friends and acquaintance, she is admired and pitied and received by them. I would she were gone to

Coppet!' Too honest not to admit that Madame de Staël 'had returned good for evil to many friends that would do any character credit', to both the d'Arblays' eternal discredit, they lacked the courage to see their old friend.[22]

In the late spring of 1802, Madame de Staël learned that her husband had suffered a stroke and was in a very bad way. She went at once to see him. Moved by pity at the lamentable state she found him in, she decided to take him to Aix for a cure and then to Coppet where he could be properly looked after, at least for a time. 'I am leaving for my six months at Coppet,' she wrote at the end of April to her friend, du Pont de Nemours, who was then in America, 'and taking M. de Staël back with me. He has a paralysis of the brain which has more or less incapacitated him. I felt I had to take him into my care when I saw that his brain no longer functioned. I hope to be able to pay off his debts without quite ruining my children. In the last ten days I have done nothing but look at accounts and meet his creditors. It doesn't help one to finish a novel'.[23]

On the night of 8 May at the Hostellerie du Grand Cerf at Poligny, in the Jura mountains, where they had stopped for the night on the way to Coppet, Staël suddenly took a turn for the worse. He was found dead by his valet the next morning. Madame de Staël set off the next day with his remains and he was buried in the cemetery at Coppet on 11 May 1802. 'I am very much affected by this death,' she wrote to a friend, 'and I will never be able to console myself for not having been able to make him happy briefly, when he had once again given himself up to me and found me again, after his false friends had abandoned him. There was also the horror of finding myself alone with his sad remains . . . If there was no hope of another life what a miserable nightmare this one would be!' she reflected.[24] The death from consumption of Gerlach, the twenty-six-year-old German tutor, soon after her return to Coppet added to her general depression.

Before she left Paris, Madame de Staël had been involved, at least tacitly, in a plot instigated by General Moreau and a few disaffected generals – among them Bernadotte – to get rid of Bonaparte. She knew that the Concordat would give Bonaparte an important ally in the Church: 'You haven't a moment to lose!', she had supposedly said to Bernadotte, 'Tomorrow the tyrant will have forty thousand priests at his service!'[25] When Bonaparte's mandate as First Consul had been renewed for ten years, she remarked: 'Here is the second step towards monarchy! I fear that with the third, this man may, like Homer's Gods, reach Olympus.'[26] Moreau's plot had been supported by Bernadotte, though he had taken good care not to be compromised. 'Throughout these very dangerous negotiations, I often saw General Bernadotte and his friends. It was more than enough to condemn me if their designs were discovered. Bonaparte already believed that people left my house less attached to him than before,' Madame de Staël wrote later.[27]

However the plot had been easily foiled and Bonaparte had been lenient. Bernadotte was married to Desirée Clary, Bonaparte's first love and sister to Joseph's wife. The First Consul merely contented himself with a warning through his brother Joseph that if Bernadotte continued to plot he would have him shot on the Place du Carrousel.[28]

In May 1802, over the heads of the Senate, registers had been opened for a vote on the question: 'Should Napoleon Bonaparte become Consul for life?' Madame de Staël had been right: Olympus beckoned. Even before the results of the vote, Camille Jordan, a former royalist deputy in the Five Hundreds, and a confidant of hers since Brumaire, anonymously published a pamphlet at Madame de Staël's suggestion, in which the author spoke out against what would be in effect a dictatorship. It was essential to establish durable and representative institutions: 'We must not consent to what was in effect a hereditary position before we have obtained an immutable bill of our rights.' But before the pamphlet appeared the whole print run was seized and destroyed, the person who had taken it to the printer imprisoned, and a search put out for its author.

Madame de Staël was kept informed of events by her friends Mathieu, Gérando and Jordan himself. A copy of the pamphlet, which had been reprinted and was being distributed clandestinely in France, was in her hands by mid-July. 'The pamphlet has had the greatest success in Paris,' she wrote, sending a copy to Henri Meister, as well as to several other friends.[29] In early August, Bonaparte was appointed First Consul for life, with the right to choose his own successor by a *senatus-consultum*, a device which made it possible for him to legislate through the Senate without any prior debate. It was accurately described by Madame de Staël as 'a farrago, a cipher, for which there is only one word: despotism'.[30]

By the time she left Paris in late April 1802, Madame de Staël no longer entertained any illusions about Bonaparte's intentions. As for

Bonaparte, he had told his brother that wherever there was any resistance to him he was sure to find Madame de Staël. It was disingenuous of her to write later that 'what shocked him [Bonaparte] even more than the opinions he supposed I held, was the number of foreigners who had come to see me. The son of the Stathouder, the Prince of Orange, had done me the honour of dining with me and had reproached him. It was an unimportant matter; the existence of a woman whom people came to see for her wit and her literary reputation, but however unimportant, it did not come from him and this was enough for him to wish to crush me.'[31]

Bonaparte knew of Madame de Staël's involvement with the Moreau plot and that she was a friend of Camille Jordan and that made him angry enough. His rage, indeed his incredulity, can only be imagined when in August the second Consul Lebrun presented him with a copy of Necker's *Dernières vues de politique et de finances*, sent by the former Minister himself. Necker had delayed publication to allow Madame de Staël to enjoy a quiet winter in Paris and was even prepared to withdraw this work. She called it his swansong and, of all his works, it was the one most in accordance with her own views. Naturally Madame de Staël wanted him to publish: 'It had seemed to me perfectly noble to speak out against the absolute power of one man . . . and I wanted more than anything this last ray of glory in the sunset of my father's life.'[32]

Necker paid fulsome compliments to the First Consul, but referred to him as *l'homme nécessaire* – the man of the hour. This particularly incensed Bonaparte, who did not see himself as a mere stop-gap. Denouncing military power as 'incompatible with our enlightened century', Necker criticized the Constitution of the Year VIII, showing it to be nothing but a step on the way to despotism. He called for a republican government: 'No form of government in which the people counted for nothing, other than fictitiously, could be called a republic'. The Consulate for life, with the option of the First Consul being able to choose his successor, was a clear introduction of the principle of heredity. While he might have favoured a hereditary and constitutional monarchy, Necker wrote: 'Bonaparte with all his talent, all his genius, all his power' could not aspire to founding his own dynasty without strong resistance from all sides. Would he then resort to military force? 'May God preserve France from such a destiny!'

Bonaparte aspired precisely to such a destiny but he did not wish his designs to be known beforehand. Attacks in the press on Necker were not slow to appear and Bonaparte's signature was all over them. Necker was ridiculed for his vanity, for being out of date and ignorant of current events; for his political incompetence and for his Anglomania. Worse, he, a foreigner, had set the Revolution in motion and then spent it peacefully by his lakeside, while heads rolled and people were ruined.[33] Bonaparte also dictated Lebrun's reply to Necker himself. Thanking him for his book and reminding him of the mistakes made during his Ministry, Lebrun suggested drily that he give up politics and put his trust in the First Consul, 'who alone was capable of governing France properly'.[34]

There was no longer any doubt about the intentions of the First Consul. In mid-August 1802 Madame de Staël learned that he had ordered her arrest and deportation if she ventured anywhere off the route between Coppet and Paris. No doubt, Bonaparte hoped that she would take the hint and stay at Coppet, saving him the trouble and embarrassment of exiling her.

Whatever Bonaparte may have believed about the true inspiration behind Necker's book, this was a God-given opportunity to rid himself of Madame de Staël. 'All that was needed on this work was her signature,' he said. Madame de Staël was indignant; 'as if one could push the pen of such a high-minded man'. But she knew that she had burned her bridges. 'He fears me,' she told Lacretelle. 'Therein lies my joy and my pride; therein my terror. I must admit to you that I am bound to be proscribed and I am ill prepared to bear the boredom of a long exile; my courage fails but not my will. I suffer but would not seek a remedy which would be degrading. I have all the fear of a woman but not such as would turn me into a hypocrite or a slave.'[35]

Was there any chance that the relationship between Madame de Staël and her great adversary might have been different? They had much in common: both were children of the Enlightenment and both believed in progress. They shared exceptional intellectual abilities, a capacity for hard work and a romantic imagination. Both had wanted to unite all Frenchmen and believed in opening up opportunities to people of talent. They were also representatives of the new rising bourgeoisie, believing that property was the foundation of social order. She had admired the young hero of the Italian campaign, attracted by a genius which she had recognized at once and by his potential for glory. They shared a love of glory and enthusiasm, believing it to be the essential life force, the mainspring of genius, but to Madame de Staël glory was but a tool in the pursuit of higher goals, whereas to Bonaparte it was always in the service of his own power. The crucial difference between them lay in her love of humanity – which he despised.

She had admired Bonaparte as a reformer, strong enough to bring together the factions dividing a France embittered and exhausted by the Terror. An activist to the core, as a woman her only hope of action was through a man, so she had hoped to know him and if possible to influence him. With Madame de Staël admiration was always akin to love and she expressed her feelings with a lack of restraint which to less hardy spirits might seem like utter folly, but to her was the only way to live life with truth and courage, with 'enthusiasm', a word she interpreted in its original Greek sense as 'God within us'. She was quickly disillusioned and not merely because Bonaparte had resisted her advances. When it became clear to her that his genius was solely in the service of his own power, 'that literature meant as little to him as religion unless they served his greatness,' that in short, as Chateaubriand was to realize as well, he was a tyrant, she could not support him. That being the case, she must oppose him. Sitting on the sidelines was never an option for Madame de Staël. In spite of moments of weakness when her love and homesickness for France and Paris almost undermined her resolve, she never gave in. Her charge against him was that he had perverted Republican liberty in France.

Bonaparte had known at once that she would be a formidable opponent. As a woman she repelled and perhaps frightened him, but he too had started off by trying to come to terms with her, offering to buy her off. She could not accept his terms even for as great a prize as permission to remain in her beloved Paris. He saw where her weakness lay and would banish her from her world. At a stroke he would satisfy his need for vengeance – Bonaparte never forgot a slight – be rid of her negative influence, and perhaps cut off the source of her inspiration. When persecution merely stiffened her spine and sharpened her pen, he determined to crush her. She feared him at first, feared above all the loss of the world she loved, but as time went by, as her own literary reputation marched in step with his growing political power, as her mind expanded with her travels, her fear turned first to resistance and then to implacable hatred and contempt for the 'little Corsican'. Yet she was anything but a hater by nature. Constant, with his extraordinary powers of analysis, who for the last ten years of their relationship filled his diary with almost daily expressions of exasperation about her, could still write: 'the two dominant qualities of Madame de Staël were love and pity. She had, like all superior minds, a great passion for glory; she had, like all elevated spirits, a great love of liberty; but those two emotions, imperious and irresistible when there was nothing to oppose them, would give way at once when the least circumstance placed them in opposition to the happiness of those she loved, or when the sight of a suffering being reminded her that there was something on earth much more sacred to her than the success of a cause or the triumph of an opinion.'[36]

She would oppose Bonaparte and what he stood for in the only way open to a woman of her talent – with words. At first she would oppose him through her books, later through visiting the princes and ministers of Europe to incite them to resist his tyranny, and finally and forever through her book, *Considérations sur la Révolution Française*, published a year after her death. The words of the modern Dutch historian, Pieter Geyl cannot be bettered: 'This woman of genius has succeeded in portraying her subject in historical perspective, which is not of course the same as saying that she has succeeded in giving the objective truth about Napoleon. But it is in her writings that for the first time it is possible to find unfavourable criticism allied to the actual events in such a way as to set one thinking. Moreover, the problems with which the liberal spirit, the spirit of belief in the rule of intellectual and moral values, must always wrestle when it comes in contact with the phenomenon of power, its rise and decline, are stated by her in such a way that it sometimes seems as if later writers, though capable of finer shades and possessing a far richer store of data, can only elaborate her themes.'[37]

Chapter 17

The Sorrows of Delphine

> 'The whole of Paris is behind closed doors reading Madame de Staël's new novel.'
>
> Roederer in the *Journal de Paris*

DELPHINE, published simultaneously in Paris and Geneva in December 1802, was dedicated provocatively '*to Silent France*'. An immediate success, the novel was the main topic of conversation in Paris despite the absence of its banished author. 'Do you know why nobody was at the theatre the day before yesterday, or why today, which is Sunday, there will be few attending Mass? . . . It is because the whole of Paris is behind closed doors reading Madame de Staël's new novel,' Roederer wrote in the *Journal de Paris*.[1]

Lady Bessborough, who was in Paris at the time, wrote to her lover Lord Granville: 'My eyes are swell'd out of my head with crying over *Delphine* and I have but just got through the 1st Vol. Pray read it if you have time and *mark*' (her italics). Some thought it had an immoral tendency, she adds, but Narbonne had defended it stoutly. She had not been able to resist saying to Narbonne that: 'She [Madame de Staël] must have suffered greatly, she writes of men's injustice too well not to have felt it personally – one cannot invent such things.' Narbonne, understanding to whom she was referring, had replied immediately: 'I assure you that she had no reasonable cause for complaint but Madame de Staël is one of those beings who loves trouble and seeks it even where none exists'.[2]

Set a decade earlier in the revolutionary years of 1790–92, the novel deals with all the most important political and social issues of the time; issues which Bonaparte particularly wished to bury. The aims and the achievements of the Revolution, the importance of political freedom, religious controversy, the problems of divorce and marriages of convenience, suicide, the role of women in general and talented women in particular, and the importance of literature, which she had already discussed in her previous book, *De la littérature* – all were there. To add insult to injury, Madame de Staël constantly praised the English.

It is not hard to imagine Bonaparte's reaction to the sentiments expressed by one of her characters, Henri de Liebensei. An English-educated, liberal Protestant, modelled on Constant, he is the voice of the future in the novel. The hero Léonce represents the voice of the past. Liebensei declares that 'Liberty is the chief happiness, the only glory of a social order' and 'the only names which ring out down the ages to generous spirits are those of people who have loved freedom'. When alluding to religion Madame de Staël makes unflattering comparisons between the freedom of the Protestant faith and what she saw as the obscurantism of the Catholic Church – in her view the religion of slaves. This was bound to infuriate Bonaparte at precisely the time when he was anxious to have the support of the Church.

Delphine is not a feminist novel in the modern sense. The heroine is brought down and punished by the society she defies. But in discussing divorce and arranged marriages she points out the hypocrisy and the misery forced, not only on women, but also on men, by the need to conform. Madame de Staël's aim was to show that in spite of the Revolution, a woman's right to an independent existence was far from won; that she was accepted only if she were submissive. Her implied criticism of such rigidity came precisely at a time when the First Consul had reversed most of the advantages gained by women, and was trying above all to ensure social conformity and stability.

In the novel she also makes clear her contempt for those aristocrats who had voluntarily left France at the beginning of the Revolution, abandoning the King to his fate. Bonaparte was making strenuous efforts to win over the royalist émigrés at this very time. Like her father, a lifelong Anglophile, Madame de Staël praised English respect for the law and for freedom at a time when war with that country was imminent. More explicitly even than in her work *De la littérature*, Madame de Staël here defined the role of the writer, not as an anarchist, but as the defender of freedom of thought, of originality, of personal liberty. This was absolute anathema to Bonaparte, to whom writers were useful only as apologists for his own views or for the amusement of the salons.

The eponymous heroine of this lively and very readable epistolary novel is a highly idealized form of Madame de Staël herself.[3] Delphine, a beautiful young widow of independent means and independent views, shares with her creator the gift of brilliant conversation, enthusiasm, a romantic and passionate nature, a belief in reason, a dislike of constraints and a love of liberty. Delphine falls in love with Léonce de Mondoville, a charismatic nobleman very like Narbonne, who loves honour and is careful of social conventions. Their mutual love is thwarted by the wiles of Madame de Vernon, Delphine's aunt. When Delphine, to protect a friend, compromises her own reputation, Madame de Vernon does not scruple to betray her and persuades Léonce to marry her own daughter. Madame de Vernon, a woman with a cold and calculating nature, irresistible charm, boundless love of power and success, and an unscrupulously Machiavellian ability to achieve her aims, is a clearly recognizable female version of Talleyrand. It was Madame de Staël's vengeance on her former friend and lover, who had not hesitated to betray her to please Bonaparte. When this was brought to his attention, Talleyrand observed languidly: 'I hear that in her novel, Madame de Staël has disguised both of us as women.'[4] Several scenes in the novel, such as Delphine's attempt to rescue Léonce from execution under the Terror, and her ostracism in the ballroom, were taken directly from Madame de Staël's own experience.

Congratulatory letters poured into Coppet from all over Europe. 'M. de Chateaubriand will be writing to thank you; unable to convert you, he must admire you,' wrote her friend Madame de Beaumont.[5] Chateaubriand did indeed write: 'I tremble that you might fall into the hands of enemies who will try to hurt you in every possible way. I will do everything I can to prevent this, but while my zeal is great, my credit is small, and I fear that hatred and party spirit will win over the warmth of friendship.'[6]

He was quite right. Orchestrated by the government, the press in Paris tore Madame de Staël apart. Fiévée, one of Bonaparte's lackeys, in one of the many vitriolic attacks on her, demonstrated that her gender was the main issue. 'Examine such women closely,' he wrote, 'you will see that they are violent in all their desires, demanding in all their relationships, and that it is even more difficult to be their friend than their lover. Listen carefully to these unhappy women; you will learn that they complain of the whole world; you will constantly hear their melancholic sighing; their hearts are forever hurt by ingratitude; they shout loudly for peace; peace which they can no longer find but in their graves. Look at them: they are big, fat, greasy and heavy.'[7] It was bad enough to be unattractive; Madame de Staël's lack of conventional morality, her enthusiasm for liberty and her defiant need to broadcast her opinions, and especially her penetrating intellect, were all unacceptable in a woman. The First Consul pronounced her novel to be immoral, anti-social, anti-Catholic, and what was worse, anti-French.

Later, in an essay entitled *Some reflections on the moral aims of Delphine*, written in answer to those charges of immorality, but not published until after her death, Madame de Staël pointed out that she had never wished to present Delphine as a role model. She had, after all, taken her mother's maxim: 'A man must know how to challenge public opinion; a woman, how to submit to it' as the epigraph to *Delphine*. 'I believe it to be useful and strictly moral to demonstrate how people of superior intelligence can make more mistakes than others . . . how a generous and sensitive heart can lead to many errors if it is not subject to strong moral principles. . . . When Richardson was asked why he had made [the eponymous heroine of his novel] Clarissa so unhappy, he replied: "because I could never forgive her for leaving her father's house".' In a similar spirit, Madame de Staël continues, she had not forgiven Delphine, but she had wanted to show that society was no less to be condemned for its harshness and hypocrisy.[8]

In his response to her critics, Constant commented: 'Delphine is forever unhappy because she refuses to conform to public opinion, Leonce is forever unhappy for failing to challenge it. But this maxim, which appears to be the real aim of the work, could well be merely the apparent aim . . . Madame de Staël's real aim was to make us feel the full injustice of the tyranny of public opinion, which makes a crime out of virtue, and ruins reputations on the mere appearance of things. Delphine and her lover are made unhappy as a result of that tyranny and not of their conduct.[9]

Bonaparte's patience was at an end. He was furious that the police had not prevented the publication of the book. When he heard that Madame de Staël was preparing to return to France, he issued an order banning 'the foreign intriguer'. If Madame de Staël dared to enter France she would be conducted back to the border at once by the gendarmes. Joseph Bonaparte again intervened on her behalf while at the same time advising her to lie low for six months. At the end of March 1803 she wrote to him that she owed him the greatest possible gratitude. If the First Consul were to allow her to return, she would not say a word, write a line nor do anything which might displease him. 'I haven't the strength to renounce my friends and my country . . . I have been told that the First Consul believes that I wish to go to England in order to be free to write on any subject. The day that I leave France will be the most unhappy of my life. Doubtless I will go to England rather than remain where I am at present. But before I leave my country, the First Consul, before the eyes of all Europe, will have to have me and my children arrested by his grenadiers and treat M. Necker's family as he has not treated France's greatest enemies.'[10] This was not quite the language of a penitent.

She was desperate after almost a year away from her friends: 'You ask me a little too lightly to bury myself alive,' she wrote to du Pont de Nemours, who had advised her to be patient. 'Coppet is like living in a convent, while Geneva is, of all the places known to me, the one most uncongenial to my tastes, my habits and my thoughts. I love my father with all my heart, but he is the first to sense that this life is odious to me . . . would you have been happy thirty years ago, or even now, you who are so young in body and soul, to resign yourself to three hours of whist a day and be unable to talk with all your heart and with all your mind to anyone outside your family circle? Please bear in mind, that I have lived among the most distinguished people, and discussed the most noble ideas since my childhood . . . My dear du Pont, life is a sad business . . . do not look on the idea of exile so lightly. Ovid died of it. Cicero preferred the dagger unable to bear even Greece. And I am not in Greece. In short, anyone born on the blessed soil of France cannot bear life elsewhere.'[11]

Unhappy that his own work had excited Bonaparte's anger against his daughter, Necker had proposed to go to France to speak to the First Consul personally. Madame de Staël was tempted at first by this last chance, but her love for her father, his infirmities, the realization that he would be exposed at best to ridicule and disrespect, led her to dissuade him. Instead, he wrote once again to Lebrun. In a letter dated 5 April 1803 and dictated by the First Consul, Lebrun replied that although when he had entered government the First Consul had been full of respect for M. Necker, and had even considered consulting him from time to time, his last work had struck him 'as inspired by motives which were not yours. . . . Madame de Staël's views, actions which were more than indiscreet by those whom we know to be her most intimate confidants, have convinced him that she had influenced you and your work'. This being the case, Lebrun concluded, any further efforts to plead her case would be wasted. 'I don't know whether time might bring about a change, but I can offer you no such hope now.'[12]

Benjamin Constant had spent the winter with Madame de Staël at Coppet, working on a history of comparative religion. Their relationship was now anything but happy. Her restlessness, her unhappiness and her constant demands made it impossible for him to get on with his work. He desperately hoped to find a wife and had thought of marrying Amélie Fabri, whom he nevertheless described as a complete zero. 'Scene upon scene and torment upon torment. Germaine has been furious for three days, and has pursued me with such invective, fury and reproaches that I myself have gone alternately from fury to indifference and from indifference to fury. It is terrible, the relationship between a man who has ceased to love and a woman who does not wish to cease being loved. As always the idea of losing me makes Germaine value me more; a long habit of disposing of my entire existence, makes her forever sure that I must come back to her . . . as I truly love her, the pain she feels when she does not find in me the feelings she desires, causes me intense pain.'[13]

In the spring he made one of his bolts for freedom, this time to a cottage at Les Herbages, not far from Luzarches, which he bought after selling the convent at Hérivaux. Madame de Staël had been angry and unhappy at his departure but had consoled herself with a brief flirtation with a married Irishman, O'Brien, which provoked gossip in Geneva. The arrival in April 1803 of two Scots – Lord John Campbell, second son of the Duke of Argyll, the future 7th Duke, and his travelling companion, Dr Robert Robertson, with whom she had a brief romance – was a further consolation. Throughout April, she entertained them to supper almost every day, travelling around Switzerland with them in May.

War was once again on the horizon. Bonaparte had recently annexed more Italian territory, and declared himself President of the Cisalpine Republic. He had intervened in Switzerland, bringing the Alpine passes under French control. These acts were not in direct contravention of the Treaty of Amiens, but the retention of troops in

Holland was, and it brought a growl of protest from the British government. When it became obvious that Bonaparte still had ambitions in Egypt, Britain (who had still not given up Malta as she was bound to do under the terms of the Treaty of Amiens) demanded an extension of ten years in compensation for France's territorial gains. At the end of April 1803, after secret negotiations with Russia, a British ultimatum effectively repudiated Amiens, and Bonaparte, who had never given up his plans to invade Britain, set about preparing a camp for this undertaking at Boulogne. Not surprisingly, there were furious personal attacks on Bonaparte in the British press. Unused to a free press and highly vulnerable to criticism, he was enraged: 'Every time Bonaparte was brought a translation of an English newspaper, he would make a scene to the British Ambassador [Lord Whitworth], who would reply coolly and reasonably that the King of England himself was not safe from the sarcasm of the gazetteers, but that the Constitution did not allow them to be silenced.' Madame de Staël added with relish: 'Bonaparte, with his dumpy little figure, would buzz angrily around the tall and handsome figure of Lord Whitworth, as if the latter were the very embodiment of the principles of English freedom; unable either to strike at it or to tolerate it.'[14]

War was declared on 18 May. A week later, news that British travellers of an age to bear arms would be interned as prisoners of war had caused panic among those in Geneva. Many families, among them Mary Berry's, hurried home, although Lord John and Dr Robertson stayed on at Coppet until the end of June and Robertson then returned to spend a few days with Madame de Staël at the beginning of July. Several letters from her to Lord John suggest that she was planning to travel to England and Scotland if she failed to return to Paris. They also suggest that, true to form, she was entertaining hopes of finding true love in Robertson's arms but 'the love of men is full of ingratitude'. Other letters soon followed in which she begged him to forget what she had written and to burn her letters.[15]

In the autumn of 1803, unable to bear life in Switzerland any longer, and believing herself forgotten by Bonaparte, who was now occupied with war, Madame de Staël crossed into France, accompanied by Mathieu de Montmorency and two of her children, Auguste and Albertine. Her father's health gave her no special worries but before she left Coppet she wrote prophetically: 'I must tell you my angel, while still under your protecting roof, that I am going to put all my strength into an effort to make a life for myself in this country, sufficiently bearable to me so that I might make you happy. These separations break my heart. Is such great pain not a warning from heaven that we should no longer part?' He must take care of his health, she urged, for she would 'die in convulsions of despair if I lost you'.[16] Though she did not know it, this was to be their last time together. Auguste, too, would always remember his last hour with his grandfather to whom he was very close and whom all the children called Papa. Necker had blessed his grandson, in whom he saw 'no serious faults', and to whom he recommended his mother: 'be her support . . . make her as happy as you can' he told him.[17]

Towards the end of September, after a brief visit, with Constant to the La Fayettes at the Château de la Grange, Madame de Staël was at Maffliers, some ten leagues (thirty kilometres) north of the capital, in a small damp house she had rented, not far from Constant's cottage. She hoped to be able to slip into Paris unnoticed and live quietly in an apartment she had rented in the rue de Lille. From Maffliers she wrote long bulletins to her father, full of political and social gossip, which she asked him to keep since they were to be a kind of journal. She wrote at length about the rising in St Domingue after the re-establishment of slavery, led by the black leader Toussaint Louverture, in whose tragic fate she would take an interest later. She reported amusing gossip: Bonaparte, in a fit of impatience with the Minister of the Interior, Chaptal, who was reading a document too slowly, seized it and slapped him on the face. Chaptal had said nothing but had gone straight to the the Minister of Justice, Régnier, and resigned. The man had insulted him, Bonaparte complained to the *Grand Juge*. He had, after all, only shown his displeasure, where he might well have deported him.

Madame de Staël, having managed to convince herself that Bonaparte did not really mean to expel her, now decided to write to him. 'Citizen First Consul, having heard last winter that my return to Paris was not agreeable to you, with no direct orders from you, I condemned myself to ten months of exile.' She hoped that she might be permitted to return for the sake of her son's education. Auguste was to sit the entrance exams for the new École Polytechnique, and she needed to settle her husband's remaining debts. She promised not to write nor to say anything about public affairs during her time in France. She would remain in the country until she was sure of being given permission to return to Paris.[18]

The First Consul could not be blamed entirely for not believing her, particularly since reports from her enemies, in this case Madame de Genlis, were reaching him that she was only six leagues from Paris, and that she was receiving a constant stream of visitors. Madame de Genlis, deeply religious and an intellectual and writer herself, had always detested Madame de Staël and was very jealous of her literary reputation. Along with the publicist Fiévée, she was employed by Bonaparte to write reports on politics, finance, literature and morals – in effect to spy for him. Bonaparte found her irritating but used her none the less. 'When Madame de Genlis speaks of virtue, she always does so as if she had just discovered it,' he grumbled to Madame de Rémusat.

In early October Madame de Staël wrote to her father that 'the worst has happened', reporting a letter from the First Consul to Régnier: 'I hear Citizen Minister that Madame de Staël has arrived at Maffliers, near Beaumont-sur-Oise. Inform her, through one of her habituées and with the minimum of fuss, that if she is still there on 15 Vendémiaire (8 October), she will be accompanied to the frontier by the gendarmerie. The arrival of this woman, like that of a bird of ill omen, has always signalled some kind of trouble. My intention is that she should not remain in France.'[19] Realizing that there was little she could do, Madame de Staël had requested a passport for Germany and permission to go to Paris for a week to settle her affairs and to take her daughter Albertine to a doctor. On the same day, she moved from Maffliers to the house of Madame de La Tour, 'a good and truly soulful woman', whom she knew only slightly but who was a friend of a friend. From there, three days later, she went to Saint-Brice, which was only two leagues from Paris, to stay with Madame Récamier, 'that woman celebrated for her face, whose character is perfectly expressed by her beauty. I had been wrong to accept, but I did not know then that I might do harm to one who was such a stranger to politics; I believed her to be safe from everything, in spite of the generosity of her character. The most agreeable society was to be found at her house, and there I was able to enjoy for the last time everything that I was to leave behind.'[20] Among the house party organized by Madame Récamier for Madame de Staël was Camille Jordan, who wrote to Lady Elizabeth Foster in London: 'If only you knew how sweet and good Juliette is! How perfect she has been towards Madame de Staël in her disgrace; what a devoted friend! Where were you during these three days we spent together at Saint-Brice, where Madame de Staël, gently consoled by all those surrounding her, gave us a firework display of all her wit, such as we had never seen. She was truly marvellous.'[21]

From Saint-Brice she wrote to her father on 10 October that she expected to be leaving in about four days. Joseph Bonaparte, who had shown himself to be 'the most generous of friends', was making one more attempt to persuade his brother to change his mind. 'My dear angel, I embrace you as my friend, as my support, as my hope and I promise to be worthy of you by my courage.'[22] Five days later, in the absence of any direct orders, and believing that Bonaparte had a great deal on his mind and had merely wished to frighten her, she returned to the house she had rented at Maffliers.

On that same day she was sitting at table with three friends in a room from which there was a good view of the long drive and the garden gate. She had just picked up a bunch of grapes in her hand when one of her guests saw her freeze. As Madame de Staël later described it: 'At four o'clock a man on horseback, dressed in grey, stopped at the gate and rang; and I was sure about my fate.' He asked for her and she met him in the garden where she had been struck by the beauty of the sunlight and the scent of flowers.

He was the chief of the local constabulary of Versailles, but he was not wearing uniform because he had been ordered not to frighten her. 'He showed me a letter . . . ordering me to withdraw to outside forty leagues of Paris within twenty-four hours, while treating me with all the consideration due to a woman who was well known.' Madame de Staël replied that twenty-four hours might be enough notice for recruits, but not for a woman with children. She suggested to the gendarme, who agreed, that he accompany her to Paris where she would need three days to make all the necessary arrangements for her departure. On their way to Paris the gendarme, whose name was Gaudriot, and who had literary interests, complimented her on her writing. He should advise any woman in his family against taking it up – look where it had landed her – she replied.[23]

After a brief stop at Madame Récamier's, where she found General Junot, who promised to make one more appeal to the First Consul, Madame de Staël went to the house she had rented in the rue de Lille. Junot, Bonaparte's aide-de-camp and close friend, did then argue in her favour, 'as if she had been his sister', as his wife recalled. Even more enraged, the First Consul saw this as further proof of Madame de Staël's influence. 'What possible interest can you have in this woman?' he roared, stamping his foot violently. 'An interest that I will always have in the weak and suffering. Besides you know that she would be your friend, if you wished it.' 'Yes, yes, I know her,' Bonaparte replied and then lapsed into Italian, 'but *passato il pericolo, gabbato il santo* [once the danger is past, the saint is forgotten (hoodwinked)] . . . No, no, there is no truce nor peace possible between us; she asked for it, let her suffer the consequences.'[24]

For the next few days, Madame de Staël entertained all her friends to dinner. Every morning, 'just like Bluebeard', the policeman would call to ask if she was ready to leave the next day, and 'each day I was weak enough to ask for just one more day'. On the penultimate day Joseph Bonaparte travelled to St Cloud to make one more appeal to his powerful sibling, but to no avail. Forty leagues from Paris was as far as Bonaparte was prepared to tolerate her. She could go to Lyons or to Bordeaux. Joseph would have called on her that evening on his return, he wrote in a brief note, but his wife had thought that had they called on her so late she would have naturally assumed that they had good news, and 'it would have been too painful for me to disabuse you. We have just returned. I will call tomorrow to say goodbye.' Joseph had invited her to stay for a few days at Morfontaine. What an odd destiny, she thought, to be exiled by one brother and invited to stay by another. At Morfontaine, in spite of her hosts' kindness, she felt very out of place, surrounded as she was by many members of Bonaparte's government. She had decided that it would be too humiliating to be forced to vegetate somewhere in the country or to return to her father, much as she was tempted to see him. She could not go to England, with whom France was now at war. She would go to Germany where her book had been very well received. 'Because of the outrageous way the First Consul had treated me, I had hoped to raise up my spirits, through the welcome that I had been promised in Germany; I wished to oppose the impertinence of one who was preparing to subjugate France to the kindly welcome of ancient dynasties. To my sorrow my pride won. I would have seen my father again had I returned to Geneva.'

Still hoping for an eleventh-hour reprieve, Madame de Staël left Paris on 25 October, travelling one last time around the outskirts of the city she loved so well but dared not enter. A last letter to her father from Bondy ends: 'Farewell, I am about to enter my carriage three leagues from Paris, seeing it before me, leaving my friends who are there – by force – ah God!'[25] The faithful Constant had once again abandoned his work and the peace of Les Herbages to accompany her and her children. 'It was neither in my character nor in my heart to abandon a woman who had been banished. I was reconciled to her and we left for Germany.'[26] There is no doubt that, however much they tortured each other, there was enduring and genuine love between them. And there was Albertine, whom Constant, while never allowed to acknowledge, loved dearly.

At Metz, a letter from her father had crossed with hers: 'My poor little one! I await your first letter with infinite impatience. I could see you getting into your carriage with your children like an exile, and my heart was torn. My dear friend, I have been unable either to prevent your pain or to protect you. I am despised in my old age, but you, so young and valiant deserved more consideration. . . . Ah! lift up your head in adversity, and never allow anyone, no matter how powerful, to hold you under his boot.'[27]

PART FIVE

Ten Years of Exile

'Exile severed the roots which bound me to Paris and I became a European.'

Madame de Staël

Chapter 18

Germany

'I can see that tempest in petticoats about to sweep across our peaceful German lands.'[1]

Heinrich Heine

MADAME DE STAËL was more than grateful for Constant's offer to accompany her, for she knew it was a sacrifice. She hated travel, 'one of the saddest pleasures of life',[2] which always intensified her loneliness and sense of isolation. Afraid of the unknown and the new, she was filled with forebodings of mortal danger for her father and her children. Parting from her friends that October 1803 had plunged her into depression. Slumped into the corner of her coach, she was absolutely dejected until they reached Châlons. Only Benjamin Constant's extraordinary talent for conversation helped to raise her spirits a little. It was as well that she did not know that she was embarking on more than ten years of exile. She would never get over a devouring homesickness for Paris and the pain of exile was to be a recurrent theme in all her works.

Although she had continued her German lessons with Wilhelm von Humboldt, the Prussian envoy to France, who had also encouraged her interest in German culture, she was still not fluent. Constant, on the other hand, was absolutely fluent in German as a result of his education at Erlangen and his years in Brunswick. His own interest in German literature and thought had whetted Madame de Staël's appetite for it. Other friends like Meister, Chenedollé, Gérando and Camille Jordan, who had taken refuge in Germany during the Revolution, had returned with new ideas. Camille Jordan's translation of the poetry of the German poet Klopstock had fired her enthusiasm. She had begun a correspondence with Charles de Villers, a Frenchman who had emigrated to Germany in 1792 and was the author of a scholarly interpretation of Kant. He was now living in Metz and it was because of him that Madame de Staël extended her stay in Metz to two weeks, as she wrote to Mathieu de Montmorency, who was now her children's guardian: 'Benjamin has been wonderful to me. Without him something awful would have undoubtedly befallen me. I ask you to love him for the good he has done me, or rather for the ill he has saved me from. I found Villers of Kant here; a most intelligent man and interesting on account of all that he believes to be true and good. He is accompanied by a fat German woman, Madame de Rodde, whose charms are not yet clear to me. The Prefect has been kindness itself, but for all that I have caused panic in town . . . in my disgrace I am like one with the plague.'[3]

The two weeks in Metz passed well enough. She had many fruitful discussions with Villers who, it seems, fell under her spell, to the displeasure of Madame de Rodde, his 'fat bunny'. Madame de Staël described the crossing of the Rhine into Germany on a dank November day as though it were the crossing of the Styx. At any moment, she wrote, she expected to hear a voice solemnly announcing 'you have left France behind', synonymous with 'you have left life behind' in her eyes.[4] From Frankfurt, she wrote to Villers: 'I had stopped at an inn in a small town, where I heard the piano being played beautifully in a room which was full of steam from woollen clothes drying on an iron stove: That seems to me to be true of everything here . . . there is poetry in their soul but no elegance of form.'[5] To her father she wrote more frankly that she was being well treated, but that Frankfurt had nothing to offer. Everything in Germany was unbearable – 'the beds, the food, the stoves' – and as for the ordinary Germans, 'they are barely human by the standards of our habits and tastes'. They couldn't be less like the English, she added, 'they lock away their opinions in a cupboard and never use them, not even on Sundays'.[6] Almost at once, five-year-old Albertine fell ill with a high fever. The famous doctor Sömmering,[7] called by Madame de Staël, announced curtly and in front of Albertine that she had scarlet fever. Madame de Staël asked in English, so as not to frighten the child who had begun to cry, whether it was dangerous, to which he replied with brutal coldness that someone had just died of it in her inn. Luckily, Albertine soon recovered. Spirited, imaginative, intelligent and very pretty, Albertine was the chief joy of her mother's life: 'My daughter is charming company, I am sometimes afraid that such an extraordinary development might be bad for her health. I assure you that she will have much more wit, and especially more grace, than me.'[8]

As soon as Albertine was fit to travel, together with Constant, who had intended originally only to see them as far as Frankfurt but had been persuaded to stay with them, Madame de Staël set off for Weimar, the real object of her journey. At the town of Fulde, where they stopped on 5 December, she wrote Constant a grateful and graceful promissory note: 'I beg Benjamin to remind me if ever I am back peacefully in Paris, that I give him the absolute right to prevent me from making any gesture from the least to the most important which might in any way compromise my peace but especially that of my generous friend.'[9] Benjamin must have known that it would have been as impossible for her to keep such a promise as for him to enforce it, but he was not sorry to have travelled with her and his adored Albertine. The journey to Weimar was to be as intellectually fruitful for him as for her.

The flat expanses of Germany in mid-winter made it look like a white sea; everything was covered in four feet of snow, she wrote to her father from Gotha. Far from certain about her reception at Weimar, she acknowledged her debt to Constant: 'It is an extraordinary sign of friendship to travel sixty leagues to Germany and back in the snow . . . disguised as a tutor and seeing not a soul.' Constant's disguise as Auguste's tutor was presumably for the sake of appearances. She goes on to report that she had just dined with Grimm. Age had not improved the eighty-year-old encyclopaedist: 'He is heavy, rancorous, without wit or measure, stupidly aristocratic in his views.' He blamed Madame de Staël and her friends for the Revolution and its consequences: 'There is nothing left of his former philosophy except a general bitterness with life.'[10]

Politically, the German lands through which Madame de Staël travelled in those first years of the nineteenth century were fragmented into tiny principalities. German culture, humbled and provincial as a result of the ravages of the Thirty Years' War over a century and a half earlier, had turned in on itself, seeking solace in religion and the spiritual life. Pietism, a branch of Lutheranism, preached simplicity, contempt for learning, for pomp and ceremony, for almost everything represented by the French Enlightenment – the world Madame de Staël had grown up in. Luther had preached that reason was a whore. God was to be reached only through faith. While German courts and society aped French fashion and manners, German thinkers rejected French civilization. France on the other hand, was largely unaware of the recent intellectual ferment, the new thinking and the new aesthetics that were being developed in Germany, which were to bring about, in Isaiah Berlin's words, 'the greatest transformation of Western consciousness, certainly in our time'.[11]

The imminent arrival of the famous Madame de Staël in the small, provincial backwater of Weimar – although it was also Germany's intellectual centre – had caused equal measures of interest and alarm. In a society which both copied and despised French culture, the arrival of the author of *Delphine*, which had sold out in three different editions, was a major event. Reports and rumours flew around: she was a bluestocking, she was the most famous Parisian salonière, she was brilliant, she was a Jacobin, she was a Republican, she was in trouble with Bonaparte; and though she was no beauty, she was a great seductress – was Constant really her lover?

Madame de Staël's arrival had been awaited with some anxiety at court too. Charles-Augustus, the Grand Duke of Saxe-Weimar, was a cultivated man who had been tutored by Wieland. Enchanted by Goethe's *Werther*, he had persuaded the great man to come to his court. Goethe had been joined by Schiller, and Herder was there too. The Grand Duke now called on them all to come and help him entertain Madame de Staël. 'I am told that intellectuals have been called to arms to receive me,'[12] she wrote to her father. In December 1803, when Madame de Staël arrived at Weimar, Herder, whose doctrines contributed so much to the Romantic movement, was dying, while Goethe had escaped to Jena. Only Schiller was still there, engaged in finishing his play, *William Tell*. Dreading the thought of being dragged into the social life of the court, of having to dress up, of having to speak French to this strange woman, he wrote anxiously to Goethe: 'Madame de Staël really is at Frankfurt and we can expect to see her here soon. If only she understood German . . . but to expound our religion and struggle against her French volubility, that will be a hard task. It won't be as easy to deal with her as it was for Schelling with Camille Jordan, who came to him armed from head to foot with Locke's principles. "I despise Locke," Schelling had said, silencing his adversary.'[13]

The Grand Duke and his Grand Duchess, Louise, preparing to be coolly correct, were immediately enchanted by their exotic visitor. Her turbans, her flowing shawls and low-cut gowns, so cruelly mocked in Paris, breathed Parisian chic and glamour in this quiet backwater. But above all it was her simplicity and directness, her warmth, her unbounded vitality and her extraordinary talent for drawing everyone in and making them shine in her presence which made her so lovable. Ordered to court, Schiller had appeared in full uniform. Madame de Staël at first mistook him for a general. But he was soon won over. As he wrote to a friend, just when he was completely absorbed in finishing his play, 'the devil brought me the French lady philosopher, who is of all the creatures alive that I have ever come across, the most gesticulating, the most combative, the most fertile in expression'. But, he admitted, 'she is also the most cultivated, the cleverest of women. Were she not truly interesting I would certainly not give up my time to her. You can imagine how such an apparition, such a mind, from the heights of French culture, which is the very opposite to ours, who appears suddenly among us from another world, contrasts with German nature, and how different it is to mine . . . I see her often, and since on top of everything else I don't find it easy to express myself in French, I have spent some trying hours! However, one is bound to respect and deeply honour this woman for her great intelligence, and her liberal spirit which is open to so much.'[14]

Madame de Staël was no less impressed by Schiller, although she had found him difficult to understand at first. But in spite of the obstacles of language she discovered him to be full of ideas, and was impressed that a man of genius was happy to engage in the hard labour of conversation when his command of the language was inadequate to his thoughts. She had been so struck by his modesty and by his animated and proud defence of what he believed to be the truth, that she 'vowed from that moment on, a friendship full of my admiration for him'.[15] But of course, it had not stopped her from arguing fiercely with him on the superiority of French drama, and to illustrate her points she had declaimed parts of Racine's *Andromache* and *Phèdre*, as well as the dream of *Athalie*, before the open-mouthed court.

Madame de Staël had been particularly anxious to meet the Olympian Goethe, whose *Werther* had marked her youth. But the old curmudgeon remained at Jena, fascinated and irritated by the goings on at Weimar, about which he was fully briefed by Schiller and his wife. He admired Madame de Staël; he had, after all, been responsible for translating her works, and would be delighted to meet her, he wrote, but she must come to him: 'as long as I have twenty-four hours' notice she will find a well furnished apartment, and good simple bourgeois cooking. We will be able to meet properly and talk together; she can stay as long as she likes. But to come back to Weimar, dress up, go to court and into society, that is quite out of the question,' he wrote to Schiller.[16] He had reckoned without the Grand Duke, however, who was now unwilling to forgo Madame de Staël's company, and summoned Goethe to Weimar. On 19 December 1803, Goethe wrote to Madame de Staël with a good enough grace to announce his arrival and Schiller wrote to Goethe to prepare and reassure him: 'Madame de Staël will appear to you as you have imagined her. Everything about her is of a piece: you will find not one thing in her which is disparate or false. That is why, in spite of the differences between her nature and ours, one is comfortable with her; one is disposed to listen to anything from her while wishing, at the same time, to tell her everything: she is the very personification, as perfect as it is interesting, of the true French spirit. In everything that we call philosophy, and therefore on the loftiest principles in all things, one is opposed to her, and that in spite of her eloquence. But her naturalness and her feelings are worth more than metaphysics, and her mind often soars with the power of genius. Wishing to explain everything, understand everything, measure everything, she will allow nothing that is impenetrable. What the light of reason cannot illuminate does not exist as far as she is concerned. That is why she has an insurmountable aversion for idealist philosophy, which in her view, leads to mysticism and superstition. There is a total absence in her of a sense of poetry as we understand it . . . she can only appreciate the general, the passionate, the rhetorical. She will never approve what is false, but she does always recognize what is true. In spite of my poor French, we manage to understand one another passably, and since you speak that language easily, I have no doubt that your conversations with Madame de Staël will be of great interest to her and to you.'[17]

Schiller was right, though Goethe and Madame de Staël made a poor start. 'Goethe ruins my ideal image of *Werther*; he is a fat man without distinction to look at, who likes to think he is a man of the world but only half succeeds, a man about whom there is nothing sensitive either in looks or thoughts or habits; but he is very strong on literature and metaphysics which preoccupy him,' she reported to her father on Christmas Day. 'In this part of the world abstract ideas predominate over positive ones.'[18] She was amazed at the provincialism around her; amazed that Wieland, Goethe and Schiller never even read a newspaper.

All in all, Madame de Staël was delighted with her reception at court to which she had a standing daily invitation and which she attended three nights a week. To her friend Claude Hochet she wrote happily that she was being treated by the court and by Weimar's men of letters 'as if she had been a sister of the First Consul!'[19] Her friendship with the Grand Duchess was real enough to be maintained by a correspondence which lasted for the rest of her life. When she was not at court, Madame de Staël was at the theatre, where the Grand Duke had ordered the performance of all the plays that she wished to see. Afterwards she would discuss them with her mentor, Schiller: 'I thirst to tell you what I thought of the play yesterday. Come and see me at half-past four. We will talk through the clouds of words which separate us.'[20]

Auguste, too, loved Germany and was now almost fluent in German. Little Albertine was thriving and giving her mother and Constant great pleasure. Madame de Staël's letters to her father, which reflected a much more cheerful frame of mind, were full of her gratitude to Constant. He also noted in his journal, which he began in January 1804, that although he had set out in a spirit of self-sacrifice he had been well rewarded. Fascinated by German philosophy, they both read voraciously while Madame de Staël continued to improve her German by translating passages into French.

'Goethe, Schiller and Wieland have more ingenuity, more depth in literature and philosophy than anyone I have ever met,' Madame de Staël wrote to her cousin: 'their conversation is all ideas. There is no question, especially in a foreign language, of witticisms, but they never leave my house without my writing down new ideas, and I think my journal will interest you and my father. . . . German drama makes one think again. Schiller and Goethe are attempting all kinds of innovations in the theatre: sometimes using a Greek chorus, sometimes writing idealist pieces. While I still think our drama superior, I like to see what it is that makes it superior. The Germans, heavy as they are, have more youthfulness than the French, because they are not yet blasé: the audience gives itself up happily to those who seek to entertain them. Their comic operas are full of apparitions and machines, which greatly please Albertine, full of romantic imagination which is allowed to develop tranquilly before a simple-hearted audience which has not yet discovered ridicule. There is much originality too, not in individuals but in literature.'[21]

Madame de Staël soon met a young Englishman, Henry Crabb Robinson, a student at Jena, whose knowledge of German culture and language made him an ideal guide. She was most grateful for his help, but when he suggested that she might find it hard to understand certain aspects of German philosophy, she put him roundly in his place. 'Sir,' she said, 'I understand everything which deserves to be understood: what I do not understand is nothing.'[22]

Goethe and Madame de Staël continued to provoke each other. He could not help but admire her verbal brilliance but was irritated and shocked by her wish to discuss everything. Unabashed, she fired volleys of questions at him. He disliked answering them, becoming deliberately obstructive or retiring huffily to his Olympian heights. She told him to his face that he was only agreeable after he had drunk a bottle of champagne. He complained of her rudeness to Schiller. To her old friend Brinkman, now Swedish ambassador in Berlin, she wrote that she would tell him about Goethe when she came to Berlin: 'but I can tell you already, that his mind and his talent seem to me of the highest order not only in Germany but in the whole of literary Europe. His talent for conversation is almost as great, which is rare. As for details of character', she wrote, perhaps unwilling to be rude in print, 'they are to be spoken of not written.'[23]

It helped that Goethe and Constant liked each other, although Constant too had been shocked by Goethe's views. Having reread *Faust*, Constant confided in his journal: 'It is a mockery of the human race and of scientists. Germans find amazing depth in it; as for me I think it less good than *Candide*. While it is as immoral, arid and lacking in feeling, there is less lightness, fewer clever jokes and more bad taste.'[24] Madame de Staël and Constant saw art as an essential means of communication and moral purification; Weimar, following Kant, believed in art for art's sake. Schelling's philosophy preached that morality lay in being in accord with oneself. Goethe, for his part, noted in his journal: 'I liked Benjamin Constant with whom I enjoyed many hours of the most pleasurable and profitable intercourse . . . if my ways of approaching art and nature were not always very apparent to him, yet the manner in which he strove in all integrity to grasp my point of view . . . brought forcibly to my consciousness all that was as yet undeveloped, obscure, misty in my method', while Madame de Staël, he admitted, aroused the devil in him and made him deliberately contradictory and obstinate.[25]

She continued to puzzle and amaze him, which made him crosser still. At supper at Goethe's one evening, when Madame de Staël was expressing her thoughts with her customary directness, he even went so far as to accuse her of having no concept of the meaning of the word 'duty'. Unabashed, she wrote to thank him the next day 'for the happiest evening which I have ever spent outside my own country, for the most brilliant which one could spend anywhere. Do not reply. I love you more than you know how to love, philosopher that you are. Farewell.'[26] On the subject of his novel, *The Sorrows of Young Werther*, Goethe had said to Constant: 'What makes this work dangerous is that I described weakness as if it was strength. But when I write something that suits me I care less about the consequences. If there are madmen who have been harmed by reading the book, then so much the worse for them.'[27]

In spite of Goethe's initial reservations, their friendship grew, bridged by intellectual curiosity and mutual admiration. He thought enough of Madame de Staël's talents to take time to check her translations. She was soon comfortable enough with him to send her 'dear Sir', as she always called him in English, teasing notes full of philosophical jargon and in-jokes about Fichte's theory of the absolute self. 'Thank you, my dear Sir,' she writes thanking him for the return of her translations, 'and please love me a little, whether empirically or in the absolute. I love you with all my being, and all my talent, if I have any.'[28]

Her departure for Berlin in March 1804, after a two-month stay, was nevertheless a great relief to the sages of Weimar. They admired her more than ever and had come to like her, but she was exhausting: 'I feel,' wrote Schiller to Goethe, 'as if I had just recovered from a severe illness.'[29] She left, however, with many recommendations to their friends in Berlin. Goethe wrote warmly of her to the composer Zelter: 'It is now four weeks since we have had the happiness of Madame de Staël's presence. This extraordinary woman is soon going to Berlin and I will give her a letter of introduction to you. Go and see her at once; she is very easy to be with, and your musical compositions will certainly give her great pleasure, although literature, poetry and philosophy and all relative things give her more pleasure than the arts.'[30]

Madame de Staël and Benjamin Constant parted warmly at Leipzig in the first week of March, after first visiting the city together. Constant, who had left France without a regular passport, felt uneasy about going on to Berlin without one, especially to court where there was a French ambassador. His plan was to return to France via Switzerland. She said goodbye to him with a heavy heart. Constant had proposed to her but although she had rejected his proposal, her fear of loneliness prompted her to make him promise not to marry anyone else. Constant, too, was moved by their parting: 'I am sad in my loneliness. Solitude is like a cold bath and very disagreeable. But I will get over it. There is nothing so good, so loving and so devoted as a woman!'[31] He was very glad to have accompanied her.

Both now had a much clearer understanding of German culture and appreciation of its enormous importance for the future. Madame de Staël had already written to her father that she proposed to write a book about Germany, which would, she thought, be of some interest adding that she had also had an idea for a novel. She wrote to her friend Gérando: 'I have studied and am still studying Kant's, Schelling's and Schlegel's. etc., new philosophy and aesthetics and would like to analyse them, but I should first like to read what you have written on them. I am not anxious to enter into metaphysics; but to give an idea of the German character and of the thinking which distinguishes their literature, it will be necessary to give a simple and readable idea of their philosophies.'[32] *De l'Allemagne*, which she was to complete after a further visit to Germany three years later, and which was to get her into even deeper trouble with Bonaparte, was to be of seminal importance for both France and Germany.

After a terrible journey through deep snow Madame de Staël reached Berlin on 8 March 1804. Her first week there was a round of frivolity and pleasure. Invited to be presented at court on 10 March, the Queen's birthday as it happened, she was obliged to have a court dress made in twenty-four hours, and spent three hours getting dressed. Two days later she described the presentation to her father: 'When the Queen entered the hall, filled with men and women covered with gold and diamonds, cymbals and trumpets heralded her arrival, the music making it all the more exciting. The Queen is charming; I am not flattering her when I say that she is the prettiest woman I have ever seen. Her jewellery is breathtaking and in the best taste, she completely dazzled me when she came up to me.' The Queen had told her that she hoped that Madame de Staël realized that they had enough good taste to admire her in Berlin, adding that she herself had longed to meet her. Needless to say Madame de Staël was delighted with her reception. She was invited by everyone to everything and hoped that news of her success would reach Paris.

While she enjoyed the intense social life for a few days, she confessed to her father that she could not have gone through the whole season of the carnival without becoming seriously exhausted. Throughout March her letters mention invitations to lunch and dinner at the various embassies as well as from luminaries such as the Duchess of Courland, all the royal Princes, the Duke of Brunswick and Prince Belmonte. Berlin buzzed with European and especially French political gossip, which she related to her father. Yet in spite of the great consideration shown her by society she did not really like Berlin. It was not the place in which to study German literature; it seemed to her that it was given up wholly to social life and it was only in Paris that social life was compatible with letters: 'The republic of German letters is truly astonishing, but I think that the aristocracy is not very cultivated; the thinkers are all underground while the grenadiers march over it.'[33]

Towards the end of March, however, she was able to tell her father that she had met a man who had more knowledge of literature than almost anyone she had ever met. His name was August Wilhelm Schlegel. 'Schlegel spoke French like a Frenchman and English like an Englishman and while he was only thirty-six, he had read everything in the world.'[34] She was doing everything in her power to persuade him to come back to Coppet with her. He was far too distinguished to come as a mere tutor but he could help Albert with his German and, above all, Madame de Staël needed to consult him on the book she was planning on Germany. She offered him very generous terms which Schlegel, who had a rather tortured private life, was considering.

The son of a pastor, August Wilhelm Schlegel and his brother Friedrich had first collaborated with Schiller on his periodical *Die Hören* and then founded their own – *Das Athenäum*. Novalis, Tieck and Schelling were regular contributors to what became the flagship of the Romantic movement first in Germany and then in Europe. Schlegel was famous above all for his masterly translations of Shakespeare's plays into German.

The American George Ticknor was present at the first meeting between Madame de Staël and the philosopher Fichte, a disciple of Kant, who had developed a theory of the *ich-ich*, or the absolute self. With a passion for perfect freedom, Fichte believed that this could never be achieved by an individual in the material world in which one was necessarily confined by the laws of nature. Perfect freedom could be achieved only through the spirit, by which he did not mean the individual soul but some kind of collective pure spirit. Ticknor had been much amused and recorded the meeting almost verbatim: 'Monsieur Fichte,' Madame de Staël had said as soon as they were introduced, 'would you be so good as to give me an idea, for say a quarter of an hour, of your system, so that I might try and understand what you mean by your *ich*; your "I", because I must admit that it is still not clear to me?' Fichte then launched into an explanation. Ten minutes into his exposition she interrupted him very amiably. 'Thank you, Monsieur Fichte. I understand; I understand you perfectly. Your system is perfectly illustrated in one of Baron Münchhausen's travel tales. When the Baron came to a river where there was neither bridge nor raft nor any means of crossing, he fell into despair. But he soon pulled himself together and seizing his own sleeve, he propelled himself to the other bank. That, Monsieur Fichte, is what you have done with your *ich;* with your "I", isn't that so?'

Fichte was furious, but there was so much truth and humour in her observation that it was irresistible to the rest of the company.[35] She would stick to Kant, she wrote afterwards to her friend Jacobi; he at least presented a happy synthesis of realism and idealism, uniting the concepts of the freedom of the individual with the needs of others.[36]

To her father she wrote her usual long letters recounting the daily round, with political gossip and comments on cultural matters as well as news of his grandchildren. Auguste was doing very well, but Albertine had disgraced them by slapping the Crown Prince at a children's ball, she wrote. The news had come to Madame de Staël via her friend Brinkman, the Swedish ambassador. Albertine had admitted as much, but had not known whom she had slapped. The King and Queen were reported as saying that this was the result of the sort of education given to children by Republicans. Mortified, but secretly amused, Madame de Staël had sent a letter of apology to the Queen, telling her that Albertine was now confined to her room and forbidden to go to any children's parties until the Queen gave her leave. The

Queen had sent a very kind reply. She much regretted that Madame de Staël had been informed of an incident of no importance, and entirely natural among children. Albertine was to come to the children's ball.[37] In another letter she recounted her first meeting with Metternich, who had charming manners.

She was tired of social life, however; she had had enough of it 'to kill two lives, but not to fill one' and was longing to return to Coppet.[38] In a long letter to her cousin, Madame Necker-de Saussure, she summed up her impressions of Berlin. Although outwardly much more like Paris than Weimar, she would not wish to live there. German thought flourished in universities, not in salons as in Paris. Intellectuals and courtiers lived quite apart. The result was that scholars could not express themselves while society was absolutely incapable of thought. Frivolity without the graceful manners of the French was quite unbearable, and 'since the Germans are not naturally frivolous, there is a kind of sadness in their attempts at gaiety which makes one want to ask "but why do it?"' Everyone drank too much, including her friend, the charming Prince Louis, who 'certainly has wit and a good Prussian figure', but who was usually incoherent after dinner, so that Madame de Staël always preferred to see him in the morning. The studious and provincial calm of Weimar suited her much better, she concluded.[39]

Two days later she was in shock after hearing of the summary execution of the Duc d'Enghien. On Bonaparte's instructions, the blameless young man, grandson of the Prince de Condé, was kidnapped in Ettenheim, near Baden, and brought to Vincennes on 20 March, where he was shot without trial on a trumped-up charge of treachery. His grave had been dug beforehand. Tired of trying to come to terms with the royalists, and in the wake of the arrests of Generals Moreau and Pichegru, as well as Cadoudal, for conspiring against him, Bonaparte had decided, with Talleyrand's and Fouché's collusion, to show the Bourbons who was in charge. The whole of Europe was outraged by this shedding of royal blood, by the violation of frontiers, and by the absence of any trial. Chateaubriand resigned his post and La Fayette refused to be named senator in the new administration. An official protest from Russia brought the public reply from Talleyrand that Tsar Alexander had no right to meddle in the affairs of France when no effort had been made to bring to trial the murderers of his father Paul. In France, however, the censored press ensured that the public would believe in the young duke's treachery. There could be no question of a restoration of the Bourbons now. Bonaparte's subsequent decision to establish a hereditary successor was supposedly intended to put an end to instability. He was encouraged in this by Fouché, who was anxious to regain favour, and by Talleyrand, who wished to keep it. Three weeks later, the tame Senate voted that the Life Consul be declared Emperor and two months later, on 18 May 1804, a twenty-one-gun salute in Paris proclaimed Bonaparte as Emperor.

In order to sever any link with the Bourbons, Bonaparte chose to call himself the Emperor Napoleon, proclaiming himself a descendant of Charlemagne and the Emperors of Rome. 'The vanity of the parvenu was combined in him with the great abilities of a conqueror,' Madame de Staël wrote.[40] And indeed the new Emperor immediately elevated two of his brothers, Joseph and Louis, now in direct line of succession, to princely rank, provoking rage in two of his sisters. Forced, for the sake of family peace, to elevate them also to Imperial Highnesses, he was reported to have complained angrily: 'anyone would think that I had been trying to deprive my family of the inheritance of the late King, our father'.

Madame de Staël's disgust at what she was to call 'the sad spectacle of the annihilation of the entire moral nature of a nation'[41] was about to be overshadowed by the greatest personal tragedy of her life. On 30 March, after a happy winter in Geneva where he had enjoyed the company of many friends, her father fell ill with erysipelas of the leg.[42] His condition deteriorated rapidly although he was able to write two more letters to his daughter, who was constantly on his mind. He knew that she would be blamed for her absence, and knew what his death would mean to her. 'It is a father's heart which judges and justifies her. It is for a father to judge his daughter. I can feel nothing but gratitude to her,' he had said to Madame Rilliet-Huber, who, together with Madame Necker-de Saussure, was nursing him devotedly. 'Tell my daughter, that she should not blame herself; had she been here she could have done nothing. I know that she loves me very much, that she has always loved me.'[43] He died on 9 April 1804.

Letters warning Madame de Staël that he was seriously ill were sent off at once. No one dared to tell her the truth. In Berlin, Princess Radziwill, accompanied by her brother Prince Louis-Ferdinand, called on Madame de Staël on 18 April, where they also found the Swedish ambassador, Brinkman, who had been warned of Necker's likely death by Constant. As soon as she saw them, Madame de Staël cried out: 'He is dead', but news of his illness, her father's letters, which were delivered to her, and her own ardent wishes, combined to restore some hope. Setting off at once on the long journey back to Coppet, she was accompanied by Schlegel, who had been unable to refuse her at such a time.

Constant had been on the point of departure for Paris himself when news of Necker's death reached him in Lausanne. Knowing how distraught Madame de Staël would be when she learned the truth, he had turned around at once to meet her on her way back from Germany: 'M. Necker is dead! What will become of his daughter?' he wrote in his journal. 'What despair for the present! What loneliness for the future! Poor unhappy woman! When I think of her pain, her anxiety two months ago! Poor thing! Death would be preferable to such suffering.'[44] At Weimar, where they were reunited on 21 April, Madame de Staël's birthday, Constant found himself unable to break the news to her, asking one of her friends, Mlle von Goechhausen, a lady-in-waiting to the Grand Duchess, to do it for him. When she heard the news that she had dreaded for so long, Madame de Staël fell to the ground, screaming hysterically, her arms flailing as she blamed herself bitterly for her absence from her father's deathbed. She was not indulging in a histrionic performance; she had never learned to contain her emotion. A doctor was called to prescribe something to calm her. Only then was she able to read the letters sent to her by Madame Necker-de Saussure and Madame Rilliet-Huber. Watched over by Schlegel, who later recalled that he had never heard such piercing screams, she spent a sleepless night. Goethe too, who called the next day to present his condolences was quite horrified at the state he had found her in. Replying to her cousin Albertine, Madame de Staël wrote 'All I can tell you, my friend, is that I am alive and that the destruction of all happiness, of all existence, of all future, of all peace, has left me, in spite of my wishes, with physical existence,' she wrote to her cousin. 'I am, as is my poor friend [Constant] quite unable to contemplate leaving for a few more days. I will write to ask you to come and meet me at Berne; I will need you with me to enter his tomb, which will be mine also. Adieu, I can bear it no more, adieu. You were with him for five months longer than me, five months lost to me! Ah if I could only die uttering those words!'[45] Replying to a message of condolence from the Duke of Saxe-Gotha, she tried to explain: 'It was not a mere father-daughter relationship: it was fraternity, love, religion, all my spiritual being.'[46]

Madame de Staël travelled home accompanied by Constant and Schlegel. The two men disliked each other heartily. The touchy, quarrelsome and rather ill-looking Schlegel was clearly in love with Madame de Staël. This annoyed Constant. They both tried to distract her with conversation, arguing fiercely about literature. Schlegel, Constant recalled, took everything personally. An argument with Madame de Staël on the question of humour, and another with Constant about Cervantes, had left him pale and tearful.[47] The party was met in Zurich by Madame de Staël's cousins and her son Albert. On 19 May, as they approached Coppet, she grew ever more agitated, repeatedly putting her head out of the window to urge the coachman to hurry. To distract her, Constant pointed to a cloud over the mountains in the shape of a great figure of a man, disappearing into the evening light. To Madame de Staël it seemed that heaven itself was echoing her loss.[48] Distraught at the thought that her father would not be there to greet her, she fell out of her carriage in a swoon and was carried lifeless to her room. A period of bitter anguish now lay ahead.

Chapter 19

~

Song of Italy

'Italy could be sung, Germany would have to be recounted.'
Madame Necker-de Saussure on *Corinne* and *De l'Allemagne*

THROUGHOUT THE SUMMER of 1804 Madame de Staël sat in her father's study, pouring out her agony on paper, remembering how even when he had been working, she had always been sure of a welcome: 'Oh! That look of his, that paternal welcome, I will never see it again. I am here in the same study, surrounded by objects which were his; all my thoughts, my whole heart calls out to him, but in vain! Oh! what then is this barrier which separates the living from those that are no more! It must be redoubtable indeed; otherwise one who was so good, one who loved me so much, seeing my despair, would surely come to help me if he were able.'[1]

On the day after her return, after first visiting his tomb, she had called for his papers. Racked with terrible guilt that she had not been with him in his last hours, she assuaged her bitter grief by writing about him. Her essay, *Du Caractère de M. Necker et de sa vie privée* (On Monsieur Necker's Character and on his Private Life) is a hymn of love and praise, but also a lament for an irreparable loss. It served as a preface to her collection of her father's unpublished writings under the title *Manuscrits de M. Necker, publiés par sa Fille* (M. Necker's manuscripts, published by his daughter), which was published in Geneva that autumn. Her eulogy of her father, which raises him to truly Olympian heights and which was to provoke much amusement in the Parisian press, was, as Constant wrote, 'entirely unaffected' and deeply moving in its sincerity. Bonstetten, who thought it the best thing she had written, recalled that she had tried to read excerpts out loud to her friends, but she could hardly do so through her sobs, while 'we were all in tears and absolutely thrilled by it'.[2]

'During the troubles in France, even when we were separated, I believed that I was protected by him, that nothing terrible could happen to me . . . When I wrote to him I always called him *my guardian angel* . . . I counted on him to make good my mistakes. Nothing seemed beyond remedy while he lived: only since his death have I known the meaning of real terror . . . In his strength I found mine; my confidence depended on his support. Is he still there, my protecting genius? Will he still tell me what I should hope for or fear? Will he guide my steps? Will he spread his wings over my children whom he blessed with his dying voice? And will I be able to gather up enough of him in my heart to consult him and hear him still?'[3]

Her father had rightly called her a child. In spite of her formidable intellect, all her life Madame de Staël's emotional responses were those of a child – often those of a spoiled child. It is the key to her passionate attachment to her father. Recalling their last parting, she wrote: 'during my absence, I was to lose my protector, my father, my brother, my friend, the one I would have chosen as the sole love of my life if fate had not thrown me into a different generation'.[4] Her often repeated wish to have been born his contemporary so that she might have married him was no more than an expression of her childlike need for his constant presence, his protection, his company, his understanding – in fact, for the unconditional love of a parent. 'Ah! one is only loved like this by a father' she writes in the same essay, 'a disinterested love, a love which makes us feel forever young, that we are loved, that the world is still ours!'[5] Necker had responded to this need with a no less tender affection, and perhaps too with his own need for approval and the adulation which flowed unceasingly from his daughter: 'Many times during our talks together, my father would complain gently of how quickly time flew – "Why am I not your brother? I would be able to protect you for your whole life!" he had said.[6]

No other man in her life had ever, or ever could, measure up to this perfect love. Madame de Staël's passionate wish to hold on to successive men in her life was not due to emotional lightness or frivolity or to a voracious sexual appetite, as some have suggested. Always unsure of her charms, often depressed, she was terrified of being left alone. It was always love that she sought, a love that would fill the emptiness in her heart, and banish the fear of old age, a love at once passionate and unrestrained, equal but submissive, protective but undemanding; an impossible love.

Madame de Staël's veneration for her father remained unchanged for the rest of her life. Twelve years after his death, and only a year before her own, she wrote: 'Every day my admiration for him grows; my memories of his mind and of his virtues serve as a comparison for the value of other men and, although I have travelled the whole of Europe, never have I met a genius of his stamp, or with a morality as vigorous as his . . . Everything that M. Necker ever said to me is firm as a rock; anything I may have acquired myself may disappear, my whole identity lies in my attachment to his memory. I have loved people whom I love no more, I have respected those I respect no longer; the tide of life has carried everything away, everything except for that great shade up there on the mountain top, which points to the life to come with his finger. I owe true gratitude on this earth only to God and to my father . . .'[7] In her mind the two were often one and the same.

At Coppet, Constant, Schlegel, Bonstetten and Sismondi, watched over her anxiously. They were to form the nucleus of what became known over the next few years as the Coppet Circle: an extraordinary and influential grouping of European talent. For the moment they were an ill-assorted group of intellectuals, united only in their love for Madame de Staël. Sismondi had come into her life some two years before. A young protégé of her father's, Charles Simonde was the son of a Swiss pastor and had spent the revolutionary years partly in England and partly in Tuscany. He had changed his name to de Sismondi, believing himself to be a descendant of a noble Pisan family of that name. An economist and follower of Adam Smith, he had recently published a treatise on Tuscan agriculture. Serious and unsure of himself, the young man was flattered and delighted by Madame de Staël's encouragement. Constant and Sismondi both disliked the touchy Schlegel, who, a stranger among them, felt more insecure and more misunderstood than ever. He had left Germany reluctantly and at the last minute, out of love for Madame de Staël, but now found himself among rivals. Constant too, had again proposed marriage to her but was refused. Their relationship, so harmonious in Germany, went steadily downhill. Although Madame de Staël had no wish to marry him, she had even less intention of letting him go.

Constant was right in believing that her father's death, while it affected her to the depths of her being, had not changed her. If anything, it had made her more demanding than ever. 'It is an extraordinary combination, this deep and heartrending suffering, coupled with the need for distraction and an incorrigible nature which has left her with all her weaknesses of character, all her susceptibilities and all her need for constant activity.'[8] She had insisted on a long discussion at one o'clock in the morning. When he complained, he was immediately accused of insensitivity. Longing for his bed, Constant, wrote bitterly: 'One must obey. I have never known a better woman, nor one with more grace and devotion, but neither have I known one more continuously demanding without being aware of it . . . every minute, every hour, every year must be at her disposal. And when she gets into one of her rages it is like an explosion of all the thunderstorms and earthquakes put together . . . I should like not to have demands for love after a ten-year affair, when we are both nearly forty and when I have told her a hundred times and long since that I have done with passion. I must detach myself from her while remaining her friend, or disappear from the face of the earth.'[9]

They were not in love with one another, yet there was between them an intellectual understanding which they had with no one else, as well as trust and emotional need. They stimulated each other's creativity as no one else could. 'No one has known Madame de Staël unless he has seen her with Benjamin Constant,' Sismondi wrote to a friend many years later. 'He alone had the power, through an intelligence equal to hers, to bring all her intelligence into play, to enhance it by competition, to kindle an eloquence, a depth of feeling and thought that she never revealed in all its brilliance except in his presence; neither was he ever truly himself except at Coppet.'[10]

Another entry in Constant's journal reads: 'Minette is angry because I refuse to stay up late. I see that I shall have to get married to be able to go to bed early.'[11] He was not joking. His only possible way of escape from Madame de Staël was through marriage. But to whom? His aunt, Madame de Nassau, and his cousin, Rosalie de Constant, were both firmly against Madame de Staël and wanted him to leave her. Weak and vacillating, Constant was unsure whether to rekindle a former love affair with Charlotte von Hardenberg, now Madame du Tertre.

So the summer passed. Madame de Staël tried yet again to return to Paris, enlisting the help of Joseph Bonaparte, now Prince Joseph and the Emperor's successor, should Napoleon fail to have a son. Joseph replied very warmly, begging Madame de Staël to think of him as a friend, urging patience and promising to do what he could with his brother; 'If I am not successful, nobody will be.'[12] Mathieu de Montmorency arrived at Coppet in July. At the end of that month Madame de Staël's uncle, M. de Germany, followed his younger brother to the grave. 'Now the last link is broken, the last being who loved me paternally . . . My poor dear cousin, so here we are, all alone,' she wrote to Madame Necker-de Saussure.[13] Unhappy and restless, Madame de Staël needed constant movement and activity. Friends from Italy and from Germany, as well as half of Geneva, made their way to Coppet, scandalizing the good burghers of Geneva, who believed that mourning should take place in a silent withdrawal from society.

But in spite of her emotional turmoil Madame de Staël's formidable mind continued to function as coolly and calmly as ever. She continued to think, she wrote and dealt efficiently with her financial affairs. Soon after Necker's death she had to settle a number of questions regarding the feudal rights at Coppet. She wrote at once to Necker's man of business in Paris, M. Fourcault de Pavant, with a series of precise questions about her father's affairs. He was to remain her accountant until his retirement a year before her own death. She was to show no less a talent in the management of all her father's investments than he had himself, leaving her children with an increased fortune at her death. Among her many holdings was land in upper New York State, bought on the advice of her old friend, Gouverneur Morris, and the bank of Le Roy and Bayard. Judge William Cooper, father of the writer James Fenimore Cooper, acted for her.

Soon after the publication of her father's writings in October 1804, and aware that for the moment there was no going back to France, Madame de Staël began to make plans for a journey to Italy. Her book on Germany would have to wait until she had had a chance to study that country further, but at Weimar an idea had come to her for a novel, which she wanted to place in Italy, a country she believed had been neglected by French writers. She had already asked Joseph Bonaparte for letters of introduction to Cardinal Fesch and his mother, who was living in Rome. Fesch was Napoleon's maternal uncle and had been made a Cardinal at the beginning of 1803. Soon after he was sent as ambassador to the Vatican.

Meanwhile, in France the situation was still unstable. The execution of the Duc d'Enghien was fresh in people's minds and the trial of General Moreau, ending in his exile to America, had been deeply unpopular. The proclamation of the Empire had caused consternation and disgust as well as much amusement all over Europe. On hearing the news, Beethoven had struck Bonaparte's name off the dedication to his Third Symphony. At the coronation on 2 December, Napoleon's short form, dressed in his glittering coronation robes, made him look like the King of Diamonds, thought Madame de Boigne. Jokes about the parvenu monarchy and the newly created princes and princesses flew around: 'the three imperial sisters who had left their laundry behind and now appeared in all their finery and diamonds to carry the train of Barras's former mistress [Josephine had been Barras's mistress when she met Napoleon]' was how one royalist contemptuously put it. Napoleon despised the old aristocracy, but he also needed them: 'I offered them places in my army, they turned them down; I offered them places in my administration, they refused them; but when I opened my antechambers, they rushed in.'[14]

'Every time that a gentleman of the old court recalled the etiquette of former times, proposed an extra curtsey, a certain way of knocking on the door of some antechamber, a more ceremonial way of presenting a dispatch, of folding a letter, of closing a letter with such and such a formula, he was received as if he had made real progress for the happiness of the human race. The code of Imperial etiquette is the most remarkable documentation of the depths to which the human race can sink,' Madame de Staël wrote later.[15]

She had written to Narbonne, to beg him not to lower himself, as so many other nobles had done, by serving the 'bourgeois and bourgeoises of Ajaccio!' She believed that she had sent her letter by a trustworthy hand, but the man in question turned out to be yet another of Fouché's spies, planted permanently around Coppet. The Emperor had gone into a furious rage when he saw the letter, threatening to clap her in prison. It was Fouché who had persuaded Napoleon to leave Madame de Staël free, arguing that she might lead them to other conspirators.[16]

Certainly the Emperor had no intention of allowing her, of all people, back to Paris where her energy and her mordant wit were bound to stir up further trouble. Only intense wishful thinking can have led her to expect anything else. She did at least see the wisdom of Joseph's advice that there was no hope at present, and that she should keep away if there was to be any chance of the return of her father's money, or indeed of her possible return to France later. For the time being she would have to remove herself from the Emperor's notice. He was more than happy that she should go to Italy, even issuing orders that she was to be treated with every consideration by his agents there. He had no wish to make a permanent enemy of her or to be seen to be persecuting a woman.

Madame de Staël had decided travel to Italy at the end of the year without Constant, who was much looking forward to six months of peace and intended to spend them writing at his house in Luzarches. Accompanied by Schlegel, and by her three children, she left Geneva at the beginning of December. Sismondi, who was working on a history of the Italian Republics, was to join them in Turin, while a thankful Constant escaped to Paris.

On the eve of her departure Madame de Staël was once again assailed by doubts and fears, not entirely misplaced this time since she was about to cross the Alps in the depth of winter, an exceptionally cold one that year. A perilous journey at the best of times, the journey through Chambéry and over the Mont-Cenis pass took nine days. Before Napoleon's new carriage road over the pass was opened in 1805, there was only a steep and narrow road overhanging vertiginous drops. Travel by carriage at six miles an hour was as exhausting as it was frightening. But worse was to come. To cross the passes the carriage was unloaded, the contents loaded on to pack mules, and the passengers carried in sedan chairs. If there was enough snow the descent was by sledge, which would first be dragged by mules and then unhitched.

Turin, when she finally got there, was cold and 'too much, or too little like France'. The only point of interest seems to have been the Arab wife of the French governor Menou: 'with her olive skin and dark eyes, her oriental sweetness which inspired both interest and pity'.[17] In Milan, she wrote at once to the poet Vincenzo Monti, to whom she had an introduction.

Italy's greatest poet since the recent death of Alfieri, and still handsome at fifty, the main body of Monti's work was already behind him. His humble beginnings, his early service as secretary to Prince Braschi, nephew of Pius VI, his political journey from his early work, *Bassvilliana*, which supported the Papacy, to lauding the Revolution and Napoleon, as well as a talent for mordant satire and a love of argument, had earned him the enmity of more than his fellow poets. He had written some bitterly critical things about the Papacy and the Catholic Church. He had just left his chair at the University of Pavia and was poet laureate and consultant on the arts to the government in Milan. His health was poor and his financial situation precarious when he met Madame de Staël. An immediate sympathy sprang up between them. To her he seemed everything a poet should be. They shared a romantic imagination and a full-blooded, unrestrained mode of expressing it. She spent most of her fortnight in Milan in his company. 'I did no more than recognize you,' she wrote on the day after her departure from Milan. 'I felt my own nature in yours. You were already a friend awaiting me, you were certainly not a new acquaintance. I feel that I have all the rights of time over you. Have our thoughts not been the same for many years? And after our liveliest arguments did we not always understand one another better than on the previous day?' She had believed every Italian to be hiding a dagger under his cloak when she entered the country, but 'The sound of your voice is forever in my heart, and Italian has been ennobled for me by the impression you made on me.'[18]

Madame de Staël had a generally poor opinion of contemporary Italian writers. Monti's influence certainly helped her to review and correct some of her ideas on Italian literature, while her responsiveness, her warmth and admiration helped him through a difficult and artistically barren time. If Madame de Staël could be tactless and demanding at times, her innate kindness and generosity enabled her to show the utmost sensitivity and delicacy when appropriate. Knowing that Monti was financially embarrassed, she sent him fifty louis before her departure, with a graceful note: 'That same goodness which is such an admirable trait of your character and your mind will forgive me for daring to write this. I believe that the floods in Ferrara and other temporary circumstances have put you in slight financial embarrassment; allow me to beg your leave to lend you fifty louis. This is no trouble to me. In ten years' time you will repay me, and tell me that you still remember my tender friendship for you. Do I need to tell you that the day when I assured you of my friendship, a most sincere and lively friendship, I did a thousand times more for you than I do through a miserable loan of money, which is only a matter of the chance of our circumstances?'[19]

This was to be the first of many letters to Monti during Madame de

Staël's travels in Italy. Her next stop was Parma, where she went sightseeing with the new French Governor, Moreau de Saint-Méry, who also accompanied her to the opera. From Bologna she wrote admiringly to Claude Hochet about the beauty of Italy, even in winter, but added that it was the easiest country to subjugate: on a scale in which it would take an hour to govern France, Italy would require four minutes. She was also put out by the general enthusiasm for Napoleon in Italy. He was hailed as a liberator. She could understand why this was so, but believed that the Italians underestimated the dangers. She too could hope for the unification of Italy, but not at the price of foreign domination. She begged Hochet not to show anyone her letter in which she had been so frank about the Italians. 'I am very anxious that my views should not be known, for they [the Italians] are very susceptible on this and reproach me often for my chapter on Italy in '*De la littérature*', she explained, adding, 'It is something to love one's country even before it exists'.[20]

Madame de Staël's initially negative views of Italy underwent a real change by the end of her stay. After visits to Modena, Ferrara and Ancona in driving rain, she finally reached Rome, which she was unable to enter for two days because the Tiber had burst its banks. Installed at last at the Hotel Sarmiento in the Piazza di Spagna on 3 February 1805, she was immediately received by no fewer than four cardinals, among them the charismatic Cardinal Ettore Consalvi, Secretary of State to the Vatican, who had been responsible for negotiating the Concordat with Napoleon. Like many other northerners, she was disappointed by her first view of Rome; shocked and saddened by the poverty and dirt she saw everywhere. Madame de Staël quotes Albertine: 'my mother only likes two things in Italy; the sea and Monti' but she would now add to this Saint Peter's and Vesuvius, teasing Monti that he and Vesuvius in any case made one, since they were so alike.

However she was not impressed by Roman society: 'Ah Monti, how I admire you to have remained yourself among all this!' She was much admired as a famous author, she wrote, although nobody had read her books: 'In truth I don't know what would have become of me, if instead of the celestial being [Necker!] who has presided over all my feelings, I had had to listen to these women without love and these men without pride, to this affected language which they think witty, and these despotic women with their slave-lovers.'[21] She was hardly more tactful in society, as is clear from Artaud de Montor, the French ambassador, in his report to his minister: 'Madame de Staël is very gay and very pleased to be in Rome . . . although unused to Roman ways. She informed M. the Cardinal de La Somaglia, one of the most devout members of the Sacred College, that he had forty days to convert her, but that if he had not managed his miracle by Easter, she would not be able to wait any longer!'[22]

Nevertheless, she was fêted everywhere. On 14 February 1805 she was received in a solemn ceremony by the Arcadian Academy at the invitation of the Roman revolutionary poet, Alborghetti. This famous literary society, founded in 1690, had degenerated into little more than a pretentious social club. As was the custom at the Academy, Madame de Staël was received as a shepherdess, with the name of Telesilla Argoica (in memory of the poetess Telesilla of Argos who had fought in the war against Sparta). She declaimed her translation of a sonnet about the death of Jesus Christ. When he heard about it, Constant remarked caustically in his journal that Madame de Staël could never resist attention, adding that he hoped that this would not become known in France where it would certainly provoke ridicule.[23] In fact, had she refused to attend, she would have caused great offence. Even Goethe had not done so. Afterwards, the other Arcadians, as well as Cardinal Consalvi, M. de Humboldt and a young man, M. de Souza, 'who is very charming', had spent the rest of the evening with her.

Rome had begun to work its magic, even on someone with as little sensitivity to the visual arts as Madame de Staël. In spite of her self-proclaimed preference for conversation and intellectual pursuits, her novel *Corinne* demonstrates again and again, both in its many allusions to works of art and in its philosophical base, how deeply she had been affected by Italian art and by the natural beauty of Italy.

From Rome Madame de Staël went on to Naples. She was instantly enchanted, though shocked, by the ragged crowds of beggars who followed them everywhere. 'The river of fire from Vesuvius whose flaming waves flow beside the sea, as if nature had wished to express the same idea in different forms, . . . this vibrant nature, these lemons, these oranges shedding their fruit in the streets with the casual indifference of abundance, everything here is admirable except for the moral climate, a reminder that one should not confuse this with paradise,' she wrote to Monti at the end of February.[24] She was unworried that her party had arrived in Naples just as the French ambassador and French officers were leaving. Together with Schlegel and Sismondi she climbed Vesuvius, an excursion made on muleback and on foot, which few women attempted then. The experience was to be described in one of the most lyrical passages in *Corinne*. She visited Pompei and Herculaneum as well as the temples in Baia, where they were carried across the sulphurous mud on the shoulders of sailors. She climbed Mount Miseno. Later she was painted by Gérard as Corinne meditating at Cape Miseno, turning the mountain into a famous landmark in Romantic travels. While in Naples, Queen Maria Carolina, sister to Marie-Antoinette, invited Madame de Staël to an informal and private meeting since she had come unprepared, without even a court dress. United by their dislike of Napoleon, the two women got on famously.[25]

On her return she found Rome depressing after the vivacity of Naples. She renewed her friendship with the sculptor Antonio Canova and the Swiss artist Angelica Kauffman, who painted her portrait (now lost) and whom she used in part as a model for *Corinne*. She went sightseeing with her old friend, Wilhelm von Humboldt, who was the new Prussian envoy. She found consolation in a romantic friendship with a young Portuguese diplomat, Don Pedro de Souza, future Duke of Palmella, with whom she strolled in moonlight among the ruins. Handsome and melancholy, the blue-eyed de Souza, also mourning the loss of his father, attracted her powerfully. Reserved by nature, but with a romantic imagination and a fine intellect, he enjoyed her company, managing to elude her more pressing overtures with great delicacy. Because of him she found it truly painful to leave Rome, sending him a long poem and a ring, and taking with her a lock of his hair. She would have stayed longer had he given her a sign, she wrote. 'How could his entirely justified reserve have decided her to leave,' he wrote back tactfully. He had merely not wished to add 'to your pain the embarrassment of having to resist my pleas'.[26]

Madame de Staël was once again longing for love. She enjoyed her intellectual affair with Monti and her romantic one with de Souza, but in Florence, her acquaintance with the Countess d'Albany, widow of Bonnie Prince Charlie, who was mourning the recent death of her lifelong lover, the dramatist Alfieri, once again reminded Madame de Staël of how love seemed forever to elude her.

In Milan, Napoleon was about to be crowned King of Italy. His brother Joseph had refused the crown, preferring to remain first in line to that of France instead. Eugène de Beauharnais, Josephine's son, would rule as Vice-Regent in Milan. Madame de Staël's plan was to see Lucien Bonaparte at Pesaro and then visit Venice before ending her Italian travels in Milan once all the fuss of the coronation was over and those 'mamelukes' had returned home. Lucien had quarrelled with Napoleon because he had refused to give up the wife the Emperor considered unsuitable. Even their mother, the formidable Madame Mère, who now lived in Rome, had been unable to reconcile them.

Madame de Staël thought Venice – then under Austrian rule – astonishing rather than pleasing. 'If one were happy, then all these mysterious customs, the gondolas, the canals, would seem poetic, but for me with nothing but regrets, both my spirit and health suffered. I will use it for the parting scene in my novel', she wrote to Don Pedro.[27] None the less, she enjoyed a flirtation with a young Austrian officer of Irish extraction, Count Maurice O'Donnell, who was to come back into her life later on. In Milan at the beginning of June, she saw several of Napoleon's ministers who had not yet left, particularly her friend Gérando. Mathieu and her other friends in Paris had suggested that she might be able to ensure the return of her money were she to see the Emperor in Milan. Even Talleyrand, she reported to Monti, had told her friends in Paris that the Emperor had softened in relation to all her interests and that she would eventually get everything she wished for. Madame de Staël had pinned her hopes on a general amnesty for all exiles to celebrate the coronation. These hopes were to be dashed but Madame de Staël reported to Joseph, that the Emperor in an unusually mellow mood, had even gone so far as to declare that had she been troubled by the Queen of Naples he would at once have sent twenty thousand men to save her.[28] Madame de Staël knew by then that, however good his mood, the Emperor would have allowed her back only at the price of her silence.

Corinne the fruit of Madame de Staël's travels in Italy, is really two separate but interdependent books. It is a *roman-à-clef* about women's role in society and about love. It is also about Italy, but it is not merely a travel novel, as La Fayette, one of her first readers, thought, but a book with a strong political content, a book which Madame de Staël hoped and intended would both awaken interest in Italy and also, by drawing attention to writers like Alfieri, act as a catalyst in Italy itself at a time of dawning national consciousness.[29] The beauty of Italy and her interest in its political future had overtaken her original idea of merely setting her novel in Italy. Italy as much as Corinne herself is the subject of this novel.

Corinne, the central figure, is an idealized version of Madame de Staël, while her lover Oswald, although the personification of English virtues – liberalism, respect for tradition, self-discipline, duty – also epitomizes all the men she had known, full of 'weakness and irresolution'. Twelve years after Madame de Staël's death, in an essay about her work, Constant wrote: 'Corinne is an extraordinary woman, a lover of the arts; of music, of painting, and above all of poetry; with an exalted imagination, excessive sensibility, easily moved and passionate; carrying within her all the means of happiness, but open at the same time to all manner of suffering; able to avoid suffering only through distractions; needing admiration because aware of her strengths, but even more needing to be loved; and so always threatened with a fatal destiny; escaping from this destiny by ignoring it, so to speak, through the exercise of her faculties; and left with no resources whenever an exclusive feeling, a single thought has taken hold of her soul.'[30]

Oswald first sees Corinne in Rome, being crowned for her talents on the Capitol. Beautiful – her looks as well as her dancing are recognizably modelled on Madame Récamier – and richly gifted, she amazes everyone with her talents as a poet, an actress, a painter and a musician. She is an *improvisatrice* (an improviser of poetry, usually female), who would declaim often to the accompaniment of a harp or lyre on any theme recalling the Sybils and priestesses of the Greek and Roman worlds. Unlike Delphine, she is not merely a free spirit, a good and idealistic woman, but a woman of genius, and as such doubly bound to come into conflict with society. Her Italian mother has endowed her with all her artistic talents as well as with imagination and a sense of personal freedom. While much happier in Italy as an artist and as a woman, Corinne, whose father is English, longs for political and social regeneration in her mother's country – not through foreign domination, but through unity and freedom – and a rediscovery of the values which had once made Italy great. She is in effect a bridge between the two cultures.

Corinne and Oswald fall in love and travel together through Italy. Oswald is shocked by the misery of the Papal States, the ignorance and superstition of the people, and the inadequacy of government (as

Madame de Staël herself had been). Corinne understands his reactions but, as she initiates him into the glories of Italian art and history, she also points out Italy's potential and longing for renewed glory. 'Italians are much more remarkable for what they were and for what they might be than for what they are at present,' she agrees, but 'A nation which under the Romans had been the most military of all, the most jealous of its freedoms during the republics of the Middle Ages, and in the sixteenth century, the most famous for its letters, science and arts: has it not pursued glory in all its forms? And now that it has none why would you not see it as the fault of its political situation, since in other circumstances she showed herself so different?'[31]

As they travel on, Oswald recognizes his emotional counterpart and allows his rigid, puritan utilitarianism to melt in the warmth of Corinne's love and the beauty of Rome and the Campagna; in the opulence of Naples, forever threatened by the elements – the fires of Vesuvius and the roar of the sea; in the grandeur and dreamy mistiness of Venice and the pure hard light of Florence. Art for art's sake, learned in Germany, is a dominant theme in *Corinne*, but Madame de Staël shows that she believes beauty to be in itself a means to moral regeneration.

In spite of his newfound happiness Oswald cannot quite shake off his misgivings about Corinne – her independence, her talents and the mystery which surrounds her. In a letter from Corinne, he learns that his father and hers had once been friends. Corinne had been intended for him, but when his father realized that she was a woman of exceptional talent, he had preferred that Oswald marry her half-sister, the pretty and conventional Lucile. The negative side of English life, as Madame de Staël had experienced it, as well as many of her mother's qualities, are represented in the character of Corinne's stepmother and Lucile's mother, Lady Edgermond, a rigid, cold and conventional woman, who had made Corinne's young life a misery before her escape to Italy. Madame de Staël's own vivid memories of the stultifying boredom of what passed for conversation among English provincial ladies, and perhaps her rejection for the sake of propriety by people like Fanny Burney, are evoked in Corinne's account of her life in England. 'What is happiness for if not the development of our abilities?' is Corinne's, no less than Madame de Staël's, true *cri de coeur*.[32]

Haunted by remorse at having failed to return to his dying father, Oswald heeds the voices of convention and withdraws from Corinne, who nobly releases him from his promises. (Madame de Staël's own abiding guilt at having failed to return to her dying father is much in evidence. In two footnotes, she uses quotations from Necker's *Cours de morale religieuse* and his *L'importance des idées religieuses.*)[33] He returns to England where he marries Lucile. When he returns to Italy with his wife and child several years later, he finds Corinne dying. She has been caught in a trap. Had she returned to England with Oswald to live a conventional life she would have lost her very self. But his absence has made her too unhappy to function as an artist. Corinne and Oswald cannot live together, but they cannot live without each other. She refuses to see him. After her death he locks himself up alone at Tivoli. For a time his reason and his life are in question, but he goes back to his wife and child in England, driven by duty. There, 'Lord Nelvil set an example of the purest and most blameless domestic life. But will he ever forgive himself for his past conduct? Will the world which approved of his action console him? Will he be satisfied with a common fate after what he has lost? I have no idea, and I have no wish to either blame him or absolve him.'[34] So *Corinne* ends, with questions rather than answers.

Corinne's tragic end demonstrates yet again that the society of the time would not tolerate such women. For one with a lifelong belief in progress, it may seem paradoxical that her heroines do not triumph over the odds. The theme of the talented person destined to remain an outsider was to be central for writers of the Romantic movement. Madame de Staël was exceptional in that she wrote about women, challenging contemporary ideas about their role in society and their intellectual capacities. In giving Corinne such a strong voice, Madame de Staël tackled head on the image of the ideal woman as a submissive creature who remained silent or at best only uttered polite commonplaces. She was to return to this dilemma in *Le Mannequin*, a short satire written in 1811 for her private theatre at Coppet. In this comedy, Sophie, the talkative and feisty heroine, persuades an unwanted suitor to fall in love instead with her pretty and demure 'cousin' who, happy to sit at the back of the room, 'would never put forward her own opinion about anything and broke none of the rules of etiquette'. She is of course, a cardboard doll – a 'mannequin' – the very thing many men desired women to be, and the fate of any woman who is denied intellectual freedom.[35]

Madame de Staël's return from Italy in the summer of 1805 coincided with the formation of the Third Coalition. Alarmed at the growth of French power in Italy, Germany, Russia and Austria joined Britain and Sweden to fight Napoleon. After a frustrating summer on the Channel coast, the Emperor had abandoned his plan to invade England, and had turned his attention to Eastern Europe. He had just completed a four-year reorganization of his armies. By a curious quirk of fate, the new techniques of warfare which he was to exploit so brilliantly, everything that made his troops more mobile – better roads, dispensing with heavy baggage trains by living off the country, the organization of armies into divisions, the concentration of artillery fire and infantry attack and the use of light field guns – he had learned mainly from the *Essaï général de la Tactique*, written by one of Madame de Staël's earliest admirers, the Comte de Guibert, in 1772.

By the end of 1805, Napoleon's armies had smashed the combined Russian and Austrian armies, led by both Emperors, at Austerlitz, forcing the Austrians to sign the Treaty of Pressburg (27 December 1805). Talleyrand had done his best to prevent the Emperor from humiliating the Austrians too much but had been overruled. The Emperor followed this victory over the next eighteen months with a series of military triumphs over Prussia and Russia at the battles of Jena, Auerstadt, Eylau and Friedland. William Pitt had predicted on his deathbed in January 1806, that the map of Europe could now be rolled up – 'it would not be wanted these ten years'. The Treaty of Tilsit, of 9 July 1807, made Napoleon master of all Europe to the west of Russia and gave him the time needed to rebuild his armies. France's borders were extended to the south to include Piedmont, Parma, Genoa and Tuscany. North-east they stretched to the Rhine and were bordered by satellite states, 'the Confederation of the Rhine'.

Napoleon returned to Paris after Tilsit at the end of July 1807, to torchlight parades and thundering cannon as the treaty itself was celebrated with as much pomp and circumstance as could be devised. The Emperor now gave himself the title of 'Grand'. That August he abolished the *Tribunat*. One man who had predicted the Emperor's move towards despotism clearly was Talleyrand, who resigned or, as Napoleon claimed, was dismissed that same month. It was the beginning of the end though the end was still far off. Over the next few months scene after scene at the Imperial court at Fontainebleau, where the Emperor lived in magnificent luxury and style, demonstrated to foreign ambassadors and his own ministers that he 'had not only ceased to recognize any limits', but had 'completely thrown off the mask', as Metternich put it.[36] As ever, marching to the sound of drums and trumpets, *Hubris* did not hear the light steps of *Nemesis* at his side.

Chapter 20

~

Corinne and the Emperor

'She will never set foot in Paris so long as I live.'
Napoleon to Auguste de Staël

THE SUMMER OF 1805 saw the beginning of the great days of Coppet with its brilliant gathering of European talent. During the following five years it was to become what Ferney had been in the time of Voltaire. The most influential people in Europe came to call on its famous chatelaine, or stayed to discuss literature and politics and to enjoy the unique atmosphere. If active politics became impossible for this group of liberals in the years 1805–10, their discussions and studies were to be put to good use after 1812, and their ideals would triumph with the generation of the 1830s. Under the First Empire, the literary output by the members of what came to be called the Coppet Group – Madame de Staël's *Corinne* and *De l'Allemagne*, Prosper de Barante's *Tableau de la littérature française du XVIII siècle*, Constant's *Wallstein* and *Adolphe*, Schlegel's *Comparaison des deux Phèdres* and his *Cours de littérature dramatique*, Sismondi's *Littérature du midi*, Bonstetten's *Le traité de l'imagination* – opened the way to a greater and wider vision of culture in Europe, the importance of which cannot be overstated.

Pluralism and openness distinguished the group from other gatherings of intellectuals, mainly because there was no intention to form any kind of group in the first place. Neither an academy nor a club, nor yet a national gathering, it proposed no particular literary style, beat no special drum. Liberty and toleration were at the very heart of the philosophy and aspirations of all its members. Whatever their political views, they all believed passionately in the value of literature, a literature which could only make progress – they were all children of the Enlightenment – in a spirit of freedom and mutual respect. Their different national backgrounds and religions ensured a diversity of views, but these views were firmly rooted in their various intellectual and cultural traditions and precluded a woolly and well-meaning internationalism. The idea was to learn from each other, to cross-fertilize rather than to follow some vague and misty European ideal. What united all these diverse spirits was of course their extraordinary hostess.

'It is remarkable,' she was to write, 'that at a certain level of all thinkers, there is not one enemy of liberty . . . From one end of the world to the other, friends of liberty communicate through knowledge as religious men do through feeling; or rather, knowledge and feeling unite in a love of liberty, as they do in the supreme being . . . A whole order of virtues, as well as ideas, seems to make up that golden chain described by Homer, which by linking mankind to the heavens, frees them from the iron chains of tyranny.'[1]

Not only did the Coppet group influence each other, but they also translated each others' works, and other major works of European literature, to make them as widely accessible as possible. Schlegel, who had already translated Shakespeare and Calderon into German, would in time translate Madame de Staël's *Considérations sur la Révolution française*. Albertine Necker-de Saussure translated Schlegel's *Cours de littérature dramatique* into French. Constant, who had translated William Godwin, adapted Schiller for the French stage. Sismondi oversaw the translation of *Corinne* into Italian, while Madame de Staël's own works are peppered with translations from European literature.

Chateaubriand came for the first time that summer, irritating his hostess because he couldn't understand how, with a château in the most beautiful surroundings at her disposal and complete financial security, she could be unhappy.[2] Another talented young man, the future historian Prosper de Barante, then twenty-three years old, son of Claude-Ignace de Barante, the prefect of Léman, who had himself been a long-time admirer of Madame de Staël, joined the ranks of the 'regulars': Constant, Schlegel, Bonstetten, his friend, the German-born Danish poet Frederika Brun, Albertine Necker-de Saussure, and Mathieu de Montmorency. (Sismondi had stayed in Italy that summer.) Several German princes whom Madame de Staël had met the previous year, together with Claude Hochet, Elzéar de Sabran, litterateur and wit, her father's old friend Meister, Princes

Pignatelli and Belmonte and of course, Vincenzo Monti, all came and went.

In the days of Madame de Staël's parents, the old, ceremonious ways of the eighteenth century had prevailed. The new chatelaine had no time for such things. Madame de Boigne, one of the most talented memoirists of her time, who was to become a friend and admirer and a regular visitor over the next few years, left a vivid description of Coppet in the years 1805–10. 'Life at Coppet was strange. It seemed as leisurely as it was unstructured. There were no rules; no one had the slightest idea where they were to be or to meet. There was no place specially designed for a particular time of day. Everybody's rooms were open. One simply pitched one's tent wherever a discussion began, and there one would remain for hours, for days, without the interruption of any of the ordinary habits of life. Discussion seemed to be everybody's chief occupation. And yet, everyone was engaged on serious work and the great number of works which issued from their pens bear witness to it. Madame de Staël worked very hard, but when she had nothing better to do, she was always ready for the slightest social pleasure. She adored acting, shopping, excursions, entertaining people, going to visit them, but first and foremost she loved to talk.'[3]

Like many others at every stage of Madame de Staël's life, Madame de Boigne admired her unique talent for bringing people out, for making them shine: 'She had so much intelligence that it overflowed in the service of others, and if after talking to her one was left in admiration for her, one was also fairly pleased with oneself . . . There was no one so stupid that she was unable to bring something out of them (at least temporarily), provided they had some social manners for she cared very much about form.'

Nevertheless Madame de Staël disliked provincial small-mindedness, and she could sometimes treat people, particularly Genevans, with the haughtiest indifference. On one occasion at a great assembly in Geneva, where everyone arrived at seven to meet her, she put in an appearance at half-past ten, surrounded by her usual escort, stopped at the door and spoke only to one or two people who had come with her from Coppet. 'She was detested by the Genevans, and yet they were almost as proud of her as of their lake. It was a title of distinction to have been received by Madame de Staël.'[4]

A prolific writer, Madame de Staël had no special study. Instead she wondered around from room to room with a small portable writing case made of green morocco leather, containing both her work and her correspondence, which she would place on her knees. She was often surrounded by people as she wrote. What Madame de Staël feared most was solitude. Boredom was the bane of her life, as it was with Chateaubriand and Byron, two other striking examples, Madame de Boigne believed, of people who would wreck their lives and turn the world upside down to escape from it.

Her children, who were brought up in the midst of these strange goings on, and who participated in everything, were none the less amazingly well educated. They spoke several languages, had a solid knowledge of European literature, and excelled at music and drawing. Madame de Boigne recalled that they were nevertheless encouraged to follow their own inclinations. Interestingly Albertine, who in many ways was not unlike her grandmother, Madame Necker, was Madame de Staël's favourite. Very pretty, lively and highly intelligent, she was interested in metaphysics, religion and German and English literature. She cared little for music and nothing for drawing. As for embroidery, 'I don't believe there was such a thing as a needle in the whole château of Coppet' wrote Madame de Boigne. Although Albertine had all the naivety and simplicity of her years, some of her expressions betrayed her parentage. Once, having been told off by her mother, which happened rarely, Madame de Boigne found her in tears. ' "What is the matter Albertine?" "Alas! They think me happy, but there is an abyss [of despair] in my heart." She was only eleven but she was already talking what I call "Coppet"! Such exaggeration was so much the language of the place that when there one naturally adopted it.' As for the boys, Albert, the only one to show no great enthusiasm for his studies, drew very well, while Auguste added a remarkable talent for music to his literary occupations.[5]

When, in the autumn of 1805, Auguste left for Paris to prepare for the entrance exams for the École Polytechnique, one of the Grandes Écoles recently created by Napoleon, he had already had an extraordinary education, mostly at the hand of his mother, although he had been boarding in Geneva since 1801. A highly intelligent and studious child, he had won first prize in Latin at the Collège de Genève at the age of eleven. He was equally at home in Greek, German and English and was highly competent in physics, chemistry and maths. A talented musician and painter, only his dancing apparently left something to be desired. His clodhopping style, his Parisian dancing master told him, 'recalled the mountains'. Perhaps the family nickname of '*pataud*' (clumsy) was deserved after all. His sister Albertine, herself a bluestocking, later recalled his extraordinary powers of concentration: 'Madame de Staël taught Auguste herself in all subjects, and she almost always did so while carrying on her other normal activities. She would give him his lessons while writing letters or giving orders to her servants, but the child, although constantly interrupted, was never distracted; his attention never wandered, and he would pick up the thread of his mother's explanations the moment she began again.'[6]

Madame de Staël hoped that her son's presence in Paris would enable her to settle close to the capital. Saddened as she was by his departure, her letters to Auguste rarely express the warmth and love which was so much a part of her letters to her father. 'Our father, or your father', as she always called him to her children, was forever held up as an unattainable example: 'Tiredness prevented me from writing to you on Wednesday evening, my dear Auguste. I had left Coppet where I find a new emptiness alongside the eternal emptiness which breaks my heart. I had your kind note from Morez, and I reflected that in just such a way I had written to your father [Necker] and that from being the one who was protected I had become the protector. All my thoughts were sad, and I don't like to express what I feel most.' Soon after his arrival in Paris, Madame de Staël wrote to Auguste, then just fifteen, instructing him as to whom he was to see and what he should say about the question of the return of her father's money and the lifting of the Emperor's ban: 'Adieu, my dear friend,' she ended, 'this is the most serious and important letter that you have ever had, as well as a challenge to your wisdom. Adieu, remember that at precisely your age, my father began to make that fortune without which we would be nothing.'[7]

She was anxious that he should meet Narbonne. It seems likely that Auguste, if he did not know then that Narbonne was his natural father, would have soon found out. In December 1805, he wrote enthusiastically to his mother: 'I have been to see M. de Narbonne, who received me wonderfully. I have never seen a man with so much grace and wit in conversation, as I well noticed in the little time we spent together. But some people arrived and I was obliged to leave. But he promised that he would come and see me this week and that we would then have time to talk. I am delighted at the prospect.'[8]

But the news from her friends in Paris was bad. Napoleon had no intention of allowing her to return there. However preoccupied, he never lost track of Madame de Staël. From the camp in Boulogne, where he was preparing for the German campaign, he had still found time to send instructions to his Minister of Police, Fouché. 'Inform her friends that she is to remain at forty leagues distance. All elements of discord must be sent away from Paris. It is out of the question when I am two thousand leagues away at the other end of Europe, that I should grant such disloyal citizens the freedom to agitate in my capital.'[9]

Madame de Staël's letters to Auguste are also extraordinarily demanding. He may have been guilty of writing in less detail than she wanted, and the timidity natural to a fifteen-year-old made him hesitant in the execution of some of her commands, but he longed to please his exacting parent. It was hardly surprising that a boy of his age should hesitate to plead her cause with Fouché, or to take letters from her to Joseph and indeed, to the Emperor himself. Her self-centredness is never more obvious than in her letters to her son, about whom she heard nothing but praise from her friends: 'I must admit, my dear Auguste, that I was not pleased that you had not spoken of me to Prince Joseph on Sunday at his house. This is an irreparable omission, and I do believe that at your age I would have been incapable of a similar fault. In general you have taken far too lightly what is a terrible sorrow to me, and I accuse not your heart, but your self-esteem, which makes you mistakenly timid.'[10]

At the beginning of October, carrying out Napoleon's instructions to the letter, in its strict enforcement of the forty leagues limit, Fouché wrote to Madame de Staël, giving her permission to stay in the south of France. Resigned, but perhaps a little less sad than she might otherwise have been because of a blossoming romance with the young Prosper de Barante, she decided to spend the winter in Geneva instead. Intelligent and attractive, the young Prosper had had his head turned by Madame de Staël's marked attention to him. To the horror of his father and the undisguised pleasure of Madame de Staël herself, he fancied himself in love. At nearly forty (though she only admitted to thirty-five) she was still longing for love. Affairs with much younger men – henceforth the pattern of her love life – staved off her growing terror of old age and perhaps suited her dominant personality. By the end of the summer they were writing notes to each other which suggest that they might have been lovers. 'Adieu, I embrace you and I love you. I am happy. Sometimes when I hold you in my arms I regret that I am not able to be yours entirely, but when I consult my heart alone, I tell myself that nothing could add to my feelings and I need nothing more to declare myself yours for ever', wrote Prosper.[11] Whether he was referring to the impossibility of marriage between them or to the non-consummation of their love is not clear.

Constantly tortured by jealousy, poor Schlegel, who must have realized by then that there was no romantic future for him with Madame de Staël, wrote an extraordinary declaration, dated 18 October 1805. 'I declare that you have all rights over me and I have none over you. Dispose of my person and of my life, command, refuse, I will obey you in everything . . . I am proud of being your property. I will make no new relationship which might detach me from you . . . you have a supernatural power over me which I would struggle against in vain. Do not abuse your power; you could easily make me unhappy, while I have no arms against you. Above all I beg you that you never banish me from your side, your slave, A. W. Schlegel.'[12] She never did. He was to remain by her side until her death. She was fond of Schlegel, respected and admired his learning, and needed his help with her German studies. She made him one of her literary executors in her will and left him comfortably provided for – but she never loved him.

Schlegel, who had studied Shakespeare in detail, and who had now turned his attention to the French classical theatre (which he did not admire), inspired Madame de Staël to organize what Constant referred to as 'a fury of spectacles'. To prove him wrong about French drama, she decided to put on several plays herself. As usual she did nothing by halves. She rented a hall in the Molard district of Geneva and transformed it into a stage. Four of Voltaire's plays – *Mahomet, Mérope, Alzire* and *Zaïre* – were followed by Racine's *Phèdre*, in which she excelled in the title role. She supervised the design of sets and costumes, she cast and directed the plays, and she even wrote one – *Agar in the desert*. Her acting was much admired by all who saw her, particularly by Schlegel, who was, after all, an expert on theatre. In a letter to a friend (herself an actress), he said that as an actress, Madame de Staël was an incomparable artist: 'she had the gift of eloquence, of versatility, of presence of mind, and an unfailing memory, exact to a syllable, unusual proficiency in poetic recitation.'

What really interests her, he continued, are the vicissitudes of life, inevitable for a sensitive heart; and she expresses its secrets and sorrows with great naturalness and simplicity. Moreover she has a rare gift of bringing out the best in everyone which puts great life into her productions, and a very good eye for stage design and costumes.[13]

In the spring of 1806, Madame de Staël decided to return to France. Prosper de Barante had left for Paris to take up his post at the Counsel of State and she was tired of Geneva. She settled in Auxerre, with Schlegel and her children, at the château de Vincelles, but she was soon bored, frustrated and bitterly unhappy. Prosper had failed to visit as often as she had expected and her correspondence with him demonstrates yet again how her intemperate demands (together with strenuous efforts made by his father to break up the relationship) hastened the end of a young man's infatuation.

This did not stop her from bombarding the unfortunate Constant at the same time with imperious letters summoning him to her side. On a visit to his father at Dôle, he was at first inclined to refuse, but had nevertheless obeyed as he must have known he would: 'With all her faults, she is superior to everyone for me – I will join her at Auxerre.' Nothing had changed. The news from Paris about her banishment was bad. Constant found her very agitated, her nerves in shreds. It was at this time that Madame de Staël, who had inherited her mother's terrible insomnia, began to take opium regularly in an effort to sleep. 'All the volcanoes put together are less fiery than she is,' Constant noted in his journal, but 'struggling tires me, let us lie down in the boat and sleep through the tempest'.[14] There was to be no sleep however. Constant was again dispatched to Paris with instructions to see Joseph Bonaparte, Fouché and Lacretelle in an effort to persuade the Emperor to lift his ban. He returned with bad news, but also with Madame Récamier, Mathieu and Adrien de Montmorency, whose presence helped temporarily to alleviate her depression and frustration.

Madame de Staël had enlisted Madame Récamier's help to bring Prosper to heel but was beginning to suspect that he was falling in love with the irresistible Juliette instead. From Rouen, to which she had moved from Auxerre, she wrote to Madame Récamier, begging her to come and visit her. 'I confess that I am afraid that you might allow yourself to be loved by him [Prosper]. It would be a mortal blow to me! Don't do it Juliette. Proscribed as I am, confiding in you as I do, and so prodigiously inferior to your attractions, generosity forbids that you allow yourself the least coquettishness with him. Not that I have much faith in his love for me. I bear the terrible sorrow of doubting it constantly. But if in addition, this unhappiness was to be caused by you it would be a terrible blow which I don't think I could bear . . .'[15]

Life was not without some satisfactions however. Don Pedro de Souza who, encouraged by Madame de Staël, had undertaken the translation of the *Lusiades* by Luiz de Camoëns, national poet of Portugal, into French, met her for a few days at Constant's farm at Argeville before he left for Portugal in September.[16] Meanwhile Madame Récamier showed her devotion to Madame de Staël by returning to spend some time with her. And a note from Auguste announced that he had passed the entrance examinations for the École Polytechnique, coming first, with the best result ever achieved in the school's history. He had been ill for two days at the thought that he might fail his mother 'in the one poor way he might be of use to you'.[17] But in the letter which followed he allowed himself a little credit: 'The examiner kept me at the board for three hours; he tried hard to trip me up, but what pleased me was that he told Garat [the senator], that he had only kept me there for such a long time for the pleasure of hearing my exposition.'[18] Yet in spite of his brilliant results the Emperor refused permission for Auguste to take up his place at the École Polytechnique, perhaps because it would have guaranteed him employment by the state and might have made his mother's return easier.

After a few quiet months in Rouen, moved by her constant pleas, Fouché allowed Madame de Staël to settle at the château d'Acosta at Aubergenville, only twelve leagues from Paris. Here, while she corrected the proofs of *Corinne*, she was joined by Constant. Emboldened by her two-month stay so near to Paris, Madame de Staël bought an estate near Franconville, only ten leagues from Paris. But once again she had not counted on the Emperor. 'Do not allow that hussy, Madame de Staël, near Paris,' Napoleon wrote to Fouché from Prussia, where he was campaigning at the end of December 1806. This was followed up by more severe instructions in March: 'You must execute my commands and ensure that Madame de Staël is not allowed within forty leagues of Paris. That wicked intriguer will in time have to learn to take the wisest course.'[19] Constitutionally incapable of learning anything of the sort, and busy with the imminent publication of *Corinne*, she insisted to Fouché that she could not leave until the end of April – her daughter was ill and she had no money.

In mid-April 1806 the Emperor wrote again to Fouché: 'It gives me pleasure that I have heard no more of Madame de Staël. If I take an interest it is because I have facts to back it up. That woman is a real crow . . .' But he rejoiced too soon. The very next day a letter from Madame de Staël to Prince Louis of Prussia, one of the coalition's most able generals, was intercepted and brought to him by one of his spies. 'You will see for yourself what a good Frenchwoman we have here,' he wrote furiously. Fouché must at once get rid 'of that whore, and an ugly one at that. I say nothing of the plans made by that ridiculous coterie in the happy event that I might be killed. A Minister of Police must surely be aware of this.'[20] Napoleon was referring to a plot by General Malet, in which he believed Madame de Staël to be involved, to set up a provisional government in case of his removal one way or another. In another letter to Fouché, evidently in reply to the latter's assurance that Madame de Staël had left Paris, Napoleon writes: 'I see from your letter of the 27 April that Madame de Staël left for Geneva on the 21st. I regret that you should be so ill informed. Madame de Staël was in Paris on the 24th, 25th, 26th, 27th, and 28th and is probably still there. She has dined with many people in the world of letters. If Madame de Staël's head had not been filled with illusions, all this nonsense would not have taken place and she would keep quiet. In not removing all hope from her of ever being able to return to Paris and begin her intrigues, you only worsen this woman's misfortune and expose her to unpleasant possibilities, for I will put her in the hands of the police.'[21]

Napoleon's spies had been right. Just before her departure for Coppet at the end of April, Madame de Staël had indeed taken the risk of slipping into Paris for a few days to oversee the printing of her book. Holed up quietly in her apartments at the rue de Lille by day, she had wandered around her beloved streets by moonlight. She had, of course, been unable to resist paying visits and receiving her friends. Someone had let the secret out.

That Napoleon, over a period of five months, in the midst of a bloody campaign and in spite of all the other business he had to attend to, should have written ten letters to Fouché alone on the subject of Madame de Staël demonstrates how seriously he took her and how much he feared her influence. Fouché had long since lost the

Emperor's confidence. Extraordinarily well informed by his own spies, Napoleon was convincd that wherever there was trouble, Madame de Staël would be at the root of it.

Corinne ou l'Italie, the fruit of Madame de Staël's travels in Italy, was published at the beginning of May 1807. It was an immediate and resounding success, so much so that henceforth she would often be called by the name of the novel's heroine. Women everywhere adopted Corinne as their model. A generation later, Sainte-Beuve called *Corinne* 'the ideal of all celebrated women'.

Letters of congratulation flowed in from all quarters of the globe. 'Rare quality of genius! To lead us in the ripe days, as love in the green ones, wheresoever it will!' Gouverneur Morris rhapsodized from America.[22] 'I swallow Corinne slowly, that I may taste every drop,' Sir James Mackintosh wrote to a friend from Bombay: 'Her picture of stagnation, mediocrity and dullness; of torpor, only animated by envy; of mental superiority, dreaded and hated without being comprehended; and of intellect gradually being extinguished by the azotic atmosphere of stupidity – is so true.'[23]

Lady Elisabeth Foster, mistress and later wife of the Duke of Devonshire, wrote to thank her for the pleasure she had felt reading *Corinne:* 'I had become so attached to poor Corinne that I dared not read too quickly for fear of separating myself from her and for the fear I felt that you had destined her to be unhappy. How did you have the courage to make her suffer so? I liked Oswald, but I cannot forgive him for Corinne's unhappiness. How well you have described the sorrows of the heart! You have painted them as faithfully as your eloquent descriptions of Italy.'[24]

Years later Byron inscribed a copy of *Corinne* which he had given to his mistress, Teresa Guiccioli, with the words: 'she is sometimes right and often wrong about Italy and England; but almost always true in delineating the heart, which is but of one nation; of no country, or rather of all.'[25] In Germany, Queen Louise had been so moved that she had been obliged to stop reading, and Goethe pronounced that in the novel, talent had been devoted to show up evil.[26]

The Napoleonic press, on the other hand, could only suggest that her ideas were sick. 'A woman distinguished by qualities other than those proper to her sex is contrary to the laws of nature,' wrote the critic of the *Gazette de France*.[27] Madame de Staël had great hopes that the success of *Corinne*, which she believed to be apolitical, would soften the Emperor's obduracy towards her. Before she left Paris, she sent him a copy, with a direct appeal. 'That madwoman, Madame de Staël has written me a six-page letter full of gibberish in which I find a great deal of pretension and very little common sense,' Napoleon wrote to Fouché.[28]

Fouché had suggested to Madame de Staël that were she to include praise of the Emperor in her book – some flattering allusion – all obstacles to her return to Paris might be lifted. But she refused to do so. At a time when hymns of praise rose from all sides to the victor of Marengo, the newly crowned King of Italy, Napoleon was displeased to find no mention in her book of himself or of French power in Italy. Instead Madame de Staël praised Napoleon's enemy, England, celebrated English liberties and expressed the hope that Italy would be united and independent. The whole novel was a celebration of idealistic fervour, of what Madame de Staël called 'enthusiasm', for independence and freedom, all of which hardly appealed to the Emperor. The characters of the Frenchmen in *Corinne*, the vain and shallow Comte d'Erfeuil and the profoundly cynical M. de Maltigues, largely based on Talleyrand, whose only values were money and power no matter how they were acquired, was hardly flattering. Madame de Staël had deliberately set out to hold up a mirror to Napoleonic France, to show the French what they had become. As the Emperor well knew, she was not anti-French, but she was against everything he stood for. The accusation of being anti-French – 'I cannot forgive Madame de Staël for lowering the French in her novel,' he had said – was as good an official reason for continuing to ban her from France as the Emperor was likely to find. But perhaps most of all, she had identified herself so well with her heroine that Napoleon simply couldn't bear to read it. Only when he was himself banished to Saint-Helena, did he feel able to acknowledge both his visceral antipathy to her and his interest in her work. 'I see her, I hear her, I feel her, I want to escape from her, I hurl the book away,' he admitted much later to Las Cases. 'However I shall persist; I want to know how it ends, for I still think it an interesting work.'[29]

Now a European celebrity, Madame de Staël spent that summer at Coppet and at Ouchy, near Lausanne, where she had rented a house. Madame Récamier joined her for what was to become the first of several summers at Coppet and where her pretty room is still named after her. She had suffered the death of her much-loved mother that

January, soon after the blow of her husband's bankruptcy. On the way to Coppet her carriage had turned over several times, two horses had been killed and a postilion injured. Although Madame Récamier had merely sprained her ankle and suffered shock, Madame de Staël had not hesitated to rush off in her own carriage to fetch her friend from Morez in the Jura where the accident had taken place. Soon after their return together news came of the death of Madame Récamier's close friend and admirer, Prince Pignatelli. To cheer her up, Madame de Staël devoted the rest of the summer to her friend, taking her sightseeing in Switzerland and resuming her theatrical activities. Madame Récamier took the title role in *Andromaque*, with Madame de Staël as Hermione, Constant as Pyrrhus and Elzéar de Sabran as Orestes. The twenty-four-year-old Prince Augustus of Prussia, who had fallen passionately in love with Madame Récamier, had a minor role, though Madame de Staël failed to persuade François Guizot, the future liberal politician, and a young American, a Mr Middleton, to take to the boards, and had to be content with having them as members of the audience.

Battered by his stormy relations with Madame de Staël, Constant had renewed his attachment to the sweet and gentle Charlotte du Tertre in October, promising to marry her when she had her divorce. He had none the less been unable to resist Madame de Staël's summons the previous winter. In January 1807, over two feverish weeks, he had written his short masterpiece, *Adolphe*, putting into this slim novel all his frustration with his exacting mistress, but above all with his own weakness. The eponymous hero was a brutally honest and absolutely recognizable portrait of himself, while the heroine Elléonore, disguised to look like Anna Lindsay, was all too obviously Madame de Staël. The novel is a brief tale of the seduction of Elléonore by Adolphe. She has given up everything for him; when he tires of her, he at first tries to do his duty but then determines to escape and is found out. Broken-hearted, Elléonore dies in his arms. It is in fact a masterly description of the tortured emotional conflict between him and Madame de Staël. 'Everything that the most implacable hatred had invented against us, we used against each other; and these two unfortunate beings, who alone really knew each other in this world, who alone could do the other full justice, understand and console one another, seemed to be two irreconcilable enemies, determined to tear each other apart,' writes Adolphe in the novel.[30]

Almost every line of the novel has its counterpart in Constant's journal. It is impossible not to recognize, as Sismondi did, 'the author on every page' – as well as Madame de Staël – 'this was their story'.[31] Madame de Staël must have recognized it too although she pretended otherwise and was always 'furious at the supposition' that she was the heroine of *Adolphe*, as Byron later recalled in a letter to Lady Blessington.[32]

Constant tried once again to make a final break. Strongly encouraged by his aunt, Madame de Nassau, his cousin Rosalie, and his father, he tried feebly to get away to join Charlotte, who was waiting patiently for him. He was tired, he said, of 'always being necessary but never enough'.[33] But Madame de Staël had no intention of letting him go. There were endless scenes, and even threats of suicide. A letter from his cousin Rosalie to her brother Charles bears witness to one such appalling outburst. 'When after a few days, he failed to arrive [Benjamin had remained in Lausanne when she returned to Coppet], she sent her horses, her carriage and her servants to fetch him,' Rosalie explained. Giving in, he returned to Coppet where once again he proposed either marriage or a friendly separation. Madame de Staël still had no wish to marry Constant. She did not wish to change a name she had made famous, nor was she in the least in love with him. Terrified of being alone, yet wanting her own freedom, she needed his love and his company, his intellectual collaboration. He had been part of her life for fourteen years, he was someone she trusted, a contemporary and one of her very closest friends. He was also the father of her beloved daughter. 'Calling her children and Schlegel,' Rosalie went on, 'Madame de Staël, pointed to Constant, exclaiming dramatically, "there is the man who would drive me to despair, or force me to compromise your name and your fortune!" Furious, Benjamin riposted "If I ever marry your mother you may think of me as the most base of men!"' Madame de Staël then had a fit of hysterics, throwing herself to the ground, shrieking and threatening to strangle herself with a scarf she had around her neck. 'In short,' Rosalie concludes, 'she made one of those scenes she is all too capable of, and which poor Benjamin is incapable of resisting.' Panic-stricken, Constant had stolen out of the house the next morning and returned to Rosalie's house in Lausanne. While he was describing the events of the previous day to his aunt and cousin, they heard screams below. Rosalie locked him into the drawing room and went downstairs. Prostrated on the staircase, her hair fanning out behind her and her bosom heaving, Madame de Staël was screaming 'Where is he? I must find him!' Benjamin drummed on the door while Madame de Staël rained insults and accusations on Rosalie. As soon as Benjamin was let out, she threw herself into his arms.[34]

Once again Constant could not resist her. 'She came, she threw herself at my feet, she uttered terrible cries of anguish and desolation. A heart of iron could not have resisted. So I have returned to Coppet with her. And Charlotte who expected me back at the end of September! Oh God, what can I do? I am trampling on my future and my happiness,' Constant wrote in his journal.[35]

Rosalie, meanwhile, had had enough and refused to ever see her again. 'Although I like her books, I have even sworn never to read anything she might write . . . A woman who puts herself in the position I saw her in, who gives herself up to such unruly passions, degrades any wits she may possess,' she wrote to her brother a month later.[36]

Assuring poor Charlotte that he would be with her in the autumn, Constant spent the next few weeks at Coppet adapting Schiller's trilogy, *Wallenstein*, for the French stage (as *Wallstein*), with Madame de Staël's help, and acting unwillingly, and by all accounts badly, in her productions of *Andromaque* and *Phèdre, Le Grand Monde* by Elzéar de Sabran, and Madame de Staël's own *Geneviève de Brabant*, which she wrote that autumn. His plan was to marry Charlotte and to make good his escape when Madame de Staël went to Vienna in December. For the moment, Madame de Staël was being 'sweet and good' and, but for the memory of former violent scenes, he might well have been tempted to renew his attachment. 'Everything is fine so long as one does exactly as she wants. Let us submit and pretend; that is the art of the weak,' he sighed in his journal.[37]

Madame de Staël's efforts to keep Constant by her side in no way prevented her from pursuing Prosper de Barante, who came and went that summer, returning to Paris at the end of October to take up a position as a deputy prefect. She agonized about their love affair, writing several letters to him and to his father. She believed that Prosper would be unhappy as a junior official and suggested that marriage to her, which he had promised in the first flush of love, would save him from an uncongenial occupation and give him the independence to write. It was precisely what his father most wished to avoid. 'The example of Benjamin Constant ought to save you by waking you up,' the elder Barante warned his son.[38] Exhausted by her demands, and convinced by his father that marriage to a much older and richer woman would make him a laughing stock, Prosper wriggled out as best he could: 'I do not believe that this union would bring happiness to either of us. You do not desire it enough and I fear it too much.'[39]

In early December 1807, accompanied by Schlegel, Albert and Albertine, Madame de Staël set out, intending to visit southern Germany and Vienna to complete her research for her book on Germany, on which she had been working continuously with Schlegel. She stopped for a week in Munich to visit the Romantic philosopher Schelling, now married to Schlegel's former wife. 'She is a phenomenon of vitality, egotism and intellectual activity,' wrote Caroline Schelling to a friend. 'Her appearance is transfigured by her soul as indeed it needs to be. She has moments, or rather clothes in which she looks like a market-woman, yet at the same time it is easy to imagine her in the part of *Phaedra*, in the most tragic sense imaginable.'[40] At the end of that month, on the very day that his mother arrived in Vienna, Auguste was received by Napoleon at Chambéry.

Hearing that the Emperor was to stop there on his way back from Italy, Auguste had gone to plead his mother's cause on his own initiative. He had waited for several days, staying at the post inn, where he asked to be warned as soon as the Emperor's couriers arrived. Early in the morning he was woken with the news that the Emperor had arrived. Dressing hurriedly he handed a note to Lauriston, one of Napoleon's aides-de-camp, begging the Emperor for an audience. Duroc, Napoleon's chief of staff, who was present when the audience took place, later recounted the story to General Bourrienne, who was so impressed that he recorded it verbatim in his memoirs.

Napoleon had been intrigued to meet Madame de Staël's son, whom Lauriston had recommended as 'very young and very interesting'. When Auguste was shown in, he was impressed that the seventeen-year-old, though respectful, was not too intimidated. Auguste had found the Emperor at table, surrounded by his aides-de-camp. For three quarters of an hour, while Napoleon had his breakfast, Auguste argued with the master of Europe for his mother's banishment to be lifted.

'Where have you come from?' Napoleon asked.

'Sire, from Geneva.'

'Where is your mother?'

'Sire, she is in Vienna or almost there,' Auguste replied.

'Very good, she is very well there, she must be pleased, she will have a chance to learn German,' Napoleon said not without irony.

'Sire, could Your Majesty really think that she could be happy, far from all her habits, her friends, her country?' the young man asked. 'If you would allow me to show you her letters you would see, Sire, how sad and miserable she is as a result of her exile!'

'Ah, bah!' said the Emperor, 'Your mother is always like that. She is not a bad woman; she is clever, she is perhaps much too clever, but she has an unbridled mind, she has never understood the meaning of subordination . . . If I allow your mother to come back to Paris she won't be there six months before I would be forced to send her to Bicêtre or put her in the Temple. It would annoy me very much to have to do this because it would cause a stir and it would do me harm with public opinion. Tell your mother that I have made my decision and it is irrevocable . . .'

'Sire,' Auguste interrupted, as Duroc and the others held their breath. No one interrupted the Emperor when he was in full flow. 'I cannot think that you would put my mother in prison if she gave you no cause.' He promised that she would see no one but a few close friends.

'She would give me ten causes,' Napoleon said shortly, but he looked amused. 'I know her well! . . . She would be incapable of not meddling. She would become a standard-bearer for the Faubourg Saint-Germain. See no one, eh? Would she be able not to? She would be visited by people, she would pay visits in her turn, she would commit a thousand follies, she would see people and make jokes. She does not take that seriously, but my government is not a joke, and I take everything seriously . . .'

Auguste tried again. Why was the Emperor so angry with her? Could it have been anything to do with his grandfather's last work? 'I swear to Your Majesty that my mother had no part in it,' he said.

Although Napoleon had softened a little, at the mention of Necker's name he roared: 'Your grandfather was an ideologist, a fool, an old maniac. At the age of sixty to try and overturn my constitution! And draw up plans for constitutions!'

Auguste tried to defend his grandfather: 'Sire, since you take my grandfather's ideas to be empty theories why do they make you so angry? There has never been an economist who did not consider constitutions.'

Napoleon brushed him aside: 'Ah yes indeed! Economists! They are all useless, they dream up plans but would be incapable of acting as tax collectors in the most remote village of my Empire! Your grandfather's work is that of an stubborn old man who died still lecturing about how to govern nations!'

'Perhaps,' said Auguste bravely, 'the Emperor had been influenced by ill wishers and hadn't actually read the work?'

'There you are wrong. I read it from one end to the other.'

'Well then, Your Majesty will have seen how much justice he did him.'

'Justice indeed! – He called me *l'homme nécéssaire*' . . . and according to his work, one must cut the throat of the "necessary man". Yes, I was necessary alright, essential indeed, to repair all the stupidities of your grandfather, to erase all the harm he did to France . . .'

'Sire, he defended the King and thereby all his wealth was confiscated!' Auguste exclaimed.

'Defended the King! A great defence! My word, Monsieur de Staël – if I fed poison to a man and then gave him the antidote, would you say that I had wanted to save him? . . . He led the King to the scaffold . . . he was responsible for the Revolution . . . yes, I tell you even Robespierre, Marat and Danton have done less harm to France than M. Necker!'

As the Emperor worked himself into a rage, Duroc and the others began to tremble for the young man, but suddenly Napoleon laughed: 'But when all's said and done, gentlemen, it isn't for me to speak ill of the Revolution, since I ended up snatching the throne.'

Looking sternly at Auguste, he warned him: 'The reign of these troublemakers is over. What I want is submission. Respect authority, because it comes from God. You are young and well brought up, get used to subordination.'

'Sire, if Your Majesty does me the honour of thinking me well brought up, he should not condemn my mother and my grandfather, for it is according to their principles that I have been brought up.'

'Well, I advise you to keep to a straight line in politics,' Napoleon told him, getting up from the table.

Auguste tried again. Could his mother not have a trial period?

Napoleon rather admired this young man for the courage with which he defended his mother. Taking him by the ear, in a sign of avuncular approval, he said: 'You are very young. When you are my age you will judge things better.' In any case, why was Madame de Staël so eager to put herself under his tyranny? Couldn't she go to Rome, to Berlin, to Vienna, to Milan, even to London? 'Only your mother could be unhappy when she had the free run of Europe . . . but Paris, you see, M. de Staël, is where I live. I don't want anyone there who doesn't like me. If I allowed her back to Paris she would commit new idiocies . . . she would promise all kinds of miracles, but she would never be able to stop talking politics.'

She might need a few days in Paris to see to 'sacred duties', Auguste persisted, referring to Necker's millions still blocked at the treasury.

'All debts are sacred to their creditors,' Napoleon replied with amusement. They would have to wait for the due process of law, he would do nothing personally.

Seeing that the Emperor was about to bring the interview to a close, Auguste made one last, desperate effort. If his mother were allowed to return to Paris, 'she would confine herself to literature', he promised.

But Napoleon knew Madame de Staël: 'Tell your mother my mind is made up. She will never set foot in Paris again, as long as I live. Besides, you can make politics by talking literature, morality, art, anything in the world. Women should stick to knitting.'[41]

Chapter 21

Notre Dame de Coppet

'If she knew how to rule herself, she could rule the world.'
Benjamin Constant

When Madame de Staël arrived at the end of December, Vienna was preparing to celebrate the marriage of the Emperor Francis to his cousin, Maria-Ludovica of Modena, which was to take place on 6 January 1808. Madame de Staël was depressed and anxious; suffering her usual sense of disorientation and gloom in a strange place. She was therefore especially grateful to see among her first visitors, the young Count Maurice O'Donnell, with whom she had enjoyed a flirtation in Venice, and the old Prince de Ligne.[1] The Austrian Minister of Foreign Affairs, Count Stadion, had called on her at once, anxious to lose no time in completing the formalities for her reception at court so that she could fully participate in the celebrations of the royal wedding. Napoleon and France were deeply unpopular in Austria, which was still smarting from the humiliation of Austerlitz, and all Vienna was anxious to meet the extraordinary woman who dared to oppose the Emperor. But when, soon after her arrival, the French ambassador, General Andréossy, gave a great dinner in her honour, she was immediately suspected of being an agent of Napoleon. Throughout her stay in Vienna, she had the honour of being shadowed by both the Austrian and the French secret services. Napoleon did not want her stirring up trouble in France but nor did he want her to stir up trouble abroad. He was as anxious not to make a victim out of Madame de Staël as she was not to look like one.

Received at court on 30 December, she wrote to Auguste that very day: 'I ask God for a thousand blessings on you at this end of year, my dear friend. I am very touched by the sentiment which made you leave for Chambéry; but I have no great hopes of it . . . I am being wonderfully treated though I don't expect to enjoy myself in my way.'[2] Two weeks later, when Auguste's letter describing his meeting with the Emperor in detail had reached her, she wrote gratefully: 'I believe, my child, that you have done everything possible, and you certainly showed a presence of mind and a thoughtfulness very superior to the common lot of men'. She was anxious, however, that Auguste should keep the Emperor's categorical refusal to allow her back to Paris secret, even from Benjamin. With Constant's help, Auguste might yet be able to secure the return of her father's money: 'I have a great need that he should support me in this – and Paris is unfortunately so necessary to him,' and besides, a great principle of success was never to look like a victim, she explained to Auguste. 'Adieu my dear friend, do not, I beg, think that success is necessary for me to feel your friendship.'[3]

Soon she was installed in an apartment where she began to give tea and supper parties. Since the French Revolution, Vienna had replaced Paris as the city most congenial to the European aristocracy. At the time of Madame de Staël's arrival it was still quite small, with more grand houses per square metre than anywhere else in Europe, all quite close to one another 'as in a small town, although there were all the advantages of a large capital city', as Madame de Staël noted in *De l'Allemagne*.[4] At its centre was the Hofburg, an enormous complex of buildings which was the imperial residence. It was a cosmopolitan, commercial and tolerant city. In addition to the many French, English, Russian and German visitors who flocked there, resident members of the various nationalities of the Habsburg Empire had been joined by Polish nobles after the third partition of Poland in 1795. There was a thriving Balkan population, a large Greek community for whom Vienna was a centre of literature and the press, a large Jewish community which was beginning to make its presence felt in intellectual life as well as in the financial sector, and so many Turks that cafés put out cushions specially for them.[5]

Madame de Staël was enchanted by the beauty of the Prater, Vienna's great park, with its magnificent trees, its green lawns rolling down to the Danube, and the view of herds of deer roaming on the other side of the river, as she later described in *De l'Allemagne*. The Viennese would gather at exactly the same time for the evening promenade 'as in Italy'. Vienna was said to consume more food per head than any other comparable city and this was particularly obvious in the Prater where huge picnics of cold ham, sausages and chicken were washed down by beer and white wine. The great families in their splendid carriages amused themselves 'by recognizing in the Prater's various drives, those they had just left in a salon'. Far from thinking the Viennese aristocracy stiff and proud, Madame de Staël found 'simplicity, politeness and loyalty' as well as a great regularity in their customs – but they bored her. She thought it a pity that, as in Berlin, there was very little contact between the aristocracy and intellectuals, to the detriment of both. Social life, which was imitative of the French, was dull and predictable.[6]

Invited everywhere, Madame de Staël rather astonished than pleased the Viennese who could not forgive her for her part in the early years of the Revolution, which had sent the Emperor's aunt to the scaffold. Her clothes were mocked as – dressed in her usual low-cut gowns, a turban placed haphazardly on her head and with shawls trailing – she swept through the salons. At court, dressed in gold-coloured satin, with diamonds and bird of paradise feathers in her jet black hair, she immediately committed a breach of etiquette when, unable to confine herself to answering questions politely, she insisted on asking some herself.

Before long she was giving theatrical performances at various soirées. She performed her own play, *Hagar in the desert* at Countess Zamoyska's on 14 February and again at Princess Fürstenberg's, with Albertine as the young Ishmael and Albert as the angel, followed by *Geneviève de Brabant* at Countess Potocki's and at Princess Liechtenstein's. Quite unaware of the adverse comments about her 'violent screaming' during the performance, or her bizarre appearance – her clothes, her red shoulders and twitching toes in their sandals were again ridiculed –[7] she wrote to Sismondi, who was soon to join her, that she and Schlegel were 'on the top of the fashion'.[8] She had persuaded Schlegel to give a series of lectures on comparative literature, which he did with the Emperor's permission, and which had enjoyed great success in Vienna's fashionable circles.

She was even able to enjoy herself 'in her way', at the house of Charles-Joseph, Prince de Ligne, closest of her new friends, a generation older and very much an eighteenth-century grandee. Born in Brabant, now part of Belgium in 1735, he had been a friend of the Empress Catherine and the Emperor Joseph, of Casanova and of Frederick the Great. A great admirer of women, he had been the lover of Madame du Barry and a confidant of Marie-Antoinette. A distinguished soldier, he was a Marshal of both the Russian and the Austrian Empires. He was also a prolific and talented writer, a famous and much-quoted wit, and a brilliant conversationalist. Close to all his children, in old age he was surrounded by an adoring family. Goethe called him 'the most cheerful man of the century', while Saint-Beuve was to describe him as 'One of the cleverest, among arbiters of taste, one of the truly most agreeable among the blessed of this earth'.[9] His modest house on the Mölkerbastei, where he had lived since the French Revolution deprived him of his fortune and his vast estates, was a meeting place of people of talent and intellect. Madame de Staël was to be found there almost every day. By tacit mutual agreement they did not discuss the Revolution. He had once even written critically about Necker! They could, however, agree on Napoleon.

To Madame Récamier she wrote that the Prince de Ligne was like Narbonne but with a heart. It was a pity he was old although she had a great affection for that generation.[10] He was enchanted by her and amused too: 'She is good, easy to be with, grateful for a nothing . . . I don't know whether her head or her heart is the most warm. Those two enemies have great difficulty in getting on together. The richness of her mind enchants and irritates, she is paradoxical in discussion and if the word sensibility is mentioned, off she goes! But what grace and kindly desire to show everyone at their best! What eloquence, what improvisation, what spirit!'[11]

Ligne's pen-portrait of her, in which she is disguised as Donna Elvira, is a familiar mixture of the admiration, affection and exasperation felt by all her friends at one time or another. 'She has more than intelligence; she has genius, or better still she is a genius. A powerful genius, a profound genius, a fertile genius, a creative genius, an improvising genius. Finally a beautiful and good genius . . . her imagination united to tact, grace and taste entrances with its unmatched eloquence. Continuous movement is accompanied by two brilliant eyes like bolts of lightning, and an agreeable though strong voice, which loses a little of its charm in dispute; but her sweetness makes one forgive her a sharpness which is neither in her heart nor in her ideas. She has more imagination than wit, more wit than learning; she cuts through, decides, piles mistake on mistake, and ends up by no longer hearing what she is saying when she speaks of the arts of which she is ignorant, or of religious feeling which she sees in everything. Her

Christianity makes one long to be a pagan, her mysticism makes one prefer dryness, and her love of the marvellous makes one like everything that is simple and vulgar, so much do exaggerations produce the opposite effect. Donna Elvira's . . . devouring flame of sensibility and fruitless search for love make her unhappy and often ridiculous; but it is compensated for by so much that is unexpected, quicksilver and inspiring that you forgive her for what in anyone else would be unendurable . . . Her nature is as pure as gold, her style as warm as her heart: she is not quite a man, nor is she quite a woman; but she is the most distinguished person.'[12]

A true man of the Enlightenment, Ligne was irritated by what he saw as Madame de Staël's mysticism. Madame de Staël undoubtedly had a religious temperament as is obvious in all her works. She retained a firm faith in God throughout her life even if her general religious beliefs altered with time. Her faith was firmly anchored in the Protestant religion of her parents, especially the tolerant, liberal piety of her father. At Coppet, she went to church regularly and read the gospels, as well as her father's works on religion and morals, to her children. Madame de Staël's attitude to the Roman Catholic Church had softened. Corinne is a Catholic and her explanations to Oswald in the novel demonstrate that Madame de Staël had great respect for the deeply held religious convictions of her Catholic friends – Prosper de Barante, Chateaubriand, but above all Mathieu de Montmorency – even if she disliked the Papacy and the power structures of the Church. But she remained a Swiss Protestant at heart. When Auguste was preparing for his confirmation, under the instruction of the mystic François Gautier, she had written: 'I do not want him to read Catholic texts; I care about our religion, that of my father and mother, and my son should not deviate from it. Let him be virtuous and pious like those respectable people and my wishes will be wonderfully fulfilled!'[13]

Her father's death had forced her to a new awareness of the limits of reason to make sense of her grief and her life and Madame de Staël had tried to find consolation in religion. But to her, religion, literature, morality were all linked and all founded on liberty. She was attracted for a while to the quietist philosophy of men like Constant's cousin, Charles-Louis de Langallerie, leader of the sect of 'Internal spirits', not so much for the sect's religious doctrines, but for their broad, ecumenical toleration which welcomed members of all faiths, and their optimistic message that one day all men will be happy, and that even the devil would return to the fold. 'There is a religious calm in the depths of your souls which I have been begging for, from the Heavens, but so far in vain,' she wrote to Gautier from Vienna. It was an inner calm which forever eluded her and that she longed for. She was anxious that her interest should not be misrepresented however. While ready to admit in *De l'Allemagne* that she had been wrong in her religious philosophy, she begged Gautier to say nothing to others about it, except to Langallerie: 'I am frightened most of all of appearing hypocritical for since I lead a dissipated life, I can only speak of religion as of an aspiration.'[14]

Madame de Staël's 'dissipated life' in Vienna was duly recorded by the security services. They soon noticed that one of her most regular visitors was a handsome young officer, Count Maurice O'Donnell von Tyrconnel, of a Viennese family of Irish descent, fourteen years her junior. Soon the police reports noted that 'Madame de Staël spends all the time when she is not out in society with him' and that he was to be seen late at night writing to her dictation![15] Madame de Staël's affair with O'Donnell followed the usual pattern: declarations of love followed by jealous scenes – he had openly flirted with Flore de Ligne, the Prince's daughter – followed by recriminations. In between she sent him oranges and broth, together with enquiries about his health – he seemed to be frequently ailing. O'Donnell, who was a perfectly conventional man, must have been embarrassed by her outlandish behaviour. She was deeply depressed: 'we seem to be drawing apart' she wrote towards the end of her stay, 'exile, my return, the solitude in my heart, the battles ahead, the pain of parting, a total lack of interest in anything which was not of the heart, no hope of happiness, in short a kind of self-disgust, a feeling which justifies Chateaubriand's dictum about those souls who are condemned to eternal solitude. I know that if someone heard me, that if I was to meet my father in his youth, I would kiss his footprints, but my spirit wears itself out against the barriers which separate us . . . I had a tender affection for you which deserved that you should not fight against my nature, but seek to harmonize with it . . . instead of seeking to clip my wings.'[16]

Whether he was touched by her genuine sorrow or relieved at the prospect of her imminent departure, O'Donnell and Madame de Staël had one last romantic outing together. They went to Laxenburg, the imperial family's summer estate, and to the Brühl valley where he carved her name on a tree. O'Donnell's kindness in these last moments unfortunately rekindled Madame de Staël's enthusiasm and her subsequent letters express her belief that he must love her, urging him not to listen to gossip about her.

From Vienna Madame de Staël corresponded frequently with Madame Récamier. Unhappy with O'Donnell, afraid that she had lost Constant, she poured out her despair: 'Benjamin tells you that I am displeased with him. My God! I have one sorrow, but such a cruel one. It is the fear of not being loved. If I believed myself to be loved, all my problems would disappear . . . I have tried to ignore these thoughts this winter as much as I could, but ignore them like an eighteen year old . . .'

In another letter she expresses her fears that Benjamin might be tempted to go to America without her. Did his heart not tell him that it would mean death for her? She begs Madame Récamier to see him often: 'there is nothing for me without the friend of all my youth, and any success – the admiration of the whole world, are not worth life at Coppet with him.'[17] To Constant she wrote just before her departure: 'I return with the same attachment to you, an attachment unaffected by any other attention to me, an attachment which compares you with no one else on earth, my heart, my life, everything is yours, if you still want it and in whatever way you wish, Think about it. I am convinced that no one could replace Albertine and me for you . . .'[18] Anyone reading Madame de Staël's flood of love letters to O'Donnell over the next few months might be forgiven for thinking her insincere or worse. In fact she was desperate, deeply unhappy, clutching at any straw, of which O'Donnell was one. Constant was her mainstay and she was terrified of losing him. With his usual clear insight he had been absolutely right to judge that 'he was always needed but never enough'. It is impossible to blame him for being tired of it. He had already taken a decision, of which Madame de Staël would be unaware until the following year. A few weeks later, on 5 June 1808, he quietly married Charlotte Hardenberg at Dôle in a simple Protestant ceremony. The marriage was not registered. His father and his new wife were delighted, but Benjamin was too terrified of Madame de Staël's imminent arrival to feel anything but panic.

On 22 May, Madame de Staël's *berline* rolled out of Vienna with

Schlegel, Albertine and Sismondi on board. Her younger son, Albert, was left behind at the military academy in Vienna. After a very brief pause in Prague, she continued her journey to Teplitz, then one of Europe's most fashionable spas, where she met Friedrich von Gentz. Prussian in origin Gentz was a famous journalist and publicist, and a bitter opponent of Napoleon, though not yet the out-and-out reactionary he was to become later, as Metternich's secretary and *éminence grise*. From there she wrote to the Prince de Ligne. 'I have met Gentz, with whom I talked until human strength was exhausted, for he is so animated, interested in everything, and would seem even more of a thinker if he did not feel obliged, as a German, to speak French at an incredible speed.' She thought him very intelligent and very learned, if not particularly original – 'but I think I have not met a man in all Germany with a greater knowledge of political France.'[19]

Madame de Staël's meeting with Gentz was duly reported to Napoleon by his spies and had serious consequences for her. Gentz was a known agent of Britain, of Prussia and then of Austria. With Austria rearming and a second front opening up in Spain, Napoleon had every right to take Gentz seriously. 'Until now I had looked on her as a mad woman, but now she is beginning to enter a coterie which is against public peace,'[20] he wrote to Fouché from Bayonne, where he had gone in May 1808 to accept the abdication of the King and Queen of Spain. The Spaniards had proved less than co-operative. Over the next seven years, the 'Spanish ulcer', which demanded an ever-increasing expenditure in men and effort, was to be one of the major factors in Napoleon's downfall.

Before she left Vienna Madame de Staël had offered to publish a selection of the Prince de Ligne's works. Together they had made a choice among a lifetime of his writings. Included were his portraits of Voltaire, Rousseau, Catherine the Great, Frederick II, Joseph II, together with various letters and *pensées*. Madame de Staël wrote a masterly foreword to the selection and had it published in Paris and Geneva in January 1809. The book was a tremendous literary and commercial success. 'My good protector!' Ligne wrote to her. 'No man is a hero to his valet. I was known to be writing, but no one read me, and few understood me. One word from you – your name, has made my fortune. If only . . . you had written a short preface to my fifteen or sixteen volumes on war I would have been given armies to command.'[21]

Madame de Staël bombarded O'Donnell with letters throughout June 1808 as she travelled to Dresden, Weimar, Erfurt, Gotha, Frankfurt, Heidelberg and Freiburg, seeing, as she wrote to Ligne, 'men of letters or intellectuals at every stop' and making notes for her work on Germany. She was back at Coppet at the begining of July where she was joined by Mathieu. There she received her first letter from O'Donnell informing her that, with war on the horizon, he had rejoined the army. Over several long letters to him she wrote that she understood his reasons for wishing to remain in Vienna but that there was nothing to prevent her from joining him. She would come to Vienna for the winter!

Constant meanwhile had been persuaded back to Coppet. Neither his aunt nor his cousin Rosalie, nor yet Madame de Staël had the slightest clue that he had married Charlotte. Charlotte was dispatched to a hotel at Neuchâtel where she was to await further news. She spent the summer touring Switzerland with an aunt. Immured at Coppet, Constant was unable to find the courage to tell Madame de Staël of his marriage. Busy with the printing of his play, *Wallstein*, he managed to escape to see Charlotte in October for a few days when Madame de Staël was in Geneva. She was beginning to suspect that something was going on but was lulled by Constant's continued presence at Coppet.

In early August, Madame de Staël received a harsh letter from O'Donnell. He was angry that she had sent him money. He believed she had trifled with him! He accused her of spreading a rumour that he had proposed to her and that she had refused him. She had made him a laughing stock in Vienna. It is evident from her reply of 14 August that he had used expressions such as 'shower of letters', 'abuse of confidence' and 'the art of dissimulation' in relation to her. An angry correspondence of counter-accusations and dramatic declarations of betrayal, ingratitude and much else besides followed in which Madame de Staël expressed her belief that, since his father had become Austrian Minister of Finance, opening the way to the possibility of jobs, appointments and an advantageous marriage for Maurice, he was now trying to get rid of her.[22] She continued in this vein throughout the autumn, but the affair was over. (On active service he distinguished himself at the battle of Aspern in the following year and was then made aide-de-camp to the Archduke Maximilian. He was reconciled with Madame de Staël after she sent him a warm and friendly letter in March 1810, following the death of his father. In

1811, when he married Titine de Ligne, the Prince's illegitimate granddaughter, Madame de Staël sent him her warm congratulations.)

In mid-August, with a group of friends and her children, Madame de Staël attended the 'shepherds gathering', the celebrations of five hundred years of Swiss independence, at Interlaken, an event which she described in a letter to Maurice O'Donnell and later in *De l'Allemagne*. Ten thousand spectators had gathered beneath the Jungfrau to watch the descent of the shepherds – Swiss from every valley dressed as they would have been five centuries before at the time of the swearing of the oath at Rutli, followed by games. The painter Madame Vigée Lebrun recalled that she and Madame de Staël had been so moved by the solemn procession that they had squeezed each other's hand wordlessly with tears in their eyes.[23] Madame de Staël and her friends also visited the Swiss educationist and philanthropist Pestalozzi at Yverdon, where he came out to greet her 'with straw in his hair and floating garments'.[24]

When she returned to Coppet in July 1808, Madame de Staël's first thought was to begin work on her book. 'I have already ordered a notebook to be sewn for my letters on Germany and I have written two lines which I re-read with a kind of fear, for I am not sure whether I will recover my talent,' she wrote to the Prince de Ligne.[25] That autumn Coppet was full of German guests. Madame de Staël spent several evenings a week reading Klopstock, Herder and Lessing with the Baron Voght, a friend of Madame Récamier. She also wrote, staged and acted in her own play *La Sunamite*, and in *Gustave Wasa* by her son Auguste, among other productions, juggled three lovers – Constant, O'Donnell and Prosper de Barante – the last two admittedly by correspondence, all amid the comings and goings at Coppet.

Among her earlier guests that summer was Madame de Krüdener. Then in her early forties, Julie de Krüdener was an attractive blonde with a racy past which she had immortalized in her very successful autobiographical novel *Valérie*, which Madame de Staël declared to be 'a caricature of the genre'. Of Latvian origin, she had recently buried a husband and had turned to religion at first through the pietist Moravian brethren who were attracting many converts, and later as a follower of Jung-Stilling, a famous mystic who preached a higher form of Ecumenical Christianity and professed occult knowledge of the imminent end of the world. Her arrival was followed by that of the poet and dramatist Zacharias Werner, whom Madame de Staël had just met at Interlaken. Unstable, hysterical, mystical, with a long bony figure and an uncontrollable lust – no housemaid was safe when he passed – he was to end up as a Catholic priest, but that summer his religious views were somewhat less orthodox. God, he explained to Sismondi, was the greatest hermaphrodite in the universe, uniting every kind of love in Himself. If one were unable to rise to the heights of religious love, carnal love would do! He called Madame de Staël, who was fond of him, Notre Dame de Coppet. Werner was a good and talented man, Sismondi remarked, but completely mad. Others who joined her familiars – Bonstetten, Sismondi, Constant, Camille Jordan, Sabran and Mathieu and his family – were, at various times, the Danish poet Oehlenschläger, Henriette Mendelssohn, the sculptor Friedrich Tieck, a young Greek called Dimitri Schinas, the former Russian Foreign Minister Count Kochubey, and the Duke and Duchess de Noailles.

All three of Madame de Staël's lovers proved a sad disappointment that winter of 1808. Her desperate fear of loneliness and old age, and her need for reassurance drove her to entertain illusions and employ unworthy tactics to keep them, all of which invariably had precisely the opposite effect. In December, Constant had gone to his house near Paris to be with his wife, though Madame de Staël was still unaware of their relationship, let alone their marriage. O'Donnell had stopped writing to her and Prosper de Barante, with whom she had vaguely hoped to rekindle her romance, had fallen in love with Madame Récamier. Madame de Staël suspected her of encouraging him, which caused a temporary estrangement. In February 1809 Madame de Staël wrote to beg her pardon. 'Forgive me for believing that it is impossible to see you and not love you,' she wrote.[26]

Meanwhile Madame de Staël continued to press for the return of her father's millions. In February 1809 she wrote to Talleyrand: 'You will be astonished to see a hand which you will have forgotten. At the distance at which we find ourselves I feel as if I am addressing you from another world. My life has changed so much that it is all too easy for me to entertain such an illusion . . . You wrote to me fourteen years ago [from America]: "If I stay here for another year I will die." I could say the same . . . the time for pity is gone, but perhaps you can do something for my children. If you can, I believe you will.'[27] But Talleyrand himself was out of favour and nothing came of it.

War was imminent. Steady rearmament, Napoleon's defeats in

Spain and Metternich's secret relations with Talleyrand in Paris (he was now Ambassador there) convinced the Austrian government that the time was right. Talleyrand did not scruple to betray Napoleon to the Austrians when he believed that the Emperor's actions were injurious to France. Austria was to do better this time but, after a hard fought campaign from April to July 1809 she was again defeated at Wagram. The Peace which followed was reinforced in 1810, when, after divorcing the ageing Josephine, who had been unable to give him an heir, Napoleon married Marie-Louise of Austria.

At the beginning of April 1809, Madame de Staël brought her son Albert back from Vienna. The coming war was not the only reason. Often in trouble – he had recently broken a front tooth brawling with a Polish classmate – Albert had resorted to a pawnbroker when he had overspent his pocket money and had been punished. She was once again deeply depressed, feeling abandoned and alone. It was her invariable reaction when returning to Coppet, until she had filled it to overflowing with friends. 'Please ask Benjamin to leave now and come to me. He has caused me enough pain this winter and must come and console me,' she wrote to Madame Récamier.[28] At the beginning of May, Constant and Charlotte arrived at Sécheron, near Coppet. Constant knew that he could not keep his marriage secret any longer but, too afraid to face Madame de Staël himself, he left poor Charlotte to break the news. Charlotte duly sent a note to Madame de Staël, begging her to call on her. She signed it Charlotte von Hardenberg. That night Madame de Staël arrived unannounced. 'I have come because you are a Hardenberg,' she announced. It was not, as some have thought, a snobbish remark, but much more likely a warning shot: that she suspected that a marriage had taken place but would not accept it. Charlotte's announcement of her marriage led to an almighty row which raged till four o'clock in the morning. To each fresh accusation against the perfidious Benjamin, Charlotte could only bleat 'but he is such a good man'.

To have this ninny preferred to her was too much for Madame de Staël. When at last Constant put in an appearance, she persuaded him to keep the marriage secret at least for six months, until her planned departure for America. Meanwhile Constant was to return with her to Coppet, while Charlotte could go to Germany and wait for him there. Charlotte agreed, no doubt to get rid of Madame de Staël, but when she had left, she refused to go to Germany. She would wait for Constant at Dôle.

When, in June, Constant escaped to Dôle to see her, Auguste was sent to fetch him back. Auguste had been in such rage at the suffering Constant had caused his mother that he had almost challenged him to a duel, Constant wrote to his aunt, Madame de Nassau, who had been doing her best to put some backbone into him. Full of excuses for his continued presence at Coppet, he explained that Madame de Staël's misery was terrible, and he was anxious not to make an enemy for life of her or her sons. There was also a question of money. He owed Madame de Staël a large sum which he was completely unable to pay back. He swore that he would return to his wife in July.[29]

Meanwhile, life went on. In June, breaking her banning order at great risk, Madame de Staël and her friends went to Lyons to see the great actor Talma. Years later Madame de Boigne recalled what had been their first meeting there. A message from Madame de Staël, who was staying in the same hotel, had been delivered to Madame de Boigne, asking whether she would receive her. Madame de Boigne replied that she would be delighted and would call later to arrange a time. Five minutes later Madame de Staël swept into her room, escorted by Constant, Camille Jordan, Mathieu de Montmorency, Schlegel, Elzéar de Sabran and Talma himself! 'I was very young then,' Madame de Boigne recalled, 'and this great celebrity with her large attendance intimidated me. Madame de Staël soon put me completely at ease.' Madame de Boigne had intended to visit Lyon that morning but Madame de Staël brushed the idea aside, telling her that all she needed to know was that it was a very ugly town between two very beautiful rivers. She had spent the rest of the morning in Madame de Boigne's room, receiving visitors and enchanting the young woman with her conversation. Forgetting her promise to dine with the prefect, Madame de Boigne dined with Madame de Staël instead. Afterwards, she recalled, they had gone to see Talma in *Manlius*, 'who acted for her more than for the public, and who was well rewarded by the delight she took in his performance'. Madame de Boigne had been startled by Madame de Staël's appearance: 'At first glance I had thought her ugly and ridiculous. A big red face without freshness, topped with hair "picturesquely arranged" but in fact ill-styled; a white muslin tunic cut very low, her arms and shoulders naked, no shawl, no scarf, no veiling of any kind. All this made for a singular apparition in a hotel room at midday. She held a small leafy twig, which she twirled constantly. It was intended, I believe, to draw attention to a very beautiful hand, but it added to the strangeness of her costume. Watching her intelligent pleasure in Talma's acting and her ability to communicate it, watching the expressiveness of her features, I was surprised into thinking her almost beautiful.'[30]

Tired of waiting for her husband, Charlotte had followed them to Lyons. She had been Madame Constant for a year and still Benjamin couldn't get rid of Madame de Staël. Writing to announce her arrival, she forgave him, blamed Madame de Staël for all their troubles and declared that she was taking poison. When the letter reached Constant, who read it with Madame de Staël, they rushed around to Charlotte's hotel where they found her writhing in agony. A doctor was called, an antidote administered and Charlotte saved. As soon as she returned to consciousness, Charlotte threatened to poison herself again if Constant did not acknowledge their marriage at once; Madame de Staël threatened to stab herself if he did. Constant could only wring his hands. In the end Madame de Staël agreed to write to 'Madame Constant' acknowledging the marriage provided they kept it quiet from everyone else for three months. After escorting Charlotte to Paris and placing her in the care of a doctor, Constant returned once again to Coppet.

Constant and Madame de Staël spent the rest of that summer of 1809, tearing each other apart. At Aix-en-Savoie in September, with Madame Récamier as mediator, Madame de Boigne witnessed 'deplorable scenes where two great minds used more wit than God has perhaps ever granted to any mortal, to torment each other mutually'. There were daily rows in the morning, followed by reconciliations in the afternoon and conversational duets in the evenings. Madame de Boigne believed that Madame de Staël had hoped that Constant would come with her to America and had been deeply hurt and put out by his secret marriage. 'There was a deep bond between them. He always behaved in an entirely paternal manner with the pretty child, [Albertine], who had been indiscreet enough to look exactly like him.'[31]

Schlegel had tried to dissuade Madame de Staël from bringing Constant back with her: 'That he is a cause of discord between you and your friends is the least of his faults. But every day you spend with him from now on is a waste of your talents and merely delays a time when you might be happy again, or at least when you regain some peace: forget, and put your noble faculties to work.' But in spite of her heartache, Madame de Staël's 'noble faculties' were never idle, and she was perfectly able to work on her book while her unruly heart played havoc with her own life and that of others. Madame Récamier's presence at Coppet that summer was a great solace. Once again, Madame de Staël staged *Phèdre* to great acclaim, with herself in the title role and Madame Récamier as Aricie. When Werner returned in the autumn – he was to remain for two months – brandishing his enormous snuffbox, his handkerchief and his play, *The twenty-fourth of February*, Madame de Staël staged it with himself and Schlegel in the leading roles.

Constant remained at Coppet until the middle of October, but throughout all the time he was there he sent batches of his papers to his aunt, in preparation for his final escape. His cousin Rosalie was incensed by his treatment of Charlotte and his inability to stand up to Madame de Staël. He tried to explain from Les Herbages that although he thought Charlotte truly angelic, yet 'I have, in the depths of my heart, I know not what kind of fatal sympathy for another person, which means that as long as I believe her to be honest about her pain or her feelings, though I might take violent action to get out of a situation which weighs on me, I fall back into a kind of agony which drives me mad and undoes everything I have done and that others have done for me.'[32] After his departure Madame de Staël wrote to Madame Récamier: 'He has been gone for eight days and never in my life have I felt such a paroxysm of sorrow. His letters since then have softened feelings which were otherwise unbearable. But misery remains, such as makes one long for the end of life. Believe me, I beg you, and encourage him to think well of me. I don't know how this might be done, but I know that I cannot live without seeing him and talking to him.'[33]

In December, Constant and Charlotte were married again in a civil ceremony in Paris. He had got around the problem of his debt to Madame de Staël by promising that he would leave the 80,000 francs he owed her to her heirs on his death. He also promised to return in February. Meanwhile, several visits from Prosper de Barante, who had come to Geneva to stay with his parents, had rekindled Madame de Staël's hopes. She wrote to Madame Récamier, begging her to keep these thoughts secret from everyone except Mathieu. She was still nervous of Madame Récamier's attraction. In the spring of 1810, after consultations with Madame Récamier and Mathieu, both of them devoted to Madame de Staël and anxious about her state of mind,

Prosper wrote a kind letter to her, which put an end, once and for all, to her delusions of any possibility of marriage to him. Clear-sightedly the young man, who was about to be appointed a Prefect in the Vendée, explained that, fond as she might be of him, 'never or at any rate rarely do you imagine an existence together with mine. You would still need travel and continuous movement.' Of course he would love to go to Italy with her (as she had suggested) but what she had to offer had nothing in common with his own ideas of 'a durable union and the establishment of a life'. 'Finally, my dear friend,' he writes, 'I love you, I am overwhelmed by the affection you show me, I believe that your character might change, as it has already; that it might lose something of its ardour and anxiety; but in the end, wonderful as your letters are, and in spite of the sentiments and the self-abnegation which move me so much, they still leave a great deal which I find alarming. I so love peace . . . my independence is so precious to me that it doesn't take much to plunge me into anxiety.'[34]

Chapter 22

~

De l'Allemagne

'*De l'Allemagne* was like a powerful instrument which drove the first breach in the wall of prejudice which had risen between us and France.'

Goethe

THE MAGNIFICENT CHÂTEAU de Chaumont with its pepper-pot turrets stands on a hilltop overlooking the Loire and the lush and fertile plains near Blois. Steeped in history, it had once been home to Diane de Poitiers and to Catherine de Medici. Madame de Staël was to spend one last summer in France in this enchanted setting, entertaining her friends and correcting the proofs of her book. Chaumont belonged to her American agent, James Le Ray, who would not be returning until the autumn, and as it lay just outside the forty-league limit, Fouché gave her permission to live there for the summer. She arrived in mid-April 1810, with the manuscript of the last part of *De l'Allemagne* and a passport for America. She had made sufficient progress on the book to be able to envisage publication that summer. After that, if Paris remained closed to her, she would go to America which, she prophesied, 'would inherit the civilization of Europe'. Moreover, she had business interests in America and from there she would be able to sail directly to England. 'Great man, good woman, luxury of the heart and the mind, Good-day!' wrote the Prince de Ligne when he heard of her plans. 'Do not go and set up a volcano in the most apathetic, the most tranquil country in the world; leave America as it is. They are merely a poor imitation of the English. If you wish to speak English we can offer you a few boring representatives of that nation here.'[1]

Most of her book was already in Paris with her publisher Nicolle, who had submitted it to the censor. In order to speed up the proofreading, Madame de Staël had arranged to have it printed in nearby Tours by Mame. The publication of all books, already under strict control, had been further regulated recently by a decree which stipulated the need for a permit in advance to be attached to the manuscript. The Director of Publications, as also the Minister of Police, had the right for 'reasons of state' to stop the printing, irrespective of the opinion of the censors. To gain time, Madame de Staël and her publisher had taken a risky decision: they would submit the text to the imperial censor in proof form, one volume at a time, as the writing proceeded. Since the Director of Publications, Joseph-Marie Portalis, was a friend of Madame de Staël and she had always got on with Fouché, she was not unduly worried.

Madame de Staël arrived accompanied by her children, Schlegel, Pertosa, a Neapolitan music master, and a new member of her household, Miss Fanny Randall. A cousin by marriage of Sismondi's, Fanny was a tall, bony, English spinster, with an unhappy past and a difficult character. Madame de Staël had engaged her as a governess for Albertine. Fanny Randall became fiercely attached to Madame de Staël and to Albertine.

Soon after Madame de Staël arrival, she was joined by Prosper de Barante and Camille Jordan; closely followed at the beginning of May by Mathieu and his cousin Adrien de Montmorency; then by Madame Récamier, surrounded by three adorers: the American Middleton, the Hanoverian Baron von Voght and the Baltic Russian Baron von Balk. Then came the Russian Prince Tuffiakin, who was joined by Prosper's father with his youngest daughter Sophie, a companion for Albertine. Elzéar de Sabran followed with a young writer, Adalbert de Chamisso, the son of a French émigré to Berlin, where he had served in one of the Russian regiments and been a page at court. Introduced to Madame de Staël by Prosper de Barante, Chamisso was a writer, poet and miniaturist, the creator of the character Peter Schlemihl in *The Man without a Shadow*, published in 1814. Constant, too, had no compunction in dumping his Charlotte and joining them. His excuse to Charlotte was that Madame de Staël needed his help with the final part of *De l'Allemagne*. It was probably partly true; they had collaborated on everything that either of them had written over the past fifteen years. The fact was he could not resist Madame de Staël or the company which gathered around her. He promised Charlotte that he would be away for two weeks. He stayed for seven.

It was a wonderfully happy and productive summer. Madame de Staël worked hard to finish her book, even shutting herself away some mornings. 'I am horrified myself by the amount of work I have done on my book,' she wrote to her father's old friend, Meister. She was not the only one – 'in every corner there is someone composing some work,' wrote Baron von Voght to Madame Récamier.[2] The group met at meals and in the evenings they made music, with Pertosa playing his guitar, Albertine on the harp, while Madame Récamier shook her tambourine prettily. Auguste fell passionately in love with Madame Récamier, as did Schlegel. Mathieu did his best to bring her to God. Chamisso fell a little in love with Madame de Staël, who did not discourage him. 'She has German gravity, southern warmth, French culture,' he wrote. He recalled that she invented a game called *petite poste* that summer, in which, sitting around a table, everyone wrote notes to each other instead of conversing. It was a splendid outlet for various flirtations, as were two of the walks in the park which were christened *L'allée des explications* and *L'allée des réconciliations*

In August this agreeable state of affairs was shattered by the unexpected arrival, a month early, of Mr Le Ray. War had been declared recently between England and America, which had made the ocean crossing more dangerous. He had therefore caught a frigate which was sailing under a flag of truce. He hoped Madame de Staël would stay on at the château. But since he was accompanied by his family and Madame de Staël by her 'court' it was not a very practical suggestion. The prefect of Loir-et-Cher, M. de Corbigny, a liberal and enlightened man and a former protégé of Condorcet, who was supposed to be watching Madame de Staël but had fallen under her spell and become a regular guest, found her other accommodation. This was a large country house at nearby Fossé which belonged to a royalist nobleman, the splendidly named Comte Charles-Marie D'Irumberry de Salaberry, a gentleman of Basque origins. Their arrival at Fossé startled the quiet neighbourhood. Pertosa had immediately started to play his guitar, Albertine strummed her harp while Madame Récamier sang, much to the astonishment of the local peasantry, who gathered around to watch the arrival of 'this group of troubadors who had come to enliven their master's solitude'. When, a few days later, Madame de Staël and her friends had walked through Blois on their way to the opera, they were followed by the entire population. Word soon came to the new Minister of Police, who complained to the prefect that Madame de Staël was surrounded by a court. 'Yes,' she had riposted to Corbigny when he informed her of this, 'but at least I don't owe my court to my power.'[3] Meanwhile, in Paris, Fouché, who had never been trusted by the Emperor, was replaced in June by General Savary, now Duke of Rovigo, the man responsible for the murder of the Duc d'Enghien, and so faithful to the Emperor that Napoleon said of him that had he ordered Savary to leave his wife and children he would have done so without hesitation.[4]

All too soon, the summer came to an end. The war had forced her to postpone her voyage to America. Madame de Staël waved a sad goodbye to her friends and settled down to correct the proofs of part three of her book, which had been submitted to the censors in the middle of September (the first two parts had already been cleared and printed). One of the censors was the poet and academician Esménard, another of Madame Récamier's admirers, who, they hoped, would do his best to ensure a smooth passage for the book. She had seldom been happier since the death of her father and once again nurtured the illusion that this book might help to have the ban on her lifted. She had sent it to the Emperor under cover of a letter begging for an audience. Madame Récamier was to give it to Queen Hortense, Napoleon's stepdaughter, who would make sure it reached the Emperor. 'Sire, I am taking the liberty of presenting my work on Germany to Your Majesty. If Your Majesty deigns to read it, he will find proof of a mind which time has matured and capable of some thought.'

She went on to point out that it was ten years since they had met and eight since she had been exiled. She was about to leave the country again and hoped that, if she were not to be granted permission to live in the country near Paris, at least her children might have this possibility. 'Those who are the objects of Your Majesty's disfavour are put in such a position in Europe that I have been unable to take a step without feeling the effects; some fear to compromise themselves if they see me, while others think of themselves as *Romans*, if they succeed.'[5]

Metternich, then Austrian ambassador in Paris, had pointed out the danger of treating such a famous woman so harshly, but once again Napoleon refused to countenance her presence. 'If Madame de Staël wanted to be a royalist or a republican, I should have no objection, but she is a machine of movement, stirring up the salons. Such a woman can only be dreaded in France, and I will not have her there,' the

Emperor told him.[6] Madame de Staël may have been subversive by nature and by conviction, but it was Napoleon himself, as Metternich had warned, who turned her into what would be known in our day as a dissident.

She described the events which followed in her autobiographical account of her travels, *Dix années d'exil* (Ten Years of Exile). 'On 23 September, I was correcting the final proofs of my book. After six years of work it was a real joy to put the words, "the end" to my three volumes. I drew up a list of the hundred people in France and in Europe to whom I wanted to send the book. I attached great importance to this book which I believed contained many ideas new to France. I felt, however, that it had been inspired by the highest intentions which were in no way hostile to the French, and that it was written in a language that was no longer spoken. Armed with a letter from my publisher in which he assured me that the censors had authorized publication, I believed that I had nothing to fear and so I left for M. Mathieu de Montmorency's estate which lay some five leagues from Blois. The house on that estate was in the middle of a forest; and I was travelling with the man [Mathieu, who had come to escort her] whom I respect most on this earth since I lost my father. The lovely weather; the magnificence of the forest; these places steeped in history, where the battle of Fréteval between Philippe Auguste and Richard Coeur de Lion had taken place; everything combined to put me in the sweetest and most tranquil state of mind.'[7]

Leaving on 26 September to return to Fossé, Madame de Staël recollected how they got lost on the vast and empty plain of the Vendômois, bare of all landmarks. At about midnight, a lone rider rode up to their carriage and, understanding their predicament, offered them shelter for the night at his mother's château. Their rescuer, the Chevalier de Conan, happened to have been born in India, and the next day Madame de Staël was thrilled to see that the house was full of exotic art and furniture which his parents had brought back from their travels. Fascinated and in no hurry to leave, she had spent the morning examining all the rare curios, and paid little attention when a letter from her son Auguste was handed to her in which he begged her to leave at once. Her book, he wrote, had run into trouble in Paris.

Auguste had returned to Fossé from Paris to warn his mother, and became anxious when she failed to return from Blois as planned.

Mounting his horse he set off to meet her, but he too got lost on the plain and by strange chance, had ended up at the same Château de Conan, where he learned that his mother and Mathieu had recently arrived but had already gone to bed. Asking for Mathieu to be woken up, Auguste explained that the entire book was now in danger. Mathieu must break the news to her in the morning while Auguste sped off back to Fossé to do what he could to save it. Here, during the night of the 26–27 September, he and Fanny Randall collected together the final proofs of her manuscripts, together with the printed copies of the first two parts, which they just managed to hide before the police came to impound her book. The next day, as they approached Fossé, afraid that the police might be waiting for her, Madame de Staël gave her travelling writing desk with all its contents to her younger son Albert, who jumped over the wall and entered the house through the garden. Meanwhile Fanny Randall came out to meet her and gave her a quick account of all that had happened.

'The Prefect of Loir-et-Cher came to ask for my manuscript. To gain time I gave him an earlier copy which I still had and with which he was satisfied.'[8] At the same time he handed her a letter from Savary, requesting her to leave the country within forty-eight hours. Deciding to use the passport she had for America, but to take a ship which stopped in England and disembark there instead, Madame de Staël informed Savary that she needed more time to make the necessary arrangements. He had already sent instructions to the police at Tours, without consulting the censors, to impound the whole print run of 10,000 copies of the first two volumes, the proofs of the final one, and the type blocks, which were broken up there and then. The printer Mame immediately complained to Portalis, the Director of Publications, who had no idea of what had occurred. He in turn protested to the Minister of the Interior, to the effect that the police had no right to seize the book until the process of censorship had been completed and a report issued.

Savary's reply made matters quite clear. He had acted on the direct instructions of the Emperor. Napoleon had read the book, although his initial intention was not to suppress the book completely.[9] 'I have sent back Madame de Staël's book to you. Is she entitled to style herself Baroness? Has she used this title in her other published works? Have the passage concerning the Duke of Brunswick [who had led a successful cavalry charge against the French and escaped to England] suppressed and three quarters of the passages in which she exalts England. This unfortunate exaltation has done us enough harm as it is.'[10]

Meanwhile Auguste and Albert left for Paris to see what they could do. There Auguste asked Savary whether his mother might at least be allowed to settle outside the forty-league limit while she awaited the decision about her book. The state needed his mother's talents, Savary replied, but she would have to proclaim herself for or against the government. She had been wrong to praise the Prussians. Madame de Staël could have a week to make her arrangements – implicitly, to repudiate publicly all she stood for – or to leave the country. The two young men then went to Fontainebleau to plead personally with the Emperor, where they were informed curtly that if they remained they would be arrested. On 3 October, Savary wrote again to Madame de Staël, a letter she would later give full public exposure to by including it in the preface to *De l'Allemagne* when it was at last published by John Murray in London in 1813:

> I have received, Madame, the letter which you did me the honour of writing. Monsieur your son will have informed you that I see no objection to your delaying your departure by a week; I trust that that will suffice for you to make all your arrangements, because that is all the time I can grant you.
>
> You should not suppose that the order I sent you was motivated by your failure to mention the Emperor in your last work; that would be an error. There could not be a place worthy of him in it; but your exile is a natural consequence of your consistent conduct over the last few years. It seems to me that the air of this country does not agree with you, and we are not yet reduced to looking for models among the countries you admire. Your last work is not French; it is I who stopped the printing. I regret the losses which will be suffered by your publisher but I cannot allow it to go ahead.
>
> You must know, Madame, that you were allowed to leave Coppet only because you expressed the desire to travel to America. If you were given permission by my predecessor to reside in the department of Loir-et-Cher, you should not have viewed this concession as a revocation of the measures taken in regard to you. Today you oblige me to apply them strictly. For this, you have only yourself to blame.
>
> I have instructed M. de Corbigny to carry out my order to the letter, on expiry of the time granted to you.

> I regret, Madame, that you have obliged me to begin my correspondence with you with an act of severity. I should have preferred to be able to offer you only the assurances of my high esteem.
>
> I have the honour, Madame, to be your most humble and obedient servant, P.S. I have good reason, Madame, to indicate the ports of Lorient, La Rochelle, Bordeaux and Rochefort as the only ports of embarkation open to you. I invite you to let me know which you have chosen.[11]

Madame de Staël noticed at once that all the Channel ports were closed to her. She knew from her friends that the Emperor suspected her of wishing to reach England, and that he was determined to prevent it. She decided then to return to Coppet. To Madame Récamier, to whom she sent a copy of Savary's letter and her own reply, she wrote that she was in such a cloud of pain that she hardly knew what she was writing. She had hoped to see Prosper at Saumur, but had been told that he would be sacked immediately if she did so. M. von Balk, the handsome Russian baron, had offered to travel with her. Could he be interested in her she wondered hopefully? At Auxerre she spent two days with Benjamin, who, she believed, still loved her and was bored with his wife. 'When I was in the greatest possible pain, he was hard, but during those months at Fossé and Chaumont when I was so happy, he felt the need of me with a passion. I too found him to be what he is: the cleverest man in the world.' It wouldn't have been surprising if Constant, with the perversity of human nature and an emotional instability equal to hers, had made overtures to her now that he felt himself to be safe, nor that she should mistake his undoubted love for her for something more passionate.[12]

Madame de Staël's *De l'Allemagne* was not to see the light of day for another three years. What was it about this book which so annoyed Napoleon, even though initially he had been inclined to allow it to be published, provided she removed the offending passages? Later, on Elba, he read the book properly, writing to his brother Joseph and charging him to repeat it to Madame de Staël, that there was nothing in it which had required it to be prohibited, and laying the blame on the censors. This was a lie; the censors had in fact been overruled by a furious Napoleon, who never hesitated to rewrite history when it suited him, and it had suited him then, to try and rally liberal opinion to his side.[13]

In the autumn of 1810, however, Napoleon was at the height of his power and he had declared *De l'Allemagne* to be anti-French. For Napoleon, who had identified himself with Louis XIV, *De l'Allemagne*, even more than *Corinne*, undermined everything he stood for, and was therefore, by his definition, against France. Moreover it praised weak and subjugated people and encouraged them to rise against their oppressors. It praised England, the great enemy. Savary had been more honest, if less subtle, when he had asked Auguste angrily why his mother had not mentioned the Emperor or his armies in her book on Germany. The work was purely literary, Auguste replied, how could she deal with such matters? 'You think, Monsieur, that we have waged war for eight years in Germany so that a person as well known as Madame, your mother, should publish a book without even mentioning us? The book will be burnt and we should have put its author in Vincennes [prison].'[14]

If Savary was crude and simplistic, Auguste was certainly being disingenuous. The Emperor was right in believing Madame de Staël incapable of writing a purely literary book. She was always an activist, a committed political thinker and an analyst of human behaviour. She was also a perceptive and exciting literary critic and she believed passionately that literature could not and should not be viewed as separate from the political, social and historical conditions in any country. *De l'Allemagne* remains a wonderful book: intelligent, stimulating, perceptive. What she has to say about Germany and German social and political thinking is, of course, of its time, but her vibrant analyses of the works of Schiller and Goethe, Wieland, Klopstock and Werner are full of insight and interest. She coined the word *romanticism* to describe the new kind of poetry she had found in Germany: a poetry rooted in Christianity and chivalry, a poetry of inspiration and natural sensibility, celebrating the individual human spirit. She terms it modern, and compares and contrasts it with the classical tradition rooted in ancient Greece and Rome, which she sees as conservative.[15] She has a genius for communicating her own enthusiasm and interest so that her reader, even if out of sympathy with a particular idea, is fascinated and engaged, made to think and eager to learn more. Her intimate knowledge of the theatre – her work as a dramatist, actress, director and designer – make her a uniquely exciting theatre critic, irresistably drawing in her audience. Two hundred years on, this still seems a remarkable achievement. The impact of her discoveries and her expositions, of her ability to seize the spirit of the time, of her translations of the German 'greats' on her French and her European contemporaries, then largely ignorant of German culture, was electrifying. She was less enthusiastic about contemporary art, and wrote very little about music, which she none the less qualifies as 'the foremost of the arts' and despite the fact that it was a central part of her life.[16] This omission was deliberate. She thought words inadequate to express the effects of music. Music was a language in itself: the language of dreams, a language closest to the infinite, a direct link to God. None the less she admired Mozart, Gluck and Haydn, although she prefered Italian music – a preference shared by many of her contemporaries.[17]

Madame de Staël's Swiss family background placed her on the natural boundary between the two cultures and her interest in Germany was there from her earliest years. Her hope of writing something about Germany began to expand as a result of her travels. Her particular attachment to Schiller, whose works gave pre-eminence to the ideal of freedom, led her directly to Kant. She had thought first to write 'a literary and philosophical journey', then an anthology of poetry and prose, preceded by a 'clear analysis of the new systems of philosophy and aesthetics' which would give a better idea of the German character.[18] But six years later, in the light of Napoleon's rise, his conquest of German lands, the progressive stifling of political and intellectual freedoms in France and her own persecution, it also turned into a clarion call to France, where dictatorship had smothered creativity, emptying literature of all meaning. She did not see herself as – nor indeed was she – betraying French culture. In introducing German culture to the French, who had largely ignored it, Madame de Staël was certainly not putting Germany forward as a model to be imitated, as Savary had supposed crassly. On the contrary, she always claimed that mere imitation led to sterility and mediocrity. She had said so in Italy and would say so again in *De l'esprit des traductions* (On the spirit of translations), an essay published in 1816, in which she urged Italians to profit from English and German translations to create their own modern literature. She would repeat it in Russia. Pushkin was to say of her that she had been the first to do justice to the Russian people.

What she did not perhaps quite realize herself was the effect that her book would have in Germany too. In 1812 in St Petersburg, the diplomat Baron Stein, one of the architects of Prussian resistance, but then a refugee at the Tsar's court, wept as he listened to a reading of the final chapters on 'enthusiasm'.[19] In 1814, Goethe was to say of *De l'Allemagne* that had it been published in 1810 as Madame de Staël had intended, recent events (the rise of German nationalism and resistance to Napoleon) would have been attributed to the book, but that now it seemed like a prophecy after the event.[20] As she explains in the preface of *De l'Allemagne:* 'It is important I think, that this book, so slandered and the source of so much trouble, be made known to the public. General Savary declared that my book was *not French*. Since I do not see him as a representative of France, it is with confidence that I address these writings to the French people as I have known them, in which I have tried to the best of my ability, to celebrate the glory of the works of the human spirit.'[21] Her love of France did not preclude an admiration for England, which 'we have seen, like a knight at arms, defending social order, preserving Europe over ten years of anarchy and ten of despotism'. The French had aspired to a similar constitutional arrangement at the outset of the Revolution, but had forgotten these aims and hopes to which Madame de Staël, however, had remained true.[22]

In 'celebrating the works of the human spirit' Madame de Staël passionately hoped to bring about a cross-fertilization of ideas. She had more or less invented the study of comparative literature in *De la littérature*. She continued to use this system in *Corinne* and she used it again in *De l'Allemagne*, not as a mere academic or intellectual exercise but in the ardent hope that new ideas might serve as an inspiration to French literature, moribund in a self-regarding classicism, silent under Napoleonic censorship, helping it to find forms of expression and thought which would be both new and French. Madame de Staël encouraged the development of a national spirit which might help each country to discover its own character and express it in its own way, thereby enriching European civilization as a whole.

The French believed that German culture was vulgar, but Madame de Staël maintained that even were it true, original thinking was more important than good taste. 'Good taste in literature', she warns, 'is, in some ways, like order under despotism: it is important to examine the price one must pay for it. M. Necker has said of politics that: "as much liberty as was reconcilable with order was desirable". I would turn that around and say that in literature, good taste is desirable in so far as it can be reconciled with genius; for whereas peace is the most important thing in the social sphere, what matters most in literature, on the contrary, is interest, movement, emotion – to all of which good taste as such, may in some cases be an enemy.'[23] The diversity of writing and ideas which she had found in German drama made it difficult to categorize, she concludes. But, 'that diversity is in itself praiseworthy, for in literature as in so many other fields, unanimity is almost always a sign of servitude'.[24]

De l'Allemagne divides into four parts. In the first its author examines the institutions, social habits and geography of the country. The second part deals with literature and the arts. In part three she discusses philosophy and ethics, with chapters also on French and English philosophy, to compare and contrast and to demonstrate the roots and the connections in the works of recent and contemporary philosophers. The final part of *De l'Allemagne* is dedicated to religion and 'enthusiasm', which she defines thus: 'Enthusiasm turns towards universal harmony; it is the love of beauty, a lofty spirit, the enjoyment of devotion altogether which gives it grandeur and peace. The Greek meaning of the word gives us the noblest definition: enthusiasm means *God within us*. Truly when man's existence is expansive, there is something divine in it.' It is quite different from fanaticism, whether religious or political, or national, which is on the contrary, exclusive and narrow, based on a specific belief.[25]

Madame de Staël had not set out to idealize Germany. Exciting and fertile as she had found German literature and philosophy, there were many aspects of German life which she found profoundly uncongenial. These she summed up as a mixture of 'stoves, beer and tobacco: a warm and heavy atmosphere', from which the people rarely emerged. There was too great a gap between classes, the aristocracy was dull and lacking in ideas, the intellectuals isolated, the people rude and crude as well as xenophobic, slow, dull and too respectful of power. 'One is constantly struck, in Germany, by the contrast between sentiments and habits, between talent and taste; nature and civilization do not seem to have amalgamated very well.'

She was astonished by the persistence of feudalism in a country of thinkers, concluding that Germans had more imagination than wit, quoting the German writer J.-P. Richter, who had said that the empire of the sea belonged to the British, of land to the French, and of the air to the Germans. Their great qualities of loyalty, perseverance and justice are paralysed by inertia: 'You will hear the words "it is impossible" a hundred times in Germany to one in France.'[26]

She thought that the shocking contrast between German intellectual originality and daring and their submissiveness to authority and acceptance of feudalism must be due, as in Italy, to an absence of a national spirit. They lacked the 'energy of action' of the British, largely because they lacked British national consciousness. She encouraged the idea of German nationalism and independence, as she had done in Italy, not merely for Germany's sake but also for the sake of Europe's equilibrium, as she explains in the Preface to *De l'Allemagne*: 'Germany's geographical position at the heart of Europe makes her independence essential for the independence of a great many other European states.'[27] But her concept of nationalism was very different to that adopted by the Prussian nationalists. It had nothing to do with the ideals of Frederick the Great, who had wanted a military state founded on blind obedience and enlightened patriotism – two irreconcilable ideas in her view. She saw it rather as an expression of the authentic spirit of each nation, and as a struggle against injustice and oppression on the British model which she had always admired so much. Even though Napoleonic conquests would actually speed up the creation of national consciousness in Germany and Italy, Madame de Staël would never give him credit for it. It was not a good that he had intended. His motives had been immoral, even if in some cases good had later come of what he had done.

Napoleon had ample reason to fear a book which in every line set out to undermine him and his authority, both in the lands he had conquered but, especially and more importantly to him and to Madame de Staël, in France. Nor was that all. In the sections on German literature, her famous portrayals of Charles V and Attila in Werner's plays were all too clearly portraits of Napoleon. Here she quotes directly from *Attila*: 'This giant of a man has no heart in his fearful breast. In his hand he grasps the thunderbolts of absolute power; but he does not know how to make love triumph. He is like the young eagle who holds the entire globe in his claws and must devour it.'[28] Describing Attila, as he appears in Werner's eponymous play, in the ruins of the town of Aquilea, which he had just sacked, Madame de Staël writes: 'He has a kind of superstitious belief in himself, he is the object of his own worship, he believes in himself, he sees himself as the instrument of Heaven's decrees, and this belief makes his crimes seem reasonable.'[29] The parallel with Napoleon's well-known belief in 'his star' couldn't be more clear.

But nothing emphasizes more the fact that the real philosophical backbone of her book on Germany is liberty than the section she devotes to philosophy, and in particular the discussion of Kant, in a chapter entitled 'Other famous German philosophers before and after Kant'. Free will was a central Kantian doctrine. No morality could exist unless man was free to choose. Therefore he rejected all determinism whether natural or social. If man is propelled blindly by nature then he is no more than a puppet, unable to make a moral choice. Man must be believed capable of making a choice and be free to make it. It follows that no form of domination by any one human being over another is permissible; human dignity and liberty are pre-eminent. What Madame de Staël particularly admired in Kant was that he treated morality, science and art as parts of a whole, and in contrast to materialist philosophy, united 'primitive truths, spontaneity of the soul and conscience as the only guide to morality and idealism in the arts'.[30]

Finally the book concludes with a direct appeal to her countrymen: 'Oh France! Land of glory and of love! If one day enthusiasm was to become extinguished on your soil, if calculation was to be everything and reason alone inspired even contempt of danger, to what end your lovely skies, your brilliant minds, your fertile nature? An active intelligence, the impetus of knowledge might make you masters of the universe; but you would leave behind nothing but the traces of torrents of sand, terrible as the seas, arid as the desert.'[31]

In the autumn of 1810, Madame de Staël travelled back to Switzerland as slowly as she dared, respecting the forty leagues limit but unable to tear herself away from her beloved France. 'I am dawdling on the journey back because leaving France hurts and Switzerland seems to me a prison,' she wrote to Madame Récamier.[32] At Coppet, to which she had returned 'like a pigeon with clipped wings', (an allusion to La Fontaine's fable *Deux Pigeons*), she saw a great rainbow 'over my father's house', which helped to raise her spirits. She was almost resigned to the idea of living quietly at Coppet for the time being and publishing nothing more when she heard that her sons too were banned from France. For the first time she felt the pain of knowing that her situation would weigh on them too.

Soon after *De l'Allemagne* was pulped, a letter from Chateaubriand informed her of the losses suffered by her publisher Nicolle. Madame de Staël repaid her advance at once but Nicolle was still forced into bankruptcy. Prosper de Barante's father, still the prefect of Leman, wrote to Savary asking whether Geneva, then a part of France, was to be included in the general ban. She was given permission to go 'only to Geneva', where she spent the winter of 1810–11.[33] Barante had also been obliged to request that she hand over any copies of *De l'Allemagne* still in her possession. Thanks to the kindness of the prefect Corbigny, and the quick-wittedness of her son and Fanny Randall, she had managed to save and smuggle out two complete printed copies of volumes 1 and 2, of her book as well as the proofs volume 3. She replied that the only remaining copies were no longer in Switzerland and she therefore could not, hand them over, nor indeed was it her wish to do so. Barante was sacked in November, and most of Geneva blamed Madame de Staël.

The deposed Empress Josephine was visiting Geneva at the time. Madame de Staël recalled that as 'dethroned powers' they had been full of courtesies to one another, the Empress sending her ladies-in-waiting to call on Madame de Staël while 'I could only reciprocate by sending my chamberlain, Schlegel'. The Empress had said a lot of very kind things about her – 'she is a person without faults except perhaps for her liking for celebrity, but it is a perfectly natural taste, given her talents'. Madame de Staël reported this remark cheerfully to Maurice O'Donnell, with whom she was now on terms of friendship.[34]

Barante was replaced in March 1811 by Capelle, a former lover of Eliza Bonaparte, now Grand Duchess of Tuscany. Madame de Staël was to describe him later as 'eminently suited to the present regime, with a great knowledge of facts in matters of government, and a total absence of any principle; a complete devotion to power, his only conscience'. She had accurately summed up a man who had once been a passionate Republican, now served the Emperor and would after the Restoration serve as a Minister under the reactionary Charles X.

The first time they met, Capelle told her that a talent such as hers was positively made to celebrate the Emperor, repeatedly urged her to write something laudatory about the regime and suggested to all her friends that they persuade her to do so. It would put an end to all her troubles, he promised. Madame de Staël tried to explain that even the Emperor might consider eulogies coming from her ridiculous in the present circumstances. Soon after the birth of the King of Rome, Napoleon's son and heir, on 20 March 1811, Capelle appeared again, suggesting that Madame de Staël might now write something to celebrate the occasion. She had no thoughts on the subject, she replied, and would merely confine herself to wishing him a good wet-nurse![35] Perhaps she remembered Napoleon's crude remarks about breast-feeding in the past. At any rate her little joke put an end to all further attempts to bring her into the fold. Capelle now tightened the screw, and in May Schlegel, who was still with her, received orders to leave Geneva. The reason given was that he was anti-French and responsible for corrupting Madame de Staël. He had written an essay, with which Madame de Staël had actually disagreed, in which he compared Racine's *Phèdre* unfavourably with *Phaedra* by Euripides. 'How nice that a Corsican monarch should be so keen to defend French literature,' Madame de Staël remarked later. The truth was that Napoleon wanted to punish and isolate this woman who refused to submit to his control. A fortnight later, when Schlegel left to visit his brother Friedrich in Vienna, he took with him a complete set of *De l'Allemagne*. Before his departure they made plans for Madame de Staël's own escape from Coppet, where she was now effectively under house arrest. She knew that somehow she must get to England.

The new year of 1811 had thus held out little promise of happiness for Madame de Staël, who had spent a miserable winter in Geneva, under constant surveillance and shunned, for fear of displeasing the Emperor, by all but her closest friends. That winter, however, the emotional stability which she had always sought was to be hers at last, not in the great love she had always dreamed of but in the shape of a most unlikely young man. Albert Jean Michel Rocca, known as John Rocca, a Swiss member of a patrician Genevese family of Piemontese origin, was then twenty-three to Madame de Staël's forty-four. After running away to join a Hussar regiment in Alsace, he had seen active service in Spain where he was seriously wounded. Very handsome, tall and slender, extremely good at all sports but no intellectual, he had a romantic disposition to match his image of the wounded young hero. He was still limping around on crutches, a result of a bullet in his thigh. Rocca had met Madame de Staël at the house of his cousins, the

Argand-Picots, in November 1810. She had addressed a few words of sympathy and gone on her way, while he fell passionately in love. 'I will love her so much', he declared, 'that she will end up by marrying me.'[36] True to his word, Rocca wooed her with romantic fervour, even training his black Andalusian horse to kneel to her while he declared his love under her window. Unable to resist being loved, and flattered by the attentions of such an attractive young man, Madame de Staël was doubly susceptible: 'this new sentiment concerns a young man of twenty-three, handsome as the day'. Writing to Madame Récamier, she added that 'his mind is not at all cultivated and there is no future in the relationship. His very noble character makes it safe, and as you know a love which one inspires has the power to console and distract one for a while.'[37] By the spring they were inseparable.

Constant had come back to Geneva with his wife in February. In April, after a dinner together, where the two old friends treated each other with all their former intimacy, a jealous Rocca challenged Constant to a duel. It was only prevented by the intervention of Madame de Staël, who had got wind of it from her son Auguste. Constant had been sufficiently worried to make a will and was no doubt relieved to leave for Germany with Charlotte in May. 'This morning at about eleven o'clock I parted with Madame de Staël on the staircase of the Crown at Lausanne, for the last time for the present. She said that she believed we would never see each other again in this life. Alas! Albertine! Alas!'[38] Prosper, too, had given in gracefully and gratefully to the new man in Madame de Staël's life. On 1 May 1811, in the presence of a Protestant pastor, Madame de Staël and Rocca affirmed their intention to marry as soon as circumstances permitted with only the devoted Fanny Randall as witness.

Madame de Boigne, who often saw Madame de Staël at that time – Madame de Staël loved her voice and often begged her to sing – found Rocca 'completely ridiculous'. Once, after she had finished singing, the inarticulate Rocca, prompted by Madame de Staël, had attempted a graceful compliment. Taking Madame de Boigne's arm as Rocca hobbled off on his crutches, Madame de Staël whispered: 'Ah! speech is not his language!' These words, Madame de Boigne remarked, 'have always struck me as a cry of pain from a clever woman who loves a fool.'[39]

In August 1811, Mathieu de Montmorency arrived to visit Madame de Staël. Together they set off on a tour. A visit to a Trappist nunnery in Fribourg shocked Madame de Staël deeply. They had arrived in violent rain and were soaked through. She rang the bell and a pale nun, who had appeared behind a grille, refused at first to let them in. Eventually they were allowed to dry off in a side room. Madame de Staël asked to be allowed to visit the convent. Only those wishing to join their community were allowed in, the nun replied. But how could she judge whether or not she had a vocation if she were not allowed to see their house? Madame de Staël countered. 'Oh, there is no point,' the nun replied, 'I am absolutely certain that you have no vocation for our way of life.' At Vespers that evening Madame de Staël was struck by the starkness of the service – their chanting had no emotion, their prayers no exaltation. But she supposed that any overt piety would have a softening effect, and 'only harsh and serious habits made it possible to bear that kind of life'. She was particularly saddened by the sight of children brought up in this way; their poor heads shaven, their young faces already lined, dressed in mortuary clothes before they had even had a chance to live or make a free choice. She felt a strong sense of revulsion at the parents who had placed them there. 'If one does not enter into such a life freely, then it inspires as much horror as . . . freely chosen it might inspire respect.'[40]

After a few days back at Coppet, Mathieu and his cousin Adrien returned to France to be summarily sent into exile from Paris. Madame Récamier, who had braved the Emperor's wrath to visit Madame de Staël a week or so later, found on her return that she too had been exiled. Napoleon rightly believed Mathieu to be a member of the Catholic opposition which was conspiring against him. The annexation of the Papal States to France and the imprisonment of the Pope – after the Emperor had declared that the Pope had better think of him as Charlemagne – had turned the aristocracy and the clergy in France against him. Madame Récamier's house had become the main liberal salon in Paris, so he had other good reasons to banish them. Their visit to Madame de Staël, which was cited as the justification of their exile, served not only to punish and isolate them but to punish her over again, both by depriving her of her dearest friends and by making her feel guilty and responsible. Beside herself with rage and sorrow Madame de Staël wrote to Madame Récamier, who was now installed at Châlons, forty leagues from Paris, where she was visited by a few friends who again admired her serenity in adversity. 'I cannot speak. I am at your feet. I beg you not to hate me! In God's name take care of your own interest so that I may live. Extricate yourself from this so that I may believe you happy, so that your admirable generosity might not have ruined you!'[41]

Madame de Staël wanted to get away but ended up spending the winter in Geneva. In spite of poor health and depression she wrote a play, *Sapho*, full of thoughts of suicide, into which she poured all her despair, and also an essay, *Réflexions sur le suicide*, stimulated by the suicide of Heinrich von Kleist in Berlin, a subject of major interest in intellectual circles in Germany at the time. In this tract, influenced by Kant, she condemns suicide where in her earlier works she seemed to condone it. Her theme was that self-improvement, not happiness, should be the chief aim of human life – overcoming suffering is a condition of moral progress.

She was also doing research for a 'historical poem' on the life of Richard Coeur de Lion. She hoped to travel to the east as part of her research for this work, because, as she wrote to Meister, 'descriptions of places unseen, are like mere rhetoric about sentiments unfelt'. It was to include four heroes: Richard I himself, Frederick Barbarossa, Philip Augustus and Saladin.[42]

More importantly she had begun work on what would be an autobiographical account of her struggle with Napoleon, *Dix années d'exil*, the second part of which was completed in Sweden in 1813. In Part I, covering the years 1797 to 1804, she gives a vibrant, eye-witness account of Bonaparte's rise to power and growing despotism. Part II covers the years 1810 to 1812 only. This book, which unfortunately she never finished but which was published by her son, did not include her stay in either Sweden or England in 1813 because she had abandoned it for her more philosophical work, the *Considérations sur la Révolution Française*. When she died in 1817, the manuscript of *Dix anñees d'exil* existed only in drafts, two of which were written in code in case they fell into the hands of the police. It was no mean feat that she had succeeded in writing the whole story in terms of Elizabethan England, with Queen Elizabeth substituted for Napoleon. Moreover the book had not been intended as an autobiography. 'It is not in order to make myself known to the public that I resolved to write the circumstances of ten years of exile. The misfortunes I suffered, whatever bitterness I experienced then are as nothing among the general disasters we have witnessed since, and it would be shameful to write of oneself if the events which concern one were not linked to the great cause of humanity under threat. The Emperor Napoleon, whose character is entirely manifest in every aspect of his life, persecuted me with punctilious care, with ever greater effort, with an inflexible harshness, and so my relations with him enabled me to understand that enigma long before Europe was able to decipher it, allowing itself to be devoured by the sphinx the while, because it was unable to discern its intentions.'[43]

But while Napoleon is as much the villain of *Dix années d'exil* as her father was the hero of *Considérations sur la Révolution française* the book was far from being merely an anti-Napoleon tract. Unable to exercise her talent for conversation or her impulse to act, henceforth all her writings would be a constant dialogue with a world from which she had been banished. Her energy, her finely tuned sensibility, her intellectual curiosity, her passionate need to communicate, all ensure that this book, particularly in the account she gives of her journey to Russia, was also to be one of the great works of travel writing.

In November 1811 Prosper de Barante was married to Mlle d'Houdetot. Madame de Staël wrote him a warm letter of congratulations to which she had a 'sad and sweet reply', she wrote to Madame Récamier, adding that she herself no longer had 'a right to a bridal veil'. She was unwell and unhappy and looked terrible.[44] She had good reason to feel unwell; she was once again pregnant. The pregnancy, much longed for by Rocca, who wanted 'a little us', but so late in life and so inopportune, had made her ill. In Geneva her swollen bulk and sallow face was disguised as dropsy for which she was supposedly being treated. The secret was admirably kept. Not one of her three children, two of whom were with her constantly, knew of her condition. The only one to know was the faithful Fanny Randall. In early April Madame de Staël returned to Coppet from Geneva, where on the night of 7 April 1812 she gave birth to a son, attended only by her Genevese doctor and Miss Randall. The birth of her child at the age of forty-six had been uncomplicated. Neither Schlegel, nor Albertine and Albert, who were all at Coppet, had any idea of it. Auguste, who was sighing after Madame Récamier and had gone to visit her at Châlons, was also completely in the dark. Three days later Rocca and Madame de Staël took the baby to the house of Pastor Gleyre in the village of Longirod near Nyon, where Louis-Alphonse was duly christened as the child of an English mother and an American father, Henriette Preston and Theodore Giles of Boston.

Only five years later, after her death in July 1817, was his presence made known to her family. Although the secret had been kept from her own children, there were some who suspected the truth, among them the prefect, Capelle, and the special commissioner, Baron de Melun, who sent back a report to Savary, full of witticisms at Madame de Staël's expense to the effect that the cure for her dropsy was a little boy. He also sent epigrams – which were doing the rounds in Geneva – back to Paris. Here is one such:

> Astonishing woman, how fertile her genius!
> Productive in all things, a woman of fame –
> Nothing is lost to posterity
> Not even her dropsy.[45]

In 1817, soon after Madame de Staël's death, Byron sent the following verses to his publisher John Murray:

> 'Tis said she certainly was married
> To Rocca – and had twice miscarried,
> No – not miscarried – I opine –
> But brought to bed at forty-nine,
> Some say she died a Papist – some
> Are of the opinion that's a hum-
> I don't know that that fellow Schlegel
> Was very likely to inveigle
> A dying person in compunction
> To try the extremity of Unction –
> But peace be with her for a woman
> Her talents surely were uncommon.[46]

The gossip must have reached Constant too. His entry for 7 May 1812 reads: 'Could Madame de Staël be pregnant?'[47] Two weeks after giving birth, to avoid further gossip, Madame de Staël was once again appearing in society. Her official marriage to Rocca was to take place later, in 1816. 'Little us' – Louis-Alphonse – was brought up secretly by the good pastor and his wife. The reason for the delayed marriage, and therefore the secrecy, was not only, as some have thought, the fear of ridicule, but was also connected with Madame de Staël's plans to escape – plans which had been delayed by her pregnancy. Barely recovered from childbirth, still unwell and terrified of travel, deprived of all her friends, Madame de Staël knew that she would have to act. She was mortally afraid of being imprisoned if caught trying to escape. But she feared even more that by remaining at Coppet she would be wrecking her sons' chances of a career or be forced to part with them for the foreseeable future. She also knew that she would be condemning her fourteen-year-old daughter to incarceration with her at Coppet. By then Madame de Staël was under virtual house arrest, forbidden any movement beyond two leagues of Coppet. Her plans were therefore made in the greatest secrecy. In mid-May news came of the Emperor's departure from Paris for Dresden, where he had convened the vassal German kings and his father-in-law, the Emperor of Austria, in readiness for war with Russia. It was clear, Madame de Staël wrote, that he intended to attack Russia to make himself master of the Baltic ports before turning his attention to Constantinople. 'I am tired of old Europe', the Emperor had said as he looked east for fresh conquests.

Tsar Alexander of Russia had been preparing for war for some time. In April 1812, accompanied by a great retinue of generals and advisers, the Tsar left St Petersburg for Vilna in Lithuania to take personal command of his troops. Napoleon dispatched a personal envoy to negotiate with the Tsar – as it happened, Narbonne, one of his aides-de-camp since 1809. The Tsar had sent Narbonne back with the message that he was willing to return to the Treaty of Tilsit, under the terms of which Russia had promised to join the continental blockade against England, on condition that the French withdrew from Prussia, Swedish Pomerania and the territories they now occupied beyond the Elbe. He knew that Napoleon would not accept the terms, but he wished to lay the responsibility of the coming war squarely on him. Napoleon had by then almost completed the enormous task of transferring half a million men to the Russian frontier. He left Dresden to review his armies while Empress Marie-Louise travelled to Prague to spend a few days with her family. Madame de Staël recalled how the Emperor, insisting on the maximum of pomp, had obliged the Empress to travel 'dressed in gold brocade, as were her ladies-in-waiting; she almost always has to wear a diamond diadem on her head, and since heaven has not endowed her with the possibility of uttering a single word of any significance, she looks exactly like a dummy of a queen, on which all the crown jewels are displayed.'[48]

Throughout the previous year Madame de Staël had pondered where she might go to escape from Coppet. She had once again requested a passport for America, but her pregnancy had put an end to any possibility of travelling so far. Italy was closed to her. England was forbidden without the express permission of the French government. But that was where she would go nevertheless: 'to those friends of all that is good and noble, with whom, even if one does not know them personally, the heart is ever in sympathy'. She knew that she could only get there via Austria, Russia, Finland and Sweden. But she would have to move quickly before war blocked all her possible escape routes.

Chapter 23

The Long Way to England

> 'There are only two kinds of people on earth: those who serve tyranny and those who know how to hate it.'
>
> Madame de Staël

On Saturday, 23 May 1812, at half-past two in the afternoon, and carrying only her fan, Madame de Staël, accompanied by her daughter Albertine and escorted by Auguste and John Rocca on horseback, climbed into her carriage as if to go for a drive. She had told her people that she would be back for dinner. While her heart was in turmoil, she had kept her customary cool head. She had already transferred ownership of Coppet to her son Auguste and equipped herself with a large sum of money in cash. She took silent leave of her father's house: 'I sat down in all the places where my father used to rest and contemplate nature; I looked once more on the beauty of the lake and the countryside which we had so often admired together', before visiting her parents' tomb where 'I spent an hour in prayer before that iron door which had closed on the remains of the noblest of human beings, and there my soul was persuaded that the time had come to go.' In her father's study she took a last look at his things all in their usual place, kissing every object. She had no idea when or if she would come back. On impulse she took her father's red coat with her for comfort and protection – 'to envelop myself in if Bonaparte's agents or death came for me'. As she turned to take a final look at Coppet, she almost fainted. Auguste took her hand, she recalled: 'Think *ma mère*, you are going to England,' he whispered encouragingly. 'These words lifted my spirit.'[1]

Although the village of Coppet was bristling with spies and informers, nobody guessed that she had flown. A few leagues from Coppet she sent back one of her grooms to tell her staff that she would not be back until the following day, and Rocca too returned to Geneva to deal with his own affairs that same evening. He would join her later on the Austrian border, after galloping through Bavaria disguised as a French courier, while Auguste escorted his mother and sister to the hamlet of Papiermühle, just outside Berne, which they reached on 25 May and where Schlegel was waiting for them.[2]

Handing her over to Schlegel's care, Auguste returned to Coppet where he had much to do on his mother's behalf. 'To have managed to leave Coppet and fool the Prefect of Geneva's spies was little; we still had to obtain visas to travel through Austria, and these visas had to be in a name that would not attract the attention of the various police forces in Germany. My mother had put this into my hands, and I can never forget my feelings at the time. It was a truly decisive moment; had the visas been refused my mother would have fallen back into a far more cruel situation. Her plans once known, any chance of escape would have been cut off and the harshness of her exile would have become more intolerable with each day.' Auguste decided to appeal to the Austrian Minister in Geneva, M. de Schraut, whom he believed to be a good and honest man. He had not misjudged him. It was not until his younger brother Albert left Coppet in Madame de Staël's travelling carriage that the Genevan police noticed her absence.[3]

Madame de Staël was resolved to go to Russia, but she had been afraid to apply for Russian visas in Geneva where, had the French ambassador got wind of it, as he surely would, she would almost certainly have been arrested. She decided to go first to Vienna and wait there for the visas, which could only be issued from St Petersburg and would take a minimum of six weeks to reach her. 'I spent my life studying the map of Europe to find a way of escape just as Napoleon studies it to make himself master of it, and my plan of campaign no less than his had Russia as its object,' she recalled in *Dix années d'exil*.[4]

In Vienna, where Madame de Staël's party arrived on 6 June, she immediately sent notice of her arrival to Count Stackelberg, Russian ambassador to Austria, requesting visas for Russia. By sheer luck, she had arrived only two hours before his courier was due to leave with letters for the Tsar, then still at Vilna. The Russian ambassador called on her immediately, promising the visas, but she would have to wait for the return of the courier.

The court was absent at the time of her arrival, summoned to

Dresden by Napoleon, but she happily renewed old friendships, visiting the Prince de Ligne and his granddaughter Titine, now Maurice O'Donnell's wife, as well as Frederick Gentz, whose help she enlisted to ensure that she was given permission to cross Galicia (then Austrian Poland). During the two months that she spent on Austrian territory Madame de Staël was under the continuous surveillance of the Austrian police, who followed her everywhere, filling 114 large sheets of paper with notes about her movements. While she waited, with no guarantee of success, and with her return route home cut off, she was obliged to make several alternative plans. One of her plans was to travel in Richard the Lionheart's footsteps, to Constantinople, via Bucharest and Odessa, and perhaps later to Syria. Should she fail to obtain Russian visas, she might go to Constantinople via Hungary. She even came to an arrangement with an Armenian who, if all else failed, had agreed to take her there through Salonika. From Constantinople, where her friend, Baron Balk was then posted, she planned to travel to England through Greece, Sicily, Cadiz and Lisbon. At last permission was granted to leave Austria either for Constantinople via Hungary, or St Petersburg via Poland, but she would have to decide which, she was told, since two exit visas could not be issued at once. Much to the relief of her family, Madame de Staël chose St Petersburg via Poland. The agent in charge of spying on her, a simple soul called Seywalt, not altogether surprisingly, was totally confused about her plans. His reports were as fantastical as they were comical. Madame de Staël, he reported, was planning to travel to England via Riga, Malta, Asia and Greece![6]

The relentless and intrusive harassment by the police decided her to leave without waiting for her Russian visas, in the hope that she might be a little freer in the provinces. Schlegel would wait for the visas in Vienna and bring them to her. Gentz, who grumbled in his journal that this time Madame de Staël's presence was more of an embarrassment than a pleasure, had managed to get her the necessary exit visas.[7] Her arrival in Brno in Moravia coincided exactly with Napoleon's crossing of the Nieman into Russia. They seemed to be moving almost in tandem. At Brno she aroused further suspicions by renewing her acquaintance with Colonel George Mills, a British secret agent who had stayed with her at Coppet. After four days the governor suggested politely that she move on, but would not allow Rocca, who was listed simply as her private secretary, to travel with her since he was not included on her documents by name. Her appeals for help to the Swedish ambassador in Vienna proved fruitless. Rocca was given permission to travel directly to Sweden via Troppau, where he might wait to see whether a visa to join Madame de Staël in Russia would be granted. Travelling through Galicia, Madame de Staël was obliged to report her presence at every police station. The police also read all her letters, reporting that they contained nothing but complaints about the absence of Rocca and the monotony of the Polish landscape.[8] She wrote to Madame Récamier from Wadowice, near Cracow: 'I am therefore alone at present, with my son and daughter in the most melancholy country in the world, where German seems like my native language, so strange is Polish to me.'[9]

In *Dix années d'exil* she writes: 'Poles love their country as one loves an unhappy friend. The landscape is sad and monotonous, the people ignorant and apathetic; they have always longed for liberty, but never known how to win it. But the Poles believe they can and should govern Poland and this is entirely natural. Yet, the education of the people has been so much neglected and they so lack industry that all trade has been taken over by the Jews who buy all the following year's harvest from the peasants in exchange for vodka . . . At every stop one sees three kinds of people: Polish beggars, Jewish peddlers and German policemen. None the less it was great sorrow for a people as proud as the Poles to be subjected to daily humiliation by their Austrian masters. There is a kind of brutality only to be found in German subalterns. Obsequious respect for power is succeeded immediately by arrogance towards the weak.'[10] The officer accompanying her would bow almost to the ground, but refuse to change his orders to the slightest degree. She was to feel the effects of this herself at Lanzut, where she had planned to rest for a few days with her friend, Princess Lubomirska. They had met in Vienna during Madame de Staël's previous visit. The Princess still wore mourning for the Duc d'Enghien, detested Napoleon and welcomed all French émigrés.[11]

Meanwhile Rocca, as resourceful as he was inarticulate, had given his spies the slip, managed to travel through Prussian Silesia and had arrived at Lanzut as prearranged with Madame de Staël. A warrant for his arrest as a French officer had been put out, in spite of the fact that he had resigned from the army and was in any case ineligible for active service as a result of his wounds. Had he been arrested and handed over to the French he would have almost certainly been shot as a deserter, Auguste wrote later in a footnote to his mother's account. When he arrived at Lanzut, seeing her carriage, the ever impulsive Rocca had ridden up joyfully to greet her. Only at the very last moment was Madame de Staël able to signal a warning to him, to get back.[12] Her genuine and well-founded terror brought on a fit of the vapours. She had to be helped out of her carriage and revived with a glass of water by the roadside, furious with herself, she wrote later, for showing such weakness in front of her odious policeman. On the other hand, fine actress that she was, she may well have created a diversion to allow time for Rocca to disappear.

At Lanzut, where she stopped for the night at Princess Lubomirska's, the same coarse officer who had been riding on her heels throughout the day declared that since his orders were never to let her out of his sight he was proposing to sleep in her room, but, he assured Albert, he would do nothing untoward out of respect for her. 'You might say out of respect for yourself,' Albert had replied, 'because if you set foot in my mother's room tonight, I will throw you out of the window.'[13] The threat seems to have worked. Madame de Staël had a long and agreeable dinner with the Princess and her nephew Prince Henry, as well as Count Potocki and Prince Adam Czartoryski, who were also staying at Lanzut, while the policeman was dispatched to the kitchens where he was plied with food and drink. He was sufficiently the worse for wear next day for her to have been able to stay longer, but she did not wish to expose her hosts to any further embarrassment, so the next morning was up at seven, to be greeted by Prince Galitzine who had just arrived. Her party left at ten, according to police records. Schlegel joined her with their Russian visas at Lemberg (today Lviv in the Ukraine), and presumably Rocca too. Here the governor, Count Jean-Pierre Goëss, an old-style Austrian gentleman, gave them their exit visas without any difficulties. Time was now running out as the Grande Armée advanced further into Russia.

'One was hardly accustomed to considering Russia as the freest country in Europe,' Madame de Staël wrote in *Dix années d'exil*, but Napoleon's tyranny had made her feel that she was in a republic when she crossed the border at Brody on 14 July 1812. Struck by the date – the anniversary of the beginning of the French Revolution – she swore that she would never enter any country subjugated to Napoleon. Would she ever see her beautiful France again, she wondered? The first man she visited in Russia was a former employee of her father's. Hearing him speak of her father with tears in his eyes, she felt that it was a happy omen, and indeed Madame de Staël's initial impression of Russia, unlike her usual very negative first impressions of other countries, was all but euphoric. She had left behind countries supposedly at peace, where one couldn't take a step without police checks, and entered Russia at a moment when the French armies had already invaded the soil: yet though she was a stranger and a Frenchwoman, nobody had bothered or persecuted her. 'I had only the noblest and sweetest impressions of that Russian Empire, so wrongly called barbaric,' she wrote. 'May my gratitude attract further blessings on these peoples and their sovereign!' The advance of the French armies made it impossible for Madame de Staël to travel directly to St Petersburg. She would have to go by way of Kiev, Tula, Orel and Moscow.

Perhaps because her spirits were so high and the country so different, Madame de Staël was extraordinarily receptive to every detail. Considering the vastness and strangeness of Russia, and the fact that she was there for a mere eight weeks, she writes with real insight and an evocative freshness and clarity about the Russians, their history, their customs and habits, and the landscape and cities.

The endless wheatfields of the Ukraine looked as if they had been cultivated by invisible hands, so sparse was the population. Kiev, seen from a distance, looked to her like a Tartar encampment, the wooden houses resembling nomadic tents among which were scattered palaces and churches, their green and golden cupolas catching the evening sun and making the city look like some kind of festival. Russians never went past a church without making the sign of the cross and their long beards gave them a particularly religious aspect, she thought.[14] Later, in reply to someone who – like all Russian westernizers since Peter the Great – expressed the wish to deprive the Russian peasant of his beard, she was to say that 'men who knew how to defend their beards would know how to defend their lives'; a quip which Pushkin, then a boy, included in a story published twenty years after her death.[15] The Russians' almost oriental love of colour, particularly noted in the peasant and merchant dress, greatly appealed to her. The landscape she thought dull except for the magnificent rivers – the great glory of Russia and historically, objects of veneration. She recounts the blessing of the waters on the Neva in January, and the fact that in the eleventh century St Vladimir had declared the waters of the Dnieper holy: it was enough to dive into them to become a Christian. Since the Orthodox baptism is by total immersion, it was a pragmatic as well as spiritual edict – thousands of men were able to convert in short order. It had been natural for the Russians to prefer the Greek rite, which Madame de Staël noted with surprise was at least as beautiful as the Catholic. The Greek Orthodox faith is poetic and full of sensibility, recalling the Orient where it originates, but because the clergy was drawn from the people rather than the upper classes, the Church enjoyed great spiritual power over the people but very little political power, she noted. Their rejection of the Pope's domain, however, gave the Russian emperors much greater autonomy and power, both spiritual and temporal. Church music was particularly lovely; pomp and ceremony appeals to the Russian soul, she reflected; art was confined to the magnificence of the icons, often studded with diamonds and rubies.

Although Madame de Staël was naturally attracted to the Russians and fascinated by everything she saw, she was far from blind to their weaknesses. At the time of her visit, the Russian aristocracy was still almost entirely French in manner and culture. Some barely spoke Russian. 'They have often been compared to the French, but it seems to me the most false of comparisons. Their flexibility makes imitation extremely easy for them; they are French, English, German in their manners and according to circumstances, while never ceasing to be Russian; that is to say, at once impetuous and reserved, more given to passion than friendliness, proud rather than refined, religious rather than virtuous, brave rather than courtly, and so violent in their desires that nothing can stop their wish to satisfy them.' She might well have been describing herself!

At Kiev she was received by the Governor, General Milarodovich, a former aide-de-camp to General Souvarov, one of Russia's greatest strategists. She thought him a true Russian, 'impetuous, brave and confident, and in no way moved by that spirit of imitation which sometimes almost deprives the Russians of their national character.'[16] On the way to Moscow, some thousand kilometres distant from Kiev, she noted that the coachmen drove at lightning speed, singing what she was assured were compliments and encouragement to their horses: 'Come, my lovely one, courage, we know each other well, go faster' and so on. She liked the polite way they doffed their hats at any passing woman, who would incline her head graciously in response.

Staring for hour after hour out of her carriage window, the uniformity of the landscape and the huge distances through which they were speeding seemed like a nightmare in which one tries to move forward only to remain rooted to the spot, Madame de Staël reflected. The country was the very image of infinite space and it seemed that one needed an eternity to cross it. From her carriage she glimpsed the Russian people: the official couriers flying along the potholed roads, sometimes bouncing several feet into the air from the little wooden seats of their carts as they hit a rut. Hooded Cossacks in grey, carrying long lances, reminded her of ghosts among the brightly coloured uniforms of the other regiments – the red of the hussars, the orange of the Uhlans, the Green of the Preobrazhensky Guard. On they sped through Kursk to Orel, where Madame de Staël was surprised and flattered to be complimented on her writings and where she was received by the governor's wife 'in oriental style with sherbets and roses' in apartments elegantly decorated with paintings and musical instruments. She was delighted by the beauty and grace of the women, the 'modest voluptuousness' of their dances, which were a mixture, like themselves, of indolence and vivacity, and overwhelmed by Russian hospitality – 'one feels close to them from the first day'.

In Russia she was struck not so much by the differences between rich and poor – she saw no terrible poverty – but by the ability of the Russians to tolerate extremes. The very rich, whose houses were full of every imaginable luxury, when they travel and not only in wartime, were prepared to put up with food that no French peasant would tolerate, as well as with every sort of physical discomfort. They seem, she reflected, not to be weakened by luxury. Their ability to endure was what had made it possible for them to sacrifice everything, even to the burning of Moscow. She admired what she called the public-spiritedness of Russians, perhaps confusing it with the Russian's blind and passionate love of country, although she admitted that 'One can never see a country under greater advantage than in times of misfortune and courage'.

'I believe that their passions when provoked may well be terrible, and as they are uneducated they do not know how to rule their passions. For the same reason they have few morals and theft is very common, but so is hospitality. They give as readily as they take, according to whether their imagination has been excited by cunning or generosity. They admire both qualities.' 'What characterizes these people,' she concludes, 'is something gigantic in every way – ordinary dimensions apply to nothing in their case. I don't mean by that that there is no true grandeur nor stability to be found there, but in the Russian imagination, which knows no limits, everything is colossal rather than proportionate, reckless rather than thought out, and if the aim is not achieved it is usually because it has been exceeded.'[17]

In many ways Madame de Staël had met her soulmates, which perhaps explains her happiness in a country so strange to her otherwise. If intellectually and culturally she was forever the child of the Western enlightenment, she responded at once to an undoubted temperamental affinity with the Russians. Like them she was excessive, passionate, vital, tyrannical but capable of immense self-sacrifice, life-loving but melancholy, impulsive, generous and brave. Nor, for all her education, had she ever learned to rule her own passions.

On 2 August Moscow's golden cupolas, visible from a great distance, at last appeared in their sight. She found the city in a ferment of war fever. Only three weeks before, the Tsar had addressed his people from the top of the Kremlin staircase of honour. A mighty roar of hurrahs from a million throats had cheered him. Two days later, at a meeting of nobles and merchants in the Slobodsky palace, huge sums were pledged as well as whole regiments. Madame de Staël was astonished by the sacrifices which the aristocracy no less than the people were prepared to make: 'A young count Mamonov raised a whole regiment for the country, but wished to serve only as a second lieutenant. A Countess Orlov, charming and rich in an oriental fashion, was giving up three quarters of her income.' Nobles pledged their serfs and although she was startled by the expression 'to give men' – 'they themselves offered their services with such ardour that in this war their masters were merely interpreting their own wishes,' she wrote.

Invited by Count Rostopchin, the Governor of Moscow, to his country estate outside Moscow she was introduced to all of Moscow society. When Napoleon invaded Moscow, Rostopchin had set fire to his own house to encourage others, an action Madame de Staël admired greatly. Her only reproach to Rostopchin was that he kept bad news of Russian reverses too long to himself, whereas 'The English, with the admirable candour which distinguishes all their actions, publicize their reversals as truthfully as their successes and enthusiasm is kept alive by the truth, whatever it may be. The Russians cannot aspire yet to such moral perfection, which is the result of a free constitution . . . Much has been made of Diderot's famous saying: *The Russians are rotten before they are ripe*. Nothing could be less true; their very vices are not a result of corruption but of violence . . . Their nature has not changed as a result of Peter I's rapid modernization: for the present it has only changed their manners. Luckily for them, they remain what we call "barbarians", that is led by their instincts which are often generous, always involuntary and in so far as they reflect on their actions at all, they do so usually on the choice of means, never to examine the ends. I say luckily, not because I applaud barbarians; what I mean by that word is a certain kind of primitive energy, which for many nations is the only thing that can act as substitute for the concentrated force of freedom.'

While much more hospitable than the French, Madame de Staël believed that the Russians had little love of conversation and, contrary to the French, gathered together as for a festival – to see a lot of people, eat rare food, listen to music and generally enjoy sensual pleasures. 'The Russian character is too passionate for them to love abstract thought and in any case ideas of any significance are always more or less dangerous at a court where there was always a great deal of envy and watchfulness,' she thought. She had a low opinion of most of the literature of the time, derivative and written in French. However, without any knowledge of the language, she guessed from its sound 'full of sweetness and variety of sounds' that it might be a wonderful language for poetry.[18] What she could not know was that she was standing on the very threshold of what came to be known as the golden age of Russian literature, and that a boy called Alexander Pushkin, and after him a wave of great writers, would create a great body of literature as Russian as it was universal.

Madame de Staël's visit to Moscow and St Petersburg caused such a stir that it resounded down the years. In one of Pushkin's stories, *Roslavlev*, a novella written in the form of a memoir by a young lady, and published in 1836, a generation after Madame de Staël's visit, he gives if not an eyewitness account, nonetheless a faithful account, as told him by Prince Viazemsky, of an evening with Madame de Staël and of the impression she made on Moscow society and her influence on a young, well-read and sensitive young woman. 'Memoirs of social life are usually vague and pointless even in those historic times,' writes the narrator, 'nevertheless the arrival of one visitor to Moscow left an indelible impression on me. That visitor was Madame de Staël. She had arrived in the summer, when most Moscovites were in the country. There was a great bustle of Russian hospitality. They didn't know quite how to receive the celebrated foreigner. Of course dinner parties were organized for her. Ladies and gentlemen gathered to gape at her. For the most part they were not pleased. They saw a fat woman of fifty, dressed inappropriately for her years. Nor did her manners please. People found her speeches too long and her sleeves too short. Polina's father, who had met Madame de Staël in Paris, gave a dinner for her, calling in all our Moscow wits. It was at this dinner that I met the author of *Corinne*. She sat in the place of honour with her elbows on the table, furling and unfurling a little tube of paper in her beautiful fingers. She appeared out of sorts, made several attempts at conversation but seemed unable to continue. Our wits ate and drank to their hearts' content, seeming more interested in the Prince's fish soup than in Madame de Staël's conversation. The ladies looked stiff and starched. The guests, convinced of the insignificance of their reflections and overawed by the presence of the European celebrity, said little. Throughout dinner Polina sat as if on tenterhooks. The attention of the guests was divided equally between the sturgeon and Madame de Staël. They were all waiting for a witticism from her. At last a *double entendre*, and a rather daring one at that, escaped from her lips. Everyone seized on it, bursting out in laughter, and a general murmur of amazement went around the table. The Prince was beside himself with joy. I glanced at Polina. Her face was burning and tears stood in her eyes. The guests rose from table entirely reconciled with Madame de Staël. She had made a pun which they skipped off to spread all over town.'[19]

In the story Madame de Staël, noticing Polina's embarrassment at her fellow countrymen's behaviour, makes a point of talking to her after dinner. Later, she sends her a letter, which the narrator of the story has in her keeping. 'Despite my curiosity Polina remained silent on any further contacts she had with Madame de Staël, but she adored this illustrious woman who was as kindhearted as she was brilliant.'[20]

Pushkin was probably inspired to write the story by a letter sent by Madame de Staël to the young Princess Zinaida Volkonsky, who was married to one of the Tsar's aides-de-camp, and close to the Tsar who had stood godfather to her son. Although the circumstances are changed – in the fictional letter Madame de Staël speaks of her own illness, whereas it was Zinaida who was recovering from a nervous breakdown at the time – there are enough similarities to justify the assumption. Pushkin, who knew Zinaida personally, would certainly have seen Madame de Staël's letter to her. Madame de Staël had written to thank the Princess for her present. The beautiful and richly talented Zinaida, already a star of the St Petersburg salons and known as the 'Northern Corinne' in Russia, greatly admired Madame de Staël. She had sent her an engraving of Coppet, together with a poem, '*Á Madame de Staël en lui renvoyant "Corinne"*,' in which she praised the author's powers of imagination, ending with the plea to 'you whose genius soars in full flight under a free sky, to go on singing'.[21]

In Pushkin's novella, when Polina is reproved by her friend for meddling in politics, she behaves exactly as Zinaida might have done later: 'Her eyes flashed. "Shame on you," she said. "Do you not think that women have a native land? Do they have no brothers, fathers, husbands? Is Russian blood foreign to us? Or do you think that we were born merely to whirl around at balls, dancing Scottish reels or embroidering little dogs on canvas at home? No! I know how much influence a woman can have on public opinion, or at least on one man. I refuse to recognize the subservience to which they relegate us. Look at Madame de Staël. Napoleon fought her as if she were an enemy force. And my uncle has the cheek to laugh at her when she is worried about the approach of the French armies. "Fear not Madame, Napoleon is fighting against Russia, not against you . . . Really! If uncle was to fall into French hands, they would probably let him walk around in the Palais Royal but if they catch Madame de Staël, she would die in a state prison."'[22]

Madame de Staël left Moscow with regret, having 'played with her *esprit*, and shown her beautiful arms', Rostopchin wrote to the Tsar.[23] The road to St Petersburg via Novgorod was flat and monotonous. 'From Novgorod on it is all marshland, so that one arrives in one of the most beautiful cities in Europe, as if suddenly an enchanter had brought forth all the marvels of Europe and Asia out of the desert.' On arrival at St Petersburg on 13 August she thanked God that she was near the sea; it made her feel more secure, especially when she saw the Union Jack, to her a beacon of freedom, fluttering on a ship on the Neva. The Russians, who Madame de Staël believed were temperamentally a southern people, lived in St Petersburg like people from the south, condemned to fighting a climate which was not their natural one. The palaces along the Neva, surrounded by huge greenhouses and orangeries, 'embellished with all the plants of the south, the perfumes of the east, the divans of Asia', created a completely artificial climate; a warm and scented buffer against the freezing northern winter.

In St Petersburg the social whirl continued in spite of the proximity of French troops. Although she was overwhelmed with invitations to all the grand houses and embassies, she managed to do a great deal of sightseeing. Accompanied by the Swiss banker Galiffe, whom she had met in Rolle and who served as her guide and interpreter – and later when she was in Sweden as her personal envoy – she set off the very next day to visit Kazan Cathedral and all the important sights of the city, describing everything with extraordinary relish, down to the great mammoth she saw in the St Petersburg museum.

The day after her presentation at court, Count Orlov invited Madame de Staël to spend the day at his summer palace on Orlov Island. 'The famous count Orlov', wrote Countess Gurjeva acidly, 'crawled on hands and knees to bring Madame de Staël to his palace, hoping to increase the celebrity of his island.'[24] When the British National Anthem was struck up, the Count announced to a group of merchants with long beards that peace with Great Britain had just been proclaimed. They crossed themselves in gratitude, Madame de Staël recalled. The economic blockade of Britain had cost them dear, severely damaging Russia's trade. Later, Madame de Staël read out the section on 'enthusiasm' from *De l'Allemagne* in the presence of Baron Stein, Arndt and the other Prussian nationalists, moving them to tears.[25]

Not far from the Orlov estate lay the magnificent palace of the Stroganovs, on Stroganov Island, which was served by 600 serfs. The palace was full of ancient sculptures – Count Stroganov was a noted collector – and the count also owned a full serf orchestra and choir. Like most visitors from the west, Madame de Staël was amazed at his way of life: 'He kept open house every day of his life. Anyone who had been introduced could return. He never invited people to dine with him on a specific date. It was simply understood that once admitted to his circle, one was always welcome. Often he did not know half the people at his table, but this luxurious hospitality pleased him as did all other forms of magnificence.'[26]

On another visit, Prince Naryshkin's love of society made even her own need for people pale into insignificance. Her host, she reflected, believed himself to be in the most silent philosophical retreat when there were only twenty people staying. She was enchanted by the beauty of the Prince's choir of serf voices. The Russian custom whereby the same person sang the same note – the so-called living organ – fascinated her. 'There goes M. Narishkin's *sol, mi*, or *re*, people would say when the serf who always sang that particular note, passed by.'

Naryshkin had proposed a toast to the success of Russia and Britain, against the tyrant, with a sign to his private artillery to fire an accompanying fusillade. Madame de Staël found herself in tears – 'that an African tyrant [Corsican, i.e. southern and by extension African] should have reduced me to wishing the defeat of the French!' 'Let us hope for the defeat of the Corsican, for the true French will triumph when the Corsicans are repelled,' she cried, and everyone drank to that.[27] Nor was this the only occasion that she was forced to face the fact that her beloved France was the enemy.

One evening, Madame de Staël was still at table with her guests when Rocca and Albert returned from the theatre where Racine's *Phèdre* was being performed, with Mademoiselle Georges in the title role. It was soon after the fall of Smolensk, and with francophobia running high, the performance had been booed, they told her. 'Barbarians!' Madame de Staël exclaimed with tears in her eyes. 'Not to wish to hear Racine's *Phèdre*!'[28]

As always she soon gathered her own salon around her. Among her English friends in St Petersburg during the month or so which she spent there, were Sir Robert Wilson, who had fought Napoleon in Egypt, served in the Russian army until the declaration of war with Britain, and would serve again, leaving a remarkable record of Napoleon's retreat from Moscow; Lord Tyrconnel, Attaché at the British embassy, sent as aide-de-camp to Robert Wilson; and Lord Cathcart, the newly arrived British ambassador. John Quincy Adams, the first American ambassador to Russia, son of the President of the United States and himself a future President, described his visit to Madame de Staël in a letter to his father. The Prussian patriots Baron Stein, the writer Arndt, who was Prince Schwarzenberg's aide-de-camp, Tettenborn, the Hessian, Colonel Dörnberg, Don Bermude, the Spanish ambassador, and Alexis de Noailles – 'the only émigré from tyranny, the only one who like me, was there to represent France' –

completed her circle. Perhaps the most politically important of all her acquaintances was General, Lord William Bentinck.[29]

If Madame de Staël was anxious to encourage the Tsar to stand firm against Napoleon, he was no less anxious to enlist her help in his dealings with General Bernadotte, whom he knew to be a close personal friend of hers. Bernadotte had been Crown Prince of Sweden since 1809, when upon the death of the heir of Charles XIII it was decided to choose a Frenchman, or at least a lieutenant of Napoleon's, to ensure French protection against Russia. Ambitious but vacillating, Bernadotte had opposed Napoleon at the end of the Consulate, though never overtly. Madame de Staël described him as having 'great courage in war, but he is prudent in all political matters'. He had accepted the future crown of Sweden with Napoleon's agreement, if not with his enthusiasm. Bernadotte had always been more or less suspect to Napoleon, who did not like to find 'a sword and an opinion in the same hand', as Madame de Staël put it. But it had suited the Emperor to have Sweden on his side in the coming war with Russia. Bernadotte, meanwhile, had quickly gone native. He had not only converted to the Protestant faith of his new country but became sincerely interested in promoting its interests and those of liberal constitutionalists – above the interests of France. Napoleon's subsequent cavalier treatment of Sweden, and of Bernadotte personally, deepened the resentment which had always existed between the two men. It was not too difficult for Madame de Staël and the Tsar to convince him that he was to be one of the saviours of Europe, and afterwards perhaps, Napoleon's successor in France. General Bentinck, one of Bernadotte's most ardent supporters, had already prepared the ground, arranging a meeting between him and the Tsar at Abo (Turku) in Finland. Madame de Staël's arrival was timely. Her hopes now lay in a war of liberation – not only of France, but of all the countries occupied by Napoleon. Her ideal, one shared by Bentinck, was not a return to the status quo ante, but to nothing less than a regeneration of Europe after the tyrant's defeat. She would make common cause with anyone to achieve that aim. Later she was to fall out with Stein and the Prussian nationalists who sought to replace one despotism with another, albeit a home-grown one. Her views on toppling Napoleon and on eventually replacing him in France with a constitutional monarchy, with Bernadotte as King, coincided exactly with Bernadotte's own hopes and those of the Tsar and Bentinck. She was on her way to Sweden and could be extremely useful there, not only in helping to secure Sweden's neutrality and renunciation of Finland in exchange for Russia's cooperation over Sweden's ambitions in Norway, but in preparing the way for a coalition against Napoleon led by Russia.[30]

Madame de Staël was presented to the Empress Elisabeth on 17 August. While taking tea with the Empress, the door opened suddenly and in walked the Tsar Alexander. She was struck by his air of goodness and dignity and very touched by the simple way in which he began at once to discuss the most important questions of the day with her. 'The Emperor Alexander, whom Napoleon has tried to misrepresent, is a man of remarkable intelligence and learning and I doubt that among the ministers in his empire there is one more capable in judging or directing public affairs than he is,' she wrote in *Dix années d'exil*. He had spoken frankly of his disappointment and regret in his dealings with Napoleon. Madame de Staël saw something noble in his initial admiration for Napoleon's qualities as a warrior – she had, after all, shown equal enthusiasm. Much more liberal at that time than most of the grandees in St Petersburg, the Emperor spoke of his wish to free the serfs. 'Sire, your character is the constitution of your empire and your conscience its guarantee!', she cried delightedly. 'If this were to be the case,' the Tsar had replied, 'it must be remembered that no man is ever more than a happy accident.' Madame de Staël was thrilled by his words.[31] She could not know then, any more than he would have known himself, that ten years later, the reformist and liberal young Alexander would turn into a dour and paranoid autocrat, or that the disappointments of his reign would culminate in the tragic and bloody Decembrist revolt.

It was not easy for Madame de Staël, who disapproved deeply of serfdom and the autocracy, to be diplomatic, but she was prepared to make allowances for a country she considered economically and socially backward. To those who asked why Alexander, supposedly a lover of freedom, did not establish a constitutional government in his own country, she replied that this was a vast country with many different nationalities and religions – a country like no other. 'There is no third estate [middle class] yet in Russia: how then can such a government exist?' Like most of the enlightened Russians she met, she believed that reform was imminent. The Tsar rightly saw the abolition of serfdom as the most important of his proposed reforms, if Russia was to consider itself a civilized country. He was at the time working with the Minister of the Interior, Mikhail Speransky, on a proposal to that effect.

Soon after his first meeting with Madame de Staël, on 20 August, the Tsar left for Finland. He hoped that his meeting with Bernadotte would give him the guarantees which he needed to bring his troops, some 20,000 men, home from Finland. (Finland had been taken by Russia from Sweden after the Treaty of Tilsit in 1808, which is why it was garrisoned.) It was while at Abo that he heard that Smolensk, the last city on the road to Moscow, had been taken by the French.

While the Tsar was in Finland, Madame de Staël was received by his mother, the Empress Dowager, Maria Feodorovna. Deeply interested in the welfare of her people, the Empress Dowager had founded and supported twenty-seven charitable institutions as well as a school for the daughters of the nobility, which Madame de Staël visited. She was very impressed by the gracefulness of Russian girls as they curtsied to her and was moved to tears when one of them recited a passage from her father's *Cours de morale religieuse*.[32]

Before going to Finland, the Tsar, somewhat against his own inclinations, had appointed the old Marshal Kutuzov to overall command of the Russian forces. Fat, lazy, blind in one eye, careless about dress, fond of women and food, the sixty-eight-year-old warrior affected an earthy populism which made him adored by his troops as much as it offended his sovereign. There was another side to him, as Madame de Staël discovered when she met him on the eve of his departure to join his troops: French-educated, he spoke French and German perfectly and had a great knowledge and love of literature. 'He was an old man with graceful manners and a lively face, although he had lost an eye as a result of the unbelievable wounds incurred over fifty years of military life. None the less, looking at him I was afraid that he might lack the strength to fight the fierce young men who were swooping down on Russia from very corner of Europe; but the Russians, courtiers in St Petersburg, become Tartars in the army, and we have seen in Souvarov how neither age nor honours sap their physical and moral energy. I was moved when I left the illustrious Marshal Kutuzov. I did not know whether I was embracing a conqueror or a martyr, but I saw that he understood the greatness of the cause which was now in his hands.'[33]

Madame de Staël and her party left St Petersburg on 7 September

1812. That day the Russian forces knelt to the famous icon of the Black Virgin of Smolensk at Borodino, some eighty miles outside Moscow. Forty-eight hours later, the legendary battle of Borodino was over and 50,000 Russians and 30,000 Frenchmen lay dead. Both sides claimed victory. Refusing to sacrifice any more men, Kutuzov ordered a retreat, thereby saving the army but abandoning Moscow to its fate.

As fear spread that Napoleon meant to march to St Petersburg, the Tsar wrote to Kutuzov: 'Tell all my subjects that when I have not one soldier left, placing myself at the head of my dear nobles, of my good peasants, I shall fight to the last man in my Empire. Now it is Napoleon or me; we can no longer reign together.' Five weeks later, encamped in a city burnt down by its own citizens, the first snows fell on the French, spelling Napoleon's doom. Napoleon ordered the Grande Armée to retreat, but harried by Cossack forces who fell on them unexpectedly from the forests and decimated by starvation, frostbite and exhaustion, the French army lost a further 30,000 men in the battle of the Beresina, Kutuzov's last. The remnants of the Grande Armée, by then only a thousand strong, recrossed the Neiman on 14 December. Napoleon who had learned of General Malet's attempt to seize power in the October conspiracy abandoned his frostbitten and exhausted troops to rush back to Paris to rally public support and raise fresh troops, travelling incognito with Caulaincourt. It was the beginning of the end, although he did not yet know it.

Madame de Staël passed through Abo, barely a fortnight after the departure of the Tsar, on her way to Sweden. Not far from Stockholm, a terrible storm forced her party to stop on the island of Aland. They disembarked and walked along the rocky shore. Only Madame de Staël could have organized amateur theatricals in such circumstances. It is at this point that Madame de Staël's own account, *Dix années d'exil* ends. She arrived in Stockholm on 24 September, preceded by the usual rumours that she was a dangerous person, an intriguer, probably also a spy of Napoleon's. The Russian ambassador had already promised her full support were she to be ill treated at court. But on the day after her arrival, she was reunited with the Crown Prince Bernadotte, who had been out of town when she arrived.

Madame de Staël and the Crown Prince spent their first meetings reminiscing happily about their common past in Paris. She even had her pamphlet on suicide reprinted with a dedication to the Crown Prince, to whom she presented it with the words: 'You have returned hope and a love of life to me; please accept this book which has saved me from the horror, which goes back to a time when life seemed a burden; at that time I was almost in favour of suicide.'[34]

She had two important reasons to remain in the Swedish capital. Her children were Swedish citizens; all Napoleonic Europe now being closed to them, she hoped to establish them there. Albert was immediately commissioned into the Hussars of the Royal Guards regiment and was to become aide-de-camp to the Crown Prince, while Auguste was later to posted to the United States as Swedish envoy, although after Albert's untimely death he did not go. Schlegel, too, was made private secretary to Bernadotte, for whom he wrote an important memorandum on the future of Germany. With such a firm base, Madame de Staël could now concentrate on a real political task, that of helping to bring Sweden firmly into the British and Russian coalition against Napoleon, a task for which she was very well equipped. Her longstanding friendship with Bernadotte and her wide international network of friendships, as well as her contacts in St Petersburg and her friend Galiffe's excellent reports from there, made her a natural go-between.

On arrival in Stockholm, Madame de Staël had been presented at court, where she was warmly received by the Swedish King, Charles XIII, and his Queen. However she didn't live up to everyone's expectations. 'All those who knew her through her works expected to meet a sweet, sensitive, modest woman; the sort who would have written *Corinne*. These high hopes were singularly disappointed,' wrote an anonymous witness. 'She was a woman all right, but badly turned out and absolutely lacking that timidity which is the ornament of her sex, who rather resembled in manner and clothes one of those crude old knights in drag. She is dark with strong colouring, and above all, seems in rude health. Her great dark eyes, sparkling with the fire of genius, intimidate rather than attract. Her hands, arms and shoulders, otherwise attractive, moved constantly when she spoke. In conversation she was surprising in her fluency, in the flood of ideas and in her animated gestures. It was obvious that all affectation and conventional habits displeased her; in Stockholm she produced more or less the effect that Queen Christina must have had on the court at Versailles.'[35]

Madame de Staël's assistance to Bernadotte not only extended to her international contacts but also her extraordinary influence on those who counted in Sweden. 'By virtue of her speeches and her brilliant flights of imagination, she contributed powerfully to shaping public opinion against Napoleon and to giving credence to ideas which the Crown Prince had not managed to make popular with the nation . . . she was a real bureau of public affairs.'[36] Her salon soon became the most brilliant in Stockholm. Not only was her conversation extraordinary – 'she never chattered, she discussed' – but she also kept a splendid table. Swedes as well as foreign diplomats and visitors flocked to it.

In Stockholm, Madame de Staël renewed her acquaintance with a very old friend, a man she had first met in her mother's salon. Field Marshal Count von Stedingk had had a distinguished career. He had recently returned from St Petersburg where he had served as Sweden's ambassador. As a young man he had done well in the American War of Independence and had come back wounded as well as inspired with ideals of liberty. In 1783 he had been one of the group of young Swedes around Marie-Antoinette. When Count Creutz, then Swedish Ambassador in Paris, had brought him to Madame Necker's salon the young Germaine had been very taken with the romantic young man on crutches, as much for his liberal views as for his handsome figure and noble manners. She had sung couplets which she composed in his honour. Germaine's marriage to the Baron de Staël had then been all but arranged. By an extraordinary quirk of fate it appears that the Duc de Broglie (grandfather to Madame de Staël's future son-in-law), who had known and liked young Stedingk, had suggested to him that he might consider a marriage with Germaine Necker and that if he liked the idea, he, Broglie, would arrange it. Staël, meanwhile, who had got wind of the possibility of being cut out of M. Necker's millions, approached Stedingk 'with tears in his eyes', begging him not to pursue the matter. Stedingk had immediately promised to withdraw his suit. His King and his ambassador were negotiating the marriage and M. de Staël, though much older than his bride-to-be and in every way less suitable as a man, was their candidate. The next day Stedingk had gone to the Duc de Broglie to tell him that he did not think after all that he wanted the matter to go any further. Stedingk himself admitted that Madame de Staël used to joke in Stockholm, that she would have done much better to marry him instead.[37]

Madame de Staël seems to have enjoyed an easy relationship with the royal couple, even if she gesticulated, laughed and asked questions in her normal way – no more able here than she had been in Vienna to maintain a respectful silence when royalty was present. This offended some of the starchier courtiers. Hauswolff, the master of ceremonies at court and a man used to the most rigid etiquette, declared that had she been a man he would have called her out. Some wit assured him that Madame de Staël would have accepted his challenge, and killed him with her caustic wit.[38] Whatever her effect on Swedish society there is no doubt that she made social life there a great deal livelier and more interesting. Her main task however was to stiffen Bernadotte's spine, and iron out whatever problems arose between him and the Tsar. Irresolute by nature, Bernadotte was well aware that he might lose Sweden without gaining France or Germany – Schlegel's idea being a united Germany under Bernadotte. Madame de Staël was constantly at his side, as was recalled by the same anonymous witness: 'One day she arrived at the palace, and asked to be announced to His Highness.

"Tell Madame de Staël," said the Prince to his Chamberlain, "that I have business for an hour with Count Engeström [the Foreign Minister] and ask her to go down to the Queen, where I will have the pleasure of joining her shortly." "No," replied Madame de Staël. She would wait where she was for M. Engeström to finish his work.

The Prince, who was usually very polite to ladies, cried: "Good God, if Madame de Staël comes here to torment me about public affairs every day, she might as well be a member of the council." But he sent M. Engeström away and asked for Madame de Staël to be shown in. After an exchange of common civilities, fixing her great dark eyes on the Crown Prince she asked him what he was waiting for. "For the Russian forces so that we can begin operating in Denmark," Bernadotte replied.

"And so you persist in wishing to begin with an operation which will deflect your forces from the great aim which is to fall on Napoleon's back and help the Germans?"

Bernadotte tried to calm her by teasing that she herself had quoted in her book, that *the land belonged to the French, the sea to the British and the air to Germany*.

"My word, Monseigneur! The poor Germans will soon be unable to breathe at all in the air that poisons their land. You have often said that Germany is the heart of Europe – you must not allow that poor heart to dry up and die. You hold the thunderbolt: when will you throw it?"

"Madame, I am not the German Jove. I am Sweden's champion, whose interests I must put first. But console your Germans. You have accepted a martyr's crown to do them justice. Their turn will come." '[39]

However much Bernadotte must have wished his old friend a thousand miles away at times, there is no doubt that most of the important negotiations between Russia and Sweden took place through the intermediary of Madame de Staël and her Swiss friend, Galiffe, through whom she was in constant touch with the Russian government. Acting as Madame de Staël's personal ambassador, he wrote to her twice a week, keeping her informed of the different stages of the Russian campaign. 'Not only are you the only one to send me news, but three quarters of the time it is you, who through me inform our admirable Prince of what is going on, since an intelligent man like you is better able to understand the situation than the ambassadors themselves,' she wrote in October.

She also attempted through him to direct the Tsar: 'Do you know what is needed at present? It is to keep the Poles out for the moment. The Emperor Alexander ought to declare himself their King so that there might be a Poland again.'[40] Galiffe not only kept her informed and acted as a channel of communication between her and the Tsar, but sometimes she commissioned him on more personal matters, such as finding the son of a friend (Constance Cazenove Arlens) who had been wounded in Russia, or the purchase of a large crimson cashmere shawl for Albertine – concerning which there was a considerable correspondence, Madame de Staël giving him precise details as to shape, colour and price.[41]

On one occasion, however, Bernadotte managed to get the better of her. Deep in conversation at a party with the Austrian ambassador, Count Neipperg, he saw her determinedly making her way towards them. Seizing her arm with great presence of mind, he propelled her towards an armchair at the other end of the drawing room. 'I can see Madame that these large gatherings tire you,' he said, remaining with her for a moment before he returned to his conversation with the diplomat. Alexander Hope, a British General sent to Stockholm at the time to conclude a treaty with the Swedes, who liked Madame de Staël very much and with whom he often discussed the war and politics, also had to take evasive action occasionally. Unwilling to discuss matters which he wished to keep secret, he pleaded exhaustion at a party and was seen to jump over a footstool in order to make a quick getaway.[42]

Despite ill-health and the rigours of the Scandinavian winter, Madame de Staël remained active in all her favourite occupations: politics, writing and social life. There were occasional problems. Albertine, though she was described as 'an angel of beauty in spite of her red hair', could be as outspoken and tactless as her mother. She had made an insulting remark about two young men who wanted to dance with her at a ball and had been ostracized. She had spent a mortifying evening quite alone. After bearing it for a while, she rushed to her mother in tears. When Madame de Staël heard the reason, she whisked her away to spare her any further pain. The next day she gave a big lunch, inviting all the young people at the ball, and apologizing on Albertine's behalf. Albertine was forgiven, and was more courted than ever thereafter.[43]

During her time in Stockholm, Madame de Staël was hard at work on two books – *Dix années d'exil*, and *Considérations sur la Révolution française* – both works of major importance, which remained unfinished at her death but were published posthumously by her son and daughter. At the same time she encouraged Rocca – who was actually not as stupid as his extreme shyness and inability to express himself made him seem – to write a memoir of the war in Spain, for which she later wrote an introduction. She was naturally believed to have written the whole thing herself. This was not to be merely an account of his own service, but was intended to inspire a horror of the Napoleonic campaigns and admiration for the Spanish resistance which Madame de Staël hoped would serve as an example to others.

In the spring of 1813 she was joined by Auguste, who had come to accompany his mother and sister to England. At the end of April, Bernadotte, with Schlegel as his secretary and Albert as one of his aides-de-camp, left for the general headquarters of the Northern army in Stralsund, in Germany. Schlegel was to continue to keep her informed of Bernadotte's plans, while Madame de Staël would keep the Prince informed through Schlegel of developments in London and continue to encourage and advise him. She wrote to Schlegel that he was to remember that he was part of her family and must return to them when his noble mission in Germany was accomplished.

Facing the terrifying thought of another journey by sea, she also wrote to Constant, to try to persuade him to join her in England – though they had been apart for two years. She hoped to involve him on Bernadotte's side in the choice which would have to be made as to who was to rule France after Napoleon. Although Rocca loved her and she loved him – grateful for his unswerving loyalty – he provided no intellectual stimulus. Constant was always her true intellectual partner and she missed him: 'For two months I have heard nothing from you. I have not seen you for two years. Do you remember saying that we would never be apart? I must honestly tell you that all other considerations apart, you have allowed a fine career to escape you . . . What is to become of me in my spiritual solitude? Who am I to talk to . . ? My eldest son is with me; he has been appointed Secretary to the [Swedish] embassy in the United States . . . My daughter will write to you from Gothenburg. It will be her last farewell and mine too; but I hope that you will still feel the need to see us and not forget that which God has given to you . . . I always keep some of your letters by me . . . My father, you and Mathieu have a place in my heart now closed for ever . . . there I live and die . . . There I suffer continuously and in new ways. Is it possible that you can have brought about such ruin? . . . Farewell, Ah! may you understand what I suffer!'[44]

He did suffer – and in the same way. Her letter, he wrote in his journal, had provoked one of the worst days of regret and self-disgust in his life. Bored with Charlotte, Constant's journal throughout that year is full of Madame de Staël: 'Excellent letter from Madame de Staël. Alas! – Who knows! – Bitter quarrel with Charlotte about politics. She cannot hold two consecutive ideas in her head . . . confounded marriage. Shall I get out of it?' Throughout the year his journal is peppered with references to Madame de Staël's movements and anxiety about her safety. On 8 June, he writes: 'Albertine's birthday. Alas! Alas! Worked badly. I am out of sorts with everything in this world!'[45]

Madame de Staël's stay in Sweden had undoubtedly been important. An alliance with Russia was viewed with great scepticism in Sweden and Bernadotte hesitated to make any move which might threaten his own still delicate position there. It was largely through her influence and contacts that the treaty with England was concluded and it was English gold which enabled him to take an army into Swedish Pomerania. Through Schlegel's many contacts in Germany, Madame de Staël also used her influence to bring Prussia into the fourth coalition. To influence Swedish public opinion, an anonymous pamphlet was published, *On the Continental System in its Relationship with Sweden*, whose authorship was acknowledged by Schlegel. Its style and content were directly attributed to Madame de Staël however.

After his return from the disastrous Russian campaign Napoleon had again managed to raise another army, and had defeated the Prussians at Bautzen and Lützen just outside Dresden in the spring of 1813. But a crippling shortage of cavalry, which coincided with Bernadotte's arrival in North Germany, forced him to agree to an armistice, brokered by Metternich. The so-called Reichenbach armistice lasted two months until the Prague conference in July, when Austria changed sides, joining in the coalition against Napoleon. By then the allies had regrouped, encouraged by a £2 million grant by Britain. Napoleon himself later acknowledged the importance of Bernadotte's intervention – in which a considerable part had been played by Madame de Staël.

A final vignette sums up Madame de Staël's effects on Swedish society. When, some years later, Bernadotte (by then King Charles-John of Sweden) read the notice of Madame de Staël's death, he turned to his chief of staff, Admiral de Gyllenskold, and, sighing deeply, exclaimed: 'Ah! May God let her soul rest in peace!' 'You should rather say, Sire, may Madame de Staël leave God to rest in peace!' the Admiral replied.[46]

Chapter 24

~

England

'That green island which has stood alone against the enslavement of Europe.'

Madame de Staël

MADAME DE STAËL's triumphal reception in London, where she arrived on 17 June 1813 with Auguste, Albertine and Rocca, exceeded all her expectations. She was to remain there for almost a year. 'On arrival in England there was no particular person that sprang to mind; I knew no one but I was coming full of confidence. I was being persecuted by an enemy of freedom; I believed myself to be certain of an honourable sympathy in a country where all institutions were in harmony with my political convictions. I was also sure that the memory of my father would protect me. I was not wrong. The waves of the North Sea, as I crossed them from Sweden, still filled me with fear, when from a distance, I saw that green island which had stood alone against the enslavement of Europe.'[1]

She arrived immediately after the armistice signed at Dresden between Napoleon and the allies. Britain was in a bad economic situation after twenty-one years of war with France, and with another war threatening. Yet on her way from Harwich to London Madame de Staël was amazed at how prosperous everything looked – the country houses with their gardens; the people almost all decently dressed; even the animals looked 'as if they too enjoyed rights in this great edifice of social order', she wrote in the *Considérations sur la Révolution française*, part four of which was dedicated to an analysis of the history and the political and social institutions of the country she most admired. 'No nation in Europe can be compared with the English since 1688: there are a hundred and twenty years of social progress between them and the continent. True liberty, established for more than a century among a great people, has led to the results we may all witness, but in the preceding history of these peoples, there was more violence, more inequality, and in some respects, more servility even than in France.'[2]

No sooner installed at Brunet's Hotel in Leicester Square, than Madame de Staël sent off letters of introduction from her Swedish friend, the diplomat Brinkman, to the Marquis of Wellesley, Wellington's elder brother, who duly invited her to dinner on 28 July. She had already warned her friend, the widowed Duchess of Devonshire, of her arrival. She was her first visitor the very next day. Fluent in French and Italian the Duchess had probably met Madame de Staël as early as 1783 on a visit to Paris. Although she was no longer mistress of Devonshire House, she had a charming house at No. 13 Piccadilly, and another at Richmond.[3] Thanks to her, in spite of the disapproval of the Regent's mistress, Lady Hertford, Madame de Staël was soon presented to the Queen, the Prince Regent, the Duke of Gloucester and the Duchess of York.

Madame de Staël took a house first at 3 George Street, near Hanover Square, later moving to Argyll Street. Politicians from both Houses of Parliament and both parties queued to meet her. 'To meet a cabinet minister one must go to Madame de Staël's,' wrote Miss Berry.[4] Her reputation as Napoleon's great opponent, her personal relations with all the powerful men of Europe, her network of correspondents almost amounting to a personal foreign service, made her an important interlocutor. Madame de Staël's chief political ambition while she was in England – apart from the final defeat of Napoleon – was to support Bernadotte as the candidate for the throne of France.

Aside from her political importance, she aroused vivid curiosity wherever she went. Before her arrival, somebody had asked at a large dinner when she was likely to come to London. 'Not till Miss Edgeworth is gone . . .' Samuel Rogers, the poet, a friend of Byron and Thomas Moore, had replied. 'Madame de Staël would not like two stars shining at the same time.' The words were hardly out of his mouth, Thomas Moore reports in his diary, when he saw a gentleman rise at the other end of the table and pronounce in a solemn tone, '*Madame la Baronne de Staël est incapable d'une telle bassesse*' (Mme de Staël is incapable of such pettiness). It was her son, Auguste de Staël, whom Rogers had never seen before.[5]

In the event, Madame de Staël made her first entrée into London society at Lord Lansdowne's town house, with Rogers at her side. Her arrival had been the main topic of gossip; people stood on chairs to see her. On 3 July she was at the opera when news was announced of Wellington's victory at the battle of Vittoria. When the Italian soprano Madame Catalani sang 'God save the King', 'all the ladies rose to their feet and prayed for their country', Madame de Staël reported to the Queen of Sweden.[6] On 9 July she attended a gala performance of *Macbeth* at the King's Theatre, with the celebrated Mrs Siddons as Lady Macbeth. Her acquaintance with Mrs Siddons and her brother Kemble, who often came to her dinners, and through them other members of literary London, gave her particular pleasure. As well as Rogers, Madame de Staël met Byron, Sheridan, Coleridge, Southey and Thomas Moore. She never met the two female literary lights of her time, Jane Austen and Maria Edgeworth. Her friend, Sir James Mackintosh, lent her one of Jane Austen's novels, but she disliked it, pronouncing it *vulgaire*. It was too close to the narrow and dull English provincial life she had so hated. There could never have been two writers of genius more temperamentally different than Madame de Staël and Jane Austen: the one used to moving forward triumphantly through the mainstream of events, cosmopolitan, committed, her brilliant all-seeing 'sense' forever at odds with her questing, passionate 'sensibility'; the other, quintessentially English, hidden, reserved, a cool observer of the private life, venturing in her incomparable novels no further than she might go in her carriage, observing the follies of the human heart with clarity and devastating humour.

Madame de Staël's greatest friend and constant companion in England, Sir James Mackintosh, whom she described as 'a universal man in his knowledge and a brilliant conversationalist', had been a friend of Benjamin Constant's from his university days in Edinburgh. He had recently returned from India to become a reforming and liberal Member of Parliament. A polymath with a lively sense of humour, Mackintosh liked eccentric foreigners. He remained unperturbed by Madame de Staël's direct ways and would say with resigned amusement that 'he would be ordered with her to dinners as one orders beans and bacon to the houses of Cabinet Ministers'. She was one of those persons, he added, 'who surpass by far, all expectations of them'.[7]

If Madame de Staël surpassed all expectations, it was not always in a way that was desirable. At Lord Wellesley's dinner one guest recalled: 'she attacked him for his speech on the Swedish treaty which he repelled with so much address that he was the admiration of the whole table. His sarcasm was so tempered with humour and politeness . . . that he could not fail to delight the entire company, while he did not in the least offend her once.' Realizing that everyone was smiling at her discomfiture, Madame de Staël cried out to Mackintosh: 'Ah! it is easy to catch me out!' She chose, however, to ignore the English custom of withdrawing with the ladies after dinner, amazing everyone by standing up and 'haranguing the men for half an hour against the peace'.[8]

Byron had not liked her at all initially but was amused by the effect she had on people. 'She interrupted Whitbread; she declaimed to Lord L.[iverpool], she misunderstood Sheridan's jokes for assent; she harangued; she lectured; she preached English politics to the first of our English Whig politicians the day after her arrival in England . . . and no less to our Tory politicians the day after. The sovereign himself, if I am not in error, was not exempt from the flow of her eloquence.'[9]

What particularly annoyed Byron and many of the reforming Whigs was Madame de Staël's passionate and uncritical admiration of England and English institutions, which seemed to include Tories, Whigs, religious forces, and intellectuals indiscriminately. Her main difficulty with the Whigs, whose political views she shared, was over their foreign policy. A number of the Liberals supported and admired Napoleon and had been strongly against the war, a position she simply couldn't understand. 'She is for the Lord of Israel and the Lord of Liverpool – a vile antithesis of a Methodist and a Tory – and talks of nothing but devotion and the ministry,' Byron wrote crossly, while Henry Crabb Robinson, whom she had met at Weimar, and who had pointed out great ills such as rotten boroughs and press gangs to her, was sufficiently exasperated to call her 'a bigoted admirer of our government which she considers perfect'.[10]

In fact Madame de Staël considered it nothing of the sort. She believed Lord Liverpool to be a mediocrity: 'Pitt and Fox were dead, and no one had succeeded them,' she wrote in the *Considérations*. What she admired was the English system of government. 'In England the institutions promote every kind of intellectual progress. Juries, provincial administration, elections, newspapers, the nation as a whole has a major role in public affairs . . . thanks to toleration, to the political institutions, and to the freedom of the press, there is more respect for religion and customs than in any other country in Europe.'[11] Sir Humphry Davy, the famous chemist and the inventor of the miner's lamp, complained on one occasion that England was losing her civic liberties. 'And you count as nothing to be able to say all that, and in front of the servants!' she exclaimed.[12]

As for Methodism, she was interested in religious idealism in general, rather than in any particular sect. She loved English writing but was less happy with the prevailing admiration for Bentham's Utilitarian philosophy. Her admiration often cut across Byron's rebellious attitude to his own country, which he saw as corrupt and stifled by hypocrisy. Sometimes he would tease her, as on one occasion he told her that her novels *Delphine* and *Corinne* were actually dangerous for young women because in representing all the virtuous characters in her novels as dull, she had struck a blow at virtue. 'She was so excited and impatient to attempt a refutation that it was only by my own volubility I could keep her silent. She interrupted me every moment, by gesticulating, exclaiming "*Quelle idée!*" "*Mon Dieu!*" "*Écoutez donc!*" "*Vous m'impatientez!*".' He was particularly amused by the thought that he of all people, generally considered as the worst of bad lots, should be giving Madame de Staël lectures on morals.[13]

Byron and Madame de Staël also differed on Napoleon. Madame de Staël had not opposed the Emperor so implacably merely because he had persecuted her. In her eyes, as she makes abundantly clear in the *Considérations*, he was the man who stole the freedoms won with so much agony in the Revolution. The young revolutionary general she had once admired had turned into a power-mad autocrat, corrupting both individuals and public life. By appealing to greed and self-interest and ruling by bribery and fear he had destroyed France, as he had the whole of Europe, with his wars of conquest. These, she believed, had not only caused the deaths of millions but had set out to destroy the cultural individuality of each nation, a pluralism she cherished. Byron too saw that his boyhood hero had changed into a tyrant, but he admitted it more reluctantly.

Madame de Staël's utter lack of decorum annoyed and amused in equal measure. On one occasion at dinner, Byron remembered, one of the whalebones in her corset lost its moorings and shot up her cleavage. After several attempts to push it back, using both her hands and growing crimson with her exertions, Madame de Staël turned to the footman behind her chair and ordered him to pull it out, which, with a mighty heave, he did! Byron was convulsed with laughter as he observed the faces of the other ladies at table. Madame de Staël, apparently quite unaware that this might be seen as odd behaviour, or that she had offended against female propriety in any way, continued with her conversation unperturbed.

At the end of July and of the parliamentary year, with most of the *ton* (the fashionable world) gone from London to their country estates, Madame de Staël moved to Richmond in Surrey, where she had taken a house near her friend, the Duchess of Devonshire. Here she worked on her two books. She scarcely noticed the beauty of the river or the surrounding countryside. All her interest was centred on politics and the defeat of Napoleon, Jean-Louis Mallet recalled.

The eldest son of the journalist and chronicler of the French Revolution, Mallet du Pan, Jean-Louis Mallet had married an Englishwoman and settled in England. His description of Madame de Staël's appearance tallies with that of her contemporaries in France and in Vienna, Moscow, St Petersburg and Stockholm – beautiful dark eyes, plump, bad complexion, badly arranged black hair, too much bare bosom and arms for a woman of her age, an agreeable melodic voice, much movement of the arms and eyes. Mallet recalled that Rocca although he was her husband, (though not officially until 1816, the year before her death) was forced to live in a hotel and would come and visit her with his hat and cane just like any other visitor, while Schlegel, who was not her lover, lived in her house when in London and sometimes in the mornings would appear in his dressing gown and slippers. Rocca's furious refusal to greet him provoked an exasperated note from her: 'I simply don't understand you. Do you wish to forbid me all literary or political discourse? Do you wish to deprive me of the most innocent pleasures of life as well as the exercise of my faculties? When a man loves a woman he seeks her happiness . . . I have given you proof of my attachment such as I have given to no one else, I prefer you to all others and I am ready to do everything for you once my daughter is married . . . I die of the need to be loved and show it to you clearly enough for you not to need to take advantage of my weakness.'[14]

Mallet was present at a dinner at Madame Achard's, to which Madame de Staël had brought her house guests. They were a Mr

William Spenser, a litterateur, M. Rocca, who Mallet thought had an interesting face and beautiful expressive eyes, and the Duc de Laval and his Russian wife. The 'little Tartar' Duchess maintained that there was no one happier or freer than the Russian peasant. 'Happy – very well,' Madame de Staël interjected, 'but free! I have never seen slavery included among all the various definitions of liberty!' She had then gone on to express herself warmly and eloquently in defence of liberty. After M. and Mme de Laval's departure she explained the history of their marriage – an arranged one – 'with much wit and little malice'.[15] The talk turned to Talleyrand. 'You know that he once loved me greatly!' Madame de Staël exclaimed in exactly the same tone, Mallet noted, that another person would have said 'we are old friends'. In the absence of any real conversation that evening, and to amuse the company, Madame de Staël recounted several anecdotes about Talleyrand, ending with the observation that she could not understand how Talleyrand had been able to marry such a very silly woman. Mallet also reported that when Talleyrand heard this he replied: 'To understand the full value of such peace of mind one would have to have lived under the same roof as Madame de Staël for a month!'[16]

While she was at Richmond she received a letter from Schlegel with the terrible news that her younger son Albert had been killed in a duel. Unlike his reliable and studious elder brother Auguste, Albert had always been wild, causing his mother and Schlegel endless trouble and anxiety. His vitality always seemed to be at cross purposes to his interests, his mother had once observed. Schlegel, who was with him in Hamburg, compared him to Hotspur, while General Hope, who had watched him gambling, predicted 'a premature and unfortunate end'. Bernadotte had made him an aide-de-camp only for the sake of his mother. Sent as a courier to Hamburg, Albert, against his mother's wishes, had remained there to serve under Colonel Tettenborn, who was in charge of the Cossack regiments occupying the city. As aide-de-camp to Tettenborn, he fought with furious and reckless enthusiasm, drinking, gambling and wenching. Bernadotte was angry enough to punish him by sending him into temporary exile at Rügen and then to Wismar, a small town near Hamburg. Schlegel reported all this to Madame de Staël, but she had refused to intervene on Albert's behalf. Escaping for a few days to the small spa of Doberan, Albert was soon at the gaming tables. A fight over a few disputed louis with a Russian officer, the Baron Ralf, resulted in a challenge to a duel. A witness who heard the clash of swords in the park arrived in time to see Albert's head being almost struck off with one blow of a heavy Prussian sword. Albert was buried at Doberan. He was not quite twenty-one. Madame de Staël admitted to Schlegel that she was completely exhausted with grief.[17]

After Albert's death, Schlegel had forwarded a number of his IOUs. Madame de Staël paid all his gambling debts. 'Poor Albert! . . . Did you cry for him?' she wrote to Constant. 'I do not want to die before seeing you again, without talking to you as in the past . . . but then I would like to die . . .'[18] News of Albert's death had been followed by that of his natural father, Narbonne. At the time of Madame de Staël's disgrace following the publication of *Delphine* in 1803, and her banishment by Bonaparte, then still First Consul, Narbonne, who had rejoined the army, wrote to him asking for a post. It was suggested to him that his friendship with Madame de Staël might be a hindrance. He was ready to serve France, he explained, but 'Accused just before the 2 September [1792], I owed my escape and therefore my life to Madame de Staël. The more she has fallen into disgrace with the First Consul, the less, I am certain, he would forgive me for denying my friendship and gratitude to her.'[19] In 1812 Narbonne had served as ambassador to Vienna. In the spring of 1813 Napoleon, who was displeased with him, had sent him to take command of his troops at Torgau. There he died of typhus.

Madame de Staël remained at Richmond until the end of September 1813, while Rocca was sent off to Bath, partly for his health but also for the sake of propriety, though nobody was fooled. Byron always referred to him as *Monsieur l'amant*. A month later, before the beginning of the winter season, she was invited to Bowood, Lord Lansdowne's magnificent house in Wiltshire. 'At Bowood I saw the most wonderful group of enlightened men that England and therefore the world has to offer,' she recalled in the *Considérations*. Apart from Sir James Mackintosh and Samuel Rogers, she met Samuel Romilly, the reforming Solicitor-General and Whig Member of Parliament who campaigned for penal reform and Catholic emancipation and against the death penalty and slavery. Madame de Staël described him as 'the light and honour of English jurisprudence, in itself an object of respect for all humanity'.[20] Here, too, she saw again her love from her time in Rome, Don Pedro de Souza, Count later Duke of Palmella. Now thirty-five, the still young and handsome Souza had joined the Portuguese army and then fought bravely under Wellington. He had married the beautiful young Dona Eugenia Telles de Gama who, with their two children, had accompanied him to England where he was now chargé d'affaires.[21] It must have been a poignant reunion for Madame de Staël.

From Bowood, Madame de Staël and Albertine went on to visit Stonehenge and Salisbury and then on to Sandhurst, where they were shown around by General Hope. It was from him that she learned of Napoleon's defeat by Russian, Austrian, Prussian and Swedish troops at the battle of the Nations at Leipzig on 17 and 18 October 1813. Madame de Staël, aware that the defeat of Napoleon would mean the defeat of France, now had two contradictory fears – Napoleon's survival and the invasion of France by foreign armies expected in early 1814.

In spite of her grief over the death of her son and her fears for France, Madame de Staël pressed on with plans to publish her book on Germany and to complete the two other books on which she was working. *De l'Allemagne* was permeated with her respect for Britain, 'that great free people'. The *Considérations sur la Révolution française* was not only an apologia of her father's political career and views but also (in the final part VI) an exposition of Britain's political and social institutions. Her intention was not just to glorify a country she admired deeply, but in making British institutions which guaranteed individual and political freedoms known and understood in France, to offer an example.

De l'Allemagne was published on 4 November 1813 by John Murray, on the same day as the victory at Leipzig was announced in England. Murray had bought it for the considerable sum of 1,500 guineas. The book sold out in three days in its French edition and sold 2,250 copies in English by the end of the year. Madame de Staël was now the literary as well as the political and social star of the season, putting Byron's nose out of joint. 'To-day received Lord Jersey's invitation to Middleton – to travel sixty miles to meet Madame de Staël! I once travelled three thousand to get among silent people; and this same lady writes *octavos* and talks *folios*,' he wrote with some irritation in his journal that autumn.[22] Yet travel he did. Lady Jersey was one of the leading hostesses of her time: her invitations were never refused.

Byron found it hard to forgive the middle-aged authoress for not being good-looking. To Lady Melbourne he declared: 'I never go near her – her books are very delightful, but in society I see nothing but a very plain woman forcing one to listen and look at her with her pen behind her ear and her mouth full of *ink*.'[23] To another friend he describes her as being 'frightful as a precipice'.[24]

No one challenged contemporary assumptions about women's intellectual inferiority, or their freedom to be what they liked, more obviously than Madame de Staël. At first acquaintance, many people, particularly men, found her overwhelming, irritating, ridiculous – or all three at once. If they could not deny her brilliance they could ridicule her appearance, her volubility, her inability to conform. Byron was no exception, but he was too intelligent, too fine an artist, not to recognize her intellectual merit. Later, when he spent a great deal of time at Coppet, he grew to like his hostess very much, recognizing her goodness as well as her genius. In late November 1813, soon after the publication of *De l'Allemagne*, he wrote to acknowledge Madame de Staël's 'very pretty billet', as he calls it in his journal, in which she had thanked him for a singular accolade. In a note to his poem *The Bride of Abydos* (canto I, stanza VI), Byron had written: 'For an eloquent passage in the latest work *of the first female writer of this, perhaps of any age*, on the analogy between painting and music, see vol. iii, cap. 10 *De l'Allemagne*. [my italics].' 'My praise', he wrote, was 'only the feeble echo of more powerful voices – to yourself any attempt at eulogy must be merely repetition – of the work itself I can only say – that few days have passed since its publication without my perusal of many of its pages.' He ended with an apology for the irregularity of his visits and hoped that 'your Goodnature [sic] will forgive my negligence & perhaps some of my faults – amongst which however cannot be numbered any deficiency in real respect & sincere admiration on the part of . . . Byron.'[25] 'I have read all her books and like all of them – and delight in the last,' he admitted to John Murray. 'I do not love Madame de Staël but depend upon it – she beats all your natives hollow as an Authoress – in my opinion – and I would not say this if I could help it.' In his diary he admitted: 'she is a woman by herself and has done more than the rest of them together, intellectually – she ought to have been a man'.[26]

Madame de Staël had been keen to meet William Godwin, the radical philosopher, who had once said: 'God Himself has no right to be a tyrant'. The widower of the famous feminist writer, Mary Wollstonecraft, and the father of Mary Shelley, he was used to strong-minded and clever women. During a discussion on Milton, Godwin defended Milton's connection with Cromwell, who he said had been a usurper, but neither cruel nor a tyrant. 'I am glad I have seen this man; it is curious how naturally Jacobins become the advocates of tyrants,' Madame de Staël remarked to Lady Mackintosh after Godwin's departure.[27]

Much was forgiven her as a foreigner, even such lapses of tact as one occasion when Lady Mackintosh appeared at Madame de Staël's dinner all in green with a bright red turban on her head. 'Ah milady! you look just like a parrot!' Madame de Staël exclaimed impulsively.[28] They knew that she meant no harm but, like a child, simply said the first thing that came into her head.

Madame de Staël admired English domestic virtues, no less than political ones. The English, she believed, were happier at home than anywhere else – hence their love of privacy. Lord Grey, whom she describes as one of the most ardent lovers of freedom in the House of Lords, she also believed to be a perfect example of domestic bliss after she stayed with him and his wife and their thirteen children. But she found English social life terribly dull, with the rare exception of a few people whose company provided 'the best and noblest forms of intellectual pleasure'. 'One is invited daily to huge assemblies . . . where women were in the majority . . ,' she wrote. Great strength was required just to cross a drawing room without being suffocated and to enter one's carriage without accident, 'but I don't see that any other talent is required for such a crowd, where a lady's visiting list might include 1,200 names . . . The lady of the house feels no necessity, as in France, to lead the conversation and especially to ensure that it does not languish. One is very much resigned to this misfortune in England, and it seems that they are much better able to bear boredom than the need to put themselves out to bring the discussion to life. Women in particular are extremely timid,' she noted sadly.[29] In spite of her admiration and gratitude she was not happy.

'The English,' she wrote, 'are at least as shy and ill at ease with each other as they are with strangers; they only speak to one another if introduced. They are extremely formal even among brothers and sisters. This formality makes for a dull life.' Their love of travel, she believed, owed at least as much to a wish to escape from such constraints as it did to a wish to escape from the fogs of their native land.[30] For all that, she had hoped that Auguste would marry an Englishwoman. In fact, as Byron was to write later: 'There was a double marriage talked of in town that season: Auguste (the present Baron) was to have married Miss Milbanke, I, the present duchesse of Broglio. I could not have been worse embroiled.'[31] Byron married Anabella Millbanke on 2 January 1815; Madame de Staël's daughter Albertine married the Duc de Broglie.

The winter of 1813–14 was nevertheless a round of social pleasures. Madame de Staël was entertained at Althorp by Lord Spencer, at Hatfield House by Lord Salisbury, and, recommended by Lady Bessborough, she also stayed at Blenheim, which struck her as being like a magnificent tomb, 'all splendour outside, but death and boredom inside'. After a luncheon served by silent servants, who communicated with her through sign language, Madame de Staël was presented to the Duke of Marlborough, a famous eccentric who had decided never to speak again. She found him sitting at a large table, upon which were scattered written signs for all the usual things he might require. He would merely hold up a sign to his servants, with no need of speech. Madame de Staël naturally took this as a supreme challenge. She bombarded the Duke with questions and compliments in English and French, with not a word out of him. It was only when she enquired after his wife who had died recently that, unable to bear it any longer, he rushed out of the room with a desperate cry of 'Let me out!' to his servants – the last words, it was said, that he uttered before his death four years later![32]

From the time of her arrival in England, Madame de Staël had been extremely keen to meet William Wilberforce, the philanthropist and 'the most respected and most loved man in England'.[33] A dinner party was arranged by the Duke of Gloucester. Deeply religious and afraid of the effects that such an evening might have on him, the great champion of the abolition of slavery had not wished to go. When Madame de Staël invited him to dinner, Wilberforce prayed for guidance. Although his carriage was waiting at the door, he decided to stay at home in further prayer and meditation. But little did he know her! His hesitations only made her more determined, and eventually he gave in. Madame de Staël had invited 'a brilliant company in rank and talent' to honour him, notably Lords Harrowby and Lansdowne and Sir James Mackintosh, as Wilberforce guiltily admitted in his journal. Afterwards, he had spent most of the night on his knees. He had found the evening intoxicating, and after wrestling with his conscience late into the night, he concluded that it had been 'true dissipation which corrupts the spirit, thought and sometimes even judgement.' The next morning he had been convinced that for the sake of his soul, he should 'withdraw from the gay and irreligious, though brilliant society of Mme de Staël and others.'[34] Fortunately, Divine guidance decreed otherwise and he did not. By the time of her return to France they were friends. Madame de Staël was to prove an active supporter of Wilberforce's struggle for the abolition of slavery. Her son Auguste, too, was to become actively committed to this cause for the rest of his life, maintaining the family connection with Wilberforce, who lived just long enough (he died in 1833) to see the wretched trade in human beings finally banished.[35]

But there were times when Madame de Staël, longed to escape. She missed Constant and Schlegel. The absence of letters when she expected them made her unhappy and reproachful. She was depressed, anxious about Rocca's failing health and about Albertine's future. Albert's death had affected her profoundly; she never fully recovered her health afterwards, and lost a great deal of weight. She had inherited her mother's insomnia and was taking laudanum in ever-increasing doses to be able to sleep at all. 'My book has been a wild success,' she wrote to Schlegel, 'but none of this can lighten the weight on my heart. Since our separation and Albert's death, my health deteriorates, in short, I am tired of life.'[36] As for Constant, they were in regular correspondence. If anything he missed her even more than she missed him. 'Charlotte is very good; I love her; but when I look at her attachment, I think of Madame de Staël's for me, and remembering her and Albertine tears me apart!' he wrote in his journal. 'Let us do no harm, but remember that I cannot live truly closely with anyone. I might have been able to do so with Madame de Staël because of her mind which is unique; I did not wish it! . . . Let me carry the pain and not punish others for my own faults.'[37]

As the Allies advanced, Madame de Staël was increasingly torn between her desire to see Napoleon finally beaten and her concerns for France. As early as September, she had admitted to Miss Berry: 'Between the Cossacks and the Corsican I see little hope of liberty for France. I don't know what to hope for, but I know well what to fear.' 'Madame de Staël is in despair about France', Miss Berry wrote to a friend in January 1814. 'She cannot bear what she calls the humiliation of the Allies marching to Paris. She wants the annihilation of Bonaparte (which she doesn't think will take place), and she doesn't want the return of the Bourbons . . . she wishes for a liberty a real constitutional liberty, for which I believe France is no more fitted than Turkey; but this she won't bear to hear.'

On 6 April 1814 'news came of the defeat of Bonaparte's army near Paris . . . we went directly to Madame de Staël . . . Madame de Staël was completely overcome. No arguments, no reply, no wit; she showed her true feeling for what she always calls her country.'[38]

The question uppermost for everyone now was who was to replace Napoleon when he was finally beaten. The choices were a constitutional monarchy under Bernadotte; a restoration of the Bourbons, favoured by the British Cabinet, the Prince Regent and British public opinion in general as well as by Talleyrand; for Napoleon to remain as ruler in France provided the French accepted him as such, a solution which the Tsar was considering; or a regency until Napoleon's three-year-old son, the King of Rome, was old enough to mount the throne. Madame de Staël believed a constitutional monarchy under Bernadotte would give the best guarantees of enlightened and liberal rule. She did not believe that a regency for Napoleon's son would last a week, and was reluctant to see a return of the Bourbons. She had seen Louis XVIII taking the waters at Bath that autumn. Shocked at the sight of the hugely overweight monarch being wheeled along in a bathchair, she wrote: 'In his wheelchair he was the image of the former monarchy, pulled from the front and pushed from behind . . . How can anyone mount the throne again, when they have need of so many arms to help them into a chair?'[39] Most of all she feared that the Allies would leave Napoleon in place.

It was a measure of Madame de Staël's power, however, that emissaries from the Bourbon camp now began to make advances to her. As it became clear that Bernadotte, afraid of losing the throne of Sweden, was not prepared to commit himself fully to the much more uncertain one of France, she thought pragmatically that she might have to make the best of a restoration. 'The Duc de Berry has come to see me and I am on reasonable terms with the Bourbons,' she wrote to Constant in late January. Constant, meanwhile, was working on a pamphlet entitled *De l'esprit de conquête et de l'usurpation*, ('On the spirit of Conquest and on Usurpation') and he sent her the first pages. Published in Hanover in January, in London in March 1814, and then in Paris, it was a resounding success. She was all admiration, congratulating him on the lucidity of his thought and style. But, she cautioned, 'One must not speak ill of the French with the Russians at Langres. May God banish me from France rather than let me return with the help of foreigners! Has not France two arms, one to punish the enemy, the other to overthrow tyranny?'[40]

The Russians were indeed at Langres. On 26 January 1814, Castlereagh, the Foreign Secretary, and Metternich, who had travelled together from Basle, called on the Tsar. They found him in a mystical mood and much inclined to talk of the Divine Will. While undecided about who was to succeed Napoleon, he was clear that there would be no negotiation until the final defeat of 'the Corsican tyrant'. Castlereagh's dispatch to Lord Liverpool speaks of the Tsar's '*chevaleresque* state of mind'. He was determined to enter Paris as a magnanimous liberator, and 'the idea that a rapid negotiation might disappoint this hope added to his impatience'.[41]

Meanwhile, leaving Paris undefended in the hands of a Council of Regency, Napoleon hurried to take personal command of his troops. With the odds heavily against him, Napoleon fought a brilliant campaign through the first half of February, beating the Prussians three times and throwing the Austrians back across the Seine. The negotiations referred to by Castlereagh were scheduled to be held at Chatillon for 3 February 1814, with Caulaincourt in charge. He had tried unsuccessfully to persuade Napoleon to accept the Allies' terms while there was still time, but the Emperor, whose recent victories had served to increase his confidence, refused to listen. On 1 March, the allied sovereigns signed at Chaumont what Castlereagh referred to as 'my treaty'. This established the Quadruple Alliance of Britain, Russia, Austria and Prussia and stipulated that the signatories would not deal with Napoleon separately and would 'concert together on the conclusion of a peace with France' for twenty years after the cessation of hostilities. Napoleon had rejected peace terms which would have allowed France to keep her 1792 frontiers. The Allies now agreed that war would be pursued until his unconditional surrender and called on France to reject Napoleon.

'I think that the Allies' decision to march on Paris wrong . . . all French hearts will be revolted . . . I myself could only think of France,' Madame de Staël wrote to Constant, pointing out that it would make Napoleon seem the champion of France's freedom. A month later, in reply to a memorandum Constant had written, she turned on him furiously. Being with the Crown Prince [Bernadotte] had turned him into a court chamberlain, she raged: 'Have you forgotten what you wrote against foreigners and can you imagine a king supported by Cossacks? . . . So you think that Bonaparte cannot appear in an assembly of princes! Forty battles are also a badge of nobility. I hate the man, but I blame events which force me at this moment, to wish for his success. Do you want France to be trodden underfoot? . . . I read your memorandum; God forbid that I should show it to anyone! I will do nothing against France; I will not turn against her in her misfortune, I will use neither my fame, which I owe to her, nor my father's name which she had loved. You are not French, Benjamin. All your childhood's memories are not attached to that land. That is where the difference between us lies – but can you really wish to see Cossacks in the rue Racine?'[42]

On Wednesday, 31 March 1814, the allied armies entered Paris, with the Emperor Alexander, flanked by the King of Prussia and Prince Schwarzenberg, representing the Emperor of Austria at their head. Britain, who had done more than any other country to bring down Napoleon, was unrepresented at the triumphant entry in Paris. There were to be victory celebrations in London in due course. Standing in the crowd, Chateaubriand – although he wanted the downfall of Napoleon – felt 'like an ancient Roman might have done at the approach of Alaric's Goths'.[43] Madame de Staël too could hardly bear it. 'This is a cruel blow, all London is drunk with joy, and I alone feel the pain in this great city,' she wrote to Auguste.[44] Congratulated by someone on the end of her exile, she had cried: 'What are you congratulating me on, pray – that I am in despair?'[45] Recognizing that Bernadotte would not succeed Napoleon, she wrote to Constant on 1 April: 'the fact is that if Bonaparte is overturned, the *ancien régime* will be reinstated. It may be for the best, but it's sad. Adieu! . . . be faithful to France and to liberty; without friendship there is nothing.'[46]

Chapter 25

~

The End of Empire

'There are three great powers in Europe: Britain, Russia and Madame de Staël.'

THE SPRING OF 1814 was particularly beautiful in Paris. Exhausted by war, her citizens awaited the end of the Empire in a strangely fatalistic mood. Napoleon, who had been on his way to Paris, had returned to Fontainebleau where, in an utterly dejected frame of mind, he had shut himself up in his study with the faithful Caulaincourt and Berthier.

The warm weather had brought all the citizens of Paris out of doors, and the city was full of pretty young women dressed in the exaggerated fashion of the day. As Madame de Boigne observed: 'Nothing in this city, neither battles, nor occupation, nor riot, nor troubles of any kind, ever stopped Parisiennes from enjoying their fashionable *toilettes*.' Dressed in the latest fashion – dresses made of material with very wide stripes and exaggeratedly high crowned hats, their tiny pokes decorated with enormous bows and bunches of flowers – they paraded along the Champs-Élysées, gawping at the Cossack troops who were encamped there. Madame de Staël's nightmare of Cossacks had come true. Madame de Boigne recalled that: 'they had neither tents, nor any kind of shelter. Three or four horses were tethered to each tree, with the horsemen sitting on the ground nearby, as they chatted to each other in soft voices and very harmonious sounds. Most were sewing: they were mending their old clothes, cutting and making new ones, mending their shoes, their horses' harness, or tailoring in their own fashion their share of materials pillaged in the previous days . . . Their uniforms were very pretty; large blue trousers, a high-collared tunic, also blue, quilted on the chest and tightly belted with a wide black patent-leather belt, buckled and ornamented with highly polished brass on which hung their weapons.'[1] The Tsar had issued the strictest instructions, and everyone testified to the impeccable behaviour of the Russian troops.

After his triumphal entry into Paris, the Tsar had dismounted outside Talleyrand's magnificent house in the rue St Florentin: 'Well here we are in Paris. It is you who brought us here, M. de Talleyrand! There are three possible solutions now: to negotiate with the Emperor Napoleon, to establish a regency, or to call back the Bourbons.'[2] As Prince of Benevento, and Vice-Grand Electeur, Talleyrand was still nominally at the top of the French hierarchy, although out of favour with Napoleon, who neither trusted nor liked him. When Paris had capitulated to the Allies on 31 March, Count Nesselrode, the Russian Foreign Minister, had called on Talleyrand to explain that the Tsar, who had been intending to stay at the Élysée Palace, had received a warning that it was mined. He had therefore decided to stay with Talleyrand. Everyone believed that it was Talleyrand himself, wishing to keep the Tsar under his own roof and under his influence, who had been the author of the warning. Talleyrand had been coaching the Tsar since Tilsit on how best to curb Napoleon's expansionist ambitions, which he strongly opposed because he believed them to be contrary to the interests of France. When in February the Allies, rattled by Napoleon's military successes, had been doubtful about their next course of action, Talleyrand had sent the royalist Baron de Vitrolles to the Tsar with a secret message. 'Would you like to see the document which determined us to advance on Paris?' Nesselrode asked Madame de Boigne, pulling a crumpled note from his pocket. Urging Alexander to make all haste to Paris, Talleyrand's note read: 'You are groping about like children: you ought to stride forward on stilts. You are now in a position to achieve anything you wish.'[3]

Talleyrand's aim was that the Empire should be replaced with a constitutional monarchy. Although he had little affection or respect for the Bourbons, only the legitimate monarchy could give France the stability she needed, he told Alexander. Britain supported the Bourbons largely because, as Lord Liverpool wrote, the people refused to countenance any peace with Bonaparte.

Napoleon abdicated at Fontainebleau on 6 April and at the end of that month he left for Elba. With the Tsar's agreement, Talleyrand became interim President of the provisional government.

Madame de Staël could now return to Paris, but the thought of the occupying foreign troops agitated her. The country must first be freed. Auguste wrote impatiently from Paris, urging her not to waste any more time: 'Everyone asks me, is Madame de Staël not coming?'[4] 'I am entirely sure that we must rally to the Bourbons,' she wrote to Constant from London at the end of April, 'and I hope that they will require the withdrawal of foreign troops, which I think is more essential to liberty than all the senates in the world. I shall come back sporting the white cockade [symbol of the Bourbons] most sincerely, and be more concerned with independence than with liberty, which in truth, the French are hardly worthy of – I am finished with politics – I shall go to Greece and write my poem on Richard's crusades.' He need not worry, she added, about Rocca's jealousy (a justified worry; Rocca had challenged Constant to a duel when they last met), and she would be delighted to receive Madame de Constant if it suited her. 'Your mind and your talents will always be the objects of my admiration and conversation with you, if you still care for my company, will always remain my chief pleasure.' Albertine continued the letter, ending: 'I am a little afraid of France, which I hardly know, but what makes me happy is the thought of seeing you again . . . You will find my mother thin and in poorer health, but you will see more clearly than ever what an admirable person she is.'[5]

On 3 May 1814, Louis XVIII returned to France with his niece, the Duchesse d'Angoulême, the last surviving child of Louis XVI. The fat and gouty King and his stiff and dowdy niece in her funny little English hat made as poor an impression on his people as they did on Talleyrand, who had wished for his return, and on the Emperor Alexander, who had not.

On 12 May, accompanied by Albertine, Rocca and Schlegel, who had joined her in England, Madame de Staël finally disembarked at Calais. 'After ten years of exile I was approaching Calais, and counting on feeling great pleasure at the sight of lovely France again, a country I had missed so much. My first impressions were quite unexpected. The first men I noticed on the quays wore Prussian uniforms: they were now masters of the town by right of conquest. Oh France! Oh France! That a foreign tyrant was destined to reduce you to this state – a French sovereign, whatever he may have been would have loved you too well to expose you to this.' As she approached Paris, all she could see around her were Germans, Russians, Cossacks and Bashkir (tribesmen from central Asia): 'They were camped around the church of Saint-Denis, where lie the ashes of the French kings . . . Was I in Germany or Russia?' Happy that the tyrant had been deposed, she felt unbearable pain at the occupation of Paris – the Opera full of 'sabres and moustaches . . . the Tuileries, the Louvre guarded by troops from the very confines of Asia, to whom our language, our history, our great men, everything, was less familiar than the last Khan of Tartary.'[6]

Madame de Staël's much longed for return to Paris left her disorientated at first. Her reunion with some of her friends had been disappointing. Mathieu de Montmorency, for example, who had always been very religious, had now also become a rabid royalist.[7] Constant, who had not seen her for three years, called on her on the day after her return. 'She is much changed, she is thin and pale,' he confided to his journal. 'I did not allow myself to show any emotion. What good would that have been? Albertine is delightful; as amusing as can be – adorable. It is her I regret. I should like to spend the rest of my life in her company.' He was back for dinner on the 15th and again on 18 May when he noted that Madame de Staël was 'distracted, utterly changed, almost arid, thinking only of herself, hardly listening to others, caring about nothing, even her daughter only from duty, and not at all of me'. At another dinner he had read her his poem: 'She obviously no longer cares for me, since she hardly praised it at all. She only praises what is part of herself – as for instance the man whom she is now keeping.'[8]

That, of course, was the real trouble. While apart, what they both remembered was the extraordinary intellectual pleasure they each found in the other's company. If Constant had found her demanding before, now he was disappointed at her matter-of-fact attitude towards him. She too found him cold and uncaring, as she explained later. When he realized that she was coming back, she had been profoundly hurt by the non-committal tone of his letters to London. 'When I returned, I found you to be like your letters, not a look not an inflection of voice betrayed in you any memories, and I sometimes admired you for being so intelligent and so uninspired all in one. I was hurt, but it was for the best, for fifteen years of such strong feeling leave a cruel wound which could be reopened all too easily.'[9] Nevertheless, Constant's journal for the next two months mentions dinner with Madame de Staël almost every other day.

By the end of May, when Madame Récamier returned to Paris from

Rome and Naples, Madame de Staël was back to her old self. 'With what feeling, my dear friend, do I see the hour of your arrival approaching! . . . You are more loved than ever by all your friends; and as for me who is responsible for your troubles, will you see me with a little of the feelings you inspire in me? I hold you to my heart.'[10] They were to see each other almost every day while Madame de Staël was in Paris.

On 25 May Madame de Staël's salon was triumphantly inaugurated at the Hotel Lamoignon. At a three-hour-long reception, she received the Tsar Alexander, the Grand Duke, Charles Augustus of Saxe-Weimar, Prince Schwarzenberg, and most of the important foreign ambassadors. The Tsar, who shared her doubts about the Bourbons, had expressed his contempt openly that evening, declaring them 'unchanged and incorrigible'. Alexander believed that the only liberal among the royals was the recently returned Louis-Philippe, Duc d'Orléans, son of the regicide prince Philippe Égalité, who was the King's cousin. He was to succeed the King's brother Charles X (Comte d'Artois in 1830.) The Tsar promised Madame de Staël, La Fayette and Constant that he would demand the abolition of slavery at the next Congress and abolish serfdom in his own Empire. For good measure he strongly criticized the reinstated Ferdinand VII for abolishing the Constitution in Spain.[11]

The Swiss Ambassador, Pictet de Rochemont, noted that among the political figures present that evening were Talleyrand and his old fellow conspirator Fouché. Madame de Staël's friendship with Talleyrand could never be rekindled but she was reconciled with him as a public figure, indeed, now the most important man in France.

Also present were several of her old political friends who were now involved in the preparations for the new constitutional charter, among them Boissy d'Anglas, the Abbé de Montesquiou, now Minister of the Interior, and Malouet, now Minister of War. There were many distinguished foreigners: the German brothers Humboldt, Frederick Gentz, Sir James Mackintosh, Lord Harrowby and Lord Canning. All her familiars were also present at that reception: Madame Récamier, Mathieu de Montmorency, Sismondi, Constant – who was now actively seeking a post – and Schlegel, whose hopes of an independent life had died with the withdrawal of Bernadotte. La Fayette, to whom she had written in 1805 that she could not despair of the human race so long as he lived, was also present.[12] Among old friends and former lovers were Mathieu's cousin, the Duc de Laval, Suard, Jaucourt, Camille Jordan, Prosper de Barante, Chateaubriand, Pedro de Souza, Lally Tollendal, the Duchesse de Duras, Elzear de Sabran and Madame de Boigne – like ghosts from the whole of her past life.

Madame de Staël had become an institution. Her political and intellectual life, spanning as it did the entire period from the *ancien régime* through the Revolution, the attempts at constitutional government, the Empire and now the Restoration, gave her a unique perspective as well as friends from every period. She also had personal links with the sovereigns and heads of government of every country in Europe. In 1814 her salon was the most important meeting place in Europe, and it was said that the three great powers in Europe were now Britain, Russia and Madame de Staël.

Madame de Staël proceeded to use that power to promote the Constitutional Charter, and was present when it was promulgated on 4 June at the château de Saint-Ouen, scene of her childhood. Although she was proud to recall that 'the declaration signed by Louis XVIII in 1814, at Saint-Ouen, included almost all the articles safeguarding liberty, which M. Necker had proposed to Louis XVI in 1789, before the Revolution had broken out', she believed it to be a great mistake that the King had chosen to 'grant' the Charter. Surely the Revolution and all that had come afterwards had established the nation as sovereign, and a truly constitutional monarchy could only be founded on a contract between the people and the monarch? The preamble had also contained glaring mistakes, such as that all authority resided in the person of the King. 'Such pretensions exposed the throne to danger even more than they threatened the nation's rights.'[13] As soon as the Charter was signed, the Tsar, accompanied by the King of Prussia and Marshal Blücher, left for the peace celebrations in London.

Madame de Staël's salon resumed not only its former brilliance but also its heterogeneity. 'She admitted all shades of opinions and all forms of expression while fighting to the last for the cause she supported. But she always ended with a courteous laying down of arms, not ever wishing to deprive her salon of any person capable of adding to the variety of opinion,' recalled Madame de Boigne.[14] But there was one notable absentee from her salon – the Duke of Wellington. Madame de Staël had still not met the Duke, the man she most admired in Europe, as he had been absent in Spain throughout her time in England. But at the end of June she was able at last to write proudly to her cousin: 'Lord Wellington spent the evening with me the day before yesterday. Of his two days in Paris, he gave me one. It is his simplicity which excites one's admiration.' Perhaps it was not only his simplicity. With great gallantry the famous warrior had knelt at her feet!

She had also seen the King alone on the previous day. He had assured her that he acknowledged her father's deposit in the state treasury and would take steps to ensure that it was paid.[15] The recovery of her father's money was more important than ever now that there was the question of Albertine's dowry. Rumours about Albertine's engagement to the young Duc de Broglie were already circulating. Of the highest rank, extremely intelligent, politically active and a liberal, Victor de Broglie was the grandson of Marshal de Broglie who, as a fervent royalist, had opposed Necker and had died in exile, refusing to return to France. His son, Victor's father, who had been a liberal, was guillotined during the Terror. Madame de Staël had helped to save his wife and son. For a time, during the Terror, when they had escaped to England, they had lived in a cottage not far from Juniper Hall in Surrey. A great friend of Auguste, young Victor de Broglie – outwardly terse and somewhat priggish, although his letters and memoirs show sensitivity, kindness and a dry sense of humour – was respected for his intelligence and was widely expected to be a minister soon. But he knew that before he could fulfil his political ambitions he would need to repair his family fortune, which had been completely ruined during the Revolution.

'Madame de Staël', he recalled in his memoirs, 'welcomed me kindly; she was fond of titles, historic names, and liberal views . . . she was resigned to the Restoration, but with no illusions, no aversions, no prejudice for or against . . . I soon saw her daily or almost; I called on her regularly in the evening or in the morning, both in Paris and at Clichy where she stayed during the summer. I was an intimate friend of her son, whose elder I was by several years. . . . I knew M. Rocca but little. When Madame de Staël came back to France he was already mortally ill and condemned to absolute isolation and silence. One only saw him from a distance. From the very few words we exchanged he left me with the impression of an original mind, abrupt and naïve . . . which must have had something singularly attractive about it.'[16]

In spite of all the newly regained pleasures of Paris, Madame de Staël left for Coppet in the middle of July because of Rocca's health. She hoped that the mountain air of his native land would do him good. Besides, she had been away for more than two years. The villagers of Coppet welcomed her back like a returning heroine with songs, flowers and fireworks. On arrival she went at once to pray at her father's tomb. She was more anxious than ever about money, anxious to get Albertine married soon, so that she and Rocca could marry and legitimize their child before one of them died. Alphonse, or 'little us', now two, was still at Longirod in the care of the pastor and his wife. Madame de Staël and Rocca paid a secret visit. The child was well, but backward and timid with an over-large head. No member of the family had the slightest idea of his existence except for the faithful Fanny Randall, who would visit him from time to time. Meanwhile Madame de Staël settled to work on her *Considérations* and on a poem, 'Richard Coeur de Lion', while Albertine enjoyed the pleasures of Coppet, which she had always loved far more than her mother.

That first summer after the fall of Napoleon, the English, deprived of foreign travel for so long, flooded the continent. Many of Madame de Staël's friends found their way to Coppet. The Mackintoshes, the Davys, Lord Canning, William Romilly, Lady Charlotte Campbell and her daughters all visited her, joining Schlegel, Bonstetten and Sismondi, the inner core of the Coppet group. Joseph Bonaparte, who had escaped to Switzerland after his brother's fall, had bought the nearby château of Prangins and the two happily renewed their friendship. One day someone came to tell Madame de Staël that Napoleon's life was in danger – assassins were on their way to Elba. Never one to bear the smallest grudge personally, she rushed around to warn Joseph. He was at dinner with the actor Talma. Perhaps overwhelmed by the drama of the situation, Madame de Stael offered to go to Elba herself. Joseph declined her kind offer, thereby depriving history of a wonderful scene – Napoleon's face at Madame de Staël's arrival! But Joseph had immediately sent off a man to warn Napoleon, who was grateful, and sent his thanks, even going so far as to admit later that Madame de Staël would have been less dangerous to him in Paris than in exile. For the time being, with Paris under occupation and the fate of France in foreign hands, perhaps Madame de Staël was able, once again, to identify Napoleon with France. Perhaps, too, the fallen and disgraced Emperor had ceased in her mind to be the Corsican tyrant and had become simply an exile and a prisoner who needed help. Madame de Staël had already intervened with the Swiss authorities who threatened to arrest Joseph, and on her return to Paris enlisted Wellington's help to ensure that Joseph was left in peace.[17]

She was back in Paris at the end of September 1814. Her early return was due to a pressing need to pursue the matter of her father's money, for Albertine could not get married without a dowry. The Duc de Broglie who, Mackintosh recalled that autumn, 'was courting Albertine more assiduously than usual', was everything Madame de Staël could have wished for. Madame de Boigne remembered Madame de Staël's happiness on being back in Paris: 'increased I think by her joy in the youthful beauty of her charming daughter. In spite of the rather daring [red] colour of her hair, and a few freckles, Albertine de Staël was one of the most ravishing young women I have ever met; her face had an angelic, pure, ideal quality which I have only seen in her. Her mother rejoiced in her and was proud of her.' Madame de Staël always said that she was determined that Albertine would not suffer the unhappiness she had suffered and, Madame de Boigne added wittily, 'she would force her daughter to marry for love!'[18]

In Paris Madame de Staël found Constant sighing over Madame Récamier. On 31 August he had noted in his journal: 'Dined at the club. Madame Récamier. Good Lord! Am I going off my head?' And a little later, 'The day was all Juliette's. I am not yet loved, but she is attracted to me; there are few women unaffected by my way of being both absorbed and dominated by them.'[19] Madame Récamier, who liked to make every man fall in love with her while remaining chastely distant, had another motive this time. She had hoped to enlist Constant's help and support to keep her friend Murat on the throne of Naples. Instead he mooned over her like a schoolboy, bombarding her with embarrassingly ardent love letters. He had been afraid of what Madame de Staël would think. To his annoyance she had not minded much, merely warning him of Madame Récamier's inability to love.

The Duke of Wellington, who had returned to Paris in August as ambassador was now installed in his splendid new embassy, the Hôtel de Charost in the rue du Faubourg Saint Honoré. The house, with a courtyard in front and a garden which then ran down to the Champs-Élysées, had belonged to Princess Pauline Borghese, Napoleon's youngest and favourite sister. Wellington had bought it for the British government complete with all its furniture. 'Lord Wellington dined with me yesterday,' Madame de Staël wrote to her cousin on 30 September 1814. 'He is very much the fashion here and his manners are simple and noble. History will only increase his greatness,' she added prophetically.[20] Constant records that they attended a ball at the embassy that day.[21] Madame de Staël and Wellington had immense respect and admiration for each other, and a genuine bond grew between them. But their relationship was not always easy. Sometimes their political disputes even reached the press.

Madame de Staël had challenged Wellington publicly over the American war of 1812–14 declared by President Madison over shipping rights and the Great Lakes, which were declared neutral territory by virtue of the peace treaty signed in Ghent on 24 December 1814. *The Times* of 14 October 1814 reported: 'Madame de Staël . . . has lately returned and resides within a mile or two of Paris, where her salon has become, as heretofore, the central point of the literary, political and fashionable world. It would appear that she has taken under her protection the United States as well as the house of Bourbon; for lately on hearing of the capture of Washington, she pronounced an oration in favour of that government which, as it happened to be in the presence of our Ambassador, seemed to be a challenge to his Grace to prove that the sword is not his only weapon. The Duke of Wellington did all that Bonaparte himself could not do – he silenced her.' Madame de Staël confirmed this in a letter to Thomas Jefferson a year later, when she mentions that she had supported 'your American cause against a very noble adversary, the Duke of Wellington'.[22]

Both *The Times* and the Duke were flattering themselves, however. She was to have plenty more to say to him, almost to her dying breath. Wellington, however tiresome he sometimes thought her, always spoke of her with the greatest affection: 'She was a most agreeable woman, if only you could keep her light and away from politics. But that was not easy. She was always trying to come to matters of State. I have said to her more than once, "*je déteste parler politique*"', the Duke recalled after her death, to which she had answered '*Parler politique pour moi, c'est vivre.*'[23]

One of Wellington's tasks in Paris was to persuade the French King to abolish the slave trade in his colonies – a matter of major importance to British public opinion. To help change views in France, Wellington enlisted Madame de Staël's help to translate, write and publish abolitionist literature. Only a fortnight after her return to Paris, Madame de Staël had written to Miss Berry, asking her to 'tell Wilberforce that the Emperor of Russia has told me that the abolition of the Slave Trade will take place at the Congress [of Vienna]'.

She now wrote a preface to a work by Wilberforce, translated into French by Albertine (who was rewarded with a gold pen by her mother), tracing the development of the political struggle which had culminated in the abolition of the slave trade in Britain in 1807. Madame de Staël and the Iron Duke were ultimately successful, at least in France, where the King promised to abolish the slave trade within five years. In Vienna, Castlereagh and after him Wellington himself, fought for worldwide abolition, achieving a declaration condemning the slave trade in the final act of the Congress which was signed in June 1815.

Albertine's engagement to the Duc de Broglie was announced on 15 February 1815. 'The courtiers say that there was but one Jacobin duke and that Madame de Staël has just got what suited both her vanity and her opinions,' wrote Lady Mackintosh. 'His fortune is very small and his manners disagreeable. But he has very considerable talents and perfectly reasonable opinions. He is forward, eager, dogmatic and disputatious.'[24] Madame de Staël was absolutely delighted. Everything about this young man suited her. 'I cannot congratulate myself enough on the marriage of my daughter. M. de Broglie really is the only Englishman in France,' she wrote delightedly to Lady Davy,[25] and to Meister: 'The Duc de Broglie has everything except fortune, he is a man of rare intelligence and admirable education.'[26]

Nor had Albertine, serious and highly intelligent, but unlike her mother cool-headed and much less romantic, needed to be 'forced'. 'My mother has given me leave to announce my forthcoming marriage to the Duc de Broglie,' she wrote to the Duchess of Devonshire: 'you were so good to me in England that I dare to hope in your continued interest in me. This marriage is entirely *English*, in that it is founded on mutual affection . . .' Her mother added a postscript: 'We are so happy and it is to M. de Blacas that we owe it, for without a very small payment, but at least a payment of some sort, we could not have made the necessary arrangements.'[27] The Duc de Blacas, Secretary of State and Minister of the King's household, had obtained a repayment of part of her father's two million, promised to her by the King.

The atmosphere in Paris was such, however, that both she and Constant thought that the tensions between Bonapartists and royalists in France could lead to full scale revolt. There was still a great deal of sympathy for Bonaparte in France, particularly in the army which was Bonapartist to a man. French resentment against the foreigners occupying their country had grown. The English, so popular in the spring of 1814, were now hated. Wellington in particular, who had been cheered when he had arrived from Spain on his way to England, was now dubbed '*Monsieur Vilainton*' for his casual manners and simple style of dress, which were seen as arrogance. Louis XVIII's anglophilia only increased his growing unpopularity. As Madame de Staël had predicted, Napoleon began to be identified not with tyranny but with the freedom and independence of France. By the spring of 1815 there were people openly wearing bunches of violets in their buttonholes – a symbol of Napoleon as opposed to the white lily of the Bourbons.

On 6 March 1815, the bombshell fell. Napoleon had escaped from Elba and was on his way to Paris. A few days later he was in Lyons at the head of the troops who had been sent to oppose him. In Vienna, the coalition which had all but dissolved, came together again and issued a proclamation that same day which read simply: 'Napoleon Bonaparte has placed himself outside the pale of civil and social relations and rendered himself subject to public vengeance.'

'No, I will never forget the moment when I learned through one of my friends on the morning of 6 March 1815, that Bonaparte had landed on the French Coast. I was unhappily able to foresee all the sad consequences of that event there and then, exactly as they have occurred since, and I believed that the earth would open up before me. For several days after that man's triumph I was completely denied even the solace of prayer and in my trouble, I felt that God had abandoned the earth and had no wish to communicate with his creatures,' Madame de Staël wrote in *Considérations*.'[28]

To the Bonapartist Comte de Lavalette and to the Prince de Beauveau, who occupied the apartments above hers at the Hôtel Lamoignon, and who were urging her not to leave, she could only say: 'Liberty is done for if Bonaparte wins – national independence if he loses.' Another friend, Villemain, who saw her that day, recalled how she had looked. She was 'not the historian [of the *Considérations*], but the victim of *Dix anńees d'exil* . . . Without her usual headdress, at once brilliant and unkempt, without that scarlet turban which half covered her thick black hair and matched the magnificent brilliance of her eyes, Madame de Staël did not seem to be the same person. Her face was drawn; it seemed sick with sorrow. That spiritual fire which usually flickered back and forth across her features, animating them with a thousand subtle expressions, was now marked by an extraordinary look of deep and penetrating anxiety; a sort of attempt to divine her own sorrow.'[29] 'Bonaparte hates me,' she had said to Lavalette; 'he hates me, my father, my friends, all our opinions, the spirit of 1789, the Charter, France's liberty and Europe's independence. He will be here tomorrow. What sort of games will he play at first? I don't know. But you know what he said at Lyons; his general promises of forgetting and his proscriptions against individuals. His claws are already fully out, before he has sprung on us. I have no army between us and I do not wish to be his prisoner for I will never be his supplicant.'[30]

She resolved to go as quickly as possible. After taking leave of the King, she had tried to persuade Madame Récamier to go with her. Madame Récamier, believing herself safe enough under the protection of her friend Queen Hortense (the Empress Josephine's daughter, who had been married against her wishes to Napoleon's unstable brother Louis, who became King of Holland), chose to remain. Hortense, while remaining a Bonapartist, was a great favourite of the Tsar, who had spent much of his time in Paris at her salon. She had been given the title of the Duchesse de St Leu at his request.

Madame de Staël left Paris for Coppet on 11 March with Albertine, Rocca and Schlegel. Auguste and Victor de Broglie were to stay to press for the return of the balance of Necker's millions, without which Albertine's marriage would have to be postponed indefinitely. Once again, just as her financial affairs were about to be settled, everything had been overturned. Her last thoughts were for Constant who had decided to remain in Paris.

In a hurried note to Madame Récamier, written on the morning of her departure, she scribbled: 'Make B. [Benjamin] leave. I am extremely anxious about him after what he has written.'[31] On 6 March, immediately after the news of Napoleon's escape from Elba, Constant had published an article in the *Journal de Paris* in favour of the Bourbons. In it he branded Napoleon forever a tyrant: 'He promises peace but his very name is a signal for war. He promises victory, yet three times – in Egypt, Spain and Russia – he deserted his armies like a coward.'

A few days later, on 19 March, as Louis XVIII's carriage lumbered out of Paris on its way to Ghent, Constant published another article in the *Journal des Débats*, praising Louis XVIII and branding Napoleon an Attila and a Ghenghis Khan, ending: 'I will not go, a wretched deserter, to drag myself from one seat of power to another; nor disguise infamy with sophism, muttering profane words in order to buy a disgraced life.'[32] The next day, 20 March 1815, the first of the hundred days left to him in France, Napoleon was back at the Tuileries.

Chapter 26

The Return of the Exile

'We were good friends and she asked for me on her deathbed.'
Wellington

MADAME DE STAËL need not have worried about Constant. Exactly a month later, in April 1815, he was helping Napoleon to draft the new Constitutional document, the *Acte additionel aux constitutions de l'Empire*. To his enemies, and to many of his friends, it seemed the action of a complete opportunist and yet there is some truth in Constant's justification of his actions in his *Mémoires sur les Cent-Jours*, published soon after Waterloo. His first impulse had been to take Madame de Staël's advice and flee. A week later, with the King gone and Napoleon back, he changed his mind. It was clear that the Emperor could not rule as a tyrant. At the beginning of April, after assurances from Joseph, Fouché and others close to the Emperor, Constant had offered his services to Fouché, who was back once again as Minister of Police. A few days later he was invited to see the Emperor. 'If there is any way of governing through a constitution so much the better,' Napoleon had said to him frankly. 'I had wanted the Empire of the world, and to get it I needed absolute power . . . but to govern France alone perhaps a Constitution would be better . . . See what you think might be possible; bring me your ideas . . . Public meetings, free elections, ministerial responsibility, freedom of the press, . . . I want all that, especially the freedom of the press . . . to silence it is absurd,' declared the new, born-again liberal. 'I am convinced of that . . . I am a man of the people, if the people truly want liberty I owe it to them. I don't hate liberty . . . I pushed it aside when it was in my way but I understand it, I was brought up in its ideals . . . I long for peace but I will only get it through victories.' Napoleon had been completely realistic: 'I have no wish to give you false hope. I am allowing them to say that negotiations are going on. There are no negotiations. I foresee a hard struggle, a long war. To sustain it I need the nation's support. But I believe that it will want freedom in exchange . . . It shall have it. This is a new situation. I am more than happy to learn. I am getting old. One is not the same man at forty-five that one was at thirty. The peace of a constitutional monarch might suit me. It will suit my son even more no doubt.'[1]

In spite of warning letters from Madame de Staël and La Fayette, Constant came out of the interview convinced, if not of the Emperor's good intentions, at least of the new imperatives. The Emperor needed the Liberals and this might be a way to establish a Constitution in France at long last. His own time had come, he believed! Napoleon could hardly have been more clear. He knew perfectly well that the real decisions about his future and that of France would be made on the battlefield. But first he must consolidate his position in France. He had been defeated not by the allied sovereigns but by liberal ideas. He accepted a two-chamber assembly, a free press and the abolition of censorship. Later, on St Helena, he admitted that his intention had been to 'sending the chambers packing' once victory was his. After a long meeting with the Emperor on 14 April, Constant wrote in his journal: 'He is an astonishing man. Tomorrow I am to bring him a draft Constitution.'[2]

Madame de Staël remained unconvinced of the Emperor's good intentions. To someone who had been sent to tell her that the Emperor had heard how generous she had been to him in his misfortune, she replied tartly that he must also know how much she detested him. Joseph Bonaparte now attempted to enlist her help. He did so with a subtle mixture of flattery, promises and the bribe of ensuring the repayment of her father's money. If Madame de Staël came back to Paris, he intimated, she would be able to speak and write freely, indeed, she would find the Emperor in agreement with views which were also shared by the nation! Fouché, too, wrote to her on 24 March, to declare his personal interest in 'the delicacy of Mademoiselle de Staël's position' and offering a peerage to her son-in-law. But she must return to Paris.[3] Madame Necker-de Saussure recalled that Madame de Staël had said to her: 'The Emperor has done without a constitution and without me for twelve years; he does not love one any more than the other.'[4]

Before the Constitution had been adopted, she wrote to Constant: 'I am not attached to the royalists. If the Emperor grants full liberty he will become the legitimate government as far as I'm concerned.' But who, she wondered, would be able to resist him if, having returned to power, he did not keep his promise? Perhaps Constant should have waited a little, but her mind, she admitted, was much more occupied with Albertine's affairs. Would Constant consider either paying back half of what he owed her (40,000 francs) to help Albertine, or engage to pay the interest on that sum monthly? She believed that if he could afford to lose large sums gambling, he could help Albertine.[5] 'A letter from Madame de Staël. She would like me to do nothing for my own fortune and to give her the little I have. Neither one nor the other!' he wrote furiously in his journal.[6]

Another letter now reminded him that he had promised to pay back half his debt on Albertine's marriage. As a well-paid Councillor of State that should present no problem, she wrote, adding: 'I passionately hope that you will be faithful to the Constitution. The respect in which you will be held will depend on it. Think of Albertine's situation, I beg you . . . all the means I have, I use for her. – Please love her – her at least.'[7]

Constant's fury was probably a measure of his own uncertainty. His vile threat in reply was that he would publish her former letters to him if she did not leave him alone. For once, fully justified, Madame de Staël blasted him by return of post, for a cad, an ingrate, a worthless gambler and a man of no principle. 'What a harpy!' he wrote in his journal. His reply, accusing her of censoriousness, brought another blast. Money alone decided his political and private conduct, she wrote. 'If you had treated the ugliest and stupidest servant girl, but one who had loved you as I loved you, as you have treated me, you would still be what you are – the most profoundly embittered and indelicate creature on earth . . . you found it necessary to tell my daughter, that you had never loved any woman for more than three months; the miserable statement of a roué, which you should have spared Albertine's innocence.' While prepared to accept his help on Albertine's behalf, she ends with the hope that she might never see him again. All her communications henceforth would be through her lawyers.[8]

Madame de Staël knew as clearly as Napoleon that the war was not yet over, but believed that he would lose it. However great her misgivings about Napoleon's return and his intentions, she cared passionately about the future of France. From Coppet, she continued to bring her considerable influence to bear on European public opinion in defence of France, writing letters to anyone who might make a difference. 'Allow me not to desire your success,' she wrote to Lord Harrowby. 'What will you do when you are in Paris once again? What will happen to us if you divide France? May God preserve us from a victory for Bonaparte! But if you become masters of France what a humiliation for that country . . . I return to the same hope I expressed in England [that Bonaparte should be] *victorious and killed.* What I mean by victorious is to defend France as she was. We cannot see her invaded by foreign troops without pain . . . I say nothing of the past, the mistakes of your Congress which played into Bonaparte's hands so well, but in the future do not dismember France, do not humiliate her! While she is very susceptible to low dealing from within, she will not bear humiliation imposed by others.' Foreign troops had made themselves hated. She had quarrelled with two of her closest friends, Constant and Sismondi, and 'the terrible alternative of betraying my country or supporting a tyrant condemns me to the most complete inactivity. I am alone here with my children. I am finishing my *Considérations sur la Révolution française*, and leaving a great empty space for whatever happens next.'[9]

Ten days before Waterloo, on 8 June 1815, she wrote to the Tsar: 'Sire, in the present crisis in Europe there will be no shortage of people to tell you that your generosity was the reason for our present sorrows . . . Were France to be dismembered in any way new troubles would arise; she would not obey any but a constitutional King, and if it was thought this time to abolish all principles of liberty, it would be like burying a volcano: the explosion would be all the more terrible afterwards.' But the mood of the Tsar was no longer what it had been in Paris in the previous year. Then he had been hailed as the liberator of Europe, now he could only wait for the outcome of the war, which was in Wellington's hands. The instability of his character was more apparent every month. Increasingly religious and superstitious, he had been reading occult works daily. His reply was polite but not encouraging. He understood that she should have occupied her spare time with such important matters, but he hoped that his contemporaries would desist from premature judgements about a period in which he had taken an active part, which was better left to history, he wrote pointedly.[10]

Napoleon's hopes of rallying liberal opinion through his Constitution were much less successful than he hoped. Fear of conscription was uppermost in every family. The elections of May 1815 had returned a Liberal, not a Bonapartist majority. His only hope now lay where he had always known it would – on the battlefield. On 12 June, with allied forces massing on the frontiers, he left Paris for his headquarters at Laon. In Brussels Wellington waited with an army of 100,000 English, Dutch, Hanoverian and Belgian troops. On 18 June, standing under a poplar near a hop field outside Ghent, during a pause in a solitary walk, Chateaubriand suddenly heard the distant thunder of cannon. It was only at one o'clock the next morning that a letter from Pozzo di Borgo, the Russian ambassador, to Louis XVIII, announced the news: Napoleon had been defeated at Waterloo by the allied armies under the command of Wellington and Blücher.[11]

Napoleon abdicated two days later. On 15 July, a hundred days after his return to France, he embarked on a British ship, HMS *Bellerophon*. Two weeks later he sailed to St Helena, and into history. The King returned to Paris in early July. Chateaubriand was there to witness the arrival of the two ministers who had been responsible for his return. He recorded it in a famous passage: 'Suddenly a door opened. Silently in came Vice, leaning on the arm of Crime. It was M. de Talleyrand, supported by M. Fouché. The infernal vision passed slowly before me, entered the King's chamber, and disappeared. Fouché had come to swear faith and allegiance to his lord. On his knees the loyal regicide placed the hands which had caused the beheading of Louis XVI into those of the martyred King's brother, while the apostate Bishop stood surety for the oath.'[12]

As a Councillor of State, Constant had seen Napoleon regularly throughout the Hundred Days. The *Acte additionel*, known mockingly as the *Benjamine*, did indeed provide for many liberal safeguards, but it satisfied no one. Constant's new position at Napoleon's court, a month after he had publicly asserted that he would rather die than join him, had provoked general derision. Under strong attack from all sides, Constant published his justification of the Hundred Days on 19 March 1815. There was still one person whose opinion mattered to him above all others. Believing that Madame de Staël would never wish to see him again, he had asked Madame Récamier to send it to her. Incapable of bearing a grudge for long, Madame de Staël wrote to him herself. 'Your justification is perfect,' she reassured him, 'but I felt shattered as I read it – there is no chance of anyone being able to attack you on legal grounds. Only your friends are saddened by the extreme unsteadiness of your character – you have perfect answers for your enemies . . . Everyone says that had you not written that article on the 19th there would be nothing to say against you. God has willed it that you should hold everything in your hands, but a bad fairy makes you throw it all away. Have courage none the less, support the French cause, do not let yourself go, and try and adopt some unshakeable principles.' Of course she would see him when she returned to Paris in the spring. Sismondi, from whom she had been estranged during the Hundred Days because of his support for Constant, was staying with her, ill and 'sad to a degree which is pitiful, but what does friendship mean except mutual support in bad times?'[13]

Madame de Staël knew that the fate of France lay in the hands of the Allies, and that it was the British who would moderate the demands for reparation. Believing that a lasting peace depended on the restoration of the Bourbons, Wellington presented the Allies with a fait accompli by bringing the King back to Paris. Madame de Staël's admiration for him, already great, now knew no bounds. In August, writing to congratulate him 'for a glory without reproach . . . recognized and felt universally', she nevertheless reminded him that 'one must not humiliate twenty-four million people if one wishes to give the world peace'. The King, she suggested, would not be able to keep his throne if war reparations were too harsh – 'do not allow your work to be undone, milord, its existence is a monument worthy of you and its duration will depend on a quick end to France's troubles.'[14]

The Tsar, in his highly religious mood, returned to Paris on 10 July. He now proposed a pact of Holy Alliance, based on the precepts of the gospels. Metternich, who had thought it empty of meaning, had craftily redrafted the Tsar's proposals to suit his own plans. Castlereagh, too, had thought it 'a piece of sublime mysticism and nonsense', to which he and Wellington had found it difficult to listen 'with becoming gravity'.[15] The more earthly Quadruple Alliance between Britain, Austria, Prussia and Russia was signed after much bargaining at the end of November. Castlereagh and Wellington had managed to temper the demands of Prussia, supported by Russia, for Alsace, Lorraine and Lille – a punitive settlement which would have undermined the second Restoration of Louis XVIII and might have led to another war. By the terms of the Treaty of Paris, signed on 29

November 1815, France would have to draw back to her 1790 borders, accept allied occupation for the time being and pay war reparations. The Congress System, as it was called, was put in place, ensuring regular meetings by the Allies. But perhaps the most painful article in the treaty and the one most discussed in the salons, was that which had proposed to return the looted treasures of Europe to their respective countries.

Rocca's health had grown steadily worse throughout the autumn and his doctors had prescribed a milder climate. In November, instead of returning to Paris, where the presence of Prussians in particular caused her acute anguish, and where, as she wrote to Madame Récamier, she would make needless enemies, Madame de Staël went to Italy where she planned to spend the winter. The end of the year found her in Pisa, with Albertine, Rocca and Schlegel. There she commissioned sculptures of her father, Albertine and Rocca from the sculptor Tieck, while she awaited the arrival of Victor de Broglie and Auguste.

After more than a quarter of a century, Necker's two million had at last been repaid. Albertine was married to Victor de Broglie in Pisa on 20 February 1816. Only two hours after the marriage ceremony, Madame de Staël wrote to Albertine Necker-de Saussure: 'Four o'clock – it is done, my dear friend. The first ceremony, the Catholic one, did not move me in the slightest . . . but when the words of the English liturgy were spoken, my heart almost broke. I was holding my father's portrait and I thought of you all the time.'[16] Rocca had just managed to attend the ceremony but looked so ill that Sismondi, who was one of the witnesses, thought he might die at any moment. Both Madame de Staël and Albertine wrote to Constant to announce the marriage. If his paternity was never referred to openly, it was always there, the unexpressed sub-text in all their dealings. He wrote to his cousin Rosalie that the Duc de Broglie 'is a man of rare honesty and with the most unprejudiced mind that I have ever seen. He is also of a rare goodness and with something very attractive in his manner. I hope that he will make Albertine happy and be happy too.'[17]

Soon after the departure of the young couple for Rome, Madame de Staël, Rocca and Schlegel went to Florence where they remained until the end of May, to give Rocca the maximum time in the sun. In Florence Madame de Staël renewed old friendships and made new ones, especially with Priscilla Burgersh, Wellington's niece. 'Italy is extremely agreeable now that the English are travelling again,' she wrote to Constant, 'one can enjoy their company and the sun, a rare combination.' To Constant, disconsolate in England for the publication of his novel, she expressed the hope of returning to Paris for the winter if Rocca's health permitted, and then there was the journey to Greece, which she still hoped to make 'so that I might write a last work before I die, which would express new ideas which I believe are still in me.' The novel, *Adolphe*, written several years before, had been published in England and Paris that summer. Everyone recognized the main characters as Madame de Staël and himself, although he had published a denial. A letter from her, which he noted with relief, 'shows that my novel has not estranged us.'[18]

Madame de Staël and her family returned to Coppet a month later, in June 1816, for what was to be her last and perhaps her most brilliant summer there, despite the weather which was memorably bad. Geneva was now free, and many of the Swiss liberals came to Coppet to discuss the future of their city, over which there was strong disagreement with many of the city fathers who were anything but liberal. Coppet, which had been the headquarters of European liberal resistance to Napoleon for the past ten years, now became 'the general headquarters of European thought', as Stendhal was to call it. 'Voltaire never had anything to compare,' he wrote. 'There were six hundred of the most distinguished people in Europe by that lakeside'; almost a court, with writers, artists, aristocrats, politicians, scholars, scientists and students among them, Italians, Germans, Swiss, French, Russians, Poles, Greeks, all flocking to see the 'Empress of thought'. Most of all there were Madame de Staël's English friends, such as the Landsdownes, the Jerseys and Henry Brougham. The latter found Switzerland intolerably boring, writing to his friend Creevey: 'It is a country to be in for two hours . . . Ennui comes on the third hour, and suicide attacks you before night. There is no resource whatever for passing the time, except looking at lakes and hills, which is over immediately. I should except Madame de Staël whose house is a great comfort.'[19]

The only absentee from Coppet was the Duchess of Devonshire, who had arrived in Florence just as Madame de Staël left. Letters between them flew back and forth however. Madame de Staël wrote to her at the end of July to announce that Albertine was pregnant and that she would have to go with her to Paris, although she would have preferred to take Rocca back to Italy that winter. The Broglie marriage was going well. Madame de Staël believed it would be a lasting one. 'He is a man, steady in every way,' she wrote of her son-in-law.

The same could not be said of Lord Byron, but 'he is the great poet I know and admire and his domestic affairs cannot concern others.'[20] Byron had escaped from England, and from the scandal following the collapse of his marriage, and was working on the third canto of *Childe Harold* at the Villa Diodati across the lake. Madame de Staël told Madame d'Albany that no one received him except her. He was to spend much time at Coppet until his departure for Italy in early October 1816. On his first visit he had found the room 'full of strangers, who had come to stare at me as at some outlandish beast . . .'. He noticed on arrival that a lady was being carried out. 'It is true that Mrs Hervey [William Beckford's sister] (she writes novels) fainted at my entrance to Coppet, and then came back again. The Duchess de Broglie exclaimed, "this is too much – at sixty-five years of age!",' he wrote to John Murray with amusement.[21] He was delighted to find himself in such congenial society – the Abbé de Brême, a friend of the Italian poet and patriot Ugo Foscolo, who was staying at Coppet, was an important influence on Byron's growing interest in the Italian revolutionary movement.

Madame de Staël also managed to involve Henry Brougham in the cause of the northern Italians, then under Austrian oppression, a cause Brougham took to his heart. In a long letter to her, which Brougham asks her to show to the Abbé de Brême, he writes: 'It seems to me quite possible to interest both Parliament and public opinion in England in favour of the Italians, and he went on to explain how the matter might be brought before the House of Commons.[22] Brougham was to become a great friend of both Auguste and Victor de Broglie, on whom he was a lasting influence. Broglie, who was involved in the reform of the French legal system and had a particular interest in the liberty of the individual, 'put his kindness to the test by questioning him on rules of procedure in England'. Brougham had produced a memorandum for him, which inspired Broglie to go to England in the early 1820s to study English law more thoroughly.[23]

Madame de Staël and Byron exchanged books and occasionally teased one another. He wondered whether Eleonore in *Adolphe* was a portrait of her – something which she vehemently denied – and lent her Walter Scott's *Antiquary*, while Madame de Staël naughtily lent him her copy of Lady Caroline Lamb's *Glenarvon*, with its highly romantic and recognizable portrait of himself. If he was in the least put out, he hid it well, even composing an epigram: 'I read *Glenarvon* too, by Caro Lamb – God damn!'. 'She has made Coppet as agreeable as society and talent can make any place on earth,' he wrote to Murray that autumn.[24] Ostracized by many of his countrymen, he was treated with almost motherly concern by Madame de Staël, who even tried to effect a reconciliation with his wife. 'To say that I am merely sorry to hear of Lady B[yron]'s illness is to say nothing – but she had herself deprived me of the right to say more,' he wrote to Madame de Staël. 'The separation may have been my fault – but it was her choice. I tried all means to prevent it and – and would do as much and more to end it – you asked me if I thought that Lady B was attached to me. To that I can only answer that I love her.'[25] From Italy, Byron wrote to Moore: 'I am indebted for many kind courtesies to Our Lady of Coppet – & I now love her – as much as I always did her works – of which I was and am a great admirer.'[26]

On 10 October, after the departure of the last of her visitors and her children, 'Anne Germaine Louise Necker, widow of the Baron de Staël-Holstein and the Chevalier (of the Légion d'Honneur) Albert Jean Michel Rocca', were secretly married at Coppet in the presence of the minister, Guillaume Gerlach. There were only two witnesses: Fanny Randall and Rocca's brother Charles. In the marriage document, signed in her new name de Rocca, though she would never use it publicly, they recognized Louis-Alphonse as their legitimate child. Two days later Madame de Staël drew up a new will. 'I look forward to seeing you, and Mathieu, despite everything, and Prosper, . . . and then the streets,' she wrote to Madame Récamier, referring to her beloved Paris, as she prepared to leave Coppet.[27]

Paris in the autumn of 1816, after Louis XVIII's second restoration, was occupied by 150,000 foreign troops. The Hundred Days had resulted in a much less moderate political scene. There were three dynastic groups: Bourbonists, Orleanists and Bonapartists, while politically there were supporters for everything from autocracy through parliamentarism to revolution, with Catholicism, militarism and nationalism for extra colour. The elections in August had swept in the Ultras, extreme royalists who were much more reactionary than the King and supported his brother Artois. Madame de Boigne, who was an Orleanist, described them as 'mad, unbalanced, ignorant, hot-headed and reactionary, dominated by the interests of their caste'.[28] The new Assembly, the reactionary *Chambre introuvable*, had proved too much to deal with, even for Talleyrand. In September it was dissolved, and Talleyrand and Fouché dismissed. In the elections that followed, the Duc de Richelieu, a man universally admired in all Europe, got a working majority. But the strongest party in parliament was still the Ultras, led by Villèle in the Chamber of Deputies, and by Montmorency, Chateaubriand and Polignac in the Chamber of Peers. Paradoxically they found themselves in opposition to the King, who was supported by the less fanatical royalists, with Richelieu on the right and Decazes, Minister of Police and the King's favourite. Constant, who was completely out of favour with the royalists following his defection to Napoloen during the Hundred Days, none the less contrived to advocate a parliamentary monarchy on the English model. He remained the chief theorist of the left, which included La Fayette and Manuel, known in the Chamber of Deputies as the Independants. The new generation of liberals on the centre left, the Doctrinaires, who now gathered around Madame de Staël, and who were to carry her political convictions triumphantly into the future, were led by her son-in-law Victor de Broglie and François Guizot, and included Camille Jordan, Prosper de Barante, Charles de Rémusat and Royer-Collard.

No sooner back in Paris and installed in the rue Royale, than Madame de Staël presented her newly married daughter at court and began to entertain all Paris in her salon. But she was far from well. Madame de Boigne remembered how exhausted she had looked: 'It was really sad to see her at the beginning of each evening party. She would arrive exhausted by her suffering [she suffered from severe and chronic insomnia] but after a while her mind would overcome her senses, and she was as brilliant as ever, as if she wanted to demonstrate her inimitable and unequalled superiority to the very end.'[29]

Wellington had been absent when she arrived. She regretted his absence both personally and for France, 'since she is so unfortunate as to depend on strangers, one must hope that the most noble among them should exercise his influence on the fate of France,' she wrote to him at the end of October. Madame de Staël knew perfectly well that the British government wanted to keep the army of occupation in France, something which she found intolerable. With Napoleon now gone, all her efforts were bent to persuading the Allies to be as liberal and as generous as possible towards France. There had been a row with Canning at her salon, which Sir Charles Stewart, the British ambassador, had naturally reported. Wellington was perfectly aware of the importance of her support for the monarchy and of her influence. After expressing all manner of regrets and politenesses he went straight to the heart of the problem in his reply. 'I have no wish to begin our disputes so soon, though your letter tempts me to greatly. It seems to me to be in the nature of a challenge . . . I cannot help observing that you refer to yourself as French, when I had thought that you were on our side. I reclaim you. You are too precious to us to contemplate losing you in this way,' he joked. 'Do you recall that I once wished you a happy old age and that you might die with your head still on your shoulders?' He hoped that she might continue to be one of them, but 'I recognize the battlefields on which we shall meet, when I once again have the pleasure of arguing with you . . . And I will make sure to be well prepared.'[30]

Her reply that same evening, in which she suggests that in the Duke's absence France was 'subjected to British influence', annoyed the Duke so much that his response by return of post is written pell-mell, half in French and half in English: 'My presence in this country is founded upon treaties; the particular object of it and the conduct I am to pursue are defined in Declarations, and Instructions, the whole of which are before the Publick, and those who walk may read, and those who read may understand that France is anything but *soumise à l'influence Anglois*.' But, 'All of you who have such short memories, and such a strong imagination, you forget everything that has brought France to the situation she finds herself in, you forget where she was last year, and the far worse situation she might have found herself in as a result, and as the English were your Ennemies [sic] or rather you the Ennemies of the English during the whole course of the Revolutionary wars, and experience has now shown that they were next yourselves your most formidable enemies, national hatred now inspires you to cry that it is to England that we owe our misfortune, and that we are under English influence.'

If only she would stick to facts instead of allowing her imagination to take flight, the Duke continues crossly, she might see things as they are. 'The facts are to be found in the treaties,' he adds pointedly; not in Parliamentary debates, nor those of your Assembly, nor in your favourite newspapers, nor in the *Edinburgh Review* nor in Sir James Mackintosh's letters, nor yet in your salons. I will go one step further and tell you that although in War I always have done and always will do as much harm to France as is in my power, I will not lend myself to be the Instrument of carrying with execution in Peace, such a system as you suppose exists.' Having got that off his chest, he repeats that his absence from Paris is a pity only because it deprives him of the pleasure of arguing with her in person, but he issues a warning: 'Permit me to tell you frankly as I would if we were sitting alone beside your fire, that you are devilishly indiscreet, that even here I am constantly hearing reports about you which will do you serious harm, certainly in relation to your position with the King.' Knowing that she is fundamentally friendly towards the King, she must beware of criticizing the government, except to her most trusted friends . . . 'be discreet therefore' he recommends.[31]

Madame de Staël was hardly going to allow this to pass without comment. Suspecting Canning of making mischief between them, she writes: 'M. Canning, whose oratorical skills, diplomatic intelligence and parvenu ambitions you will be aware of, has played a less than worthy role here.' She had put it to Canning that France would never be at peace so long as she was occupied by foreign armies, that the war was fought against Bonaparte, and that it was unfair to treat France as Bonaparte had treated Prussia, to which Canning replied: 'We have conquered France, she is ours by right of conquest and we wish to exhaust her so that she might keep quiet for at least ten years.' 'In that case you are less generous than the Emperor of Russia who is proposing to withdraw thirty thousand men, something which would give us back hope and save us money', and this would speed up war reparation payments, she had retorted.

'You remind me of France's faults,' she continued passionately, addressing Wellington directly. 'I grant them – but the Bonapartist generation is withdrawing and the Jacobins are finished . . . If in the time of Charles II, Louis XIV's regiments had camped in Hyde Park, would there have been one Englishman, be he a Cromwellian, a Puritan or a Royalist who would not have felt despair? . . . I am French, the daughter of a man who most loved France, and the fate of Poland [partition] for my country fills me with horror . . . If I had the honour of being English, I think that I would not have wished the destruction of a nation which for five hundred years has been a worthy opponent of England, and which on the fields of Waterloo showed you milord, that at least, she knew how to die.'[32]

Letters – sometimes exasperated, but always respectful on his part; always putting the case for France but full of affectionate respect and admiration as well as political news on hers – flew back and forth between Wellington at his headquarters at Cambrai and Madame de Staël. Before his return, Wellington had been certain that the growing resentment against the army of occupation, and especially against England, precluded any possibility of a reduction in the number of troops. When he returned to Paris in the New Year of 1817, he saw for himself how seriously the situation had deteriorated. The harvest had failed, following an unusually cold and wet summer. There was widespread disaffection. Even the army of occupation was seriously affected by a shortage of forage. France's finances were at breaking point.

No sooner had news of his arrival reached her than Madame de Staël sent a note to the Duke. Wellington was now living around the corner from her at the Élysée. 'The same old story of the English, that the French are not made for freedom and must be governed with a rod of iron,' Madame de Staël had scribbled privately in a notebook that winter.[33] If Richelieu's government was to survive – which was what both she and the Duke wanted – troop reductions might give it a little popularity, she argued. It was largely through her influence that the Duke changed his mind. Their hopes for France were the same: a constitutional monarchy, supported by Parliament. In early January, Villèle, President of the Chamber of Deputies, was able to write: 'Wellington is decidedly on the side of the government through the good offices of Madame de Staël, who has played a great role here this year.'[34] In early January he had not only arranged loans for France with Barings Bank but had also persuaded the standing conference of the four ambassadors that troop reductions should begin to the tune of 30,000 men by April of that year. Nor did Madame de Staël hesitate to beg him to intercede on behalf of various friends, even though she knew well that she was running a risk of using up her credit with him.

Madame de Staël's health had been precarious for the past two years, and now took a turn for the worse. The same illness that had attacked her mother now tormented her, and she suffered with constant painful nervous cramps of the limbs which prevented her from getting any sleep unless heavily drugged. On 21 February, she attended a reception with her son-in-law (Albertine was in the ninth month of pregnancy) at the house of Decazes, Louis XVIII's chief minister. She had been particularly witty that evening, but while descending the stairs on the way out, she fell back senseless into Broglie's arms. She was carried to her coach and then to her bed where an attack of hydropsy (a probable stroke) was diagnosed, which quickly gave way to almost total paralysis. She was even unable to squeeze Rocca's hand to reassure him. Her legs were very swollen, and her skin darkened as she lay in a fever for the next two weeks.

Her friends gathered around her, first and foremost Mathieu de Montmorency, who, all political differences forgotten, hovered anxiously and guiltily around her. Madame de Boigne called on her before leaving Paris: 'The last time I saw her was in the morning; I was leaving the next day. For some days, she was not able to rise from her sofa; livid spots with which her face, her arms and her hands were covered told of a decomposition of the blood. I felt the sadness of an eternal parting, while her conversation was all about future plans.'[35]

Only Benjamin Constant, once the nearest and dearest of all her friends, was refused permission to see her. Was it Madame de Staël herself who did not wish it or was it her children, angry at the pain he had caused their mother, or perhaps worried that his presence might prove too much for her? 'Others see her, does she not wish to see me? Believe me the past is a terrible spectre when one fears for those to whom one has caused suffering . . . If it were to do her no harm please arrange for me to see her,' he begged Schlegel.[36]

On 1 March, Albertine de Broglie gave birth to her first child, Pauline. Madame de Staël, who had wanted to be with her for the birth of her first grandchild, was unable to move, but she sent a portrait of Necker for Albertine to look at while in labour, 'so that the new mother and child could feel his protection'. A fortnight later her fever had gone, and friends and family were able to announce the beginning of what they hoped was a recovery. La Fayette wrote reassuringly to Bernadotte that although Madame de Staël had been dangerously ill she was now recovering. No sooner was she a little better than she insisted on being dressed and carried to a sofa where she received her callers for part of the morning. Sometimes she would give dinner parties, with her children doing the honours. She was still paralysed but undaunted, making all sorts of plans for the summer. 'A truly awful accident has overcome me as a result of my illness, my dear friend,' she wrote to Miss Berry in May, 'which is that I am unable to make almost any use of neither my hands or feet, because of the cruelly painful cramps I suffer. I have been obliged therefore to lie on my back for some ninety days like a turtle, but with much more agitation and suffering of the imagination than that animal.'[37]

Soon after she was stricken down, a letter arrived from the Tsar, who did not know of her illness, in which he spoke of her 'enlightened mind, her love of good, which no circumstances altered', which he knew would make her share his hopes of an established order for France.[38] Wellington's niece, Priscilla Burgersh, herself barely recovering from a very serious miscarriage and the medical treatment of those days, wrote warmly to enquire after her health, ending with 'You know how much I love you'.[39] The Duke had been a daily visitor while he was in Paris. Their correspondence resumed when he returned to Cambrai. Madame de Staël could no longer write – Albertine was now her faithful secretary. Her mind was as clear as ever, however, and her interest in politics undiminished. The Duke had grown used to her 'talking politics' and relied on her acute powers of observation and her detailed and informed knowledge of the political scene. Visitors and friends from all sides of the political spectrum called on her. One of them was Chateaubriand: 'Good morning, my dear Francis,' she greeted him from her bed: 'I am in great pain but that does not prevent me from being very fond of you.'

In the spring, with the arrival of warmer weather, the Broglies decided to move Madame de Staël from her apartments at the rue Royale to a charming house with a garden in the rue Neuve-des-Mathurins. Here she could be wheeled out into the garden to enjoy the sun. Madame Récamier, who lived nearby, called every day, as did many of Madame de Staël's old friends, among them Mathieu, Talleyrand, Schlegel, Sismondi, Barante, Wellington, La Fayette and occasionally a new one – the young American scholar, George Ticknor, to whom she had apologized sadly for being so diminished. She was a shadow of her former self, she told him, a shadow which might disappear at any moment, but she prophesied, referring to America, 'You are the vanguard of the human race. You are the world's future.'[40]

Chateaubriand came again at the end of May, but by then Madame de Staël was too ill to see anyone but her very closest friends. Invited to stay for dinner, he found himself sitting next to Madame Récamier, whom he knew only slightly. It was the beginning of a love affair which meant more than any other to these two friends of Madame de Staël and which was to last until the end of Chateaubriand's life. He recalled how Rocca had looked that day: 'His face caved in, his cheeks hollow, his eyes dim, his skin colourless, leaning against the wall, his eyes fixed interminably on Madame de Staël with an anxious, begging stare.'[41] She treated him with maternal solicitude, making sure that he had taken his medicine and asking for a fire to be lit in his room, although by then the cold was inside her.

Madame de Staël's sufferings were so great throughout June that her children decided to call on Dr Jurine, who had been with her at the birth of Alphonse in Geneva. He arrived at the beginning of July, but was able only to give her some relief by curing her bedsores with the help of mustard plasters. 'Madame de Staël's condition is much the same,' wrote Madame Récamier to Constance d'Arlens in Geneva; 'there is no immediate danger but no hope of a cure. She is sick at heart too. It is impossible to see her without despairing of her state. She now only sees her intimate friends and even then cannot see them for long; but in the midst of all her suffering she has kept the grace of her mind. Her wish to make others happy at a time when it would be natural to think only of oneself, is moving beyond words.'[42]

Madame de Staël, who had always feared old age, was now more afraid of physical disintegration than of her death. 'My father is waiting for me on the other side,' she would say. Towards the end she was heard to murmur: 'I think that I know what it is to pass from life to death, and I am sure that the Good Lord makes it easier for us. Our mind becomes clouded and suffering is not so very great.'[43] Her illness was now beyond remedy, as signs of gangrene appeared on her body. Albertine and Miss Randall took turns in the sick room while Auguste and Victor de Broglie slept on sofas in the drawing room to be on call. On 13 July 1817, a Sunday, Madame de Staël spent the afternoon in the garden where she received the Duc d'Orléans and distributed roses to the friends who had come to see her. She dictated a last letter to Wellington, asking him to call on her. 'We were good friends,' Wellington later told Stanhope, 'and she had asked for me on her deathbed, but I was then out of Paris.'[44]

That evening she asked Miss Randall for a larger than usual dose of opium to help her sleep. In spite of doctor's orders, Fanny Randall gave it to her, holding her hand while she fell asleep. Later, she dozed off herself, still holding Madame de Staël's hand. Albertine settled down on a folding bed at the foot of her mother's bed, while Auguste stretched out on a sofa outside; Schlegel and Rocca retired to their rooms. Victor de Broglie lay down on his bed fully dressed. Early in the morning of 14 July, he awoke suddenly and went into Madame de Staël's room. Fanny Randall, asleep in her chair, still held Madame de Staël's hand, but the hand was now cold.[45] Madame de Staël had died on the anniversary of the Fall of the Bastille. She was just fifty-one years old.

Later that morning, after the first explosion of grief had given way to a exhausted depression, and when the laying out of the body had been completed, Broglie accompanied Auguste, Albertine, Rocca, Schlegel and Miss Randall to his house at the rue d'Anjou, coming back 'to the house of death for the night'. Benjamin Constant, 'touched to the quick and sincerely moved', was at last admitted into Madame de Staël's presence. Throughout that night, as they kept watch over her body, they talked, first of her and of their personal memories, and then of serious issues.[46]

It was a fitting tribute to Madame de Staël, the most brilliant conversationalist, the most steadfast liberal thinker and one of the most important writers of her age, that these two great liberal thinkers and politicians, Constant and Broglie, should have held one more important discussion in the presence of a woman whose influence on their age and on their personal and professional lives had been so great. For Madame de Staël, the word was always the beginning and the end. It was life itself.

Epilogue: On Death and Immortality

> 'Nothing that has come from her, can be compared to her own self'
>
> Albertine Necker-de Saussure

MADAME DE STAËL's death was announced first to her friends and then to the world, followed by a flood of obituaries. Inconsolable for days, Madame Récamier's beautiful eyes were red with crying. Benjamin Constant fell into such depression that Sismondi hardly recognized him. To Madame Récamier he wrote: 'I am sad but above all indifferent to everything else. However much I exhort myself to some interest, it doesn't work. Neither success nor failure moves me; I am no longer irritated with those who wish me ill, nor grateful to those who are good to me, . . . All in all, I no longer live.'[1]

Madame de Staël had always wanted to be buried with her parents. Her body was embalmed and taken to Coppet by Auguste and Schlegel while the Broglies, Rocca and Miss Randall went on ahead. Sismondi and Bonstetten were there among the silent villagers to see the black carriage carrying her coffin enter the gates of Coppet on 26 July. The heavy, lead-lined coffin covered with a pall was placed on the floor in the middle of a room decorated with the portraits of her parents. Dressed in deepest mourning, Albertine and Fanny Randall threw themselves on their knees, their arms on the coffin, sobbing uncontrollably.[2]

Victor de Broglie asked one workman only to break open the door into the mausoleum, posting a guard at the entrance to prevent the curious from entering. Broglie had found the burial chamber empty, except for the large open basin of black marble, still half-full of spirits: 'The two bodies lay side by side, covered by a red pall. Madame

Necker's head had slipped under the cover; I did not see her face; M. Necker's face was uncovered and perfectly preserved,' he recorded in his memoirs.[3]

Madame de Staël's funeral was held on 28 July 1817 and attended by her family, her closest friends and by all of Genevan society, represented officially by Counsellors of State dressed in mourning and wearing their swords, headed by the eighty-year-old Duc de Noailles. Her coffin, carried by Auguste, Victor de Broglie and four others, was placed, according to her wishes, at her parents' feet. The door – surmounted by a bas-relief by Tieck, commissioned by Madame de Staël – (it represented Necker being drawn up to heaven by his wife, looking back and stretching out his hand to his daughter, weeping by his tomb) – was shut. The mausoleum was then walled up forever, never to be opened to this day. Around it, in a small enclosed area, lie Auguste with his eighteen-month-old son Victor-Auguste, and his wife, Madame de Staël-Vernet, who long outlived him; Louis-Alphonse Rocca; the Countess d'Haussonville, née Louise de Broglie, and her infant sister Béatrice de Broglie, who died at birth.

The following day the family met for the official reading of the will. Her children had already learned of their mother's marriage to Rocca and of the existence of their little half-brother, Louis-Alphonse, from a preliminary reading of her will on the day after her death in Paris:

> I commend my soul to God, who has bestowed so many benefits on me chiefly through my father, to whom I owe what I am and what I have, and who would have spared me all my faults had I never turned away from his principles. I have only one piece of advice for my children; it is to always keep in mind my father's conduct, virtues and talents, and to try and imitate him, each according to his abilities. I know no one in this world to have equalled my father and every day my respect and my tenderness for him are etched more deeply into my soul. Life teaches us much, but for all those who think, it brings us ever closer to God's will; not because one's faculties weaken, but on the contrary, because they become greater.

After sharing her fortune proportionately between her three children and Rocca, she asks her children to look after their young half-brother of whom his father, Rocca, is to have custody: 'I know all three well enough to be certain that they will always treat their mother's husband, one who has loved her and protected her so well in her misfortune, as a friend, and that they will think of their mother's legitimate child as their brother.'

There were several smaller bequests: a life pension for Miss Randall, 'her excellent and faithful friend'; a portrait of her by Madame Vigée Lebrun and 12,000 francs 'to the friend I regard as my sister', Madame Necker-de Saussure; 1,000 écus to her son-in-law, Victor de Broglie, begging him to buy something 'in memory of one who is full of respect for his character and confidence in the happiness which he will give to her beloved daughter'; To Schlegel she left not only a pension of 3,000 francs per annum but also his apartments at Coppet – 'a house which is honoured by his presence' for his lifetime; and to her childhood friend, Madame Rilliet-Huber, 2,000 French francs and 'whichever of my shawls she prefers, certain that she will prefer one I have worn'. She also asked Auguste to have a portrait of her made for Mathieu de Montmorency in memory 'of a friendship which I hope is unalterable'. Then followed bequests, pensions and keepsakes to her servants, as well as her clothes and linen to her maid, Marie, and a sum of money to the pastor to be distributed to the poor. Schlegel and Auguste, helped by Albertine, were to be her literary executors.[4]

John Rocca barely survived her: 'I had hoped to die in her arms, it would have been sweet. Now I would like to escape to a desert,' he confided to Bonstetten. 'What am I now? Who could ever replace that elevated soul for me? People who come to see me speak of my inheritance. Miserable creatures! Did I not enjoy all her fortune during her lifetime? What is this money to me now?'[5] In the last stages of consumption, he spent the rest of the year first in Italy and then in Hyères, in the south of France, where he died on 30 January 1818. Their young son, Louis-Alphonse, a timid and backward child with a limp and a head too large for his body, was brought up by the Broglies with their own children. He was greatly loved by all his family and by Miss Randall who lived with the Broglies for the rest of her days. In spite of his unpromising beginnings he grew to adulthood, marrying, by another strange turn of fate, Narbonne's granddaughter, Marie-Louise de Rambuteau. He died without issue at the age of thirty.

Madame de Staël was remarkably lucky in her two older children. 'As soon as possible, she placed herself on equal terms with her children, and told them that not only did she need their love, but also their support,' her daughter wrote to her earliest biographer;

'Nothing can ever give a just impression of that mixture of dignity and confidence, of feeling and reserve which was part of her way with her children . . . No one had more natural dignity than she had, which enabled her to allow her children to be on terms of the utmost familiarity with her. She sometimes even inspired in them a pity for her sorrows, without them ceasing to revere her. Never has a mother been more confiding and more imposing at the same time.'[6]

All the same, she cannot have been an easy parent. Apart from her turbulent private life, Madame de Staël, like her own mother, was a better daughter than a parent. She retained the emotional vulnerability and demanding nature of a child all her life. She lived life entirely on her own terms and while her children, dragged along willy-nilly in her wake, had as interesting a life as one could imagine, they may well have wished for more normality and stability. On the other hand, they probably had far more personal attention from her than was customary in those days. Auguste and Albertine proved their devotion to her memory and their fidelity to her wishes after her death. Not only did they bring up their frail, young half-brother lovingly but they ensured the publication of Madame de Staël's major works: her unfinished *Dix années d'exil*, and the *Considérations sur la Révolution française*. They also published her collected works, commissioning Madame Necker-de Saussure to write an introductory biographical sketch. It was a happy choice. Her intimate knowledge of her cousin, her own fine intellect, humour and acute powers of observation, bring Madame de Staël to life with honesty and grace, even if most of the 'warts' were excised by the family.

The times were changing. A more religious and less permissive atmosphere now prevailed; one more in keeping with the temperaments of Madame de Staël's children and son-in-law. Out of devotion to their mother's memory, Albertine de Broglie made colossal efforts to get back as much of Madame de Staël's correspondence as she could over the next few years, destroying or locking up in the family archives everything which was too intimate or in any way threatening to her mother's memory. Most of Madame de Staël's correspondence with Constant, with Prosper de Barante and several others, disappeared in this auto-da-fé. We owe the survival of some letters to Narbonne, to Madame Récamier and to O'Donnell to the refusal of their owners to part with them, or to the family's ignorance of their existence. Auguste even sanitized Madame de Staël's texts in the *Considérations* and *Dix années d'exil*. Certain unflattering allusions to people like Talleyrand, now back in power, were excised, while others were toned down out of a natural desire to protect Victor de Broglie's burgeoning political career. Sainte-Beuve, who was an unqualified admirer and wrote a glowing essay about Madame de Staël and her work in 1832, was none the less denied permission to see some important correspondence.

Highly intelligent and deeply religious, Albertine de Broglie also had beauty and grace, which made her much admired. Like her mother and grandmother before her, she held an important salon in Paris to the end of her days. Her marriage to the austere Victor de Broglie lasted until her premature death in 1838. It had turned out to be all that her mother had hoped. Intelligent and reserved, Broglie's high-mindedness did little for his popularity, although his letters and journal betray a sense of humour and a much warmer heart than was apparent to his contemporaries. Seen whispering tenderly into his bride's ear soon after their marriage, gossip had it that he was telling her about a treatise on the salt tax!

As a leading light of the Liberals, Broglie was the true heir to Madame de Staël's political ideas, which triumphed under Louis-Philippe. In August 1830, when he became Prime Minister, Wilberforce wrote to congratulate him: 'What may the friends of justice and humanity not be able to hope for when they see the present King on the throne of France, and the Duc de Broglie as Prime Minister? May Almighty God grant you a long life, rich in services rendered and crowned with honours, followed by a still better world to come.'[7] Broglie enjoyed a brilliant political career as Minister for Foreign Affairs, Prime Minister, and then as Ambassador to London. He died in 1870. Of his and Albertine's five children, Pauline the eldest, born just before Madame de Staël's death, died in her fourteenth year, Béatrice died in infancy, Louise married the Comte d'Haussonville, and was herself an author. It is their distinguished progeny who have carried the family's brains and talents down through the generations to our own day. Their elder son Albert, Duc de Broglie, had a distinguished career in public service, dying in 1901. Their youngest, Paul, who began life as a sailor, entered holy orders, becoming a professor at the Catholic University of Paris. He was killed by a madwoman in 1895.[8]

Madame de Staël's eldest son Auguste, as serious, intelligent and religious as his sister, divided his time between Paris and Coppet. He took a great interest in politics and in Protestant issues, as well as in humanitarian causes, particularly the abolition of slavery. In 1825, after a visit to England, he published his *Letters on England*. In the same year he married Adélaide Vernet, daughter of the Genevese patrician banking family who had once employed his grandfather, Jacques Necker. Back at Coppet, he greatly extended the estates, setting up a model farm where he concentrated on cattle and long-haired sheep, and taught local farmers new systems of agriculture. He also instituted regular 'agricultural lunches' at which he brought together men of all classes. His only son died in infancy a year after his own untimely death from a sudden illness in 1827 at the age of thirty-seven. His widow, Madame de Staël-Vernet, survived him for many years, leaving Coppet of which she had been an excellent caretaker, to Albertine's daughter, Louise d'Haussonville. Their descendant, Comte Othenin d'Haussonville, is the present master of Coppet, himself a writer and President of the Society of Staëlien studies.

Albertine Necker-de Saussure, Madame de Staël's beloved cousin, found consolation in writing Madame de Staël's first biography. Later she wrote an important volume on progressive education. Increasingly deaf in old age, she died in 1841.

Of Madame de Staël's closest friends, Mathieu de Montmorency, once a revolutionary, finished his days politically as a fervent Ultra in the reign of Charles X (formerly Comte d'Artois who succeeded his brother Louis XVIII in 1824). Always deeply religious, he practised his Christian values supporting several Catholic charities. Simple in manner and style, he was much loved by all his friends. In spite of the great gulf between their political opinions he and Madame de Staël remained true to their friendship, which he would recall every anniversary of her death by writing something about her. He died on Good Friday, 24 March 1826, while praying at the foot of the cross in the church of St Thomas Aquinas in the Faubourg Saint-Germain.

Constant kept in close touch with Madame de Staël's children until his death in December 1830. The 'schoolmaster of liberty', as he called himself, was one of the Deputies – he had been elected for Alsace – who signed the address which led to the July Revolution. 'For forty years', he wrote, 'I have fought for the same principle: liberty in all things, in religion, in philosophy, in literature, in industry, in politics. By liberty, I mean the triumph of the individual, as much over the government which seeks to rule by despotic methods as over the masses who seek to render the minority a slave of the majority. Despotism has no rights at all.'[9] He died respected as one of the greatest political thinkers and writers of his time and laden with honours by the monarchy to which he had been midwife. He was given what amounted to a state funeral on 12 December 1830, his pall-bearers being the Prime Minister, the President of the Chamber of Deputies, the Prefet of the Seine and General La Fayette. A friend of Miss Berry's described to her how he had been followed by so many people to the grave that eight or nine processions at a time had crossed the Tuileries Gardens, headed by tricolour flags, with his name and 'Liberté et Droit' written upon them.[10]

As one of Madame de Staël's literary executors, Schlegel was eased out gently by her family, renouncing his rights to all her 'printed or unpublished material and all other literary papers'. The sole beneficiary of the royalties of the first edition of the *Considérations*, the taint of his being anti-French was considered too great for his name to appear. He lived with the Broglies in Paris until 1818, when he left for Germany. There he married Sophie Paulus, a young woman of twenty-seven, but they were divorced six months later. He died in Bonn in 1845 after a distinguished academic career.[11] Sismondi too enjoyed a distinguished career as a writer. He died in 1842. Prosper de Barante, laden with honours, died in 1866. In the autumn of 1832, Madame Récamier and Chateaubriand were travelling together in Switzerland. Finding themselves very near Coppet, Chateaubriand recalled Madame Récamier had wanted to pay one more visit to the house where she had spent such happy summers. It was late September and the house was closed for the winter. After walking around the empty rooms, scene of so many memories, they went out into the park. Madame Récamier alone had permission to enter the wood and the small enclosure around the tomb. Chateaubriand waited, sitting on a bench overlooking the lake and the distant Alps: 'Golden clouds extended along the horizon behind the dark line of the Jura; like a glory rising above a long coffin. I could see Lord Byron's house on the other side of the lake, its rooftops gilded by the setting sun. Rousseau was no longer there to admire the scene; while Voltaire, gone long since, had never bothered to do so. It was at the foot of Madame de

Staël's tomb that so many illustrious names who had once lived here, now dead, flooded my memory: it was as if they had come to seek the ghost of their equal, and to fly to heaven with her, escorting her through the night. At that moment, much like a ghost herself, pale and in tears, Madame Récamier came out of the silent wood. If ever I have felt the vanity and the truth of fame and of life, and understood what it is to be truly beloved, it was at the entrance to that silent wood, dark and unknown, where sleeps one who was so brilliant and so celebrated.'[12] Chateaubriand and Madame Récamier both outlived their friend by more than thirty years. He died in July 1848, to be followed by Madame Récamier in May 1849.

The publication of the *Considérations sur la Révolution française* in April 1818, which sold out almost at once in its first edition of 60,000 copies,[13] ensured Madame de Staël 'a brilliant and public funeral', as Sainte-Beuve called it.[14] It was the first important book of the nineteenth century to examine the causes, the course and the aftermath of the French Revolution, a work as much of political science as a history. It secured Madame de Staël a place as one of the founders of nineteenth-century liberalism in France, just as *Delphine, Corinne* and *De l'Allemagne* ensured her place as the herald of French Romanticism.

Madame de Staël always believed that the Revolution had been betrayed by Robespierre and the Terror. She never repudiated its initial aim, which was to overturn the injustices of centuries of oppression and ignorance; indeed she believed that the excesses of the Terror, while due to political fanaticism, had their roots in centuries of brutalization. Faced with its unspeakable and unfathomable horrors, she hoped that the Terror had been an exception, an aberration never to be repeated. It was as well that she could not see into the future. She hated violence as much as fanaticism and often quoted Rousseau's words that 'It was not permissible for a nation to buy the most desirable Revolution with the blood of a single innocent'. No end could ever justify the means. Long before George Orwell, she understood how language could be perverted for political aims; how noble motives could be ascribed, post hoc, to ignoble actions. 'When . . . they had wanted to sanction every crime, they called the Government the Committee of Public Safety; thereby proclaiming the well-known maxim, that the security of the people is the supreme law. The supreme law is justice.' And 'those guilty of doing harm in every period, have tried to attribute some generous pretext to themselves to excuse their actions; there are almost no crimes in existence which their perpetrators have not attributed to honour, religion or liberty.'[15]

To Madame de Staël, politics was, above all, about moral government, as represented by her father. 'Liberty', she wrote, 'is nothing other than morality in government.' Against that – in her writing, as in her life – stands Napoleon, the fallen angel. In *Dix années d'exil* he is judged in a more immediate and personal way; in the *Considérations sur la Révolution française*, Madame de Staël views him in the context of his times.

Stendhal, who admired Napoleon, dubbed Madame de Staël 'the chief talent of the age'. Byron echoed this, calling her 'the first female writer of our age perhaps of any age', but he also had this to say of the woman: 'The mother tenderly affectionate and tenderly beloved, the friend unboundedly generous, but still esteemed, the charitable patroness of all distress, cannot be forgotten by those whom she cherished, and protected and fed. Her loss will be mourned the most where she was known the best; and to the sorrows of her many friends, and more dependants, may be offered the disinterested regret of a stranger, who amidst the sublimer scenes of the Leman lake, received his chief satisfaction from contemplating the engaging qualities of the incomparable Corinna.'[16]

Finally, the man who knew her better and longer than any other, Constant, wrote immediately after her death: 'But it was to her that her friends should have said how much they loved her; we never managed to convince her enough. We were afraid of the effects that such emotion might have on a body which had become so frail, an emotion which perhaps her soul needed . . . All those who knew her, have kept indelible memories of her. No one came to her in misfortune but they found help, no one unhappy, but they found consolation, no one proscribed but they found asylum, no one oppressed whose cause she would not plead, no superior mind which was not captivated by hers, no powerful man worthy of his power, who did not recognize and respect her superiority. No one could have spent an hour with her without according that hour a special place in his memory; and her life was necessary to those who had known her, even if they no longer saw her.' Twelve years later, in an expanded memoir, he wrote: 'The dominant qualities of Madame de Staël were affection and pity. She had, like all superior minds, a great passion for glory; she had like all high-minded souls, a great love of liberty; but those two sentiments, imperious and irresistible when they were unchallenged by others, gave way immediately, when the slightest circumstance pitted her against those she loved, or when the sight of a suffering being reminded her that there was something much more sacred than the success of a cause or the triumph of an opinion . . . people of all shades of opinions who had fallen from grace found in her more zeal to protect them in their misfortune than to oppose them when they were powerful. Her house was their asylum, her fortune their resource, her activity their hope.'[17]

Madame de Staël herself explained the mainspring of her character with the simple words: 'My passion is my genius'. Just before her death, almost as if writing her own epitaph, she said to Chateaubriand: 'I have always been the same; lively and sad. I have loved God, my father and liberty.'

~

Notes

1 Madame Necker's Salon

1. Vicomte d'Haussonville, *Le Salon de Madame Necker*, 2 vols, Paris, 1882, vol. 2, p. 222.
2. Beatrix d'Andlau, *La Jeunesse de Madame de Staël*, Paris-Genève, 1970, p. 11.
3. Their name was Albert not d'Albert, her paternal grandfather having been a lawyer from Montélimar. De Nasse is also unsubstantiated. See d'Haussonville, *Le Salon de Madame Necker*, vol. 1.
4. Ibid., vol. 1, p. 11, footnote.
5. Lucien Perey and Gaston Maugras, *La Vie intime de Voltaire aux Délices et à Ferney*, Paris: Calmann Lévy 1885, quoted by Lady Blennerhassett in *Madame de Staël: Her Friends and her Influence in Literature*, 3 vols, London, 1889.
6. Edward Gibbon, *Memoirs of My Life*, London, 1984, p. 92.
7. Ibid., p. 105.
8. J. E. Norton (ed.), *The Letters of Edward Gibbon*, London, vol. 1, p. 106.
9. Abbé E. Lavaquery, *Necker, Fourrier de la Révolution*, Paris, 1933, p. 37, quoted by Ghislain de Diesbach in *Necker ou la faillite de la vertu*, Paris, 1978, p. 44.
10. d'Haussonville, *Le Salon de Madame Necker*, op. cit., vol. 1, pp. 60–61.
11. Ibid., pp. 62, and Françis de Crue, *L'Ami de Rousseau et des Necker: Paul Moultou à Paris en 1778*, Paris, 1926, p. 34.
12. Comte Fedor Golovkine, *Lettres diverses recueillies en Suisse*, Genève et Paris 1821, p. 8.
13. Françis de Crue, op. cit., p. 47.
14. d'Haussonville, *Le salon de Madame Necker*, op. cit., vol. 1, p. 102.
15. Ibid., vol. 1, p. 105.
16. Ibid., pp. 107–8.
17. Ibid., p. 106.
18. Ibid., pp. 109–10.
19. Golovkine, *Lettres diverses recueillies en Suisse*, op. cit., p. 292.
20. d'Haussonville, *Le Salon de Madame Necker*, op. cit., vol. 1, pp. 113–14.
21. Letter to Madame Pathod, 9 July 1765, Coppet archives, cited by B. d'Andlau in *La Jeunesse de Madame de Staël*, op. cit., p. 17.
22. d'Haussonville, *Le Salon de Madame Necker*, op. cit., vol. 2, p. 5.
23. Madame Necker-de Saussure, *Notice sur le caractère et les écrits de Mme de Staël*, p. xviii, *Oeuvres complètes de Mme la baronne de Staël publié par son fils*, Paris, Strasbourg & London: Treuttel & Würtz 1821.
24. Madame Necker's papers, Coppet archives, cited by B. d'Andlau in *La Jeunesse de Madame de Staël*, op. cit., p. 28.
25. Pierre Kohler, *Madame de Staël et la Suisse*, Lausanne & Paris: 1916, p. 27, citing Golovkine, letter to Madame de Brenles, 1765, pp. 264–5.

26. *Memoirs of the Baroness d'Oberkirch*, 3 vols, London, 1852, vol. 1, p. 3.
27. *Oeuvres complètes Du caractère de M. Necker et de sa vie privée*, vol. 17, p. 11.

2 Minette

1. Madame Necker-de Saussure, *Notice sur le caractère etc.* op. cit., p. xxiij.
2. Protestants still had no formal legal status in France.
3. Golovkine *Lettres diverses etc.* op. cit., p. 292.
4. d'Andlau, *La Jeunesse de Madame de Staël*, op. cit. p. 20.
5. Kohler, *Madame de Staël et la Suisse*, op. cit., letter to Mme Reverdil, p. 31, quoted by d'Andlau in *La Jeunesse*, op. cit., p. 21.
6. Ibid., p. 23.
7. The house was destroyed to make way for the rue de Mulhouse, see d'Andlau, op. cit., p. 28.
8. Montesquieu's *De l'esprit des Lois* was published in 1748, La Mettrie's *L'Homme machine* in the same year, Buffon's *Histoire naturelle* and Diderot's *Lettres sur les aveugles* in 1749, Condillac's *Traité des sensations* of 1754, all works which were essentially empirical in their view. It was Diderot who conceived the idea of a complete *Encyclopaedia* of which he was editor, intended to cover all knowledge and publicize these new ideas. The first volume appeared in 1751. Rousseau wrote on music, Marmontel on comedy, Buffon on natural history, Holbach on chemistry, Quesnay on agriculture, Montesquieu and Turgot covered history and politics, Condorcet, Helvétius and Voltaire contributed articles, while d'Alembert, a gifted mathematician, was also the assistant editor.
9. The daughter of one of the Dauphine's servants, the beautiful and intelligent orphan was married at fourteen to the fifty-year-old François Geoffrin, a rich manufacturer of glass.
10. d'Haussonville, op. cit. vol 1, p. 163.
11. Melchior Grimm, German in origin, who together with Diderot became the editor of the *Correspondance littéraire*, Reynal's monthly review of Parisian events for foreign royalty.
12. d'Haussonville, p. 165.
13. Madame de Staël, *De l'Allemagne, Oeuvres complètes*, vol. X, p. 169, also quoted by d'Andlau in *La Jeunesse de Mme de Staël*, op. cit., p. 27.
14. Lavaquery, *Necker*, op. cit., p. 88, cited by Ghislain de Diesbach, *Necker ou la faillite de la vertu*, op. cit., p. 97.
15. d'Andlau, *La Jeunesse*, op. cit., p. 43.
16. Mme de Staël, *Journal de Jeunesse*, Occident, 15 October 1932 cited by B. d'Andlau, op. cit.
17. d'Haussonville, op. cit., vol. 1, p. 10.
18. M. de Lescure (ed.), *Correspondance complète de la marquise du Deffand avec ses amis: Président Hénault, Montesquieu, d'Alembert, Voltaire, Horace Walpole*, 2 vols, Paris 1865, Letter of 6 June 1769.
19. Much resented forced labour imposed on commoners and used mainly for road-building. Peasant farmers who desperately needed manpower on their own farms could buy themselves off, but rarely had the money to do so.
20. *Oeuvres complètes publiées par son petit-fils le baron de Staël*, 15 vols, Paris, 1820, vol.1, p. 145, quoted by Ghislain de Diesbach, *Necker* op. cit., p. 125.
21. d'Haussonville, op. cit., vol. 2, p. 137.
22. Kohler, op. cit., p. 53.
23. Lescure, *Correspondance complète*, op. cit. vol. 11, p. 365.
24. Gibbon, *Memoirs of My Life*, op. cit., p. 160.
25. d'Haussonville, op.cit., vol. 2, pp. 34–7 and Madame de Staël, *Correspondance*

générale, Notes and Commentary by B. Jasinski, J. J. Pauvert (ed.), Paris, 1962, 1777–August 1788, vol. 1.

26. Mme Necker-de Saussure, *Notice*, op. cit., p.xxij.
27. *Correspondance générale* op. cit., vol. 1, p. 7, letter of spring or summer 1778 or 1779.
28. For all letters from Mme Necker, see d'Haussonville, op. cit., vol. 2.
29. De Crue, *L'Ami de Rousseau*, op. cit., p. 73.
30. Catherine Rilliet-Huber, quoted by d'Andlau in *La Jeunesse*, op. cit., p. 31.
31. The Comtesse de Genlis was part of the household of the Duc de Chartres, and educated his children – among them the future King, Louis-Philippe. A prolific writer and lifelong supporter of the standards of the *ancien régime*, she hated the *philosophes*.
32. Ibid., p. 32.
33. Ibid., cited by d'Andlau, *La Jeunesse*, op. cit., pp. 36–7.
34. The line in brackets was scratched out in the original and the rest of the paragraph torn. See d'Andlau, op. cit., pp. 46–8.
35. Ibid., citing Coppet Archives, footnote 7, p. 48.
36. d'Haussonville, op. cit. vol. 2, p. 48.
37. Saussure, *Notice*, op. cit., pp. xliij–xliv.
38. Ibid., pp. xxxj–xxxij.
39. d'Haussonville, op. cit. vol. 2, p. 49.

3 Monsieur Necker's Daughter

1. Mme de Staël, *Considérations sur la Révolution française*, Paris 1983, 2000, p. 101. The *Taille* was a feudal levy, applied mainly in rural areas, raised from those sections of the population exempted from military service. Nobles, the clergy and the holders of various offices were exempted from paying it.
2. d'Haussonville, *Le Salon de Madame Necker*, op. cit., vol. 2, p. 118.
3. Ibid., p. 104.
4. Jean-Denis Bredin, *Une Singulière Famille*, Paris 1999, p. 109.
5. d'Haussonville, op. cit., vol. 2, p. 119.
6. de Staël, *Considérations*, op. cit., p. 106.
7. Ibid.
8. d'Haussonville, op. cit., vol. 2, p. 167.
9. Lavaquery, *Necker*, op. cit., p. 207; also cited by Diesbach in *Necker*, op. cit., p. 227.
10. Béatrice Jasinski, *Correspondance générale*, op. cit., vol. I, p. 20, citing *Memoirs of William Beckford of Fonthill*, 2 vols, London 1859, vol. II, p. 353.
11. Baronne D'Oberkirch, *Mémoires sur la Cour de Louis XVI et la Societé française avant 1789*, Paris, 1989, vol. 1, p. 254.
12. Mme de Staël, *Journal de Jeunesse*, Occident, no. 3/4, Paris, 1932, p. 240.
13. Madame de La Tour du Pin, *Mémoires d'une femme de cinquante ans*, Paris: Chapelot, 1914.
14. d'Andlau, *La Jeunesse*, op. cit., p. 115, citing Madame de Genlis, *Mémoires*, vol. III, Paris, 1831, p. 315.
15. Ibid., unpublished papers, Coppet, p. 113.
16. Ibid., pp. 113–14.
17. d'Haussonville, op. cit., vol. 2, pp. 54–5, see footnotes. The proposal is mentioned both in Lord Stanhope's history of William Pitt and in Wilberforce's memoirs.
18. de Staël, *Journal de Jeunesse*, op. cit., p. 238.
19. d'Haussonville, op. cit., vol. 2, pp. 55–8.
20. d'Haussonville, *Madame de Staël & M. Necker d'après leur correspondance inédite*, Paris, 1925, pp. 58–9.

21. d'Haussonville, *Le Salon*, op. cit., vol. 2, pp. 59–60.
22. Ibid., p. 178.
23. d'Andlau, *La Jeunesse*, op. cit., p. 142.
24. Ibid., letter of 23 December, 1784, p. 143–4.
25. d'Andlau, *La Jeunesse*, op. cit., p. 76.
26. Mme de Staël, *Mon journal*, 29 June 1785 in Occident, no. 3/4, Paris 1932.
27. d'Andlau, *La Jeunesse*, op. cit., August 1785, Appendix IV, pp. 158–9.
28. Ibid., pp. 88–91.
29. de Crue, *L' Ami de Rousseau et des Necker*, op. cit., letter of 19 August 1785, pp. 179–80.
30. Comtesse J. de Pange, *Monsieur de Staël*, Paris 1932, p. 41.
31. de Staël, *Journal de Jeunesse* op. cit., Occident no. 3/14, 15 October 1932, pp. 236–7.
32. d'Andlau, *La Jeunesse*, op. cit., p. 100.
33. de Crue, op. cit., letter of 23 October 1785, p. 181.
34. Ibid., pp. 181–2.
35. A. Grot (ed.), *Lettres de l'Impératrice Catherine II à Grimm, 1774–96*, St Petersburg 1878, p. 30.
36. A. Vivie, *Lettres de Gustave III à la comtesse de Boufflers*, Paris, p. 368, quoted in Diesbach, op. cit., p. 68.
37. *Correspondance Générale*, op. cit., vol. 1, p. 50.
38. d'Andlau, *La Jeunesse*, op. cit., p. 101.

4 Marriage

1. *Correspondance générale*, vol. 1, part 1, p. 58, letter to her mother, 29 January 1786.
2. Ibid.
3. Mercier Sébastien, *Tableau de Paris*, 12 vols, Amsterdam, 1782–88, vol. II, p. 173.
4. Françis de Crue, op. cit., p. 184.
5. d'Haussonville op. cit. vol. II, pp. 185–6.
6. Baronne d'Oberkirch, *Mémoires sur la Cour de Louis XVI*, op. cit., p. 442.
7. Hero of *A History of Sir Charles Grandison*, a portrayal of male virtue by Samuel Richardson.
8. *Correspondance générale*, Letters of Mrs Adams, the wife of John Adams, Boston Wilkins, Carter & Co., 1848, vol. 1, part 1, footnote 4, pp. 42–3.
9. Baron de Frénilly, *Souvenirs du Baron de Frénilly*, Paris: Plon-Nourrit, 1909, p. 207.
10. Ibid.
11. Vivie, *Lettres de Gustave III*, op. cit., p. 386.
12. d'Haussonville, op. cit., vol 2, p. 184.
13. Ibid., pp. 17–18.
14. Mme Necker-de Saussure, *Notice*, op. cit., p. xxxiv.
15. Ibid.
16. Ibid., pp. xxxviij–xxxix.
17. In which he had recognized that in the future wars would be waged in a completely different way, not with troops lined up in ranks on battlefields as they had been hitherto, but spilling out of them into regions and even countries. In 1788 he completely reorganized the army, military engineering and field logistics to prepare for these differences. He was greatly admired by Napoleon who put many of his ideas into practice.
18. A love rhapsodically recorded in the many letters she wrote to him, which he kept and which his wife later published.

19. Simone Balayé, *Madame de Staël Lumières & Liberté*, ed. Klincksieck, Paris, 1979, pp. 28–9.
20. *Correspondance générale*, vol. 1, part 1, p. 81.
21. Mme de Staël, *Préface à la première édition en 1788 aux Lettres sur les écrits et le caractère de J. J. Rousseau, Oeuvres complètes*, vol. 1, pp. 3–4.
22. Mme de Staël, *Préface 1814 aux écrits sur . . . J.-J. Rousseau*, op. cit., pp. 4–8.
23. Ibid., p. 36.
24. *Correspondance générale*, footnote 7, p. 146, letter from Mme Necker-de Saussure to her mother.
25. Ibid., pp. 149–50
26. Mme de Staël, *Oeuvres complètes*, op. cit., vol. 17, *Du caractère de M. Necker et de sa vie privée*, pp. 34–5.
27. *Correspondance générale*, op. cit., vol. 1, part 1, footnote 1, p. 153.
28. Mme de Staël *Considérations*, op. cit., p. 128.
29. *Correspondance générale*, op. cit., vol. 1, part 2, pp. 239–40.
30. Ibid., pp. 255–6.
31. Ibid., pp. 257–8.

5 A Salon in the Rue du Bac

1. Mme de Staël, *Considérations*, op. cit., p. 136.
2. The two which preceded it were *Essai sur les privilèges* (Essay on Priviledge) and *Vues sur les moyens d'exécution dont les représentants de la France pourront disposer en 1789* (Thought on the means of implementation available to the representatives of France in 1789). E. Sieyès, *Qu'est ce que c'est que le Tiers État?*, ed. E. Champion, Paris, 1888, pp. 123–97.
3. Arthur Young, *Travels in France and Italy during the Years 1787, 1788 & 1789*, New York.
4. The Marquis de La Fayette, a friend and protégé of George Washington, had, as a twenty-year-old volunteered in Washington's army and was a veteran of the American Revolution. He revered Washington, to whom he sent the key to the Bastille after its fall, putting it in the hands of Thomas Paine with the message that he was sending it 'as a missionary of liberty to its Patriarch'. Married to the all-powerful Noailles family he helped to draft the Declaration of the Rights of Man and was made Commander of the newly created National Guard on 15 July 1789, immediately after the fall of the Bastille.
5. Gouverneur Morris, *Diaries and Letters*, 2 vols. edited by Anne Cary Morris Kegan, London, 1889, vol. 1, pp. 68–9.
6. Ibid., p. 44.
7. Marquis de Ferrières, *Correspondance inédite, 1789, 1790, 1791*, edited by H. Carré, Paris, 1932 pp. 37–41.
8. Philippe, duc d'Orléans, member of a cadet branch of the Bourbons, was in direct line of succession after Louis's sons and brothers. At court the d'Orléans, who were immensely rich and powerful, had always been in opposition to the King. Philippe, a dissolute libertine, had at first taken up the liberal cause. He belonged to the Society of Thirty and later as Philippe Egalité was a member of the Jacobin Club.
9. G. Morris, op. cit, vol. 1, p. 73.
10. *Considérations*, op. cit., p. 139.
11. Ibid., p. 140.
12. Ibid., p. 141. Honoré-Gabriel Riqueti, comte de Mirabeau, was a member of the Provençal nobility. His huge size and brutish appearance had not prevented him from becoming a notorious libertine. His scandalous private life had precluded his election as deputy to his own estate but he was elected by the Third Estate. He was a brilliant orator and journalist.

13. *Memoirs of Madame de La Tour du Pin*, edited and translated by Felice Harcourt, London, 1985, pp. 105–6. Born Henriette-Lucie Dillon in 1770, Madame de La Tour du Pin married the Comte de Gouvernet, later the Marquis de La Tour du Pin, in 1787. She was a member of Marie-Antoinette's household and was at Versailles during the events of 1789. She wrote her memoirs after 1820.
14. G. Morris, op. cit., vol. 1, p. 75.
15. *Considérations*, op. cit., p. 141.
16. G. Morris, op. cit., vol. 1, pp. 75–6.
17. Ferrières, op. cit., letter of 6 May 1789, pp. 45–6.
18. *Considérations*, op. cit, pp. 141–2.
19. Ibid., p. 142.
20. Ibid., p. 160.
21. Jean Égret, *Necker, Ministre de Louis XVI, 1776–1790*, Paris, 1975, p. 442.
22. Mme de Staël, *Oeuvres complètes*, op. cit., vol. 17, *Du caractère de M. Necker et de sa vie privée*, pp. 44–5.
23. *Considérations*, op. cit. p. 160.
24. O. Browning (ed.), *Despatches from Paris 1784–90*, London, 1910, vol. II, Camden Modern Series xix, pp. 238–42.
25. *Correspondance générale*, op. cit, vol. 1, part 2, pp. 314–15.
26. Mme de Staël, *Du caractère de M. Necker*, op. cit., pp. 52–3.
27. The King's brother Artois, the Prince de Condé, the Duc d'Enghien, and the powerful Conti and Polignac clans left immediately after the fall of the Bastille, blaming the King and Queen for weakness and abandoning them to their fate.
28. *Considérations*, op. cit. p. 168.
29. Jacques Necker, *Sur l'Administration de M. Necker par lui-même*, Paris, 1791, p. 128, cited in *Correspondance générale*, vol. 1, part 2, p. 316, footnote 4.
30. Ibid., letter of 16 August 1789, pp. 325–30.
31. *Considérations*, op. cit., p. 210–11.
32. Born in Liège, the beautiful, dark-haired Théroigne had arrived in Paris in 1788 under the protection of the marquis de Persan. She became the symbol of revolutionary women and although she denied it, she was described by subsequent writers as present or leading everything from the storming of the Bastille to the women's march on Versailles. Romantic descriptions have her dressed in a blood-red habit, her sabre at her side and two pistols at her waist (Lamartine, *Histoire des Girondins*). Carlyle saw her as both Pallas Athene and Joan of Arc. See also Linda Kelly's excellent *Women of the French Revolution*.
33. Thomas Carlyle, *The French Revolution*, Oxford 1989, p. 265.
34. Linda Kelly, *Women of the French Revolution*, London, 1989, pp. 15–16.
35. *Memoirs of Madame de La Tour du Pin*, op. cit., p. 134.
36. *Considérations*, op. cit., p. 213.
37. Madame de La Tour du Pin, op. cit., p. 136.

6 Hopes of Boundless Happiness

1. *Considérations*, op. cit., part 2, ch. XVI, p. 226.
2. Ibid., p. 214.
3. G. Morris op. cit., vol. 1, p. 188.
4. Ibid., p. 225.
5. *Extracts from the Journals and Correspondence of Miss Berry, 1783 to 1852*, edited by Lady Theresa Lewis, London, 1866 (3 vols), vol. 1, p. 370.
6. *Correspondance générale*, p. 331, footnote 2.
7. Paul Gautier, *M. de Montmorency et Madame de Staël d'après les lettres inédites de M. de Montmorency à Mme Necker-de Saussure*, Paris, 1908, cited B. W. Jasinski in *Correspondance générale*, p. 388.

8. *Memoirs of Madame de La Tour du Pin*, op. cit. p. 119.
9. *Mémoires de la Comtesse de Boigne*, vol. 1, *Mercure de France*, 1999, p. 254.
10. *Correspondance générale*, op. cit., vol. II part 1, letter to Narbonne, of 21 April 1794, p. 278.
11. *Memoirs of Madame de La Tour du Pin*, op. cit, p. 97.
12. *Correspondance générale*, vol. 1, part 2, p. 352.
13. Ibid., pp. 356–7.
14. G. Morris, op. cit., pp. 220–1.
15. Comtesse Jean de Pange, *Monsieur de Staël*, Paris 1932, pp. 135–7.
16. Mme de Staël, *Oeuvres complètes*, vol. 17, *Du caractère de M. Necker*, op. cit. p. 67.
17. Ibid., p. 66.
18. G. Morris, op. cit., pp. 278–9.
19. *Considérations*, op. cit., part 2, ch. XVI, p. 226.
20. Mme de Staël, *Oeuvres complètes*, vol. 17, *Éloge de M. de Guibert*, pp. 295–6.
21. P. Kohler, *Madame de Staël et la Suisse*, op. cit., letter of 4 December 1789, p. 91.
22. Rivarol, *Le petit dictionnaire des Grands Hommes de la Révolution*, Paris, 1956.
23. *Memoirs of Madame de La Tour du Pin*, op. cit., p. 142.
24. Ibid., p. 144.
25. *Considérations*, op. cit., p. 227.
26. *Correspondance générale*, op. cit., vol. 1, part 2, footnote 4, p. 364.
27. Ibid., letter of 11 September 1790, p. 365.
28. d'Haussonville, op. cit., vol. 2, p. 243.
29. *Correspondance générale*, op. cit., vol. 1, letter of 19 October 1790, p. 370.
30. Ibid., letter of 15 October 1790, p. 369.
31. Ibid., p. 372.
32. d'Haussonville, op. cit., vol. 2, p. 249.
33. *Correspondance générale*, op. cit., vol. 1, part 2, p. 373.
34. Ibid., p. 392.
35. Ibid., p. 403.
36. Ibid., p. 419.
37. Ibid., p. 420.

7 From Constitution to Revolution

1. G. Morris, op. cit., vol. 1, p. 371.
2. Ibid., p. 376.
3. *Considérations*, op. cit., part 2, ch. XIX, pp. 233–4.
4. Ibid., part 3, p. 268.
5. *Correspondance générale*, op. cit., vol. 1, part 2, p. 421.
6. Adélaïde de Rohan-Chabot, a friend of Madame de Staël who was married to the Comte de Castellane, a deputy of the Constituent Assembly.
7. *Correspondance générale*, op. cit., vol. 1, part 2, p. 423.
8. Ibid., p. 426.
9. *Considérations*, op. cit., part 2, ch. XX, p. 238.
10. Ibid., p. 237.
11. *Oeuvres complètes*, op. cit., vol. 17, pp. 318–30, also cited by B. Jasinski in *Correspondance générale*, vol. 2, pp. 312–13.
12. A disciple of Voltaire and Diderot, the mathematician and philosopher Condorcet was a leading member of the Constituent Assembly. A libertarian, he had campaigned for civil rights for Protestants and the abolition of slavery and the slave trade.
13. Kelly, *Women of the French Revolution*, op. cit., p. 37, and Lacour-Gayet, *Talleyrand*, Paris, 1933, 4 vols, vol. 1, p. 139.

14. *Correspondance générale*, op. cit., vol. 1, part 2, pp. 427–8.
15. Ibid., p. 444.
16. The Feuillant club was founded on the 15 July 1791, taking its name from the convent of the same name which became its headquarters.
17. Mme de Staël still believed at this stage that the King's flight had been successful and that her husband might have to live in the counter-revolutionary camp in Germany, where the French royal family were to have joined Gustavus III.
18. *Correspondance générale*, op. cit., pp. 449–50.
19. Ibid., letter of 28 June 1791, pp. 450–1.
20. Ibid., pp. 465–6.
21. Ibid., pp. 470–1.
22. H. Walpole, letter of 5 September 1791, in *Extracts from the Journals and Correspondence of Miss Berry*, op. cit., vol. 1, p. 362.
23. *Correspondance générale*, op. cit., vol. 1, part 2, pp. 489–91.
24. R. M. Klinckowström (ed.), *Le Comte de Fersen & la Cour de France*, 2 vols, Paris, 1877, vol. 1, pp. 208–9.
25. *Considérations*, op. cit., part 2, ch. XXIII, pp. 248–50.
26. The King's brothers, the Comtes Artois and Provence, together with other Princes of the Blood, were then based at Coblenz, where they were assembling an émigré army.
27. G. Morris, op. cit., vol. 1, pp. 456–9.
28. Ibid., Morris.
29. Alma Söderjhelm, *Fersen et Marie-Antoinette*, 1930, p. 227.
30. B. Jasinski, Introduction to *Correspondance générale*, op. cit., vol. 2, part 2, p. 310.
31. Ibid., vol. 1, part 2, letter of 12 December 1791, p. 527.

8 War

1. *Correspondance générale*, op. cit., vol. 1 part 2, p. 527.
2. Talleyrand and all Madame de Staël's moderate friends were members of this club. She herself must be considered an honorary 'Feuillante'.
3. Morris, op. cit., vol. 1, p. 509.
4. Alfred Cobban, *A History of Modern France*, 3 vols, London, 1963, vol. 1, p. 190.
5. Verdi's opera *Un Ballo in Maschera* faithfully represents the circumstances of the assassination of King Gustavus III of Sweden.
6. Georges Solovieff, *Madame de Staël, ses amis, ses correspondants, choix de lettres, 1778–1815*, presenté et commenté par Solovieff, preface de la comtesse Jean de Pange, Paris, 1970, p. 17. Comtesse Jean de Pange, *Monsieur de Staël* op. cit., p. 159, letter of 16 January 1792.
7. Unhappily, in 1798 Necker burnt all Madame de Staël's letters – those that covered events in France and her own views of them – which she had written to him during these dangerous times, as she destroyed most of hers on his instructions.
8. *The Letters of Edward Gibbon*, edited by J. E. Norton, 3 vols, London, 1956, vol. 3, pp. 252–3, letter of 4 April 1792, cited by B. Jasinski, *Correspondance générale*, vol. 2, part 2, p. 352.
9. *Correspondance générale*, op. cit., vol 2, part 1, commentary by B. Jasinski.
10. Morris, op. cit., vol. 1, letter of 17 March 1792 to George Washington, pp. 522–3.
11. *Correspondance générale*, op. cit., vol. 2 part 2, p. 354.
12. *Considérations*, op. cit., part 3, ch. V, p. 270.
13. Inspired by the *pileus*, the headgear of enfranchised Roman slaves, the *bonnet rouge* became an essential part of *sans-culotte* dress, like the trousers they wore

instead of the knee-breeches (culotte) which were associated with the *ancien régime*.

14. *Correspondance générale*, op. cit., vol. 2 part 2, p. 354.
15. Ibid., p. 276.
16. Ibid., p. 278.
17. Morris, op. cit., vol. 1, p. 569.
18. *Considérations*, op. cit. ch. IX, p. 279.
19. Ibid.
20. Simon Schama, *Citizens – A Chronicle of the French Revolution*, London, 1989, p. 615.
21. *Considérations*, op. cit., pp. 279–80.
22. Twenty years later, Madame de Staël was much amused by the amazing fact that her desperate invention had turned out to be prophetic. As a result of Napoleon's victories, Lubeck and Swedish Pomerania then belonged to France.
23. *Considérations*, op. cit., ch. X, pp. 280–1.
24. *Lettres de Mme de Staël à Narbonne*, Introduction, notes et commentaires par Georges Solovieff, Paris, 1960. *Récit du sauvetage de Narbonne par E. Bollmann*, translated and edited by G. Solovieff, ibid., pp. 48–9.
25. Ibid., pp. 50–7.
26. *Correspondance générale*, op. cit., vol. 2, part 1, letter of 25 August 1792, pp. 1–3.
27. Morris, op. cit. pp. 576–7.
28. *Correspondance générale*, op. cit., vol. 2, part 2, p. 357, footnote 3.
29. *Considérations*, op. cit., part 3, pp. 282–3.
30. Ibid., p. 283.
31. Ibid.
32. *Correspondance générale*, op. cit., pp. 13–14.
33. Ibid., p. 14.
34. Pauline Chapman, *The French revolution as seen by Madame Tussaud; Witness Extraordinary*, London, 1989, p. 122.
35. *Considérations*, op. cit., pp. 283–6.

9 Burning Letters

1. *Correspondance générale*, op. cit., vol 2, part 1, preface, p. xii. When Narbonne left France, he gave his letters from Madame de Staël for safekeeping to his friend d'Arblay, who had married Fanny Burney. They disappeared for many years, turning up eventually among a collection of Fanny d'Arblay's papers. On the folder containing them, Fanny had written: 'Burning letters for burning – a fine moral lesson too.' Fortunately, she did not take this extreme measure. The papers were later sold to the Berg collection of the New York Public Library.
2. Ibid., letter of 7 September 1792, p. 16.
3. Ibid., pp. 17–18.
4. Ibid., p. 18.
5. Kohler, *Mme de Staël et la Suisse*, op. cit., p. 126.
6. *Correspondance générale*, op. cit., vol 2, part 1, letter of 18 September 1792, p. 22–3.
7. Ibid., letter of 19 September 1792, pp. 23–4.
8. *Extracts from the Journals and Correspondence of Miss Berry*, op. cit., vol. 1, p. 381.
9. The radical Thomas Paine had written this pamphlet in response to Burke's attack on the Revolution. It became a runaway bestseller. In August 1792, the Legislative Assembly accorded him honorary French citizenship for services to the cause of freedom, along with several others, among them William Wilber-

force, Jeremy Bentham and George Washington. He was elected to the Convention as a member for the Pas-de-Calais where he sat with the Girondins.
10. Ibid., Miss Berry letter of 19 September 1792, pp. 24–7.
11. *Diary and Letters of Mme d'Arblay*, London, 1854, vol. 5 p. 283.
12. Ibid., p. 299–301.
13. Ibid.
14. *Correspondance générale*, op. cit., vol. 2, p. 29.
15. Ibid., letter of 2 October 1792, pp. 35–7.
16. Ibid., letter of 13 October 1792, p. 45.
17. Ibid., letter of 15 November 1792, pp. 65–7.
18. Ibid., letter of 27 October 1792, p. 55.
19. Ibid., p. 31.
20. *Considérations*, op. cit. Part III, ch. XII, p. 288.
21. *Correspondance générale*, op. cit., letter of 12 November 1792, p. 64.
22. Solovieff, *Lettres*, op. cit. p. 152. The reforming and radical Gracchi brothers, Tiberius and Caius, were members of the Roman Liberal aristocracy in the last century of the Republic. Their mother Cornelia, herself daughter of Scipio Africanus, had given her sons an education such as would make 'her two jewels' worthy of her father's great name. Guibert had composed a tragedy on the subject which Madame de Staël, in her *Éloge de Guibert*, had called 'the most republican play we have'. André Chénier had also written a tragedy – *Caius Gracchus*, – which had been very succesful early that year.
23. *Correspondance générale*, op. cit., vol. 2, part 2, p. 369.
24. Ibid., letter of 23 December 1792, pp. 90–1.
25. Ibid., letter of 26 December 1792, pp. 95–6.
26. Ibid., vol. 2, part 2, letter of 28 December 1792, pp. 374–5.
27. Kohler, op. cit., p. 133.
28. The same man who had protected Madame de Staël's coach from looters outside the Hôtel de Ville during the September massacres, was now commander of the National Guard.
29. Morris, op. cit., vol. 2, p. 31.
30. *Memoirs of Madame de La Tour du Pin*, op. cit., p. 177.

10 Juniper Hall

1. Madame d'Arblay, *Diary and Letters*, edited by her niece, 7 vols, London 1845, vol. V, 1789–93, p. 365.
2. Ibid., letter of 28 January 1793, vol. V, p. 325.
3. *Correspondance générale*, op. cit., vol. 2, part 1, letter to Narbonne of 24 January 1793, pp. 101–2, and vol. 2, part 2, letter of same date to Lord Grenville, pp. 380–1. Letter from Lally-Tollendal to Lord Grenville from the manuscripts of J. B. Fortescue, Esq., preserved at Dropmore, vol. III, pp. 478–9. Quoted in *Correspondance générale*, p. 380, note 4.
4. D'Arblay, *Diary and Letters*, op. cit., vol. V, pp. 329–30.
5. Ibid., pp. 330–1.
6. Ibid., letter of 22 February 1793, pp. 339–42.
7. Ibid.
8. *Lettres de Mme de Staël à Narbonne*, op. cit., pp. 203–4.
9. *The Journals and Letters of Fanny Burney (Madame d'Arblay)*, edited by Joyce Hemlow, 12 vols, London, 1972–84, vol. 2, p. 31.
10. Ibid., p. 32.
11. *Correspondance générale*, op. cit., vol. 2, part 2, p. 408.
12. d'Haussonville, *Souvenirs et mélanges*, cited by Ghislain de Diesbach in *Histoire de l'Émigration 1789–1814*, Paris, 1984, p. 289.

13. Diesbach, ibid., p. 288.
14. *Lettres à Narbonne*, op. cit., pp. 498–9.
15. *Correspondance générale*, op. cit., vol. 2, part 2, p. 408.
16. *Lettres à Narbonne*, op. cit., pp. 498–9.
17. *Private Letters of Edward Gibbon* edited by R. E. Prothero, London, vol. II, letters of 15 March 1793, p. 375 and 26 March 1793, p. 377, quoted in *Correspondance générale*, op. cit., vol. 2, part 2, p. 410.
18. d'Arblay, *Diary and Letters*, op. cit., vol. V, pp. 345–6.
19. Ibid.
20. *Correspondance générale*, op. cit., vol. 2, part 2, pp. 413–14.
21. d'Arblay, *Diary and Letters*, op. cit., vol. V, p. 346.
22. *Moniteur*, 5 April 1793, cited by B. Jasinski, p. 420.
23. *Parliamentary History*, vol. XXX, pp. 194–258.
24. Mme de Staël, *Considérations*, op. cit., part III, ch. XVI, p. 300.
25. *Correspondance générale*, vol. 2, part 2, letter of 25 April 1793 to Gibbon, pp. 422–9.
26. *Correspondance générale*, vol. 2, part 2, letter of 8 May 1793, pp. 437–8.
27. d'Arblay, *Diary and Letters*, op. cit., vol. V, p. 348.
28. Ibid., p. 353–4.
29. Ibid., pp. 351–3.
30. d'Arblay, *Diary and Letters*, op. cit., vol. V, p. 365.

11 Scarlet Woman and Scarlet Pimpernel

1. *Considérations*, op. cit., part 3, ch. XVIII, pp. 311–12.
2. Ibid., part 3, ch. XVI, p. 303.
3. This populist paper, aimed at the *sans-culottes*, was published by Jacques René Hébert between 1790 and 1794. It was named after a fictional character who smoked a pipe and talked the coarse language of the streets.
4. *Considérations*, op. cit., p. 309.
5. *Correspondance générale*, op. cit., vol. 2, Part 1, letter of 2 June 1793, pp. 113–14.
6. Ibid., p. 455 and footnote 9.
7. Ibid., letters of 10, 11, 15 June 1793, pp. 121–7.
8. Ibid., pp. 127–30.
9. Ibid., p. 144.
10. Ibid., p. 465.
11. Jules Michelet, *Histoire de la Révolution française*, 2 vols, Paris, 1952, vol. 2, pp. 645–6.
12. Madame de Staël, *Réflexions sur le procès de la Reine*, in *Oeuvres complètes*, op. cit., vol. 1, pp. 1–33.
13. A Söderhjelm, *Fersen et Marie-Antoinette*, op. cit., p. 303.
14. Ibid., p. 468, footnote 8.
15. Ibid., letter of 21 September, 1793, p. 163.
16. Ibid., p. 166.
17. Ibid., pp. 169–71.
18. d'Arblay, 7 vols, London, 1854, op. cit., vol. 6, pp. 10–11.
19. *Correspondance générale*, op. cit., vol. 2, part 1, pp. 172–3.
20. Ibid.
21. Ibid., p. 179. Charlotte Corday had recently assassinated Marat. Madame de Staël must have been thinking of her when she made her threat.
22. Ibid., letter of 13 December 1793, pp. 209–10.
23. Ibid., vol. 2, part 2, letter of 19 November 1793, p. 490.
24. Ibid., letter 1 December 1793, p. 509.
25. Ibid., letter 13 December 1793, p. 526.

26. Ibid., letter of 30 December 1793, pp. 542–3.
27. Ibid., letter of 18 January 1794, pp. 550–53.
28. Ibid., vol. 2, part 1, letter of 21 February 1794, p. 229.
29. Ibid., p. 237.
30. Ibid., p. 253.
31. Ibid., letter to Ribbing of 29 April 1794, pp. 631–4.
32. Mme de Staël, *Oeuvres complètes*, op. cit., vol. 17, *Du caractère de M. Necker*, pp. 88–90.
33. Coppet Archives, Madame Necker's papers cited by B. d'Andlau, in *La Jeunesse* . . . op. cit., p. 50.
34. Ibid., p. 90.
35. F. Golovkine, *La Cour et le Règne de Paul per*, Paris 1905, pp. 314–16.
36. *Correspondance générale*, op. cit., vol. 3, part 1, letter of 10 September 1794, p. 101.

12 Benjamin Constant

1. Madame de Staël, *De l'Influence des passions sur le bonheur des individus et des nations*, Paris, 2000, p. 125.
2. *Correspondance générale*, op. cit., vol. 3, part 1, p. 103.
3. Ibid., p. 117.
4. P. Godet, *Madame de Charrière et ses amis*, 2 vols, Geneva 1906, vol. 2, pp. 163–4, letter of 24 September 1794.
5. *Lettres de Benjamin Constant à sa famille*, edited by J.Menos, Paris, 1888, letter of 18 February 1788.
6. *Correspondance générale*, vol. 3, part 1, p. 149.
7. Ibid., letter of 30 October 1794, p. 170.
8. Jasinski, *L'Engagement de Benjamin Constant*, op. cit., pp. 16–17.
9. Coppet Archives, *Madame de Staël et L'Europe*, Bibliothèque Nationale catalogue no. 146 (1966) quoted by B. Jasinski in *L'Engagement de B. Constant*, Paris 1971, p. 13.
10. Ibid., pp. 17–18.
11. Simone Balayé, *Madame de Staël*, Paris 1797, pp. 34–5, footnotes 4 and 5.
12. Benjamin Constant, *Amélie et Germaine Ma Vie – Cécile*, ed. P. Delbouille, Paris 1989, pp. 183–4.
13. *Correspondance générale*, vol. 3, part 1, op. cit., letter of 22 October 1794, p. 158.
14. Benjamin Constant, *Journal intime*, cited by B.Jasinski, *L'Engagement* . . ., op. cit. pp. 19–20.
15. *Correspondance générale*, op. cit., letter of 1 March 1795, p. 264.
16. J. M. Norvins, *Mémorial*, 3 vols, Paris, 1896, vol. II, cited by B. Jasinski in *L'Engagement* . . ., op. cit., p. 10.
17. Madame de Staël, *Oeuvres complètes*, op. cit., vol. II, pp. 36–95.
18. Ibid., Preface, p. 36.
19. *Parliamentary History*, vol. XXXI 1345–1413, speech of the Rt. Hon. Charles James Fox in the House of Commons on Tuesday, 24 May 1795.
20. *Correspondance générale*, op. cit., vol. 3, part 1, pp. 322–3.
21. Madame de Staël, *De l'Influence des passions sur le bonheur des individus et des nations*, Paris, 2000, p. 76.
22. *Lettres inédites de Madame de Staël à Henri Meister*, edited by P. Usteri and E. Ritter, Paris 1903, pp. 126–7.
23. Kohler, *Madame de Staël et la Suisse*, op.cit., pp. 181–2.
24. Léouzon Le Duc, *Correspondance diplomatique du baron de Staël-Holstein 1783–1799*, Introduction, cited by Lady Blennerhassett, *Madame de Staël and her influence in politics and literature*, 3 vols, London 1889, vol. 2, pp. 238–9.

13 The New Republicans

1. *Lettres inédites de Madame de Staël à Henri Meister*, op. cit., p. 134.
2. *Correspondance générale*, op. cit., vol. 3, part 1, *Journal des Lois de la République française*, 26 April 1795, cited by B. Jasinski, p. 316.
3. Ibid., p. 317.
4. Ibid., p. 321.
5. Ibid., p. 3, Jasinski citing diplomatic correspondence between France and Prussia in 1795.
6. *Lettres inédites à H. Meister*, op. cit., pp. 45–9.
7. *Considérations*, op. cit., part III, ch. XX, p. 316.
8. *Correspondance générale*, op. cit., vol. 3, part 2, p. 8
9. *Oeuvres complètes*, op. cit., vol. II, p. 113.
10. *Considérations*, op. cit., part III, ch. XX, p. 317.
11. *Lettres de Mme de Staël à Ribbing*, edited by S. Balayé, Paris 1960, Appendix, p. 416.
12. J. Mallet du Pan, Correspondance avec la Cour de Vienne, *Mémoires et Correspondance de Mallet du Pan*, 2 vols, Paris 1851, p. 333, cited by Blennerhassett, op. cit., p. 253.
13. *Correspondance de Napoléon 1er rassemblée dans les ouvrages publiés par les soins de Napoléon III 1858–69*, Paris 1858.
14. Ibid.
15. *Considérations*, op. cit., part III, ch. XX, p. 317.
16. *Correspondance générale*, op. cit., vol. 3, part 2, p. 22, letter of 27 June 1795.
17. *Considérations*, op. cit., ch. XX, p. 316.
18. B. Jasinski, *L'Engagement de B. Constant*, op. cit., p. 108.
19. Ibid., pp. 110–125.
20. Ibid., pp. 128–9.
21. J. Mallet du Pan, Correspondance inédite, *Mémoires*, op. cit., vol. ii, p. 10, cited by Blennerhassett, op. cit., vol. 2, p. 253.
22. *Correspondance générale*, op. cit., vol. 3, part 2, article of 26 August 1795, cited by B. Jasinski, p. 43.
23. *Lettres à Ribbing*, op. cit., article of 2 September 1795, pp. 328–9.
24. *Correspondance générale*, op. cit., vol. 3, part 2, op. cit., letter to Ribbing of 31 August 1795, p. 46.
25. Lacretelle, *Dix années d'épreuves*, Paris 1938, p. 248, cited by S. Balayé, p. 333.
26. Comtesse Jean de Pange, *Madame de Staël et François de Pange*, Paris 1925, p. 124.
27. *Considérations*, op. cit., part III, ch. XXI, pp. 321–2.
28. *Correspondance générale*, vol. 3, part 2, op. cit., letter of 13 January 1796, pp. 114–15.
29. Ibid., letter of 25 January 1796, pp. 119–21.
30. Benjamin Constant, *De la force du gouvernement actuel de la France et de la nécessité de s'y rallier*, Paris 1988.
31. Mme de Staël, *De la Littérature*, Paris 1991, p. 88, and *De l'influence des passions sur le bonheur des individus et des nations*, Paris 2000, p. 26.
32. Ibid., p. 54.
33. Ibid., p. 23.
34. Ibid., pp. 133.
35. Foreign Affairs archives, vol. 103, fo. 375, Paris, cited by B. Jasinski in *Correspondance générale*, vol. 3, part 2, letter of 12 February 1796, pp. 135–6.
36. Ibid., pp. 135–7 and Comtesse de Pange, op. cit., pp. 201–6.
37. P. Gautier, *Mathieu de Montmorency et Madame de Staël*, Paris 1908, p. 68 cited by S. Balayé in *Lettres à Ribbing*, op. cit. p. 357.

38. Ibid., pp. 365–6.
39. *Correspondance générale*, op. cit., vol. 3, part 2, letter of 12 February 1796, pp. 135–6.
40. B. Jasinski, *L'Engagement de Benjamin Constant*, op. cit., p. 27.
41. *Lettres à Ribbing*, op. cit., Appendix VII, pp. 420.
42. *Correspondance générale*, op. cit., vol. 3, part 2, letter cited by B.Jasinki, p. 225.
43. Ibid., p. 230.
44. Ibid., pp. 259–60.
45. Ibid., letter of 1 October 1796, pp. 244–50.

14 From Fructidor to Brumaire

1. Letter of 18 or 19 December 1796, p. 16.
2. Ibid., citing *Journal général de France* of 9 January 1797.
3. Kohler, *Madame de Staël et la Suisse*, op. cit., p. 234.
4. *Correspondance générale*, op. cit., vol. 4, part 1, letter to Pictet-Diodati of 6 February 1797, pp. 34–5.
5. Ibid., letter of 11 February 1797, pp. 38–9.
6. B. Constant, *Des effets de la Terreur* from *Les Oeuvres de Benjamin Constant*, ed. A. Roulin, Paris 1957.
7. *Correspondance générale*, vol. 4, part 1, letter of 22 April 1797, pp. 59–60.
8. Benjamin Constant, *Lettres à sa famille*, edited by Jean Menos, Paris 1888.
9. Kohler, *Madame de Staël et la Suisse*, op. cit. p. 232.
10. *Correspondance générale*, vol. 4, part 1, letter of 20 June 1797, pp. 73–4.
11. *Mémoires de Barras membre du Directoire*, edited by G. Dury, Paris 1895–96, 4 vols, vol. 2, chs XXX–XXXI, pp. 448–65.
12. *Memoirs of Madame de La Tour du Pin*, op. cit., pp. 304–5.
13. *Correspondance générale*, vol. 4, part 1, p. 83.
14. *Memoirs of Madame de La Tour du Pin*, op. cit., p. 305.
15. Ibid., p. 306.
16. Ibid., p. 313.
17. *Correspondance générale*, vol. 4, part 1, letter of 20 September 1797, pp. 92–5.
18. B. Constant, *Mémoires sur les Cent Jours en formes de lettres* in *Les Oeuvres de Benjamin Constant*, op. cit.
19. *Considérations*, op. cit., part 3, p. 334.
20. Ibid., p. 343.
21. Ibid., p. 337.
22. Ibid.
23. Blennerhassett, *Madame de Staël . . .* op. cit., vol. 2, op. cit., letter to Meister of 24 July 1797.
24. *Fingal, an ancient epic poem*, actually by James Macpherson, but purporting to be a translation by him of an ancient Gallic epic by Ossian, son of Fingal, was published in 1762. It had became famous and all Europe was convinced of its authenticity, including Hume and Adam Smith, Goethe and Schiller, Madame de Staël and Napoleon, who numbered it among his favourite works.
25. Emmanuel de Las Cases, *Mémorial de Sainte Hélène, 1823–1824*, Paris 1968, vol. II, pp. 195, 18–20 January 1816, and General Bourrienne, *Mémoires*, 10 vols, Paris 1829, vol. VI.
26. Paul Gautier, *Madame de Staël et Napoléon*, Paris 1903, letter of 1 October 1797.
27. *Considérations*, op. cit., pp. 338–9.
28. Ibid.
29. Ibid., p. 339.

30. Lucien Bonaparte, *Mémoires*, vol. II, p. 231, cited by Paul Gautier in *Madame de Staël et Napoléon*, Paris 1903, p. 8 and Arnault, *Souvenirs d'un Sexagénaire*, vol. IV, p. 24, cited by G.de Diesbach, *Madame de Staël*, op. cit.
31. Lucien Bonaparte, *Mémoires*, Ibid., p. 342.
32. Bourrienne, *Mémoires*, op. cit.
33. *Considérations*, op. cit., p. 343.
34. Ibid., pp. 344–5.
35. d'Haussonville, *Madame de Staël et Necker*, Paris 1925, p. 82.
36. Ibid., letter of 4 May, p. 88.
37. Madame de Staël, *Des Circonstances actuelles qui peuvent terminer la Révolution et des principes qui doivent fonder la République en France*, edited by Lucia Omacini, Paris-Genève 1979, p. 122.
38. d'Haussonville, *Madame de Staël et M. Necker*, op. cit., letter of 20 April 1799.
39. *Correspondance générale*, vol. 4, part 1, p. 374.
40. Ibid.
41. *Considérations*, op. cit., part 4, ch. 2, p. 357.
42. d'Haussonville, *Madame de Staël et M. Necker*, op. cit., pp. 101–2.

15 The First Consul

1. Madame de Staël, *Dix années d'exil*, edited by Simone Balayé and Mariella Vianello Bonifacio, Paris 1996, Part I, p. 84.
2. d'Haussonville *Mme de Staël et M. Necker*, op. cit., pp. 102–3.
3. Ibid., p. 105.
4. Albert Vandal, *L'Avènement de Bonaparte*, Paris 1903, vol. II, pp. 31–42. Constant's speech in *Écrits et discours publiques de Benjamin Constant*, Paris, vol. I, pp. 139–153.
5. d'Haussonville, *Mme de Staël et M. Necker*, op. cit., p. 121.
6. Gautier, *Mme de Staël et Napoléon*, op. cit., p. 39, footnote 3.
7. *Dix années d'exil*, op. cit., p. 85.
8. *Correspondance générale*, op. cit, vol. 4, Part 1, p. 250, footnote 3.
9. Ibid., letter of 9 January 1800, pp. 250–2.
10. *Dix années d'exil*, op. cit., p. 89.
11. Ibid., p. 84.
12. Ibid., p. 88.
13. d'Haussonville, *Mme. de Staël et M. Necker* op. cit., p. 121.
14. *Correspondance générale*, op. cit, vol. 4, Part 1, p. 257, and Comtesse Victorine de Chastenay, *Mémoires*, Paris 1896, vol. I, pp. 419–20.
15. *Correspondance générale*, op. cit, p. 257.
16. Gautier, *Mme de Staël et Napoléon*, op. cit., pp. 45–6.
17. Mme de Staël, *De la littérature*, edited by Gérard Gengembre and Jean Goldzink, Paris 1991, ch. III, p. 87.
18. Ibid., cited by Simone Balayé in *Madame de Staël*, Paris 1797, pp. 81–8.
19. *De la littérature*, op. cit., p. 205. Montesquieu had paid the English a similarly backhanded compliment. The English dislike of autocracy is strong, he wrote in *the Spirit of the Laws*, because: 'In a nation so distempered by the climate as to have a disrelish of everything, nay even life, it is plain that the government most suitable to the inhabitants is that in which they cannot lay their uneasiness to any single person's charge.' As for political progress he wrote: 'Slavery is ever preceded by sleep. But a people who find no rest in any situation, who continually explore every part, and feel nothing but pain, can hardly be lulled to sleep.' Book XIV, ch. 13.
20. Ibid., p. 211.
21. C-A. Sainte-Beuve, *Portraits de femmes*, Paris 1998, p. 103.

22. Ibid., pp. 114–19.
23. Ibid., pp. 121–3.
24. *Dix années d'exil*, op. cit. p. 94.
25. Lucien Bonaparte, *Mémoires*, Paris 1836, vol. II, p. 242, cited by Gautier in *Mme. de Staël et Napoléon*, op. cit. p. 58, footnote 1.
26. Comtesse d'Hautefeuille, cited by H.Noel Williams in *Mme Récamier and her Friends*, London and New York 1901, p. 331.
27. Mme Lenormant, *Souvenirs et correspondance de Mme Récamier*, Paris 1859, vol. I, p. 24.
28. Benjamin Constant, *Portraits, Mémoires, Souvenirs*, 'Les Mémoires de Juliette', Paris 1992, p. 282.
29. *Dix années d'exil*, op. cit., p. 94.
30. *Considérations*, op. cit. p. 377.
31. Comte de Las Cases, cited by Jasinski in *Correspondance générale*, op. cit., vol. 4, part 1, p. 274.
32. Ibid., letter to Baron de Gérando of 29 Floreal Year VIII (19 May 1800), pp. 274–6.
33. Mme. Necker-de Saussure, *Notice sur le caractère*, op. cit., pp. 242–9.
34. Ibid., pp. 251–2.
35. *Correspondance générale*, op. cit, vol. 4, Part 1, letter of mid-June 1800, p. 288.
36. Ibid., letter of 17 August 1800, p. 305.
37. Ibid., letter of 8 October 1800, pp. 328–9.
38. Ibid., p. 306, footnote 5.

16 The Empress of the Mind

1. Th. Jung, *Lucien Bonaparte et ses mémoires, 1775–1840*, 3 vols, Paris, vol II, p. 233
2. Madame de La Tour du Pin, *Memoires*, op. cit., p. 346.
3. *Dix années d'exil*, op. cit., p. 95.
4. Ibid., pp. 101–2. In fact sixty-eight were sent to the Seychelles and twenty-six to French Guiana. More than half died in exile. (Georges Lefebvre, *Napoléon*, p. 122).
5. Ibid., p. 110.
6. Madame de La Tour du Pin, *Memoirs*, op. cit., pp. 346–7.
7. Lucien Bonaparte, op. cit., vol. II, p. 255; also Général Bertrand, *Cahiers de Sainte Hélène*, Paris 1951–9, vol. I, p. 358, see *Dix années d'exil*, op. cit., p. 49, footnote 5.
8. Comtesse Jean de Pange, *Monsieur de Staël*, op. cit., pp. 233–5.
9. *Memoires et correspondance du roi Joseph par le Baron du Casse*, Paris 1856–69 vol. I, p. 190, letter of 19 March.
10. *Correspondance générale*, vol. 4, part 2, letter of 3 Germinal (24 March 1802), pp. 358–60.
11. Ibid., letter of 11 Germinal (1 April 1800).
12. *Dix années d'exil*, op. cit., p. 105.
13. Ibid., p. 118.
14. B. d'Andlau, *La jeunesse de Madame de Staël*, Paris-Genève 1970, p. 114.
15. *Correspondance générale*, op. cit., vol. 4, part 2, letter of 13 November 1801, p. 426.
16. Ibid., letter of 8 December, p. 440.
17. Jung, *Lucien Bonaparte*, op. cit., p. 484.
18. Ibid., p. 237, also cited by Gautier, *Madame de Staël et Napoléon*, op. cit., p. 71.
19. *Dix années d'exil*, op. cit., p. 124.
20. *Considérations*, op. cit., p. 375.

21. *Dix années d'exil*, op. cit., p. 127.
22. Madame d'Arblay, *Diary and Letters*, vol. 6 op. cit., pp. 152–3.
23. *Correspondance Générale*, vol. 4, part 2, letter of 5 Floreal (25 April 1802), pp. 493–5.
24. Ibid., letter of 12 or 19 May 1802, p. 506.
25. Comte E. de Las Cases, *Mémorial de Sainte Hélène*, Paris 1948, chapter V, cited by Gautier, *Mme de Staël et Napoléon*, op. cit., p. 80.
26. Ibid., p. 83.
27. *Dix années d'exil*, op. cit., p. 130.
28. *Lucien Bonaparte et ses mémoires*, op. cit., vol. II, p. 107.
29. *Correspondance générale*, op. cit., vol. 4, part 2, letter of 4 August 1802, pp. 542–3.
30. Ibid., letter of 12 August 1802 to C. Hochet, pp. 543–4.
31. *Dix années d'exil*, op. cit., p. 131.
32. Ibid.
33. Gautier, *Mme de Staël et Napoléon*, op. cit., pp. 90–96.
34. Ibid. Lebrun's letter to Necker of 23 Thermidor Year X 9, (15 August 1802).
35. Madame de Staël to Chateaubriand, cited by Madame Necker-de Saussure, *Notice sur la caractère*, op. cit., vol. II, p. 53.
36. Constant, *Portraits, Mémoires, Souvenirs*, op. cit., 'De Madame de Staël et de ses ouvrages', p. 213.
37. Pieter Geyl, *Napoleon For and Against*, London 1965, p. 23.

17 The Sorrows of Delphine

1. P. L. Roederer, *Oeuvres*, Paris 1853–59, vol. V.
2. Lord Granville Leveson-Gower, *Private Correspondence*, ed. Countess Granville, 2 vols, 1916, vol. 1, p. 380, reported conversation with Narbonne (translated from the French by the author).
3. Madame de Staël, *Delphine*, introduced by Béatrice Didier, 2 vols. Paris 2000.
4. Gautier, *Madame de Staël et Napoléon*, op. cit., p. 103.
5. d'Haussonville, *Mme de Staël et M. Necker*, op. cit., p. 213.
6. Archives de Broglie cited by Gautier in *Madame de Staël et Napoléon*, op. cit., p. 116.
7. Ibid., p. 117.
8. *Delphine*, op. cit, vol. II, 'Quelques réflexions sur le but moral de Delphine', Annexes, pp. 363–77.
9. Benjamin Constant, 'Compte rendu de Delphine', published in *Le Citoyen Français*, 10 January 1803; see Annexes, *Delphine*, op. cit., vol. II, pp. 379–83.
10. *Correspondance générale*, op. cit., vol. 4, part 2, letter of 27 March 1803, pp. 601–4.
11. Ibid., p. 596.
12. d'Haussonville, *Mme de Staël et M. Necker*, op. cit., pp. 240–1.
13. Benjamin Constant, *Amélie et Germaine, Ma Vie – Cécile*, edited by Paul Delbouille, Paris 1989, p. 59.
14. *Dix années d'exil*, op. cit., p. 143.
15. *Correspondance générale*, op. cit., vol. 4, part 2, letters of 22 and 23 July 1803, pp. 646 and 650.
16. Ibid., vol. 5, part 1, letter of 15–16 September 1803, pp. 14–15.
17. *Correspondance générale*, Vol. 5, p. 54, footnote 5.
18. Ibid., letter of 23–24 September 1803, pp. 18–19.
19. Ibid., letter of 7 October 1803 and p. 52, footnote 5.
20. *Dix années d'exil*, op. cit., p. 157.

21. Leonce Pingaud, *Camille Jordan and Lady Elizabeth Foster*, Paris 1904, cited by Jasinski, *Correspondance Générale*, op. cit., vol. 5, part 1, p. 56.
22. Ibid., letter of 10 October 1803, p. 57.
23. *Dix années d'exil*, op. cit., p. 153.
24. Duchesse d'Abrantès, *Mémoires*, 12 vols, Paris 1838, cited by Gautier, *Mme de Staël et Napoléon* op. cit., p. 137.
25. d'Haussonville, *Mme de Staël et M. Necker*, op. cit., p. 335.
26. Constant, *Amélie et Germaine*, op. cit., p. 193.
27. d'Haussonville, *Mme de Staël et M. Necker*, op. cit., letter of 28 October, p. 336.

18 Germany

1. Cited in *Correspondance générale*, op. cit., vol. 5, part 1, introduction.
2. Mme de Staël, *Corinne*, book I, ch. II, cited by Simone Balayé in *Madame de Staël: Écrire, Lutter, Vivre*, Droz 1994, p. 55.
3. *Correspondance générale*, op. cit., vol. 5, part 1, letter of 29 October 1803, pp. 86–7.
4. Mme de Staël, *De l'Allemagne*, Paris 1968, vol. 1, ch. XIII, p. 115.
5. Ibid., letter of 14 November 1803, p. 104.
6. Ibid., letter of 15 November 1803, p. 109.
7. Sömmering was an anatomist, famous for declaring that following decapitation, the severed head remained alive and conscious of pain for a while longer – a subject not without interest after the French Revolution.
8. Ibid., letter of 10 December 1803, p. 136.
9. Ibid., p. 132.
10. Ibid., p. 134.
11. Isaiah Berlin, *The Roots of Romanticism*, London 1999.
12. Mme de Staël, *De l'Allemagne*, op. cit., p. 142.
13. *Madame de Staël et la Grande Duchesse Louise – Coppet et Weimar*, par l'auteur des Souvenirs de Mme Récamier, Paris 1862, p. 35.
14. Ibid., letter of 4 January 1804, Schiller to Koerner, pp. 36–7.
15. Ibid., pp. 38–9.
16. Ibid., pp. 39–40.
17. *Madame de Staël et la Grande Duchesse Louise*, op. cit., pp. 40–42.
18. *Correspondance Générale*, op. cit., vol. 5, part 1, pp. 162–4.
19. Ibid., p. 173.
20. Ibid., p. 166.
21. Ibid., pp. 187–8.
22. Henry Crabb Robinson, *Diary, Reminiscences and Correspondence*, edited by Thomas Sadler, 2 vols, Boston 1869, vol. 1.
23. *Correspondance générale*, letter of 5 February 1804, p. 220.
24. B. Constant, *Journal intime*, edited by Ed. du Rocher, Monaco 1946, entry for 12 February 1804, p. 160.
25. Goethe's diary, 1804, cited by H. Nicholson in *Benjamin Constant*, London 1949, p. 163.
26. *Correspondance générale*, op. cit., vol. 5, part 1, letter of 17 February 1804, p. 234.
27. Constant, *Journal intime*, op. cit., p. 161. There had been a wave of suicides in imitation of Werther's after the publication of the book.
28. *Correspondance générale*, p. 224. German philosopher, follower of Kant, whose theory of the *absolute ego* as opposed to the *empirical ego* was metaphysical enough to amuse even Goethe and Schiller. For a clear exposition of Fichte's theory and its implications for the Romantic movement as well as for his influence on German romantic philosophy, see Isaiah Berlin's *The Roots of Romanticism*.

29. Nicholson, *Benjamin Constant*, op. cit., p. 162.
30. Charles-Augustin Sainte-Beuve, *Portraits de femmes*, citing letter of 27 February 1804, p. 140.
31. Constant, *Journal intime*, op. cit. p. 165.
32. *Correspondance générale*, op. cit., vol. 5, part 1, pp. 247–8.
33. Ibid., letter of 11 March 1804, pp. 265–7.
34. Ibid., letter of 23 March 1804, pp. 284–6.
35. *The Life, Letters & Journals of George Ticknor*, 2 vols, Boston 1880, vol. 1, pp. 497–8, cited by B. Jasinski in *Correspondance générale*, op. cit., vol. 5, part 1, pp. 293–4.
36. Ibid., letter of 31 March 1804, pp. 296–7.
37. Ibid., letter of 27 March 1804, pp. 290–3.
38. Ibid., letter of 31 March 1804, p. 300.
39. Ibid., letter of 1 April 1804, pp. 306–10.
40. *Considérations*, op. cit., part IV, p. 398.
41. *Correspondance générale*, op. cit., vol. 5, part 1, p. 391.
42. A usually fatal streptococcal infection which manifested itself as an inflammation of either the face or the leg. Easily cured with penicillin, it is almost unknown today but was fairly common at the time. The patient rarely survived for more than a week.
43. d'Haussonville, *Mme de Staël et l'Allemagne*, Paris 1928, pp. 262, 265.
44. Constant, *Journal intime*, op. cit., p. 172.
45. *Correspondance générale*, op. cit., vol. 5, part 1, p. 337.
46. Ibid., pp. 337–8.
47. Constant, *Journal intime*, op. cit., p. 179.
48. Mme de Staël, *Dix années d'exil*, op. cit., p. 175.

19 Song of Italy

1. Mme de Staël, *Du caractère de M. Necker et de sa vie privée*, op. cit., p. 107.
2. Kohler, *Madame de Staël et la Suisse*, op. cit., p. 451.
3. Mme de Staël, *Du caractère de M. Necker* . . . op. cit., pp. 105–6.
4. Ibid., p. 105.
5. Ibid., p. 111.
6. Ibid., p. 118.
7. *Considérations*, op. cit., part IV, ch. X, p. 393.
8. Constant, *Journal intime*, op. cit., pp. 181–2.
9. Ibid., pp. 187, 190.
10. C. L. Simonde de Sismondi, *Fragments de son journal et correspondance*, Geneva 1857, letter of 13 December 1830.
11. Constant, *Journal intime*, op. cit., p. 194.
12. Letter of 1 August 1804 from the military camp of Outreau, Broglie Archives, cited by P. Gautier in *Madame de Staël et Napoléon*, op. cit., p. 163.
13. *Correspondance générale*, op. cit., letter of 31 July 1804, p. 395.
14. Gautier, *Madame de Staël et Napoléon*, op. cit., p. 166.
15. *Considérations*, op. cit., p. 398.
16. Gautier, *Madame de Staël et Napoléon*, op. cit., p. 168.
17. *Correspondance générale*, op. cit., commentary by B. Jasinski, pp. 469–70 and letter of 14 January 1805, p. 475.
18. Ibid., p. 474.
19. Ibid., letter of 23 January 1805, pp. 480–1.
20. Ibid., letters of 6 and 7 February 1805, pp. 492, 493–5.
21. Simone Balayé, *Les Carnets de voyage de Madame de Staël*, Genève 1971. Madame de Staël must have been referring to the practice of cicisbeos, or walkers,

who invariably accompanied married Italian ladies and who affected an air of slavish adoration.

22. Cited by Ch. Dejob, *Mme de Staël et L'Italie*, Paris 1890.
23. Constant, *Journal intime*, op. cit., p. 232.
24. *Correspondance générale*, op. cit., vol. 5, part 2, pp. 504–5.
25. Benedetto Croce, *La signora di Staël et la regina Maria Carolina di Napoli in Uomini e cose della Vecchia Italia*, Bari 1956, p. 187.
26. *Correspondence générale*, op. cit., vol. 5, part 2, letter of 26 May, pp. 511–14.
27. Ibid., letters of 2 July, p. 612.
28. Ibid., letter of 14 June 1805, p. 594.
29. Colloque de Coppet 1966, *Madame de Staël et l'Europe*, Carlo Pellegrini, 'Corinne et son aspect politique', pp. 265–74.
30. Constant, *Portraits, Mémoires, Souvenirs*, op. cit., Paris, p. 220.
31. Mme de Staël, *Corinne ou l'Italie*, preface by S. Balayé, Gallimard, folio 1985, ch. 3, p. 160; see also Pellegrini, note 29 above.
32. Ibid., p. 365.
33. Ibid., footnote 19, p. 590 and 26, p. 592.
34. Ibid., p. 587.
35. Mme de Staël, *Oeuvres complètes, Le mannequin*, For English translation, see Vivian Folkenflik, *Major Writings of Madame de Staël*, New York 1987, p. 325.
36. Lefebvre, Georges, *Napoleon*, 2 vols, translated by J. E. Anderson, London 1969, vol. 2, p. 8.

20 *Corinne* and the Emperor

1. *Considérations*, op. cit., part IV, ch. XII, cited by S. Balayé in *Le Groupe de Coppet* op. cit., 1977.
2. François de Chateaubriand, *Mémoires d'outre- tombe*, 2 vols, Paris 1989, vol. 1, p. 583.
3. *Mémoires de la comtesse de Boigne*, 2 vols, Paris 1999, vol. 2, p. 242.
4. Ibid., pp. 248–9.
5. Ibid., pp. 249–51.
6. Duchesse de Broglie, *Notice sur M. le baron Auguste de Staël*, Albertine de Broglie's introduction to *Oeuvres diverses de M. le baron Auguste de Staël*, Paris 1829, vol. I, pp. i, ii, cited by Othenin d'Haussonville in *Auguste de Staël et ses parents.*
7. *Correspondance générale*, op. cit., vol. 5, part 2, p. 643, letter of 16–18 August 1805.
8. Othenin d'Haussonville, *Auguste de Staël et ses parents*, Paris 2002, *Cahiers Staëliens*, No. 53, pp. 145–64.
9. *Lettres inédites de Napoléon Ier An VIII (1815)*, edited by Léon Lecestre, 2 vols, Paris 1897, vol. I, pp. 57–8, cited by Jasinski in *Correspondance générale*, op. cit., vol. 5, part 2, p. 661.
10. Othenin d'Haussonville, *Auguste de Staël*, op. cit., letter of 5 December 1805, p. 149.
11. Baronne de Barante, *Lettres de Claude-Ignace de Barante à son fils Prosper . . . de Prosper de Barante à son père – de Prosper de Barante à Madame de Staël*, Paris 1929, p. 118.
12. Comtesse Jean de Pange, *Auguste-Guillaume Schlegel et Mme de Staël*, Paris 1938, p. 122.
13. Blennerhassett, op. cit., vol. 3, pp. 193–4, citing A. W. Schlegel, *Collected Works*, Leipzig 1848, vol. IX, pp. 266–81.
14. Constant, *Journal intime*, op. cit. p. 242.
15. *Lettres de Mme de Staël à Mme Récamier*, edited by Domat, Paris 1952, pp. 101.
16. *Correspondance, Mme de Staël et Don Pedro de Souza*, edited by B. d'Andlau, Paris

1979. Luiz de Camoëns (1525–79), national poet of Portugal and author of the *Lusiades*, an epic tale of Portuguese history and of the adventures of Vasco de Gama.
17. Othenin d'Haussonville, op. cit., p. 159.
18. Ibid., p. 146.
19. *Lettres inédites de Napoléon Ier*, op. cit., letter of 31 December 1806, cited by Gautier in *Madame de Staël et Napoléon*, op. cit., p. 185.
20. Ibid., letter of 15 March 1807, p. 186.
21. Ibid., letter of 19 April 1807, p. 187.
22. Gouverneur Morris, *Diary and Letters*, London 1889, vol. 2, p. 509.
23. *Memoirs of the Life of Sir James Mackintosh*, vol. I, London p. 405, cited by Blennerhassett, op. cit., vol. 3, p. 185.
24. Victor de Pange, *Le plus beau de toutes les fêtes, Correspondance inédite de Mme de Staël et d'Elizabeth Hervey, Duchesse de Devonshire*, Paris 1980, letter of 6 June 1807, pp. 37–8.
25. Thomas Moore, *Letters & Journals of Lord Byron*, London 1830, p. 407.
26. Blennerhassett, op. cit., vol. 3, p. 184.
27. S. Balayé, *Madame de Staël: Lumières et Liberté*, Paris 1797, p. 152, footnotes 93 and 94.
28. Gautier, *Madame de Staël et Napoléon*, op. cit., pp. 189–90.
29. *Correspondance générale*, op. cit., vol. 6, p. 295, commentary and footnote 1.
30. Benjamin Constant, *Adolphe*, Paris 1965.
31. Sismondi, *Fragments de son journal et correspondance*, op. cit., letter of 13 December 1830 to Mme de Sainte Aulaire, pp. 122–3.
32. *Byron's Letters and Journals*, edited by Leslie Marchand, London 1975, 12 vols, vol. 10, p. 167.
33. *Mémoires de la comtesse de Boigne*, op. cit., p. 243.
34. J. Menos, *Lettres de B. Constant à sa famille, 1775–1830*, Paris 1888, p. 42.
35. Constant, *Journal intime*, op. cit., p. 249.
36. Menos, *Lettres*, op. cit., letter of 6 October 1807, p. 42.
37. Constant, *Journal intime*, op. cit., p. 250.
38. Baronne de Barante, *Lettres de Claude-Ignace de Barante*, op. cit., p. 25.
39. Ibid., p. 308.
40. Blennerhassett, op. cit., vol. 3, p. 216.
41. M. de Bourrienne, *Mémoires*, 10 vols, vol. VIII, Paris, 1829, pp. 101–16 and *Oeuvres diverses de M. le baron Auguste de Staël*, op. cit., vols I, XXXI

21 Notre Dame de Coppet

1. *Correspondance générale*, op. cit., vol. 6, letter of 29 December 1807, p. 352.
2. Ibid., letter of 30 December 1807, pp. 353–4.
3. Ibid., letter of 18 January 1808, p. 363.
4. Madame de Staël, *De l'Allemagne*, 2 vols, Paris 1968, ch. VIII, p. 89.
5. Frances Trollope, *Vienna and the Austrians*, 2 vols, 1938, vol. 1, p. 317, cited by Philip Mansel, *Prince of Europe: Life of Charles Joseph de Ligne*, London 2003, p. 150.
6. *De l'Allemagne*, vol. 1, op. cit., pp. 90–1.
7. *Madame de Staël et Maurice O'Donnell 1805–17*, Paris 1926, pp. 40–4.
8. *Correspondance générale*, op. cit., letter of 1 April 1808, p. 398.
9. Prince de Ligne, *Mémoires, Lettres et Pensées*, edited by François Bourin, Paris 1989, pp. 814, 816.
10. Ibid., pp 774–5.
11. Ligne, *Fragments de l'histoire de ma vie*, vol. II, p. 59, cited by S. Balayé, *Mme de Staël: Lumières et Liberté*, op. cit. p. 158.
12. Ligne *Mémoires, Lettres*, op. cit., pp. 774–5.

13. *Correspondance générale*, op. cit., vol. 6, letter of 27 February 1807, pp. 203–4 and Colloque de Coppet, 1966, edited by Klincksieck, Paris 1970; Henri Perrochon, 'Les sources de la religion de Madame de Staël', pp. 5, 6.
14. *Correspondance générale*, op. cit., letter of 28 April 1808, and Perrochon op. cit.
15. *Madame de Staël et Maurice O'Donnell*, op. cit., p. 74. He was writing things down which she needed for *De l'Allemagne*.
16. Ibid., p. 96, also *Correspondance générale*, op. cit., vol. 6, op. cit., letter of May 1808 and p. 420, footnote 6. Chateaubriand addresses her directly in his *Lettre à M. de Fontanes*. 'You seem unhappy: you often complain in your work of the absence of a heart which might hear yours. You must know that there are certain souls who seek in vain for those with whom they might be united, and who are condemned by the Almighty to a kind of eternal widowhood.'
17. *Correspondance générale*, op. cit., vol. 6, letter of 30 April 1808, pp. 410–11.
18. Ibid., letter of 15 May 1808, pp. 420–1.
19. Ibid., letter of 28 May 1808, p. 435.
20. Lecestre, *Lettres inédites de Napoléon I, en An III (1815)*, Paris 1897, letter of 28 June 1808, cited by P. Gautier, *Mme de Staël et Napoléon* op. cit., p. 225.
21. Ligne, *Mémoires, Lettres et Pensées*, op. cit., pp. 611–21.
22. *Correspondance générale*, op. cit., vol. 6, letters of 5, 6, 14, 16 and 18 August 1808, 13 and 22 September 1808, 4 October 1808 and 9 February 1809.
23. Madame Vigée Lebrun, *Souvenirs*, 3 vols, Paris 1835–7, vol. II, p. 214, *De l'Allemagne*, vol. 1, ch. XX, pp. 151–5; see also Kohler, *Mme de Staël et la Suisse*, op. cit.
24. Kohler, *Mme de Staël et la Suisse*, op. cit., p. 548.
25. *Correspondance générale*, op. cit., vol. 6, p. 475.
26. Maurice Levaillant, *Une amitié amoureuse: Madame de Staël et Madame Récamier*, Paris 1956.
27. *Correspondance générale*, op. cit., letter of 28 February 1809.
28. Ibid., letter of 14 April 1809, p. 619.
29. *Lettres de B.Constant à sa famille*, Paris 1931, letters of 12, 13 July 1809, pp. 324–5.
30. *Mémoires de la Comtesse de Boigne*, op. cit., pp. 241–3.
31. Ibid., pp. 244–5.
32. *Lettres de B. Constant*, op. cit., letter of 14 November 1809, pp. 386–7.
33. *Letters de Madame de Staël à Mme Récamier*, op. cit., p. 154.
34. Baronne de Barante, *Lettres*, op. cit., p. 389.

22 *De l'Allemagne*

1. Ligne, *Mémoires, Lettres* op. cit., pp. 617–18.
2. Blennerhassett, vol. III, op. cit., letter to Meister of 25 May 1810, p. 306 and Voght's letter, p. 305. See also Prince J. de Broglie, *Madame de Staël et sa cour au Château de Chaumont*, Paris 1936, p. 255 and Levaillant, *Une amitié amoureuse*, op. cit.
3. Mme de Staël, *Dix années d'exil*, op. cit., p. 195.
4. Mme de Rémusat, *Mémoires*, Paris 1879–80, vol. II, p. 245.
5. Blennerhassett, op. cit., vol. III, p. 316, citing Metternich's Posthumous Papers, vol. III, p. 447.
6. Ibid.
7. *Dix années d'exil*, op. cit., pp. 196–7.
8. Ibid., pp. 197–9, see also p. 197, footnote 3, and p. 198, footnote 2. Madame de Staël gave this account to protect Corbigny who had in fact helped to save the final version of her book. He was to fall foul of the Emperor anyway, not only for his negligence in watching Madame de Staël but for his leniency towards several other nobles.

9. S. Balayé, 'Madame de Staël et le Gouvernement impérial en 1810', *Cahiers Staëliens*, no. 19, December 1974, p. 38.
10. Lecestre, *Lettres inédites de Napoléon Ier*, op. cit., vol. II, p. 74.
11. *Dix années d'exil*, op. cit., pp. 200–1.
12. *Lettres de Madame de Staël à Mme Récamier*, op. cit., pp. 179.
13. Balayé, *Madame de Staël*, op. cit., p. 195, and *Madame de Staël et le Gouvernement impérial en 1810.*
14. *Dix années d'exil*, op. cit., p. 201.
15. *De l'Allemagne*, Introduction by S. Balayé, Paris 1968, vol. 1, part. II, ch. XI, pp. 211–14.
16. Ibid., vol. 1, part I, ch. II, p. 58.
17. Balayé, *Madame de Staël*, op. cit., pp. 175–6.
18. *De l'Allemagne*, op. cit., Introduction, citing letter to Jacobi, 1 January 1804, letter to Hochet of 3 February 1804 and to Gérando, 26 February 1804.
19. S. Balayé, *Les Carnets de voyages de Mme de Staël*, Genève 1971, p. 305.
20. Blennerhassett, op. cit., vol. III, letter from Goethe to Mme Grothius of 17 February 1814.
21. *De l'Allemagne*, op. cit., vol. 1, part II, ch. IV, p. 248.
22. Ibid., ch. XXV.
23. Ibid., Préface, p. 41.
24. Ibid., p. 40.
25. Ibid., vol. 2, part IV, ch. X, p. 301.
26. Ibid., vol. 1, part I, ch. II, pp. 55–64.
27. Ibid., vol. 1, Préface, p. 41.
28. Ibid., part II, ch. XXIV, p. 370.
29. Ibid., p. 374.
30. Ibid., vol. 2, part III, ch. VI, pp. 127–40; cited by S. Balayé, *Madame de Staël*, op. cit., p. 191.
31. Ibid., vol. 2, p. 316.
32. Ibid., pp. 179–81.
33. Balayé, *Mme de Staël et le Gouvernement impérial en 1810*, op. cit., p. 64.
34. J. Mistler, *Madame de Staël et Maurice O'Donnell 1805–17*, Paris 1926, letter of 19 October 1810, pp. 269–73.
35. *Dix années d'exil*, op. cit., pp. 206–7.
36. Kohler, *Mme de Staël et la Suisse*, op. cit., p. 596.
37. Levaillant, op. cit., p. 281.
38. Constant, *Journal intime*, op. cit. p. 108.
39. *Mémoires de la Comtesse de Boigne*, op. cit., vol. 1, p. 252.
40. *Dix années d'exil*, op. cit., pp. 212–13.
41. Letter of 3 April 1812 cited by Balayé, *Madame de Staël*, op. cit., p. 202.
42. *Dix années d'exil*, part I, p. 45.
43. *Dix années d'exil*, part 1, ch. 1, p. 1.
44. *Lettres à Mme Récamier*, op. cit., p. 202.
45. Kohler, *Mme de Staël et la Suisse*, op. cit., p. 603. Lines translated by the author.
46. *Byron's Letters & Journals*, edited by Leslie Marchand, London 1924, vol. 5, pp. 260–1. Schlegal had by then converted to Catholicism.
47. Constant, *Journal intime*, op. cit., p. 269.
48. *Dix années d'exil*, op. cit., p. 239.

23 The Long Way to England

1. *Dix années d'exil*, op. cit., p. 228.
2. S. Balayé, *Les carnets de voyages de Madame de Staël*, op. cit., p. 265; Comtesse J. de Pange, *Auguste Guillaume Schlegel et Madame de Staël*, Paris 1938, p. 374.

3. *Dix années d'exil*, op. cit., pp. 229–30, footnote 6.
4. Ibid., p. 210.
5. Ibid., p. 242.
6. Mistler, *Mme de Staël et M. O'Donnell*, op. cit., p. 287.
7. M. Ulrichova, 'Mme de Staël et Fréderick Gentz,' Colloque de Coppet, *Mme de Staël et l'Europe*, op. cit., p. 89.
8. *Dix années d'exil*, p. 299.
9. *Lettres à Mme Récamier*, op. cit, pp. 236–7.
10. *Dix années d'exil*, pp. 247–8.
11. Ibid., p. 253.
12. Ibid., pp. 252–3, footnote 2.
13. Ibid., p. 253.
14. Ibid., pp. 255–60.
15. Alexander Pushkin, *Polnoye Sobraniye Sochinenii* (complete works) 10 vols, Leningrad 1978, vol. 6, *Roslavlev*, pp. 132–41, 135.
16. *Dix années d'exil*, pp. 261–71.
17. Ibid., p. 267.
18. Ibid., pp. 271–80.
19. Pushkin, op. cit., vol. 6, p. 134.
20. Ibid., p. 135.
21. Maria Fairweather, *The Pilgrim Princess*, London 1999, letter from Mme de Staël, St Petersburg, 8 August 1812, p. 214.
22. Pushkin, *Roslavlev*, op. cit., p. 137.
23. F. V. Rostopchin, Russki Archiv, 1875 vol. II, letter of 26 July 1812, p. 400.
24. Shchukin (ed.), *Bumagi otnoschayesya do otechestvennoy voyni 1812 goda*, Moscow 1905, vol. IX, p. 303.
25. Balayé, *Carnets de voyages de Mme de Staël*, op. cit., pp. 294–321.
26. *Dix années d'exil*, op. cit., p. 288.
27. Ibid., pp. 294–5.
28. Arndt, *Erinnerungen*, cited by Gautier, *Madame de Staël et Napoléon*, op. cit., p. 315.
29. Ibid., pp. 308–9, see also footnotes; Balayé, *Carnets de voyages*, op. cit., pp. 300–11 and *Memoirs of John Quincy Adams*, Philadelphia 1874, vol. IV, pp. 450 ff., also cited in Gautier above.
30. *Madame de Staël et l'Europe*, Colloque de Coppet, 1966, Norman King, *Mme de Staël et la chute de Napoléon*, p. 63.
31. *Dix années d'exil*, op. cit., p. 291.
32. Ibid., p. 302.
33. Ibid., pp. 307–8.
34. *Cahiers Staëliens*, no. 48, Sheilagh Margaret Riordan and Simone Balayé, *Un Manuscrit inédit sur le séjour de Mme de Staël à Stockholm*, p. 76.
35. Ibid., p. 73.
36. Ibid., p. 94.
37. Ibid., pp. 77–82.
38. Ibid., p. 85.
39. Ibid., pp. 86–8.
40. Kohler, *Madame de Staël et la Suisse*, op. cit., p. 616.
41. Ibid., pp. 618–19.
42. *Cahiers Staëliens*, no. 48, *Mme de Staël à Stockholm*, op. cit., pp. 99–100.
43. Ibid., pp. 100–1.
44. Baronne de Nolde, *Lettres de Madame de Staël à Benjamin Constant*, Paris 1928, letter of 20 May 1813, pp. 39–41.
45. Constant, *Journal intime*, op. cit., pp. 285–7.
46. *Cahiers Staëliens*, no. 48, *Madame de Staël à Stockholm*, op. cit., p. 102.

24 England

1. *Considérations*, op. cit., part VI, ch. III, pp. 523–4.
2. Ibid., p. 513.
3. Victor de Pange, *Le plus beau de toutes les fêtes*, op.cit., p. 63.
4. Lady Theresa Lewis, *Extracts from the Journals & Correspondence of Miss Berry 1783 to 1852,* London 1866, vol. II, p. 538.
5. *Lettres inédites de Madame de Staël à Hedvig, reine de Suède*, edited by Lucien Maury, Paris 1953, p. 93, cited by Victor de Pange in *Le plus beau . . .* op. cit., p. 59.
6. Thomas Moore, *Letters and Journals of Lord Byron*, London 1830, p. 232.
7. James Mackintosh's memoirs are cited by Victor de Pange in *Le rêve anglais de Mme de Staël*, pp. 173–89 in Colloque de Coppet, 1966, *Madame de Staël et l'Europe*, 1970.
8. Ibid., p. 178 and footnote 5, citing Emma Darwin's *A Century of Family Letters*.
9. Lord Byron, *The Complete Miscellaneous Prose*, edited by A. Nicholson, *Some Recollections of my acquaintance with Madame de Staël* (1821), Oxford 1991 pp. 184–6.
10. *Byron's Letters & Journals* op. cit., vol. III, p. 66.
11. *Considérations*, op. cit., part VI, pp. 543, 550.
12. Victor de Pange, *Le rêve anglais*, op. cit., p. 174.
13. *Byron's Letters & Journals*, op. cit., vol. III, p. 66.
14. Comtesse de Pange, *Le dernier amour de Madame de Staël*, Genève 1944, p. 165.
15. Mallet du Pan's *Memoirs*, pp. 622–3, cited by Kohler, *Mme de Staël et la Suisse*.
16. Ibid., p. 624.
17. Ibid., p. 621; Comtesse Jean de Pange, *A-G Schlegel et Madame de Staël*, op. cit., p. 436.
18. Baronne de Nolde, *Lettres de Mme de Staël à Benjamin Constant*, Paris 1928, letter of 30 November 1813, pp. 43–5.
19. Georges Solovieff, Introduction to *Lettres à Narbonne*, op. cit., citing letter from Narbonne to the First Consul of 2 Nivôse Year XII (24 December 1803), p. 29.
20. *Lettres de Madame de Staël à Meister*, op. cit., p. 263.
21. *Considérations*, op. cit., part VI, ch. VI, p. 562.
22. D'Andlau, *Mme de Staël et Don Pedro de Souza*, op. cit., pp. 112–13.
23. Norman King, *Le Séjour de Madame de Staël en Angleterre*, in *Les Carnets de voyages*, op. cit., ch. 5.
24. *Byron's Letters & Journals* op. cit., vol. IV, letter of 1 January 1814, p. 19.
25. Ibid., vol. IV, letter of 8 June 1814, p. 122.
26. Ibid., vol. III, letter of 30 November 1813, pp. 184–5, p. 184, footnote 1.
27. Ibid., vol. III, p. 226, entry for 30 November 1813.
28. Henry Crabb Robinson's *Diary, Reminsiscences and Correspondence*, Boston 1869, pp. 269–71, cited by Blennerhassett, vol. III, p. 456.
29. Victor de Pange, *Le rêve anglais*, op. cit., p. 178.
30. *Considérations*, op. cit., part VI, ch. VI, p. 556.
31. Thomas Medwin, *Conversations of Lord Byron*, London 1824, p. 273.
32. Norman King, *Les Dernières paroles d'un duc*, *Cahiers Staëliens*, no. 10, June 1970.
33. *Considérations*, op. cit., part VI, ch. III, p. 529.
34. Victor de Pange, *Le rêve anglais*, op. cit., p. 182.
35. Ibid., p. 181 and Madame de Staël, *Oeuvres complètes*.
36. *Considérations*, op. cit., part VI, ch. VI, p. 557.
37. Blennerhassett, op. cit., vol. III, letter of 30 November 1813.
38. Nolde, *Lettres de Mme de Staël à Constant*, op. cit., letter of 12 December 1813, p. 45, and letter of 8 January 1814, p. 47.
39. Unpublished letter from Etienne Dumont to Maria Edgeworth, 1 November

1813, cited by Norman King, *Mme de Staël et la chute de Napoléon*, Colloque de Coppet, 1966, p. 65.
40. Nolde, *Lettres à Constant*, op. cit., letter of 23 January 1814, pp. 57–62.
41. *Correspondence, Despatches & other papers of Viscount Castlereagh*, vol. IX, despatch of 30 January 1814, p. 212.
42. Nolde, *Lettres à Constant*, op. cit., letters of 27 February 1814 and 22 March 1814, pp. 62–6.
43. François de Chateaubriand, *Mémoires d'outre-tombe, Napoléon*, Paris 1989, p. 270.
44. *Notice de Mme de Broglie*, introducing *Oeuvres diverses d'Auguste de Staël*, cited by Gautier in *Mme de Staël et Napoléon*, op. cit., p. 355.
45. Blennerhassett, op. cit., vol. III, p. 504.
46. Nolde, *Lettres à Constant*, op. cit., pp. 66–8.

25 The End of Empire

1. *Mémoires de la Comtesse de Boigne*, op. cit., vol. I, pp. 324–5.
2. Ibid., pp. 321–2; also Maria Fairweather, *The Pilgrim Princess*, op. cit., ch 4.
3. *Mémoires* . . . ibid., pp. 326–7.
4. Victor de Pange, *Le plus beau de toutes les fêtes*, op. cit., p. 96.
5. Nolde, *Lettres à Constant*, letter of 24 April 1814, pp. 69–71.
6. *Considérations*, op. cit., part V, ch. VI, pp. 459–62.
7. The leader of a royalist and Catholic secret society, the *Chevaliers de la Foi*, aide-de-camp to the King's brother Artois, and chamberlain to the Duchesse d'Angoulême, Montmorency was to become Prime Minister under the Ultras, the party of reactionary legitimists who stood for the purest ideals of the counter-revolution. They were well to the right of the King.
8. Constant, *Journal Intime*, op. cit., entries of 13, 18, 19 and 24 May 1814, pp. 307–8.
9. Nolde, *Lettres à Constant*, op. cit., p. 74.
10. *Lettres à Mme Récamier*, op. cit., p. 249.
11. Blennerhassett, op. cit., vol. III, citing Pictet de Rochemont's letter in *Fragments de lettres*, 1840, p. 63, at Bibliothèque Publique et Universitaire de Genève, p. 505.
12. Ibid., p. 506.
13. *Considérations*, op. cit., part V, ch. VII, p. 463.
14. *Mémoires de la Comtesse de Boigne*, op. cit., vol. 1, p.392.
15. Kohler, *Mme de Staël et la Suisse*, op. cit., letter of 21 June 1814, pp. 630–1.
16. Victor de Broglie, *Souvenirs*, Paris 1886, vol. 1, cited by André Lang, *Une vie d'orages: Germaine de Staël*, Paris 1958, p. 238.
17. Kohler, op. cit., p. 637.
18. *Mémoires de la Comtesse de Boigne*, op. cit., vol. I, p. 391.
19. Constant, *Journal Intime*, op. cit., 31 August 1814, p. 313.
20. Kohler, op. cit., p. 639.
21. Constant, *Journal Intime*, op. cit., p. 414.
22. Victor de Pange, *Mme de Staël et le Duc de Wellington, Correspondance inédite 1815–1817*, Paris 1962, p. 37, footnote 3.
23. Blennerhassett, op. cit., vol. III, citing Stanhope *Notes of Conversations with the Duke of Wellington*, London 1818, vol. 3, p. 507.
24. Victor de Pange, *Le plus beau*, op. cit., p. 112.
25. Victor de Pange, *Le rêve anglais*, op. cit., p. 189.
26. *Lettres inédites de Madame de Staël à Meister*, op. cit., letter of 28 February 1815.
27. Pange, *Le plus beau*, op. cit., letter of 18 February 1815, pp. 114–15.
28. *Considérations*, op. cit., ch. XIII, part V, p. 494.

29. S. Balayé, *Madame de Staël*, p. 220, footnote 98.
30. Ibid.
31. *Lettres à Constant*, op. cit., p. 257.
32. Harold Nicholson, *Benjamin Constant*, London 1949.

26 The Return of the Exile

1. Benjamin Constant, *Mémoires sur les Cent-Jours in Les Oeuvres de Benjamin Constant*, op. cit.
2. Constant, *Journal Intime*, op. cit., p. 348.
3. Gautier, *Mme de Staël et Napoléon*, op. cit., citing Archives de Broglie, p. 383.
4. Mme Necker-de Saussures, *Notice sur le caractère*, op. cit., p. cxci.
5. Nolde, *Lettres à Constant*, op. cit., letter of 17 April 1815, pp. 84–6.
6. Constant, *Journal Intime*, entry of 20 April 1815, p. 349.
7. Nolde, *Lettres à Constant*, op. cit., 30 April 1815, pp. 89–93.
8. Ibid., letters of 28 May 1815 and 12 June 1815, pp. 96–104.
9. A. Lang, *Une vie d'orages*, op. cit., pp. 264–5.
10. Ibid., pp. 265–7.
11. Chateaubriand, *Mémoires d'outre-tombe*, op. cit., vol. 2, pp. 679–80.
12. Ibid., p. 703.
13. Nolde, *Lettres à Constant*, op. cit., letters of 1 and 3 September 1815, pp. 108–13.
14. Victor de Pange, *Madame de Staël et le Duc de Wellington*, op. cit., letter of 9 August 1815, pp. 40–1.
15. Castlereagh, *Correspondence, Despatches and other papers of Viscount Castlereagh*, London 1852, vols IX and X.
16. Kohler, *Mme de Staël et la Suisse*, op. cit., pp. 657–9.
17. Benjamin Constant, *Lettres à sa famille*, Paris 1888, letter of 17 July 1816, pp. 542–4
18. Nolde, *Lettres à Constant*, op. cit., 30 May 1816, pp. 120–3.
19. Victor de Pange, *Le plus beau*, op. cit., p. 189, footnote 32, citing Creevey Papers, p. 258.
20. Ibid., letter of 30 July 1816, pp. 181–3.
21. *Byron's Letters and Journals*, op. cit., vol. IV, pp. 300–1.
22. Pange, *Le plus beau*, op. cit., pp. 191–3.
23. Ibid., pp. 190–1.
24. *Byron's Letters and Journals*, op. cit., vol. V, p. 109.
25. Ibid., p. 88.
26. *Byron's Letters and Journals*, op. cit., vol. IV, pp. 300–2.
27. *Lettres à Mme Récamier*, op. cit., p. 271.
28. *Mémoires de la Comtesse de Boigne*, op. cit., vol. II, pp. 512–13.
29. Ibid., p. 706.
30. Victor de Pange, *Mme de Staël et le Duc de Wellington*, op. cit., letters of 23 and 29 October 1816, pp. 55–6, 61–2.
31. Ibid., letter of 27 November 1816, pp. 74–8.
32. Ibid., letter of 1 December 1816, pp. 87–95.
33. Ibid., unpublished Broglie Archives, p. 102, footnote 1.
34. Comte de Villèle, *Mémoires et Correspondance*, Paris 1898–1901, p. 159, cited by Lang, *Une vie d'orages*, p. 290.
35. *Mémoires de la Comtesse de Boigne*, vol. II, pp. 706–7.
36. Lang, *Une vie d'orages*, op. cit., p. 290.
37. *Extracts from the Journals and Correspondence of Miss Berry*, op. cit., vol. 3, 26 May 1817, pp. 125–7.
38. Lang, *Une vie d'orages*, op. cit., letter of 24 February 1817.

39. Victor de Pange, *Mme de Staël et le Duc de Wellington*, op. cit., letter of 12 April 1817.
40. *The Life, Letters & Journals of George Ticknor*, Boston 1880.
41. Lang, *Une vie d'orages*, p. 295.
42. Ibid.
43. Broglie, *Souvenirs*, op. cit.
44. Pange, V.de, *Mme de Staël et Le Duc de Wellington*, op. cit., footnote 3, p. 130
45. Broglie, *Souvenirs*, op. cit., vol. 1, p. 383.
46. Lang, *Une vie d'orages*, op. cit., p. 297.

Epilogue: On Death & Immortality

1. B. Constant, *Lettres à Madame Récamier 1807–1830*, Paris 1882, letter of July 1817, p. 313.
2. Kohler, *Mme de Staël et la Suisse*, op. cit., p. 670, citing Victor de Broglie, *Souvenirs*, op. cit., vol. 1, p. 383.
3. Lang, *Une vie d'orages*, op. cit., p. 301.
4. Kohler, op. cit., pp. 672–5.
5. Comtesse Jean de Pange, *Le dernier amour de Mme de Staël*, Geneva 1944, op. cit., p. 207.
6. Madame Necker-de Saussure, *Notice sur le caractère*, op. cit., p. cc lij.
7. A. Lang, *Une vie d'orages*, op. cit., pp. 305–6.
8. Kohler, op. cit., p. 525.
9. Nicholson, *Benjamin Constant*, op. cit., p. 253.
10. *Extracts from the Journals and Correspondence of Miss Berry*, op. cit., vol. 3.
11. Kohler, op. cit.
12. Chateaubriand, *Mémoires d'outre-tombe*, op. cit., vol. 2, p. 606.
13. Reissued immediately, then again in 1820, and in the same year included in Madame de Staël's complete works, to be reissued regularly throughout the rest of the nineteenth century.
14. Charles-Augustin Sainte-Beuve, *Portraits de femmes*, Paris 1998, p. 214.
15. *Considérations*, op. cit., p. 603.
16. Byron, *Poetical Works*, vol. II, pp. 490–1, note to *Childe Harold* cited by Victor de Pange in *Mme de Staël et le Duc de Wellington*, op. cit., p. 72.
17. B. Constant, *De Madame de Staël et de ses ouvrages* in *Portraits, Mémoires, Souvenirs*, ed. E. Harpaz, Paris 1992, pp. 204–54.

Bibliography

Primary Sources

Madame de Staël's Complete Works: *Oeuvres complètes de Mme la baronne de Staël publié par son fils*, Paris, Treuttel et Würtz, 1821
Madame de Staël works in separate publications
—— *Delphine,* B. Didier, 2 vols, Flammarion, Paris, 2000
—— *Corinne ou l'Italie*, Simone Balayé, Gallimard, Paris, 1985
—— *De l'Allemagne*, intro Simone Balayé, 2 vols, Flammarion, Paris, 1968
—— *Des Circonstances actuelles qui peuvent terminer la Révolution et des Principes qui doivent fonder la république en France*, ed. critique Lucia Omacini Lib. Droz, Paris-Genève, 1979
—— *De La Littérature*, Flammarion, 1991, ed. établie par G. Gengembre & J. Goldzink
—— *De l'influence des passions sur le bonheur des individus et des nations suivi par Réflexions sur le suicide*, préface Chantal Thomas, Payot & Rivages, Paris, 2000
—— *Considérations sur la Révolution française,* présenté par Jacques Godechot, Tallandier, Paris, 1983
—— *Dix années d'exil,* ed critique par Simone Balayé et Mariella Bonifacio, Fayard, 1996

Correspondence

Correspondance générale de Madame de Staël
Texte établi et présenté par Béatrice W. Jasinski, Jean-Jacques Pauvert, Paris
Tome II *Lettres de Jeunesse 1777–1788*
vol ii 1788–1791
Tome II vol i *Lettres inédites à Louis Narbonne*
Tome II vol ii *Lettres Diverses 1792–15/5/1794*
Tome III vol i *Lettres de Mézery et de Coppet 16/5 1794–16/5 1795*
Tome III vol ii *Lettres d'une nouvelle Républicaine 17/5 1795–fin Novembre 1796*
Tome IV vol i *Du Directoire au Consulat 1/12/1796–15/12/1800*
Tome IV vol ii *Lettres d'une républicaine sous le Consulat 16/12/1800–31/7/1803*
Tome V vol i *France et Allemagne 1/8/1803–19/5/1804*
Tome V vol ii *Le Léman et L'Italie 19/5/1804–9/11/1805*
Tome VI *De Corinne vers de l'Allemagne 9/11/1805–9/5/1809*
d'Andlau, B., *Correspondance de Madame de Staël et Don Pedro de Souza*, Preface, introduction, commentaires et notes par Beatrix d'Andlau, Gallimard, Paris, 1979
Balayé, S., *Lettres de Mme de Staël à Ribbing*: Préface de la Comtesse Jean de Pange introduction & notes by Simone Balayé, Gallimard, Paris, 1960
Lenormant, C., *Madame de Staël et la Grande Duchesse Louise*, Michel Lévy Frères, Paris, 1862
Léouzon Le Duc, L., *Correspondance diplomatique du baron de Staël Holstein, ambassadeur de Suède en France et de son successeur comme chargé d'affaires, le baron Brinkman. Documents inédits sur la Révolution (1783–1799)*, Hachette, Paris, 1881
Loménie E. B de, *Lettres de Madame de Staël à Madame Récamier* présentées et annotées par E. Beau de Loménie, Ed., Domat, Paris, 1952

Luppé, Robert de, *Madame de Staël et J.B.A. Suard*, Correspondance inédite 1786–1817, Lib Droz, Genève, 1970
Mistler J., *Madame de Staël et Maurice O'Donnell 1805–1817*, d'après les lettres inédites, Calmann-Lévy, Paris, 1926
Nolde, baronne de, *Lettres de Madame de Staël à Benjamin Constant*, Kra, Paris, 1928
—— *Lettres à Madame de Staël*, Putnam, Paris, 1907
Pange, Victor de, *Le plus beau de toutes les fêtes:* correspondance inédite de Mme de Staël et d'Elizabeth Hervey, Duchesse de Devonshire, Editions Klincksieck, Paris, 1980
—— *Madame de Staël et le Duc de Wellington*: Correspondance inédite 1815–1817, preface Comtesse Jean de Pange, Gallimard, Paris, 1962
Lettres à John Rocca, Revue de Genève Juillet-Dec, 1929
Schilder, Gen., *Lettres au Tsar Alexandre Ier* publiées par le General, Schilder Revue de Paris, Paris, 1897
Solovieff, G., *Lettres de Madame de Staël à Narbonne*
Préface Comtesse Jean de Pange; Introduction, notes & commentaires Georges Solovieff, Gallimard, Paris, 1960
Usteri, P. & Ritter, E., *Lettres inédites de Madame de Staël à Henri Meister*, Hachette et cie, Paris, 1903

Books and academic articles about Madame de Staël and her family

Occident et Cahiers Staëliens 1930–1939 which include the *Journal de jeunesse de Louise-Germaine Necker, 1785* published in June 1930, July 1931 & October 1932 and *Notes sur l'enfance de Madame de Staël* by Catherine Rilliet-Huber, June 1933 & March 1934
Cahiers Staëliens The volumes 1–53 published by the Société des études staëliennes founded in 1929, and published by Éditions Honoré Champion, Paris, contain the most important body of work since 1962, on Madame de Staël, her work and her family
Colloque de Coppet 18–24 Juillet 1966 published Éditions Klincksieck, 1970: *Madame de Staël et l'Europe*, contributions from various authors. Specific papers cited in endnotes where appropriate
Colloque de Coppet Juillet 1974: Champion Paris & Slatkine Genève 1977: *Le Groupe de Coppet*, contributions from various authors. Specific papers cited in endnotes where appropriate
d'Andlau, Beatrix, *La Jeunesse de Madame de Staël*, Librairie Droz, Paris-Genève, 1970
Balayé, Simone, *Madame de Staël: Lumières & Liberté*, Klincksieck, Paris, 1797
—— *les carnets de voyages de Madame de Staël*, Droz, Genève, 1971
—— *Écrire, Lutter, vivre*, Droz, Genève, 1994
Many articles in the *Cahiers Staëliens* see above
Barante, Baronne de, *Lettres de Claude-Ignace de Barante à son fils Prosper . . . de Prosper de Barante à son père de Prosper de Barante à Madame de Staël*, Clermond Ferrand, 1929
Blennerhassett, Lady, *Madame de Staël and her influence in politics & Literature*, 3 vols, Chapman & Hall, London, 1889
Bredin, Jean-Denis, *Une singulière famille Jacques Necker, Suzanne Necker et Germaine de Staël*, Fayard, Paris, 1999
Broglie, duc V. de, *Souvenirs*, Paris, 1886
Broglie, Prince J. de, *Madame de Staël et sa cour au château de Chaumont*, Plon, Paris, 1936
Broglie, duchesse de, *Notice sur M. le baron Auguste de Staël* as preface to *Oeuvres diverses de M. le baron Auguste de Staël*, see below
Constant, Benjamin
—— *Amélie et Germaine, Ma Vie, Cécile,* Texte établi par Paul Delbouille, H. Champion, Paris, 1989
—— *Adolphe*, Flammarion, Paris, 1965
—— *Journal intime* and *Le Cahier rouge* edited by Jean Mistler, Éditions du Rocher, Monaco, 1945
—— *Portraits, Mémoires, Souvenirs,* Textes établis etc par E Harpaz, Lib H. Champion, Paris, 1992

—— *Lettres à Rosalie de Constant,* Nouvelle revue, October 1903
—— *Lettres à Madame Récamier,* Calmann Lévy, Paris, 1882
—— *Lettres de Benjamin Constant à sa famille 1775–1830*, Menos, Jean-H, Albert Savine, Paris, 1888
Croce, Benedetto, *Uomini e cose della Vechia Italia, La Signora di Staël et la regina Maria Carolina di Napoli*, G. Latrza, Bari, 1956
Crue, Françis de, *L' Ami de Rousseau et des Necker – Paul Moultou à Paris en 1778*, Lib. Honoré Champion, Paris, 1926
Dejob, C., *Madame de Staël et l'Italie*, Paris, 1890
Diesbach, Ghislain de, *Madame de Staël,* Lib académique Perrin, Paris, 1983
—— *Necker ou la faillite de la vertu,* Lib. académique Perrin, Paris, 1978.
Folkenflik, V., *Major Writings of Madame de Staël*, Columbia University Press, NY, 1987
Gautier, Paul, *Madame de Staël & Napoléon*, Plon, Paris, 1903
—— *M. de Montmorency et Madame de Staël, d'apres les lettres inédites de M. de Montmorency à Madame Necker-de Saussure*, Plon, Paris, 1908
Goldsmith, M., *Madame de Staël: Portrait of a liberal in the revolutionary age*, Green & Co., London, 1938
Gribble, F., *Madame de Staël and her Lovers*, Nash, London, 1907
Guillemin, H., *Madame de Staël, Benjamin Constant et Napoléon*, Plon, Paris, 1959.
Gutwirth, M., *The Twilight of the Goddesses*, N. Brunswick, 1992
Hasselrot, Bengt C.G., *Nouveaux Documents sur Benjamin Constant et Madame de Staël*, Ejnar Munksgaard, Copenhagen, 1952
d' Haussonville, comte, *Le Salon de Mme Necker*, 2 vols, Calmann Lévy, Paris, 1882
—— *Mme de Staël & Necker*, Calmann-Lévy, Paris, 1925
—— *Madame de Staël et l'Allemagne,* Calmann-Lévy, Paris, 1928
d'Haussonville, Othenin, *Auguste de Staël et ses parents, Cahiers Staëliens* No 53, 2002, pp. 145–164
—— *Coppet et la Révolution de Suisse 1797–1805*, Forum Européen de Coppet, 2003
Herold, Christopher, *Mistress to an Age: A Life of Madame de Staël*, Hamish Hamilton, London, 1958
Jasinski, Béatrice, *L'engagement de Benjamin Constant,* Minard, Paris, 1971
Kelly, Linda, *Juniper Hall: an English Refuge from the French Revolution*, Wiedenfeld & Nicholson, London, 1999
—— *Women of the French Revolution*, Hamish Hamilton, London, 1987
Kohler, Pierre, *Madame de Staël et la Suisse*, Payot & Cie, Lausanne, Paris, 1916
Lacretelle, J-C-D, *Madame de Staël et les Hommes*, Grasset, Paris, 1938
Larg, David, *Mme de Staël – La Vie dans L'oeuvre, 1766–1800*
—— *La Seconde Vie 1800–07,* Birkbeck College Publications, London, 1928
Lavaquery, Abbé, E., *Necker, fourrier de la Révolution*, Plon, Paris, 1933
Lenormant, Charles, *Weimar & Coppet: Madame de Staël et la Grande-Duchesse Louise*, Michel Lévy Frères, Paris, 1862
Levaillant, Maurice, *Une amitié amoureuse: Madame de Staël et Madame Récamier*, Hachette, Paris, 1956. English translation – *The Passionate Exiles*, Allen & Unwin, London, 1958
Maury, Lucien, *Lettres inédites de Mme de Staël à Hedvig, reine de Suède*, Mercure de France, Paris, 1953
Pange, Comtesse J. de, *Madame de Staël et François de Pange*, Plon, Paris, 1925
—— *Auguste-Guillaume Schlegel et Madame de Staël*, Editions Albert, Paris, 1938
—— *Monsieur de Staël*, Les Portiques, Paris, 1932
—— *Le dernier Amour de Mme de Staël*, La Palatine, Genève, 1944
Pellegrini, Carlo, *Madame de Staël: il gruppo cosmopolita di Coppet, l'imfluenza delle sue idée critiche*, Firenze, 1938
Saussure, Madame Necker-de, *Notice sur le caractère et les écrits de Mme de Staël, Oeuvres Complètes de Mme la baronne de Staël*, Treuttel & Würtz, Paris, 1821
Sorel, A., *Madame de Staël*, Hachette, Paris, 1890
Staël, baron Auguste de, *Oeuvres diverses de M. le baron Auguste de Staël*, Treuttel & Würtz, Paris, 1829

—— *Jacques Necker: Oeuvres Complètes publiées par son petit-fils*, 15 vols, Treuttel & Würtz, Paris, 1820
Wilkes, Joanne, *Lord Byron and Madame de Staël – Born for Opposition*, Ashgate, 1999
Winegarten, Renee, *Madame de Staël*, Berg Women's series, Leamington Spa/Dover, 1985

General Sources

d'Abrantès, duchesse de, *Mémoires de la duchesse d'Abrantès*, 12 vols, Paris, 1835
Adams, John Quincy, *Memoirs of J.Q. Adams comprising portions of his diary 1795–1848*, Lippincott, Philadelphia, 1874
Adams, *Journal & correspondence of Miss Adams, daughter of John Adams, second President of the United States, written in France & England in 1785*, Wiley & Putnam, 1841
Adams, *Letters of Mrs. Adams, the wife of John Adams*, Boston, Wilkins, Carter & Co., 1848
d'Arblay, Madame, *Diary and Letters, edited by her niece*, 7 vols, H. Colburn 1854
—— *The Journals & Letters of Fanny Burney (Madame d'Arblay)* edited by Joyce Hemlow, 12 vols., London, 1972–84
Aroutounova, Bayara, *Lives in Letters: Princess Zinaida Volkonsky and her Correspondence*, Slavica Pub. inc., 1994
Beckford, W., *Memoirs of William Beckford of Fonthill*, 2 vols, Charles J. Skeet, London, 1859
Berlin, Isaiah, *The Age of Enlightenment*, OUP
—— *The Roots of Romanticism*, Chatto & Windus, 1999
Bernard J.F., *Talleyrand: a biography*, Collins, London, 1973
Berry, *Extracts from the Journals & Correspondence of Miss Berry 1783 to 1852 edited by Lady Theresa Lewis*, 3 vols, Longmans, Green & Co., London, 1866
Bertrand, Général, *Cahiers de Sainte-Hélène*, Paris, 1951–59
Boigne, *Mémoires de la Comtesse de Boigne*, 2 vols, Mercure de France, Paris, 1999
Bonaparte, Lucien, *Mémoires de Lucien Bonaparte, Prince de Canino écrits par lui-même*, Gosselin, Paris, 1836
Bonaparte, Napoléon, *Correspondance de Napoléon Ier rassemblée dans les ouvrages publiés par les soins de Napoléon III*, Paris, 1858–69
Bourrienne, M. de, *Mémoires*, 10 vols, Ladvocat, Paris, 1829
Browning, O., ed., *Despatches from Paris 1784–1790*, Camden Modern Series, London
Bruce, Evangeline, *Napoleon & Josephine: An Improbable Marriage*, Weidenfeld & Nicholson, London, 1995
Burghersh, Lady, *Journal and letters of Lady Burghersh*, ed. Lady Rose Weigall, J. Murray, London, 1897
Burke, Edmund, *Reflections on the Revolution in France*, Penguin Classics, London, 1988
Byron, Lord, *Byron's Letters & Journals edited by Leslie Marchand*, 12 vols, John Murray, London, 1924
—— *The Complete Miscellaneous Prose*, ed. A. Nicholson, Clarendon Press, Oxford
Carlyle, Thomas, *The French Revolution*, World's Classics OUP, 1989
Casse, baron du, *Mémoires et correspondance du roi Joseph*, Paris, 1856–69
Castlereagh, *Correspondence Déspatches & other papers of Viscount Castlereagh*, vol. IX, William Shobel, London, 1852
Catherine II of Russia, *Lettres de l'Impératrice Catherine II à Grimm 1774–96*, A.Grot, St. Petersbourg, 1878.
Caulaincourt, Gen de, *Mémoires du Général de Caulaincourt*, 3 vols, Plon, Paris, 1933
Chapman, Pauline, *The French Revolution as seen by Madame Tussaud; Witness Extraordinary*, 1989
Chastenay, Comtesse Victoire de, *Mémoires*, Plon, Paris, 1896
Chateaubriand, François de, *Mémoires d'outre-tombe*, 2 vols, Garnier, Paris, 1989
—— *Napoléon* Egloff, Paris, n.d.
Cobb, Richard, *The French and their Revolution*, ed. David Gilmour, London, 1998
Cobban, Alfred, *A History of Modern France*, 3 vols, Pelican, London, 1969
Cooper, Duff, *Talleyrand*, Jonathan Cape, London, 1947

Craveri, Benedetta, translated by Teresa Waugh, *Madame du Deffand and her World*, Peter Halban, London, 2002
Creevey, Thomas, *The Creevey Papers*, ed. John Gore, John Murray, London, 1948
Dallas, Gregor, *1815 – The Road to Waterloo*, Richard Cohen Books, London, 1996
Davies, Norman, *Europe: a History*, OUP, 1996
Diesbach, Ghislain de, *Histoire de L'Émigration 1789–1814*, Perrin, Paris, 1984
Égret, Jean, *Necker, Ministre de Louis XVI, 1776–1790*, Paris Lib. Honoré Champion, Paris, 1975
Fairweather, Maria, *The Pilgrim Princess*, Constable, London, 1999
Ferrières, Marquis de, *Correspondance inédite, 1789, 1790, 1791*, H. Carré ed., Paris, 1932
Foreman, Amanda, *Georgiana Duchess of Devonshire*, HarperCollins, London, 1998
Fraser, Antonia, *Marie Antoinette*, Weidenfeld & Nicholson, London, 2001
Frénilly Baron de, *Souvenirs du baron de Frénilly*, Plon-Nourrit, Paris, 1909
Furet, François, *La Révolution*, 2 vols, Hachette, 1988
Garde-Chambonas, comte de La, *Souvenirs du Congrès de Vienne 1814–1815*, Henri Vivien, Paris, 1901
Geyl, Peter, *Napoleon: for and against*, Penguin Books, London, 1965
Gibbon, Edward, *Memoirs of my life*, Penguin, London, 1984
—— *The Letters of E. Gibbon*, ed. By J.E. Norton, London
Golovkine, F., *La Cour et le régne de Paul I*[er], Paris, 1905
Hardman, John, *Louis XVI*, Yale University Press, 1993
Harman, Claire, *Fanny Burney*, Harper Collins, London, 2000
Hellegouarc'h, Jacqueline, *L'esprit de société*, Ed. Garnier, Paris, 2000
Hobsbawm, E.J., *The Age of Revolution 1789–1848*, Cardinal, London, 1988
Horne, Alistair, *Napoleon: Master of Europe*, Morrow, NY, 1979
—— *How far from Austerlitz? Napoleon 1805–1815*, Macmillan, London, 1996
Johnson, Paul, *Napoleon*, Phoenix, London, 2003
Jones, Colin, *The Great Nation*, The Penguin Press, Allen Lane, London, 2002
Klinckowsröm, R.M. ed., *Le Comte de Fersen & la Cour de France*, 2 vols, Paris, 1878
Knapton, Edith, *The Lady of the Holy Alliance*, NY, 1939
Lacour-Gayet, G., *Talleyrand*, 4 vols., Payot, Paris, 1933
Tour du Pin, Marquise de La, *Mémoires d'une femme de cinquante ans*, Chapelt, Paris, 1914.
—— *Memoirs of Madame de La Tour du Pin*, translated by Felicity Harcourt, Century Publishing, Toronto, 1985
Lanson, G., *Histoire de la Littérature française*, Lib. Hachette, 19eme éd., Paris
Las Cases, Emmanuel de, *Mémorial de Sainte-Hélène*, 2 vols, Ed du Seuil, Paris, 1968
Lecestre, Léon, *Lettres inédites de Napoléon Ier III, (1815)*, 2 vols, Plon, Paris, 1897
Lefebvre, Georges, translated by Harry Stockhold, *Napoleon*, 2 vols, Routledge & Kegan, London, 1969
—— *La Révolution française* Presses, Universitaires de France, Paris, 1957
Lenormant, Madame, *souvenirs et correspondance de Madame Récamier*, Paris, 1859
Lescure, *Correspondance complète de la Marquise du Deffand avec ses amis le Président Hainault, Montesquieu, d'Alemberet, Voltaire, Horace Walpole*, Paris, 1865
Ligne, Prince de, *Mémoires*, 2 vols, Paris, 1899
—— *Mémoires, Lettres et Pensées*, préface Chantal Thomas, ed. François Bourin, Paris, 1989
Longford, Elizabeth, *Wellington: The Years of the Sword & The Pillar of State* Weidenfeld & Nicholson, London, 1972
Lukács, Georg, *Goethe & his Age*, translated by Robert Anchor, Merlin Press, London, 1968
MacCarthy, Fiona, *Lord Byron: life and legend*, J. Murray, London, 2002
Mallet du Pan, J., *Mémoires et correspondance de Mallet du Pan*, 2 vols, Crapelet, Paris, 1851
Mansel, Philip, *Prince of Europe, the life of Charles Joseph de Ligne*, Weidenfeld & Nicholson, London, 2003
—— *Paris between Empires 1814–1852*, John Murray, London, 2001
—— *Louis XVIII*, Blond & Briggs, London, 1981

Marchand, Leslie, *Byron: a Portrait*, Futura Publications, 1976
Medwin, Thomas, *Conversations of Lord Byron*, Coburn, London, 1824
Meister, H, *Souvenir de mon dernier voyage à Paris 1795*, Elbez, Orell, Gessner, Fussli, Zurich, 1797
Mercier, Sébastien, *Tableau de Paris*, 12 vols, Amsterdam, 1782–88
Michelet, *Histoire de la Révolution française*, 2 vols, Pléiade, Gallimard, Paris, 1952
Moore, Thomas, *Letters and Journals of Lord Byron*, London, 1830
Morris, Gouverneur, *Diary and Letters*, 2 vols, edited by Anne Cary Morris, Kegan, Paul, Trench & co., London MDCCCLXXXIX
Nicholson, Harold, *The Age of Reason*, Constable & Co., London, 1960
—— *The Congress of Vienna*, Constable, London, 1946
—— *Benjamin Constant*, Constable, London, 1949
Norvins, J. de, *Mémorial*, 3 vols, Plon, Paris, 1896
Oberkirch, Baronne d' *Mémoires sur la cour de Louis XVI et la societé française avant 1789*, 2 vols, Paris, 1989
—— *Memoirs of the Baroness d'Oberkirch*, 3 vols, Colburn & Co Publishers, London, 1852
Palmer, Alan, *Metternich: Councillor of Europe*, History Book Club, London, 1972
Parliamentary History, vol. XXXI, nos 1345–1413, London
Pushkin, Alexander, *Polnoye Sobranie Sochinenii (Complete Works)*, 10 vols, ed. Nauka, Leningrad, 1978
Reid, Loren, *Charles James Fox: A Man for the People*, Longmans, London, 1969
Rémusat, Madame de, *Mémoires*, Calmann Lévy, Paris, 1879–1880
Rivarol, *Le Petit Dictionnaire des Grands Hommes de la Révolution*, Paris, 1956
Robinson, Henry Crabb, *Diary, Reminiscences & Correspondence*, pp Th. Sadler, 2 vols, Fields, Osgood & Co., Boston, 1869
Russki Archiv 1875, Vol II, *Rostopchin's letters*, Moscow
Sainte-Beuve, Charles-Augustin
—— *Portraits de femmes*, Folio classique, Gallimard, Paris, 1998
—— *Pour la critique*, Folio essays Gallimard, Paris, 1992
—— *Nouveaux Lundis*, M. Lévy, Paris, 1870
Schama, Simon, *Citizens; a chronicle of the French Revolution*, Viking, London, 1989
Shchukin ed., *Bumagi otnoschayesya do otechestvennoy voyni 1812 goda*, vol IX, Mamontov, Moscow, 1905.
Sieyès, E., *Qu'est ce que c'est que le Tiers État?* Ed, Champion, Paris, 1888
Sismondi, C.L. Simonde de, *Fragments de son Journal et Correspondance*, Genève, 1857
Söderhjelm, Alma, *Fersen & Marie Antoinette*, Paris, 1930
Stanhope, Earl, *Life of the Rt Hon. William Pitt*, 4 vols, John Murray, London 1867
Talleyrand, Prince de, *Mémoires*, 5 vols, Calmann Lévy, Paris, 1891–92
Ticknor, *The Life, Letters & Journals of George Ticknor*, 2 vols, Houghton Osgood & Co., Boston, 1880
Tocqueville, Alexis de, *L'Ancien régime et la Révolution*, O.C.
Trollope, Frances, *Vienna & the Austrians*, 2 vols, London, 1938
Vigée-Lebrun, Madame Elizabeth, *Souvenirs de Madame Vigée-Lebrun*, 3 vols, Paris, 1835–37
Villèle, comte de, *Mémoires et Correspondance*, 5 vols, Paris, 1898–1901
Vivie, A., *Lettres de Gustave III à la comtesse de Boufflers et de la comtesse au roi*, Paris
Wagener, Francoise, *Mme Récamier*, Flammarion, Paris, 2000
Webster, Sir Charles, *Documents on British Foreign Policy*, 1924
Wellington, Duke of, *Despatches*, 13 vols, London, 1834–39
Wilberforce, R. & S., *The life of William Wilberforce*, London, John Murray, 1838
Wilson, Sir Robert, *Narrative of Events During the Invasion of Russia*, John Murray, London, 1860
Young, Arthur, *Travels in France & Italy during the Years 1787, 1788 & 1789*, Th Okey, NY
Zamoyski, A., *Holy Madness: Romantics, Patriots & Revolutionaries 1776–1871*, Weidenfeld & Nicholson, London, 1999

Index

Where Madame de Staël is referred to in sub-entries her name is abbreviated to 'de S'.